THE SANTS

In Memoriam
K. Kailasapathy
(1933-1982)

CONTENTS

NOTE ON TRANSLITERATION

The scheme of transliteration which has been followed here is the standard system internationally used for Sanskrit and for Perso-Arabic languages, with a few modifications designed to make the text less forbidding and to reflect the pronunciation of modern North Indian languages. Thus, all proper names appearing as part of the English text are given in their generally accepted Anglicized form (e.g. Kabir, Vaishnava, Ram, Shiva) as are Indian words which have come into general English usage (e.g. guru, bhakta, mantra, dharma, yoga). Only italicized words are formally transliterated. In order to bring the transliteration visually closer to the pronunciation, the palatal consonant *c* and its aspirate *ch* have been rendered, respectively, as *ch* and *chh* (e.g. *chaupāī* and *chhand* instead of *caupāī* and *chand*), except in pure Sanskrit or Tamil contexts, where the older standard pattern is retained. A nasal before a consonant (*anusvāra*) is rendered by the nasal homorganic stop for that consonant's class (*ṅ* for gutturals, *ñ* for palatals, *ṇ* for cerebrals, *n* for dentals, *m* for labials, *ṃ* for sibilants and aspirates). Nasalization of vowels is indicated by *ṅ* (e.g. *meṅ, haiṅ*). In transliterating words which are current in the present-day languages of North India, the final *a* is omitted except where preceded by a double consonant (e.g. *nām* and *darśan*, but *śabda* and *yantra*). A certain latitude has been observed, however, in the case of certain technical terms (e.g. *nirguṇa*, *vinaya*, *sahaja*), and where lines or phrases from actual Sanskrit or medieval texts are quoted. Finally, when italicized words embedded in the English text have been pluralized, the *s* has been added to the word but not italicized (e.g. *bhagat*s, *bānī*s, *dohā*s).

INTRODUCTION

THE SANT TRADITION IN PERSPECTIVE

KARINE SCHOMER

The devotional transformation of medieval Hinduism known as the bhakti movement was a phenomenon of crucial importance in the history of Indian religion. Starting in the Tamil South in the seventh century, gradually spreading northward through Karnataka and Maharashtra, and sweeping over North India and Bengal from the fifteenth century onward, the impulse toward a personal devotional faith profoundly changed both the quality and the structures of religious life. From ritual observance and the performance of prescribed duties, or alternately, ascetic withdrawal in search of speculative knowledge of the divine, the heart of religion became the cultivation of a loving relationship between the individual and a personally conceived supreme god. Salvation, once considered unattainable except by men of the three upper castes, came to be seen as the prerogative of all, and spiritual leadership shifted from the Brahman priest knowledgeable about ritual and Sanskrit scriptures to the figure of the popular poet-saint who composed fervent songs of devotion in the regional vernacular.

As an expanding movement energized by fresh leadership and generating new ideas, bhakti reached its zenith between the fifteenth and the seventeenth century. As a legacy and an ongoing tradition, however, it is still very much alive today, permeating all facets of Hindu religious life. The songs of the poet-saints, their adaptations of Sanskrit religious texts, their sayings and the legends of their lives are the "classics" of the different vernacular literatures, and the principal source of religious inspiration for most ordinary worshippers. Many of the current practices of popular Hinduism, from the forms of home and temple ritual, festivals and pilgrimages to activities such as repeating the divine name and community devotional singing, have their origin in the bhakti movement and devotion as their central motivation. In addition, most of the organized religious communities that evolved out of the followings of particular poet-saints or groups of poet-saints continue to exist as independent traditions with their distinctive patterns of belief and practice. Above all, it is the ideas and attitudes of the bhakti movement that live on, giving present-day Hinduism its emotional texture, its spiritual and social values, and its basic philosophical assumptions.

Analogous in many ways to the Protestant Reformation of Christianity, the bhakti movement was equally diverse. Though the poet-saints were kindred spirits moved by similar devotional fervor, the expression of this devotion took a variety of forms. Some poets were devoted to Shiva, others to Vishnu or one of his incarnations, yet others to the goddess in one or another of her forms, while some worshipped a supreme god transcending all these concrete manifestations. Besides differing in the object of their devotion, the poet-saints and the movements they inspired also espoused a wide range of philosophical positions, from strict dualism to the absolute monism of *advaita* Vedanta. At the level of doctrine and social ideology, there were varying degrees of opposition and accomodation to the orthodox tradition's insistence on the revealed status of the Vedic scriptures, the priestly role of Brahmans, and the observance of caste duties and restrictions. In matters of devotional practice, finally, one finds both the rejection of all external forms of worship and the most elaborate kinds of idol worship and temple ritual.

Indeed, while it is customary to discuss the bhakti movement from an overall perspective, stressing its underlying unity and the role of the poet-saints as religious and cultural integrators, it is equally if not more appropriate to conceive of it as a cluster of individual bhakti groups, each with its particular emphases. These groups are strongly regional, moreover, so that they are distinguished not only by their doctrinal content but by their separate histories. Thus, under the rubric of bhakti, one finds traditions as different as the orthodox Shri Vaishnava and Saiva Siddhanta schools of the Tamil South, the non-conformist Virashaivas of Karnataka, the worship of the goddess Kali in Bengal, the widespread North Indian cult of devotion to Ram, the exclusively Krishnaite sects of Vallabha in Western India and Chaitanya in Bengal, and the tradition which is the subject of this book: the Sants.

The tradition of the Sants is one concerning which there are differences of opinion, both among scholars of Indian religion and within the Indian bhakti tradition itself. The difficulty begins with the term *sant* itself, which has several overlapping usages. Derived from Sanskrit *sat* ('truth, reality'), its root meaning is 'one who knows the truth' or 'one who has experienced Ultimate Reality', i.e. a person who has achieved a state of spiritual enlightenment or mystical self-realization;

by extension, it is also used to refer to all those who sincerely seek enlightenment. Thus conceptually as well as etymologically, it differs considerably from the false cognate 'saint' which is often used to translate it. Like 'saint', '*sant*' has also taken on the more general ethical meaning of the 'good person' whose life is a spiritual and moral examplar, and is therefore found attached to a wide variety of gurus, 'holy men' and other religious teachers. Historically, however, 'Sant' is the designation given to the poet-saints belonging to two distinct, though related devotional bhakti groups. The first is that of the non-sectarian Vaishnava poet-saints who flourished in Maharashtra from the thirteenth to the eighteenth century, devotees of the god Vitthala or Vithoba at Pandharpur. The second group, spanning the Hindi-speaking area, Punjab and Rajasthan, and active from the fifteenth century onward, was a loose fellowship of believers in a supreme god conceived as beyond all qualifications (*nirguṇa*). Rejecting all concrete *saguṇa* ('qualified') manifestations or incarnations of the divine, and mystics as much as devotees of a personal god, the North Indian Sants defy classification within the usual categories of Hindu bhakti; it has become customary, however, to describe them as proponents of '*nirguṇa* bhakti'. The majority of the papers in this volume are concerned with this second group of Sants.

The concept of '*nirguṇa* bhakti' as a distinct devotional mode contrasting with '*saguṇa* bhakti', and of the Sants constituting a separate devotional tradition, is relatively new. The idea that there is a coherent body of Sant teachings (*sant mat*) and that individual Sants belong to a common spiritual line of descent (*sant paramparā*) distinct from that of sectarian Vaishnavas did not become fully crystallized until the mid-nineteenth century. Originating in certain late esoteric Sant circles more self-conscious about belonging to a tradition than were the earlier Sants, it has however gained general acceptance among the members of Sant panths (communities of shared belief and practice). In the past fifty years, it has also been given currency in scholarly circles, replacing the older understanding of the Sants as "reformed" or "syncretistic" Vaishnavas. The pioneering works in this regard were Pitambar D. Barthwal's *The Nirguṇa School of Hindi Poetry* (1936) and Parashuram Chaturvedi's historical study published in 1952, *Uttarī Bhārat kī sant-paramparā* (The Sant Tradition of North India). The more recent work of Charlotte Vaudeville and W.H. McLeod also reflects this point of view, as does the present volume.

Who then belongs to the *sant paramparā*? In the case of the tradition in Maharashtra it is quite clear. All the Marathi-speaking poets of the Vithoba cult and those following their teachings have been integrated since the thirteenth century into a single panth, called the Varkari or pilgrims' panth because of the annual pilgrimage to Pandharpur that is its central focus. The Varkaris recognize a succession of some fifty poet-saints over a period of five hundred years, all of whose lives are recorded in a standard hagiographic work of the eighteenth century. Among them, the most important are four: (1) Jnaneshvar (Dnyandev), who is usually credited with founding the panth and wrote a commentary on the *Bhagavad-Gītā*, the *Jñāneśvarī*, that is a fundamental text of the panth; (2) Namdev (1270-1350), whose forceful championship of the panth helped spread its influence in Maharashtra, and whose travels to North India established a link between the two regional Sant traditions; (3) Eknath (1548-1600), an erudite scholar who, in addition to composing devotional lyrics, adapted many important bhakti works into Marathi; and (4) Tukaram (1598-1649), composer of the most beloved lyrics of the panth.

The Sant tradition of the North presents a more fragmented picture. Instead of a single panth there are many, each with its separate history going back to a particular founding figure. In addition to these, there are a large number of Sants who were neither the founders of panths nor affiliated to any panth, but are still regarded as being part of the tradition. What binds the North Indian Sants together is neither an historical connection nor an institutional focus, but the similarity in their teachings. That they themselves perceived this commonality is clear from the numerous references in their poetry to both "the Sants" as a spiritual fellowship and to specific historical Sants. Not only this, but one of the major genres of North Indian Sant literature is anthologies compiled from the songs and utterances of different Sants, the most important of which have attained the status of canonical scriptures. Despite the institutional fragmentation, there is thus a strong sense of spiritual unity.

The earliest Sants of the northern *paramparā* are said to have been disciples of Swami Ramanand, a Vaishnava reformer who lived in Banaras some time between the fourteenth and the third quarter of the fifteenth century. According to Vaishnava hagiography, Ramanand was in the direct line of descent from Ramanuja, the great teacher of the southern Shri Vaishnavas, but came to disagree with the sect's strict dietary restrictions and caste exclusiveness. Breaking away from his own teacher, he founded the Ramanandi sect, which was more liberal

An assembly of dervishes, with Sufi saints in the background and a group of Sants and Yogis seated in the foreground. Mughal, mid-seventeenth century. (Victoria and Albert Museum, London, I.S. 94-1965)

frontispiece

THE SANTS

STUDIES IN
A DEVOTIONAL TRADITION OF INDIA

EDITED BY

Karine Schomer

AND

W. H. McLeod

MOTILAL BANARSIDASS
Delhi Varanasi Patna Madras

First Published: *1987*

MOTILAL BANARSIDASS
Bungalow Road, Jawahar Nagar, Delhi 110 007
Branches
Chowk, Varanasi 221 001
Ashok Rajpath, Patna 800 004
120 Royapettah High Road, Mylapore, Madras 600 004

ISBN: 81-208-0277-2 AACR 2

Library of Congress Cataloging in Publication Data
Library of Congress Card Number: 83-72272

PRINTED IN INDIA

BY JAINENDRA PRAKASH JAIN AT SHRI JAINENDRA PRESS, A-45 NARAINA INDUSTRIAL AREA, PHASE I, NEW DELHI 110 028 AND PUBLISHED BY NARENDRA PRAKASH JAIN FOR MOTILAL BANARSIDASS, DELHI 110 007.

and worshipped Ram as its supreme deity. Out of his teachings, two divergent schools of bhakti arose. The first, more conservative, held to the doctrine of incarnation and worshipped the *saguṇa* Ram and his consort Sita; its greatest exponent was Tulsi Das, the author of the Hindi *Rāmāyaṇa*. The second school was that of the Sants, who completely rejected orthodox practices, and worshipped under the name 'Ram' the transcendent and formless *nirguṇa* aspect of divinity; greatest among this group was Kabir, the preeminent figure of the northern Sant tradition.

Recent scholarship has tended to doubt this whole interpretation of the origins of the northern Sants. It is rejected, first of all, on chronological grounds: it is simply not possible for Ramanand to have had all the disciples attributed to him. Secondly, it is pointed out, nowhere in the preserved utterances of the early Sants is there any mention of Ramanand, or of any other human guru. Instead, the Sants appear as independent figures whose spiritual awareness is based on personal mystical experience alone. What is likely is that later tradition invented the connection with Ramanand in order to give them Brahmanical respectability by affiliating them with the orthodox mainstream of the bhakti movement; because of his liberal views, he was at least a plausible guru for these largely low-caste men and women. The popular legend that Kabir, as a Muslim, had to trick Ramanand into accepting him as a disciple, is also highly suggestive in this regard.

Little is known about the very earliest northern Sants—the predecessors and contemporaries of Kabir. The names of some of them (Sena, Pipa, Dhanna, Sadhana, Raidas, etc.) have come down to us in the traditional list of disciples attributed to Ramanand, and the Sikh scriptures (the *Ādi Granth*) contain some of their utterances as well. A few panths may have developed among their followers, but they soon decayed and are no longer in existence today. It is to Kabir that all later tradition looks back as the fountainhead of the Sant movement. Though he never intended to found a panth, and there is no direct historical connection between him and later Sants, all of them consider him their spiritual ancestor. Beyond the Kabir-panth and the Sant tradition as a concrete historical movement, moreover, Kabir's influence has spread throughout the northern part of India, his sayings so widespread that they are part of proverbial lore and his name virtually a household word.

In the century and a half following Kabir, two Sants stand out most prominently: Nanak (1469-1539), founder of the panth that evolved into the Sikh religion, and Dadu Dayal of Rajasthan (1544-1603). Both were unquestionably influenced by Kabir's thought, even though they reworked it in unique ways of their own. In both the Dadu-panth and the Sikh tradition, moreover, Kabir himself is accorded a position of great honor. Among other things, he is the most prominent of the early Sants or 'Bhagats' included in the *Ādi Granth*, as well as one of the five revered Sants figuring in the devotional *Pañchvāṇī* anthologies of the Dadu-panth.

Kabir, Nanak and Dadu are thus the major figures of the northern Sant tradition in its formative years. The panths they founded or inspired are also the oldest surviving Sant communities today. The Sikh community is by far the most important, now over 13 million in number and with a distinct religious way of life that has not only removed it from the Hindu fold but also distanced it considerably from its Sant origins. The Kabir-panth, currently estimated to have around 2.5 million adherents, is active in several areas, particularly Madhya Pradesh and eastern Uttar Pradesh, as a religious community of the dispossessed. The Dadu-panth, numerically less strong than the other two panths, is nevertheless influential in Rajasthan because of a special historical connection with the Jaipur state. All three Sants and the panths claiming them as founders are examined in this volume.

Though the time period in which Kabir, Nanak and Dadu flourished was the most creative phase of the northern *sant paramparā*, the tradition continued to expand during the seventeenth and eighteenth centuries. Besides the consolidation and growth of the established panths, there was a proliferation of new ones as well. Most of the Sants who appeared during this period have yet to be studied in depth, though texts containing their utterances have been coming out for some time and the work of Barthwal and Chaturvedi has provided at least an overview of their history and interrelationships. Among these late medieval Sants, some of the most noteworthy are the following: (1) Malukdas (1573-1671), a Sant who was associated especially with the area around Allahabad and Lucknow; (2) Prannath (1617-1693), who lived in Bundelkhand, had the famous Bundel raja Chhatrasal as a disciple, and was known for his extreme religious eclecticism; (3) Dharanidas and Dariya Sahib, two influential Sants of Bihar who lived at the turn of the eighteenth century and whose followers are numerous even today; (4) Jagjivandas (1669-1760), who revived the earlier Satnami panth and propagated it among Untouchables in northeastern Uttar Pradesh; (5) Charandas (1702-1781), who tried to harmonize *nirguṇa* teachings with the worship of Radha and Krishna, and was especially influential around Delhi and in eastern Punjab; and (6) Paltu Sahib, a late eighteenth-century Sant who lived in Ayodhya and came into conflict with the Ramaite ascetics there because of his fierce condemnation of idol worship and caste exclusiveness.

For all the religious traditions of India, the nineteenth century was an age of rationalistic reform, during which the attempt was made to systematize beliefs and make practices consistent with doctrines. Tulsi Sahib of Hathras (ca. 1760-1843) was at once heir to certain esoteric tendencies in later Sant tradition and a precursor of the new spirit. Stressing the unity of the Sants as a *paramparā*, he taught what he believed to be the common core of doctrines implicit in all the Sants (*sant mat*), and tried to reverse the spread of *saguṇa* beliefs and practices among the followers of *nirguṇa* panths. Heavily indebted to him was Shiv Dayal Singh (1818-1878), founder of the modern Radhasoami movement. This growing movement, which is especially popular among the educated middle classes of North India, regards itself and is regarded by many as the principal manifestation of the northern *sant paramparā* in the present age.

To what extent is it justifiable to speak of the *sant paramparā* as distinct from the Vaishnava devotional tradition? Although there are clear differences between the religious outlook of the Sant poets and that of poets associated with the *saguṇa* worship of the incarnations of Vishnu, there are also many important points on which they coincide. Thus the northern Sants use Vaishnava names for their *nirguṇa* deity, while the god Vithoba of the Maharashtrian Sant tradition is considered to be a form of Vishnu. Sants also share with Vaishnavas a belief in grace and the power of the divine name, the idea that the relationship between the human soul and God is that of lover and beloved, an emphasis on the pain of separation (*viraha*) as leading to spiritual enlightenment, and the view that salvation is attainable by all. Sants and Vaishnavas also share common ethical ideals. Their similarities have been further emphasized by the North Indian tradition of Vaishnava hagiography that developed from the sixteenth century onward, which has consistently included the major Sants as Vaishnava devotees.

Despite these important areas of commonality, however, there are significant differences as well—especially marked in the case of the northern Sants. Thus while the Sants use Vaishnava names for God, they do not worship the incarnations of Vishnu or accept the Vaishnava scriptures, and are not affiliated to any of the orthodox bhakti schools or *sampradāys*. They are also indifferent to the authority of the Vedas, reject the priestly prerogatives of Brahmans and oppose the outer forms of devotion associated with *saguṇa* bhakti. Finally, while the orthodox Vaishnava tradition has affirmed at the level of doctrine that salvation is open to all regardless of social status, ritual barriers between high and low castes have not really been challenged at the level of practice, and leadership has remained almost exclusively in the hands of Brahmans. The Sants, by contrast, have been uncompromising in their opposition to caste hierarchy and exclusiveness, and the great majority of the leading figures in the tradition have been from lower castes.

In many ways, the Sants are closer in spirit to the heterodox religious traditions of India—the Buddhists, the Jains and the esoteric Shaivite tradition of the Nath Yogis—than they are to the orthodox mainstream of Vaishnava devotional religion. In the case of the Naths, there is a clear continuity of attitudes and themes, and the general scholarly consensus is that the Sants represent a synthesis of Vaishnava bhakti and elements from the tradition of the Naths. The Sants also have many points of commonality with the Islamic Sufis, who were present in India from the twelfth century onward and contributed to the religious environment in which the Sant tradition evolved.

As a non-conformist 'counter-tradition' that transcended established religious categories and challenged many of the beliefs and practices of orthodox bhakti, the Sants are also close in spirit to certain non-sectarian movements and figures in other regions of India. Two of these, the Bauls of Bengal and the Tamil Siddhas, are discussed in this volume. Others include the Virashaivas of Karnataka, the tradition of Shaiva bhakti associated with the great Kashmiri mystic Lal Ded, and independent figures such as the Gujarati poet-saint Narsi Mehta.

While the historical Sant panths of North India, the Varkari panth of Maharashtra and spiritually kindred movements elsewhere continue to function as organized religious communities in the present, their influence extends far beyond them, diffused throughout the contemporary religious culture of India. Their radical form of bhakti has been especially attractive to modern intellectuals and social reformers, for whom an interior religion of the heart combined with ethical behavior and egalitarian social values is more congenial than the complexities of divine incarnations, image worship, temple ritual, orthodox rules of behavior and the intermediary role of the Brahman priesthood. In every region, the 'counter-tradition' has been a rallying point for those challenging the status quo and its injustices. Rabindranath Tagore was a great admirer of both Kabir and the Bauls, while for Mahatma Gandhi, Kabir, Narsi Mehta and the Sant tradition as a whole were both a source of inspiration and a medium through which he articulated his message to the masses.

To explore aspects of the Sant tradition and related movements, a conference was held in Berkeley, California in May 1978. Jointly sponsored by the Graduate Theological Union and the Center for South and Southeast Asia Studies at the University of California, the conference brought together scholars from several disciplines and countries currently working on the Sants or other non-conformist bhakti traditions. Scholars of the classical orthodox heritage were also present to help place the Sants in perspective. The majority of the papers included in this volume were originally prepared for the conference.

The papers are grouped into four sections. Those in the first provide background perspectives for the more specialized contributions that follow. The second group deals with the literature of the Sant tradition, the third with the organized communities that have evolved out of the teachings and followings of the Sants. The fourth section is devoted to related movements.

Background

Charlotte Vaudeville introduces the subject matter of this volume by presenting an overview of Sant religious attitudes and spiritual practices as a blend of Vaishnava bhakti and the esoteric Tantric tradition mediated through the Nath Yogis. She argues that the core of Sant teaching is heterodox and not assimilable to Vaishnava bhakti, yet the sensibility and ethical ideals of Sants and Vaishnavas are very close. Likewise, while the Sants direct their devotion to a *nirguṇa* deity that is beyond the qualifications of concrete personality, they express it through the familiar love symbolism of the *saguṇa* Vaishnava tradition. Finally, the Sants reject the outer forms of Vaishnava practice (idol worship, temple ritual, pilgrimage, etc.) and advocate an interiorized Yoga, but share the Vaishnava belief in the saving power of the divine Name and the spiritual benefit of keeping company with true devotees.

The next two papers situate the paradoxical Sant concept of *nirguṇa* bhakti within the broader perspective of philosophic and popular Hinduism. *Frits Staal*, equating the *nirguṇa* god of the Sants with the ineffable *nirguṇa* Brahman or Absolute-without-qualities of the monistic Vedanta tradition, demonstrates that *nirguṇa* bhakti is a logical impossibility. Yet mystical traditions everywhere have sought and affirmed the possibility of a relationship with the ineffable. Therefore, he concludes, in India as elsewhere, devotion and philosophical reflection are not compatible activities. *Wendy O'Flaherty* suggests that the concept of a *nirguṇa* god is a creation of monistic philosophers and fundamentally at odds with the natural bhakti impulse of the Hindu masses, which has always been resolutely *saguṇa.* There exists in Hinduism, as is clear from the Epic and Puranic texts as well as the structure of temple architecture, an unresolved tension between *nirguṇa* and *saguṇa* images of deity. The contribution of the Sants was to challenge the whole distinction with a conception of deity that transcends it.

Andrew Rawlinson concludes this section by proposing a topology of bhakti according to which the Sant tradition can be situated as a religious system. The various schools of bhakti that preceded the Sants can be ranged between the poles of love and meditation, or conceptions of God as a person and as a state of being. Along another axis, they can also be placed on a continuum between structured and unstructured paths to salvation. The genius of the Sants was to have blended together all these dimensions of bhakti while at the same time rejecting the peripheral trappings of the concrete historical traditions that had been their carriers.

Literature

The first two papers in this section explore particular literary genres. *Karine Schomer* focuses on the *dohā* couplet used by the North Indian Sants. Particularly suited to aphoristic statement, it has a long history among the Jain, Buddhist and Nath Yogi predecessors of the Sants as a vehicle for the propagation of religious teachings. Traditionally, it also serves to express intense feeling, particularly in women's folksongs on the theme of *viraha* or separation. Fusing these two streams, the North Indian Sants developed the *dohā* into a characteristic form for the expression of their religious ideas and sensibility, investing it with the status of *sākhī* or authoritative utterance. Examining the *dohā*s of the Sants as poetic statements of a generalized nature, Schomer stresses the need to study the different rhetorical contexts in which they can occur: as the original utterances of particular Sants in response to specific situations, as verses incorporated into later written texts governed by ordering principles of their own, and as units of speech available for use in present-day discourse situations.

Whereas Schomer deals with one of the major genres of North

Indian Sant poetry, *Eleanor Zelliot* focuses instead on a minor genre of the Maharashtrian Sants that has not been studied so far. The *bhāruḍ*, a kind of drama-poem that puts the Sant message in the mouths of different types of low-caste, low-status people, is atypical in that Sants usually restrict their poetry to the expression of their own experience. Full of vulgar speech and describing in graphic detail the life of the lowly, these poems are even more surprising as the compositions of Eknath, who was a Brahman and a scholar. Intended to instruct the lowest levels of society in the way of bhakti, Eknath's *bhāruḍ*s reveal in a dramatic manner the Sants' spiritual egalitarianism and concern to make salvation available to all.

The next three papers deal with the towering figure of Kabir. *Linda Hess* begins with a comparative study of the three principal written traditions of Kabir: the Kabir-panthi tradition of the East preserved in the *Bījak*, and the Sikh and Dadu-panthi traditions of the West. Two different Kabir personae emerge from the comparison: in terms of language, attitudes and themes, the Western Kabir is more devotional, while the Eastern Kabir is more harsh and intellectual. Challenging present scholarly concensus on the priority of the Western tradition, Hess makes a case for the Eastern tradition based on the congruency between its pungent style and the forceful personality universally attributed to Kabir. In a second paper, Hess analyzes the style of the *Bījak* more closely, presenting Kabir as a master of the "rough rhetoric" of challenge and assault. Contrasting his blunt immediacy and radical honesty with the idealized world-view of classical Indian poetry, she finds him the most "modern" of pre-modern Indian poets. The particular genius of his poetry, she says, lies in its power to jolt listeners into facing the truth about themselves and the world, pushing them to the brink of the mystical realization they both fear and long for.

Vijay Mishra takes up the problem of translating Kabir and critiques Rabindranath Tagore's well known *One Hundred Poems of Kabir.* By closely analyzing one poem, he demonstrates that Tagore makes Kabir conform to his own personal religiosity and the monotheistic reinterpretation of Hinduism characteristic of the Indian Renaissance. Tagore transforms Kabir stylistically as well, using as his model the loose mystical verse of the late Romantics and early Yeats rather than a more direct and forceful style such as that of the Metaphysicals. Tagore's translation is an example of what happens when the poetic tradition of the receptor language is given more importance than that of the source language, or when the translator makes an inappropriate choice of stylistic period from within the receptor tradition.

Turning from poetic to hagiographic literature, and from literary to textual problems, *Winand Callewaert* surveys the sources available for the life of the Rajasthani Sant Dadu in an attempt to uncover the kernel of truth out of which later traditions grew. The problems and patterns he encounters are characteristic of Indian hagiographic texts in general and biographies of the Sants in particular. First, all later accounts are based on just a few early sources that are usually very scant. Second, alteration and embellishment begin very soon after the initial composition. Finally, changes are influenced by both sectarian motivations and by archetypes for the life and behavior of a Sant. Thus in later sources, Callewaert finds Dadu's low-caste status deliberately obscured, clear suggestions that he was of divine origin, and typical incidents such as a visit from the emperor Akbar.

In the final contribution to this section, *John Hawley* examines the *vinaya* poems (songs of petition and self-remonstration) of the famous Krishnaite poet Surdas, and finds in them many of the themes usually considered characteristic of Sant religion. In manuscripts predating the recasting of Surdas to conform to the beliefs of the Vallabha sect, these poems appear as an integral part of Sur's message, rather than being relegated to the "pre-conversion" phase of his life. This suggests that in the period before the rise of the Krishnaite sects of North India, the distinction between Sants and Vaishnavas was not as marked as it later became. The theological distinction between *saguṇa* and *nirguṇa* conceptions of deity should not obscure the thematic connections that bind Sants and Vaishnavas together as part of a single overall movement. There is a Sant side to Sur's religious sensibility, and indeed, tc that of every Vaishnava bhakta.

Movements

In the first paper of this section, *Charlotte Vaudeville* examines the Sant tradition of Maharashtra from the point of view of its indebtedness to the older Shaiva, in particular Nath Yogi, religious substratum of the region. Though the Sants of Maharashtra tend to be viewed as essentially Vaishnava, they are a result of the interpenetration of the Nath Yogi tradition and a nominal kind of Vaishnavism. The blurring of sectarian lines is seen in the spiritual lineage of Jnaneshvar, the founding figure of the tradition, and in his *Jñāneśvarī*, the fundamental text of the Maharashtrian Sants. It can also be seen in the icon of the god Vitthala, and in both the biography and the poetry of other Sants, in particular Namdev and Narsi Mehta of Gujarat. This ecumenical attitude is typical of the early Sants and persists to a large degree in later tradition as well.

The next three papers focus on the Sikhs. *W.H. McLeod* begins by tracing the evolution of the Sikh Panth from the standard early Sant pattern of a loose cluster of disciples to its present status as a clearly defined community recognized as a separate religion. Factors contributing to this unique line of institutional development include Nanak's appointment of a successor and hence the establishment of a clear line of Gurus, the largely uni-caste constituency of the Panth, the compilation of the *Ādi Granth*, contests over succession to the Guruship, the experience of external attack, the emergence of the Khalsa as an armed brotherhood and the definition of orthodoxy in terms of adherence to that brotherhood's code of conduct, the modern reform movement's drive to bring about greater consistency in doctrine and practice, the pattern of political involvement of recent years and, finally, the experience of the Sikh diaspora. In the process of this evolution, the interior religion preached by Nanak and the Sants has been overlaid by an emphasis on external forms, and loyalty to the Sant heritage exists side-by-side with a militant sectarian identity.

Within the context of this shift to outward standards of piety, McLeod examines next the emergence of a new kind of religious figure among the Sikhs: the modern Sant. Devout men with a militant sense of religious duty, Sikh Sants live in rural establishments called *ḍerās*, where they impart instruction in Sikh belief and practice, providing the faithful with personal religious leadership and attracting permanent followings. They thus represent a tradition of subsidiary master-disciple relationships within the Sikh Panth. Though the use of the title 'Sant' is a recent phenomenon, the role is to be found in the earlier history of the Panth as well, and has its ultimate antecedents in India's ancient tradition of reverence for individuals distinguished by pious behavior. The modern Sant is not necessarily a person who has experienced spiritual enlightenment, and is thus of lesser stature than the early Sants and the Sikh Gurus. The distance which the term *sant* has travelled from its original meaning to present-day Sikh usage is a reflection of the evolution of the Panth itself.

Since the late 1960s, modern Sants have begun to make periodic appearances in Sikh communities overseas. On the basis of field work among the Sikhs of northern California, *Bruce LaBrack* examines the role visiting Sants play in the life of these communities. He finds that behavior and attitudes towards Sants are not the same as in India. Overseas, the Sant receives more overt attention, but engenders less personal commitment. Furthermore, he is valued less for his message than for his function as a cultural representative and as a symbol of the Sikh faith. Finally, his presence serves to make a statement about the image of itself which the community wants to present. As a result, the choice to invite a particular Sant, and the Sant's words and behavior during his visit, can frequently exacerbate already existing divisions within the community.

Next after the Sikh panth in numerical strength and social importance is the Kabir-panth. *David Lorenzen* examines its present-day structure and recent history in order to determine in what ways the element of social protest in Kabir's teachings has been used by its adherents. The Kabir-panth's recruitment has been primarily from two economically and socially marginal groups: tribals and low-caste Hindus. In both cases, membership in the panth has made possible greater personal dignity through rejection of caste hierarchy at an ideological level, but at the same time has facilitated de facto accomodation to it by encouraging the adoption of higher-status 'Sanskritic' behavior (i.e. vegetarianism and abstention from alcohol). Thus it would appear that, instead of challenging the whole system, Kabir's social protest has been modified to meet the more immediate ideological and cultural needs of the panth's followers.

The last two papers in this section deal with the modern Radhasoami movement. Two complementary perspectives are presented: *Daniel Gold* takes the point of view of Radhasoami doctrine to interpret the Sant tradition as a whole, while *Mark Juergensmeyer* examines the Radhasoami movement from the point of view of the earlier Sants. The problem Gold addresses with the help of Radhasoami perceptions is how such a disparate group of individuals as the Sants can be said to form a coherent tradition. Using metaphors from the world of biological kinship and its extension in the world of medieval feudal relations, he sees the Sant tradition as held together by two principles: a concept of organic relationship between guru and disciple which generates *lineages*, and a sense that genuine Sants of any lineage form a vaguely related spiritual *clan*. The Sant at the head of any lineage is a living embodiment of the divine and a mediator of spiritual power, which is passed on like a physical substance through the lineage's succession of gurus. In this sense, each lineage is unique, but at the same time, there is a recognition of the gurus of other Sant lineages as transmitters of the same *kind* of spiritual substance, and therefore as worthy of veneration and a source of secondary inspiration.

Looking at the Radhasoami movement itself, Mark Juergensmeyer asks whether its claim to being a modern revival of the Sant tradition is justified. All the major elements of Sant doctrine are present, but each is developed in a unique way: the *nirguṇa* object of worship is given a name, the interior path of spirituality is mapped out in great detail, and the concept of *satsaṅg* or spiritual companionship takes on a meaning akin to 'church'. The most far-reaching departures, however, are in the exalted concept of the human guru as mediator of spiritual power or transmitter of secret knowledge, and in the elaboration of a complex cosmology. In these as in several other matters, the Radhasoamis are indebted to an esoteric strand of Sant belief that developed during the eighteenth century in one of the branches of the Kabirpanth. It is this late tradition that is being revived by the Radhasoami movement rather than the tradition of the early Sants.

Related Traditions

The tradition most consistently linked to the Sants in popular belief is that of the Indian Sufis, but scholarly opinion is divided over the nature and the extent of the interaction. *Bruce Lawrence* opens this section with an assessment of the various possible grounds for claiming Sufi influence on the Sants. First, there are the encounters with Sufis related in Sant hagiographics; mostly fictional, they only prove that the theme of encounter served some kind of legitimizing function. Secondly, there is Sant use of Sufi technical terms, but it is a negligible factor. Third, there is the appearance of hagiography as a literary genre, an event likely to have been inspired by the well developed Sufi tradition of religious biography. The most convincing argument, however, is the presence in Sant poetry of numerous affinities to the Sufi outlook: the rejection of ceremonial and scriptural authority, the interior vision of an ineffable God, the emphasis on intense pain in man's love relationship with the divine, and the vision of suffering as necessary to an understanding of the true meaning of love.

Arguments about Sufi influence also exist in relation to the Baul poets of Bengal. Challenging the dominant view of the Bauls as being primarily influenced by Vaishnava bhakti, *Edward Dimock* shows that they are equally indebted to Sufism and to the esoteric tradition of Tantric Yoga. Like the Sants of North India and Maharashtra, the

Bauls exist at the confluence of three powerful currents of religious feeling and expression, and draw freely on the imagery and vocabulary of all three. Like the Sants as well, the Bauls are ultimately committed to an interior religion of the heart that transcends the outer aspects of all historical traditions.

The major medieval 'counter-tradition' of the Tamil area is that of the Siddhas or Cittars. In the last paper of this section, *K. Kailasapathy* presents an outline of their ideas, history and literature. Though emerging out of Shaivism rather than Vaishnavism, and on the whole less devotional in tone, the Siddhas can rightly be considered a southern analogue of the Sants. Like the Sants, they were mostly from low castes, had a connection with the Naths, held to an abstract idea of the divine, opposed idol-worship and temple ritual, challenged the authority of scriptures, and rejected caste hierarchy. As poets too, they resembled the Sants in that they composed in a rough popular idiom, using folk forms. Where they differed to a certain extent was in having a more pronounced esoteric component to their teaching, and in the cultivation of a practical tradition of astrology, medicine and alchemy. The legacy of the Tamil Siddhas, like that of the northern Sants, has made itself felt far beyond their immediate followings and belongs to the culture as a whole.

In an appendix, *Elinor Gadon* offers comments on the Mughal miniature painting reproduced as frontispiece to this volume. A seventeenth-century work of unknown authorship, it expresses a vision of the commonality between Hindu and Muslim mystics by portraying together in a single scene the great saints of Sufism and the major figures of the Sant tradition. Gadon theorizes that the painting may have been produced under the patronage of the Mughal prince Dara Shikoh, who was famed for his broadness of religious outlook and his interest in building bridges between the two religious communities. Finally, as an aid to readers, W.H. McLeod has compiled a glossary of unfamiliar Indic terms, and Karine Schomer an annotated bibliography on the Sants and related traditions. Prepared with the help of recommendations by contributors to this volume, the bibliography includes primary sources and translations as well as secondary works.

The editors of this volume would like to express their appreciation to Professor Bruce Pray, former director of the University of California's Center for South and Southeast Asia Studies, for his support of the 1978 conference, and to Professor Mark Juergensmeyer of the Graduate Theological Union for his help in organizing the conference and his guidance in the preparation of the volume for publication. We also appreciate the editorial, typing and coordinating assistance given by Anita Miller and Lucinda Glenn Rand. We are grateful to the Victoria and Albert Museum in London for permission to reproduce the miniature painting used as frontispiece and on the dust-jacket.

The Sants is dedicated to the memory of K. Kailasapathy. As a participant in the 1978 conference and a Visiting Professor at Berkeley during the spring of that year, he made himself beloved to both colleagues and students by his combination of scholarly integrity, intellectual enthusiasm and personal warmth. His sudden death in 1982 was a shock to all of us and a great loss to the scholarly world.

SECTION I

BACKGROUND

SANT MAT: SANTISM AS THE UNIVERSAL PATH TO SANCTITY

CHARLOTTE VAUDEVILLE

Who were the Sants ?

From the fourteenth century onwards, in northern and central India, there is an efflorescence of religious poetry whose authors are known as Sants or 'poet-saints'. Mostly Hindus, some of them Muslim-born, the Sants cannot be easily classified from a metaphysical or religious point of view. There is no adequate translation of the expression *sant mat* (literally the 'mind' or 'point of view' of the Sants), which has sometimes been referred to as 'Santism'. The 'tradition of the Sants' (*sant paramparā*) is essentially non-sectarian, though a number of Sant poets have been considered the founders of sects which bear their name but have developed after them. Moreover, the Sant tradition is the only one in medieval and modern India which has crossed the frontier between the Hindu and the Muslim blocks and, to some extent, has established some bridges between the two communities.

Who were the Sants? Socially, they belonged to the lower strata of Hindu and Muslim society: nearly all were Shudras, some of them even Atishudras, i.e. Untouchables. They were poor, mostly uneducated or even illiterate; quite a few were women. They had no access or right to Brahmanical knowledge, were not acquainted with Sanskrit and could only express themselves in the local languages of the people, the archaic Indo-Aryan vernaculars of Hindustan and central India. With the possible exception of Marathi,[1] these languages were still in a state of infancy, apparently not suited to the expression of metaphysical or mystical truth. The poetry of the Sants largely contributed to the

1. The poet Jnaneshvar or Jnandev, considered by the Maharashtrian Sants as their *ādi-guru*, was the author of the *Bhāvārtha-dīpikā* (better known as the *Jñāneś-varī*), a versified commentary in Old Marathi on the *Bhagavad Gītā*; this monumental work was completed in 1290 A.D. The language of the *Jñāneśvarī* is definitely much more archaic than the language of the *abhaṅg* literature composed by Namdev and the other Sants of Maharashtra, including a number of *abhaṅg*s attributed to Jnaneshvar himself and to his brothers and sister. About that chronological problem, see Charlotte Vaudeville, *L'Invocation: Le Haripāth de Dnyāndev* (Paris: École Française d'Extrême-Orient, 1969), pp. 1-3.

development of the northern vernaculars into 'literary' languages. It was especially the case with Hindi, which was to become the national language of India in modern times.[2]

The *sant paramparā* may be divided into two main groups. The northern group of Sants includes poets from the northwestern provinces of Punjab and Rajasthan and from the Gangetic valley, including eastern Uttar Pradesh. The poets of that group, whose figurehead is Kabir, express themselves in a rough form of archaic Hindi which was apparently used as a kind of *lingua franca* for popular preaching by itinerant holy men. The southern group's language is archaic ('Middle') Marathi, used by Nama or Namdev and the other Sants of Maharashtra from the fourteenth century onwards.

Addressing themselves to the common folk, the Sants expressed themselves in oral style. Their compositions took the form of short utterances. In the north, these were distichs (*dohā*s) or short rhymed poems (*pad*s) with a refrain. The *dohā*, a meter inherited from Apabhramsa, is mostly a didactic form; in the Sant tradition, it is usually referred to as *sākhī*, literally 'witness'. The *pad* is a short lyric set to a musical mode (raga) and meant to be sung, the refrain (*ṭek* or *dhruva*) being repeated in a chorus between each verse. The *pad* form is closely linked to folk song: many *pad*s composed by the Sants look like folk songs with a religious or ethical message. Similarly, in the Deccan, the Marathi *abhaṅg*s, based on the ancient folk form known as *ovī*, appear as a close equivalent of the northern *pad*. Both the *dohā* and *pad* of northern India and the *abhaṅg* in the Deccan have remained very popular forms down to this day, since they are perfectly adapted to the ear and taste of the common people, who are able to memorize them easily. Practically the whole of early Sant poetry was transmitted orally, at least until the beginning of the seventeenth century.[3]

Heterodoxy and Non-Conformity

The Sants are non-sectarian and do not hold a body of doctrine in common. Yet in spite of differences between the two main groups and

2. The contribution of the northern Sants — themselves preceded by the Shaiva Nath-panthis or Gorakhnathis, the disciples of Gorakhnath — to the development of the Hindi language has been considerable. Kabir himself has been heralded as 'the founder of Hindi poetry'.

3. The first collection of Sant poetry which bears a definite date is in the *Ādi Granth* or *Gurū Granth* of the Sikhs, compiled by Guru Arjan in 1603-04.

between individual poets within each group in matters of religious belief, they have certain characteristics in common which mark them as distinct from 'learned' poets on the one hand and sectarian religious poets on the other. Sant poetry as a whole has strong anti-Brahmanical overtones. As Hindus, and even more as Muslims, the Sants appear more or less heterodox. In so far as orthodoxy, in a Hindu context, may be defined in terms of acceptance of the authority of the Veda and the Brahmanical tradition as a whole, the Sants appear as some kind of 'heretics'. The Maharashtrian Sants, however, remain rooted within the Hindu fold. They do not formally reject the great Vedantic tradition or the authority of the Veda, but occasionally pay lip service to it. They retain a strong link with the Bhagavata or non-sectarian Vaishnava tradition and claim to be the descendants of all the great bhaktas of old whose heroic lives are narrated in the Puranas and the spiritual heirs of the great saint Jnandev (Jnaneshvar). On the other hand, the northern Sants, led by Kabir, appear as extremists: they reject the Veda altogether and make fun of all Vedic teaching, rituals and knowledge. The Muslims among them, especially Kabir, reject the authority of the Qur'an as well. Actually it is not simply *śruti* and *smṛti* which they reject or disregard, but the authority of Scripture as such— the value and prestige of 'the Book', which, in Hinduism, remains the privilege of the Brahman pandit. Not only do the Sants as a whole contest that privilege, but they hold that man has no need of 'holy books' to attain salvation, nay, that such books are an obstacle in the spiritual path. In the words of Kabir:

> Reading book after book the whole world died
> and none ever became 'learned' (*paṇḍit*)!
>
> *KG sākhī* 33.3[4]

Though the Sants are not considered *nirgrantha* (literally 'book-

4. *KG* refers to the edition of the *Kabīr-granthāvalī* established by P.N. Tiwari (Allahabad: University of Allahabad, Hindi Parishad, 1961); *sākhī* refers to the *sākhī* collection in the same edition, the first number corresponding to the chapter [*aṅga*] and the second to the verse number. The translations are culled from Charlotte Vaudeville, *Kabīr*, vol. 1 (Oxford: Clarendon Press, 1974); *pad* refers to the *pad*s found in the same P.N. Tiwari edition. *AG* refers to the *Ādi Granth* or *Gurū Granth*, published in Amritsar by the Shiromani Gurduara Parbandhak Kamiti and constantly reprinted as the only authoritative text. *BI* refers to the edition of the *Bījak* known as the 'Barabanki edition': Hansdas Shastri and Mahabir Prasad, eds., *Kabīr sāhab kā bījak* (Barabanki: Kabir Granth Prakashan Samiti, 1950). All the translations from *KG*, *AG* and *BI* are by the author.

less') as were the Jains, in practice they are as detached from scriptural authority as were the early Buddhists and Jains. They consider meaningless the Brahmans' pretensions to superior knowledge. The pandit's 'holy books' are compared to "a cell made of paper" in which to imprison fools.[5] In vain do naive folk look up to the Brahman for guidance:

> The Brahman is the guru of the world
> but he is not the guru of the devotees—
> He got entangled in his four Vedas
> and there he died!
>
> *KG sākhī* 21.4

The Sants deny the value of Brahmanical sacrifices and Brahmanical rites. As a whole, they reject idol-worship. They scoff at the Brahman in his role as performer of Hindu rites (*karamiyā*) and even more as *pujārī*, performer of the *pūjā* offering to the various Hindu divinities. Killer of human beings (in the animal sacrifices he performs), worshipper of stones, "the Brahman of this Kali age is a buffoon"—he has lost all dignity. His ignorance and his greed make him a laughing stock.[6]

In the matter of caste too, the Sants as a whole are resolutely nonconformist. The Brahman's pretension to perfect purity and his obsession with pollution are turned into ridicule by Kabir:

> Hey, pandit! Beware of that water you're drinking!
>
> *BI śabda* 47

Even the poor Chokhamela, the Untouchable poet of Pandharpur in Maharashtra, proclaims that the whole world is deep in filth and contests the claim of the Brahmans to purity:

> The body itself is the very source of filth.
> At the beginning and at the end, it is full of filth:
> Who is it then who could get pure? I do not know!
>
> In impurity they were born, in impurity they died:
> Steeped in impurity, all of them passed away![7]

5. *KG sākhī* 26.2.
6. *KG sākhī* 21.20. See also *sākhī* 21.21; on idol-worship, see *sākhī* 26.
7. Nanamaharaj Sakhare, ed., *Sakalasantagrantha* (Poona: India Printing Press, 1961), vol. 1, *abhaṅgs* 84, 83. The translations are by the author. About Chokhamela, see also Charlotte Vaudeville, "Cokhameḷā: An Untouchable Saint of Maharashtra," in *South Asian Digest of Regional Writing*, vol. 6 (Heidelberg: University of Heidelberg, 1977), pp. 67 ff.

Ritual barriers between the castes, based on the notion of pollution, are considered purely artificial and totally irrelevant to the man who seeks salvation. So are all the common practices of popular Hinduism, such as pilgrimage to holy spots (*tīrtha*) and holy baths supposed to wash away man's sins. Moreover, all magical performances, especially those connected with witchcraft and animal sacrifices or with immoral practices, such as those of the *vāmamārga* Shaktas, are emphatically condemned. The position of the Sants in these matters is identical to that of the Buddhists and Jains of old. Believing in the endless transmigration of souls (*jīva*) through the illusory world of *saṃsāra* they adhere to strict *ahiṃsa*, hold all living beings in reverence and reject all kinds of *pūjā*—even of flowers:

The gardener's wife picks flowers,
each flower is alive—
But that idol for which she picks them
is a lifeless stone!

AG Āsā 14

The only dignity the Sants recognize in the scale of living beings is that of being born a man, for a human body is "the boat to cross the Ocean of Existence"—and this chance is unique:

A human life is hard to get
and it comes only once:
The ripe fruit fallen on the ground
will never return to the branch!

KG sākhī 5.5

It is this belief in the uniqueness of human life, the intense awareness of the shortness of that lifespan in which salvation can be achieved and the hovering presence of death (*kāl*) which give to the warnings of Kabir their tragic intensity:

The mourners have died
and so have the pallbearers,
The weepers too have died:
to whom shall I cry for help?

KG sākhī 16.23

Today or tonight or tomorrow,
he will strike you on the way:

Man is the sparrow and *kāl* is the hawk,
suddenly, he strikes!

KG sākhī 16.28

This overpowering presence of death, in the Sants' view, negates all the pretensions of the Brahmans and those of the great and rich of this world:

Kabīr, for a little bit of life
people make a grand display—
Yet they all stand on the same road,
be they sultan, prince or tramp!

KG sākhī 15.43

Kabīr, do not pride yourself:
kāl holds you by the hair.
Who knows where he will strike you,
whether at home or abroad?

KG sākhī 15.44

Today or tomorrow or in five days
you will rest in the jungle:
Cattle will stray over your head
eating the grass.

KG sākhī 15.67

The Sants as Adepts of 'Nirguṇa *Bhakti'*

Rejecting as they do the plurality of gods as well as the Vaishnava doctrine of the avatars of the supreme Lord, the Sants appear as seekers of the Absolute, conceived as the One Godhead, the Ultimate Reality. In Indian tradition, *sant mat* has been equated with '*nirguṇa* bhakti', a term which would seem to define bhakti according to its objective: the non-qualified (*nirguṇa*) aspect of the supreme Brahman, the One non-personal, all-pervading, ineffable Reality which can only be spoken of in negative terms. This notion of the Absolute as *nirguṇa* coincides with the Upanishadic concept of the Brahman-Ātman and the *advaita* (monistic) interpretation of the Vedantic tradition, which denies any real distinction between the soul and God and urges man to recognize within himself his true divine nature. The northern Sants, led by Kabir, mostly seem to adopt this stance, speaking of merging or re-absorption of the finite soul, the *jīva,* into the infinite ineffable reality — or state — which is the ultimate goal:

The jar is in the water, the water in the jar:
Inside and outside, nothing but water!
KG pad 194

Actually, if we admit that there can be no real bhakti (from *bhaj°*, 'to participate' or 'to adore') without some distinction between the Lord (Bhagvan) and the devotee (bhakta), the very notion of '*nirguṇa* bhakti' seems to be a contradiction in terms.[8] If it signifies the abolition of all distinctions and the thorough merging of the illusory *jīva* into the One Reality so that all identity is lost forever, then '*nirguṇa* bhakti' would bring about the abolition of bhakti itself.

This monistic view of salvation as a total merging of the finite soul into the One Being, however, does not represent the prevailing view of the Sant poets as a whole. Kabir himself, the most *nirguṇī* of them all, is far from being consistent in this matter.[9] Most of the Sant poets express views which imply that they seek union with, rather than merging into, the One Being. Conceived as formless (*nirākāra*) and even devoid of qualities (*nirguṇa*), the supreme Being they worship or yearn for seems to be conceived more or less as Ishvara, the personal (though purely spiritual) aspect of the Godhead. For the Sants already, as for earlier Shaiva and for later Vaishnava bhaktas, *nirguṇa* is a somewhat magic word. They would talk of the ultimate object of their own bhakti as *nirguṇa*, but for them, *nirguṇa* should not be interpreted as 'that

8. For a discussion on this point, see Frits Staal, "The ineffable *Nirguṇa Brahmaṇ*," below in this volume.

9. The various collections of the 'Words of Kabir' (*Kabīr-vāṇī*) show considerable discrepancies, not only in language and expressions but also in doctrinal contents. The 'Western recension' includes both the Rajasthani (originally Dadu-panthi) recension, printed under the name *Kabīr-granthāvalī* on the one hand and the Punjabi recension, which corresponds to the verses attributed to the *bhagat* Kabir in the *Gurū Granth* of the Sikhs (see note 3). The 'Eastern recension' represents the various forms of the *Bījak*, a collection of *Kabīr-vāṇī* held as authentic by the sectarian Kabir-panthis, and compiled in eastern Uttar Pradesh in various forms at an unknown date. The comparison of the two main recensions shows that the *Bījak* emphasizes the *nirguṇa* aspect of the supreme Reality and borrows heavily from the tradition of Tantric Yoga, whereas both the *Kabīr-granthāvalī* and the *Gurū Granth* emphasize the bhakti element and show Vaishnava leanings, though maintaining a strong monotheistic attitude. Though neither of the two main recensions can claim total authenticity, and in the absence of ancient manuscripts (prior to the compilation of the *Gurū Granth*), the comparison of texts suggests that the original message of Kabir must have undergone a process of 'Vaishnavization' in the West before the beginning of the sixteenth century A.D. See Linda Hess's discussion of this process in her essay "Three Kabir Collections: A Comparative Study," below in this volume.

which is deprived of qualities' but rather as 'that which is beyond the three *guṇas*' (inherent to material nature, *prakṛti*) and even beyond the traditional distinction between the *nirguṇa* and the *saguṇa* aspects of the Godhead. This supreme Godhead is conceived as inaccessible to the senses, beyond all names and forms (*nāma-rūpa*), ineffable and essentially One. In the words of the Shaiva Kashmiri mystic Lal Ded:

> May He take from me, sick woman as I am,
> the disease of the world,
> Whether He be he, or he, or he, or he...[10]

With the exception of Kabir himself, who sometimes refers to the ultimate State or Reality as 'the Void' (*śūnya*), a view inherited from Tantric Buddhism,[11] the prevailing attitude of the Sants is monotheistic. They believe in one, absolute, ineffable Reality which transcends all the attributes and the whole world of transmigration, yet can be perceived and apprehended within the heart of the true seeker. It is to that Reality that the Sant should dedicate his own soul:

> As elusive as the path of a bird, as the track of a fish is He,
> says Kabir, as he ponders;
> The Highest Being ('Person', *puruṣottama*) is beyond the beyond
> (*aparampārapāra*):
> To this Form (*mūrti*) alone I dedicate myself!
>
> *KG pad* 108

Even the assertion of pure monotheism which characterizes *sant mat* as a whole ought to be qualified in connection with the religious attitude of the southern (Maharashtrian) Sants, all of them devotees of the god Vitthala (or Vithoba) of Pandharpur, in whom they contemplate a *svarūpa*, ('own form') of the god Vishnu-Krishna, the supreme Being, manifested in Pandharpur for the sake of his beloved bhaktas. The devotees of the god Vithoba are Vaishnava bhaktas—and they pride themselves in being called 'true Vaishnavas'. They do not hesitate to worship the 'body' of the Lord manifested in Pandharpur, in which they recognize a manifestation of the One, the eternal Godhead. This is true not only of Jnaneshvar, their earliest and foremost Sant, but of

10. *Lallā Vākyānī or the Wise Sayings of Lālded a Mystic Poetess of Ancient Kashmir*, trans. G. Grierson and L.D. Barnett (London: Royal Asiatic Society, 1920), *pad* 22, p. 10.

11. Allusions to *mukti* achieved in 'the Void' are frequent in the *Kabīr-vāṇī*: see *KG sākhī* 5.7; 9.18, 21, 31; see also Vaudeville, *Kabīr*, introduction, pp. 124-25.

Namdev too, who is earlier than Kabir and to whom Kabir refers with veneration. Yet, as a whole, in spite of their ardent devotion for the visible Vithoba, Namdev and his spiritual descendants tend towards a monotheistic type of bhakti, which is essentially '*prema*-bhakti', even while sharing most of the views and spiritual attitudes of the northern Sant poets.

Prema-*Bhakti*: *the Way of Love*

Prema-bhakti, 'tender devotion' for Lord Vithoba, characterizes the attitude of the Maharashtrian Sants, who call their Lord 'father and mother' — but mostly see him as a tender Mother, often addressing him in the feminine (*Viṭhe* instead of *Viṭho*). This tender devotion is only a reflection of God's own love for his bhaktas — a love so powerful that he was driven to Pandharpur and there remained forever 'standing on the brick' for the sake of his bhaktas. When away from their Lord, the Maharashtrian Sants experience the pangs of separation (*viraha*) and so does the Lord away from them. But the relationship always remains that of a child to his father or mother: bridal symbolism is nearly unknown in Maharashtrian bhakti.

Prema-bhakti, or more commonly *bhāva*-bhakti, is not unknown to the northern Sants. The supreme Being or ultimate Reality is symbolized by the beloved lord, master or husband and the human soul, the *jīva*, by his eternally wedded wife, pining for union with her inaccessible, though ever-present, spouse. The pangs of *viraha* experienced by the bereaved soul — so long as she has not learned to discover him and unite with him within her own self — are depicted by Kabir and the northern Sants with a remarkable intensity of feeling, in simple and touching words, which recall the pathetic *virahiṇī* songs sung by village women especially during the rainy season. So sings Kabir:

O Beloved,
        come to my house!
Away from you
        my body aches!

They'll say I'm your wife
        yet I have my doubts:
If one doesn't sleep united on the couch
        what kind of love is that?

KG pad 13

Away from Ram
    my body burns for ever —
In water itself
    a blaze has broken out!

You are the Ocean
    and I the fish in water;
In water I live
    yet for water I pine!

KG pad 9

In their illustrations of *bhāva*-bhakti, mostly under its *viraha* aspect, the Sant poets are in keeping with the ancient tradition of both Shaiva and Vaishnava bhakti. At least from the time the *Bhāgavata Purāṇa* was composed, and even earlier with the Tamil Alvars and Nayanars, bhakti was conceived as an intense love relationship between the soul and God, in which the yearnings of the soul brought about a sublimation of the love relationship, so that the bhakta ultimately could accede to a perpetual union with and participation in his God. The northern Sants go a step further in describing the torments of the bereaved soul. For Kabir especially, *viraha* is a spiritual martyrdom which only the heroic soul can endure — but it is also the path which leads to union with the Lord:

Do not abuse that *viraha*
    for *viraha* is a King:
The body that contains not *viraha*
    is for ever a burning-ground!

KG sākhī 2.16

The final reunion of the wife-soul with her eternal husband is expressed by Kabir in terms of 'merging':

You search, you search, O my friend,
    but Kabir has disappeared:
The drop has merged into the ocean,
    how then could it be found?

You search, you search, O my friend,
    but Kabir has disappeared:
The ocean has merged into the drop,
    how then could it be found?

KG sākhī 8.6-7

If love symbolism, especially on the *viraha* theme finds its roots in Hindu tradition, more precisely in the tradition of folk songs, the place given by Kabir and his followers to the *viraha* theme, with its suggestion of martyrdom, is in keeping with the great Sufi tradition, very much alive in India at the time of Kabir.[12]

The Sant Sādhanā

The two groups of Sants may differ on metaphysical grounds, the northern group, with Kabir and Dadu, hovering between staunch monotheism and some form of pantheism verging on nihilism or *śūnyavāda* and the southern group, with Namdev and the Maharashtrian Sants, clinging to a purified form of Vaishnavism which implies a permanent love relationship between the soul and God. Both groups however agree in practice on the *sādhanā*, i.e. on the means to achieve *mukti*. Whether they be born Shaiva, Vaishnava or Muslim, all the Sant poets stress the necessity of devotion to and practice of the divine Name (*nāma*), devotion to the Divine Guru (*satguru*) and the great importance of the 'company of the Sants' (*satsaṅg*). The Name, the Divine Guru and the *satsaṅg* are the three pillars of the Sant *sādhanā*.

Whereas traditional Hinduism conceives God (or gods) as endowed with both 'name' and 'form' (*nāma-rūpa*) as objects of bhakti, the Sants as a whole reject the cult of the 'form' (with the exception of the god Vithoba for the Maharashtrian Sants, as mentioned above) to cling to the sole Name as the hypostasis of the supreme Being.[13] The form of

12. See Bruce B. Lawrence, "The Sant Movement and North Indian Sufis," below in this volume. The resemblance is even more striking in the description of the torments of the soul yearning for union with God. There is hardly any doubt that in this Kabir was influenced by Indo-Persian poetry. On the equivalence between the Sanskrit word *viraha* and the Arabic *ishq* in the Avadhi work *Padmāvat* composed by the Chishti poet Muhammad Jayasi, see Charlotte Vaudeville, "La conception de l'amour divin chez Muhammad Jayasī: *virah* et *ishq*", *Journal Asiatique* 1962, pp. 351-67.

13. The most lucid and complete exposition of the doctrine of the Name of Ram as the hypostasis of the supreme Being is found in the prologue of the famous *Rāmcharitmānas* of Tulsi Das; see the English translation by W.D.P. Hill, *The Holy Lake of the Acts of Rāma* (London: Oxford University Press, 1952), Childhood, stanzas 19-27, pp. 14-18. Tulsi Das, a non-sectarian Vaishnava, accounted as an illustrious champion of Rama bhakti, does not hesitate to vindicate the superiority of the Name over the *nirguṇa brahmaṇ* and over the *saguṇa* (visible) form of Ram himself:

"Thus the power of the Name is immeasurably greater than the impersonal prayer advocated is *sumiran* (Sanskrit *smaraṇa*), absorption in the 'remembrance' of God through the Name. It may be done by vocal repetition (*jap*) of the Name 'with the tongue' or by voiceless repetition (*ajāpajap*), mental concentration on the divine Name beyond all mental representations. All Vaishnava bhaktas practice *sumiran*, though they may also meditate on the divine form (*mūrti*) of their God and worship him within their heart in that very form. For the Sants however, at least for the northern Sants, such a representation is meaningless since the supreme Lord is conceived as essentially formless.

The divine Name is conceived as unique, though the actual names by which the supreme Lord is called are many. In the *Jñāneśvarī*, Jnaneshvar, who stands as the *ādi-guru* of all the Maharashtrian Sants,[14] exhorts the devotees to call upon the Name "whether Shaiva or Vaishnava."[15] The Sants, however, in contrast with the related poet-saints of the Kashmir Shaiva tradition or the Virashaivas of the Kanarese area, cling exclusively to the Vaishnava names of God such as Ram, Hari, Govinda, Mukunda, Madhava, Murari, Sarangapani — with a special emphasis on the name of 'Ram'. This 'Ram' however, has nothing to do with the divinized hero of the *Rāmāyaṇa* or with the god Vishnu, but connotes the all-pervading Being whom the Bhagavata tradition calls *ātmarāma:* besides Ram, the word *ātmarāma* is commonly found in Sant poetry referring to the supreme Reality.[16] It appears that for

(*nirguṇa*); and I declare that in my judgment the Name is greater than Rāma too."

[*dohā* 23]

"Therefore the Name is greater than both the Absolute (Brahma) and than Rāma and blesses even those that bless."

[*dohā* 25]

"But why should I any more extol the Name? Rāma himself cannot sing the full perfections of the Name!"

[*chaupāī* 26]

For a commentary on this passage of the *Rāmcharitmānas*, see Charlotte Vaudeville, *Etude sur les Sources et la Composition du Rāmāyaṇa de Tulsī-dās* (Paris: Adrien-Maisonneuve, 1955), pp. 11-14.

14. See above, fn. 1.
15. *Jnānesvarī* 17.223 (on *Bhagavad Gītā* 17.15).
16. e.g. *KG pada* 174:

kā nāṅgeṅ kā bāṅdheṅ chāṅma
jau nahiṅ chinhasi ātamarāṅma
"What's the use of denuding one's skin or covering it,
so long as one has not recognized *ātmarāma* [within]?"

Ātmarāma literally means 'he who finds joy in his own self', but in the whole of the Sant and Vaishnava literature, beginning with the *Jñāneśvarī*, the word takes on the

the Sant tradition as a whole, and for Kabir in particular, 'Ram' (*Rāmā*) and 'the Name' (*nāmā*) are interchangeable — so much so that one of the terms is often found in place of the other in variants of the same line. Ram is the divine Name *par excellence*. In the Sant literature as a whole, and in common parlance down to this day, Ram simply means 'God'. Kabir himself states that there is no difference between the Hindu 'Ram' and the Muslim 'Rahim' or 'Khuda':

> For the Hindu and for the Turk there is but one Way
> which the Satguru has shown.
> Says Kabir, O Sants, listen:
> what matter if one calls 'Ram' or 'Khuda'?
>
> *BI śabda* 10

Along with the cult of the divine Name, the cult of the *satguru*, the Perfect Guru who speaks within the heart of man to awaken the soul and lead it on the way to *mukti*, is also characteristic of the Sant *sādhanā*. The cult of the guru is ancient in India, where the spiritual guide who shows the way to salvation is usually conceived as the very embodiment of perfect spiritual knowledge and God-imparted wisdom. It is the guru's priviledge to confer initiation on his disciple by imparting the mantra to him in a confidential manner, through whispering it into his ear.

The *satguru* or Perfect Guru, however, need not assume a human form: he can be interiorized. In Shaiva tradition, especially in the Tantric schools, the guru tends to be divinized and held identical with Paramashiva, the *ādi-guru*; the Word (*śabda*) he utters within the soul is the highest revelation, which releases the soul from the bonds of *māyā*. Yet, to be without a visible guru (*nirguru*) is not respectable in the Hindu tradition as a whole since it is nearly universally admitted that a man cannot achieve salvation without a proper initiation imparted by a human guru.

The position of the Sants on this matter is somewhat ambiguous. Some of them allude to a human guru, but they do not name him. Later tradition, especially sectarian traditions issued from the teachings of a particular Sant, have usually tried to make up for that silence by attributing to him a reputed religious figure as a guru. In this way, the prestigious — and rather mysterious — figure of Ramananda was attributed to Kabir as his human guru for having unwittingly imparted the

meaning of 'the All-pervading', 'he who is immanent in all beings'. See Vaudeville, *L'Invocation*, pp. 63-64 and fn. 2, p. 63.

mantra '*Rām-Rām*' to him. Yet it is clear that, by and large, the Sants have been very reluctant to name their human guru — if they had one. On the other hand, it is clear that the one guru consistently claimed and revered by all the Sant poets is the supreme Being as *satguru:*

The grandeur of the *satguru* is infinite,
infinite his bounty:
He opened my eyes to the Infinite
and showed me Infinity.

KG sākhī 1.13

The initiation that the *satguru* confers on the worthy soul does not take the form of a spelled word mantra, whispered in the disciple's ear: it takes the form of a sudden, fulgurant revelation referred to as the Word, *śabda*, and often compared to an arrow:

The *satguru* is the true hero,
who loosed off a single *śabda:*
The moment it struck, I fell to the ground
and a wound opened in my breast.

KG sākhī 1.9

Though *śabda* itself, like a number of other words commonly used by the Sants, is borrowed from the language of Tantric Yoga, the Sants themselves reject both the theory and the practices of Hatha Yoga. For them true Yoga is of the spirit, not of the body: *kāyā-sādhanā* is of no avail, all truth and salvation should be realized within, in the depths of the soul. This permanent insistence on inwardness is characteristic of the Sant *sādhanā* as a whole. This attitude is common to them and to that of the Muslim Sufis: both groups are fervent adepts of 'interior religion'.[17]

In the Sant tradition, the 'true Sants' are extolled just like the Perfect Guru, as so many manifestations of the divine in human form. Who they are is not said, though some lists include a number of 'great devotees' (*mahābhakta*s) of the mythical past and a few great Sants of the Kali age such as Jayadeva and Namdev.[18] It is clear that the 'true Sants' are great devotees of the divine Name, entirely permeated by the love of Ram and wholly detached from the world. Needless to say, such

17. See above, fn. 12; see also Charlotte Vaudeville, "Kabīr and Interior Religion," *History of Religions* 3:2 (1964), pp. 191-201.

18. See *KG pada* 45 (*Jaideuṅ Nāṅmāṅ bipa Sudāṅmāṅ*), 48 (*Sanaka Sanandana Jaideu Nāṅmāṅ*), 198 (*kali jāge Nāṅmāṅ Jaideva*); also *AG Bilāval* 7; *Gauṛī* 36.

perfect Sants, just as a good human guru, are hard to find, and Kabir proclaims that he has never met one:

Such a one cannot be found
to give us initiation
And pull us out by the hair
as we sink into the Ocean of Existence.
Such a one cannot be found
who can guide us all the way to salvation...

I wander in search of one who loves
but I can find no true lover...
KG sākhī 5.3, 7, 10

A few less exalted Sants must be found anyhow — men of noble heart and upright behavior, ardently devoted to the divine Name — since 'the company of the Sants', *satsaṅg*, is held by all the Sant poets as a powerful means of purification and a way to salvation. Association with true Sants is often compared to pilgrimage to the Hindu *tīrtha*s accompanied with a purificatory bath: the Sants themselves stand as the true *tīrtha*s. This belief is common to the Sants and to Hindus in general[19] though the northern Sants do not countenance the common Hindu practice of *tīrtha-yātrā*. The 'true Sants', in that context, mean 'the Just' or even 'the genuine *bhagat*s' (bhaktas) of the one Ram — those very chosen souls whom Kabir often addresses as Sants — or even as Vaishnavas: they are the very people who delight in joining together to sing the Name of Ram in the traditional performance of *bhajan* and *kīrtan*, so dear to all Vaishnavas.

The beneficial character of *satsaṅg*, and of its corollary *bhajan* or *kīrtan* — admittedly a Vaishnava practice — is stressed by Kabir:

I have two companions with me,
one is Ram, the other is the Vaishnava:
One is the Bestower of salvation
the other makes me invoke the Name.
KG sākhī 4.5

19. According to the *Skanda Purāṇa*, a spot hallowed by being a resort of holy men is called a *tīrtha*; the main thing is to go to (i.e. associate with) holy men; pilgrimage itself is only a secondary object. See P.V. Kane, *History of Dharmaśāstra* (Poona: Bhandarkar Oriental Research Institute, 1930-62), vol. 4, p. 155.

The Sant Ideal of Sanctity: Sants and Vaishnavas

The various elements which appear as characteristic of the Sant *sādhanā* can be traced to various traditions, especially to the Vaishnava tradition. The cult of the Name as an hypostasis of the supreme divinity and especially of the Name of Ram, though it probably owes much to the Tantric tradition, is present in most forms of Vaishnava bhakti at least from the time of Jnaneshvar.[20] The extreme importance attributed to the 'company of the Sants' (*satsaṅg*), with the Sants themselves taking the place of the Hindu *tīrtha*s, is commonly held by all Vaishnavas. On the other hand, the exaltation of the guru as the interiorized *satguru*, whose powerful mantra is conceived as the mysterious 'Word' (*śabda*) which provokes the disintegration of the soul itself and its instant re-absorption into the undifferentiated Reality or State, is clearly a Yogic concept unfamiliar to the southern Sants who retain a link with traditional Vaishnava bhakti. The Sant *sādhanā* or the Sant ideal of sanctity therefore may be viewed as a subtle blending of two main traditions of Hindu mysticism, apparently antagonistic to each other: Vaishnava bhakti and an esoteric Tantric tradition, whose most popular representatives are Gorakhnath and the Nath Yogis, often referred to by Kabir and his followers.[21]

What seems to distinguish the Sants is their advocating a path to 'holiness', and ultimately to salvation, open to all creatures. Indian languages as a whole have no dearth of terms to qualify 'holy men'. The Sant is a 'holy man' of a somewhat special type, who cannot be accomodated in the traditional categories of Indian holy men — and he may just as well be a woman. The Sant is not a renunciate, neither a Shaiva *sanyāsī* nor a Vaishnava *vairāgī*. He has not necessarily received an initiation — except in some cases what is known as *nāma-dīkṣā*, 'initiation through the Name alone'. He is not one of those wandering holy men known as 'sadhus' who go about dressed in various attires, living on begging and actually making a show of holiness to earn their daily pittance. He is neither a Yogi nor a Siddha, practices no *āsana*s, boasts of no secret *bīja-mantra* and has no claim to magical powers. The true Sant wears no special dress or insignia, having eschewed the social consideration and material benefits which in India attach to the profession of asceticism. Typically, the Sant is a layman, mostly a Shudra,

20. See above, p. 32 and fn. 15.

21. About Nathism as a kind of half-Buddhistic creed widespread among weavers and some other low artisan castes, see Vaudeville, *Kabīr*, introduction, pp. 87-88.

sometimes even an Untouchable, or even a Muslim-born *mleccha*—and he is supposed to support himself and his family on his own traditional skill or trade. Though he has not cut ties with his family and caste, he is totally detached at heart from such ties, which he bears as a heavy burden. He is usually reproached and ridiculed by his own people for his strange behaviour, his contempt for money and all material things, his absorption in the Name of God. On the whole, he is considered a social misfit and is not recognized as a man of God until God himself vindicates his saintliness through some striking miracle, which the Sant himself neither begs for nor expects.[22] The Sant ideal of sanctity is a lay ideal, open to all; it is an ideal which transcends both sectarian and caste barriers. It testifies to a rather modernistic view of sanctity which has captivated the heart of the common people, and remains very much alive in modern India while the traditional gurus continue to ply their trade, more and more oriented towards their middle-class patrons.

According to the Indian literary tradition, the Sants are supposed to be adepts of the *nirguṇa* aspect and the Vaishnavas adepts of the *saguṇa* aspect of the supreme Being. In practice, however, it is difficult to draw a hard and fast line between the two groups, at least up to the beginning of the sixteenth century, which saw the development of the two main modern Krishnaite sects in northern India, the Vallabhas and the Chaitanyas (or Gaudiyas), both of them oriented towards a dualistic conception of God and the soul, in spite of the fact that the Vallabhas claim for their system the label of *śuddhādvaita*, 'pure monism'.

It is a striking fact that most medieval texts inspired by non-sectarian Bhagavatism or Vaishnava bhakti do not seem to distinguish between the terms *bhakta* (*bhagat*), *sant* and *Vaiṣṇava*. In the *Gurū Granth* of the Sikhs, the Sant poets are referred to as *bhagat*s and even the *Bhaktamāl* ("The Garland of [Vaishnava] Devotees") composed by Nabhaji around 1500 includes the biographies of a number of Sant poets as if they were just a variety of the so-called 'Vaishnava bhaktas'.

As we have seen, a number of elements entering into the Sant *sād-*

22. The Maharashtrian poet and chronicler Mahipati relates at length the story of the miracle wrought by the god Vithoba of Pandharpur for his devotee Sant Tukaram: envious of Tukaram's poetical gift, a wicked Brahman had ordered the Sant to throw his manuscripts of *abhaṅg*s into the river — an order to which Tukaram submitted meekly but with deep sorrow. After thirteen days, the Lord appeared in a vision to Tuka's friends and showed them the manuscripts floating dry on the river. See Justin E. Abbott, trans., *The Poet-Saints of Maharashtra*, vol. 7 (Poona: Scottish Mission Industries, 1930), pp. 203-15. This volume, *Tukaram*, is a translation from Mahipati's *Bhaktalilāmṛta*.

hanā can be traced to the non-sectarian Vaishnava tradition. Both Sants and Vaishnavas are either antagonistic or indifferent to Vedic orthodoxy and Vedantic learning. Both are disdainful of caste barriers and expect little — or nothing at all — from bookish knowledge and learned discourses, all despicable *pāṇḍitya*. Both insist on some form of bhakti, essentially a love-relationship between the human soul and God as a means towards salvation. Both see in the experience of *viraha*, 'love-in-separation', the highest religious experience and the door to the ultimate illumination of the soul. Both have a total faith in the power of the sacred Name to achieve salvation, even in the absence of any other practice or means. Both hold the conviction that God is infinitely merciful and that he will, whenever he chooses, remove the veil of darkness which covers the eyes of the wife-soul and grant her the bliss of eternal union with himself. Both hold that the path to salvation is open to all, including Shudras and women, and even to those Untouchables who will never have access to Vaishnava temples — actually Brahman fortresses.

The northern Sants however — and especially Kabir — seem to have gone a step or two further than even the most liberal of the ancient Bhagavatas and of the southern Sants as a whole by actually breaking with the Brahmanical tradition altogether. Kabir does not only reject idol-worship and ridicule the vain pretensions of the Brahmans and the hypocrisy of swamis and Yogis. He and his followers do not look upon themselves as Hindus or Muslims, but reject all religions based on revelation, advocating a purer, higher form of religion which actually does away with God — at least with a personal God. It is what Rabindranath Tagore — who owes much to Kabir — would call 'the Religion of Man'. Kabir sometimes adopts a monotheistic stance, but in many of his *sākhīs* and *pads*, he adopts a nihilistic attitude and his utterances come nearer to the teaching of the Siddhas and Naths of yore, who were the propagators of the Tantric Yoga later taught by the Shaiva Nath Yogis. And the fact is that such utterances can hardly be reconciled with Vaishnava bhakti.[23]

If we give priority to Kabir and the northern Sants — as most Hindi critics have done—we must admit that the hard core of Sant teaching is not assimilable by true Vaishnavas, even by the most liberal among them. This is true on the doctrinal or metaphysical plane, but on that plane only. In their religious sensibility, as well as in their ethical views,

23. See above, fn. 9.

Sants and Vaishnavas remain very close to each other. They share a pessimistic view of mundane life and of family ties, dominated by self-interest. They cordially despise and fear women, whose lures are the main obstacle to spiritual life (woman, in the words of Kabir, is "a pit of hell"). They insist on sexual restraint, even to the point of extreme puritanism, yet they reject the traditional Hindu forms of professional asceticism and even the traditional opposition between home and forest, *vana* versus *gṛha*: on the spiritual plane, nothing more can be achieved in the forest than in the home; all that pertains to salvation is achieved within the heart of man himself. As laymen, both Sants and Vaishnavas cordially despise *veṣa*, the outward attire and paraphernalia of the professional Yogis and sadhus, whom they see as hypocrites.

The highest virtue cultivated by both groups is *ahiṃsā*, 'non-violence', which implies absolute respect for life, and strict vegetarianism, but extends further to include the Buddhistic virtues of self-restraint, humility, compassion, gentleness and reverence for all, since "the heart of the Sants is soft as butter." Never uttering a harsh word, the Sant should suffer slander and persecution without retaliating, nay with gratefulness. As Kabir says wryly:

Keep the slanderer near you,
    build him a hut in your courtyard—
For without soap or water
    he'll scrub your character clean!

KG sākhī 23.4

That common ideal of the 'true Sant' who is also a 'true Vaishnava' is well exemplified by the often-quoted *pad* by the Gujarati poet Narsi Mehta, one of Mahatma Gandhi's most beloved hymns, which expresses in simple and moving words this lay ideal of sanctity:

Vaiṣṇava jana to tene kahie
Call that one a true Vaishnava
    who feels the suffering of others,
Who seeks to relieve others' pain
    and has no pride in his soul (Refrain)

He bows respectfully to the whole world,
    he talks ill of no one;
He remains steadfast in mind, words and actions:
    blessed, blessed be his mother!

He is impartial to all, he has renounced all greed,
he sees another man's wife as his own mother,
His tongue speaks no lie,
he does not touch another man's property.

He remains unaffected by *māyā* and *moha*,
in his soul is total detachment;
He remains absorbed in meditation on Ram's Name,
within his body, all the *tīrtha*s are found!
Without cupidity or guile is he,
without lust or anger.
Says Narsaiyo, by the mere view of such a Sant,
seventy-two generations find salvation![24]

24. This *pad* is included in the *Āśram-bhajanāvali* (Ahmedabad: Prakashan Press, n.d.), no. 102, p. 135. It is the first in the section "*Gujarātī bhajan.*" Translation by the author.

THE INEFFABLE *NIRGUṆA BRAHMAN*

FRITS STAAL

Everyone has heard *of* the *nirguṇa brahman*, but I don't think anyone has heard anything *about* it. For being ineffable, there is nothing which can be said about it. Therefore, if I had any sense I would keep silent. Not only many ancient philosophers, even Wittgenstein wrote: "What we cannot speak about we must pass over in silence."

But I am not keeping silent. This is because there are several ways of getting around this ineffability of the *nirguṇa brahman*. Some are more general, and others are more technical. Both should be considered, for, if one wishes to find out whether *nirguṇa bhakti* makes any sense, one had better know first whether its predecessor, *nirguṇa brahman*, makes any sense.

In general terms, it is possible to *try* to say something about the *nirguṇa brahman*, or Absolute-without-qualities; only we must realize that whatever we say is applicable only to the *saguṇa brahman*, or Absolute-with-qualities. As soon as we try to talk about the *nirguṇa brahman* we are in fact talking about the *saguṇa brahman*.

The more technical procedure one can adopt starts from the observation that if you cannot express (*vācayati*), you can still indicate (*lakṣayati*). The *nirguṇa brahman*, therefore, can have definitions (*lakṣaṇa*) which, however, involve implication (*lakṣaṇā*). The main question regarding these possible definitions is whether they imply the primary sense of the term. There are three possibilities:

(1) They include the primary sense; this is called *ajahallakṣaṇā*; an example is: *chattriṇo yānti*, 'the people with umbrellas are going'. The people are implied here, but the umbrellas themselves, the primary sense of the term *chattriṇaḥ*, are also included since the people are carrying them. We find this also in the Agnicayana ritual: *sṛṣṭīr upadadhāti*, 'he puts down the *sṛṣṭi* bricks', which refers to bricks deposited in the altar to the accompaniment of mantras which contain the term *sṛṣṭi*. The bricks are implied, but the *sṛṣṭi* mantras are also included.

(2) They exclude the primary sense; this is called *jahallakṣaṇā*; an example is: *gaṅgāyāṃ ghoṣaḥ*, 'the village is on the Ganges', meaning:

'the village is on the banks of the Ganges'. Here the primary sense 'Ganges' is excluded since the village is not mysteriously suspended on the waters of the Ganges river itself. Another example is *dvirepha*, which literally means: 'a word with two *r*'s', but which does not refer to such a word but only to the bee which is also called *bhramara*, which *is* a word with two *r*'s.

(3) They include and exclude the primary sense: *jahadajahallakṣaṇā*, for example: *grāmo dagdhaḥ*, 'the village is burnt', which does not mean that all of the village is burnt, but implies that at least a part of it is burnt. This third type of implication is applicable to the *nirguṇa brahman*.

The *jahadajahallakṣaṇā* type of implication is applied to statements about the Absolute in the following manner. In such sentences as *tat tvam asi*, 'you are that', or *ahaṃ brahmāsmi*, 'I am brahman', the Absolute is indicated but as stripped of all its qualifications. Similarly, the 'you' refers not to Svetaketu, son of Uddalaka, as we all know him, but to that same person, stripped of all qualifications, especially the *dvandva* pairs such as intelligence/stupidity, love/hatred, pride/humility, etc. In this way, then, the Absolute is, if not referred to, at least indicated.

There is another way of dealing with definitions of *brahman*. We distinguish accidental definitions (*taṭastha-lakṣaṇa*) which are given from without, from essential definitions (*svarūpa-lakṣaṇa*) which are given from within. An example of the former is: '*brahman* is the cause of the origination, preservation and cessation of this world'. Since the *nirguṇa brahman* cannot enter into any relationship, these definitions are not applicable to it and need not concern us here. A *svarūpa* definition is to say that *brahman* is *sat* ('being'), *cit* ('spirit'), and *ānanda* ('bliss'). Note that these three concepts are not synonymous. And yet, in each case, definiens and definiendum coincide. For example, *sat* is not a property of *brahman*; it is not in, or a part of it; it *is brahman*. The same holds for the other two. There is no contradiction here; it is the same thing approached from different directions.

The implications are clear. According to the *Taittirīyopaniṣad*, *brahman* is that 'from which all words return; not within reach of the mind' (*yato vāco nivartante; aprāpya manasā saha*). We keep sending words that way; this may throw some light on us, on the words, or on the sending; it certainly throws no light on *brahman*.

As I shall prove a little later, there are identical implications in connection with *nirguṇa bhakti*. Assuming for the moment that *bhakti* means 'love' — which I leave for the experts to decide — all I can say is that I might love something with bad qualities, but shall certainly not love something without qualities. The expression may say something about the loving and the lovers; it is unlikely that it would convey information about the beloved. Incidentally, the issue is not about personal versus impersonal. One can easily love something impersonal, e.g., music, mathematics, or the Communist Party. The issue is about *nirguṇa* versus *saguṇa*. One cannot love something without qualities.

If we wish to save the term *nirguṇa bhakti*, is there a grammatical way out? I can think of three ways of analyzing the compound (assuming it to be a compound). If it is a *tatpuruṣa* compound with *nirguṇa* as the object (which, incidentally, is not in accordance with Panini's rules), meaning 'loving *nirguṇa*', it makes no sense since we love only things with qualities. If it is a *tatpuruṣa* compound with *nirguṇa* as subject, meaning 'love by *nirguṇa*', it makes no sense because if you have no qualities you cannot love. And if it is a *karmadhāraya* compound meaning 'love which is without qualities', it is self-contradictory because love is not without qualities.

You might still think that there must be a way out of this by tinkering or tampering with the term *guṇa*. I am afraid there isn't if we stay within the traditional framework of any of the systems of Indian philosophy. For they all accept as a starting point the logical analysis of the Nyaya, according to which *guṇa* is 'that which is located in a locus' (*āśraye ya āśritaḥ sa guṇaḥ*), which itself is the counterpart of the definition of *dravya* ('substance') as *guṇāśrayaḥ* (locus of *guṇa*'s'). If you use *nirguṇa* and *bhakti* in a meaningful way, the compound *nirguṇa-bhakti* makes no sense. If you don't use them in a meaningful way, of course, it makes no sense either.

Much of what I have said is generally known. It can be found in the handbooks, and it has been described in greater detail, in a style ranging from the obscure to the relatively clear, by De Smet, T.R.V. Murti and Kunjunni Raja.[1] The rest of what I have said, which has not been said before, follows from what *has* been said before. Now we come to

1. Richard V. De Smet, *The Theological Method of Saṃkara* (Louvain: Pontificia Universitas Gregoriana, 1954); also in *Revue Philosophique de Louvain* 52 (1954): 31-74. T.R.V. Murti, "The Two Definitions of Brahman in the Advaita," *Krishna Chandra Bhattacharyya Memorial Volume*, Amalner Indian Institute of Philosophy, 1958. K. Kunjunni Raja, *Indian Theories of Meaning* (Madras: Adyar Library, 1963).

something which has not, to my knowledge, been satisfactorily explained. Why do people all over the world (for this occurs not only in Hinduism, but also in Taoism, Christianity and Islam) have a strong desire to go back to something ineffable? Looking at it in the light of reason this is certainly surprising. People could be expected to desire things which tell, give, promise or at least remind them of something. The ineffable does none of these things.

One explanation which looms round the corner is the psychoanalytical explanation. It theorizes that people wish to go back to an infantile stage, characterized by the fact that there was oral fixation, but no speech. I don't believe that anybody in his right mind wishes to go back, consciously or subconsciously, to the pre-linguistic state of the babbling baby. Of course, that I don't believe it is taken as positive evidence that it is the case by psychoanalysts—but only by them. However, I think that the Freudian hypothesis points in the right direction; only we have to go much further, and extend our perspective from the ontogenetic to the phylogenetic. In so doing we can incidentally explain the psychoanalytical explanation. I believe that this curious desire for the ineffable is a desire for the pre-linguistic state of mankind, a kind of nostalgia not for our childhood, but for the childhood of the race before it spoke. This explains the archaic features of all mysticisms of the ineffable: they point to a golden age, an original paradise, or at least a distant past.[2]

I mean to take this hypothesis seriously. There is a tradition in Western thought, culminating with Herder, that language defines man. If that were true, pre-linguistic would mean pre-human. The way I visualize man's evolution—without attempting to be at all precise in chronological terms—admits of many more qualifications. I would imagine Zinjanthropus mostly silent, Peking Man humming and babbling; by the time we arrive at Neanderthaler, we have songs and mantras; with Cro-Magnon, if not earlier, we get language. When Cro-Magnon wishes to be Peking Man—which is like Malraux dreaming of China—we witness the origin of the desire for the ineffable.

I admit that this is pure speculation, but hasten to add that the speculations of the so-called professionals are equally pure. Those who make much of the upright position of man as a determining cause of the shape of his vocal tract[3] put the origin of language millions of years

2. Frits Staal, *Exploring Mysticism: A Methodological Essay* (Berkeley: University of California Press, 1975), p. 58.

3. E.g., W.S. Smith, "Messages of Vertebrate Communication," *Science* 165 (1969): 145-50.

earlier than others who do not accept this hypothesis and place it in the Upper Paleolithic.[4] My evidence from the ineffable is certainly no worse than this. For consider how we are supposed to reach the ineffable. The answer is: by silence, silent meditation, mantras, and many forms of exercise which are partly like language or which occupy an intermediate position between silence and mantras. All the religious uses of language retain a pre-linguistic flavor, and many involve expressions which are language-like but meaningless. Mantras themselves are meaningless sounds. In Vedic and other Indian forms of ritual, recitations and chants are prescribed which are *anirukta* ('un-enunciated'), *upāṃśu* ('inaudible') or *tūṣṇīm* ('silent'). There is also *vāgyamana* ('retention of the voice, i.e., of speech'), which means that the consecrated person 'retains his voice' (*vācaṃ yacchati*) for a prescribed period of time, and then 'releases his voice' (*vācaṃ visṛjate*). We also meet with *japa* ('muttering'), and also *tūṣṇīṃjapa* ('silent muttering').[5] Parallels to this are found in all the religions of mankind. All these curious facts fall into place when we assume that meaningless syllables preceded meaningful language, which is another way of saying that men hummed, babbled and sang before they talked. Such a theory of the origin of language provides an explanation of the desire for the ineffable as a bonus.

I am now approaching my final conclusion. There is one thing that certainly does *not* lead to the ineffable: talking, which includes meetings and conferences. The same holds for the *nirguṇa bhakti* — as all true bhaktas have always realized. I shall corroborate this by providing the promised proof that *nirguṇa brahman* and *nirguṇa bhakti* are the same.[6] The proof proceeds by *reductio ad absurdum*. Let us assume that they are different. If they are different, they must differ at least in one respect, which means that they must differ at least with respect to one *guṇa*. But then they cannot both be *nirguṇa*. Since they *are* both *nirguṇa* by definition, the original assumption leads to a contradiction. Hence it cannot be valid, so that the two cannot be different. Hence they must

4. See M. Swadesh, "Linguistic Overview," in Jesse Jennings and Edward Norbeck, eds., *Prehistoric Man in the New World* (Chicago: University of Chicago Press, 1964), and F.B. Livingstone, "Genetics, Ecology and the Origins of Incest and Exogamy," *Current Anthropology* 10 (1969): 45-62.

5. See L. Renou, "La valeur du silence dans le culte védique," *Journal of the American Oriental Society* 69 (1949): 11-18, and L. Renou and L. Silburn, "*Nirukta* and *Ánirukta* in Vedic," *Sārupa Bhārati*: *Dr. Lakshman Sarup Memorial Volume*, (Hoshiarpur: Vishveshvaranand Indological Series, 1954), no. 6, pp. 68-79.

6. This proof was independently arrived at by Hilton Yee.

be the same. This shows, incidentally, what curious things they are, and it also explains why I and *brahman* are the same as soon as you strip us of all our qualities.

What follows from this? At least two things. A bhakta may indulge, but not in *pāṇḍitya*. And a person who writes about the ineffable should not write too much.

THE INTERACTION OF *SAGUṆA* AND *NIRGUṆA* IMAGES OF DEITY

WENDY DONIGER O'FLAHERTY

The hypothesis of this essay is that the *nirguṇa* image of deity is an embarrassment to Puranic and temple Hinduism, that the *nirguṇa* line has been force-fed to grass-roots Hindus with a strictly limited degree of success. Charlotte Vaudeville has elegantly and clearly stated the Sant paradox which is at the heart of this problem: the Sants not only wavered between *nirguṇa* and *saguṇa* images of deity, but purposely challenged the very distinction between these categories.[1] The logical outcome of merging with a *nirguṇa* deity — *mokṣa* — would be the disappearance of bhakti. This conflict results, at least in part, from the merging of several different Indian traditions (Sanskrit Vedanta, vernacular bhakti, other traditions) — a merging that was not always willing or conscious. For *nirguṇa* bhakti is an Irish bull (or, as the Hindus say, *vandhyāputra*, '[as meaningless as] the son of a barren women'). It is a concoction of monistic scholars, artificially imposed upon Sant traditions. Indeed, one might even go farther and say that the idea of a *nirguṇa* deity itself was imposed by monistic Hindu philosophers upon a *saguṇa* bhakti tradition that managed, somehow, to absorb it.

It is difficult to imagine a deity who cannot, by definition, be imagined; it can be done, but it is difficult. Hindu philosophers have much more practice, and can bring it off; but what about the rest of India? Nowhere on earth can one find a people more eager than the Hindus to revel in specific, concrete, multitudinous detail. This is immediately obvious from a brief glance at any Sanskrit *kāvya* or Puranic *stotra* — the descriptions of jewelery and of trees, the lists of attributes, the enumeration of physical qualities. And in temple architecture, the epitome of *saguṇa* deity is surely the South Indian *gopuram* with its staggering, overwhelming baroque superabundance of detail that so nauseated the early European observers with their cool Greek ideals.

Where, then does the *nirguṇa* image play a role in this side of Hinduism? It begins in the *Ṛg Veda*, with the hymns of the late tenth book

1. See Charlotte Vaudeville, "*Sant Mat*: Santism as the Universal Path to Sanctity," earlier in this volume.

beginning to play word-games with the ineffable that is neither being nor non-being: "Who is the god who was there before all the other gods?" asks the sage, in genuine wonder.[2] But the down-to-earth Hindus were quick to turn the *nirguṇa* question into a *saguṇa* answer: Yes indeed, they replied, 'Who' (Ka, cognate with Latin *quis*) is indeed the god who was there before all other gods; and Ka is Prajapati, who once fought a battle with the god of death, and who has two breasts, and who desired his daughter, and on and on — who is, in brief, a god with specific qualities. Vedic speculation was of course fruitful of *nirguṇa* lines of thought in other areas, but the point I wish to make is merely that the minute it was tried out on the early Vedic worshippers, it met with a counter-attack.

In Epic and Puranic Hinduism, one finds numerous examples of resistance to the *nirguṇa* ideal. Avatar is a prime example. Theoretically, one cannot reconcile *nirguṇa* deity with avatars; yet the Kabirpanthis tended to treat Kabir as a kind of avatar. Avatar tends to color even the *nirguṇa* Sant tradition, both in the tendency to divinize Sants and in the magnetic attraction of the name of God, a cult which impinges upon the very *mūrti*-worship and celebration of incarnation that is elsewhere sharply mocked by the Sants. This tension is even more evident in the Puranas, where the Brahman authors attempted to channel the emotional current of *prema bhakti* into the classical furrows of *advaita* monism, stubbornly ignoring their basic incompatibility. (The philosopher Ramanuja tackled the problem in a far more sophisticated way; though the Puranas do not quote him as much as they quote a kind of third-rate version of Shankara, Puranic thought owes much to Ramanuja's resolution of *saguṇa* with *nirguṇa*.)

The avatar is constantly bumping into his own *nirguṇa* image; the texts never fully accept this resolution of the *nirguṇa-saguṇa* tension. When, in the *Bhagavad Gītā*, Arjuna naively requests Krishna to demonstrate his full *nirguṇa* form and Krishna complies, Arjuna quickly begs him to turn back into the aspect he can handle — his old pal Krishna, the tricky charioteer. This request is couched in terms of striking intimacy and specificity, the essence of the *saguṇa* deity, in sharp contrast with the *nirguṇa* god that he has just praised:

> Your strength is infinite, and your power is infinite;
> You achieve everything; you are everything.

2. *Ṛg Veda* with the commentary of Sayana, 6 vols. (London: Oxford University Press, 1890-91), 10.121.

It was madness of me to think of you as a friend,
to say, "Hey, Kṛṣṇa, Hey Yādava, Hey friend!"
I did this because I did not know how great you are—
or else, perhaps, in carelessness because I love you.
Sometimes I would tease you when we were joking,
either at table, or sitting, or resting, or playing,
when we were alone, or together with others.
Forgive me for that, you who cannot be measured.[3]

Arjuna begins and ends with praise of the *nirguṇa* god; in between, he lapses helplessly into the *saguṇa* idiom, to justify himself, to reassure himself, and to remind the god that he loves him.

When, in the *Bhāgavata Purāṇa*, Krishna's mother sees the *nirguṇa* Krishna inside her child (the *saguṇa* Krishna), she cannot stand it, and Krishna lovingly deludes her with the emotion of maternal love, giving her back the specific, complicated little boy she adores in place of the ineffable God she cannot understand.[4] Tulsi Das, too, is irresistibly drawn by the magnet of the *saguṇa* deity: though he begins his invocation to Shiva as *nirguṇa*, *nirvikalpa*, etc., he ends up by describing him as having matted locks, the Ganges in his hair, etc.[5] And this same tendency may also be seen in the relentlessness with which the Puranas attribute to their gods details so minute as to border on the banal, and to contrast these details specifically with the *nirguṇa* image.[6]

Despite this bias, the *nirguṇa* philosophy is expounded at great length from time to time in the Puranas, in the typically Puranic *Reader's Digest* version of Vedantic philosophy. But these speeches never seem fully integrated into the main plot-lines; they do not affect the characters who speak them, or cause them to exchange their world-attached, earthy goals for the high ideals inspired by the *nirguṇa* deity. Like the *Reader's Digest*, the Puranas are not *by* common people but *for* common people; they are manipulated by Brahmans to inculcate people with ideas that Brahmans think people should have. The Sants, on the

3. *Bhagavad Gītā*, with a commentary based on the original sources, by R.C. Zaehner (London: Oxford University Press, 1969), 11.40-42.

4. *Bhāgavata Purāṇa* with the commentary of Sridhara (Bombay: Venkateshvara Steam Press, 1832), 10.8.21-45. (Rept. Motilal Banarsidass, Delhi 1983).

5. Tulsi Das, *Rāmacaritamānasa*, translated by W.D.P. Hill as *The Holy Lake of the Acts of Rāma* (London: Oxford University Press, 1952), Sanskrit invocation.

6. I have expanded this idea in chapter 3, "The Shazam Syndrome, or, The Banalization of the Hindu Gods," in my *Sexual Metaphors and Animal Symbols in Indian Mythology* (Delhi, Motilal Banarsidass, 1982).

other hand, *choose* to mix *nirguṇa* and *saguṇa*; theirs is a free choice, as they have no canon or priesthood.

One can see a similar interaction in the structure of the Hindu temple, in shrines as far removed and different in form as the Minakshi temple at Madurai or the caves at Elephanta in the North. On the outermost periphery, the quintessence of worldliness is expressed in a mind-blowing variety of detail: the temple market, the piles of vermillion powders and rows of shining brass pots, brilliant flowers and garish post cards, the chaotic and noisy world of profane life. But even here there is a sacred tug: for what is being sold is food for gods (*prasāda*), and vessels for holy water; this is the borderline of the two worlds. Immediately afterwards, in South India, one encounters the incredible *gopuram*, the epitome of *saguṇa* detail; now nothing is being bought and sold, and the detail is all God's detail, not man's. But detail it certainly is: we have moved a little farther into the center, and the theological strip-tease is beginning to take place. We enter the next courtyard and encounter less color and shape than in the *gopuram*, but still a lot: carved pillars, images depicting mythological scenes, and the actual human and animal activity of the temple — painted elephants, strange beggars, chanting priests. At Elephanta, we see the elaborate panels depicting the marriage of Shiva and Parvati, their quarrels at dice, Shiva squashing Ravana under Kailasa, Shiva in Yogic meditation, the Ganges descending on Shiva's head, the androgynous form of Shiva and Parvati, Shiva impaling the demon Andhaka, Shiva dancing to create the universe, Shiva dancing to destroy the universe — one's head begins to spin, the mind boggles, the eye cannot absorb it all.

Overwhelmed by these *saguṇa* manifestations, one flees gratefully to the still center of the temple, the *garbha-gṛha*, the innermost shrine, *sanctum sanctorum* — and here one encounters the *nirguṇa* god. At Elephanta, it is the great Maheshvara image which, whatever it may mean (and no one has ever convinced me that they really understand it), is certainly most striking in its simplicity and lack of detail, in contrast with the surrounding panels. Here is a god who has gathered all his action into himself and remains completely latent, potential; one cannot tell what he is thinking, what he is about to do, or indeed if he has ever done anything or ever will; he is a complete enigma. In the South Indian temples, too, one encounters the simplest of images in the *garbha-gṛha*, usually a Shiva-*liṅga* or Vishnu's *śālagrāma* stone, sometimes a small icon completely mummified in layers of cloth, a sinister image but one without qualities, *nirguṇa*. This stark, aniconic symbol is usually very old, worshipped from time immemorial, far older than anything else in the temple; but in its original existence, outside the temple, it had particular meanings associated with various local cults, a name perhaps, a mythology, a specific function to procure specific human desiderata for the villagers who worshipped it. Only when it was later incorporated into the temple and subjected to Brahmanical reinterpretation did it take on the meaning of *nirguṇa* deity.

And although one has moved from a large physical space (the outer boundary of the temple) to a small physical space (the small cave, cool and dark, reeking of bat urine), the feeling is that one has been moving *outward* all the time, spiritually, into larger and larger spaces, until one encounters in the still center the *nirguṇa* image that is the totality of the universe. (Similarly, at the end of the Narnia books, C.S. Lewis describes the end of the world, and the entry of the elect into a tiny stable, in which there is a larger garden, in which there is a larger mountain, and so on, until the Faun explains, "The farther up and the farther in you go, the bigger everything gets. The inside is larger than the outside."[7]) This is the triumph of *nirguṇa* deity in the Hindu temple.

But it is not a lasting triumph. Again and again one encounters a kind of backlash against the serenity and finality of the metaphysical stasis of the central image in the *garbha-gṛha.* For one thing, people keep taking it and playing with it, and banalizing it as they do the Puranic gods: this mysterious, unearthly 'thing' that lurks under the ancient wrappings is changed, fed, and treated with almost insulting intimacy — given qualities which make it possible for the worshipper to demonstrate his love for it. In a similar way, an eye-less, face-less, naked, feature-less ancient Teddy bear, reduced by years of hard play to a *nirguṇa* lump, may be wrapped up in a cloth (like the image in the temple) and *imagined* to have all the qualities the child desires.

The excursions to which the *garbha-gṛha* image is subjected may range from the daily routine to the annual festival — the great ceremony of the *ratha* carrying the image outside the temple. (George Michell has referred to the temple *ratha* as a 'mobile temple', in contrast with the 'minimal' temple represented by the formless roadside shrine of rock or tree.[8] The 'minimal' temple is *nirguṇa*; the orthodox temple is *saguṇa*; and the 'mobile' temple mediates between them, giving quali-

7. C.S. Lewis, *The Last Battle* (Harmondsworth, Middlesex: Penguin Books, 1964), p. 162.

8. George Michell, *The Hindu Temple: An Introduction to Its Meaning and Form* (London: Elek, 1977), pp. 184 and 64.

ties to the formless central image.) Even here, the austere splendor of the veiled deity is tempered by the need for anthropomorphic detail. In the temple of Kataragama in Ceylon, the god is taken out once a year; in an inspiration of true anthropomorphism, he is carried past the house of his long-suffering wife and left instead in the house of his mistress, where he spends the night and emerges next morning in a better mood, more inclined to grant favors to his devotees.[9] And what are these favors? Not *mokṣa,* nor enlightenment, nor any of the stock-in-trade of the *nirguṇa* deity; but the small, worldly needs that animate his worshippers: a clear skin after smallpox, a decent crop after a failed monsoon, a husband, a healthy child—all the *details* that make life precious to the Hindu. And these details are reflected in the very image of the god, a god endowed with specific qualities, *saguṇa,* by the mind of the worshipper if not by the hand of the sculptor.

9. See the film, "Kataragama: A God for All Seasons," made under the supervision of Gananath Obeyesekere for Granada Television in London.

LOVE AND MEDITATION IN THE BHAKTI TRADITION

ANDREW RAWLINSON

The aim of this paper is to provide a general conceptual framework that will enable us to grasp the ramifications of bhakti in all its complexity. In effect, I am proposing to examine the dimensions or topology of bhakti as a counterweight to historical analysis of the tradition. For it is only when we have such a topology that we can explain *why* certain historical factors had the influence they did, for historical influences are structured by religious dimensions as much as religious dimensions are formed by historical causes. This is particularly true of the Sant tradition, whose complex antecedents are extremely difficult to untangle. Part of the logic of the model I shall be proposing is that, if the main contours of the central experience of bhakti are drawn, then the few remaining ones can be filled in from almost any source and even with the most tenuous historical connections.

What I want to show is that different ways of talking about God and the relation he has with individuals and with the world have their own internal logic, which inevitably affects such key notions as salvation, grace, effort, duty, the reason for the existence of the world, etc. Not only this, but these different ways of talking — i.e. the localization of concepts within a religious topology — can be combined to provide various flavors and textures. The situation is rather like the mixing together of the four elements, the irreducible raw stuff of which all complexities are made. Earth and water, which are complementary, can give us the seashore or the mountain top (depending on their relative proportions); fire and water, which are antagonistic, can give us a thunderstorm or a cup of tea.

The two basic images within the bhakti tradition are love and meditation. Both these terms have a great variety of meanings and can be associated with very different metaphysical systems. What I want to make clear is that this range of meanings is due to a tension within each of them and how, by a seeming paradox, this tension can be relieved by borrowing elements from the other.

The essential characteristics of the two trends are summarized in the diagram below:

	LOVE stress on relationship with God	MEDITATION stress on God as a state of being
U N S T R U C T U R E D P A T H S	ECSTATIC *Key terms*: intimacy, bliss *Psychological aspects*: lost in love *Cosmological aspect*: the Beloved is everywhere *Main themes*: (1) God as Beloved (2) relationship tends to identity with the Beloved; intimacy, cheek (3) world seen from God's point of view ⟶ grace, ⟶ spontaneity *Examples*: Chaitanya, Nataraja Shiva	NIRGUṆA *Key terms*: merging, pure essence *Psychological aspect*: discrimination *Cosmological aspect*: māyā *Main themes*: (1) God as *līlā* (2) God and the soul are identical (3) world seen from God's point of view ⟶ effortlessness, ⟶ purposelessness *Examples*: Vallabha, Kashmir Shaivism
S T R U C T U R E D P A T H S	NUMINOUS *Key terms*: dependence, strength *Psychological aspect*: obedience to the Lord *Cosmological aspect*: everything is God's doing *Main themes*: (1) God as King (2) relationship always separate; distance, awe, fear (3) world seen from man's point of view ⟶ effort, ⟶ purpose *Examples*: ch. 11 of the *Gītā*, Mahakala Shiva	SAGUṆA *Key terms*: separation, manifestation *Psychoiogical aspect*: disciplined practice *Cosmological aspect*: the universe as God's attribute *Main themes*: (1) God as Ordainer (2) the soul is a mode (*prakāra*) of the Lord (3) world seen from man's point of view ⟶ *samucchaya*, ⟶ *prapatti* *Examples*: Ramanuja, *Śiva-jñāna-bodha*

I hope it is apparent that, although there are obvious similarities between the two types of love bhakti (i.e. the ecstatic and the numinous) and the two types of meditational bhakti (i.e. the *nirguṇa* and the *saguṇa*), there are also obvious differences. In the same way, although there are obvious differences between ecstatic and *nirguṇa* meditational bhakti, there are equally obvious similarities, and an analogous relation exists between numinous and *saguṇa* meditational bhakti. The reason for these similarities and differences is that both ecstatic and *nirguṇa* meditational bhakti are examples of *unstructured* paths, while numinous and *saguṇa* meditational bhakti are examples of *structured* paths. And the inherent logic of these two kinds of paths acts as a bond between teachings that are in fact based on opposing images (namely, love and meditation). The result of this cross-fertilization is a sort of creative tension, a multi-dimensional topology.

The basic difference between love bhakti and meditational bhakti is that for the latter, bhakti is *viśeṣa-jñāna*. In fact, this is another way of expressing the conception of God as a state of being. On the whole, meditational bhakti is much more explanatory than love bhakti; it justifies a practice or a cosmology by reference to a framework of doctrines. This is a necessary aspect of all *jñāna*-like paths since their basis is clear awareness. By contrast, love bhakti is much richer in its descriptions of the nature of love or the relationship with the Beloved; it tends to subordinate doctrine to these descriptions. In other words, exuberance takes precedence over simplicity, or aesthetics over logic.

But it is the cross-fertilization between the love and meditational poles that is most interesting. Here are a few examples:

(a) The true discrimination of God's attributes (as in Ramanuja: *saguṇa* meditational bhakti: structured) is equivalent to the true understanding of the relationship between God and the devotee (as in numinous bhakti: structured); the obliteration of all attributes (Kashmir Shaivism: *nirguṇa* meditational bhakti: unstructured) is equivalent to the merging of the devotee in the Beloved (Chaitanya: ecstatic bhakti: unstructured).

(b) God has laid down certain laws that men must obey in order to gain God's grace (Ramanuja and numinous bhakti: both structured); there are no laws (ecstatic bhakti and *nirguṇa* meditational bhakti: both unstructured) because the concept 'law' is antithetical to the concepts of 'that which acts without constraint' (ecstatic bhakti) and 'that which has nothing outside it' (*nirguṇa* meditational bhakti).

(c) Both ecstatic and *nirguṇa* meditational bhakti regard the world as *līlā* — the former because it bubbles out of God uncontrollably, the latter because there is no reason for it at all; both numinous and *saguṇa* meditational bhakti regard the world as having a purpose — the former so that souls may be liberated, the latter because God wishes to express his nature.

(d) Ecstatic and *nirguṇa* meditational bhakti support a *vivarta* type of causation theory; numinous and *saguṇa* meditational bhakti support a *pariṇāma* type of causation theory.

(e) Since neither ecstatic nor *nirguṇa* meditational bhakti is interested in forms, neither is very concerned about morality or duty; but numinous and *saguṇa* meditational bhakti insist on both.

(f) Ecstatic bhakti is tolerant of human failing (because ultimately God is responsible for it: *doṣabhoga*), but intolerant of any method other than pure bhakti as a means of salvation (because love is the means as well as the goal and no substitutes are acceptable to God); in contrast, numinous bhakti is intolerant of human failing (because God expects man to make an effort to avoid *doṣa*), but tolerant of other methods (because the means can be discarded once the goal is reached). (This is a typical unstructured versus structured tension and is reflected in meditational bhakti: the *nirguṇa* type holds that knowledge of God is both means and goal, and nothing else will do; the *saguṇa* type is very eclectic.)

As opposed to cross-fertilization, an extreme polarization is found in the practice of repetition. In ecstatic bhakti (unstructured love) it means repetition of the name(s) of God (e.g. Chaitanya); in *saguṇa* meditational bhakti (structured meditation) it means *mantra-yoga* (e.g. *so'haṃ* in the *Śiva-jñāṇa-bodha*). This, incidentally, shows that the greatest dissimilarity exists between the opposite corners of the diagram—i.e. between ecstatic and *saguṇa* meditational bhakti on the one hand, and between numinous and *nirguṇa* meditational bhakti on the other. This is simply because neither of these pairs shares either of the two dimensions of love/meditation or structured/unstructured.

Now that this topology of bhakti has been sketched, how does it dovetail with the history of the bhakti movement in India? I think we can show that it is very relevant to the development of Vaishnavism and Shaivism.

Early Vaishnavism can be regarded as a fusion of two quite distinct trends: Bhagavata Vaishnavism and Pancharatra Vaishnavism. The Bhagavatas were non-Vedic and non-Brahmanical; they evolved around the personalities of Vasudeva and Krishna who were transformed from warrior heroes to supreme deities (*devadeva*). I regard the *Bhagavad Gītā* as a Krishnaite (*Kārṣṇa*), not a Vaishnava, work, and chapter eleven as an excellent example of numinous bhakti. Pancharatra Vaishnavism, on the other hand, is Vedic. It is centered on Narayana who performs the *pañcarātra* sacrifice in the *Śatapatha-Brāhmaṇa* and is identified with *puruṣa* or *mahāpuruṣa*; the *Mahā-Nārāyaṇa-Upaniṣad* identifies *puruṣa, brahman* and Vishnu with Narayana; in the *Nārāyaṇīya* section of the *Mahābhārata*, Narayana is called *devadeva*. Generally speaking, Pancharatra Vaishnavism is strongly influenced by the *jñāna-mārga* of the Upanishads; and both it and Bhagavata Vaishnavism have adopted the *pariṇāma* theory of causation from Samkhya.

The Bhagavatas represent numinous bhakti and the Pancharatras *saguṇa* meditational bhakti. At some point, Vishnu did a take-over of both of them and thereby united them under the single rubric of Vaishnavism. Later still, the Alvars provided the ecstatic dimension with their constant emphasis on the need to abandon oneself to the Beloved. (In fact, Tamil bhakti provides the first example of the description of the devotee's feelings being more important than the attributes of the Beloved — compare the Alvars with Arjuna's confrontation with the numinous *aiśvārya-rūpa* of Krishna in chapter eleven of the *Gītā*.) The *nirguṇa* meditational dimension took a long time to evolve: it does not really make its appearance until Vallabha.

As for Shaivism, the numinous aspects of Rudra-Shiva are well known. The ecstatic dimension developed under the influence of the Tamils, where the unbridled power and bliss of the northern tradition is softened by the tenderness of the Nayanars. Shiva the *mahāyogin*, surrounded by silence, developed into Kashmir Shaivism (aided by Vedanta, no doubt — as Vallabha also was, of course), thus providing the *nirguṇa* meditational dimension. *Saguṇa* meditational bhakti is perhaps the weakest side of Shaivism, but Yoga will always spill over into this category since it is concerned with the gradual removal of impurities; and cosmologically, this form of bhakti places great stress on the manifestations of the Lord in forms that are appropriate to the level of the devotee. The *Śiva-jñāna-bodha* has both of these characteristics, and this is why I have given it as my Shaivite example.

Naturally, I do not want to insist on the way I have divided up Vaishnavism and Shaivism between the categories of my model. These are more complex matters and I am sure others would do it differently. But I do hope to have shown that my model delineates some of the basic contours of the bhakti tradition.

The relevance of this to the Sant tradition is two-fold. First, this tradition partakes of all four dimensions of bhakti; in other words, it is a rich tradition. Secondly, the four traditions that preceded and, from the historical point of view, helped to form the Sant tradition — namely, Vaishnavism, Shaivism, Tantra and Sufism — are also rich traditions. We have already shown this for the first two, and it is true of Tantra and Sufism also. Tantra has the bliss attribute of ecstatic bhakti as well as the terrible, awe-inspiring aspect of numinous bhakti; in this, it is very much like Shaivism. On the other hand, Tantra's monistic tendencies fit well with *nirguṇa* meditational bhakti; at the same time, the one Reality reveals itself in various forms (whether the guru or a mantra) that may be used to gain *sahaja*, and this is typical of the manifestation attribute of *saguṇa* meditational bhakti. The God-intoxication of the Sufis is well known (ecstatic dimension), though naturally the more restrained devotionalism of conventional Islam is not far away (numinous dimension). Sufism's monistic sympathies are also obvious (*nirguṇa* meditational dimension), while its contemplative practices make it akin to Yoga (which is the psychological/behavioral aspect of the *saguṇa* meditational dimension), and its doctrine of 'stations' make it akin to Tantric cosmology.

The Sants are therefore the center of a confluence of rich traditions. Looked at purely from the point of view of its religious dimensions, the Sant tradition is not so different from the other four traditions we have mentioned. The real difference is that these four traditions have developed a considerable variety of peripheral trappings which the Sants assiduously reject. It is therefore misleading to see the Sants as syncretists — i.e. as deliberately fusing diverse traditions — or as being unconsciously influenced by those traditions and producing a distinctive combination by a sort of religious genius analogous to artistic genius. The traditions that preceded the Sants were their raw materials, but the guiding force that enabled them to unite the disparate terminologies and teachings was an understanding of the dimensions of bhakti based on their personal experience.

SECTION II

LITERATURE

THE *DOHĀ* AS A VEHICLE OF SANT TEACHINGS

KARINE SCHOMER

It is common for studies of religious literature to focus almost exclusively on the doctrinal, ethical or mythological content of texts, and to relegate the literary form of these texts to a position of relative inconsequence. In the case of Sant religion, the aim is usually to construct a coherent picture of Sant beliefs, values and ideas, with verses or lines quoted as illustrations. This lack of attention to form is unfortunate, for the conventions of literary forms and genres are the structural framework that shapes and transmits thought content and, as such, are an integral part of any text being studied. "Message" and "medium" are not really separable. Thus, in trying to understand 'the way of thinking of the Sants' (*sant mat*) and 'the tradition of the Sants' (*sant paramparā*), a knowledge of the literary forms in which the Sants expressed themselves and through which their thought is remembered, i.e. the forms of 'the utterances of the Sants' (*sant bānī*), is one of the utmost importance.

This paper is a contribution to the study of the Sants through the examination of Sant literary genres. It focuses on the particular kind of poetic utterance most characteristic of the North Indian Sants: the *dohā*, also referred to in Sant literature as the *sākhī*.[1] First, some general observations will be made about the *dohā* as a Hindi verse form,[2] concerning its metrical structure, the kinds of syntactic patterns dictated by the metrical form, and the poetic devices used to re-enforce them. Then a brief history of the *dohā* genre prior to its adoption by the medieval Sants of the Hindi area will be sketched, including its possible origins,

I would like to thank the following people for their comments on the ideas expressed in this paper: Prof. Kali Charan Bahl of the University of Chicago, my colleague Prof. Amin P. Sweeney, and Linda Hess. I would also like to thank Dr. Premlata Sharma of Banaras Hindu University for having introduced me to the musical performance of Sant-*bānī*.

1. For the notion of *sākhī*, see below, pp. 24-26. The other principal genre of Sant-*bānī* is the *śabda* or *pad* (lyric).

2. 'Hindi' refers here not to the modern speech alone but to the entire community of dialects which have been carriers of the Hindi literary tradition.

its importance in Apabhramsa literature,[3] its primary functions, and its use in the Jain, Buddhist, Siddha and Nath Yogi traditions. The use of the *dohā* by the Sants themselves will be examined next, which will entail discussing the particularly close association that developed between the *dohā* and *nirguṇa* teachings, the conception of *dohā*s uttered by Sants as '*sākhī*s', and what the expression and transmission of Sant teachings in the *dohā* form implies for their status and role in the society. Finally, I will propose a rhetorical approach to the study of Sant *dohā*s or *sākhī*s which takes into account the different contexts in which they can occur.

The Dohā *as a Verse Form*

The *dohā* is a couplet, the meaning of which is complete in itself—a verse form which Indian literary tradition would classify as *muktaka* ('independent verse'). To simply say that the *dohā* is a couplet is not enough, however, for there are many different kinds of couplets, each with its formal characteristics. A very popular *dohā* of Kabir may serve as an illustration:

Jahāṅ dayā tahāṅ dharma hai, jahāṅ lobha tahāṅ pāpa
Jahāṅ krodha tahāṅ kāla hai, jahāṅ khimāṅ tahāṅ āpa[4]

Where there is compassion, there is dharma,
where there is greed, there is sin.
Where there is anger, there is death,
where there is forgiveness, there is the Self.

The first obvious observation is that it is an extremely short verse form. A standard *dohā* has only 24 *mātrā*s or morae in each line,[5] which makes it one of the shortest quantitative meters of Hindi. Furthermore, each line forms a complete sentence. This means that the *dohā* requires

3. Apabhramsa: collective name for the middle Indo-Aryan dialects which evolved from the various forms of Prakrit between the sixth and tenth centuries A.D.

4. Parasnath Tiwari, ed., *Kabīr-granthāvalī* [hereafter *KG*] (Allahabad: University of Allahabad, Hindi Parishad, 1961), 15.23. All references to verses in this text are to the *sākhī* section. All translations in this paper are by the author.

5. The standard form of the *dohā* was specified for the first time in the *Prākṛta paiṅagalam*, a fourteenth-century treatise on poetic meters. In that text, 23 different kinds of *dohā*s are mentioned. Even today, the *dohā* in oral tradition does not rigidly conform to the standard form. For a technical discussion of *dohā* meter, see Shivanandan Prasad, *Mātrik chhandoṅ kā vikās* (Patna: Bihar Rashtrabhasha Parishad, 1964), pp. 387-88.

extreme succinctness of expression. Only the bare essence of a thought is expressed: elaboration is impossible. A closer look at the metrical structure reveals further characteristics of the *dohā*: (a) it is a *rhyming* couplet (with, as is usual in Hindi, rhyme in the last *two* syllables of each line); (b) there is a clearly marked caesura or rhythmic break (*yati*) in the middle of each line (after the thirteenth *mātrā*), which also marks a syntactic break in the sentence; and (c) within each half-line, there is a tendency for a rhythmic pause after the first six *mātrā*s, a pause which also marks the end of a phrase or clause within the sentence. Thus, the *dohā* is a verse form that has all the requirements for oral composition and memorization: strict end rhyme, division into smaller rhythmic units, and a close relationship between rhythmic units and units of meaning. It is thus not only brief, but also easy to remember. A final formal characteristic is the irregularity of the sequence of long and short *mātrā*s within each line and, indeed, of the overall *mātrā* count. (This particular *dohā* has 23 instead of 24 *mātrā*s in each line.) Instead, what gives the couplet its rhythmic regularity is a pattern of four stresses per line. This is a musical rhythm created by the regular beat of a musical *tāl* or rhythmic cycle. The *dohā* is thus a form intended to be sung as well as spoken.

If one turns to the syntactic structure of the *dohā*, one can see that the metrical form dictates a certain sentence pattern. Because of the sequence of binary structures created by the two-line couplet, the mid-line caesural break and the regular rythmic pause in the half-lines, there is a tendency for parallelisms and simple either/or oppositions. Here we have parallelisms within parallelisms. At the level of the smaller units, there is a series of balanced, formulaic "*jahāṅ...tahāṅ...*" ("where... there...") constructions in each half-line, while at the overall level there is a reverse parallelism between the first and the second line: positive-negative, negative-positive. Furthermore, the logic of the whole statement is one of oppositions: compassion vs. greed, dharma vs. sin, anger vs. forgiveness, death vs. the Self—made all the more sharp by a certain amount of alliteration (*dayā...dharma, krodha...kāla*, etc.) and the rhyming of *pāpa* and *āpa*. Though this particular *dohā* is especially schematic, the same simple logic of parallelism and opposition is characteristic of *dohā*s in general. This kind of structure is typical of proverbial utterances, and the *dohā* is in fact one of the favorite meters of Hindi proverbs and folk sayings.[6] Thus the *dohā* is not only brief and easy to

6. On the popularity of the *dohā* as a metric form for Hindi riddles as well, see Alan Dundes and Ved Prakash Vatuk, "Some Characteristic Meters of Hindi Riddle

remember, but also highly persuasive, carrying about it an aura of traditional wisdom and universal truth.[7]

The Dohā *before the Sants*

The oldest surviving instance of a *dohā* is in the Northern recension of Kalidasa's *Vikramorvaśīya.* In this recension of the Sanskrit drama, the fourth act contains a few passages in Western Apabhramsa, including one *dohā.*[8] Though these passages are without doubt later interpolations, perhaps of the eighth century, scholarly opinion agrees that there was some form of Apabhramsa literature by the sixth century A.D., and that the *dohā* was from the beginning the major poetic meter of this literature.[9]

The *dohā* appears indeed as a new kind of verse form closely associated with the rise of Apabhramsa. Not only is it hardly found at all even in late Sanskrit and Prakrit literature, but its formal principles differ radically from those of Sanskrit and Prakrit meters. Whereas the latter are rigid syllable-counting meters with a fixed order of feet within each line, the *dohā,* as has been demonstrated above, is an extremely flexible meter based on *mātrā* or moraic count alone. Furthermore, while in most Sanskrit and Prakrit meters end-rhyme is something optional, it is a fundamental defining feature of the *dohā* and other meters of Apabhramsa origin. Finally, the *dohā* is distanced from Sanskrit and Prakrit meters by the fact that its form suggests oral composition and sung performance. Despite the fact that the word '*dohā*' may be derived from Sanskrit *dodhaka, dvipadī* or *dvipathaka* (all names of

Prosody," *Asian Folklore Studies* 33:1 (1974), pp. 124-46. For a general discussion of proverb structure, see Roger D. Abrahams, "Proverbs and Proverbial Expressions," in Richard M. Dorson, ed., *Folklore and Folklife* (Chicago: University of Chicago Press, 1972), pp. 117-27.

7. Equivalent "proverbial" folk meters in other regions of India include the Tamil *kanni,* the Kannada *tripadi* and the *vākh* of Kashmir. For the *kanni* as a verse form of the Tamil Siddhas, see K. Kailasapathy, "The Writings of the Tamil Siddhas," below.

8. C.R. Devadhar, ed., *Vikramorvaśiyam* of Kalidasa, 2nd revised ed. (Delhi: Motilal Banarsidass, 1966), 4.7, p. 169.

9. For the history of Apabhramsa literature, see Richard Pischel, *Materiellen zur Kentniss des Apabhramsa* (Berlin: Weidmann, 1902), Ludwig Alsdorf, *Apabhramsa-Studien* (Leipzig: Deutsche Morgandlandische Gesellschaft, 1937) and Ramsingh Tomar, *Prākṛt aur Apabhraṁśa sāhitya tathā unkā Hindī sāhitya par prabhāv* (Allahabad: University of Allahabad, Hindi Parishad, 1964).

Sanskrit couplet forms),[10] the form itself is most probably of popular, non-Sanskritic origin. A theory first propounded by Hermann Jacobi, and still given general credence, is that there may have been some connection between the *dohā* (and end-rhyming poetic meters in general) and the foreign peoples who entered India from the north-west during the early centuries of the Christian era. The Abhirs are specifically suggested in this connection because of their widespread political power, their role in the development of the Krishna cult, and their undoubted influence on the evolution of Apabhramsa as a language.[11] This supposition is further supported by the fact that there is a reverse *dohā* (in which the 24-*mātrā* line is broken after the eleventh instead of the thirteenth *mātrā*) which is called *soraṭhā*, a name which suggests a link with Saurashtra, to which the Abhirs were long connected.

Whatever the exact origin of the *dohā*, it became the dominant poetic meter of Apabhramsa, just as the *gāthā* was the dominant meter of Prakrit and the *śloka* of Sanskrit. According to Hazariprasad Dvivedi, the term *dūhāvidyā* ('the science or art of *dohā*'), found in several texts, was practically a synonym for Apabhramsa literature.[12] Indeed, the *dohā* is prominent in all of the different kinds of Apabhramsa literature that have come down to us: grammars and works on metrics, Jain didactic anthologies and religious narratives, secular love narratives, the utterances of the Buddhist Siddhas, doctrinal works of the Kashmir Shaivas, the vernacular literature of the Nath Yogis and, finally, poetry in praise of kings, including the early *rāso* literature of Rajasthan.[13] Furthermore, it came to be used in a great variety of formal contexts. Thus, in both Apabhramsa and medieval Hindi literature, one finds *dohā*s as: (a) independent verses quoted in other works; (b) independent verses gathered together in collections; (c) building blocks around which longer narrative cycles (*prabandha*) are constructed; (d) the concluding verses for stanzas in other, narrative meters; (e) refrains (*ṭek*) for sung

10. For a summary of opinions on the derivation of the word *dohā*, see Krishna Bihari Sahal, *Dholā-Mārū rā dūhā: ek vivechan* (Delhi: Atmaram and Sons, 1965), pp. 210-14.

11. For a recent statement of this theory, see Hazariprasad Dvivedi, *Hindī sāhitya kā ādikāl*, 3rd ed. (Patna: Bihar Rashtrabhasha Parishad, 1960), pp. 99-100 and Shakuntala Dube, *Kāvyarūpoṅ ke mūlsrot aur unkā vikās* (Varanasi: Hindi Pracharak Pustakalay, 1964), p. 374.

12. Dvivedi, *Ādikāl*, p. 99.

13. For a survey of Apabhramsa works in *dohā* meter, see Prasad, *Chhandoṅ kā vikās*, pp. 390-95. *Rāso* is a genre of heroic narrative written by the court poets of the Rajput kings to glorify their patrons and their patrons' lineages.

lyrics (*pad*); (f) lines of song lyrics; and (g) combined with other meters to create new metric forms.[14]

Thus, like the *śloka* and *gāthā* before it, the *dohā* became an omni-purpose meter. It became especially associated, however, with two principal functions, which are also its predominant functions in the folk environment.[15] The first is that of compressed aphoristic statement, i.e. proverbial utterance or folk saying. The didactic *dohā*s of the Jains, Siddhas, Naths and Sants belong in this tradition. The second function is one which most likely evolved out of women's folksongs. It is the lyrical evocation of intense feeling, particularly the feeling of *viraha*, the pain of separation from one's beloved. In adopting this theme, central to all medieval Indian love poetry, as a symbolic expression of the soul's yearning for God, the Sants became part of this second major tradition of *dohā* composition as well.

The tradition of didactic *dohā*s is preserved primarily in collections. Such collections of independent verses are a standard Indian literary genre going back to religious anthologies such as the Buddhist *Dhammapada* and the secular epigram collections (*subhāṣita-koṣa*s) of Sanskrit. In Prakrit the secular tradition was most evident, works such as the *Gāthā-saptaśati* of Hala and the *Vajjālaga* of Jayavallabha being collections of *gāthā*s on a wide variety of worldly subjects.[16] In Apabhramsa, on the other hand, collections of *dohā*s were primarily religious and a tradition of the heterodox religions: Jainism and Buddhism. Only later, with the Sanskrit-imitating *rīti* movement of Hindi poetry in Braj, are secular *dohā* collections such as Bihari's *Satsaī* once again prominent.[17] The tradition of *dohā* compilation to which the Sant anthologies belong is one whose primary purpose was the exposition of philosophic doctrines and the transmission of moral and spiritual teachings.

The similarities in tone and content between the didactic *dohā*s of the Sants and those of their Jain and Buddhist predecessors are remarkable. The Jain *Pāhuḍadohā* of Ramasimha (ca. 1000 A.D.), for instance,

14. Prasad, *Chhandoṅ kā vikās*, pp. 400-10.

15. On this point, see Richard A. Williams, "The *Ḍholā-Mārū rā Dūhā* and the rise of the Hindi Literary Tradition," unpublished Ph.D. dissertation (University of Chicago, 1976), pp. 115-16.

16. For a discussion of these two works, see Tomar, *Prākṛt aur Apabhraṃśa sāhitya*, pp. 22-29.

17. See Barron Gregory Holland, "The *Satsaī* of Bihārī: Hindī Poetry of the early *Rīti* Period," unpublished Ph.D. dissertation (University of California, Berkeley, 1969).

condemns empty book-learning in words very close to those of Kabir. Ramasimha:

bahuyaiṅ paḍhiyaiṅ mūḍha para, tālū sukkai jeṇa
ekku ji akkharu taṅ paḍhahu, Sivapuri jammai jeṇa[18]

You've read a lot, your mouth is dry,
but you're still a fool:
Read only that one letter
which takes you to Shiva's abode!

Kabir:

pothī pothī paṛhi jaga muvā, paṇḍita bhayā na koi
ekai ākhara prema kā, paṛhai so paṇḍita hoi (*KG* 33.3)

Reading books, the whole world died,
and no one became learned:
Read just one letter of the word 'love',
then you'll be a pandit!

Other familiar themes also appear, such as the condemnation of hypocrisy and the call for inner purity:

abbhitarichitti vi mailiyaiṅ, bāhiri kāiṅ taveṇa
chitti ṇirañjaṇu ko vi dhari, mucchahi jema maleṇa[19]

If there's filth in your thoughts,
what good outward austerities?
Hold the Immaculate One in your mind:
then you'll be free of filth.

When we turn to the *dohā* collections (*dohākoṣas*) of the Buddhist Siddhas (eighth to eleventh centuries A.D.), the sense of family resemblance is even more striking.[20] Indeed, there is a strong line of thematic

18. Hiralal Jain, ed. and trans, *Pāhudadohā of Ramasimha Muni* (Karanja, Berar: Karanja Jaina Publication Society, 1938), *dohā* 97. For a more recent translation of this text, see Collete Caillat, "L'offrande de distiques (*Dohāpāhuḍa*): traduction de l'apabhraṃśa," *Journal Asiatique* 264 (1976), pp. 63-95.

19. *Pāhuḍadohā*, *dohā* 61. *Nirañjaṇu* (*nirañjan*), 'the Immaculate One', is a term for the Supreme Being found in Tantric and Nath-panthi vocabulary.

20. For studies and translations of the literature of the Buddhist Siddhas, see Muhammad Shahidullah, trans., *Buddhist Mystic Songs: Oldest Bengali and Other Eastern Vernaculars*, 2nd revised ed. (Dacca: Bengali Academy, 1966); Dharmvir Bharati, *Siddha sāhitya*, 3rd ed. (Allahabad: Kitab Mahal, 1968); Herbert V. Guen-

continuity linking the utterances of the Siddhas and those of the Sants. Many of the attitudes and central concepts of the Siddhas were carried over into Sant religion.[21] Like the Sants, for instance, the Siddhas had a strong critical attitude towards established religions and their representatives, particularly Brahman priests. This attitude is frequently expressed in their *dohās*. In the *Dohākoṣa* of Saraha, one finds the following verse which could easily have been uttered by Kabir:

brahmaṇehi ma jānanta hi bheu, evai paḍhiau e chaubeu
maṭṭī pāṇī kusa lai paḍhante, gharahiṅ basasī aggi huṇantaṃ[22]

The Brahmans don't know the truth,
but they recite the four Vedas;
They mutter over earth, water and kusha-grass,
and sit at home kindling their fire.

The Siddhas also shared the Sants' mistrust of the written word, (i.e. religious scriptures), seeking mystical experience beyond the reach of words. This common motif of Kabir's is expressed in another *dohā* of Saraha:

Akkhara-bādhā sāla jagu, ṇāhi ṇirakkhara koi
Tāba se akkhara gholiyā, jāba ṇirakkhara hoi[23]

The whole world is bound by words,
no one is free of words:
Only when you're free of words
will you make sense of words.

The spiritual discipline of the Siddhas was a form of Tantric Yoga. Their quest was for the experience of *sahaja*, the Ultimate Reality within, and their method for attaining it involved arresting the functions of

---

ther, *The Royal Song of Saraha* (Seattle: University of Washington Press, 1969); and Per Kvaerne, *An Anthology of Buddhist Tantric Songs* (Oslo: Norwegian Research Council, 1977).

21. See Shashibhusan Dasgupta, *Obscure Religious Cults*, 3rd ed. (Calcutta: K.L. Mukhopadhyay, 1976), pp. 345-66.

22. P.C. Bagchi, ed., *Dohākoṣa of Saraha* (Calcutta: Calcutta Sanskrit Series, 1938), *dohā* 2. It should be noted that this verse is not actually a *dohā*: though the dominant couplet form in the *dohākoṣas* was the *dohā*, other verse forms belonging to the "*dohā* family" (see Bharati, *Siddha sāhitya*, p. 295) are also to be found, and are treated by the tradition as if they were in fact *dohās*.

23. Bagchi, *Dohākoṣa*, *dohā* 88. I follow Shahidullah in translating '*akkhara*' as 'word'.

the mind by Yogic techniques.[24] Though the Sants tended to reinterpret this goal symbolically, Sant *dohā*s expressing the experience of the Ultimate barely differ from those of the Siddhas.
Sahara:

jahi maṇa pavaṇa ṇa sancharai, ravi sasi ṇāha pavesa
tahi beḍha chitta visāma kuru, Saraha kahi uesa[25]

Where mind and vital breath can't go,
where sun and moon can't enter —
There put your consciousness to rest,
this is the teaching of Saraha.

Dadu:

chala Dādū tahāṅ jāie, jahāṅ chanda sūra nahīṅ jāi
rāti divasa kī gami nahīṅ, sahajaiṅ rahe samāi[26]

Come, says Dadu, let's to go that land
where neither moon nor sun can go,
Where neither night nor day can enter
and all is merged in *sahaja*.

This Yogic element in the utterances of the Sants did not come to them directly, but was mediated through the Nath Yogi tradition, which had spread all over India by the tenth century and was quite influential among the lower classes of society.[27] The Naths appear as heirs to both the ancient Hindu tradition of Shaivite asceticism and the esoteric practices of the Buddhist Siddhas. Their teachings are similar in many ways to those of the Siddhas, though there is greater emphasis in their spiritual discipline on breath control and physical methods for the attain-

24. For the Siddha *sādhanā*, see Dasgupta, *Obscure Cults*, pp. 101-28.

25. Bagchi, *Dohākoṣa, dohā* 25. In Yogic symbolism, the sun and the moon stand for the right and left *nāḍī*s or 'channels' (called *iḍā* and *piṅgalā*) through which the 'vital breaths' (*prāṇa*) circulate in the body. When the Yogi succeeds in stopping his breaths and stilling his mental processes, the *kuṇḍalinī* or 'serpent-force' coiled up in the *chakra* or 'nerve-plexus' at the base of his spine rises through the central 'channel' (called *suṣumnā*), and eventually bursts through the highest *chakra*, throwing the Yogi into the state of trance in which *sahaja* is experienced.

26. Parashuram Chaturvedi, ed., *Dādūdayāl granthāvalī* (Varanasi: Nagaripracharini Sabha, 1965), *sākhī* 16.22.

27. For the Nath Yogi tradition, see George Weston Briggs, *Gorakhnāth and the Kānphaṭa Yogīs*, reprint ed. (Delhi: Motilal Banarsidass, 1973) and Hazariprasad Dvivedi, *Nāth-sampradāy* (Varanasi: Naivedya Niketan, 1950).

ment of mental states (i.e. Hatha Yoga) and they rejected the erotic ritual of the Siddhas. Their influence on the Sants was less in their actual practices, however, but as transmitters of heterodox attitudes towards established religion and in their emphasis on values of bodily purity and self-control. In addition, the Sants inherited all the technical vocabulary and mystical symbolism of the Naths and tried to give it new meaning.

The literature of Gorakhnath, the reputed founder of the Nathpanth, is considerable. Most of these works are in Sanskrit, and are technical treatises on Hatha Yoga practice.[28] However, a number of texts have been found which set forth his popular philosophical and moral teachings in a language described as "recently forged out of Sanskrit, Paisachi, Apabhramsa and the Desi languages of the Punjab,"[29] and very close to the mixed language of the North Indian Sants. The most important of these texts is a collection of aphoristic sayings referred to as *śabdīs*.[30] Though most of them are in meters other than *dohā*, they are generally couplets, and function like *dohā*s. Thematically, as well as in their imagery and vocabulary, they are clearly a link in the tradition of didactic *dohā*s which culminates in the Sants. Some of these *śabdī*s are found only slightly altered in the later Sant anthologies. For example, Gorakhnath says:

hindū ākhaiṅ rāṅma kauṅ, musalamāna khudāi
jogī ākhaiṅ alakha kauṅ, tahāṅ Rāma achhai na khudāi[31]

The Hindu calls on Ram,
the Muslim on Khuda,
The Yogi calls on the Invisible One,
in whom there is neither Ram nor Khuda.

In Kabir, this *dohā* has become:

hindū mūā Rāṅma kahi, musalamāna khudāi
kahai Kabīra so jīvatā, jo duhuṅ kai nikaṭi na jāi (*KG* 20.9)

28. For a survey of these works, see Briggs, *Kānphaṭa Yogis*, pp. 251-57.

29. Mohan Singh, *Gorakhnath and Medieval Hindu Mysticism* (Lahore: Oriental College, 1937), p. 38. This work contains a translation of the fourteenth-century *Gorakh-bodh*, which is a dialogue between Gorakhnath and his teacher Matsyendranath.

30. It is included in Pitambar D. Barthwal's critical edition of the Hindi texts of Gorakhnath, *Gorakh-bāṇī*, 4th ed. (Allahabad: Hindi Sahitya Sammelan, 1979), pp. 1-83.

31. Ibid., *śabdī* 69. *Khudāi* (*khudā*) is a Muslim (Persian) term for 'God'. *Alakh*, 'the Invisible One', is a Tantric and Nath-panthi term for the Supreme Being.

The Hindu dies saying 'Ram',
the Muslim 'Khuda'.
Says Kabir: one lives
when one goes to neither.

Again, describing the mystical trance or state of *sahaja* as experienced by the adept of Hatha Yoga, Gorakhnath says:

nīṅjhara jharaṇaiṅ aṅmīrasa pīvaṇāṅ, ṣaṭadala bedhyā jāi
chanda bihuṇāṅ chāṅdiṇāṅ tahāṅ, dekhyā Gorakha rāi[32]

The spring has burst forth, I have drunk the nectar of immortality,
I have pierced the thousand-petalled lotus;
Where there is moonlight without the moon,
there I saw Lord Gorakhnath.

The same *dohā* is found in Kabir, relieved of some of its more technical Hatha Yoga vocabulary:

mana lāgā unamanna sauṅ, gagana pahūṅchā jāi
chāṅda bihuṇāṅ chāṅdiṇāṅ, tahāṅ alakha nirañjana rāi (*KG* 9.8)

My mind has entered the state of reversal,
I have scaled the vault of the sky;
Where there is moonlight without the moon,
there reigns the Invisible, Immaculate One.

The principal, and crucial difference between the *dohā*s of the Sants and the *śabdī*s of Gorakhnath is the presence of the new emotional element of bhakti.[33] While, in their philosophical and moral teachings, the Sants have much in common with the Naths, as well as with their Buddhist and Jain predecessors, there is nothing in the works of these earlier traditions to compare with the Sant expression of loving devotion to their Lord and the pain of separation from that Lord. This aspect of Sant religion links them to the older bhakti tradition of the Alvars and Nayanars of Tamilnad and the *Bhāgavata Purāṇa*. The expression of this *prema-bhakti* nevertheless also takes the form of *dohā*s, and thus links the Sants to the second major tradition of *dohā* composition, that connected with women's folksongs on the theme of *viraha*. This tradition has been preserved in written texts such as the

32. Ibid., *śabdī* 171. For the esoteric symbolism, see footnote 25, above.

33. Cf. the notion of Sant religion as a synthesis of bhakti and Yoga. Pitambar D. Barthwal, *Traditions of Indian Mysticism Based upon Nirguna School of Hindi Poetry*, reprint ed. (New Delhi: Heritage Publishers, 1978), pp. 197ff.

Ḍholā-Mārū, a love narrative compiled in the sixteenth century but on the basis of *dohā*s that had been in oral circulation long before that time.[34] Examining the *dohā*s in such texts should enable us to see how closely the expression of *viraha* by the Sants echoes that of the lyrical folk tradition. In the *Ḍholā-Mārū*, there are in fact 14 *dohā*s which are nearly identical to those found in the standard text of the Rajasthani recension of Kabir.[35] Two of these will suffice to make the point. *Ḍholā-Mārū*:

supanai prītama mujha miḷyā, hūṅ galī laggī dhāi
ḍarapata palaka na chhodahī, mati supanau hui jāi[36]

I met my beloved in a dream
and ran to embrace him;
I kept my eyelids closed,
fearing it was just a dream.

Kabir:

Kabīra supinaiṅ Hari milā, mohiṅ sūtāṅ liyā jagāi
āṅkhi na mīchauṅ ḍarapatā, mati supināṅ hoi jāi (*KG* 2.42)

Kabir: I met Hari in a dream,
he woke me from my sleep;
I didn't open my eyes,
fearing it was just a dream.

Ḍholā Mārū:

yahu tana jārī masi kurūṅ, dhūṅmā jāhi saraggi
mujha priya baddaḷa hota kari, barasi bujhāvai aggi[37]

Let my body burn and become embers,
let it go up in smoke to the sky,
So that my beloved, like a cloud,
might rain down on me to quench the fire.

34. For a study of this text's composition and its relation to oral *dohā* tradition, see Williams, "The *Ḍholā-Mārū rā Dūhā*," especially chapters 3 and 4.

35. A list of these is given by the editors of the *Ḍholā-Mārū*. Ramsingh, Suryakaran Parik and Swami Narottamdas, eds., *Ḍholā-Mārū rā Dūhā*, 3rd. ed. (Kashi: Nagari Pracharini Sabha, 1962-3), pp. 168-78. For the different recensions of Kabir, see Linda Hess, "Three Kabir Collections: A Comparative Study," later in this volume.

36. Ramsingh *et al.*, *Ḍholā-Mārū*, *dohā* 503.

37. Ibid., *dohā* 181.

Kabir:

yahu tana jālauṅ masi karūṅ, jyūṅ dhuvāṅ jāi saraggi
mati vai Rāma dayā karaiṅ, barasi bujhāvai aggi[38]

Let my body burn and become embers,
let it go up in smoke to the sky;
Perhaps then Ram will have mercy,
and rain down on me to quench the fire.

The Dohā *and the Sants*

By the late fourteenth century, when the earliest of the North Indian Sants began to preach their message of *nirguṇa* bhakti, the *dohā* was already established in the literary tradition of the Hindi area. Not only in Apabhramsa, but also in medieval Hindi, the *dohā* was the most popular poetic meter, a status which it retained until the twentieth century. As we have seen, it was used for both secular and religious literary expression but, as an independent aphoristic verse, it was primarily a religious genre. As the bhakti movement in its various forms spread over North India in the fifteenth and subsequent centuries, inspiring creativity in all the medieval literary dialects of Hindi, it might have been expected that *all* the bhakti poets would make use of the aphoristic *dohā* for the propagation of their teachings. However, it tended instead to remain the special province of the *nirguṇa* Sants, and never became an important genre of either Ramaite or Krishnaite *saguṇa* bhakti.

Two explanations suggest themselves readily. In the first place, the previous history of the *dohā* as a vehicle of religious teachings had been primarily associated with heterodox religious traditions. For the Sants, who were spiritual heirs to these traditions, continued use of the *dohā* genre was only natural. Orthodox Vaishnava *bhakta*s, on the other hand, may have had some uneasiness about using a mode of expression associated with heterodox teachings. Tulsidas, in a *dohā* of his own which condemns the heterodoxy represented by the Sants, specifically mentions the *dohā* (or *sākhī*) as a verse form associated with it:

sākhī śabdī doharā, kahi kahanī upakhāna
bhagati nirūpahi adhama kavi, nindahi Veda Purāṇa[39]

38. Shyamsundar Das, ed., *Kabīr granthāvalī*, 14th impr. (Varanasi: Nagari Pracharini Sabha, 1976, *sākhī* 3.11.

39. Ramchandra Shukla *et al.*, eds., *Tulsī granthāvalī*, 4 vols., reprint ed. (Varanasi: Nagari Pracharini Sabha, 1973-74). vol. 2, *Dohāvalī*, *dohā* 554.

By means of *sākhīs*, *śabdīs*, *dohās*,
tales and stories,
These vile poets expound bhakti,
while scorning the Vedas and the Puranas.

Beyond the historical associations of the *dohā*, however, there is a second factor which is one of poetics. Kenneth Bryant has made the important observation that the difference between *saguṇa* and *nirguṇa* bhakti has a literary as well as a theological aspect. Whereas *saguṇa* poetry is based on a story, the only basis for *nirguṇa* poetry is the poet's personal experience. Therefore, while the *saguṇa* poet presents a narrative or a drama, all the *nirguṇa* poet can present is moments of realization or commitment.[40] The *dohā* form, with its conciseness and intensity, is admirably suited for the latter, but too brief for the former.

Though the *dohā* as an independent verse is a typically Sant genre, it is not entirely absent as a metrical form from the poetry of the *saguṇa* poets. It occurs in several of the formal embedded contexts described earlier: as a meter in song lyrics (*pad*), in the position of refrain and, most notably in Tulsi's *Rāmcharitmānas*, as the concluding verse of stanzas in narrative *chaupāī* meter. The concept of combining a narrative meter with a summarizing couplet goes back to Apabhramsa Jain narratives.[41] *Chaupāī* stanzas are to be found in the literature of the Siddhas, Naths and Sants, though without concluding *dohās*. The actual combination of *chaupāī* and *dohā* is first found in Kabir, where it serves an expository purpose and is called a *ramainī*,[42] and in the allegorical love narratives of Indian Sufis like Mulla Daud and Malik Muhammad Jayasi (fifteenth century), where the purpose is narrative.[43] In all of these,

40. Kenneth E. Bryant, "*Sant* and *Vaiṣṇava* Poetry: Some Observations on Method," in Mark Juergensmeyer and N. Gerald Barrier, eds., *Sikh Studies: Comparative Perspectives on a Changing Tradition* (Berkeley: Berkeley Religious Studies Series, 1979), pp. 65-74.

41. The Jain *Rāmāyaṇa* of Svayambhu (ca. 800 A.D.), for instance, was composed of stanzas made up of *paddhaṛiyā* meter and a concluding *dhattā* couplet. For a discussion of this stanzaic form as a prototype of the *chaupāī-dohā* stanza, see Parashuram Chaturvedi, *Sant-kāvya*, 3rd ed. (Allahabad: Kitab Mahal, 1967), pp. 30-31.

42. The origin of the term *ramainī* is obscure. For a discussion of the problem, see Parashuram Chaturvedi, *Kabīr-sāhitya kī parakh*, 3rd ed. (Allahabad: Bharati Bhandar, 1972), pp. 193-95.

43. For Mulla Daud's *Chāndāyan*, see Mataprasad Gupta, ed., *Chāndāyan* (Agra: Pramanik Prakashan, 1967); for Jayasi's *Padmāvat*, see Vasudevsharan Agrawal, ed., *Padmāvat* (Jhansi: Sahitya Sadan, 1955). Both works are in the Avadhi dialect, as is Tulsi's *Rāmcharitmānas*.

the *dohā* serves to summarize, shift the perspective or state a general truth. What is striking about the *dohā*s in the *Rāmcharitmānas*, however, is that they frequently have a Sant-like "ring" to them, breaking into the very midst of the *saguṇa* narrative with a statement of *nirguṇa* reality.[44] Typically, they express devotion to the Name of Ram (*Rām-nām*) rather than to Ram, the son of Dasaratha:

> *Brahma Rāma teṅ nāmu baṛa, baṛa dāyaka baṛa dāni*
> *Rāmacharita sata koṭi mahaṅ, liya Mahesa jiyaṅ jāni*[45]
>
> The Name is greater than both the Absolute and Ram,
> it blesses even those that bless.
> Knowing this Mahesa chose it
> from among the thousand million verses.

That Tulsidas, who sought to harmonize under the aegis of Rama-bhakti most of the major religious ideas of his time, should have had a *nirguṇa* aspect to his thinking is not surprising.[46] The point to be stressed here is that it was most frequently expressed in *dohā*s.

It thus seems clear that there is a close association between the *dohā*, especially the aphoristic or didactic *dohā*, and the *nirguṇa* form of North Indian bhakti. *Dohā* collections therefore came to be one of the principal kinds of literary texts produced by the Sant movement. The earliest collections were simply lists. This is the pattern in the *Ādi Granth* of the Sikhs and in the *Bījak* of Kabir.[47] At some point, perhaps as a convenience for devotional study and recitation,[48] it became the practice to organize the *dohā*s by thematic categories referred to as *aṅga*s ('limbs'). This tradition may have had its origin in the Dadu-panth; in any case, it was Rajjab, the chief disciple of Dadu, who developed this mode of compilation most systematically. The 37 *aṅga* headings under which he grouped the *dohā*s uttered by his master represent,

44. See, in this connection, Wendy O'Flaherty's essay on "The Interaction of *Saguṇa* and *Nirguṇa* Images of Deity" earlier in this volume.

45. Tulsidas, *Rāmcharitmānas, Bālakāṇḍa, dohā* 25.

46. A Sant element is to be found in the poetry of Surdas as well. See J.S. Hawley's "The Sant in Surdas," later in this volume.

47. For a discussion of the *Bījak*, see Hess, "Three Kabir Collections," below, pp. 112-15 and *passim.*

48. This is the purpose suggested by W.G. Orr in *A Sixteenth-Century Indian Mystic: Dadu and His Followers* (London: Lutterworth Press, 1947), p. 81. In confirmation of this supposition, Daniel Gold has informed me that in present-day Sant *akhāṛā*s (residential centers where the followers of a particular Sant lineage gather), there is regular chanting from the printed texts of Sant-*bānī*. Personal communication

with some variation, the standard list of major Sant themes, while the 193 categories into which his own *dohās* are arranged provide an exhaustive catalogue of themes both major and minor.[49] These same categories and headings are found not only in Rajjab's other major work, the *Sarvāṅgī*,[50] and in the *Pañchvāṇī* manuscripts of the Dadu-panth,[51] but in later Sant texts as a whole, both manuscript traditions and popular *bānī* collections. They have thus become a kind of standardized "index" to Sant teachings.

Different texts and different Sant lineages or panths[52] may order the thematic *aṅga*s differently, excluding some or adding others, and may give varying degrees of emphasis to particular themes.[53] In spite of such minor variations, however, there is a general consensus in the tradition as to what the most important thematic categories are. Thus, in a rough statistical survey of the standard editions of Kabir, Dadu and Rajjab, and popular pamphlet editions of the *bānī* of twelve later Sants, I found ten major thematic headings not only present in all three of the Dadu-panthi texts, but also prominent in all the popular editions:[54] (1) *satguru*

49. For a list of the *aṅga* headings in the Dadu-*bānī*, see Orr, *Sixteenth-Century Mystic*, pp. 81-82. The *aṅga* headings for Rajjab's own *bānī* are listed in the table of contents of Swami Narayandas, ed., *Śrī Rajjab vāṇī* [hereafter *RV*] (Ajmer: Narayansingh Shekhavat, n.d., 1967?). All references to verses in this text are to the *sākhī* section.

50. The *Sarvāṅgī* is an anthology containing the utterances of around a hundred *nirguṇa* religious poets (manuscripts differ in the total number of poets included). Of the 144 *aṅga* headings into which the *dohās* in this text are grouped, 102 are identical to those in Rajjab's *bānī*. See Winand M. Callewaert, "Life and Works of the Dādū-Panthī Rajjab,", *Orientalia Lovaniensia Periodica* 4 (1973), pp. 141-53. For a list of the *aṅga* headings in the *Sarvāṅgī*, see Winand M. Callewaert, *The Sarvāṅgī of the Dādūpanthī Rajab* (Leuven: Department Orientalistiek, Katholieke Universiteit, 1978), pp. 430-33.

51. The *Pañchvānī* is a manuscript tradition containing selected utterances of five Sant poets especially honored in the Dadu-panth: Dadu, Kabir, Namdev, Raidas, and Haridas.

52. For the concept of the *panth*, see W.H. McLeod, "On the Word *Panth*," *Contributions to Indian Sociology*, new series, 12:2 (1978), pp. 287-95; also Mark Juergensmeyer, *Religion as Social Vision*: *The Movement against Untouchability in 20th-Century Punjab* (Berkeley: University of California Press, 1982), pp. 2, 6, 87.

53. The degree to which different lineages within the Sant tradition stress certain themes more than others is a question which deserves further study. I have made an attempt in this direction in "Kabir in the *Gurū Granth Sāhib*: An Exploratory Essay," in Juergensmeyer and Barrier, *Sikh Studies*, pp. 75-86.

54. The texts surveyed were: (a) *KG*, which represents the Rajasthani recension of Kabir (see Hess, "Three Kabir Collections," below, pp. 114-41 *passim* and fn. 5); (b)

mahimā, the greatness of the *satguru*, (2) *biraha*, separation, (3) *sādh mahimā*, the greatness of Sants, (4) *satsaṅg*, the companionship of Sants, (5) *binatī*, supplication, (6) *sūrātan*, heroism, (7) *chetāvanī*, admonition, (8) *māyā*, illusion, (9) *man*, the mind, and (10) *besās*, faith.[55] In addition, the three Dadu-panthi texts shared another eleven *aṅga*s in common: (1) *sumiran*, remembrance, (2) *pīva pichhān*, recognition of the Beloved, (3) *parachā*, the experience of spiritual knowledge, (4) *sāragrāhī*, grasping the essence, (5) *nirapakha madhi*, the impartial inner [path], (6) *sajevanī*, the root of immortality, (7) *vichār*, right thinking, (8) *patibratā*, the faithful wife, (9) *nindā*, slander, (10) *kāl*, death, and (11) *samarthatā*, the omnipotence [of God].[56]

These two lists are based on a relatively small number of Sant texts and obviously do not exhaust the *aṅga* headings found in Sant *dohā* collections. The first list, however, does cover the most common ones, those likely to be found wherever there is a thematic organization of Sant *dohā*s. What then do these headings signify? How are they to be interpreted? In most accounts of Sant religion, the *aṅga* headings are hardly dealt with at all, and certainly not interpreted in any way. This is a factor of the theological, as opposed to literary, approach taken towards the study of Sant texts. If, however, as I have suggested, understanding the "message" of the Sants requires an understanding of the various "media" in which it is expressed, then the genre of the *dohā* collection and its thematic headings can no more be ignored than the *dohā* genre itself. As A.K. Ramanujan has pointed out in his analysis of the Kannada *vachana*s of the Virashaiva saints, even the most spon-

Chaturvedi, *Dādūdayāl granthāvalī*; (c) *RV*; and (d) the following texts from the *Sant-bānī pustak mālā* series of Belvedere Press, Allahabad: *Bhīkhā sāhab kī bānī* (1974), *Bullā sāheb kā śabdasāgar* (1973), *Dayā bāī kī bānī* (n.d.), *Dharanīdās jī kī bānī* (n.d.), *Dūlandās jī kī bānī* (1964), *Garībdas jī kī bānī* (1969), *Gulāl sāheb kī bānī* (1971), *Jagjīvan sāheb kī śabdāvalī*, vol. 2 (1966), *Mahātmā Dhanī Dharmadāsjī kī śabdāvalī* (1971), *Malūk dāsjī kī bānī* (1971), *Palṭū sāhib kī bānī*, vol. 3 (1973), and *Sahajobāī kī bānī* (1975). In most of these, the *aṅga* headings are found only for the *dohā*s, but in some they are found for the *śabda*s as well or, in a few cases, only for the *śabda*s.

55. Alternate forms for some of these headings: (1) *gurudev* (the guru), (2) *prem biraha* (love and separation), (3) *sādh* or *sādhu* (Sants), (4) *sādhu saṅgati*, (5) *vinati*, *vinay*, *binay*, also *dīnatā binatī* (humility and supplication), (6) *sūr* (the hero), (7) *upadeś chetāvanī* (exhortation and admonition), (10) *bisvās*, *viśvās*, also *viśvās santoṣ* (contentment in faith).

56. Alternate forms: (1) *sumiran bhajan mahimā* (the greatness of remembrance and worship), (2) *piu pahichānibe*, (3) *jñān parichay*, (5) *niṣpakṣa madhya*, (6) *sajīvan*, (11) *saṅrathāī*.

taneous of literary utterances have their "repertoire of structures."[57] What the *aṅga* categories make clear for us is that Sant *dohās* are structured not only by metrical form, but by topical convention — merely implicit in the earliest Sants, but made explicit and systematic by the later anthologizers. The best way to interpret the *aṅga* categories, I propose, is as conventional poetic topics of the Sant *dohā* genre.[58]

To illustrate this aspect of the tradition of Sant *dohā* composition, I have chosen to examine the treatment of topics on the "short list" in the *dohās* of Rajjab. Whether Rajjab, as the great promoter of the *aṅga* organization of *dohās*, was more conscious than others of composing within a tradition of conventional topics is a matter of conjecture and not particularly relevant. Though each Sant naturally exhibits a certain amount of individuality in the way he treats the common themes, the role of the traditional schemata in shaping their utterances is of paramount importance.[59]

Topic 1: *satguru mahimā* (the greatness of the *satguru*)

sadguru vāika bīja hai, prāṇa puhami meṅ boya
Rajjaba rākhe jatana kara, mana vāṅchhita phala hoya (4.38)

The *satguru*'s word is the seed,
which is planted in the soil of the soul.
Says Rajjab: if you nurture it with great care,
You'll get fruit from it whenever you want.

This is the most universal topic of Sant *dohās*, present in every collection and almost always in first place. There is some variation in the degree to which the *satguru* is identified with any particular guru,[60]

57. A.K. Ramanujan, *Speaking of Siva* (Baltimore: Penguin Books, 1973), p. 39.

58. The importance of conventional subject matter as well as rhetorical devices in structuring traditional literary expression has been brilliantly analyzed by Ernst R. Curtius in his *European Literature in the Latin Middle Ages*, trans. Willard R. Trask (Princeton, N.J.: Princeton University Press, 1953); see especially his stress on the notion of *topoi* or commonplaces (p. 25). In "The *Ḍholā-Mārū rā Dūhā*," Richard Williams argues convincingly that this is no less true for medieval Indian literature (pp. 21ff).

59. For the notion of conceptual 'schemata' and their role in shaping artistic expression, see E.H. Gombrich, *Art and Illusion: A Study in the Psychology of Pictorial Representation* (Princeton: Princeton University Press, 1960).

60. Rajjab, for instance, frequently refers to Dadu by name (see 4.14 for example), while in Kabir, the *satguru* is unequivocally the interiorized guru who is the Lord himself (*KG* 1.28).

but regardless of this *dohā*s on this topic speak of the absolute necessity of the *satguru*'s role, initiative and guidance (4.32; *KG* 1.25) and exhort seekers to worship him (4.171). Different aspects of the *satguru*'s role are set forth, by means of traditional metaphors such as the "seed and field" one in the *dohā* just quoted,[61] or even the more common one of the archer who shoots the arrow of his Word (*śabda*) into the heart of the devotee (*KG* 1.9, 21, 23).

Topic 2: *viraha* (separation)

virahani bihare raina dina, bina dekheṅ dīdāra
jana Rajjaba jalatī rahai, jāgyā viraha apāra (10.5)

The *virahinī* wanders about day and night
without seeing her Beloved.
Says the devotee Rajjab: she burns,
for the boundless pain of *viraha* has arisen in her.

This topic provides the most powerful means for the expression of fervent devotion. In most collections, it follows shortly after the *aṅga* on the greatness of the *satguru*. As in the folk tradition of *dohā*s on the theme of *viraha*, there are poignant descriptions of the anguish of the *virahinī* (the woman separated from her lover). She is shown with her eyes glued to the road, anxiously waiting for her lover to come (*KG* 2.18, 36, 39), crying her heart out (*KG* 2.9, 48) or, as in the *dohā* just quoted, wandering about distracted in search of her beloved. Typical metaphors for the pain of *viraha* include that of a fire which is lit in the heart and consumes the body (10.7; *KG* 2.7), and that of snake bite (10.4; *KG* 2.2). Despite the pain, however, *viraha* is cherished and called a "friend" (10.35), for by awakening longing in the heart it becomes a means to enlightenment and union with the Lord.

Topics 3 and 4: *sādh mahimā* and *satsaṅg* (the greatness of Sants and the companionship of Sants)

sādhu ābhe sārikhā, sadā śūnya meṅ vāsa
Rajjaba āvahiṅ puhami para, niṣkāmī ru nirāsa (32.32)

Sants, like clouds,
always remain in the sky.
Says Rajjab: if they do come down to earth,
it is without attachment or desires.

61. For a discussion of the 'seed and field' metaphor, see Daniel Gold, "Clan and Lineage among the Sants: Seed, Substance, Service," later in this volume.

Rajjaba palaṭe jīva sudha, sādhu sangati āya
pārasa lohā pahupa tila, sraka chandana vana rāya (31.15)

Says Rajjab: even ordinary souls can change
when they come into the presence of Sants,
Like iron touched by the philosopher's stone, oil by the extract of flowers, and garlands or groves by the scent of sandalwood.

These two topics often overlap. The first describes the character of true Sants: they are tender-hearted and compassionate (32.20), immersed in bhakti (32.38), in but not of this world. Keeping company with them is stated to be of utmost benefit, almost a necessity for spiritual liberation (31.8, 24). Those who come into contact with them are automatically transformed (31.2; *KG* 4.1).

Topic 5: *binatī* (supplication)

bālaka ke bala roja kā, paṛi luṛi kare pukāra
Rajjaba suta meṅ śakti yahu, samartha sirajanahāra (45.16)

An infant, who has only the strength to cry,
lies there calling out for a lump of sugar.
Says Rajjab: your son too has only that much strength,
O all-powerful Creator!

In *dohā*s on this topic, what is expressed is the devotee's need for divine grace. Often, as in the *dohā* quoted here, the Sant compares himself to a helpless child. There is also self-reproach (45.90; *KG* 6.4), and remonstration against the Lord for his failure to bestow his grace (45.107).[62]

Topic 6: *sūrātan*; (heroism)

piṇḍa prāṇa saṅkalpa kara, śūra chaḍhai saṅgrāma
jana Rajjaba jaga ko tajai, gṛha dārā dhana dhāma (71.20)

Ready to give up body and life,
the hero goes into battle.
He abandons the world, says the devotee Rajjab,
forsaking wife, wealth and home.

62. See J.S. Hawley, "The Sant in Surdas," later in this volume, for the similarities between Surdas and the Sants in this theme of *binatī* or *vinaya*.

satī sindhaurā hātha le, kāṭya moha arāva
jana Rajjaba piva ko milī, dekho deha jarāya (71.9)

The *satī* takes the vermillion in her hands
and cuts the root of infatuation.
Says Rajjab: see, by burning her body,
she has met her Beloved.

The subject dealt with here is the difficulty of the way of faith, and the need for great courage. The overall metaphor is that of the spiritual quest as a prolonged struggle against powerful impediments. The one who persists is like a hero in battle who gives his all and has no fear of death. An equally powerful metaphor used in the treatment of this topic is that of the *satī* or faithful wife who bravely mounts her husband's funeral pyre and never turns back.

Topic 7: *chetāvanī* (admonition)

re prāṇī pāsā paṛyā, minakha dehī māṅhiṅ
jana Rajjaba jagadīśa bhaja, yahu avasara bhī nāṅhiṅ (82.4)

O creature, the roll of the dice has come around:
you are now in a human body.
Says the devotee Rajjab: worship the Lord of the Universe,
for this opportunity won't last long.

*Dohā*s on this topic admonish listeners to waste no time in seeking salvation, for it can only be obtained during this hard-won human birth (82.2, 6; *KG* 15.5, 6). Seekers are reminded of the brevity of human life (*KG* 16.21), the inevitability of death (*KG* 15.66, 67) and the illusoriness of this world (82.167). In light of this, all pride in youth, wealth or power is stated to be futile (82.138; *KG* 15.21-24, 42, 45).

Topic 8: *māyā* (illusion)

māyā mārai mīcha hvai, bina bāṅchhī hī āya
Rajjaba sidha sādhaka ḍase, so ṭālī nahiṅ jāya (107.10)

Illusion comes without being desired,
and strikes like death.
Says Rajjab: it bites even accomplished spiritual seekers, and
can't be averted.

The subject here is the power of *māyā*, which is so all-pervasive that there is no escaping it. It is portrayed as a harlot (*KG* 31.18) and an enchantress (*KG* 31.17), or as a great tree whose branches spread in all directions (107.13; *KG* 31.31). Only the Sants, who have taken refuge in the Lord, have any power to withstand it (*KG* 31.5).

Topic 9: *man* (the mind)

kūkara kāka karaṅka pari, pāka pūri taji jāṅhiṅ
tyoṅ Rajjaba mana kī virati, taji amṛta viṣa khāṅhiṅ (152.12)

Dogs and crows throw themselves on dead carcasses,
ignoring vessels full of cooked food.
Says Rajjab: such is the tendency of the mind,
which gives up nectar and eats poison.

The subject dealt with here is the perverseness of the mind. It is portrayed as blinded by *māyā* (152.5), fickle (152.56), uncontrollable, and full of tricks. It relentlessly pursues its own desires (*KG* 29.15), and knowingly does wrong (*KG* 29.8). Only by overcoming it can one obtain salvation.

Topic 10: *besās* (faith)

Rāma kāja jinake karai, tinake kāraja siddha
jana Rajjaba viśvāsa pari, bana āī saba viddha (112.48)

He succeeds whose work is done by Ram,
so says the devotee Rajjab.
Keep your faith,
and all will go well.

Dohās on this topic are comforting statements reassuring devotees of the Lord's care for those who have faith in him, and expressions of the Sant's own contentment and reassurance in his faith.

The *dohās* of the North Indian Sants are almost universally referred to as *sākhīs*.[63] Like the *dohā* form itself, however, the term *sākhī* predates the Sants. Derived from the Sanskrit *sākṣin* ('witness'), it is used by the Buddhist Siddhas in its primary sense, i.e. to refer to a person who has directly experienced enlightenment and can therefore speak with authority about spiritual truth. Gradually, especially in the Nathpanthi literature, it comes to refer to the *words* of the enlightened person. Thus if *śabda* is the inner revelation of the *satguru*, *sākhī* is the authori-

63. See below, p. 83 for the exception to this pattern among the Sikhs.

tative utterance that testifies to this inner revelation and leads others towards it.[64] This is the concept of *sākhī* in the Sants as well:

> *sākhī āṅkhī jñāna kī, samukhi dekhu mana māhiṅ*
> *binu sākhī saṃsāra kā, jhararā chhūṭata nāhiṅ*[65]

> *Sākhī*s are the eyes of wisdom,
> understand them and look into your heart;
> Without *sākhī*s, there's no end
> to the struggles of this world.

> *Harijī yahai bichāriyā, sāṣī kahau Kabīra*
> *bhausāgara maiṅ jīva haiṅ, je koi pakaṛai tīra*[66]

> Reflecting on Hari,
> Kabir utters *sākhī*s,
> And a few of the creatures in the ocean of existence reach the shore.

By the time the term *sākhī* reached the Sants, however, it had become so closely associated with the *dohā* form that the two words were practically synonymous. *Sākhī* thus comes to be a formal designation for one of the two major genres of *sant bānī* in North India, the other being the sung lyric, called either *śabda* or *pad*.

There is one important exception in the Sant tradition to this use of the term *sākhī* to designate utterances in *dohā* form: the Sikh scriptures. In the *Ādi Granth*, the *dohā*s composed by the Sikh Gurus and earlier Sants are called not *sākhī*s, but *salok*s (Sanskrit *śloka*). The term *sākhī* is used instead in connection with another scriptural genre: the traditional accounts of Guru Nanak's life, called *janam-sākhī*s. These accounts take the form of a series of separate incidents, each of which is referred to as a *sākhī*. For Sikhs, thus, the ultimate 'witness' to spiritual truth is not the authoritative utterances of enlightened Sants, or even of the Sikh Gurus, but the person and life of Guru Nanak.[67] This usage, while highlighting the distinctiveness of Sikhism within the Sant tradition, also helps make clear the basic meaning of the term *sākhī*—

64. For a discussion of the concepts of *śabda* and *satguru*, see Charlotte Vaudeville, "*Sant Mat*: Santism as the Universal Path to Sanctity," earlier in this volume, pp. 33-34. For the evolution of the concept of *sākhī* see Dvivedi, *Ādikāl*, p. 112.

65. Shukdev Singh, ed., *Bījak* (Allahabad: Nilabh Prakashan, 1972), *sākhī* 353.

66. Das, *Kabīr granthāvalī*, *sākhī* 34.1.

67. For a study of the Sikh *janam-sākhī*s, see W.H. McLeod, *Early Sikh Tradition: A Study of the Janam-sākhīs* (Oxford: Clarendon Press, 1980).

a meaning which is sometimes obscured by the equation of *sākhī* with the *dohā* form.

Yet *dohā* and *sākhī* have in fact become synonymous. Though the *pad* and other genres of *sant bānī* also express the spiritual experience and teachings of the Sants, it is only the *dohā* which is called *sākhī*. This becomes especially clear if one moves from the written texts of the Sants to the living religious culture in which their various kinds of utterances exist as oral traditions. The *pad*s of the Sants, like those of the *saguṇa* bhakti poets, are almost always sung,[68] usually in religious settings and often with great musical artistry; their function is to induce an attitude and mood of devotion, and their impact is diffuse, emotional, and partly non-verbal. *Dohā*s, by contrast, are more commonly recited or chanted, often simply spoken, and the purpose is not so much to establish a mood as it is to persuade the listener to believe in the truth of the proposition being stated. Furthermore, while only people with a certain taste and aptitude for singing know many *pad*s by heart, Sant *dohā*s are widely known not only among the followers of particular Sant lineages, but throughout the society.

All this suggests that the status of the *sākhī* as a religious utterance is different from that of other Sant genres in that its statement of Sant teachings and themes is accepted as particularly authoritative. Indeed, the function of Sant *sākhī*s in popular religious culture may best be understood by analogy to the *sūtra*s of the classical philosophic texts. Like the philosophic *sūtra*s, *sākhī*s are considered revealed aphorisms on the subject of spiritual truth, are meant to be preserved in the mind as succinct statements going to the heart of the matter at hand, and are capable of being elaborated upon as the context demands. Thus, although the *sākhī*s of the North Indian Sants (and their equivalents in areas outside North India) are part of the general folk wisdom of the culture, they are on a different level from that of ordinary proverbial sayings. While general proverbial lore transmits practical wisdom for daily life, *sākhīs* express, teach and keep alive the spiritual vision and high moral ideals preached by the Sants. Thus they function in the culture as an oral "wisdom literature" which provides guidance and inspiration and is the common property of all.

68. For the *śabdas* in Kabir's *Bījak* as an exception to this pattern, see Hess, "Three Kabir Collections," below, pp. 115-19.

Rhetorical Contexts for the Dohā

The *dohā*s of the Sants, like other *muktaka*s or independent verse forms, are poetic utterances of a generalized nature which embody beliefs, values and conceptions widely accepted by the culture. As such, they are context-free units of poetic discourse available to be interpreted in different ways, elaborated on, and used in a variety of different situations.[69] What this implies for the study of the Sant *dohā* and related genres is that they cannot be properly understood without taking into account the multiplicity of contexts in which they can occur. These are of three kinds: contexts of original utterance or composition, contexts of compilation and written preservation, and contexts of present-day oral communication.

1. *Contexts of composition*

These contexts are naturally the most difficult to ascertain, as there is no reliable record of the exact situation in which an historical Sant first uttered a particular *dohā*. But at least the *kind* of situation it was can be envisioned by analogy to present-day verbal interactions between religious teachers and their listeners and from accounts of typical interactions preserved in hagiographic texts. It is a common feature of Indian religious discourses that they are punctuated by frequent verse quotations; and if the speaker is himself a poet, he may compose fresh verses of his own as he goes along. Moreover, this use of verse is not restricted to public addresses, but is also characteristic of private discussions with small groups of religious seekers and one-to-one exchanges between teachers and those they encounter in the course of their normal activities.

In the Sikh *janam-sākhī*s, this pattern can be seen very clearly, with one situation after another calling forth commentary by Guru Nanak in verse form. For example, he is shown responding to Sultan Ibrahim Lodhi's desire to bestow a gift on him with the following *salok*:

> *Nānaka bhukha khudāya dī, viā be paravāhī*
> *asāṅ talaba dīdāra hī, biā talaba na kāhī*[70]

69. For a discussion of the concept of *muktaka* in Indian poetic tradition, see Williams, "*The Ḍholā-Mārū rā Dūhā*," chapter 3.

70. *Śrī Gurū Nānak Dev jī kī Bhāī Bāle vālī janam sākhī* (Amritsar: Bhai Jawahar Singh Kripal Singh, n.d.), p. 311.

Nanak's hunger is for God
he cares for nothing else;
His search is for the vision of God,
he seeks nothing else.

Whether such incidents occurred or not is irrelevant. Their importance lies in the patterns of discourse they exemplify — one in which the original utterance of a *dohā* or other aphoristic verse is a Sant's response to a specific situation and an act of face-to-face communication. In every instance, someone was being addressed. Because of the brevity of the *dohā* form, interlocutors are seldom mentioned specifically, but the content of the *dohā* often gives a hint of who they were:

ūṅche kula kyā janamiyā, je karanīṅ ūṅchi na hoi
sobrana kalasa surai bharā, sādhuna nindā soi (*KG* 33.7)

So you were born in a noble family?
What of it, if your behavior is vile?
If your gold vessel is filled with liquor,
a Sant will only despise it!

sādhu bhayā tau kyā bhayā, mālā melī chāri
bāhari ḍhola hīngalā, bhītara bharī bangāri (*KG* 25.2)

You've become a sadhu: so what?
You've put on four rows of beads...
Your outer body is wrapped in ochre,
but inside you're full of garbage!

Most of the time, the audience being addressed was probably a small group of disciples and other sympathetic listeners gathered informally around the Sant to listen to his words. As in present-day gatherings of this nature, the Sant would have been touching on a wide range of themes and speaking in a variety of tones. In this setting, he could have uttered *dohā*s in response to questions, as commentary on the immediate or the general contemporary scene, to emphasize certain points, to exhort, inspire or condemn, to summarize truths, and to try to convey his own spiritual experience. Thus the following *sākhī* of Kabir is most likely to have been composed in the context of a discussion about the nature of the mystical experience:

Kabīra kanvala prakāsiyā, ūgā niramala sūra
raiṅni andherī miṭi gaī, bāga anahada tūra (*KG* 9.36)

Kabir says: a lotus bloomed,
a pure sun arose:
The night's darkness vanished,
the trumpet of the Unstruck Sound rang out.

By contrast, a *sākhī* such as the one below implies a situation in which Kabir is commenting either on the general breed of false gurus or, possibly, on some particularly successful religious opportunist of his day:

svāṅmīṅ hūvā senta kā, paikākāra pachāsa
Rāṅma nāṅma kāṭhaiṅ rahā, karai sikhāṅ kī āsa (*KG* 21.7)

He became a swami on the cheap,
got fifty people to serve him;
Ram's name got stuck in his throat,
and his hope is in his disciples.

Our understanding of *dohās* as poetic utterances can only be enriched by such envisioning of their original rhetorical context. One of the important tasks of the textual interpreter is thus to construct plausible pictures of the communication context in which given *dohās* might have first been uttered.

2. *Contexts of compilation*

The second kind of rhetorical context in which Sant *dohās* are found is that of the texts in which they have been collected and preserved in written form. The most important type of text, the *dohā* or *sākhī* collection, has been discussed at some length, and reference has been made to the ordering of *dohās* by thematic categories or *aṅgas* in the majority of such texts. It has been suggested that the purpose of these compilations may have had to do with devotional ritual, and that both the choice of material and the ordering of *aṅga* sections may have been influenced by the thematic emphases of the different Sant lineages. Finally, it has been proposed that *aṅga* headings should be looked at as an index to conventional poetic topics in the Sant tradition.[71]

All this points to, but does not directly state, a textual rhetoric. The assumption is still that these compilations have no internal logic of their own, but are just miscellaneous lists of *dohās* grouped under a conventional list of headings. But no poetry anthology is ever put to-

71. See above, pp. 75-76.

gether without some ordering principles and an overall rhetorical purpose. In addition to the historical question of why compilations of Sant *dohā*s were made at all, there is also the literary question of why they were made in the way they were. What was the *literary*, as opposed to the religious, purpose of the various compilers? And what were the ordering principles that followed from this rhetorical intent?

Sant *dohā* compilations, I would suggest, are texts designed to illume the principal themes of Sant religion by bringing together in one place all the best sayings on these themes by a particular Sant or group of Sants. Beyond mere doctrinal exposition, the purpose is to convey a full and subtle religious sensibility by showing each theme from as many angles as possible. In this context, a *dohā*'s rhetorical impact comes from its contribution to the overall effect of a given *aṅga* and that of the compilation as a whole. Thus both the inclusion of *dohā*s within particular *aṅga*s and their ordering within these *aṅga*s are significant, as it is by their proximity to other similar *dohā*s that they serve their purpose of highlighting different facets of a theme. It is important to realize in this connection that Sant themes are not rigidly demarcated categories, but closely interrelated, and that a given *dohā* may touch on several themes at once. Thus the inclusion of a given *dohā* under one thematic heading rather than another acts as a defining factor, making the *dohā*'s import more specific. In the same way, the specific position of a *dohā* within a thematic *aṅga* can narrow or broaden its meaning with reference to the surrounding sequence of *dohā*s.

The definition and ordering of the *aṅga*s within compilations is also significant, as each configuration expresses a slightly different sense of thematic priorities and interrelations, and thereby creates a portrayal of the Sant sensibility that has unique contours. Thus, although virtually all Sant *dohā* collections organized by *aṅga*s begin with the *satguru mahimā* category, and most of the major thematic categories follow shortly after, the order varies; and when it comes to minor themes, the variation in both the boundaries of the categories and their ordering is considerable.

Besides being brought together in collections, Sant *dohā*s have also been preserved as the initial or concluding verses of other kinds of Sant compositions. Two of these are most prominent: the *ramainī*, found primarily in the texts of Kabir, and the *vār*, a verse form of the *Ādi Granth*. In the *ramainī*, a single *dohā* follows a number of lines in *chaupāī* meter, and serves to summarize or state the essence of the more discursive matter preceding it.[72] The *vār* is a lyric form made up of a number of stanzas, each of which is preceded by a subsidiary stanza consisting of a number of *dohā*s or *salok*s; the purpose of this *dohā* stanza is to set the tone for the lyric that follows.[73] In both of these embedded contexts of written preservation, the import of the *dohā* is governed by the rhetoric of the larger verse form of which it is a part. As with the genre of the *dohā* collection, we find the *dohā*'s independent significance as a generalized statement both constrained and augmented by the meaning it derives from its position in the written text.

3. *Contexts of oral communication*

The third contextual framework in which *dohā*s are found is actually an extension of the first. Though the *dohā*s of the Sants were originally composed in very specific communication situations, they are utterances of a generalized nature that are available for all sorts of new situations. Furthermore, because of the appeal of the Sant religious message and the popularity of the *dohā* form, they have become an integral part of the proverbial lore and linguistic repertoire of the speech community, sayings that come up for use in the proper context just as the appropriate idiom or expression does. Thus there is yet another rhetoric to be examined: that of the Sant *dohā*s as they occur embedded in present-day discourse.

The use of *dohā*s in the context of formal religious discourse has already been referred to above. But *dohā* quotation is not restricted to bracketed occasions of religious instruction. Like proverbs, Sant *dohā*s come up daily in the course of normal conversational situations — to make a point in an argument, to express a feeling, to comment on persons or situations, to congratulate, to give advice, to console in times of trouble, to make a request or ask for a favor, etc. This widespread use of Sant *dohā*s in everyday oral communication is attested by their inclusion in all North Indian proverb collections. S.W. Fallon's pioneering 1886 collection, for instance, includes many Sant *dohā*s — both recognized *dohā*s by particular Sants and *dohā*s of unknown origin expressing common Sant themes. Commenting on them in the preface, R.C. Temple says that "they are habitually used on every possible occasion of daily life, especially in seasons of trouble."[74] This obser-

72. See above, p. 74.

73. McLeod, *Early Sikh Tradition*, p. 287.

74. S.W. Fallon, *A Dictionary of Hindustani Proverbs*, edited and revised by R.C. Temple, with the assistance of Lala Faqir Chand (London: Trubner and Co., 1886), preface, p. ii.

vation is as valid today as it was a hundred years ago, especially in rural areas where ordinary speech continues to be larded with proverbs and proverbial phrases, and appeal to proverbial wisdom is still highly persuasive. Even among the modern urban dwellers of North India, it would be difficult to find anyone who did not know and occasionally quote at least a few *sākhīs* of Kabir.

These living contexts in which Sant *dohās* are found today are in many ways the most important, for they are the patterns of oral communication through which the teachings of the Sants continue to be transmitted and kept alive. Unless we can become as familiar with them as we are with the written texts of the Sant tradition, our understanding of the Sant *dohā* and its role as a vehicle of Sant teachings will remain incomplete.

EKNATH'S *BHĀRUḌS*: THE SANT AS LINK BETWEEN CULTURES

ELEANOR ZELLIOT

Shri Eknath Maharaj, one of the four major figures in the seven hundred year old bhakti tradition of Maharashtra, was a link figure in many ways. Born in the sixteenth century,[1] he revitalized the bhakti tradition which had begun in the thirteenth century, preparing the way for the greatest of the Sant poets, Tukaram, in the seventeenth. He also served as a link to bhakti in northern India by including Kabir and Raidas[2] in his listing of Sants as if they were an intrinsic part of his own tradition. A third role is that of the bridge between the Sanskritic tradition and the non-Sanskritized lower classes, for Eknath was a proper Brahman scholar who lived in the orthodox center of Paithan, and yet he not only translated Sanskrit devotional material into Marathi but also wrote songs and poems clearly intended for the ears and the minds of the lowly.

A section of Eknath's work in the last genre, drama poems called *bhāruḍs*, which actually put the message of bhakti in the mouths of a varied group of low-caste, low-status characters, is the facet of Eknath's various roles that I want to explore in this paper. A great many of Eknath's three hundred *bhāruḍs*[3] are in the persona of Untouchables, passing Muslim fakirs, acrobats and travelling entertainers, religious personages from unorthodox sects, prostitutes and unhappy women — a wide sweep of the non-Sanskritic world around Eknath. These charac-

Basic work on the *bhāruḍs* of Eknath was done with the invaluable help of Poona scholars P.N. Joshi and S.G. Tulpule. I am also grateful to Jayant Karve for aid in polishing the translations and to A.K. Ramanujan for enhancing their poetic quality. Any faults in translation are, of course, my responsibility.

1. Eknath's dates are variously given as 1528-1599, 1533-1599, and 1548-1609. The middle date seems to be the one now most commonly accepted.

2. The Marathi spelling for this Chamar Sant of the north is Rohidas.

3. The word *bhāruḍ* has no accepted etymology and no one clear definition. *Bhāruḍs* have no standard form, but all adopt some conceit — animal, human, or work-a-day action — as the subject or speaker of the drama-poem. The *bhāruḍ* is often acted out, not sung in the devout manner of other bhakti songs. An *abhaṅg* (unbroken) is the more common form of Maharashtrian bhakti poetry. It is generally composed of four lines in an ABBC rhyme-plan. See pp. 451-52 in Shankar Gopal Tulpule's *Classical Marāṭhī Literature* (Wiesbaden: Otto Harrassowitz, 1979).

ters use their own images and symbols, even at times their own language, but speak the message of bhakti.

It is a common benchmark of bhakti poetry for the Sant to use images of daily life and work as metaphors for religious experience. Eknath goes beyond this to create a vivid description of the varied life all around him as others practised it. He abandons the normal Sant reliance on personal experience to allow his characters to relate *their* experiences, and this is done with an observing eye for detail and an ear for all the varieties of speech heard in the busy temple-trading center of Paithan. The *bhāruḍs*, it might be argued, are not true bhakti poetry; they certainly are not typical bhakti poetry. But it seems to me that the empathy they exhibit carries to a dramatic climax the Maharashtrian bhakti ideals that all the truly devout are equal and that any true bhakta can speak the bhakti message.

Since the *bhāruḍs* are a minor part of Eknath's work, it would be well to record his historic place in the still living Marathi bhakti tradition. An *abhaṅg*, the more common form of Marathi Sant poetry, relates the work of the four major Sants:

> By the grace of the Sant the building is complete.
> Dnyandev laid the foundation and raised the temple frame.
> His servant Nama filled out the temple structure.
> Janardan's Eknath put up the column of the *Bhāgavata*.
> Sing *bhajan* at peace: Tuka has become the pinnacle![4]

Dnyandev (1275–1296) wrote the *Dnyāneśvarī*,[5] an extensive commentary on the *Bhagavad Gītā*. One of the earliest works in the Marathi language, it is still the most highly respected popular religious text in Maharashtra. There is no question but that the *Dnyāneśvarī* is the foundation of the bhakti tradition in Maharashtra, a tradition so long and so continually creative that, although it has no overall formal organization, it could properly be called a bhakti *movement*. The message and the language of the *Dnyāneśvarī* are on the lips of all Maharashtrian bhaktas. But the practices of those same bhaktas are not found in the *Dnyāneśvarī* nor in the life of Dnyandev. Maharashtrian bhaktas are

4. *Abhaṅg* 4488 in *Viśvavandh Śrītukārāmmahārāj yāñchī sampūrṇa abhaṅg gāthā*, edited by Narhari Vishnushastri Panshikar (Pune: Panshikar Prakashan, 1968.) Although the *abhaṅg* is credited to Tukaram in this edition of his work, it is the opinion of S.G. Tulpule that Tukaram's disciple Bahinabai is the more likely author.

5. See the translation by V.G. Pradhan, edited by H.M. Lambert: *Jnāneshvari* (*Bhāvārthadīpikā*), 2 vols. (London: George Allen and Unwin, 1967-1969).

known as *vārkarīs*; (pilgrims) and the place of the important annual pilgrimage is Pandharpur. Vitthala or Vithoba is the reigning deity of the Pandharpur temple, and neither his name nor that of the town of Pandharpur appear in the *Dnyāneśvarī*.

The second Sant in the *abhaṅg* given above, Nama or Namdev (1270–1350), was probably responsible for Dnyandev's thought becoming the focus of a long-lived panth or *sampradāy*.[6] Namdev lived in Pandharpur but travelled widely, even according to legend, to the Punjab; songs by a Namdev who by tradition is the Maharashtrian Namdev appear in the *Granth* of the Sikhs. Namdev probably began the singing sessions called *kīrtan*, using his own and others' songs, including *abhaṅg*s attributed to Dnyandev. He is certainly responsible for the idea of a company of Sants, a pantheon of poets who knew each other and the Sants of the past. The line of Maharashtrian Sants who also were poets is such a dominant part of the Marathi literary tradition that the term *sant-kavi* is used by literary historians to mark the entire period from the end of the thirteenth to the middle years of the seventeenth centuries. Namdev seems to have known the multitude of *sant-kavi*s from all walks of life and all castes who joined in the worship of Vithoba during his long lifetime. He considered Chokhamela, an Untouchable Mahar, the very essence of devotion; his serving maid, Janabai, wrote *abhaṅg*s and was considered a Sant; he knew Savata the gardener, Gora the potter, Narahari the goldsmith, Sena the barber, Kanhopatra the dancing girl, as well as Dnyandev himself. Namdev himself was of the *śimpī* or tailor caste; his songs do not display Dnyandev's Brahmanical learning, but are enormously popular.

The fourth Sant in the poem above, and the most beloved of all Sant poets, is Tuka, or more commonly Tukaram (1598–1649). A Maratha by caste, Tukaram is not only the most beloved Sant in the *vārkarī*-panth but by far the most important poet of the entire period in the minds of modern readers of Marathi literature.[7] Tukaram was born in the decade of Eknath's death, and it is probably due to Eknath's

6. Both *panth*, which is usually translated cult or sect, and *sampradāy*, which simply means tradition, are used in Marathi for the *vārkarī* or bhakti tradition. The implication of *sampradāy* is that the tradition is passed down through a series of gurus, but this seems not to have always been the case in the Marathi series of Sants.

7. The *Dnyāneśvarī* of Dnyandev, the *Eknāthī Bhāgavata*, and Tukaram's *abhaṅg*s are said to be the three 'Bibles' of contemporary bhaktas. Of the many translations of Tukaram, the spirited versions of Arun Kolaktar, first published in *Poetry India* 1:1 (1966) and reprinted in the *Journal of South Asian Literature* 17:1 (1982) are the most interesting.

work that the then three hundred year old bhakti tradition could produce and nourish its major poet.

For two hundred years after Namdev was buried before the great door of the temple in Pandharpur, the bhakti movement produced few important Sants, but we know at least some elements of the tradition were alive. The story of Bhanudas (1448–1513), who was Eknath's great grandfather, is part of the *vārkarī* tradition. In the recorded legend, Bhanudas went to Vijayanagar and brought back the image of Vithoba which had been taken there by King Ramaraja. As the image was reinstalled in Pandharpur, "saints, Vaishnavas and pilgrims all felt the joy of the occasion."[8]

Eknath was certainly aware of a living tradition. He mentions some fifty Sants in his various works; wrote songs in praise of Dnyandev and his brothers and sister, Nivritinath, Sopandev and Muktabai; and composed biographies of four other Sants of the first great generation: Namdev, Gora the potter, Savatamali and Chokhamela. Perhaps even more important, he gathered the various versions of the *Dnyāneśvarī* extant in the sixteenth century and edited what he felt to be the authentic version. It is Eknath's edition of the *Dnyāneśvarī* which is honored today.

Eknath also translated and commented upon the eleventh *skandha* of the *Bhāgavata Purāṇa*, known to all *vārkarī*s as the *Ekanāthī Bhāgavata.*[9] It is typical of Maharashtrian bhakti that Eknath chose the stern morality of the eleventh *skandha* over the erotic devotion of Krishna and the *gopī*s in the tenth book of that Purana which was so important to Bengali bhakti and to Vallabhacharya. The translation of a Purana into a vernacular was evidently an unusual thing in the sixteenth century, since tradition claims that Eknath was summoned to appear before the pandits of Banaras to defend his translation of the early chapters. This he did successfully and stayed on in Banaras to complete the translation and commentary in 1573.

The connections between the Marathi-speaking area and the north seem to have been strong at this time. Eknath had made the pilgrimage

8. *Bhanudas*, a translation from the *Bhaktavijaya* of Mahipati, by Justin E. Abbott. *The Poet-Saints of Maharashtra*, vol. 1. (Poona: Scottish Mission Industries Co., 1926), p. 48. Mahipati's eighteenth-century version of the legend contains an error, since it was Krishnadevaraya (1510–1539) who took the Pandharpur image of Vithoba to Vijayanagar.

9. The twenty-third chapter of the *Ekanāthī Bhāgavata* has been translated by Abbott as *Bhikshugita: The Mendicant's Song. The Poet-Saints of Maharashtra*, vol. 3 (1928).

to the north evidently expected of the devout, and in the words of the eighteenth-century biographer of all the Sants, Mahipati, "Thus having visited the northern *tīrtha*s thoroughly, and having seen the twelve chief Shiva shrines, and the seven chief cities, he danced in the fulness of his joy."[10] It is not recorded that Eknath was in contact with northern bhaktas during this pilgrimage or during his stay in Banaras; his knowledge of Kabir and Raidas seems to have come through stories of their lives rather than through direct experience with their followers. One senses that the idea of a company of Sants was all-inclusive on a rather intellectual level but that there was no real meeting of one bhakti group with another across language lines.

The *Ekanāthī Bhāgavata* is clearly Eknath's most important work, but a listing of his other translations and commentaries is necessary to establish his scholarly character. He composed the *Bhāvārtha Rāmāyaṇa*, a Marathi version of the Valmiki *Rāmāyaṇa*; the *Chatuśloki Bhāgavata*, a commentary on the strictly Vedantic ninth chapter of the second *skandha* of the *Bhāgavata Purāṇa*; a philosophical work called the *Hastāmalaka*; a commentary on eight Sanskrit *śloka*s, the *Śukāṣṭaka*; and a number of other highly philosophical works. He is also said to have written some four thousand of the devotional *abhaṅg*s which are the traditional form for Marathi *sant-kavi* songs. In discussing Eknath's work in his volume on Marathi mysticism, R.D. Ranade states: "It was principally Eknatha who made the ideas of Vedanta familiar to the men in the streets."[11]

The appearance of the vigorous, dramatic, somewhat fundamentalistic and occasionally vulgar *bhāruḍ* in the midst of Eknath's Brahmanical scholarship and traditional piety is something of a surprise. In the context of his life as a Brahman householder in Paithan, however, they become an understandable and quite fascinating aspect of his total philosophical view. Paithan was an ancient Maharashtrian capital and an old but still prosperous market center on the trade route from the north to the sea. It was near the capital of the then recently formed Ahmadnagar Sultanate, a kingdom which allowed far more Maratha[12]

10. Verse 106, chapter 15, in Mahipati's *Srī Eknāth charitra*, chapters 13 to 24 of the *Bhaktalīlāmṛta*, as translated by Abbott in *Eknath. The Poet-Saints of Maharashtra*, vol. 2 (1927), p. 54. Mahipati specifically mentions Mathura, Gokul, Vrindavana, Varanasi, Prayag, Gaya, Kashi, Ayodhya, Badrinath and Dvarka in this chapter.

11. R.D. Ranade, *Pathway to God in Marathi Literature* (Bombay: Bharatiya Vidya Bhavan, 1961), p. 205. Ranade himself was a bhakta.

12. Maratha is used as an adjective to indicate things Maharashtrian as well as a specific caste name for the dominant land-owing caste.

participation in governance than had the earlier Bahmani Empire with its center in Gulbarga.

Eknath combined his scholarly Brahman role with an acute sense of the bustling life around him. He was aware of the customs of speech of the varied layers of society and he seems to have been concerned to put the philosophical tenets of Vedanta, stories from the Puranas and the Epics, and an understanding of the strict morality of dharma into varied forms of Marathi prose and poetry so that all could be enlightened. The *bhāruḍ*s speak to the lowest level, and yet contain elements of Vedantic non-dualism, references to the Puranas, and injunctions to be moral, all within the bhakti framework of devotion to God and the Sants.

Paithan was considered the Banaras of the Marathi-speaking area and its Brahmans the voice of orthodoxy. Dnyandev had been asked by the orthodox Brahmans of his town of Alandi to go to Paithan to secure a certificate of purity since he was the son of a *sanyāsī*, and according to legend he did this. Eknath maintained his status there in spite of his unorthodox behavior by a combination of flawless piety and a few timely miracles. Paithan orthodoxy, however, was not the only influence in Eknath's life. His guru was Janardan, a little known swami who lived in Devagiri, the old capital of the last Hindu empire of the area, the Yadava. Janardan combined his religious role with that of a commander in the army of the Muslim ruler of the area, and this curious dual occupation seems to have troubled no one. Eknath undoubtedly received some of his breadth of vision from Janardan. Recent scholarship indicates Janardan's guru was a Sufi.[13] Janardan himself was of the Dattatreya *sampradāy*, the tradition of the god Datta, not a member of the *vārkarī* panth. Eknath's initiation by his guru Janardan came through a vision of Datta, who appeared before the two as a Muslim fakir and at Janardan's request assumed "the beautiful Sagun form six armed, of elongated eyes, his face the ornament of the universe."[14] All Eknath's *bhāruḍ*s end with the signature *Ekā-Janārdan*, as if he were inseparable from his guru.

In addition to this exposure to Muslims and to the Datta tradition, Eknath may have been influenced by yet another tradition, that of the Naths. He carries the sign of this northern sect in his name, as did Dnyandev's older brother, Nivritinath. But the connections between

13. Tulpule, *Marāṭhī Literature*, p. 353.

14. Mahipati, *Eknath*, trans. Abbott, p. 21. (Verse 202, chapter 13, of Mahipati's *Bhaktalīlāmṛta*.)

the *vārkarī* and the Nath *saṃpradāy*s are not at all clear.[15] While the *vārkarī* is today the strongest panth in Maharashtra, the Nath tradition survives only at a folk level of stories of nine Naths and their miracles. What is important about all these possible influences is that Eknath seemed able to work all sorts of religious figures and ideas into his bhakti themes, not scorning them but bending them to yet other expressions of bhakti ideals.

My interest in the *bhāruḍ*s began when I discovered that Eknath had written some forty *bhāruḍ*s as if he were a member of the Untouchable Mahar caste which I had been studying, and that these drama-poems indicated the status and traditional duties of that caste in the sixteenth century. Further study of the three hundred *bhāruḍ*s indicated that one could do something of a social history of the Paithan world through an analysis of the characters of the *bhāruḍ*s. About a third of the *bhāruḍ*s are in the mouths of a throng of characters ranging from the low status *jośī* (astrologer) to the *hapsī* (Muslim Ethiopian migrant to the Maharashtrian coast). Sixteen are in a corrupt form of Hindustani; Telugu and Kannada phrases appear in others. The various forms of the goddess, from Mahalakshmi to the cholera goddess Mariai, are represented, as well as the servants of the Maharashtrian god Khandoba and other local gods, but no high-caste male figure appears, not even the dominant Maratha farmer, and no *bhāruḍ* sings chiefly the praises of Vishnu or Shiva. Eknath seems to have deliberately chosen non-orthodox characters for this form of message: the blind, crippled, deaf and dumb; animals and birds; prostitutes, soldiers and the town thug; and more *bhāruḍ*s in the mouths of the Untouchable Mahars than of any other group.

The *bhāruḍ* form in which the Sant writes in another persona had been used by earlier *sant-kavi*s. Dnyandev wrote songs entitled "Blind," "Blanket" and "Crow" and Namdev had written as if he were a hypnotizer in one case and a lisper in another. A Karnataka poet, Purandara Dasa, who lived some time before Eknath, wrote at least two songs which use the voices of the lowly, a Bairagi who takes *bhāṅg* and a vendor of sweets,[16] but there is no indication that Eknath was aware of him. Eknath, however, wrote far more extensively in this genre than any other Sant. He was also far more inclusive in his use of other sects

15. Peter Gaeffke of the University of Pennsylvania has told me that the subjects and form of the *bhāruḍ*s strongly suggest Nath influence.

16. These two songs are translated by V. Raghavan in *The Great Integrators: The Saint-Singers of India* (New Delhi: Ministry of Information and Broadcasting, Publications Division, 1964), pp. 38-39.

and of specific castes as well as occupations. There is a sense of the total society in his work, an ethos that is concerned to draw up others, whoever they are, into the morality of bhakti and into an understanding of the saving value of devotion.

The following *bhāruḍs* have been chosen for variety, their intrinsic interest and their readability in English. There is no critical edition of Eknath's *abhaṅgs* and *bhāruḍs*; I have included the title, number and the first line in Marathi as given in the Sakhare collection.[17] Since the language of this genre is quite spare at times, I have indicated controversial points of translation in the notes.

A woman's plea to the Goddess for deliverance from husband and in-laws is one of Eknath's most popular *bhāruḍs* today — in spite of the fact that it counters the image of the devoted wife! The *bhāruḍ* can be interpreted in metaphysical terms as an allegory for casting off various sins and worldly attachments. It can also be interpreted as a comment on the necessity for women bhakti Sants to give up husbands and homes to achieve the freedom to devote themselves to the worship of their Lord, as A.K. Ramanujan has pointed out. The Eknath touch is that it also reads as a married woman's bitter, ironic and quite funny cry for release. Both Amba and Bhawani are common Maharashtrian names for the Goddess.

Aṃbā (satvar pāv ge malā) 3920

Save me now, Mother —
  I'll offer you bread, Bhawani. (1)

Father-in-law is out of town —
Let him die there. (2)
  I'll offer you bread, Mother Bhawani.*

Mother-in-law torments me —
Kill her off. (3)
  I'll offer you bread, Mother Bhawani.

Sister-in-law nags and nags —
Make her a widow. (4)
  I'll offer you bread, Mother Bhawani.

Her brat cries and cries —
Give him the itch. (5)

17. *Śrī Eknāth Mahārāj yāñchyā abhaṅgāñchī gāthā*, collected and edited by Brahmibhut Shrinanamaharaj Sakhare (Pune: Indira Prakashan, 1952), pp. 350-416d.

I'll offer you bread, Mother Bhawani.
I'll give my husband as a sacrifice!
Free me, Mother! (6)
I'll offer you bread, Mother Bhawani.

Eka-Janardan says,
Let them all die!
Let me live alone! (7)

*The refrain is not in the text, but is always included when this *bhāruḍ* is sung.

Another *bhāruḍ* spoken by a woman is entitled "*Kaikāī*," after the wandering fortune tellers from the south. In the course of her fortune telling, the *kaikāī* (or *kaikāy*) invokes all gods as Mother. She also speaks some lines in an imitation of Kannada and some with a Telugu flavor, but no speaker of these languages has been able to make sense of them. I leave them as a sort of incantation, with any recognizable word translated into English.

Kaikāī (*Śrīkṛṣṇa māyā jī pāhe*) 3732

Look, by the grace of Mother Shri Krishna
I have become a *kaikāy*.
Kaikāy is a limb of the body of God.
Kaikāy became the world.
Karma is part of Brahma.
From that I came to know the dear Mother. (1)

White Mother, dark Mother, O little Mother of the good name,
O Mother of the beautiful shape, O sweet Mother. (2)

Mother Fish, Mother Tortoise, Mother Boar,
O Mother who was Lion-Man,
Mother who was '*Vāman*', Mother who was Dwarf,
Mother Rama-of-the-Axe, Mother Rama,
Mother Krishna, Mother Buddha, Mother Kalki-yet-to-come. (3)

Mother Ganga, Mother Bhaga, Mother Renuka,
O Mother Confusion,
Mother Changuna, Mother Tuka, O dear Mother.[18] (4)

18. Here Eknath invokes the rivers; the Maharashtrian Goddess Renuka who was Eknath's own family deity; Mother *gaḍbaḍ* or confusion, which may at the time have had a religious meaning; Mother-of-the-good-qualities; and Mother Tuka, or Tukai, a local god.

Look, the fear that's always on your mind
  you don't speak, you don't tell, lady.
I'll tell you what is in your soul.
I'll tell you whatever you ask.
I'll tell you what's in your mind.
What's under the seven nether worlds —
  that's in you and that's in me.
How dare you defy it, defiant girl!
I'll best even your husband in the game,
  and I'll take hold of the burning lamp's bowl.
I will spit in your face, I will spit on your greed.
I will tell your fortune—listen to it.
Mother Kalika[19]—O Little Mother. (5)

Many women have asked for a child
  and they have been set right —
I am not that kind of fortune teller.
I am a basket of self-knowledge,
Mother Kalika, O Little Mother! (6)

Hail to Kannada speech —
Listen, be alert!
Listen to the omen, listen to the omen, praise the Lord!
  siḍ biḍ hope
  biḍ hyāḷāvā
  ganmoḍ will come, Little Mother! (7)

  gaṇdine dhanānne taminne gaoïne hāḍavyāṇ
  āḍāvyāḍā moho śāi tuḍā
  Black Mother, O Little Mother! (8)

Hail to the direction of Telengana — rough rough speech!
  sarāve musaḷ llope, Little Mother! (9)

  mitti khannāḷū kaḍyaḷū
  inyāḷū
  sakhaṭhāye
  Black Mother, O Little Mother! (10)

Kaikāy, kaikāy!
I will tell your fortune — listen!
Kaikāy, kaikāy — Brahma and all those gods do not know —

19. Kalika is a form of the name of the goddess Kali.

This *kaikāy* business is a fake.
Kaikāy, kaikāy!

I will tell you one true thing:
Soul and God have become One.
A hundred million belong to Eka Janardan.
Mother Kalika, O Little Mother! (11)

Another character from the south is the *jaṅgam*, priest of the Vira-shaiva or Lingayat sect. Eknath does not seem to be aware of the poetic heritage of the Lingayats, only of the *jaṅgam* as one more religious figure in his world. The images, however, are correct descriptions of the *jaṅgam*'s appearance and practice. Notice that Eknath has made the *jaṅgams* Vaishnavas with the phrase "Hari's names" in the first line of the third verse.

Jaṅgam (*bhāv tochi bhagavā chirā*) 3737

Feeling is the brick-colored clothing,
The basic thread is Shiva's cord.
The *liṅga* of the self is *pūjā* enough.
Friends, I have come to your door. (1)

Friends, the guru's way is the rice we beg,
The Absolute is our rite of entry.

The body's discipline is the staff in the hand,
We burn desire and wear the sacred ash
Of mercy, forgiveness and peace.
In these ways we are *jaṅgams*, friends. (2)

Friends, the guru's way is the rice we beg,
The Absolute is our rite of entry.

Hari's names are the garlands we wear,
Guru-dīkṣā our festival.
Sages and saints know the beauty of it.
Friends, the Innocent One [Shiva] is in Eka-Janardan. (3)

Friends, the guru's way is the rice we beg,
The Absolute is our rite of entry.

One of the most popular cults among the peasant groups of Maharashtra is that of Khandoba, whose chief place of pilgrimage is Jejuri. The practice of dedicating children to Khandoba, either through a vow or out of poverty, is an ancient one. The males become *vāghyā*, servants of Khandoba and travelling beggars; females become *muraḷī*, companions of the *vāghyā* and sometimes prostitutes. The *bhāruḍ* opens with *ahaṃ vāghyā sohaṃ vāghyā*, a combination of highly Sanskritic Vedantic thought and the name of this low-status religious practitioner. The images and the phrases that follow are accurate depictions of the Khandoba cult's current practice.[20] Malhari and Khanderav are both names for the God Khandoba.

Vāghyā (*ahaṃ vāghyā sohaṃ vāghyā premnāgara vārī*) 3743

I am a *vāghyā*, I am He, a *vāghyā*,
  pilgrim to the City of Love.
Take care! Sing songs for my God!
  Make Him your protector.
Alms for the Lord! Alms for my Lord Malhari!

Don't oggle at desire, the *muraḷī*,
  or you will fall through hell's door.
Pour oil from your spouted cup of awareness,
  light the lamp of knowledge at the Great Door.
Let each one cool the bread of self-surrender
  in his own basket.
  Eka-Janardan is fulfilled.
  His offering — waving the fan over Khanderav.

The Mahanubhavs, a heterodox sect which arose in Maharashtra shortly before the time of Dnyandev, had become a persecuted and isolated body by the time of Eknath. Their black-clad priests and nuns, however, still appeared in public to beg for alms. The Mahanubhavs were iconoclastic and anti-caste. They worshipped the names of Krishna, Dattatreya and their own gurus, but eschewed images, and this facet of Mahanubhav belief is basic to Eknath's poems in their persona. Eknath uses a now somewhat derogatory form of their name, Manbhav, perhaps unwittingly, although he also reflects the suspicion that the Mahanubhavs may be licentious, a belief that still clings to their image.

20. While *ahaṃ sohaṃ* is not part of the *vāghyā*'s cry for alms, other phrases in this poem evoke the *vāghyā*'s present practices and the spouted cup and basket for bread are still used. Professor John Stanley has found another *vāghyā bhāruḍ* in current use by Khandoba worshippers which is clearly Eknath's, although it is not to be found in any published edition of his work.

Nevertheless, there is an identification of Eknath and his guru Janardan with the Mahanubhav. The echo formation 'ocher-bocher' (in Marathi, *śendre-hendre*) is a commonly used light touch in Marathi.

Mānbhav (*jhālo āmhī mānbhāv*) 3735

We have become Manbhavs.
In our bodies, innocent devotion. (1)

Among us, there is no mine, no yours.
We laugh and play together anywhere. (2)

We always chant the name of Krishna.
Nothing more is needed. (3)

We make merry.
We slap Yama's face. (4)

Those ocher-bocher gods —
Who the hell cares about them? (5)

Eka-Janardan's shelter —
We have become Manbhav. (6)

There is only one *bhāruḍ* sung by a Mang, the lowest of Maharashtra's three chief Untouchable castes (and none by the third Untouchable caste, the Chambhar, although Eknath was well aware that Raidas was a member of the northern leather-working caste with a related name, the Chamar. The metaphor of this *bhāruḍ* is one found in many of Eknath's *bhāruḍ*s which are sung in the persona of the largest of the Untouchable castes, the Mahars. The village is the body, the *pāṭil* or the village chief is the mind or soul, the *pāṭil*'s wife is illusion or desire, and she must be kept in control or the village-human will become chaotic and confused. The opening and refrain, *hayāt, māybāp, hayāt*, may be translated "Long life, master, long life." An early nineteenth-century Marathi dictionary[21] notes that the Arabic word *hayāt* was used by members of the Mang caste as a form of written address. As in some of Eknath's other *bhāruḍ*s, any solemn message in the poem is concealed in wry humor.

Māṅg (*hayāt māybāp hayāt*) 3910

Hayāt, māybāp, hayāt!
There was a village, it fell into ruins.

21. James T. Molesworth, *A Dictionary: Marathi and English* (Pune: Shubhada-Saraswat, 1975). It was first published in 1831.

There was a house, it went up in flames.
There were shoes, but the thorns pricked—
they were found in the hem of my *dhotī*.[22]
Hayāt, māybāp, hayāt! (1)

The village chief died,
his wife put on bangles.
The bastions of the great house tumbled down—
they were found on a little thief. [23]
Hayāt, māybāp, hayāt! (2)

Mang at the feet of Eka-Janardan says:
Patil, tell this to your wife.
If you tell her, the work is done,
if not, hang from an upside-down tree![24]
Hayāt, māybāp, hayāt! (3)

The largest section of the *bhāruḍ* collection which is in one voice is that of the *johār* poems. *Johār* was the form of address to a superior used exclusively by the Mahars until modern times. The traditional work of the Mahar was as a village servant: the person at the beck and call of the *pāṭīl* or any passing official, the groom for their horses, the watchman at the gate, the mender of the village wall, the carrier of messages, the remover of cattle carcasses from the village, the bringer of firewood to the burning ground. Eknath's Mahar does all these traditional duties; he also serves as a warning voice in the village, or as conscience in the metaphor of the village and its people as one human life. At times, Eknath simply uses the Mahar's work in a metaphysical extension, as in *bhāruḍ* 3866:

I sweep the four Vedas,
I collect the rubbish of the six Shastras,
I gather together all the Puranas,
I bring this to the street of the Sants. (3)

In *bhāruḍ* 3892, however, a long and somewhat obscure poem, the

22. This line might also be translated "they were found in my hedge."

23. This line might also be translated "that child/son was found thieving."

24. The "upside-down tree" may be a reference to the eternal tree described in the *Bhagavad Gītā*, 15.1-2, whose roots are above and branches below. It would be in character for Eknath to include a classical reference in this otherwise riddle-like poem.

Mahar of Eknath stops in the midst of telling the villagers how desire and corrupt religion have ruined the town (i.e. the human body and mind) and justifies his preaching with words that indicate the ability of Eknath to actually put himself inside the mind of the Mahar:

...don't give me that scornful sidelong glance! (15)

I do more than my routine work,
I answer to anyone who comes or goes,
I guard the houses of all the villagers.
  Is this hard life such a small thing,
  O my masters? (16)

I must get firewood for so many people,
It's me who supplies the bones and the horns,
I suffer the yoke of the dirtiest of work.
  Is all this such a small thing,
  O my masters? (17)

My fate is tethering pegs, hobbles, feed bags.
Soul weary in this forced labor,
I roam eighty-four hundred thousand villages!
  Is this sorrow such a small thing,
  O my masters? (18)

This fragment from a longer *bhāruḍ*, which seems to be the only one in which the Mahar asks for recognition of his hard life, also introduces us to another common feature of the *johār* or Mahar *bhāruḍ*s: the expression of the difficulty of living through the eighty-four hundred thousand births that are required of a being before he achieves mokṣa, freedom from rebirth. The true bhakta, however, is not reborn. One who lives in the company of the Sants and according to the morality of bhakti, eschewing hypocrisy, passion, anger, greed, pride, envy and egoism, will not be reborn. Rebirth leads to sorrow, old age, death, and a common feature of many of the *johār* poems is a graphic description of the difficulty of life and the deterioration of the body in old age, as well as the suffering of the soul as Yama punishes it on the way to hell. In the following *bhāruḍ*, Eknath's Mahar describes the problems of old age in very down-to-earth, even vulgar, speech.[25] The purpose of

25. There is quite a bit of down-to-earth, what might be called vulgar, speech in Marathi literature. Little of the erotic that marks Bengali bhakti can be found in Marathi bhakti poetry, or indeed in any other pre-modern Marathi genre.

such descriptions seems to be a sort of threat, similar to the threat of hell in Christian fundamentalism. Only the *johār bhāruḍs* are marked by this threat of continual old age, death and rebirth. Only the Untouchable Mahar, scorned and feared, delivers this harsh phase of the bhakti message.

Johār (*johār, māybāp, johār; mī sūryavaṃśīchā mahār*) 3887

Johār, māybāp, johār.
I am Lord Rama's Mahar.
I do all the work of the village.
Listen carefully, *kī jī māybāp.*[26] (1)

The village was filled with the five elements
But the twenty-five became the masters.[27]
Each one was entangled in his own vices,
They completely forgot the Lord. (2)

The Lord made over that village to them,
But they forgot that.
In the end Yamaji's hard strokes
Will fall on their asses. (3)

As long as the village is filled with its people
You should look after your welfare.
When old age comes
You can do nothing about it. (11)

The doors of the eye-village will close.
Snot will drop from the nose-city.
The thirty-two little hamlets
Will abandon your mouth-village. (5)

The neck-village will wobble.
The stomach-village will touch the spine.
The elbow-joint village will break.
You will be disgraced. (6)

26. *kī jī māybāp*: *māybāp*, literally 'mother-father', here means 'masters'. the *kī jī* has been added for rhythm; the words themselves are meaningless here.

27. The five elements (*pañchbhūt*) are earth, water, light, wind and sky; the twenty-five are those elements, subtle divisions as they appear in men. Eknath's *johār* poems are full of this kind of reference to numbers. evidently understood in the metaphysical sense by all who heard them.

The buttocks will wither.
The bowel-village will flow.
The penis will hang down
Like a dead dog's. (7)

The city of the knee-cap breaks.
The feet-village tremble in motion.
The hand-cities are dry.
What remedy is there? (8)

So the village was ruined.
I felt pity when I saw it.
So by means of a medicinal herb
I made the village prosperous. (9)

Drawing a potion of bhakti,
I gave that concoction to them.
Compounding the memory of the Name,
I gave the remedial antidote. (10)

Eka takes refuge in Janardan.
The remedy is divine.
Breaking the bondage of the worldly,
I made you an inhabitant of Vishnu's heaven.
Kī jī māybāp. (11)

All in all, Eknath wrote forty-seven *bhāruḍ*s as a Mahar, a *mahāriṇ* (female Mahar), or a *veskar* (the Mahar as gatekeeper). This is one-sixth of the total, far more than for any other character type or caste. Perhaps one reason was that the ubiquitous Mahar, who made up almost ten percent of the population and was present in every village in the Marathi-speaking area, could serve as a visible reminder of the difficulty of this life and the rebirths to come. Also, by using a Mahar as spokesman, Eknath seems able to be harsher, earthier in his images, and dramatic as well. It may be that Eknath had a genuine concern to save the Mahar, a special feeling for the many rebirths such a low caste must endure.

But in addition to all these reasons for the large number of *johār*, *mahāriṇ* and *veskar* poems, there is a clear indication of Eknath's conviction that a Mahar could be a true bhakta. The legends of Eknath's life, one of which involves his eating at the home of a Mahar bhakta because of his worthiness, tell us that Eknath honored all the truly devout and admitted all to his *bhajans*. Another *bhāruḍ*, perhaps the best known of all, specifically points to the Mahar as the teacher of the Brahman! In this translation, the speaker of each line has been added for clarity.

Johār (*kā re mahārā madamastā*) 3862

Brahman:	Hey you! Arrogant Mahara![28]
Mahar:	Yes, Brahman-baba? Why do you speak that way?
Brahman:	Why not? Do you think I'm afraid of your father?
Mahar:	My father and mother are yours too.
Brahman:	Look here, don't say things like that!
Mahar:	But all of us come from the One without qualities.
Brahman:	How do you know about the One without qualities?
Mahar:	Anyone may look into the nature of his soul.
Brahman:	We don't understand the nature of the soul.
Mahar:	If you don't, why not go to the feet of the Sants?
Brahman:	If we go to the Sants, then what?
Mahar:	You will escape eighty-four hundred thousand lives!
Brahman:	Who taught you this knowledge?
Mahar:	It came by Janardan's grace says Eka.

It is difficult to know what to make of all of Eknath's empathy. One cannot judge by the use of the *bhāruḍs* today. A few are sung on All-India Radio or by *bhajan* groups. The *vāghyā* of the Khandoba sect do know Eknath's songs, reports John Stanley, but a *vāsudeva*, one of the last of the watchmen-singers whom I met in Poona, had never heard of the songs Eknath had put in the mouths of sixteenth-century *vāsudevas*. We do not know if the Mahars of Eknath's day or in the ensuing centuries were drawn to bhakti through the *bhāruḍs* in their name, although we do know of quite a few Mahar bhaktas.[29] The large-scale rejection of Hinduism by Mahars in 1936 and the conversion of nearly

28. The addition of a long *ā* to the caste name Mahar, along with the initial *kā re* of the poem, indicate a very derogatory tone.

29. Untouchables could not go into the temple at Pandharpur until 1947, but had to stop at the *samādhi* of Chokhamela at the foot of the steps of the Great Door. Nevertheless, there are indications in such works as the Gazetteers of the nineteenth century that a good many Mahars were *vārkarīs*. Other Untouchable castes still march in the procession to Pandharpur, although always in a separate section. The mass conversion to Buddhism in 1956 led by Dr. B.R. Ambedkar, a much revered leader, removed all but a faithful few Mahars from this panth.

eighty per cent of the caste to Buddhism in 1956 has almost completely broken the earlier connection of Mahars to the *vārkarī* tradition. Many Buddhists know of Eknath's sympathy with the Mahar; few are as interested in Eknath as they are in Chokhamela, a genuine Mahar and a *sant-kavi* of the fourteenth century.

Many have claimed that a spirit of tolerance, an early manifestation of a democratic spirit, stems from the bhakti movement, and that Eknath personifies this. Such claims are difficult to prove. It is interesting that a widely supported Maratha kingdom rose in the century after Eknath which had what might be called a proto-nationalistic character. One can only wonder about the background which prepared the area for the unified thrust of empire under Shivaji. And one can only wonder at the knowledge, the concern, the humor and the inclusive spirit of the sixteenth-century Sant Eknath, who certainly attempted to link all the cultures in the varied world around him in a great devotional circle of belief.

THREE KABIR COLLECTIONS: A COMPARATIVE STUDY

LINDA HESS

A ton of tangled thread
that won't go straight...[1]

Kabir's description of an individual's karma, growing more and more complicated in birth after birth, could just as well be applied to the Kabir texts. Though a famous couplet asserts that the fifteenth-century sage never touched ink or paper,[2] his followers have been zealous writers of manuscripts and printers of books. A few of the hundreds of volumes attributed to Kabir draw from the still flourishing oral tradition; but most are based on the three principal written traditions, which originated in three widely separated regions and are associated with three sects.[3]

The earliest, and the only one to which a definite date can be assigned, is the collection of Kabir works found in the *Ādi Granth* or *Gurū Granth Sāhib* (*AG*), sacred book of the Sikhs, put into its present form

An earlier version of this essay appeared as chapter 2 of my Ph.D. dissertation, "Studies in Kabir: Texts, Traditions, Styles and Skills" (University of California, Berkeley, 1980).

1. *Bijak*, ed. Shukdev Singh (Allahabad: Nilabh Prakashan, 1972), *śabda* 85, p. 139. All references to the *Bījak* will be from this edition unless otherwise indicated. The line quoted is literally, "nine *mana* of tangled thread," a *mana* being 40 kilograms. There may also be a punning association with *mana*, mind.

2. *Bījak*, *sākhī* 187, p. 163.

3. The most important source for discussions of the collections and the issue of authenticity are the following:

(a) Charlotte Vaudeville, *Kabīr*, vol. 1 (Oxford: Clarendon Press, 1974), pp. 49-80.

(b) P.N. Tiwari, *Kabīr-granthāvalī* (Allahabad: University of Allahabad, Hindi Parishad, 1961). The nearly 300-page introduction is full of detailed information regarding texts and editorial choices. But the table of contents breaks it down so that one can seek out the parts one is interested in.

(c) Parashuram Chaturvedi, *Kabīr sāhitya kī parakh*, 3rd ed. (Allahabad: Bharati Bhandar, 1972), pp. 81-96.

(d) Shukdev Singh, ed., *Bījak*, introduction, especially pp. 30-79.

by Guru Arjan, the fifth Sikh Guru, in 1604. The *Granth* was compiled in the Punjab.[4]

The second important set of Kabir manuscripts comes from Rajasthan. The chief source to date has been the *Pañchvāṇī* (*PV*), a collection of sayings by five Sant poets compiled by members of the Dadu-panth, probably in the late seventeenth century.[5] A much shorter collection, the *Sarvāṅgī*, promises to be a more authentic source for the Rajasthani tradition of Kabir's sayings; but the *Sarvāṅgī* has not yet been published.[6]

The third major source for Kabir is the *Bījak* (*BI*), sacred book of

4. The standard text for the Kabir materials in the *Gurū Granth* (or *Ādi Granth*) is *Sant Kabīr*, ed. Ramkumar Varma (Allahabad: Sahitya Bhavan, 1966). A new version of the text, with corrections of errors in the Varma edition, is in the process of publication at the time of this writing. *Kabīr Vānī*, edited by Charlotte Vaudevile and published in Pondicherry, India, presents in one volume the Hindi texts of Kabir's works in Tiwari's *Granthāvalī* and the *Gurū Granth*. It includes an introduction in both French and English.

5. The *Pañchvāṇī* contains utterances of Dadu, Kabir, Namdev, Raidas, and Haridas. Supposedly Dadu himself ordered the compilation, but no individual is associated with the editorial work, and the process of accretion must have gone on long after the guru's death. This collection was not famous until S.S. Das's discovery of two old manuscripts which he edited and published in 1928 as the *Kabīr-granthāvalī*. Das was the head of Banaras Hindu University's Hindi Department and a powerful figure in the academic world. He announced that one of his manuscripts had been written in Kabir's own lifetime, and the *Granthāvalī* became the "Received Standard" in academic circles. Later the 1504 colophon was proved false, but the *Granthāvalī* still reigns supreme in the universities.

The Rajasthani collections have generally been called *Granthāvalī* since Das's publication in 1928. But the title creates confusion, especially since the 1961 publication of P.N. Tiwari's *Kabīr-granthāvalī*, which is not at all the same collection. Charlotte Vaudeville skirts the confusion by consistently saying "Rajasthani tradition" (rather than *Granthāvalī*) when comparing those texts with the *Gurū Granth* or *Bījak*. Using the early title, *Pañchvāṇī* or "Words of the Five," eliminates ambiguity.

6. The *Sarvāṅgī*, compiled by Dadu's disciple Rajjab (ca. 1570-1680), anthologizes the work of 107 religious poets. Mingled with the rest, under 146 topical headings, are 337 poems attributed to Kabir (1 *ramainī*, 155 *pad*s, 181 *sākhī*s). All the poems, with the exception of six *sākhī*s, are found in *PV* (Tiwari, *Kābir-granthāvalī*, p. 146). According to Vaudeville, the *Sarvaṅgī* contains "an epitome of what is generally called the Dādū-panthī or 'Rājasthānī' tradition of Kabīr's verses" (*Kabīr*, p. 60). Much work on Dadu-panthi literature has been done in recent years by Winand M. Callewaert of Leuven, Belgium. Results of his studies and manuscript searches have been published in English in *Orientalia Lovaniensia Periodica* in 1973, 1974, and 1977. A partial translation has appeared under the title *The Sarvāṅgī of the Dādū Panthī Rajab* (Leuven: Department Orientalistiek, Katholieke Universiteit, 1978).

the Kabir-panth, compiled in eastern Uttar Pradesh and/or Bihar, probably also in the late seventeenth century, though no early dated manuscripts have been reported.

All three collections show influence from the local language, from the sects that produced them, and from regional religious trends. All developed independently, but there are intricate interrelations among them. The *Pañchvāṇī* and *Gurū Granth* seem to be much more closely related to each other than either is to the *Bījak*, a distinction Charlotte Vaudeville has formalized by speaking of the western corpus and the eastern corpus of Kabir's sayings.[7] The western collections have many poems in common, whereas they share relatively few poems with the *Bījak*. Further, the poems differ in content and feeling: a portrait of the author of the *Bījak* will have subtly different colors, tones, and lines than a portrait of the poet canonized in Rajasthan and the Punjab. On the other hand, the language of the *Gurū Granth* is closer to that of the *Bījak* than to that of the *Pañchvāṇī*.[8]

Though these complications alarm the textual critic, they allure the comparativist. The three major Kabir collections provide a rich field for comparative study, a special opportunity to consider the question of authenticity and the means by which oral compositions were set down and transmitted in medieval India. This essay will describe the three collections, highlight the ways in which they resemble and diverge from each other, provide a statistical study of key words, analyze and compare individual poems, and reflect on the meaning of the information uncovered. The statistical data presented here relates only to the songs or *pad*s (also called *śabda*s; lyric poems in varied meters, usually six to eighteen lines long) and not to the *sākhī*s (also called *dohā*s or *śalok*s; rhymed couplets containing four *charaṇ*s or half-lines, often translated as quatrains). The *sākhī*s are important and are likely to yield a different kind of information than the *pads*.[9] But even without

7. Vaudeville, *Kabīr*, p. 77.

8. This point is made by Shukdev Singh, *Bījak*, pp. 44 ff., and Tiwari, *Granthāvalī*, pp. 80-81. See also Hess, "Studies in Kabīr," pp. 12-14.

9. Vaudeville notes: "It is a fact that, on the whole, the language of the dohās differs from that of the padas and ramainīs. As already noted by Barthwal, 'the style is more archaic in the dohas (or sakhis), a metre natural to Apabhramsa'. Western dialectal forms (Kharī Bolī, Rājasthānī, and a few Panjābī forms) are more numerous in the sākhīs, whereas Braj tends to dominate in the padas.... An interesting point is that the dialectal difference between the dohas and padas attributed to Kabīr corresponds to the difference noted between the languages of the Dohā-kosas and Caryā-padas composed by the Sahajiyā Siddhas" (*Kabīr*, p. 65).

them, the study is revealing. The *pads*, being musical, are more fluid; their structure is looser, more amenable to alteration. So they should demonstrate more dramatically the kinds of changes to which Kabir-attributed materials were subjected as they passed from place to place, hand to hand, lip to lip.

The overwhelming majority of the poems in all three collections are in the *pad* and *sākhī* forms mentioned above. A form called *ramainī*—a lyric in *chaupāī* meter usually concluding with a *dohā*—appears in *PV* and *BI*. All three have a version of an acrostic called *chauṅtīsā* or *bāvan akharī*. Finally, there are some miscellaneous forms found in the *Bījak* alone. The size, format, and order of the three collections are as follows:

Gurū Granth[10]

1. 226 *pads*, all but one distributed among sixteen sections with raga headings. The numbers of *pads* under each heading vary widely. The largest number (77) is under *Gauṛī*, the smallest (1) under *Tilaṅg*.
2. 237 or 239 *śaloks* (*sākhīs*), not subdivided.

Pañchvāṇī[11]

1. 810 *sākhīs* divided into 59 sections by topic or *aṅga*.
2. 384 *pads* divided into 16 raga sections, the longest (*Gauṛī*) containing 150 poems and the two shortest (*Sāraṅg*, *Kalyān*) containing

---

Dr. Mahendra speaks of differences in the poetic devices used in *pads* and *sākhīs*, mentioning that *ulaṭbāṃsī* and Yogic metaphors, common in the former, are almost nonexistent in the latter (*Kabīr kī bhāṣā* (Delhi: By the Author 1969), p. 207). Significant to the present study its the fact that the incidence of Krishnaite names in the western collections is radically lower in the *sākhis* than in the *pads* (see below for discussion of names of Krishna in the *pads*).

10. Kabir's *pads* do not appear all together in *AG*. W.H. McLeod explains how they are distributed: "The *Ādī Granth* includes 226 *śabads* by Kabīr. Of these 225 are to be found in the *bhagat bani* at the end of the various *rāgs*, and the remaining one is included among the works of Guru Arjan (*Bhairo* 3, *AG*, p. 1136). The total number of Kabīr *sloks* included in the *Ādī Granth* is either 237 or 239. . . . There are also three longer works: the *Bāvan Akharī* (AG, pp. 340-43), the *Thinti* (pp. 343-44), and the 'Seven Days' (pp. 344-43)." *Gurū Nānak and the Sikh Religion* (Oxford: Clarendon Press, 1968), p. 156, n. 3.

11. The edition I have used is Mataprasad Gupta's *Kabīr-granthāvalī* (Allahabad: Lokbharati Prakashan, 1969). Gupta's commentary was useful to me, as I suspect it will be to other western readers. The numbering is a bit different from the older and more widely used *Granthāvalī* edited by S.S. Das; but it is not too difficult to find the corresponding poem within the appropriate raga or *aṅga*. Concordances in Varma and Tiwari refer to Das's edition.

1 each. 11 of the ragas match up with the headings of the *AG* sections. Vaudeville says that some *PV* manuscripts have the *pads* divided into *aṅgas* rather than ragas.[12]

3. 43 *ramainīs* under 7 headings, which indicate the number of poems in each subdivision (e.g., *satapadī ramainī* contains 7 poems; *bārahapadī ramainī* contains 12).

Bījak

1. 84 *ramainīs* with no subdivisions.
2. 115 *śabdas* (*pads*) with no subdivisions.
3. 353 *sākhīs* with no subdivisions.
4. 34 miscellaneous poems under 8 headings, most of them identified with eastern folk song forms.[13]

From these summaries certain differences can be observed before a single poem is read. Most obvious is size: *AG* and *BI* are similar in length, while *PV* has roughly twice as many *pads* and three times as many *sākhīs* as either of them.[14]

After numbers, one notices organization. The *pads* and *sākhīs* of the standard *Bījak* have no subdivisions.[15] The *sākhīs* of the *Gurū Granth* are unclassified, while the *pads* are divided into ragas. The *Pañchvāṇī* is most elaborately subdivided of all, with musical ragas for the *pads* and topical *aṅgas* for the *sākhīs*. More significant are the musical designations, which seem to hint at the ways in which the lyrics were actually performed and spread.

Music

It is usually assumed that the *pad* form is meant to be sung, and that Kabir probably sang his own compositions. Some people claim that he

12. Vaudeville, *Kabīr*, p. 61.

13. In some versions of the *Bījak* this miscellaneous section precedes the *sākhīs*. The names of the forms are *kaharā*, *basant*, *beli*, *birahulī*, *chānchari*, *hiṇdolā*, *chauṅtīsā*, and *vipramatīsī*. Different recensions of the *Bījak* may have 112 instead of 115 *sabdas*, and as many as 481 *sākhīs*.

14. For this study, *pads* and *ramainīs* are grouped together under the heading '*pads*'. If the shorter *Sarvāṅgī*, rather than the *Pañchvāṇī*, were taken to represent the Rajasthani tradition, the differences in size would not be so great (see n. 6 above).

15. There is evidence of a rudimentary organization in the *Bījak*, as poems beginning with the same address (*santo*, *Rām*, *paṇḍit*, *Hari*, *bhāī*, etc.) are grouped together. The order is different in the older Bhagatahi recension, in which, according to Tiwari, the *pads* are arranged more thoughtfully, by subject. On the recensions of the *Bījak* see Hess, "Studies in Kabir," pp. 17-20, and n. 51.

knew enough music to sing in ragas, and that the raga divisions in the collections can be traced back to the poet. It makes more sense to attribute the choice of specific ragas to the anthologizers.[16] Parashuram Chaturvedi, in a chapter called "Kabir Literature and Music," cites various uses of musical language in Kabir's poetry, references to instruments, playing, singing and dancing, metaphors of the body as a musical instrument.[17] But as Chaturvedi himself recognizes, use of such images does not make Kabir a musician any more than metaphors from agriculture, commerce, and the kitchen prove that Kabir was a farmer, businessman, or housewife. Chaturvedi also says that the practice of organizing *pad* collections by ragas long predates Kabir. The *pads* of Jayadeva's Sanskrit *Gīta Govinda* (1200) are so organized, as are the old Bengali *pads* of the Buddhist Siddhas (ca. eleventh and twelfth centuries)[18] and the *Gorakh-bāṇī* (ca. eleventh century).[19] The compilers of *AG* and *PV* must have been following this tradition in applying raga headings to the *pads* of Kabir.

But the relevance of music in comparing the three collections goes deeper than the raga headings. Several kinds of evidence indicate that the western collections are linked to music as the *Bījak* is not. A glance at the *pads* of *PV* suggests that they are, in general, more obviously suitable for singing than those of the *Bījak*. The opening verses (one to four half-lines) of each poem, which include the *ṭek* or refrain that is repeated throughout the song, are more prominent in the *Pañchvāṇī* and are even marked *ṭek* in the text. Sometimes they are distinct in mood and content from the rest of the poem.[20] The *PV* poems contain more obvious singing devices, such as the addition of a syllable at the end of every line (*re*, *jī*, *ho*, *ho Rām*), or repetition of a line or phrase in every stanza ("Mother, who will weave?", "I won't go back to the world-ocean!")[21], or a long and euphonious verb—ending throughout (for example, *Gauṛī* 148).

16. *Sant Kabīr* has a concordance of matching *pads* in *AG* and *PV*. Of the 39 pairs listed, 22 are categorized under the same ragas, 17 under different ragas.

17. Chaturvedi, *Kabīr sāhitya*, pp. 180-90.

18. On the dates of the Buddhist Siddhas, see Per Kvaerne, *An Anthology of Buddhist Tantric Songs* (Oslo: Norwegian Research Council for Science and the Humanities, 1977), p. 7.

19. See *Gorakh-bāṇī*, ed. P.D. Barthwal, 2nd ed. (Allahabad: Hindi Sahitya Sammelan, 1946). On Gorakhnath's dates, see G. W. Briggs, *Gorakhnath and the Kānphaṭa Yogīs* (Delhi: Motilal Banarsidass, reprint ed., 1973), p. 250.

20. Examples: *PV Gauṛī* 4 and 75, *Rāmkalī* 6 and 26, *Āsāvarī* 44.

21. The lines cited are from *PV Gauṛī* 19 and 31. See also *Soraṭhī* 13, *Basant* 11, *Bilāval* 11.

The *Gurū Granth* is also arranged with the needs of singers in mind. A large number of poems rhyme *charaṇ*-to-*charaṇ* instead of line-to-line, making for short, highly flexible units. The hymns in the *Granth* were collected to be sung, and group singing was the main activity at gatherings of Nanak's followers:

> The pattern of teaching through the composition and communal singing of hymns was continued by Nānak's first four successors and reached a climax in the work of Arjan, the fifth Gurū (died 1606).[22]

But the most notable element of "singability" has to do with theme and mood. This aspect will be presented more systematically when we come to the statistical analysis. Here it may be noted that the greatest overall difference between the *Bījak* and the two western collections is that the latter are infused with bhakti feeling and language, while the former has practically none. By "bhakti feeling and language" I mean Vaishnava (especially Krishnaite) names for God that are linked with personal worship and devotional fervor; and themes that stress emotional surrender in one of the standard bhakti modes: as servant, child, parent, or lover in union or separation. The western traditions also have numerous poems of ecstatic realization, in which the poet may or may not be in the role of a lover.

The *Bījak*, on the other hand, tends to be more harsh and intellectual. Its satire is more pervasive and unmitigated. There is a greater emphasis on *nirguṇa* expression of truth by negation, riddle, and teasing mental challenge. Such lyrics are not as appealing to the singer or to the singer's audience as those that emphasize worship and emotion. There is, it is true, a tradition of '*nirguṇa bhajans*', especially active in villages of eastern U.P. and Bihar, concentrating on the themes of death and transience, "the vanity of life and the pernicious effect of worldly enjoyment and...[the] path for escaping death and decay and for attaining liberation."[23] This style was popularized by the Nath Yogis between the tenth and fifteenth centuries. But its present popularity is limited, and it is almost exclusively associated with Kabir.[24] Anyone who has

22. W.H. McLeod, "Sikhism," in A.L. Basham, ed., *A Cultural History of India* (Oxford: Clarendon Press, 1978), p. 298.

23. S.B. Dasgupta, *Obscure Religious Cults*, 3rd ed. (Calcutta: Firma K.L. Mukhopadhyay, 1969), p. 370.

24. In 1978 Dr. Edward Henry (an anthropologist specializing in North Indian folk music) went in search of *jogīs*—"householders of low Muslim caste," with both Hindu and Muslim characteristics, who are the "prime transmitters of the *nirgun*

listened to *bhajan*-singing in North India, whether in a temple or a home, at a concert or on the street, knows that the bhakti mode overwhelmingly dominates.

An anecdote will underline my point about the *Bījak* and its peculiar unmusical quality. In 1976, the Kabir Chaura temple in Varanasi published a new edition of the popular *Śabdāvalī*, a collection of *pad*s especially meant for singing (the largest section of the book is entitled "*Bhajan*"). I had been looking for lyrics in the *Bījak* that might be set to music, and had been having difficulty finding any that seemed especially suitable. So, when the monk who had edited the *Śabdāvalī*'s eleventh edition presented me with a copy, I asked him to show me which songs came from the *Bījak*. "Oh, there aren't many, "he said, "maybe only three or four."

"Please show me those three or four."

"Perhaps there's only one or two."

"Oh. Well anyway, I'd like to see the one or two."

"Actually there aren't any *pad*s from the *Bījak* in this book."

So I learned that I wasn't the only one who found the *Bījak* unmusical, and it occurred to me that the lack of raga divisions in the *Bījak* was not coincidental. Though no systematic survey was made, a quick glance through the *Śabdāvalī* did reveal a number of poems from the western collections.

Of course it would be foolish to suggest that the *nirguṇa* and satirical poems were not amenable to transmission by singing. If that were true, how could they constitute so large a proportion of the western collections as they do? They were Kabir's characteristic utterances, and they were certainly transmitted. But they were sometimes "devotionalized",

---

[*bhajan*] tradition" in U.P. and Bihar. The *jogī*s were hard to find, but Dr. Henry encountered some in his travels among villages and recorded *bhajan*s by them and others. Of the seventeen *bhajan*s he has transcribed and translated, fifteen are attributed to Kabir. One has no attribution, and only one bears the name of another composer ('Bhairo'). *Nirgun bhajan*s are popular primarily among low-caste Hindus (Henry mentions Musshars, Kohars, Kahars, Ahirs, Chamars, and Dhobis), and comparably low Muslims. They are vestiges of a time when Nath influence was much more widespread in northeast India. Henry cites S.B. Dasgupta's account of how, from about the fifteenth century, bhakti displaced Yoga as the matrix of popular religion: "The gradual revival of Hinduism in Bengal, with the Caitanya movement as a main thrust, introduced Sanskritic and Puraṇic elements which were more attractive to the caste Hindus, leaving the *nirguṇ* songs to be preserved only among Muslims and low-caste Hindus." The above information, including quotations, is from a draft of an article which Dr. Henry has kindly let me read.

especially in opening and closing lines.[25] There was, as will be demonstrated, a tendency to add passages or whole poems of a devotional nature to the lyrics attributed to Kabir, as they were passed westward by singers.[26]

Key Words

Seeking methods to test precisely the difference in tone and emphasis between the *Bījak* and the two western collections, I began by culling out 'key words' — words that stand for the supreme being or ultimate experience of reality, or (in the case of 'guru') the means by which it becomes available. The many possible key words that presented themselves — including proper and common nouns, verbs, adjectives, and phrases — were eventually narrowed down to about fifty terms, all nouns. Only positive uses of those terms were counted: if Kabir refers to the guru as the source of truth, it has been counted; if he attacks false gurus, or denies that there is any guru in the ultimate, non-dual experience, it has not been counted. Only one occurrence of each key word has been counted in each poem. So if '*Rām*' is mentioned twice in the same *pad*, I have marked only one occurrence of '*Rām*'. (But if two names of Krishna, such as Govinda and Murari, appear, they have been counted separately.) My broad aim has been to see, in terms of numbers of poems, which key words dominate in each collection and how the proportions compare among the three. Although the *pad*s and *ramainī*s are not quite the same, I have regarded them as similar enough to be grouped together in making these statistics. So the total number of '*pad*s' included from the *Pañchvāṇī* is 427 (384 *pad*s plus 43 *ramainī*s). The total for the *Bījak* is 199 (115 *pad*s plus 84 *ramainī*s). For the *Gurū Granth* it is 223 (226 minus the long poems, obviously of a different type

25. Here are some examples, taken only from the *Gauṛī* section of *PV*. 79, on universal suffering, burning pain, despair, has a *vinaya* closing: "I bow to your feet; give me a home, O Paramananda." 46, on death and transiency, says in the *ṭek* that death is sweet for one who dies by the guru's grace. 85, the first half focuses on transiency, the second half on singing Govinda's praise in the company of saints. 87, a violent repudiation of sense pleasures, ends with an admonition to worship Murari's feet. 4, discussed on p. 116 above. 109, on transiency and rebirth, turns to *vinaya* in the last line: "I beg one gift, Kamalakanta: Remove Kabir's grief, O infinite one." 40 has 'love' (*prema*) where *BI* has 'Ram' (*Rāma*). 34 has 'guru's grace' where *BI* has 'Ram'.

26. On the question of how Kabir's verses spread across the country — whether he travelled himself, or whether the verses all started in the east and were carried westward by others — see Hess, "Studies in Kabir," chapter 1, especially pp. 2-12.

than the rest, based on the days of the week, the days of the lunar fortnight, and the letters of the alphabet).

Although the list of key words is long, much has been left out. Particularly, the *nirguṇa* evocations of the supreme are omitted. These include negative descriptions (*nirākāra*, *avigata*, *agama*, *agochara*, etc.), abstract references to state, essence, place (*gati*, *sāra*, [*parama*, *amara*] *pada*, etc.), and whole poems or passages which define by negation in the Upanishadic tradition of 'not this, not this'. For this comparative study, the positive terms are more useful, and are certainly sufficient to reveal the broad differences between the texts.

After tallying the occurrences of key words in 849 lyrics, I distributed the 50-odd terms among fifteen headings and worked out some percentages. The process is obviously rough and approximate; but the approximate figures are good enough to show the kinds of trends we are looking for. The tables that follow give more detailed information on the ten groups that appeared most frequently.

Table I. Occurrence of Key Words in Pads[27]

No.—number of *pads* in which key words appear.
%—percentage of *pads* in which key words appear.

	PV		*AG*		*BI*	
	No.	%	*No.*	%	*No.*	%
Ram	220	51.64	112	50.22	49	24.62
Hari	109	25.59	72	32.29	24	12.06
Guru	75	17.6	68	30.49	19	9.55
Name/Word	95	22.3	83	37.22	30	15.08
Bhakti	203	47.65	127	56.95	19	9.55
Krishna	71	16.67	33	14.8	0	0
Vishnu	13	3.05	18	8.07	2	1.0
Lord/Master	35	8.22	35	15.7	7	3.52
Lord of Universe/Creator	40	9.39	14	6.28	11	5.53
Muslim	32	7.51	15	6.73	6	3.02
Total Key Words	1008		654		197	
Total *Pads*	427		223		199	
Average No. Key Words per *Pad*	2.37		2.93		.99	

27. Some of these categories include a number of terms. For example, 'bhakti' includes various words for love and devotion. Names of Krishna include Mohan, Gopal, Govinda, Madhav, Murari, and several others. Charlotte Vaudeville has commented to me that 'Govinda' is not exclusively applied to Krishna but is a general Vaishnavite name. My observation is, however, that it is overwhelmingly associated with Krishna in popular culture. Dictionaries confirm this, always giving 'Shrikrishna' as the first definition and sometimes not mentioning 'Vishnu' at all. For more figures and details on these categories, see Hess, "Studies in Kabir," pp. 38-40.

Table II. Order of Frequency of Major Key Words in Each Collection

Pañchvāṇī	%	*Gurū Granth*	%	*Bījak*	%
1. Ram	51.6	1. Bhakti	57.0	1. Ram	24.6
2. Bhakti	47.7	2. Ram	50.2	2. Word/Name	15.1
3. Hari	25.6	3. Word/Name	37.2	3. Hari	12.1
4. Word/Name	22.3	4. Hari	32.3	4-5. Guru &	
5. Guru	17.6	5. Guru	30.5	Bhakti	9.6
6. Experience	16.9	6. Experience	20.6	6. Experience	6.0
7. Krishna	16.7	7. Lord/Master	15.7	7. Lord of Universe	5.5
8. Lord of Universe	9.4	8. Krishna	14.8	8. Purusha	4.0
9. Lord/Master	8.2	9. Vishnu	8.7	9. Lord/Master	3.5
10. Muslim	7.5	10. Muslim	6.7	10. Muslim	3.0

Before describing the differences between the three collections, particularly between eastern and western traditions, I would like to point out some ways in which the collections are alike. All contain large numbers of poems which emphasize what may be called "delusion". This group includes the well-known attacks on Hindus and Muslims, hypocrites and idiots, the violent and the greedy. It also addresses inner delusion, the mind's endless capacity for deceiving itself as well as others. Another theme running strongly through all the collections is death, which, in its "inescapable, frightful, tragic character," as Vaudeville says, "appears to be at the core of Kabir's thought."[28] A third type unquestionably linked with Kabir is the *ulaṭbāṃsī* or poem of 'upside-down language', paradoxes, enigmas, strange images sometimes traceable to Tantric sources, sometimes apparently products of Kabir's own imagination or of local popular tradition. And there are other modes common to all traditions (such as the 'not-this' method of indicating truth, or the liberation poem using Yogic symbols). A formula by which one can calculate 'similarity', applied to the figures on occurrence of key words, revealed that the similarity of *AG* to *PV* is 88%; that of PV to BI is 66%; and (it so happens) that of *AG* to *BI* is also 66%. A mathematician friend pointed out that 66% still represents a high degree of similarity.[29]

As to differences, the statistical study did confirm my major expectation: that the chief distinguishing factor between the *Bījak* and the western collections had to do with bhakti content. Another result emer-

28. Vaudeville, *Kabīr*, p. 147.

29. For this formula and much help in assembling all the statistical information, I am grateful to Dr. Harold Nathan.

ged which was not anticipated: the *Bījak* is much below the other two collections not just in bhakti terms but in *all* positive terms for the supreme. Even '*Rām*', which is far ahead of other key words in the *Bījak*, occurs only in about 25% of the *pads*. In contrast, the figures for the two top categories in the *Gurū Granth* and *Pañchvāṇī* are between 47% and 57%. The fifth item on the *AG* list occurs significantly more often than the first item on the *BI* list. Table II shows how low the *Bījak* figures are in all categories. Table I shows the average number of key words per poem: about 2.4 for *PV*, 3 for *AG*, and 1 for *BI*.

It was interesting to discover that the *Gurū Granth* is the most devotional of the collections by the measure being used here; that the terms associated with bhakti are at the top of the *AG* list, occurring even more frequently than '*Rām*'. It was also possible to note differences between the two western collections. The *Gurū Granth* percentages were higher than the *Pañchvāṇī*'s in two-thirds of the categories. But they were *very much* higher in just a few; and those few represent the interests and beliefs of the founders of the Sikh panth. One such category is 'Guru', for which the frequency in *AG* is nearly twice that in *PV*. Another is 'Lord/Master' (*prabhu*, *svāmī*, *ṭhākur*), where again the *AG* figure is almost double that of *PV*. The third is 'Name/Word', where the figures are 37% for the *Granth* and 22% for *PV*. These emphases, along with the bhakti terms of grace and surrender, conform with what W.H. McLeod describes as fundamental tenets of the early Sikh faith. Talking of Guru Angad, the second Sikh Guru and successor to Nanak, McLeod says:

> [I]n the manner of his own preceptor he insists that only through regular meditation on the divine Name can one attain to purity and salvation. To find and follow this path of salvation one must depend upon the grace of the Gurū.[30]

Elsewhere McLeod gives a more detailed exposition of original Sikh principles:

> Nānak's teachings concerning the way of salvation are expressed in a number of key words which recur constantly in his works. God, being gracious, communicates his revelation in the form of the *śabad* (*śabda*, 'word') uttered by the *gurū* (the 'preceptor'). Any aspect of the created world which communicates a vision or glimpse of the nature of God or of his purpose is to be regarded

30. See McLeod, "The Development of the Sikh Panth," below, p. 233.

> as an expression of the *śabad*. . . . Any means whereby spiritual perception is awakened can be regarded as the activity of the *gurū*. ...Everywhere there can be perceived a divinely bestowed harmony. Salvation consists in bringing oneself within this pattern of harmony.
>
> This requires an explicit discipline, the practice of *nām simaranā* or *nām japanā*. The word *nām* signifies all that constitutes the nature and being of God, and the verb *simaranā* means 'to hold in remembrance'. The alternate verb *japanā* means literally, 'to repeat...[31]

The key words McLeod identifies with Guru Nanak correspond closely with the key words which characterize Kabir in the Sikh scripture, and which distinguish the Kabir of the *Granth* from the Kabir of Rajasthan.

Krishna in Kabir?

While in two-thirds of the categories the *Pañchvāṇī* is lower than the *Granth*, it is higher on 'Krishna' (16.7% to 14.8%). Most remarkably, the figure for the *Bijak* on this item is zero.[32] This is a very interesting point. Did the Kabir-panthi editors edit out references to Krishna? Did the Dadu-panthis add the Krishnaite names? Or is there some other way to account for their conspicuous presence in the west and absence in the east? As usual, we can only conjecture on this matter; and to begin to conjecture, it is useful to imagine the circumstances in which the events took place.

At the time when these poems were being anthologized, and in most of the areas where they were circulating, Krishna bhakti reigned supreme. With two exceptions (Kabir and Nanak), the famous bhakti poets of North India from 1200 to 1500 were all worshippers of Krishna.[33] But it was in the century after Kabir's death that Krishna's popularity became at once overwhelming and institutionalized — mainly through the activities of Chaitanya and Vallabha and their followers. Chaitanya died in 1533, Vallabha in 1531. The former had already sent his emissaries to Braj to establish Krishna religion and theology; the latter's son and successor also fixed himself in Braj. From both fountainheads issued great Krishna sects, and with them a flood of poetry, swelled

31. Idem., "Sikhism," in Basham, *Cultural History*, p. 297.
32. The name Gopal appears in *śabda* 42, but in a satirical context.
33. These include Jnaneshvara in Maharashtra, Narsimha Mehta in Gujarat, Vidyapati and Chandidas in Bengal-East Bihar, and Mirabai in Rajasthan.

above all by Sur Das and the *aṣṭachhāp*.[34] Their songs, along with Mira's, were on millions of tongues and hearts through most of Uttar Pradesh and Rajasthan by the end of the sixteenth century.

But in the belt between Bengal and the Punjab, there was one region where Krishna bhakti never became dominant. Its center: Varanasi. In eastern U.P. and western Bihar, there was no Krishna bhakti poet whose name is even remembered. Kashi was Shiva's town, and Shiva recited the name of Ram.[35] Kashi was the place where Ramananda had settled, teaching a bright array of disciples to rely on the name of Ram. And it was in Kashi in 1584 that Tulsi Das completed the *Rāmcharitmānas*, in which Shiva declares that none can know him without adoring Ram, and Ram returns the compliment, saying that devotion to him is impossible for one who doesn't worship Shiva.[36]

Now we return to the imagined movement of Kabir's sayings from the Varanasi area to points west. They would have had to pass through an atmosphere saturated with fervent Krishna bhakti. And how did they pass? On the lips of devotees. They were sung, along with the body of devotional songs already popular in those regions. Is it not likely that the deeper they penetrated into Krishna country, the more they became colored by Krishnaite feeling and language?

If this were so, one sort of evidence might be available. The most portable, alterable parts of a *bhajan* are the opening and closing, the *ṭek* and *bhaṇitā*. Each has a kind of independent existence. The *ṭek* is repeated over and over as a refrain, with little regard to the stanzas it comes in contact with. The *bhaṇitā* is even more formulaic, half of it usually filled with, "Kabir says, listen saints," or something similar. These signature lines are often interchangeable; it is easy to make them up or substitute them.

My hypothesis was that the occurrences of Krishna in the western collections should be concentrated in *ṭek* and *bhaṇitā*. A review of the

34. This is the title given to eight preeminent Krishna bhakti poets by Vitthalnath, son of Vallabhacharya and founder of the Pushtimarga (Vallabhite sect) in Vrindavan. The eight poets are: Sur Das, Kumbhan Das, Chitaswami, Paramananda Das, Krishna Das, Govindaswami, Chaturbhuja Das, and Nanda Das.

35. See, for example, *Rāmcharitmānas*, *Bālakāṇḍa dohā* 74, *chaupāī* 4: "He [Shiva] continually repeated the name of Raghunāyak, and in this place and that listened to the tale of Rāma's virtues." Translated by W.D.P. Hill, *The Holy Lake of the Acts of Rama* (London: Oxford Univerisity Press, 1952), p. 40.

36. Ibid., *Laṅkākāṇḍa dohā* 1, *chaupāīs* 3-4: " 'None is so dear to me as Śiva,' said the Lord [Ram]; the man who is opposed to Śiva and is called my worshipper can never dream of winning to me; the enemy of Saṁkara who aims at faith in me is fit for hell, a fool of little understanding." Hill, *Holy Lake*, p. 367.

pañchvāṇī revealed this to be the case.[37] Of 70 instances of Krishna names, 48, or 68%, were in the *ṭek* or the *bhaṇitā*. In all but two of these instances, the Krishna names appeared where there was no mention of Krishna in the body of the poem. 68% is quite a high proportion; it will seem even higher when we consider that the total number of lines in the bodies of poems is much greater than in *ṭek*s and *bhaṇitā*s. If the names were scattered randomly, they would occur a great deal more often in the bodies than in the openings and closings. In many cases the Krishna names occur as the poem's first or last word, or both—the easiest places to insert them. Thus an opening line which in the *Bījak* is, "*Rāmura chale bināvana mā ho,*" appears in *PV* as, "*Mādhava chale bunāvana mā ho.*" *AG* has simply, "*Gaī bunāvana mā ho.*"[38] Another *Bījak pad* begins, "*Kabīra tero bana kandalā meṅ,*" while *PV* has, "*Govyande tumhāre bana kandali.*"[39]

Sometimes the appearance of Krishna seems oddly out of place, as in a *PV pad* that is a typical warning about death and the transitory character of life. After nine *charaṇ*s in the grim and austere vein so familiar in Kabir, we come upon a closing half-line straight out of the opulent imagery of Krishna bhakti:

> *Kṛṣṇa kavala dala bhavara Kabīra.*
> Krishna the lotus petals, Kabir the bee.[40]

Another example is *PV Gauṛī* 4, a Tantric poem of realization through the eight *chakra*s, with technical details about the numbers of petals, the deities and symbols associated with each lotus, introduced by a Vaishnava bhakti *ṭek* which has nothing to do with the rest of the poem:

> *Mana ke Mohana Mīṭhulā, yahu mana lāgau tohi re.*
> *Charaṇa kaṅvala mana māṅniyā, aura na bhāvai mohi re.*
>
> Heart's Mohan, Vitthal,[41] this heart has clasped you.
> My heart is given to your lotus feet, no other pleases me.

Other instances could be given of revealing variations from one collection to another (as when *AG* has *ṭhākura* or *satiguru* in place of

37. The *ṭek* is usually printed as the first line, but can include the second line. *Bhaṇitā* refers to anything that comes after "Kabir says"—usually the last line. *AG* has not been surveyed because it places the *ṭek* after the first stanza.

38. *PV Rāmkalī* 41, *AG Gauṛī* 54, *BI śabda* 15.

39. *BI śabda* 87, *PV Āsāvarī* 8.

40. *PV Gauṛī* 4.

41. Gupta glosses *mīṭhula* as '*Bīṭhula*'—Vishnu.

PV's Krishna). But enough has been said to make plausible the theory that the names of Krishna were often added as the songs travelled west, rather than that the Kabir-panthi editors removed them. The fact that the figures for Krishna names in both western collections are rather low (14-17%, as opposed to Ram, over 50%) also suggests that they could have been added. Finally, it should be noted that the names of Krishna are much rarer in the *sākhī*s than in the *pad*s. From one of Vaudeville's notes it appears that Govinda is the only name found in the *sākhī*s of the Tiwari *Granthāvalī*, and that name occurs only in three out of 247 *sākhī*s.[42] All three of these *sākhī*s are found only in Rajasthani sources, not in the *Gurū Granth* or *Bījak*.

Separation, Supplication, Ecstasy

The names of Krishna provide one clear index of the features that distinguish the western collections from the *Bījak*. But they are only part of a more general trend toward personal devotion, suggestions of anthropomorphism in the projected deity, which open the way to different emotional ranges, more personal and extreme expressions of feeling by the devotee. These tendencies are revealed in certain types of poems and poetic devices. For example, the poet takes a role in the conventional bhakti drama: child relating to God as father or mother,[43] wife relating to husband,[44] servant relating to master,[45] young woman describing her feelings to a companion.[46] Or he emphasizes *darśan*: he wants to *see* God, and prays for the vision.

Some types of poems representing these attitudes have become subgenres in bhakti poetry, with their own long traditions. One such type is the poem based on *viraha*, the theme of separation from the beloved. *PV* has a section of 55 *sākhī*s (*aṅga* 2) devoted to *viraha*. By now no one will be surprised to hear that the theme is rare in the *Bījak*, and that where it does occur it is usually a more general kind of separation having nothing to do with a 'beloved'.[47] Interestingly, it is even rarer in *AG*, at least among the *sākhī*s: of those grouped under "*viraha*" in *PV*, nine are found in *BI*, only five in *AG*. These figures again reflect regional

42. Vaudeville, *Kabīr*, p. 155, n. 30.
43. Examples: *AG Āsā* 3, *PV Bhairūṅ* 32 (father), *AG Āsā* 12, *PV Gauṛī* 110 (mother).
44. Examples: *AG Āsā* 24 and 30, and many *viraha* poems.
45. *PV Gauṛī* 112, 121.
46. *PV Kedārau* 3.
47. See, for example, *BI sākhī*s 72, 73, 97, 99.

influence: *viraha* is especially dominant in Rajasthani folk poetry, the example always cited being the popular *Ḍholā-mārū rā dūha*. Vaudeville notes: "the Rajasthani influence is particularly clear in the passages in which Kabir makes use of the folk-song style and imagery, as in *KG*, aṅga 2."[48]

Another sub-genre, close in feeling to *viraha*, is *vinaya* or supplication. The worshipper feels helpless, lost in sin or ignorance, cut off from living intimacy with the God who could save him; so he prays, cries out, demands, begs, sometimes merely thrashes like a fish out of water. The *viraha* and *vinaya pad*s lend themselves well to singing, as they are very emotional. The *Bījak* has almost no *pad*s in the *vinaya* mode (or none, depending on debatable points of interpretation and classification). It tends rather to emphasize the strength and responsibility of the devotee, the necessity for honesty. It gives the impression that one does not need to flail and cry, but simply to face the truth, to face oneself. Though all the collections attack delusion and dishonesty, the *Bījak* is the most urgent and insistent on this theme.

A third category which illustrates the difference between western and eastern traditions may be called 'ecstatic realization'. There are some poems of "realization" in the *Bījak*, and many references to it. But a certain kind of emotional abandonment to the experience is peculiar to the West.

Two Kabirs

King Ram, here's my condition —
I can't drop worldly ties.
A bird that flies to the sky
but holds to its hopes — so I
can't drop hope, won't break
the rope. How can I fly?
I try for joy, but find
sorrow. I can't
express it.
Like elephant and musk-deer,
we defeat ourselves.
Kabir says, I'm powerless.
Hear me, Lord Murari:

48. Vaudeville, *Kabīr*, p. 64, n. 4.

Terrified of Death's messengers,
I take your refuge.

PV Soraṭhī 5

It is unthinkable for the Kabir of the *Bījak* to be terrified of death. He tries constantly to wake people up to the immanence of death;[49] but he himself is always on the far side of the terror he perceives in others.

It is equally out of the question for the *Bījak*'s Kabir to present himself as powerless. The *Bījak* poems are nearly all post-enlightenment, the utterances of a man who knows, who plunges into discourse with people who are confused but is not confused himself:

Pandit, do some research
and let me know
how to destroy transiency.
Money, religion, pleasure, salvation —
which way do they stay, brother?
North, south, east or west?
In heaven or the underworld?
If Gopal is everywhere, where is hell?[50]
Heaven and hell are for the ignorant,
not for those who know Hari.
The fearful thing that everyone fears,
I don't fear.
I'm not confused about sin and purity,
heaven and hell.

BI śabda 42

A few poems in the *Bījak* express fear or difficulty. But they are very far in tone from the expressions of helplessness and self-abasement that can be found in the western collections:

What can I do, how can I cross,
the world-ocean is terrible.
I take your refuge, Kesava, save me, save me, Murari...
There's no giver like you, no sinner like me.

PV Rāmkalī 26
AG Bilāvalu 3

49. For example, *BI śabdas* 61, 99; *ramainī* 21; *sākhīs* 132, 103.
50. See n. 32 above.

You, the holy, supreme joy —
If sages and prophets seek your refuge,
what of me, poor and filthy?

PV Toḍī 1

Kabir says, I'm the house slave.
As you please, let me live
or kill me.

AG Gauṛī 69

In contrast, here is a poem from the *Bījak* in which the poet says he is afraid of Hari the trickster or cheat (*ṭhag*):

The trickster Hari roves through the world
pulling tricks, and saying
nothing. Oh childhood friend,
when you left me,
where did you go that morning?
You're the only man,
I'm your woman.
Your footstep is heavier than stone.
The flesh is clay, the body air.
I'm afraid of Hari's tricks, says Kabir.

BI śabda 37

Compared to the outbursts in the western collections, this is cool, almost aloof. He doesn't cry, doesn't shiver, doesn't shout *mea culpa*. Yet the feeling of being bereft is not less intense. There is something simpler, emptier, more impersonal in this experience of "separation." The feeling can be demonstrated further in another comparison.

How can I see you today?
Without seeing you, how can I believe?
Was I a bad servant? Were you unaware?
Between the two of us, Ram,
who's to blame?
They call you king, lord
of three worlds, fulfiller
of all hearts' desires.
Hari, let me see you!
Either call me, or come yourself.

PV Bhairūṅ 33

Once again a fish in the water.[51]
In the last life I was drunk
on austerity. With heart detached
I renounced family, repeating only
Ram, Ram. I renounced Kashi,
became a fool.
Lord, where am I now?
Was I a bad servant?
Were you unaware?
Between the two of us, God,
who's to blame?
I came for your refuge
but couldn't find your feet.
I've come to you!
Now the servant Kabir
is truly hopeless.

BI śabda 108

The poems are identical in the questions they pose at the center, ending with "who's to blame?" But the two Kabirs, facing the same spiritual problem, solve it in different ways. Rajasthani Kabir demands *darśan*, a word that occurs three times (twice in line 1 and in the last line as *daras*). Eastern Kabir demands nothing; he describes his situation in a tone of bleak objectivity edged with a growing desperation that finally invades the poet's voice and ends where it has to end: *nirāsa*, hopelessness, the last word of the poem. One thinks of the times when Kabir has said that it is necessary to give up hope: as long as one keeps hoping for things, the deepest truth will never be known.[52] To be without hope is to be without support—another characteristic of Kabir's truth-knower.

Of the sourceless state, what to say?
No town, nowhere to stay;
seen without a trace;
what do you call that place?

BI ramainī 7

To be without support is to enter *sahaja, śunya*—

51. Two lines in this *BI pad* appear in *AG Gauṛī* 15. *Bahuri* ('again') in the Shukdev Singh *Bījak* is *bāhari* in *AG*, so in the latter we have a fish out of water instead of a fish again in the water.

52. See for example, *BI śabdas* 77, 108, 89; *sākhīs* 227, 298.

Remembering the empty, the easy,
a light broke out.
I offer myself to a being
based
on nothing.

BI ramainī 6

The western poet's solution is easier: a prayer for *darśan*. In the prayer he gets an emotional release. He has hope. Our easterner, here at least, gets no release. He has tried everything and nothing worked. He has thrown out his questions but received no answers. He experiences despair.

Bhakti and Bhakti

One of the *Bījak sākhī*s begins: "Between word and word, plenty of difference. Churn out the essence-word."[53] And another goes:

Everyone says words, words.
That word is bodiless.
It won't come
on the tongue.
See it, test it, take it.[54]

So one might try out the statement: "Everyone says bhakti, bhakti. That bhakti is bodiless."

Without joining the debate over whether '*nirguṇa* bhakti' is possible or is a contradiction in terms, I will assert that Kabir practises it, as do Nanak and other poets of the Sant school. This kind of bhakti is present, in fact omnipresent, in the *Bījak*. It is a more elemental devotion, a one-pointedness, an unwavering dedication to the single supremely important knowledge. Is Kabir's God "personal"? There is no need to debate that either. Often the poet won't let us be comfortable with a yes or a no answer:

If I say one, it isn't so.
If I say two, it's slander.
Kabir has thought about it.
As it is,
so it is.

BI sākhī 120

53. *BI sākhī* 5.
54. *BI sākhī* 35.

In a similarly disconcerting way he tells us to see, test, and take the word that is bodiless. He continually chips (or hacks) away at our compulsive duality-making, yet comes back innumerable times to the exhortation *Rām bhajo*: worship Ram, adore Ram.

The best-known use of the word 'bhakti' in the *Bījak*, in the first poem of the *śabda* section, is revealing:

Seekers, bhakti came from the Guru.
A woman bore two men —
get this, pandits and sages.
A rock broke open, out came a Ganges —
on all sides, water, water.
Two mountains hit the water,
stream entered wave.
A fly flew up, perched in a tree,
and spoke one word.
A female fly without a male,
she swelled up without water.
One woman ate up all the men,
now I alone remain.
Kabir says, if you understand this,
you're guru, I'm disciple.

BI śabda 1

The first line announces that the poem is about bhakti. But here is no lover or beloved, no divine master or supplicant. Instead we have a poem in *ulaṭbāṃsī* or upside-down language, a series of riddles that seem to pose the question: what is bhakti? And at the end the wise teacher pulls a typical impish escape: if you understand now, you're guru, I'm disciple.

There is bhakti in the *Bījak*. If we examined all the occurrences of the word 'bhakti', I think we would find that, where the poet is not using the word ironically, he is using it in a strikingly impersonal context, in connection with Ram's name (that great abstraction), or with some elemental 'force'. There seems to be no *person* at the other end of this love:

Ram's bhakti is dear
as a fire is dear.
It burns down the whole town,
still they beg for more.

BI sākhī 267

The bhakti found only in the western collections is what we more commonly understand as bhakti. To recapitulate: it differs from the devotion of the *Bījak* in its dramatization of the relation between devotee and God; fervent prayers to the personalized God, who has power to save, as opposed to the devotee, who is powerless; and emphasis on typical *saguṇa* themes like *viraha* and *darśan*.

Hazariprasad Dvivedi emphatically believes that both bhaktis belong to Kabir. First he argues (as I do) that *nirguṇa* bhakti, far from being impossible or absurd, is a viable, venerable path, and is in fact Kabir's path:

> Love for a formless being is not impossible, and it is not opposed to a monist attitude....The proof is seen in Tulsi Das, Shankaracharya, and many other Shaiva and Tantric *sādhaka*s. According to this attitude the individual is God's own form, and only by illusion believes itself to be separate. The effort made by this 'part' to know its own natural form again is an attraction based on original oneness... Masters of bhakti believe that God's form is not within the realm of human reflection. It is beyond thought. Its power is endless and its image unattainable....
>
> Devotees also make this claim that what is called in the Vedanta 'inquiry into Brahma' or 'the desire for knowledge of Brahma' is in fact only bhakti.... The greatest point is that until faith and love are very strong, there can be no desire for knowledge or inquiry....Acharya Naraharipada has also said that what is called direct experience in Vedanta is in fact the result of loving devotion. And in the *Bhāgavata* the fruit of bhakti that is without motive and without result is called detachment (*vairāgya*) and wisdom (*jñāna*), which is also the goal in Vedanta.[55]

The chapter that contains this discussion takes its title from the *Bījak* poem quoted above: *Santo bhakti satoguru ānī*, "Seekers, bhakti came from the Satguru." But the *Bījak*'s relevance seems to end with the title. To demonstrate the quality and power of Kabir's bhakti, Dvivedi quotes many passages from western collections. Nearly all are intense expressions of *viraha* or *vinaya*; nearly all figure God as the beloved with whom the female soul burns to unite. Then Dvivedi comments:

55. Hazariprasad Dvivedi, *Kabīr*, 2nd ed. (Delhi: Rajkamal Prakashan, 1973), pp. 152-55.

> This is that unique absorption, motiveless love; unreserved belief and sole allegiance that is the single condition of bhakti. Kabir doubtless believed in a God who is beyond conflict, who is beyond parties, remarkably dual-and-single, without the three qualities, "the great being beyond boundaries and beyond beyond," inexpressible, flawless, transcendent. But what devotee does not believe in such a God?[56]

For Dvivedi the difference between the harsh, cutting Kabir and the expansive, loving Kabir is explainable biographically. The crucial event in Kabir's life, Dvivedi says, is when he met Ramananda and burst beyond the Yogic views inherited from his family, beyond the merely harsh and abrasive style that links him to the Naths.[57] Having made this point, Dvivedi concludes his chapter with an emotional crescendo, energized by a famous enlightenment poem that he quotes in full:

> Kabir leaned toward the path of Yoga. That path was established in his family and in the family guru tradition. Later he became involved with Ramananda. It is not impossible that before coming under Ramananda's influence he wrote many poems in which only the roughness attained in the Yoga tradition was preserved, and there was no trace of bhakti flavor. A free spirit like Kabir, once he understood something was wrong, was not one to stick to it till the end of time just because it belonged to the family tradition....
>
> So from the day the *satguru* gave Kabir the potion of bhakti, from the day he took the initiation of *sahaja samādhi*, he took leave of the encumbrances of shutting eyes and blocking ears, he said goodby to the slavery of gesture and posture. His very walking had become circumambulation, daily life had become service . . ., and in a wave of elation he declared:
>
> Sadhus, the simple awakening —
> wonderful!
> Since the Guru's glory arose,
> wherever I roam, I'm circling the holy place,
> whatever I do I'm serving,
> when I sleep, I'm bowing,
> I worship no other gods.

56. Ibid. "The great being . . ." is quoted from *BI śabda* 24.

57. On Kabir's relation to Nathism, see Hess, "Studies in Kabir," pp. 122-25. See also Vaudeville, *Kabīr*, pp. 85-89.

When I speak it's the Name, when I hear
it's Remembrance, eating and drinking
are worship. A home and a desert
are one to me, I have no second thought.
I don't shut my eyes, don't block my ears,
don't torture my body.
With open eyes I recognize and laugh, gazing
at the beautiful form.
The Word is fixed in my mind forever,
I've thrown away shabby desires.
Sitting, rising, it never leaves me,
the crossing is complete.
Kabir says, brother, when abiding stillness
reveals itself, then beyond joy and grief
to the highest place: there
you enter and stay.

Śabdāvalī, śabda 30

Praise to that guru! He is truly like the bee who, forcing the insect to pay constant attention, turns it to a bee. The worm has become a butterfly, new wings have burst, new color spreads, new power throbs. He doesn't perceive caste, doesn't think of family. He has become one with himself. The water of the culvert has entered the Ganga and become the Ganga. Kabir on meeting the guru has become like him. Praise to you, guru: you have crippled the restless mind, within substance you have shown what is without substance, the bound one has become unbound, you have shown the steps to the unattainable. You have taught only one lesson of love, but amazingly the rain from this cloud of love has drenched the whole body. In the soul wet with *rasa* the green sprout of bhakti rises flourishing.[58]

The Case for the Western Persona

Dvivedi's argument is convincing. Even though his emotionality may put off western critics who are accustomed to a different style, his theory is psychologically and intellectually satisfying. And his view does not require us to believe that Kabir and Ramananda were contemporary, were in fact disciple and teacher. Any guru (including the inner guru) would do.

58. Dvivedi, *Kabīr*, pp. 159-60.

One can imagine reasons why the Kabir-panth might have trimmed away evidences of the more emotional, abandoned personality. Kabir was their founder, very nearly their god. Perhaps they wanted to make him a more stern and magisterial figure, one who didn't betray human weakness.

Today the panth has become Hinduized and Sanskritized.[59] They have opened Sanskrit schools, produced a Sanskrit translation of the *Bījak*, written learned tomes; they invite pandits to speak at their functions.[60] Yet the *Bījak* is vehement against Brahmans and their ways, even in larger measure than the other collections. It may be that the exaggerated odium for Brahmans has its mirror image in the Kabir-panthis' eagerness to Brahmanize themselves and to excel in panditry. It may also be that the desire to become established in the classical tradition has led to the presentation of a more 'Upanishadic' Kabir.

Further, the oldest and apparently least tampered-with collection — the Sikh *Granth* — is richly imbued with bhakti content, in the broader sense of bhakti, the bhakti that is missing in the *Bījak*. Is this not a powerful argument that such bhakti represents the real Kabir?

It is hardly necessary to defend Dvivedi's view at length, for it is everyone's view. Everyone (except the Kabir-panthis) accepts the western collections as most authentic, and considers the poems of *vinaya*, *viraha* and ecstasy essential to the Kabir corpus. Dvivedi is simply the most thoughtful and eloquent spokesman for this viewpoint.

The other viewpoint, being less popular, will be given a more detailed exposition.

The Case for the Bījak *Persona*

The search for the personality of Kabir may hinge on the question: What was unique about him? What was his unduplicatable quality?

59. This process has been described by David Lorenzen in his paper "The Kabir Panth: Heretics to Hindus," in David N. Lorenzen, ed., *Religious Change and Cultural Domination* (Mexico: El Colegio de Mexico, 1981), pp. 151-71.

60. On one memorable occasion I heard a pandit from the Sanskrit University deliver a discourse in a celebratory function at the Kabir Chaura *maṭh*. He wore a Vaishnava *tilak* and said there was no conflict between Kabir's teaching and Vaishnavism, *nirguṇa* philosophy and image worship, belief in the Vedas and belief in Kabir. He spoke at length, regaling us with orthodox Hindu terminology and classifications. Finally he gave a Sanskrit derivation for the name 'Kabir', proving that it meant "one who gives encouragement or inspiration to those who search for Brahman."

In *Gurū Nānak and the Sikh Religion*, W.H. McLeod systematically explains the Sikh founder's teachings.[61] Item by item, he could be expounding the teachings of Kabir. Often the very lines he quotes echo familiar passages from the *Bījak*. In fact all the poets roughly classified as Sants would sound more or less the same if reduced to their 'messages'.

But we know that Kabir was different. He had a special personality, spoke in a special voice, left a special imprint on the minds of later generations. What made him *Kabir*? Dvivedi answers that it was bhakti, or the unique combination of bhakti and the *nirguṇa* God:

> [T]he reader ot Kabir knows that in his poetry there is something extraordinary which cannot be found in the pugnacious expressions of the Siddhas and Yogis, in the shrilly argued volumes of the Vedantins, in the breast-beatings of the social reformers. Something extraordinary. What is it? And what was obtained from Ramananda which turned a reckless, independent man like Kabir into his debtor? The answer to both questions is the same. It is bhakti....When he found this utterly marvellous jewel, Kabir was fulfilled. Bhakti to whom? To Ram! .... Ramananda transmitted this bhakti of Ram devoid of the three qualities and beyond *māyā*. Ram and his bhakti—these were Ramananda's gifts to Kabir. These two things separated Kabir from the Yogis, Siddhas, pandits and mullahs. When he obtained them, Kabir become a 'hero'—apart and above, the most remarkable, most pungent, and most brilliant of them all.[62]

I shall propose another basis for the unique flavor and potency of Kabir: his style. There is a force in his poetry, as there must have been a force in his presence, that is shattering. Everyone who has written about Kabir, from 1600 to the present, has testified to this personal force, this inimitable voice.[63]

61. See McLeod, *Gurū Nānak*, pp. 163-227.

62. Dvivedi, *Kabīr*, pp. 147-48.

63. "More so with Kabīr than with any other Indian author, the extraordinary quality of his style seems to reflect an outstanding and somewhat mysterious personality. Indifferent to tradition, apparently unconcerned with the pleasure or displeasure of his audience, Kabīr fearlessly voices his inner convictions. His blunt language and rough words, his bitter irony, bespeak ardent indignation, but also a desperate effort to awaken his dumb, sleepy fellow men, who remain unaware of their impending doom" (Vaudeville, *Kabīr*, p. 69).

"[We must note] the amazing force and originality of Kabir. For sheer vigor of thought and rugged terseness of style, no later bhakti writer can be brought

The lines of Kabir's unique personality begin to emerge as he is compared with other Sants. McLeod speaks of how he differs from Guru Nanak:

> Kabīr's thought . . . is by no means as consistent doctrinally as that of Gurū Nānak. . . . Kabīr was above all a mystic. . . . The result is both profundity and obscurity.[64]

> No reader can possibly misunderstand [Kabīr's] emphasis upon religion as a wholly inward experience, and the imprecations which he bestows upon all who trust in pride of birth or in outward ceremony have lost nothing of their mordant effect. Gurū Nānak [though equally clear on these points] does not manifest the same pugnacity.[65]

W.G. Orr marks out the differences between Kabir and Dadu:

> In Dadu there is less of the fierce iconoclast, and more of the quiet mystic; less fondness for the bold conceit and startling paradox . . . The *Bani* of Dadu is an intimate personal record; it reflects, to an extent greater than can be said of the poems of Kabir, the author's own spiritual struggles and victories. . . . It is as a controversialist that Kabir rises to his supreme heights. . . One has difficulty thinking of Kabir, for all his ardent declaration of the doctrine of human brotherhood, earning for himself the title of "Dayal", the tenderhearted, the pitiful. It is in this character that Dadu won a unique place.[66]

---

into comparison with him" (W.G. Orr, *A Sixteenth Century Indian Mystic* (London: Lutterworth Press, 1947), p. 74).

"Kabīr had a vehement power over language. He was a dictator of words. Whatever idea he wanted to express, in whatever way — he would just make language say it that way: if possible, straightforwardly; if not, then by jolts and bruises. Language cast a sort of helpless gaze at Kabir, as if it lacked the courage to refuse anything to this carefree swaggerer. . . . For giving form to the untellable story, for making it beautiful, there is a power in Kabir's language such as is found in very few writers. . . . Then for mockery and sarcasm, he has no rival. Pandit and *qāzī mullā* and *maulvī* — all writhe under his taunts. In infinitely simple language he deals such blows that those who take the blows have no choice but to brush off the dust and shuffle away" (Dvivedi, *Kabīr*, pp. 221-22).

64. McLeod, *Gurū Nānak*, p. 149.

65. Ibid., p. 208.

66. Orr, *Sixteenth Century Mystic*, p. 78.

Nabhaji's thumbnail sketch, probably written before 1600, begins and ends with "Kabir refused." Though it does give importance to bhakti and *bhajana* in Kabir's teaching, this could well be the simpler, more limited bhakti I have associated with the *Bījak*. What Nabhaji stresses above all, as Vaudeville points out, is the poet's "extraordinary independence of character."[67]

Kabir is famous for his solitariness, vigor, fearlessness, and iconoclasm; for his swift and original mind that pierces dark places with sudden probes of light and finds a natural idiom in paradox and obscure metaphor.

This is the Kabir who is highlighted in the *Bījak*: who shouts and attacks, challenges and teases; who spins out mysterious allegories and tosses off bizarre images; who is strong and self-reliant, dares everyone to be strong and self-reliant, and never takes a stance that emphasizes the individual's weakness and impotence.

Yet the *Bījak*'s Kabir does not come across as a man who has never suffered or struggled. One of his hardest tasks is the effort to communicate. Even after going through the difficulties of putting the unsayable into words, Kabir has to address himself to an audience who despise, deny, misinterpret, or ignore his message. Repeatedly he says, "Nobody listens, nobody believes me, they're happy only if I lie."[68] He refers to his loneliness, to the rarity of individuals who can understand him, to the joy of meeting now and then a kindred spirit.[69] He indicates the great difficulty of the path, the choices he has made and must keep making, the unremitting effort.[70] And he presents the dilemmas that face the seeker at every stage, the thing in the throat (as a Zen koan puts it) that you can't swallow and can't spit out.[71]

67. Here is the whole passage from the *Bhaktamāl* as quoted in Vaudeville's *Kabīr*, p. 30:

> "Kabīr refused to acknowledge caste distinctions or to recognize the authority of the six Hindu schools of philosophy nor did he set any store by the four divisions of life (*āśramas*) prescribed for Brāhmaṇas. He held that religion (*dharma*) without devotion (*bhakti*) was no religion at all (*adharma*), and that asceticism, fasting, and alms-giving had no value if not accompanied by adoration (*bhajana*). By means of *ramainīs*, *śabdīs*, and *sākhīs*, he imparted religious instruction to Hindus and Turks alike. He showed no partiality to either but gave teaching beneficial to all. With determination he spoke and never tried to please the world. Kabīr refused to acknowledge caste distinctions and the six systems of philosophy."

68. E.g., *BI śabda*s 4, 9, 113.
69. E.g., *BI śabda* 26, *ramainī* 17, *sākhī* 121.
70. E.g., *BI sākhī*s 31, 40.
71. E.g., *BI*, *sākhī*s 118, 100.

If the songs of ecstatic realization in *AG* and *PV* have almost no parallel in the *Bījak*, the realization is nevertheless present at every turn. It finds a more austere expression — negative, oblique, sometimes with a grave and haunting beauty, sometimes sauced with a sharp challenge to his old foils the pandits, sometimes miraculously sketching, in swift, simple language, the place of enlightenment.[72]

The *Bījak* poet has yet other ways of expressing his experience of liberation. In the *ulaṭbāṃsī* poems he may do it with crazy exuberance.[73] At other moments he does it with mischievous humor.[74] In fact as one becomes more familiar with his mind, one finds the realization everywhere, informing his efforts to teach and awaken, giving shape to his images, impetus to his dares and admonitions. He lives in his truth, his "heart and mouth are one,"[75] and everything he does expresses it.

The *Bījak* has a narrower emotional range than the western collections. Joy and grief are muted. The tones are more sober, the bursts of color more jagged and primary. The author's personal drama has receded to the background. Whatever he had to go through to achieve his understanding is finished. Now he is fully engaged in his present activities: communicating, teaching (in which a vivid and dramatic personality does emerge), expressing truly his own experience whether others hear him or not.

Conclusion

I have demonstrated that the two western collections of Kabir's sayings are strikingly higher than the *Bījak* in bhakti content, as indicated by language, attitudes, and themes. And I have suggested that the circumstances of transmission of *pad*s would tend to increase devotional elements, both because they are more congenial to music than the harsher, more austere eastern style, and because bhakti — especially Krishna bhakti — dominated the regions through which the material moved. In the case of Krishna names, I have given objective evidence that they may have been added by singers as the material spread through the country. The virtual absence of Krishna names from the *sākhī*s supports this theory: *sākhī*s are tight, terse, unlyrical, pleasingly aphoristic, therefore less amenable to 'creative' change than the loose *pad*.

72. E.g., *BI śabda*s 67, 106, 80; *sākhī* attached to *ramainī* 7.
73. *BI śabda* 62.
74. *BI śabda* 74.
75. *BI śabda* 79, *sākhī*s 29, 265.

I have delineated two personalities that emerge from the western and eastern collections, and have shown how a proponent of each might defend him as the authentic Kabir. The reader may choose between them, or may decide that they represent two streams of tradition wherein the real Kabir is diffused like milk in water, unextractable except by some as yet unknown swan of scholarship or mystical insight.

Finally I have suggested that the best way to approach the particularity of Kabir is by a study of his style, his peculiar modes of expression. Elsewhere I have undertaken such a study, taking my examples from the *Bījak*.[76] If the *Bījak*'s range is narrower than that of the western collections, it can be regarded as an authentic core in this sense: it contains what is universal and typical, what is present, even dominant, in all three collections.

76. See my article "Kabir's Rough Rhetoric" in this volume; see also appendix on "Upside-down Language" in my book *The Bījak of Kabir* (San Francisco: North Point Press, 1983), pp. 135-61.

KABIR'S ROUGH RHETORIC

LINDA HESS

> Why bump that shaven head on the earth,
> why dunk those bones in the water?...
> Why wash your hands and mouth, why chant
> with a heart full of fraud?
> Why bow and bow in the mosque, and trudge
> to Mecca to see God?..
> Search in the heart, in the heart alone:
> there live Ram and Karim!
>
> *śabda* 97[1]

Kabir is persuasive. But can he be called a rhetorician? Does the word not suggest a refinement and self-consciousness quite foreign to this shouting illiterate?

All who study the 'grassroots' vernacular religious poetry of medieval India are indebted to A.K. Ramanujan for introducing the idea of 'spontaneous rhetoric' and for demonstrating how it works in the Kannada *vachanas*, or sayings, of the tenth-to-twelfth-century Virashaiva saints.[2] The rhetoric of spontaneity — natural, inseparable from the function of language — exists before the invention of the word 'rhetoric'. Historically it changes to what is more commonly understood by rhetoric. Systematizers shift from description to prescription, devising elaborate categories and laws. Their systems become powerful tools, like the laws and models of science. Writers are taught to write with them and critics to analyze with them. Thus rhetoric becomes associated with artificiality, calculation, non-spontaneity.

But science begins with the naive study of nature, and scientists must

An earlier version of this essay appeared as chapter 3 of my Ph.D. dissertation, "Studies in Kabir: Texts, Traditions, Styles and Skills" (University of California, Berkeley, 1980). It is also included in the introduction of my book, *The Bījak of Kabir* (San Francisco: North Point Press, 1983).

1. All of the quotations from Kabir in this essay are from the *Bījak*, ed. Shukdev Singh (Allahabad: Nilabh Prakashan, 1972). For discussion of the relationship of the *Bījak* to other Kabir texts, and questions of authenticity, see my "Three Kabir Collections: A Comparative Study" in this volume; and "The Textual Tradition," the first chapter in my "Studies in Kabir."

2. A.K. Ramanujan, *Speaking of Śiva* (Baltimore: Penguin, 1973), pp. 37-47.

preserve their capacity for an elegant naivete if they are to discover anything new. So the critic must discover 'for the millionth time' the simple principles of how poems work (an inquiry that will continually throw light on how systems of rhetoric were born). Kabir — on one side a careless, contemptuous poet who thinks nothing of literary rules or the people who make them; on the other a vigorous, muscular poet, who gets his fingers into our minds, manages to mold and shake us — is a good subject for such a study.

Many scholars have noted Kabir's odd combination of crudeness and potency. Charlotte Vaudeville observes that while Kabir is undoubtedly rude, crude, vulgar, and prosaic, he is at the same time eloquent, exciting, dazzling, and unforgettable.[3] P.D. Barthwal finds Kabir's crudeness a grave defect and accounts for his power only by resorting to an awkward separation of form and content:

> How earnestly one wishes that these Nirgunis knew and cared for the ordinary rules of grammar and prosody if not of rhetorics [sic]. Even a little bit of polish would have immeasurably enhanced the charm of their utterances...In the Nirgunis, it is not only the inadequacy of language, but the total disregard of form that one deplores to find... But it is not for the beauty of expression that one ought to go to the mystic...[T]hough there is not beauty of form in their utterances, beauty of content there is....And it is in the content and not the form that the real poetry consists.[4]

Other Indian critics have tried, like royal messengers trying to cram the stepsisters' big feet into Cinderella's dainty slipper, to fit Kabir's utterances into the categories of classical Indian poetics.[5] Some have told me confidentially that Kabir was not a poet at all, but a social reformer.

Kabir was a poet, and a radical reformer, though society was only the outermost skin of what he wished to reform. What makes his rough verses so strong and memorable? The question points to a study of style.

The problems involved in using translations to analyze the style of a medieval Indian poet for a twentieth-century western audience are minimized in Kabir's case, for he is the most translatable of the non-

3. Charlotte Vaudeville, *Au Cabaret de l'amour* (Paris: Gallimard, 1959), pp. 20-21.

4. P.D. Barthwal, *The Nirguṇa School of Hindi Poetry* (Benares: The Indian Bookshop, 1936), pp. 222-23.

5. See, for example, Dr. Mahendra, *Kabīr kī bhāṣā* (Delhi: By the Author, 1969), part 2.

modern Indian poets.[6] This is, first, because of the simplicity and bluntness of his style; and further, because of a way of looking at and speaking of things that is more modern than classical, more individual than idealized.

Leonard Nathan, a recent translator of Kalidasa's *Meghadūta*, has discussed the difficulties a Western audience may have in understanding the assumptions that underlie the Sanskrit poet's world-view.[7] One such assumption is that the empirical world, being impermanent and disordered, is unreal. Art is meant to reflect not this chaos of passing forms, but the harmonious reality beyond them. The poet, using the language of permanence and perfection (classical Sanskrit), composes the elements of the empirical world into an endlessly elaborated unity in which everything reflects everything else; or more exactly, reflects and gathers itself in perfect order around the human. So Kalidasa's 'cloud messenger' turns the whole subcontinent into an image of itself:

> [M]ountains and rivers are invested with feeling and their beauty charged with sexual attraction; trees and flowers become their ornaments. Animals evoke human beauties. . . [E]ven the great rains act out the release of pent-up passions.[8]

Classical Indian art, as Nathan describes it, is a ceremony celebrating in minute detail the unity and ideality of the world beyond appearances.

There may be unity underlying Kabir's vision, but he does not take the route of the classical poet to reveal it. Unceremoniously, he shows us actual human feeling, surrounds us with the experience of delusion, makes vivid the fragmented nature of ordinary life. What unity there may be comes forth in flashes, or in leaps from the disordered surface of the world to a momentary recognition: it is here, in every body (*ghaṭa ghaṭa meṅ*); something simple (*sahaja*); a single word (*śabda*). He does not, like Kalidasa or the Hindi classicist Tulsi Das, anthropomorphize flora, fauna, and the elements to reflect ideal human feeling.

The 'modernity' that many readers have remarked on in Kabir may be better understood through a passage in which Nathan contrasts Western and Indian expectations of poetry:

6. Kabir can be called the most translatable except, that is, for problems raised by archaic, unsystematic language forms and obscure expressions which trouble Indians as well as foreigners.

7. Leonard Nathan, *The Transport of Love* (Berkeley: University of California Press, 1976), Introduction.

8. Ibid., p. 2.

> Where we look for close adherence to psychological and physical reality, the Indian poet rigorously excludes verisimilitude. Where we expect the poet to speak in his own voice — a voice that should be at once close to common speech and yet identifiably original—the Indian poet stays far behind his subject and strives at every turn for uncommon eloquence which yet deliberately echoes the voices of his tradition. Where we are prepared for, if not direct conflict, at least strong tension needing drastic resolution, the Indian poet gives us the slow unfolding of a foregone conclusion. Where we might hope to feel the pleasure of new insight, the Indian poet wants his audience to experience the delight of a foreknown universal sentiment.[9]

In every one of these contrasting pairs Kabir fulfills the expectation not of the Indian audience, but of the Western.

"*Fat! Fat! Fat! Fat! I am the personal.*"[10]

Wallace Stevens's fusillade of 'Fats!' is aimed at a brilliant, vainglorious rooster with a long aristocratic name, like the names given to prize dogs in dog shows:

> Chieftain Iffucan of Azcan in caftan
> of tan with henna hackles, halt!

In the scheme of Stevens's "Bantams in Pine-Woods" this bird is the poet of the universal, sporting his grand truths like tailfeathers of which he is unspeakably proud:

> Damned universal cock, as if the sun
> was blackamoor to bear your blazing tail.

No one is more blinded by the cock's splendor than he himself. But Stevens, poet of the particular and personal, is not impressed:

> You ten-foot poet among inchlings. Fat!
> Begone! An inchling bristles in these pines,
>
> Bristles, and points their Appalachian tangs,
> and fears not portly Azcan nor his hoos.

An earlier incarnation of Stevens's universal cock is Kabir's pandit.

9. Ibid., pp. 2-3.

10. Wallace Stevens, *Poems*, ed. Samuel French Morse (New York: Vintage, 1959), p. 25.

Kabir even uses staccato repetitions, like Stevens's 'Fat!, to startle or stun an opponent:

> Puff! Puff! Puff! Why do you strut? (*śabda* 73)

The image of gurus swollen with pride is a common one:

> Proud of your quality, great with authority... (*ramainī* 35)

> They buzz their mantras from house to house puffed with pride...
> (*śabda* 4)

Nor do Muslim moralizers escape:

> Qazi, what book are you lecturing on?
> Yak yak yak, day and night.
> You never had an original thought. (*śabda* 84)

Although his *nirguṇa* God or supreme truth seems impersonal when compared with the anthropomorphic Ram and Krishna, Kabir can be described as the most personal of all bhakti poets: not because he dwells on his private experience, exposes his own quivering heart; but because he gets very personal with us, the audience.

Stylistically this factor most clearly distinguishes Kabir from his famous colleagues Sur, Tulsi, and Mira: they are primarily addressing God; he is primarily addressing us. Even when Sur and Tulsi sing in their own person of the Lord's wondrous doings on earth, the implicit relationship in the poem is between poet and God — a relationship often made explicit in the signature line where the devotee turns to God with a prayer or other fervent expression of feeling. It is a convention of revery, ecstasy, longing, in relationship to God. The reader or listener is present only as eavesdropper.

The reader[11] is central in Kabir. Nearly everyone in North India is familiar with the formula *kahai Kabīra suno bhāī sādho* — "Kabir says, listen brother sadhu!" — or *suno ho santo* — "Listen oh saints!" It is Kabir's trademark. But far more than a formula, it signifies Kabir's passion to engage, to wake people up, to affect them. This power to affect through language is fundamentally what we mean when we speak of rhetoric.

11. Kabir's original audience was composed entirely of listeners; his present audience is composed largely of readers. I have used 'reader' and 'listener' interchangeably when talking of audience response, as I have freely alternated 'song', '*pad*', and 'poem' in referring to Kabir's compositions.

Address and Assault

In his mastery of the vocative, Kabir is unique among the bhakti poets. Not in the *saguṇa* devotees, not in *nirguṇa* Dadu or reformer Nanak, not in the radical Bengali Buddhist poets, the iconoclast Gorakh or the surreal Bauls, whatever else they may have in common with him, do we find the intense bearing down upon the listener that is so prominent in Kabir. It shows itself first in the array of addresses he uses to seize our attention: Hey Saint, Brother, Brahman, Pandit, Yogi, Hermit, Babu, Mother, Muslim, Creature, Friend, Fool! Many poems are simply directed at 'you'. But titles or pronouns of address are only the beginning. Kabir pounds away with questions, prods with riddles, stirs with challenges, shocks with insults, disorients with verbal feints. It seems that if one read him responsively one could hardly help getting red in the face, jumping around, squirming, searching, getting embarrassed, or shouting back.

For a taste of the style here is a pastiche of lines from various poems:

Pandit, you've got it wrong.

Monk, stop scattering your mind.

Pandit, do some research
and let me know
how to destroy
transiency.

Now you, Mr. Qazi, what kind of work is that,
going from house to house
chopping heads?
Who told you to swing the knife?

Pandit, think
before you drink
that water!
Think! Think! Figure it out!

Saints and reverences —

Morons and mindless fools —

Enchanted madman —

Look in your heart!

You simple-minded people . . .

The vocative sabotages passivity. If someone shoots you a question, you immediately look for an answer. If someone sneaks behind your chair and whispers, 'Why are you slouched over?", before thinking about it you will straighten your back. If someone calls you a lunatic you may be angered or amused, but you will certainly be interested. Addressed affectionately, you will soften and begin to trust — which may just prepare the way for a new, unexpected blow.

The vocative creates intimacy. "Where did two gods come from?" might be a good opening to a polemical poem. But how different the effect when he says, "Brother, where did your two gods come from? Tell me, who made you mad?" (*śabda* 30). The vocative draws the reader, as participant, into highly charged dialogues:

> Saints, once you wake up don't doze off. (*śabda* 2)
>
> Pandit...
> tell me where untouchability
> came from, since you believe in it. (*śabda* 41)

Sometimes an intimate address turns out to be a brazen trick: "Where are you going alone, my friend?" the poet begins softly in *śabda* 99. A few lines later we realize that he is addressing a corpse.

The address may become so aggressive that it must be called an assault, complete with abuses that no decorum moderates:

> You go around bent! bent! bent!
> Your ten doors are full of hell, you smell
> like a fleet of scents, your cracked
> eyes don't see the heart, you haven't
> an ounce of sense.
> Drunk with anger, hunger, sex,
> you drown without water. (*śabda* 72)

In one shocking opener Kabir calls his listener the 'son of a slut! Then stepping out from behind this attention-getter, he proceeds with his poem:

> Son of a slut!
> There: I've insulted you.
> Think about getting on the good road.... (*śabda* 102)

Kabir's provocations often taken the form of questions, skillfully inserted to ruffle us up or draw us out. Questions are used in a variety of ways — in openings or conclusions, singly or in series, as bait or goad, as funnel to point our inquiry. Sometimes a single question comes like a sudden jab: "When the pot falls apart, what do you call it?" (*śabda* 75). The jab may be just a setup: when we rise to it, a hard slap may hit us from another direction. Sometimes questions are shot in rapid series, like blows from a boxer, left, right, left, right. When they end we may find ourselves staggering:

> Who's whose husband? Who's whose wife?
> Death's gaze spreads — untellable story.
> Who's whose father? Who's whose son?
> Who suffers? Who dies? (*śabda* 36)

> If God wanted circumcision,
> why didn't you come out cut?
> If circumcision makes you a Muslim,
> what do you call your women? . . .
> If putting on the thread makes you Brahman,
> what does the wife put on?
> That Shudra's touching your food, pandit!
> How can you eat it?
> Hindu, Muslim — where did they come from?
> Who started this road?
> Look in your heart, send out scouts:
> where is heaven? (*śabda* 84)

In quieter poems questions are a way of approaching an experience that is not accessible to direct statement. In certain cases questions seem to open a space at the end of a poem that is wide and silent (for example, *śabda* 67, discussed at the end of this paper; and *ramainī* 7).

The intimacy created by Kabir's style is not always obvious or entirely conscious, because the audience would often prefer not to identify with his addressees. As readers or listeners, we are more inclined to identify with Kabir. When he conjures up a comic pandit, we laugh. When he exposes the greedy and hypocritical, we scorn. When he reveals the incredible blindness of people who won't face death, we applaud. The use of stock characters allows us to maintain a sense of detachment. We know what a Brahman priest looks like: he has a shaved head, paints marks on his forehead, dresses in a white pleated loincloth, counts his beads, and sits among his paraphernalia of brass trays, sandalwood paste, scriptures and bells, squeezing coins out of hapless pilgrims. A Yogi wears a patchwork cloak and drinks out of a cup made from a skull. A merchant sits amid his wares in the bazaar and holds up his scales, two round plates suspended from strings. These are not descriptions of *us*.

But gradually something begins to gnaw at our consciousness. It occurs to us that pandits can wear other costumes besides the white *dhotī* and rosary of *tulsī* or *rudrākṣa* beads, can sit under other umbrellas than those that front the Ganga at Varanasi. It is relatively easy to notice panditry in the universities, violence in government, greed in the market place, phoniness in religion. Then we can spot signals closer at hand, in the gestures and voices of our neighbors. But Kabir's power is most tellingly revealed when his words reverberate in our own skulls, and we see the succession of disguises under which we live our daily lives:

> Dropped from the belly at birth,
> a man puts on his costumes
> and goes through his acts. (*ramainī* 1)

Riddles and Surprises

One set of formulas in Kabir clusters around the word *acharaj* — surprise or amazing thing — and *adbhuta* — wonderful, marvellous, strange (for example, *śabda*s 5, 6, 46, 82, 101). Formula or not, the promise of amazement stirs up our interest and gives Kabir a further chance to play with us:

> Saints, here's a surprise for you.
> A son grabbed his mother
> while a crazy virgin fell for her father,
> dropped her husband but went
> to the in-laws.
> Think of that! (*śabda* 6)

Related to the 'surprise' formula is the 'Who will believe it?' formula:

> Who can I tell?
> And who will believe it?
> When the bee touches that flower,
> he dies. (*śabda* 63)

The opening questions are teasers, designed to make the reader volunteer, "Tell *me*. I'll believe it!" The sudden injection of "that flower"[12]

12. The demonstrative pronoun ('that') does not appear in Hindi; but the effect is much the same, as Hindi syntax allows the sentence to begin with 'flower'.

again elicits a curious response — "what flower?" — and the poet is set up for his main exposition:

> In the middle of the sky's temple
> blooms a flower....

The poem could easily have begun at this point. But the experience is quite different when it begins with the rhetorical questions and the dramatic introduction of flower and bee.

Sometimes 'surprise' and 'who will believe it?' are linked, and the interplay darts from line to line:

> Saints, a huge surprise:
> If I tell, who will believe it?
> Just one man, just one woman —
> imagine that! (*śabda* 5)

From surprises and incredibilities it is a short step to the pure riddle. A number of poems are framed explicitly at riddles:

> Think, pandit, figure it out:
> male or female? (*śabda* 44)

> What will you call the Pure?
> Say, creature, how will you mutter the name
> of one without hand or foot,
> mouth, tongue or ear? (*śabda* 94)

> Sadhu, that Yogi is my guru
> who can untie this song. (*śabda* 24)

> Is there any guru in the world wise enough
> to understand the upside-down Veda? (*śabda* 111)

As the last example suggests, from the riddling poems it is just another small leap to *ulaṭbāṃsī* — the 'upside-down language' of paradoxes and enigmas which Kabir inherited from the Sahajiyas and Naths and adapted to his own purposes:

> The cow is sucking at the calf's teat,
> from house to house the prey hunts,
> the hunter hides. (*śabda* 31)

> Sprout without seed, branch without trunk,
> fruit without flower, son born
> of a sterile womb, climbing a tree
> without legs... (*śabda* 16)

It's pouring, pouring, the thunder's roaring,
but not one raindrop falls . . .
frog and snake lie down together,
a cat gives birth to a dog,
the lion quakes in fear of the jackal —
these marvels can't be told. (*śabda* 52)

There is a great diversity in the interpretation of the *ulaṭbāṃsī* poems. It has been questioned whether they are authentic, whether their symbols have the same meaning in Kabir as in the Tantric tradition, or whether they have any meaning at all. For the purpose of our brief rhetorical inquiry it is enough to note that these poems fascinate while they perplex the reader, that the images stick in consciousness even when their meaning eludes the mind, initiating a dialogue not only between reader and poet, but between the reader and himself, which may go on for years. Riddles and their extension, the paradoxes and enigmas of *ulaṭbāṃsī*, besides being effective rhetorical devices, are teaching devices, comparable to the Zen koan — a problem the student can't solve and can't escape, a matrix of verbal impossibilities in which a transparent truth lies hidden — or perhaps, as the Rig-Vedic hymn has it, does not.[13]

Structures

It is hazardous to analyze a *pad* by Kabir as if the structure had some kind of inevitability. The same song might turn up in another collection in fragments, or with its stanzas reshuffled like a deck of cards. Still, certain principles of structure are apparent; once spotted, they can be recognized again and again. And many poems are clearly unified. They may consist of an extended metaphor, an unfolding argument, a dialogue between poet and audience, or a dramatic monologue. These structures reveal both how songs in general are organized for oral performance, and how Kabir particularly organized his utterances to produce the effects he wanted to produce.

Several typical patterns in Kabir depend on repetition with variation. Some poems comprise a series of negations whose syntax can be varied for pleasing effects in sound and rhythm (*śabda* 43, *ramainī* 6). Some are built on anaphora — repetition of a word at the beginning of each line

13. Refers to the closing of *Ṛg Veda* 10.129, a famous poem sometimes called "Hymn of Creation" in English. For an extended discussion of upside-down language, see Appendix A of my book, *The Bījak of Kabir*.

(*ramainī*s 3, 7; *śabda* 71). Or the repeated word may be scattered in different positions ('died' in *śabda* 45, 'look' in *śabda* 104). The repeated element may be a grammatical structure, like the if-then clauses of *śabda*s 40, 42, and 84, the parallel sentences of *śabda* 59, the jabbing questions of *śabda*s 98 and 84.

Some poems are catalogues — of Vishnu's incarnations, famous sages, stereotyped fools (*śabda*s 8, 12, 92, 38). One trick of Kabir's is to take a literary convention and turn it upside-down. Other poets use the 'ten-avatar' sequence to glorify Vishnu's descents; Kabir uses it to ridicule them (*śabda* 8). The rainbird (*chātaka*) is normally presented as a touching symbol of longing and devotion. Kabir conjures her up to point out her delusion (*śabda* 71).

Many poems are constructed as dialogues or monologues (for example, *śabda*s 103, 75, 62, 35). Sometimes a single figure is developed throughout a poem—the cow, the shawl, the swan, the jewel, the musical instrument, the flower, the Yogi, the con-man.[14] Sometimes a series of parallel examples will be brought together in a conclusion, much as a sonnet may in successive quatrains give illustrations that are summed up in the sestet or couplet (e.g., the dog, lion and elephant of *śabda* 76).

Perhaps the most consistent structural device in the lyrics is that of the strong 'opener' and 'clincher' lines that keep Kabir rhetorically in control. We have seen how proficient he is at seizing the audience's attention with intriguing, challenging, shocking addresses at the beginning. He is just as adept at twisting our noses at the end, summing up the poem in a peculiarly powerful way, turning things around unexpectedly, making a wry comment, or jamming on the brakes with a suddenness that sends us hurtling forward into the darkness.[15]

A simple example of Kabir's effectiveness in framing his song with rhetorical devices at beginning and end may be seen in *śabda* 43 — a straightforward catalogue of negatives stating, in Upanishadic fashion, what the experience of truth is not:

> There's no creation or creator there,
> no gross or fine, no wind or fire,
> no sun, moon, earth or water,
> no radiant form, no time there,
> no word, no flesh, no faith,
> no cause and effect, nor any thought

14. These figures are found, respectively, in *śabda*s 28, 81, 34, 7, 69, 63, 65, and 36.

15. A good example is *śabda* 75, discussed further on in this paper.

of the Veda. No Hari or Brahma,
no Shiva or Shakti, no pilgrimage
and no rituals. No mother, father
or guru there...

The poem is musical and memorable, with the repetitious pattern finely modulated to avoid monotony. The whole piece could have been done in this style. But Kabir has another way. Characteristically, he opens with a sharp challenge: "Pandit, you've got it wrong" (literally, "your ideas are false"). Before we know what the poem is about, there is an engagement. We picture a pandit, Kabir's antagonist. He's got something wrong. What is it? From here on all the negatives also call forth the preaching of the pandit, who is fond of talking of creation, the elements, the heavenly bodies, Vedas, deities, karma, dharma. Behind the negatives is a shadowy foil who is being continually silenced just as he is about to open his mouth.

The flowing pattern of negative statements is broken abruptly in the middle of the penultimate line with a shooting question: "Is it two or one?" The question snaps us out of the lyrical mode, enclosing in its few syllables the whole point of the dispute between pandits and what is beyond panditry. Without a moment's pause, Kabir concludes: "If you understand now, you're guru, I'm disciple." Now, in immediate response to "two or one?", you can understand what the gurus have wrong. To understand is to know very personally the meaning of the negatives: guru bows to disciple, identities are exchanged, distinctions erased.[16]

Actually these last paraphrases are lame, piling words on words. But the sharp formula, "You're guru, I'm disciple," sticks in consciousness, revealing its meaning and appropriateness as the song is heard once, twice, or many times.

Śabda 41 provides a more complex example of a unified poem in which a single metaphor is developed to the point of allegory, and the poet plays certain tricks as he moves from opening to closing:

Pandit, look in your heart for knowledge.
Tell me where untouchability

16. There is another level of meaning for *jo aba kī būjhai*—'(the one) who understands now'. Since the postposition *kī* cannot stand alone, the feminine noun *bāt* is mentally inserted after it. *Bāt* means matter, point, subject. "If you understand the 'matter of now'," can mean not only "If you understand what I just said," but also, "If you understand *nowness*."

came from, since you believe in it.
Mix red juice, white juice and air —
a body bakes in a body.
As soon as the eight lotuses
are ready, it comes
into the world. Then what's
untouchable?
Eighty-four hundred thousand vessels
decay into dust, while the potter
keeps slapping clay
on the wheel, and with a touch
cuts each one off.
We eat by touching, we wash
by touching, from a touch
the world was born.
So who's untouched? asks Kabir.
Only he
who has no taint of *māyā*.[17]

The first line presents a typical challenge which (as Kabir's openings are wont to do) cuts the props out from under the addressee. "Pandit, look in your heart for knowledge" — not in your scriptures and commentaries, not in disputations with your friends. The pandit is crippled: if he follows this initial stricture, he won't be a pandit anymore. But Kabir goes on talking in a reasonable fashion. "Tell me where untouchability came from, since you believe in it." Another step is taken to lock the listener into the argument on Kabir's terms: "Well, yes, I do believe in it," the pandit is bound to say, which obliges him somehow to answer the question, "Where does it come from?" He is used to answering questions — that is his stock-in-trade — but here his usual mode of discourse has been cut off in advance by the injunction, "Look in your heart."

17. *Ghaṭa*, with the conventional double meaning of 'body' and 'clay pot', initiates the metaphor of potter and clay which is worked out in this poem in detail. The potter is considered untouchable in North India, and clay vessels are unclean, the cheap unbaked ones being thrown away after one use. The body is commonly referred to as a pot — one whose clay, as the poet points out here, surrounds the eight lotuses or *chakras*, channels of spiritual energy. The 'vessels' of line 10 (*bāsana*) have the secondary meaning of 'passions' (*bāsanā*); one finds the word printed both ways. The potter's wheel has been inferred from *pāṭa* which is sometimes used for a washerman's stone slab or a millstone, but which basically means any level surface. Shukdev Singh informed me that in the Bhojpuri area a term of abuse for potters is *garakaṭṭa*, 'neck-cutter'.

Ostensibly we have begun a dialogue; but in fact (as is often the case with Kabir), the primary speaker has a hammerlock on the argument. Or, to use another combative metaphor, the interlocutor receives two swift blows at the start. While Kabir continues the discussion in a leisurely tone, the pandit gasps, holding his solar plexus.[18]

The next couplet demonstrates the illusoriness of untouchability. All bodies are made of the same essential substances; each body is sealed within another body during its formation. At what point can touch, or defilement, take place? These verses create a very interesting picture of the emergent human being: a clay vessel, a string of lotuses. The lotuses are the *chakras*, which one almost has to imagine as luminous in the dark hollow of clay. They represent the uniqueness of the human being, the road of liberation, within a creature who otherwise is just an earthy paste of sperm, blood, and breath, like all creatures.

From this image of an individual person's birth, the poet suddenly shifts perspective to the vast turning of births and deaths in the universe. Millions of clay pots crumble, all have been set up on the same stone wheel, and all are cut off with a touch. 'Cutting off' is birth, the separation of the individual.[19] Now the meaning of touching widens. Everything we do in this world is touching, creation itself is a 'touch'. The word has come to denote duality: it takes two to touch.

The argument in this *pad* turns on Kabir's manipulation of the word *chhūti.* (modern *chhūt*), which is used eight times in seven-and-a-half lines. Basically it means 'touch', but in common usage it also means 'defiled touch', thence untouchability. By playing on the whole range of possible meanings, Kabir seems to reverse himself: in the first half he says, 'No one is touched'. In the second half he says, 'No one is untouched'. The common argument against untouchability — that everyone is made in the same way from the same stuff, and Shudras are therefore not polluted in relation to Brahmans — receives an uncommon twist. In the new and larger sense of the word *chhūti*, the Brahmans are polluted, along with everyone else.

Coming and going, Kabir has proved a radical equality: not only of all people, but of all substances and interactions. The point he makes

18. Socrates, most famous of dialoguists, tends to have the same sort of hammerlock on his conversations. It often seems that his young interlocutors are there only to say, "Certainly, Socrates," "That is beyond doubt," or "It seems impossible to avoid that conclusion."

19. Indian readers will also be aware of the significance of saying eighty-four hundred thousand vessels: only once in that many lives does the *jīva* attain human birth, the unique opportunity to become liberated.

is no longer social or moral, but ontological. *Chhūti* signifies the nature of phenomenal existence, transiency, desire, confusion of birth and death. The only way to be free of that defilement is to end one's contact with *māyā*.

Śabda 41 is only one of many *pad*s whose metaphors and movements could be analyzed closely. Staying with the same general theme, we could find many poems with imagery emphasizing the essential equality of all beings (all pots are made of one clay, all ornaments are made of one gold, all men and beasts have red blood).[20] *Sākhī* 107 affirms that as long as truth is not realized, "all four castes are untouchable." *Śabda* 47 again has a strong personal opening and closing, develops a central metaphor (the river), and works with 'clay' and untouchability.

Śabda 75 shares the themes of 41 and 47, but operates on the audience in a more dramatic fashion. It is one of the most extreme examples of abrupt changes, rushing tempo, careening stops, barrages of words that land like blows, sudden questions that set you spinning and are followed (just as you might be opening your mouth to reply) by assaults that turn you upside-down.

It's a heavy confusion.
Veda, Koran, holiness, hell — who's man? who's woman?
A clay pot shot with air and sperm.
When the pot falls apart, what do you call it?
Numskull! You've missed the point.

The diction as well as the structure is bruising; it *hurts*, it is designed to *break* something.

It's all one skin and bone,
one piss and shit,
one blood, one meat.
From one drop, a universe.
Who's Brahman? Who's Shudra?

This is not argument, but a direct assault on the structures of belief and self-image. The point that is being hammered across reaches its culmination in "From one drop, a universe" (reminiscent of "From a touch the world was born"). The line has several levels of meaning. It suggests not only a universal substance of creation (which is rather a remote, abstract idea), but also an event or experience that breaks through time: creation is instantaneous, a single act fills the universe,

20. See *śabda*s 30 and 70.

a single thought fills consciousness. Not giving the reader a chance to catch his breath after this climax, Kabir shoots another question: "Who's Brahman, who's Shudra?" The next verse may be temporarily comforting, for it is a rote repetition of the Brahmanic 'party line' about the three *guṇa*s and their association with the three great gods:

> Brahma *rajas*, Shiva *tamas*, Vishnu *sattva*...

But he has opened this line of thinking only to cut it off the more forcefully:

> Kabir says, plunge into Ram!
> There: No Hindu. No Turk.

If you reduce the universe to a drop, then remove (or plunge into) the drop, what do you have? Darkness. No distinctions.

Kabir as the Good Physician

Stanley Fish, in *Self-Consuming Artifacts*, describes an aesthetic which he traces originally to Plato and Augustine and demonstrates at length in the works of several seventeenth-century English authors.[21] Though Fish treats the metaphor of the good physician as "one of the most powerful in western literature and philosophy," the aesthetic he elaborates from it is universally applicable. Students of Kabir will vividly recognize their poet in Fish's account of the verbal good physician, who is characterized (in terms based on Plato's *Gorgias*) as a 'dialectician' rather than a 'rhetorician':

> A dialectical presentation... is disturbing, for it requires of its readers a searching and rigorous scrutiny of everything they believe in and live by. It is didactic in a special sense; it does not preach the truth, but asks that its readers discover the truth for themselves, and this discovery is often made at the expense not only of a reader's opinions and values, but of his self-esteem.
>
> ...[T]he end of a dialectical experience is (or should be) nothing less than a *conversion*, not only a changing, but an exchanging of minds. It is necessarily a painful process... in the course of which both parties forfeit a great deal; on the one side the applause of a pleased audience, on the other, the satisfactions of listening to the public affirmation of our values and prejudices.

21. Stanley Fish, *Self-Consuming Artifacts: The Experience of Seventeenth-Century Literature* (Berkeley: University of California Press, 1972).

...The good physician may be philosopher, minister, teacher, or even deity, but whatever his status, his strategy and intentions are always the same: he tells his patients what they *don't* want to hear in the hope that by forcing them to see themselves clearly, they will be moved to change the selves they see.

...The end of dialectic is not so much the orderly disposition of things in the phenomenal world, as the transformation of the soul-mind into an instrument capable of seeing things in the phenomenal world for what they really are (turning things upside-down)....[22]

So Socrates asks in the *Gorgias:*

To which treatment of the city do you urge me? ...Is it to combat the Athenians until they become as virtuous as possible, prescribing for them like a physician; or is it to be their servant and cater to their pleasure....?[23]

Fish comments that Socrates is here articulating the choice of motives that faces every would-be teacher, writer, or leader:

... whether to strive selfishly for a local and immediate satisfaction or to risk hostility and misunderstanding by pursuing always the best interests of his auditors....[24]

Socrates's choice penetrated his acts as well as his words. With clear understanding he risked and incurred hostility, and finally died for his teaching.

Kabir's attitude is the same. He does not hesitate, in the holiest Hindu city, to attack the kingpins of Hindu society ("Seekers, the Brahman is a slicked-down butcher"); or, in a country ruled by Muslims, to ridicule the religion of the Emperor (the Turk "crows 'God! God!' like a cock"). If someone tries to smooth over his insults, saying "No offence," he will cry like Hamlet, "Yes, but there is, and much offence too!"[25] And he will continue to offend. Though he did not, like Socrates, have to die for his outrages, he does speak of being beaten for telling the truth, and he often alludes to his isolation, the difficulty of finding anyone who will listen or understand. His constant effort was to strip away disguises, force confrontations, expose lies, promote honesty at

22. Ibid., pp. 1-7.
23. Ibid., p. 20.
24. Ibid., p. 21.
25. *Hamlet*, I.5.136-37. In Shakespeare, *Complete Works*, ed. W.J. Craig (London: Oxford University Press, 1922), p. 1015.

every level. His social-satirical poems, his psychological probes, his poems about death, his crazy and paradoxical and "mystical" poems, do not inhabit separate categories. They are unified by a principle of radical honesty that sweeps through marketplace, temple, body and mind, that will no more allow you to delude yourself than to cheat others, to hack up the truth than to sever the head of an animal.

Kabir's abrupt and jagged style is a technique to jolt and shock people into facing things, to push them over the edge into an understanding that they fear and yet profoundly long for. It also corresponds to, and tones the mind up for, the actual experience of a sudden, unifying insight in the midst of chaotic temporal events.

Concluding Questions

> A self-consuming artifact signifies most successfully when it fails, when it points *away* from itself to something its forms cannot capture.[26]

Kabir may seem to harangue in his more vehement poems against Hindu and Muslim hypocrisy, stupidity, violence, greed. Some of these poems are bound to be inauthentic, for the mode of satirical attack is one of the easiest to imitate. But the variety of Kabīr's rhetorical modes, and the integrity of the personality that informs them, are not easy to imitate. In this rhetoric, the question is as important as the exclamation. We can assemble another pastiche of lines, this time all questions:

For one who doesn't know the secret,
what's the way out?

How to escape the spear?

On this riverbank, saints or thieves?

The three worlds whirl in doubt.
To whom can I explain?

...the sky is ripped.
Can a tailor mend it?

What color is a living being?

Where do the senses rest?
Where do the Ram-chanters go?
Where do the bright ones go?

26. Fish, *Artifacts*, p. 4.

. . . parrot-on-a-pole,
who has caught you?

At whom is Kabir shouting?

In his definition of the dialectical process, Fish describes a change in consciousness of a sort usually spoken of in religious contexts:

> In a dialectical experience, one is moved from the first [discursive or rational way of thinking] to the second way, which has various names, the way of the good, the way of the inner light, the way of faith; but whatever the designation, the moment of its full emergence is marked by the transformation of the visible and segmented world into an emblem of its creator's indwelling presence..., and at that moment the motion of the rational consciousness is stilled, for it has become indistinguishable from the object of its inquiry.[27]

Though Fish avoids the troublesome word, what he is talking about is often called mystical experience. When the distinction between subject and object disappears ("consciousness ... indistinguishable from the object of its inquiry"), the self disappears. We say this coolly, though in fact we have said nothing. It is an unabstractible, indescribable experience. That a person should drop, even for a moment, the conviction of separate selfhood, is the most unlikely eventuality in the world. Any author who can lead his audience to the edge of such an experience has proved himself skilful indeed.

Discussing Augustine, Fish further describes this transformation of consciousness:

> [T]he Christian rhetorician believes in a world everywhere informed and sustained by God's presence..., a world that, because it is without parts, is without hierarchies, either of persons or actions. Techniques for dividing and distinguishing, including the rules of rhetoric, are therefore antithetical to his purpose, which is not to persuade to a point, but to a vision in which all points are one (he works to turn the world, as we naturally know it, upside-down)....[28]

"Dividing and distinguishing" is the chief activity of the mind and its most powerful tool. It is also, in the view of Fish's authors, and of

27. Ibid., p. 3.
28. Ibid., p. 39.

Kabir, the chief barrier to our understanding things as they actually are. The elaborate tension that Fish so skillfully illuminates in Herbert, Bunyan, and other English authors reflects the interesting fact that the mind is — or seems to be — the only means we have for understanding the truth, even if the truth we are reaching for includes the realization that the mind and its ways of perceiving are false. One thinks of Heisenberg destroying the myth of the precise observations of science by proving that the observations are irredeemably distorted by the interference of the measuring device. The dialectician (a word that sounds more rational than 'mystic') responds to the problem by trying to create awareness of the process of dividing and distinguishing, somehow causing the mind to mirror itself, so as initially to engender a doubt about the reliability of our perceptions, and ultimately to dissolve the tight network of divisions and categories in which we are ensnared.

It is one of Kabir's specialties to raise the problem of distinction. He asks, "Is it two or one?" He hovers over boundary lines, or imagined boundary lines — especially those that have to do with our sense of identity.

> Kabir says, how to work it out —
> I — he — you? (*sākhī* 312)
>
> . . . if you understand now,
> you're guru, I'm disciple. (*śabda* 1)

He circles around the question of origin, differentiation, the existence of any separate entity, prodding us to determine priority. Which is greater? Which came first? To answer that we have to determine which is which. In *śabda* 112 he treats this profound metaphysical question as if it were the stuff of a children's argument:

> This is the big fight, King Ram.
> Let anyone settle it who can.
> Is Brahma bigger or where he came from?
> Is the Veda bigger or where it was born from?
> Is the mind bigger or what it believes in?
> Is Ram bigger or the knower of Ram?
> Kabir turns round, it's hard to see —
> Is the holy place bigger, or the devotee?

The questions all ask us to solve the problem of differentiation. At what point in consciousness is something 'born'? When does it separate from 'what it was born from'? Where is the line between knower and known?

Mind and what is believed in? Outside (holy place) and inside (devotee)?[29]

In one *sākhī* he settles the question in an unsettling way:

> If I say one, it isn't so.
> If I say two, it's slander.
> Kabir has thought about it.
> As it is,
> so it is.
>
> (*sākhī* 120)

Where assertions are inescapably false, questions are conclusions. Kabir opens *śabda* 67 with a question to end questions:

> If seed is form is god,
> then, pandit, what can you ask?

If source is the same as realization, conception not separate from creation, and will or creator not separable either ("from one drop, a universe"), then . . . ? Kabir goes on with more questions, but now they seem like mere echoes of the pandit's untenable distinctions, borne away with the breath of Kabir's "where? . . . where?:

> Where is the mind?
> Where is the intellect?
> Where is the ego?
> The three qualities,
> *sattva, rajas, tamas*?

29. Another wonderful example of this sort of questioning discourse is in the *Granthāvālī, Rāmkalī* 12 in the Gupta edition. A rough translation follows:

> King Ram, I don't know how the unmanifest manifests.
> Tell me how to speak of your form.
> Was sky first or earth, lord,
> Was wind first or water?
> Was moon first or sun, lord?
> Which was first, all-knower?
> Was breath first or body, lord,
> Was blood first or semen?
> Was man first or woman, lord,
> Was seed first or field?
> Was day first or night, lord,
> Was sin first or merit?
> Kabir says, where the pure one dwells,
> is there something there, or nothing?

In the next line — "Nectar and poison bloom, fruits ripen" — the poet evokes the whole process of birth, death, karma, recalling lines from the first *ramainī*:

> No one knows this ineffable movement.
> How could one tongue describe it?
> If any man has a million mouths and tongues,
> let that great one speak.

Then, in the same sweeping, unexplained style, there is a reference to the possibility of freedom from the interlocking causes and effects of karma:

> The Vedas show many ways
> to cross the sea.

Finally, in a line that seems to focus on the pronouns 'you' and 'me', but where these are marvellously balanced, as a juggler balances balls, with other pronouns ("I . . . who . . . who"), the poet asks his most revealing and most conclusive question:

> Kabir says, what do I know
> of you and me,
> of who gets caught
> and who goes free?

TWO TRUTHS ARE TOLD: TAGORE'S KABIR

VIJAY C. MISHRA

"The poetry of mysticism might be defined on the one hand as a temperamental reaction to the vision of Reality: on the other, as a form of prophecy." So wrote Evelyn Underhill in her introduction to Rabindranath Tagore's *One Hundred Poems of Kabir*, quite possibly claiming that Kabir was a mystic poet and by extension implicitly identifying all Hindu bhakti poetry with what may be broadly termed 'mystical' verse.[1] *One Hundred Poems of Kabir* was first published in 1915 and has been reprinted ever since at regular intervals. In 1974, Samuel Weiser issued the first paperback edition of the poems under the title *Songs of Kabir*.[2] For almost sixty years, therefore, Tagore's translation has been the most readily available edition of Kabir's poems in the Western world.[3] Its inadequacies have rarely been questioned, though since the appearance of Parasnath Tiwari's edition of *Kabīr-granthāvalī*,[4] some first-rate work, especially by Tiwari himself and by Charlotte Vaudeville, has been done on the whole problem of the 'authenticity' of texts used in translating Kabir.[5] These studies have naturally cast some doubt on what is, by any standards, some of the best translation of bhakti verse into English.

A considerable body of scattered commentary may be collated to show that genuine critical opinion has not been ignorant of the shortcomings of the Tagore translation.[6] What has not been properly ans-

This is a slightly modified version of a paper published in *South Asia* (New Series) 1:2 (September 1978), pp. 80-90.

1. Rabindranath Tagore, *One Hundred Poems of Kabīr* (London: Macmillan, Pocket Editions, 1973), p. 7.

2. *Songs of Kabīr* (New York: Samuel Weiser, 1974).

3. See Charlotte Vaudeville, *Kabīr* (Oxford: Clarendon Press, 1974), p. 339, for a list of English translations of Kabir.

4. Parasnath Tiwari, *Kabīr-granthāvalī* (Allahabad: University of Allahabad, Hindi Parishad, 1961).

5. Especially Parasnath Tiwari, *Kabīr-vāṇī-sudhā* (Allahabad: Raka Prakashan, 1976) [reprint of his *Kabīr-vāṇī-saṅgrah* (1970)], and Vaudeville, *Kabīr*.

6. Notably F.E. Keay, *Kabir and His Followers* (Calcutta: Association Press, 1931), pp. 58 ff; W.H. McLeod, *Gurū Nānak and the Sikh Religion* (Oxford: Clarendon Press, 1968), pp. 155 ff.

wered are two related queries which have consistently bedevilled scholars for over half a century now. These questions may be formulated in the following fashion. First, what kinds of 'theological' assumptions did Tagore bring to bear upon the verses of Kabir? And, second, which of the hundred poems translated by Tagore may be called 'authentic'? Within the broad parameters of these questions, this paper proposes to re-examine some aspects of Tagore's translation very carefully and, in the process, offer tentative insights into the poetry of perhaps the finest poet of the so-called Sant tradition of India.

One of Kabir's better known 'authentic' poems is the following:

bālama āu hamāṅrai greha re:
tumha bina dukhiyā deha re.
saba koi kahai tumhārī nārī mokauṅ yaha andeha re;
ekameka hvai seja na sovai taba lagi kaisā neha re.
anna na bhāvai nīnda na āvai griha bana dharai na dhīra re;
jyauṅ kāṅmīṅ kau kāṅmini pyārī, jyauṅ pyāse kau nīra re.
hai koi aisā para upagāri Hari sauṅ kahai sunāi re;
aba tau behāla Kabīra bhae haiṅ binu dekheṅ jiu jāi re.[7]

As the rest of this paper is based on a close analysis of the meanings of specific words and their poetic significance, I give below a literal translation of the poem, following as far as possible the word and line order of the original.

Beloved (*bālama*) come (*āu*) to my/mine own (*hamāṅrai*) house (*greha*) [vocative particle] (*re*); without you (*tumha bina*) afflicted/in agony (*dukhiyā*) my body is (*deha re*).

Everyone (*saba koi*) says (*kahai*) [I am] your woman (*tumhārī nārī*) why am I (*mokauṅ*) of this (*yaha*) in doubt (*andeha re*)? [for unless] we become joined into one (*ekameka hvai*), sleep on the same bed (*seja na sovai*), then (*taba*) has struck (*lagi*) what kind of (*kaisā*) love (*neha re*).

Food (*anna*) I dislike (*na bhāvai*), sleep (*nīnda*) doesn't come to me (*na āvai*), within my house (*griha*), outside (*bana*), stable/peaceful (*dharai*) my mind is not (*na dhīra re*); as the lover (*jyauṅ kāṅmīṅ*) desires his beloved (*kau kāṅmini pyārī*), as (*jyauṅ*) the thirsty (*pyāse*) desires water (*kau nīra re*).

7. Tiwari, *Kabīr-granthāvalī*, Poem 13, p. 9; Tagore, *Kabīr*, Poem XXXV, pp. 45-46.

Isn't there someone (*hai koi aisā*) benevolent enough (*para upagārī*) the Lord (*Hari*) to tell (*sauṅ kahai*) to listen (*sunāi re*)? for now (*aba tau*) afflicted/'unconscious' (*behāla*) is Kabir (*Kabīra bhae haiṅ*) without seeing [the Lord] (*binu dekheṅ*) he expires/languishes (*jiu jāi re*).

The poem of Kabir begins with the word *bālama*, 'lover or beloved', and is written in the *bhāva* which evokes this special relationship between Kabir and Hari, his Lord. Based on the literal translation of the poem already given, the following paraphrase may be offered.

> Beloved, come within my house, my body yearns for you, Everyone says I am your woman, yet of this I have no assurance. For until we have slept in one bed, this love of ours remains unconsummated. I cannot eat, I cannot sleep; I am restless within and without. As a woman to a lustful man, as water to someone thirsty [so are you to me]. Isn't there any helpful soul who could take these words of mine to Hari? For now Kabir is delirious and expires without seeing him.

On a purely surface level the general meaning of the poem is clear from this paraphrase. But what is lost is not just the overall phonetic and semantic connections being made in the poem but also the patterning and somewhat Tantric symbolism which Kabir employs.

While metrical problems in Kabir inevitably remain insurmountable, it is nevertheless easy to demonstrate how his elusive style, his *sandhā-bhāṣā*,[8] stresses associative relationships between words within the poem

8. See Mircea Eliade, *Yoga: Immortality and Freedom*, Willard R. Trask, trans. (London: Routledge & Kegan Paul, 1958), pp. 249-54. Eliade translated *sandhyā-bhāṣā* (*sandhā-bhāṣā*) as 'intentional language'. I translate it as 'twilight language'. Unlike the metaphysical conceit (which it superficially resembles), its inherent paradoxes cannot be resolved through a breakdown of it into 'disambiguous sentences'. *Sandhā-bhāṣā*, in terms of literary criticism, requires a total hermeneutic of reading, an awareness in fact of the total religious and philosophical structures which infuse it.

Sandhā-bhāṣā may take the 'form' of *ulaṭbāṃsī*, the poetics of inversion. See Parashuram Chaturvedi, *Kabīr sāhitya kī parakh* (Allahabad: Bharati Bhandar, 1964), pp. 154 ff. for an extended discussion. A summary of the crucial paragraph may be useful:

> It is difficult to say with any certainty when the term *ulaṭbāṃsī* was first used. Clearly Gorakhnath used *ulaṭī charachā* ('inverted expression') in its place... From this it is clear that it is a style in which a point is made through unusual comparisons. Consequently, *ulaṭbāṃsī* may be interpreted as a word composed of two segments: *ulaṭā* ('inverted') and *aṃśa* ('aspect' or 'part').

A proverbial Hindi *ulaṭbāṃsī* is *barsai kambal bhījai pānī* ('It rains blankets and the rain gets wet').

and the esoteric systematization of Tantric symbolism. In the *ṭek* or refrain line, for instance, an exact parallel is developed.

bālama	*tumha*	(lover	you)
āu	*bina*	(come	without)
hamāṅrai	*dukhiyā*	(mine	sad)
greha	*deha*	(house	body)
re	*re*	(vocative particle)	

It is clear from the foregoing that Kabir completely identifies the 'body' with 'house'. What is not so evident is the implied connection between the body waiting to be aroused and Tantric beliefs wherein the areas of potential cosmic energy — the *chakras* (lit. 'wheels'), the *maṇḍalas* (lit. 'orbits') — must be aroused by the *kuṇḍalinī* (the coiled serpent at the base of the spine) for the body's total mystical rejuvenation.[9] Yet the implied mysticism, "the ebullition of feelings of attachment to God," to use S.N. Dasgupta's helpful phrase,[10] is couched in raw, everyday imagery. Sometimes this sense of the concrete takes the form of *ulaṭbāṃsī*, 'inverted language', suffused with heavy ironic overtones characteristic of what Mammatacharya called *vyaṅgya*.[11]

It is only after the first series of metaphors in the poem that the language acquires a certain degree of potency, of passion, and the *viraha* becomes sexually charged. This process is interesting and requires a fuller comment. Central to this change is the intrusion of the figure of the *kāṅmīṅ* and yet, true to Kabir's style, the corresponding image of the thirsty going to water remains common-place. However, *kāṅmīṅ*, I take it, is not just any man — he could have used any number of words here if this were his intention — but the vigorous, lustful man, and evokes

9. See Eliade, *Yoga*, chapter 6.

10. S.N. Dasgupta, *Hindu Mysticism*, reprint ed. (Delhi: Motilal Banarsidass, 1982), p. 123. Dasgupta's division of mysticism into five basic types (sacrificial, Upanishadic, Yogic, Buddhist and bhakti) is followed by R.C. Zaehner, *Hindu and Muslim Mysticism* (London: The Athlone Press, 1960).

11. *Mammaṭāchāryā kāvyaprakāśaḥ*, ed. Acharya Vishveshvar (Banares: Jnanmandal Limited, 1960). The importance of Mammatacharya's work lies in the fact that as a much later and more codified work of Sanskrit poetics than those it supplanted, it must have had a considerable influence upon later Sanskrit and medieval Hindi bhakti verse.

In Kabir, *vyaṅgya*, or the suggestive meaning, often takes the form of irony which, in a good many cases, operates within an overall language of inversion. It could be argued that the entire technique of *ulaṭbāṃsī* and *sandhā-bhāsā* may be explained with reference to Mammatacharya's poetics. See *pad* 188 in Tiwari's *Kabīr-granthāvalī*.

the dark figure of Shiva himself. Not only does the pedestrian train of images get a jolt here but an inversion is at work as well. Instead of the *virahiṇī* passively waiting, she becomes the active ravisher, the *kāṅmīṅ*, the Kamadeva (*kāma-deva*) of Hindu mythology who constantly desires his *kāṅmini*. However, this collocation (*kāṅmīṅ kau kāṅmini pyārī*) has a somewhat more profound and perhaps even disturbing philosophical implication. If Parasnath Tiwari's interpretation is correct, then the use of *kāṅmini* and its implied connection with the Lord (the *virahiṇī* awaits the Lord throughout the poem) reflects the extent to which Kabir quite effortlessly oscillates between Shankara's *advaita* (non-dualism) and Ramanuja's *viśiṣṭādvaita* (modified non-dualism). Tiwari in fact writes: "*Kabīr kā māyāvād Upaniṣad, Gītā tathā Śaṅkarāchārya ke māyāvād se hī prabhāvit hai,*" and on the same page adds, "*Kabīr kī uktiyoṅ par vichār karne se jñāt hotā hai ki unhoṅne māyā ko avidyā — viśeṣatayaḥ kanak kāminī — se alag karke nahīṅ dekhā...*"[12] In other words, Tiwari claims not only that Kabir was influenced by the concept of *māyā*[13] as enunciated in the Upanishads, the *Gītā* and by Shankara but that he also positively associated *māyā* with *avidyā* (absence of knowledge) and identified both (as indicated further in another line of Kabir which Tiwari quotes) with the notion of the *kāminī*. Tiwari's insistence upon the strong impact of Shankara's *advaita* Vedanta cannot be disputed, but the evidence in the poem in front of us does present another enticing possibility which Tiwari overlooks. Within the Shankara system, *māyā* and *brahman* are by definition mutually exclusive: to reach the Supreme Reality, a transcendence of *māyā*, the principle which creates the 'unreal world', must be achieved. Yet the other important Hindu speculative system — that of Ramanuja (eleventh century) — attests to the possibility of co-existence and stresses that *māyā* may well be a principle which eminates from *brahman*, so that the question is not simply one of non-dualism, but of a far more subtle 'modified' non-dualism. Now in the poem of Kabir under discussion, '*kāṅminī*' as *māyā* is being associated with the Lord, albeit through a process of poetic inversion and metaphorical extension. And the point here is that Kabir did not see himself as being bound by any set of beliefs or philo-

12. Tiwari, *Kabīr-vāṇī-sudhā*, p. 56. "Kabir's conception of *māyā* was modified by *māyā* as offered in the Upanishads and the *Gītā*, and by Shankara. ... If we consider Kabir's verses very carefully, we realise that he did not see *māyā* in terms other than those associated with *avidyā* ('ignorance') and the *kanak kāminī* ('deceitful woman')."

13. '*Māyā*' is often unsatisfactorily translated as 'illusion', 'the unreal', etc., but it is perhaps closer to the idea of a 'structuring principle'.

sophical system. True, a strong sense of the non-dualistic is evident in him, but he attempts to slip out of this category precisely when we are sure that he fits into it. I cannot go into the overall poetic ramifications of the tripartite concept of *māyā*, *kāminī* and *brahman*, but it is significant that Tulsi Das, the bhakta *par excellence*, uses another version of the *kāminī*—the *nartaki*, the dancer—to press home a similar point.[14] Part of our difficulty with Kabir arises from the fact that he is a poet who is hardly ever discursive; his linguistic economy and poetic terseness create the possibility of an 'ironic' world-view all the time. And though I may well have laid a somewhat excessive stress here, it is nevertheless evident that the image of the *kāṅmīṅ* and *kāṅminī* is different: a sense of action strongly underlines the metaphor and the 'stasis' is momentarily, and only momentarily, transformed into a stronger Tantric awakening of the *kuṇḍalinī*.

Normally Kabir's *pads* have a formulaic ending which begins with *kahai Kabīra* ('says Kabir') and is called a *bhaṇitā*. Here there is an exception. The passivity is maintained, for Kabir replaces *kahai* by *bhae haiṅ*, a condition of being, for *bhae* in the context acts very much like a reflexive verb. I suspect that the other effect achieved here is that of *muktaka*, a certain degree of detachment from the poem which is normally cancelled out by the *bhaṇitā* beginning with the slightly more 'active' *kahai Kabīra*. Two other significant departures from the normal techniques of Kabir must be mentioned as well. First, the poem does not fully introduce us to the peculiar mixture of *nirguṇa* (the Lord as the One) and *saguṇa* (the Lord as the Many) bhakti which is found elsewhere. Second, we do not get any real inkling of Kabir's religious syncretism, his merging of eclectic Sufism with orthodox Hindu bhakti. A final point ought to be mentioned as well. Kabir consciously refuses to use *alaṅkāra*, those intricate ornamentations which were the hallmark of Sanskrit and many vernacular literatures. Possibly because of this absence, the vigor and vitality of Kabir's verse are considerably enhanced.

One of the reasons I have written at some length about this poem is that it is one of the only *six* 'authentic' Kabir poems, or partial poems ('fragments') found in Tagore's *One Hundred Poems of Kabir*. In a descending order of 'authenticity' these are (with verse numbers from the

14. The seventh book of Tulsi Das's *Rāmcharitmānas* is devoted mainly to the ways in which a triumph over *māyā* can be established. Throughout the work, however, Tulsi Das emphasizes the superiority of bhakti over all other paths of salvation. For the poetic intricacies of the *māyā-nartaki-Sītā* symbolism see *Uttarakāṇḍa*, *chaupāī* 114 ff.

Tiwari edition given in parentheses): XXXV *vālama, āwo hamāre geh re* (*13—bālama āu hamāṅrai greha re*), LXIX *jo khudā masjid vasat hai* (*177 — Allah Rāṅm jiūṅ terai nāṅīṅ*, couplets 4-6 only), XV *jānh khelat vasant riturāj* (*149 — jahaṅ satagura khelata ritu basanta*), XCIX *Nārad, pyār so antar nāhī* (*35 — Nārada sādha sauṅ antara nāṅhīṅ*), XXXIV *mohi tohi lāgī kaise chuṭe* (*18 — mohiṅ tohiṅ lāgī kaisai chhūṭai*), XXXII *nāco re mero man, matta hoy* (*14 — nāchu re mana mero naṭa hoi*).[15] The order must be re-examined very carefully as what is really established here is not Tagore's relationship to the 'original' but, rather, the relationship of one corrupt text from which Tagore worked to a re-creation of the original recensions (*mūl pāṭh*) arrived at by Tiwari.[16] Whatever criteria we employ, it is clear enough that the Kshitimohan Sen edition used by Tagore was itself based upon corrupt Kabir-panthi interpolations. Sen had presented Kabir in Bengali characters and had given a useful paraphrase of the poems. His collection contained 341 poems and as F.E. Keay observed about fifty years ago, "The hundred poems translated [by Tagore] are taken from the first three [of the four] volumes, which contain only 264."[17] Sardar Ja'fri's *Kabīr bānī* contains 128 of these poems, exactly in the versions offered by Kshitimohan Sen (including 98 found in Tagore) and may be used to re-examine the texts used by Tagore for his translations.[18] In any case, it seems to me that Tagore could read the original, though in a different script, and check his own knowledge of Hindi against the paraphrase given. It is not too

15. In the version of this paper in *South Asia*, I had discovered five 'authentic' Kabir poems in the Tagore translation. I have since located a sixth poem, which is only partially translated as poem LXIX by Tagore. The version in the Kshitimohan Sen edition is also a 'fragment'. This particular poem was noticed by the Rev. Ahmad Shah, a point mentioned in F.E. Keay, *Kabīr*, pp. 62 ff. A transcription of the first lines of these poems as found in Tiwari's *Kabīr-granthāvalī* is given in brackets after the verse number and 'title' found in Tagore.

For a full concordance of six separate translations with Tiwari's text as the 'reconstructed original' see Vijay C. Mishra, "The Devotional Poetics of Kabir: A study of Kabir's Poetry and its Tradition with an Annotated Translation of His Songs," unpublished Ph.D. dissertation (Australian National University, Canberra, 1981). 2 vols.

16. This particular excercise in translation aesthetics (poetics?) is complicated by the fact that Tagore had access only to a corrupt version of Kabir. I have read the translations against Tiwari's re-constructed texts and not against those in the Kshitimohan Sen edition. This method may have influenced my judgement. Kshitimohan Sen, *Kabīr* (Calcutta: The Association Press, 1910).

17. Keay, *Kabīr*, p. 62.

18. Sardar Ja'fri, *Kabīr bānī* (Bombay: Hindustan Book Trust, n.d., 1965?).

clear how he in fact made use of the two 'sources' of information in front of him. One fact is certain, however: Tagore did have access to the 'original', however corrupt Sen's texts may have been. With this evidence, students of literary translation would naturally recall Ezra Pound who used Fenellosa for his Chinese and his own knowledge of Old English for the *Seafarer*. This analogy is significant on another level. As practising poets, both demonstrated a dislike for transliteration and always showed a strong intuitive feel for the *bhāva* of the original language from which they were translating.

Tagore's translation of *bālama āu hamāñrai greha re* is as follows (Poem XXXV):

> My body and my mind are grieved for the want of Thee;
> O my Beloved! come to my house.
> When people say I am Thy bride, I am ashamed; for I have not touched Thy heart with my heart.
> Then what is this love of mine? I have no taste for food, I have no sleep; my heart is ever restless within doors and without.
> As water is to the thirsty, so is the lover to the bride.
> Who is there that will carry my news to my Beloved?
> Kabir is restless: he is dying for sight of Him.

Very generally, I think there are three 'principles' at work in Tagore's translation. First, there is a strong identification of the 'Lover' (*bālama*, the *nāma* or name, and Hari, the Lord — the two modes of apprehending the All-knowing) with a monotheistic God who, as the translation is in English, along with 'Thee', 'Thy' and a bold 'Him', emerges as a Christian God. Secondly, and this is purely conjectural, there is a location of the text within the tradition of Western mystical poetry with the word 'bride' playing a prominent role.[19] Finally, there is a general dilution or toning down of the powerfully present and explicit sexual imagery, even a certain denial of its presence, so that the content does not 'collide' with the tradition of verse to which it belongs. More specifically, if we wish to explore the diachronic structure of this translation further, then I suspect we must take into account the transformation in the tenor of devotional poetry in English which took place from, say, the time of Richard Rolle to that of Yeats. In between occurs the poetry of the Metaphysicals, some of which comes very close to Kabir.

19. Pierre Pourrat, *Christian Spirituality*, trans. W.H. Mitchell and S.P. Jacques, 3 vols. (New York: P.J. Kennedy and Sons, 1922-27). Vol. 4, trans. D. Attwater (Baltimore: The Newman Press, 1955).

A Divine Poem of John Donne such as "Batter my heart, three person'd God..." is filled with the same kind of energy, urgency and resonance which one finds in Kabir's verse.[20] In one respect, this tradition of devotional poetry does give the poem a contextual patina, a referential context which embodies a "cumulative tradition."[21] Out of this patina, however, Tagore selects the loose 'mystical' verse of the late Romantics and (unfortunately) the very early Yeats as his 'model'.

On linguistic grounds our exploration can be more rewarding. The 'verbal respectability' which Tagore attempts to give to Kabir's rather earthy use of language is itself a major transgression. Furthermore, it gives the impression of religious conformism and stylistic organization when in fact Kabir's verse is marked precisely by their absence. Devotional pronouns such as 'Thee', 'Thy' and so on tend to 'stabilize' the writings of bhakti poets and impose a sense of order and 'absolute signification' which may well have been lacking in bhakti poetry generally. It could be that the strong late nineteenth-century style made it difficult for him to confront Kabir's language as it was; or, conversely, Kshitimohan Sen may have done the toning down for him in his paraphrase. Whatever the reason, the absence of a sense of 'unmediated' *encounter* takes its toll in the translation, as we shall now see.

Tagore begins by reversing the order of the original lines. In doing so he begins with the condition of the 'I' instead of Kabir's *bālama*. Furthermore, he employs a passive construction to demonstrate the 'detachment' of the *virahiṇī*: "My body and my mind are grieved for the want of Thee." And something of this passive *aspect* is present also in the rather awkward use of 'want'. The use, however, has the effect of completely distancing the *virahiṇī* from her *bālama* and tends to give the two lines of the original an unnecessary, and quite spurious, gloss. In the bhakti tradition of verse, *bālama* has a wide synecdochic function. On the surface level it is another word for 'husband', 'beloved' or swami, but on another and more significant level it has the effect of a *śabda* or 'word' such as *Rām-nām*, the name of Ram. It should be noted that an alternative reading of the text begins with the Lord *bālhā* ('Vallabha', which is another name for Vishnu).[22] In this respect it is a

20. See also Rolle's poems of 'love-longing' such as "Jesu my lefe, Jesu my love, Jesu my covetynge" (Bodleian MS, Don. C. 13, f. 166r). *The Divine Poems of John Donne*, Helen Gardner, ed. (Oxford: Clarendon Press, 1952), p. 11.

21. George Steiner, *After Babel* (Oxford: Clarendon Press, 1975), p. 349.

22. See S.S. Das, *Kabīr-granthāvalī*, reprint ed. (Banares: Nagari Pracharini Sabha, 1975), p. 142. S.S. Das, very helpfully, classifies Kabir's poems on the basis

more truly 'mystical' concept — and many bhakti words do possess this special polysemy which is lacking in other traditions of devotional verse. Consequently the conventional home-coming notion present in the original (*bālama āu hamāṅrai greha re*) possesses elements of what may be called, in Kabir's poetics,[23] *parachā* (*parichay*) *bhāvanā* (the encounter of recognition), and it begins the search for spiritual awareness which comes only through *direct experience.*

Perhaps a much more alarming criticism is the conscious 'insertion' of the metaphysical component "My body and my mind . . ." within the poem. Did Tagore believe that Kabir was a complete dualist? Or do we see here an imposition of a personal religiosity upon Kabir, the kind of religiosity which makes itself abundantly manifest in Tagore's *Gītānjali* for instance? Kabir, as we have seen, worked much more solidly within the prevailing speculative systems of the times and his acceptance of Shankara's *advaita* was somewhat more embracing than has hitherto been acknowledged.[24] At any rate, it is a very self-conscious use of the expansionist latitude which indicates that for Tagore the tradition of the 'receptor language' is much more important than that of the 'source language'.

The 'alternative' and somewhat personal religiosity with which Tagore invests Kabir's verse continues almost throughout the translation. Kabir's line *saba koi . . . andeha re* emerges as: "When people say I am Thy bride, I am ashamed." In Tagore the sense of impassioned involvement found in Kabir (which is both physical and Tantric, the beginning of the movement towards the *sahaja* state, the easy state, which is part of bhakti) gets dissociated from the context, and this dissociation continues right from the first line of the translation where he makes the *act* of waiting for the mystical trance (*samādhi*) merely one of passive grief. This naturally results in a further

---

of established raga forms. This poem is classified as raga Kedarau (*kedārā*—literally 'a field full of water'). The word *śabda* (in Gurumukhi *śabad*) is viewed as an axiomatic truth, an internally coherent verbal testimony. Within the Tantric methods of meditation, the *śabda* is itself 'divine', equivalent to and analogical with *brahman.* The two related words which occur in Kabir are *nāda* (and its cognate *anāhata*), resonance or vibration; and *bindu*, the still point arrived at after the experience of *nāda.* See A.K. Bannerjea, *Philosophy of Gorakhnath* (Delhi: Motilal Banarsidass 1982).

23. For a concise account of Kabir's poetics see R.K. Varma, *Kabīr kā rahasyavād*, reprint ed. (Allahabad: Sahitya Bhavan, 1972).

24. Tiwari, *Kabīr-vāṇī-sudhā*, p. 61.

removal of the lover from his/her object. The addition of a causal connection with "When" destroys the highly cryptic nature of Kabir's verse. In one way the expansionist leeway that Tagore grants himself locates connections which by their very nature work contrary to Kabir's style and purpose. Nowhere is this more obvious than in "I am ashamed," Tagore's translation of *mokauṅ yaha andeha re*. In the original, however, Kabir never uses any version of the Hindi word for 'ashamed' (*lajjit*); nor is the word given in any of the other recensions quoted by Tiwari. Indeed, all the variants given by Tiwari indicate that the words used in the various manuscripts are versions of the modern Hindi *sandeh*, self-doubt. Kabir's *andeha* is an Eastern variety of the Western Hindi *andes* and the Persian *andeśā*.[25] Quite possibly, Kshitimohan Sen himself worked from a corrupt text or the transcription into Bengali characters resulted in another word which means 'ashamed'. Yet 'ashamed' by itself does ameliorate the almost a sexual tone of the translation. Read as *lajjit* the word is very successful in evoking that precise degree of action and detachment which is obviously present in the *virahiṇī*.

The break in the linear progression of Kabir's thoughts would be a minor point were it not for the disjunction which almost invariably occurs whenever Tagore does this. For instance, the *ardhālī* (half-couplet) *ekameka hvai...neha re* is broken into two and Tagore gives the first half to one 'stanza' and the other half to another. But by doing so he disconnects the relationship which exists between the desire for *saṃyoga* (sexual union) and the condition of the *virahiṇī*, for whom the alternation between a sense of fulfilment and its opposite is equally important.[26] The powerful connection made between the sexual act and the

25. *Kabīr koś,* ed. Parashuram Chaturvedi and Mahendra (Allahabad: Smriti Prakashan, 1973), p. 9.

26. In Tiwari's *Kabīr-granthāvalī*, *pad* 11, this feeling of perpetual alternation, *in medias res*, finds a most succinct formulation. The idea also reflects a strong Sufi influence on Kabir. Originally, within Sufism, as in the poems of Rumi for instance, the poetic sensibility adumbrates God-woman and devotee-man. It is the devotee-man who languishes for love, wishes that he could drink heavenly wine from the goblets of God-woman and at her door begs entry. Obviously, this is a clear inversion of the processes at work in Kabir's poetics, his *rahasyavād*. God-woman was replaced by Lord-husband and devotee-husband by devotee-bride.

R.K. Varma states the transformation somewhat enthusiastically as "the God-woman of Sufism bowed in front of the Lord-husband of *advaita*" (Varma, *Rahasyavād*, p. 50). The relationship between love as union and *viraha*, separation, is one of the most important motifs in bhakti literature. The essence of 'harmony' inheres in the total 'immersion' of the soul into the *act* of alternation. The *samādhi* which arises is frequently the purer because of it.

mystical trance is therefore lost in the 'unqualified' monotheistic spirituality endorsed by Tagore. In a way what happens here is that the translator suggests his own *paramparā*, his own tradition, and the sense of *alaukik* (the other-worldly) manifested here is not Kabir's but Tagore's own. Tagore not only interprets, he also 'inter-penetrates': he posits an alternative text for Kabir. As a result, the conventions of Kabir—his undercutting, his verse as an evocation of 'absences', a sense in fact of incompletion—are lost.

The only other point which should be made relates to words already discussed: *kāṅmīṅ* and *kāṅminī*. Tagore, obviously, feels that the words *nārī* and *kāṅminī* (he translates both these words as 'bride') are synonymous. But in the original, Kabir uses the words *kāṅmīṅ* and *kāṅminī* within a specific collocation which, being more potent in its sexual symbolism, suggests that at least the woman implied here is not the same as the *nārī* of the previous couplet. The larger metaphorical matrix within which the words occur establishes a metonymic relationship between them: their separate identities are just as important as their contiguity. Tagore maintains an absolute correspondence between the two substantives and does not give due weight to their difference. The poetic principle of *mādhurya bhāva* (the lover-beloved mood) upon which the entire *pad* is based considers such symbolism part of the overall convention.[27] The 'pain of separation' as a consequence is akin to a charged, enervating particle, the occasional glimpses of which we get in the verse of Gerard Manley Hopkins. And the overall ethos in Kabir is precisely that of the delicate balance of the alter-fulfilment (the images in the poem attempt to replace the absence with palpable sexual union) and the perpetual condition of the *virahiṇī*. Quite possibly, Tagore's strong sense of affirmation, of didacticism even—he himself writes very much within the tradition of *dāsya bhāva*, that of the servant before the master—intrude, and the 'reciprocity'[28] he attempts to give belongs to a different order of poetics.

What interests Tagore is really the personal mystical awareness of the Supreme Reality without the intervention of an *avatārik* form which he finds in the essentially *nirguṇa* bhakti of Kabir. In this, he overlooks the very considerable evidence of *saguṇa* bhakti found in his poetry.[29] One is led to believe that Tagore was convinced of Kabir's monotheism

27. See Acharya Viveshvar, trans. and V. Snatak, ed. *Bhaktirasāmṛtasindhu* (Delhi: Delhi University, 1963).

28. Steiner, *After Babel*, p. 395.

29. Tiwari, *Kabīr-vāṇī-sudhā*, pp. 78-94.

and saw his god as not being different from the God of the Bible. More to the point, Tagore was obviously attracted by Kabir's strong religious syncretism and quite possibly saw in Kabir elements of the kind of monotheistic reinterpretation of Hinduism which occurred in Bengal during his own lifetime — the cultural renaissance of which he was the apotheosis. So Tagore's 'sacralization' (as perceived in the translation) is not the bhakti sense of the sacred but a recognition of the sacred as the antonym of the profane. In Mircea Eliade's words, then, Kabir's verse would be 'hierophanic'.

> Man becomes aware of the sacred because it manifests itself, shows itself, as something wholly other than the profane. To designate the act of manifestation of the sacred, we have proposed the term *hierophany*.[30]

Yet a translation based upon these affirmations, upon sympathetic historicity alone, overlooks not just the pre-eminent sense of individuality in Kabir, but also his slightly unusual conception of bhakti in which ultimate liberation comes through death alone, through *jīvanmṛta* ('living as if dead').[31] Hence in the final cry of the *virahiṇī*, *binu dekhen jiu jāi re*, there is a kind of raw 'paganism' at work as well which Tagore does not acknowledge. The cry recalls all those images of 'absence' in Hindu iconography — the *satī* burning on the pyre, the child bride who remains a virgin forever, and so forth.

What the translation must achieve is a condition in verse where these things remain latent, as they indeed are in the original in the *sandhā-bhāṣā*, the twilight language, employed by Kabir. The translator must in turn select that 'stylistic period' within the tradition of the 'receptor language' which comes closest to the 'source language'. My own

30. Mircea Eliade, *The Sacred and the Profane*, trans. Willard R. Trask (New York: Harcourt, Brace & World, 1957), p. 11.

31. See Tiwari, *Kabīr-granthāvalī*, *sākhī* 19 *Jīvata mṛta kau aṅga*. The first *dohā* reads:

> *maratāṅ maratāṅ jaga muvā,*
> *muvai na jāṅnāṅ koi;*
> *dāsa Kabīrā yauṅ muvā,*
> *jyauṅ bahuri na maranāṅ hoi.*

> Dying, dying, the world dies,
>   who knows how to die?
> The servant Kabir died in such a way
>   that he'll never have to die again.

feeling is that Tagore's translation, effective as it is given the *a priori* problem of translating from a language belonging to a completely different culture, would have better captured the overall *bhāva* of the original if he had chosen an earlier period within the contextual patina — the language, for instance, of the Metaphysical poets, more specifically of John Donne in the Divine Poems. The later outgrowth of that tradition of devotional poetry — through the pantheism of the Romantics, to the aestheticism of Rossetti, Swinburne and the very early Yeats — is a *paramparā* which is quite alien to Kabir and to bhakti verse generally. During Kabir's own lifetime and soon after his death a similar process was at work in India. A tradition of Hindu hagiography claimed a place for the Julaha of Kashi, the weaver Kabir, within the Brahmanical orthodoxy. Yet Kabir, as Kabir-panthis never cease to point out, escaped this judgement not because the orthodox spared efforts to claim him as theirs by right but because Kabir held to truths which were his own, not those which could be re-slotted into the conventions of others.

DADU AND THE DADU-PANTH: THE SOURCES

WINAND M. CALLEWAERT

During the past few decades some lengthy studies have been devoted to Dadu Dayal and the Dadu-panth.[1] However, when writing the biography of Dadu, the authors give a list of the sources without apparently having consulted the works they mention, with the result that most literature on the subject available now is to a great extent the result of copying from a few earlier writers.[2] Often, a mass of details about Dadu is given without a clear distinction being made between the early documents and the later information from tradition. In most cases, however, the composition of an original work was followed by a wave of sectarian historians who indulged in laudatory embellishments to the point of the most fanciful miracle-mongering. For most sectarian biographers, Janagopal's account (*Dādū janma līlā*, ca. 1620, discussed below) has served as the basic source. For the history of the Dadu-panth written by English authors, the basic source is an article written by H.H. Wilson in 1828 (discussed below). In its basic data it has been copied again and again with only minor additions and changes.

When trying to find the kernel of truth from which later Dadu traditions grew, it is necessary to consider the two following factors: (a) the

1. In Hindi: Vasudev Sharma, *Sant-kavi Dādū aur unkā panth* (New Delhi: Shodhaprabandha Prakashan, 1969) and K.P. Simha, *Dādūpanth evaṃ uske sāhitya kā samīkṣātmak adhyayan* (Banaras: Kashi Vidyapith, 1971). In English: W.G. Orr, *A Sixteenth-Century Indian Mystic* (London: Lutterworth Press, 1947).

2. Orr applied a critical test to some oral traditions about Dadu and gave a summary and analysis of Dadu's teaching, with a translation of many representative verses. His study of Dadu's life is divided into two parts. In the first part, "The Life of Dadu in Tradition" (pp. 26-44), the narrative "is based almost entirely on a little work entitled The Life Story of Dadu" (p. 26). Although he observes that "this poem has undergone considerable revision at the hand of later editors" (p. 26), he fails to distinguish the earlier accounts from those of later editions. In the second part (chapter 4) Orr critically examines the historicity of four points which have given rise to some debate: (1) Dadu's birthplace, (2) his caste and profession, (3) his religious teacher, (4) his interview with Akbar. The abundance of additional information which Orr includes seems to be presented with a critical mind, but would have been much more valuable if the sources had been mentioned regularly. It seems as if he has gathered most of his information from oral informants who in turn relied mainly on sectarian sources and oral traditions.

time-lag between the life of Dadu and the date of compilation of his biography, and (b) the tendency of both oral and written traditions to conform to certain archetypes for the behavior of Sants, telling us how they *should* have acted. To give only one example, illustrating the last factor: even if it is not true that Dadu was invited by Akbar and went to see him in Fatehpur Sikri, it was fitting that such an incident be recorded, since many other Sants were said to have been invited by Akbar. Thus, an examination of the sources must consider not only their date of composition, but their sectarian assumptions as well.

Sectarian Sources

The earliest source for the biography of Dadu (1544-1603) is the *Dādū janma līlā* written by his disciple Janagopal, probably soon after Dadu's death. (A critical edition and English translation of this work will be appearing shortly.) Orr remarks that "the original Life Story may perhaps be dated between 1610 and 1620 and its final revision about 1720-30."[3] The work was edited "on the basis of seven mss." and published by Sukhdayal Dadu (Jaipur, 1947), hereafter referred to as '*Sukh*'.

During my search for Dadu-panthi manuscripts in North India,[4] I copied several manuscripts of the *Dādū janma līlā*, on the basis of which I am now preparing a critical edition. Though they may not be quite reliable, the following dates were found in the manuscripts:

Manuscript *A*	A.D. 1653
Manuscript *B*	A.D. 1654(?)
Manuscript *C*	A.D. 1658
Manuscript *D*	A.D. 1666
Manuscript *E*	A.D. 1739
Manuscript *F*	A.D. 1700(?)

Without going into details, I can mention that the number of verses in manuscripts *A*, *C* and *D*, in manuscripts *B*, *E* and *F*, and in *Sukh* vary considerably.

3. Orr, *Sixteenth-Century Mystic* p. 209.

4. See W.M. Callewaert, "Search for Manuscripts of the Dādūpanthī Literature," *Orientalia Lovaniensia Periodica* 4 (1973), pp. 155-67; 8 (1977), pp. 305-08. Also, "Microfilms of Hindi Literature," *Orientalia Lovaniensia Periodica* 9 (1978), pp. 185-88. A list (with indexes) of the manuscripts available on film with me is published in Winand M. Callewaert and Lieve de Brabandere, "Nirguṇa Literature on Microfilm in Leuven, Belgium," *IAVRI* (International Association of the Vrindavan Research Institute) *Bulletin* 9 (1980), pp. 28-48.

	Manuscripts	No. of verses
Chapter I	*A,C,D*	18
	B,E,F	44
	Sukh	67
Chapter II	*A,C,D*	18
	B,E,F	21
	Sukh	26
Chapter III	*A,C,D*	25
	B,E,F	29
	Sukh	37
Chapter IV	*A,C,D*	22
	B,E,F	48
	Sukh	59
(Total: 16 chapters)		

Important intentional variants in chapters I—IV of *BEF* and *Sukh* also show that the original text has been tampered with, especially with regard to the delicate questions of Dadu's non-Brahmanic origin and his occupation as a cotton carder. The earliest version (*ACD*) clearly and merely states that Dadu was born in Ahmedabad and that he was working as a cotton-carder (*dhuniyā*). Thus in verse I.6 of *ACD* we read: "There was great joy in the house of the *dhuniyā* [at his birth]." In *BEF* and *Sukh*, however, we read: "All were overjoyed." Then follows an interpolation in both *BEF* and *Sukh* telling the story of the Brahman merchant in Ahmedabad who found a baby in a river. In *Sukh*, we are told that this merchant's name was Lodiram. This name is also found in the Raghavadas *Bhaktamāl* (discussed below). The terms used in the interpolation of *BEF* to denote Dadu's birth clearly suggest that he was of divine origin: "He transformed His body and appeared in the form of a child," "He descended (*avatār lenā*)." Likewise, in verse I.7 of *ACD* we read, "When he was eleven years old, Baba Budha gave him *darśan*," while *BEF* and *Sukh* say, "When he was eleven years old, Hari appeared in the form of *būḍhā*." The latter may be used in its literal, non-specific sense meaning 'an old man', it may be an actual name, or it may designate a particular person bearing the name as a title of respect. There is no certainty about the identity of this person, but there is definitely a difference between the reading 'Baba Budha' and a literal reading of *būḍhā*. This difference is emphasized by the fact that Dadu's second-generation disciple Sundaradas, when tracing the origin of the Dadu-panth back to Brahma, calls Dadu's preceptor Vriddhananda. Discussing the identity of Dadu's spiritual preceptor, Orr remarks: "the belief that Buddhan was a historical person is very general among members of the Pantha... We have incontrovertible evidence of the presence in Sambhar [where Dadu stayed at one time] in the time of Akbar, of a Muhammedan saint of this name, whose lineal descendants still have their home in Sambhar."[5] The answer may perhaps be that the name 'Budha' was conferred as a title of respect on Dadu's preceptor, whoever he may have been.

Yet another example of variant readings is in the context of a burglary in Dadu's house. In verses III.9-10 of *ACD* we read: "When the thief found threads [of cotton]...the family awoke; [Dadu's] mother and wife said..." In *BEF* and *Sukh* we find instead: "When the thief found books, the saints awoke; the saints and disciples said,..." Verse IV. 5b in *ACD* ("he went on carding cotton") is missing in both *BEF* and *Sukh*.

The second (early?) source for Dadu's life is the *Sant guṇ sāgar* by Madhavadas, who may have been one of Dadu's disciples. Information about this work (two thousand verses, not edited) was given to me for the first time in 1973, by Mr. Sukhdayal Dadu of Delhi, who attributed it to Madhavadas. According to him, the work was composed in A.D. 1604, i.e. one year after Dadu's death. If this were true, then most of the fanciful details in the later *Dādū janma līlā* would have their origin in the *Sant guṇ sāgar*. However, P.H. Sharma of Jaipur has already expressed his doubts about the authenticity of this date.[6] The doubt was confirmed by the octogenarian Dadu-panthi sadhu Swami Narayandas of Ajmer, who writes that many manuscripts of this work have now been found, but that none is dated before 1910 A.D.[7] He refers briefly to the details about Dadu's life in the *Sant guṇ sāgar* which differ from Janagopal's account and presumes that the work was written at the beginning of the twentieth century.

Orr also refers to the *Sant guṇ sāgar* when he writes: "A second Janmalila [after Janagopal's] on much the same lines is ascribed to another of Dadu's disciples, Madhu Das. This too is probably a re-edited version of a genuinely early work. In its present form it can hardly

5. Orr, *Sixteenth-Century Mystic*, p. 54.

6. Purohit Harinarayan Sharma, *Sundar-granthāvalī*, 2 vols. (Calcutta: Rajasthan Research Society, 1936), 1:3, 93, 129.

7. Svami Narayandas, ed., *Śrī Dādū charitāmṛt*, 2 vols. (Jaipur: Mantri, Svami Jayaramadas Smriti Granthamala, 1975), pp. 5-6.

be placed earlier than 1800."[8] Considering the uncertain date of composition, however, I classify the information found in this biography as a recent, sectarian tradition.

A third early source is the *Bhaktamāl* by Jagga, one of the first generation of Dadu's disciples. In verses 33-69, a description is given of Dadu and his disciples. The work was edited by A. Nahata in his edition of the Raghavadas *Bhaktamāl*, (discussed below).[9] Unlike both the early and later versions of Janagopal's *Dādū janma līlā*, verse 34 in the present work already makes mention of Dadu's foster-father "by the name of Lodi." This seems to indicate that the change in the account about Dadu's origin was brought about at an early stage in the tradition.

Rajab's *Sarvāṅgī*, a fourth major source, contains an important variant reading concerning Dadu's *dhuniyā* origin. In the fourteenth verse of the *Grantha sādha mahimā* chapter (following chapter 22, *Bhajana pratāpā*) the texts of all the manuscripts used in our edition except *F* and *J* agree in writing *dhuniyā grahe utapanno Dādū mahāmuni*.[10] This verse is often quoted in the controversies about Dadu's origin and can be translated in two ways, on account of the double meaning of *dhuniyā*: "Dadu was born in the womb of a *dhuni*-woman," or "Dadu was found in a river." Two manuscripts (*F* and *J*, dated A.D. 1790) give a different reading: *dariyā madhye utapanno mahāmuni*, in which *dariyā* can only be translated as 'river'.

The *Bhaktamāl* of Raghavadas (A.D. 1720), with a *ṭīkā* or commentary by Chaturadas (A.D. 1800), is a gigantic work dealing with about twelve hundred Sants and devotees. The Nabhadas *Bhaktamāl* mentions only about six hundred Sants. Orr gives the following description of the work:

> The Bhaktamal, completed in 1713, is one of a number of similar works modelled on the more famous Bhaktamāl of Nābhājī, written about a century earlier. Ragho's poem, like the original, is often concise to the point of obscurity, and assumes on the part of the reader some previous knowledge of the events related. It is in fact, as its name suggests, an aid to memory, being primarily intended as a devotional manual. It has indeed another purpose — namely, to give Dadu his rightful place in the roll

8. Orr, *Sixteenth-Century Mystic* p. 209.

9. Agarchand Nahata, ed., *Rāghavadāskṛt bhaktamāl* (Jodhpur: Rajasthan Prachya Pratishthan, 1965), pp. 275-79.

10. Winand M. Callewaert, *The Sarvāṅgī of the Dādūpanthī Rajab* (Leuven: Dept. Orientalistiek, Katholieke Universiteit, 1978), p. 81.

> of saints. The main body of the work is non-sectarian, the bulk of its material being borrowed from Nabhaji; but interest naturally centres in Dadu and his followers, and the subsequent history of the Pantha...[The Commentary of Chaturadas] is now generally incorporated in modern versions of the Bhaktamāl; but copies of the older work without commentary may still be seen.[11]

The work was edited by A. Nahata (Jodhpur, 1965), mainly on the basis of two manuscripts dated A.D. 1804 and 1829 respectively. The text has both the original version of Raghavadas and the commentary by Chaturadas.[12] Another edition (Pushkar, 1969) was prepared by Swami Narayandas with his own commentary "because the first edition appears to be full of mistakes." Narayandas used nine manuscripts, dated between A.D. 1783 and 1879. In my report on my search for Dadu-panthi manuscripts, I have given A.D. 1720 as the date of compilation of the Raghavadas *Bhaktamāl.*[13] The date *saṃvat satrah sai satrahotarā* at the end of the work[14] was translated by Sharma as Samvat 1770 (A.D. 1713) instead of Samvat 1777 (A.D. 1720).[15] Both editors of the *Bhaktamāl* translate *satrahotarā* not as 77 but as 17, which would make the work much earlier, i.e. Samvat 1717 or A.D. 1660. This early date (1660) looks improbable, and is also contradicted by the following discipleship lineage given by Narayandas: (1) Dadu, (2) Bare Sundaradas, (3) Prahladadas, (4) Haridas, (5) Raghavadas. The details about Dadu's origin, caste, etc. are in agreement with the enlarged version of Janagopal's *Janma līlā.*[16]

In *The Sarvāṅgī of the Dādūpanthī Rajab*, I have listed a total of twenty-three works dealing with biographical data about Dadu.[17] They range from ca. A.D. 1620 to A.D. 1912. As stated above, most of these works repeat what Janagopal wrote, but they also add a few further details. Only one example will be given to illustrate this. In Janagopal's works, it is only said that Dadu was born in Ahmedabad in A.D. 1544. Nowadays, a big annual festival is held at Naraina on the birthday anniversary of Dadu, which is said to be the eighth day of the bright half of

11. Orr, *Sixteenth-Century Mystic*, pp. 213-14.
12. Nahata, *Bhaktamāl*, pp. 1-278.
13. Callewaert, "Search for Manuscripts," p. 157.
14. Svami Narayandas, ed., *Śrī Rāghavadās jī virachit bhaktamāl* (Jaipur: Shri Dadudayalu Mahasabha, 1969), p. 898.
15. Sharma, *Sundar-granthāvalī*, introduction, p. 2.
16. Narayandas, *Bhaktamāl*, p. 8.
17. Callewaert, *Sarvāṅgī*, pp. 22-29.

Phalgun, i.e. about the end of February. However, the accurate date (*phālguṇ śukalā aṣṭamī*) appears for the first time in Atmabihari's *Śrī Dādū charitra* (about A.D. 1830).

Non-Sectarian Sources

Besides the sectarian works which have been discussed above there are several sources which were composed outside the Dadu-panth. They are among the earliest sources available and the information they give about matters such as Dadu's profession as a cotton-carder is all the more important since these sources seem to be free of all sectarian bias. What is probably the first reference to Dadu outside the Dadu-panthi literature is found in a verse of Eknath and is quoted in the Marathi work *Sakal sant gāthā*. In his poem on the Nanak-panthis, Eknath says: *Nānakā ghara Dādū piñjārī nāma japana*...[18] This can be rendered as: "The *piñjārī* Dadu is like Nanak in the meditation on the Name..."

The second non-sectarian reference to Dadu is found in *abhaṅg* 4299 of Tukaram's *Gāthā*.[19] The dates of Tukaram are generally taken as A.D. 1598-1650. Since Dadu died in 1603, the year 1635 seems to be a reasonably approximate date for this piece of information. It begins with the statement "Pride of caste has never made any man holy, says Tuka. The untouchables have crossed the ocean of life by God-devotion, and the Puranas sing their praise." Then follows a list of those who were saved in spite of their low caste or different religious faith. The list includes Gora the potter, Rohidas (Raidas) the cobbler, Kabir the *momin* (weaver), Latif the Muslim, Sena the barber, Kanhopatra the daughter of a concubine, *Dadu the cotton-carder*, Chokhamela and Banka the Untouchables, Jani the maidservant and Mairala, the low-caste woman. The *abhaṅg* is supposed to be authentic. In it, Dadu is specifically mentioned by Tukaram as a *piñjārī*, one engaged in the profession of carding (or rather loosening or breaking up of) cotton.

Another early reference is found in a Persian work called the *Dabistān-i-mazāhib*, written in the mid-seventeenth century A.D. If the work was written about A.D. 1665, as maintained by Blochmann, it is a relatively close witness:

> Another sect is that of the Dādū Panthians. Dādū was one of the cotton-carders in the village Narainā, in the district of

18. T.H. Avate, ed., *Sakal sant gāthā*, (Poona: 1924), No. 3964.

19. Tukārām, *Śrī Tukārāmāñchāgāthā*. 2 vols. (Bombay: Government Central Press, 1950), 1:594.

> Marwar. In the time of the Padshah Akbar (who inhabits heaven) Dādū devoted himself to the state of a Durvesh, and assembled many disciples about him. He prohibited his followers to worship idols, to eat the flesh of any animal or to hurt any living being; but he did not order them to abandon woman and wife or to withdraw from all business of the world; but he left it free to anyone to give up or to cultivate the connection and the intercourse with men.[20]

The quotation not only confirms the statement in Tukaram about Dadu being a cotton-carder, but also throws light on the already existing sect, known to outsiders for its rules governing external behavior.

Western Sources

The first known account about the Dadu-panth written by a Western author is in H.H. Wilson's "A Sketch of the Religious Sects of the Hindus."[21] The note by the editor introducing Wilson's account in the *Journal of the Asiatic Society of Bengal* (1837) says that Wilson's "notice of the sect was chiefly obtained from Lieut. Col. Smith and partly from verbal information at Benares, where the elder branch of the same dissenters, the Kabirpanthias, have a principal establishment."[22] This account by Wilson is very important since the data given in it ("at Benares") will be found in most subsequent articles on Dadu in English, for nearly a century, with only a few minor additional details. In *The Sarvāṅgī of the Dādūpanthī Rajab*, I refer to twenty-four such works or articles published after Wilson's article, which give descriptions of the origin of the Dadu-panth, the contemporary situation and the growth of the military branch of the Dadu-panth (the Nagas).[23] Wilson calls the Dadu-panth "one of the direct ramifications of the Ramanandi stock; its founder is said to have been a pupil of one of the Kabir-panthi

20. D. Shea and A. Troyer, eds., *Dabistān-i-mazāhib*, 3 vols., (Paris, 1843), 2:233.

21. H.H. Wilson, "A Sketch of the Religious Sects of the Hindus," *Asiatic Researches* 16 (1828), pp. 79ff, quoted as a preface to the contribution made by G.R. Siddons, "Extract and Translation of one of the Granthas, or sacred Books, of the Dadupanthi Sect," in *Journal of the Asiatic Society of Bengal* 6 (1837), pp. 481-87 and pp. 751-56. These excerpts are the first known English translation of any Dadupanthi literature. Wilson's article was later reprinted in H.H. Wilson, *Religious Sects of the Hindus* (London, 1861; reprinted, Calcutta: Sushil Gupta, 1958), pp. 57-58.

22. *Journal of the Asiatic Society of Bengal* 6 (1837).

23. Callewaert, *Sarvāṅgī*, pp. 34-56.

teachers, and to be the fifth in descent from Ramananda, viz. 1. Kabir; 2. Kamal; 3. Jamal; 4. Bimal; 5. Buddhan; 6. Dadu."[24]

Conclusions

On the basis of my research on the sources for the biography of Dadu and the history of the Dadu-panth, I have reached the following conclusions:

1. The earliest biography of Dadu (Janagopal's *Dādū janma līlā*) has been changed and enlarged in a very early stage after its composition. Most interpolated details are encomiastic and more miraculous. This fact emphasizes the need to work on reliable manuscripts.
2. Later biographies only add more details, which clearly grew out of the oral tradition. These additional elements seem to conform to an Indian archetype for the behavior of Sants, which involves the performance of miracles in order to impress their audiences—even the Emperor Akbar.
3. In the early hagiography of Dadu, we notice a tendency towards Brahmanization. Although Dadu himself stressed that caste in fact was not important, later disciples in the sect tried to hide his (possible) Muslim origin and Muslim preceptor (?) and invented an explanation for his connection with the *dhuniyās* (cotton carders).
4. The basis for English writings (and recent Hindi writings) on the subject of Dadu and the Dadu-panth is Wilson's article of 1828. Relying mainly on informants in Banaras, Wilson started the tradition of calling Dadu a disciple in the lineage of Ramananda and Kabir.

24. Quoted in Siddons, "Extract and Translation," p. 480.

THE SANT IN SUR DAS

JOHN STRATTON HAWLEY

Sur Das is justly famous for the *bhramargīt* poems in which his *gopīs* lash out against Udho, the messenger of Yoga and *nirguṇa* religion. Here, seemingly, is one Vaishnava bhakta who cannot possibly be identified with the Sants and what they are usually said to stand for: bhakti in the *nirguṇa* mode. In the essay that follows, however, I hope to make a case for the reality of this unlikely creature, the Sant in Sur Das. I will do so by exploring certain themes in his *vinaya* poetry, the songs of petition and self-remonstration that most directly resemble the utterances of poets who are more customarily called Sants than Sur. As we shall see, however, salient differences do remain. For instance, although Sur assumes communities of Sants (*satsaṅg*) as part of his world and labels them as such, indicating that he participates in the general Sant milieu, he accords little significance to such communities. What matters instead is a direct confrontation with the divine. Even this radical message, however, allies him in surprising ways with Sants such as Kabir, for in his own way Sur proclaims a message of unqualified faith that is no less stringent than that of the great Sant. It would be confusing, no doubt, to call this an expression of *nirguṇa* bhakti, for that label could hardly mean what it does when applied to a Sant like Kabir; but Sur's stance is closely analogous and no less extreme.

A Spectrum of Sants

The familiar taxonomy for popular devotion in medieval North India rests on a theological distinction between *nirguṇa* and *saguṇa*. *Saguṇa* bhaktas worship through the attributes of the objects of faith, hence in the nature of the case they can easily enough be distinguished not only from *nirguṇa* bhaktas but also from other members of the *saguṇa* camp according to their emphasis on either Ram or Krishna. By the same token this theological rubric suggests that there is no further need to differentiate among *nirguṇīs*. As worshippers of a God whose formlessness is his most significant property (the term and the ranking are, of course, misleading), they too resist formal differentiation. Still, they are allied with one another not only on the basis of what they lack, a consistent Krishnaite or Ramaite orientation, but on the basis of certain shared emphases: an inward faith, the conviction of the importance of the guru (whether external or internal), sometimes an explicit social protest, and ever so occasionally the mention of one by another.

The contrast between Sants and Vaishnavas, *nirguṇī*s and *saguṇī*s, however, is not always so neat as this taxonomy would imply. This is clearly evident in the social arena. One might logically predict that Vaishnava religious movements claiming one or more of these bhakti figures as their founders or inspirers would have a clearer organization than their Sant counterparts, since the community could be so directly shaped around a specifiable, 'qualified' (*saguṇa*) object of devotion, Ram or Krishna. Scholarship in Hindi typically speaks of a rather ill-defined Sant persuasion (*sant mat*) for just this reason. The fact is, however, that religious movements representing this Sant persuasion bear organizational patterns no less definite than their Vaishnava counterparts. The Dadu, Kabir, and Nanak (i.e., Sikh) panths are as well articulated as the Gaudiya, Vallabha, and Radhavallabha *sampradāy*s. Indeed, it is the Ramaite component of medieval bhakti, not the Sant, that has failed more than any other to spawn clearly recognizable sectarian communities, with the case of the Ramanandis as the single notable exception and even that a bit mystifying.[1]

Such difficulties of classification are fortunate, for they alert us to the likelihood that the religious world in which the medieval bhaktas participated and which they so shaped was much more fluid in its organization than that of subsequent generations.[2] To divide the principal figures of this period (ca. 1400-1650) into Ramaite and Krishnaite bhaktas on the one hand and Sants on the other is to run the risk of obscuring the important connections that related them to one another and made them in significant ways part of the same movement.[3] There

1. On problems relating to the connection between this sect in its more recent forms and the shadowy Ramananda, however, see Charlotte Vaudeville, *Kabīr*, vol. 1 (Oxford: Clarendon Press, 1974), pp. 113-14.

2. See Wilfred Cantwell Smith, "The Crystallization of Religious Communities in Mughul India," in Mojtaba Minovi and Iraj Afshar, eds., *Yād-nāme-ye Irāni-ye Minorsky* (Tehran: Tehran University, 1969), pp. 1-24.

3. In what follows I will occasionally have to refer to the movement as a whole, and will call it the bhakti movement, reserving the term Sant for a stream within the whole. This usage, though conventional and in accord with the precedent set long ago by Nabhadas, can be misleading. I must ask the reader to remember that if one gave greater weight to what its participants called one another, the term Sant would be equally appropriate as a designation of the whole.

were differences, of course: the *bhramargīt* poems of Sur Das and Nanda Das plainly make fun of the *nirguṇa* position, at least insofar as yogic, ascetic types are understood as its spokesmen. The remarkable thing, however, is that someone like Kabir, who is normally classed as *nirguṇī* and on occasion uses a Nath Yogi term of address, *avadhūt*, in a roughly collegial sense, is scarcely less sparing in his criticism of Yogis. Or to take the contrary case, while Kabir was uncompromising in his opposition to worship through images, some of the most forceful poems attributed to the supposedly like-minded Namdev associate him with a particular manifestation of divinity, Lord Pandurang of Pandharpur—and do so in '*nirguṇī*' terms!

We are forced to conclude, at the least, that we ought to think of the most influential poets of this early period as arrayed in a spectrum rather than clumped together in well-defined camps. Kenneth Bryant's distinction between Sants and Vaishnavas in rhetorical terms provides one way of describing the extremities of the spectrum: Kabir's appeal is to personal experience, particularly on the basis of his own, whereas Sur's appeal is to a shared dramatic legendry.[4] One will find more explicit reference to features of the everyday world, therefore, in the poetry of Kabir, Dadu and Namdev than in Sur or Tulsi, and there is a strong suggestion that such '*nirguṇīs*' inherit much from the emphases of the Nath Yogis.[5] Yet they share a surprisingly similar range of perspectives. In almost all cases, not just at the Vaishnava extreme, *viraha*, separation from the Lord, is interpreted as the true and rigorous form of Yoga; the Kabir who speaks in the *Bījak* is the only exception that comes to mind.[6] And the yogic goal of *mukti*, release from this world as such, is at some level called into question by all. To be sure it is Namdev, Kabir, Nanak, and Dadu who speak most familiarly of the *satguru*, but Mira does as well and there is even a hint or two in the poetry attributed to Sur. Sur, Tulsi, and later Tukaram make a great

4. Kenneth E. Bryant, "*Sant* and *Vaiṣṇava* Poetry: Some Observations on Method," in Mark Juergensmeyer and N. Gerald Barrier, eds., *Sikh Studies: Comparative Perspectives on a Changing Tradition* (Berkeley: Berkeley Religious Studies Series, 1979), pp. 67-68.

5. In regard to Kabir see Vaudeville, *Kabīr* 1:120-48. Also P.D. Barthwal, *The Nirguṇa School of Hindi Poetry* (Banares: Indian Book Shop, 1936), pp. 140-52. In regard to Nanak, see W.H. McLeod, *Gurū Nānak and the Sikh Religion* (Oxford: Clarendon Press, 1968), pp. 157-58.

6. See Linda Hess, "Studies in Kabir: Texts, Traditions, Styles and Skills," unpublished Ph.D. dissertation (University of California, Berkeley, 1980), chapter 2, section 7, pp. 49-51.

deal of the fact that the Lord has represented himself as a savior of sinners—but so does Namdev near the other end of the spectrum. And of course the hallmark of the whole group, from Sur to Kabir, is a trust in the absolute power of the name of God as such; and all agree that whatever designations are also possible, that name can be called Ram.

Later generations, with more narrowly defined loyalties, were often forced to awkward extremes in accounting for the catholicity of their revered predecessors. The case of Kabir is well known. The puzzle was how Kabir, as a member of a caste which had embraced Islam, could have sung the name of Ram, for by 1700 or so that name had come to be thought of as a particularly Vaishnava province. Hence one has, in Priya Das's commentary on the *Bhaktamāl*, the story of how Kabir, the Julaha, elicited an inadvertent initiation from Ramananda.[7] And later, as so often, a tale develops that establishes that Kabir was really a Brahman all along, and Julaha only by adoption, which makes the whole affair impeccably legitimate—or would if it were not for Kabir's own disdain for Brahman pretensions. Similar chroniclers evidently wondered how Namdev could have been at once a bhakta of Pandurang (Krishna) and at the same time capable of condemning sectarian allegiances of all sorts. Namdev was primarily remembered as a *nirguṇī* Sant, so the solution was to periodize his life in such a way that he grew away from his attachment to the Lord of Pandharpur and adhered to a more strictly interior religion.[8]

In the case of Sur the interested parties were *saguṇī* rather than *nirguṇī*, so the opposite transformation was effected. At the hands of the Vallabha *sampradāy*, Sur's life was demarcated into two phases separated by an encounter with Vallabha which entirely reoriented his perspective.[9] The poems of Sur that did not describe the sports of

7. Nabhaji, *Śrī bhaktamāl* (Lucknow: Tejkumar Press, 1961), *tīkā kavitt* 328, p. 481.

8. I am not sure what is the earliest attestation of the story of Namdev's devotion to Pandurang and subsequent *dīkṣā* at the hands of Sant Vithoba Khechar. It does not appear in the *Bhaktamāl*. Standard works report it without citation, e.g., Ramchandra Mishra, *Sant Nāmdev aur Hindī sāhitya* (Farrukhabad: Sailendra Sahitya Sadan, 1969), p. 61, and Parashuram Chaturvedi, *Uttarī Bhārat kī sant-paramparā* (Allahabad: Leader Press, 1972), p. 110.

9. *Chaurāsī Vaiṣṇavan kī vārtā*, with the commentary of Hariray (Mathura: Shri Govardhan Granthamala Karyalaya, 1970), pp. 405-08. English translation, omitting the poetry, in Richard Barz, *The Bhakti Sect of Vallabhācārya* (Faridabad: Thomson Press, 1976), pp. 112-14.

Krishna then become the documents of his life before enlightenment, and the Krishna poems followed. It was inconceivable to the Vallabhite theologian(s) who shaped the *Chaurāsī Vaiṣṇavan kī vārtā* that the two could mix.

But in fact, as I would like to show, they did. In the poems of Sur which have come to be called collectively his *vinaya* poems, it becomes clear that even the poet who held up the *nirguṇī* position to such ridicule in his *bhramargīt* poems has a dimension that brings him into the company of the Sants.

Sur's Vinaya *Poems: Old Collections*

In the edition of the *Sūr sāgar* that is currently standard, that of the Nagari Pracharini Sabha (NPS), one locates Sur's *vinaya* poetry—his poems of petition, his prayers—with considerable difficulty. The reason is that the manuscript that was evidently a principal model for the Sabha editors (NPS 269/26, dated Vikram 1850 [A.D. 1793]) went even farther in its attempt to cast Sur in the Vallabhite mold than had the *Chaurāsī Vaiṣṇavan kī vārtā* itself. It categorized the whole of Sur's poetry in such a way that each poem would fit (sometimes awkwardly) into one of the episodes described in the twelve books of the *Bhāgavata Purāṇa*. The *vinaya* poems are distributed among several headings appropriate to the first two books.

In the earliest manuscripts of Sur's poetry—Kenneth E. Bryant and I have studied those dated before about A.D. 1700—there is only the scantest reference to the *Bhāgavata Purāṇa*, and nothing to suggest a particular debt to it, as in some later poems, or a knowledge of its organization.[10] Quite the contrary, these poems, once collected, were organized either by theme (most commonly), by raga, or by loose alphabetical groupings. Like most poetry to come out of the bhakti movement, then, these were occasional poems later collected.

10. For details see Hawley, "The Early *Sūr Sāgar* and the Growth of the Sur Tradition", *Journal of the American Oriental Society* 99:1 (1979), pp. 64-68, and *Sūr Dās*: *Poet, Singer, Saint* (Seattle: University of Washington Press, 1984), chapter 2. The system for enumerating manuscripts that is followed here and is adopted in the latter work, was originally suggested by Bryant, "Toward a Critical Edition of the Sursagar," (unpublished paper delivered to the international conference on Sur Das, Calcutta, December 1978). I regret that a number of the judgements I make in the current article must remain somewhat tentative until the completion of a full critical edition of the *Sūr sāgar*, a task in which Bryant and I are now engaged.

This is the case with Sur's *vinaya* poems as well, and early manuscripts do not agree about what they should be called. The *vinaya* label that has become current recently (in the Gita Press edition, for instance) seems to have been borrowed by analogy from the first great collector of poems of this type, Tulsi Das. His *Vinaya patrikā* was largely a reworking of earlier poems which he, like Sur, had composed independently.[11] The term *binatī* (or *vinatī*, 'prayer, petition'), a close relative of *vinaya*, does indeed occur in early Sur poems of this genre, but as it happens, none of the early scribe-editors seized upon it to characterize the group as a whole.[12]

Of the seven manuscripts that provide substantial collections, four omit any designation at all. In two cases the poems are distributed through the manuscript according to their ragas (Bikaner 2, Jaipur 2); in the others (Jaipur 5, Allahabad 1) they are numbered in separate series and then listed one after another, but without headings. Udaipur 1 is the first manuscript to provide headings, and it does so by distinguishing ten poems of petition voiced by figures in the *Mahābhārata* and the twenty-five couplets called *Sūrpachīsī* from the general mass, 137 poems called *bhagat* because they have to do with bhakti.[13] At almost the same time, the scribe of Bikaner 4 (or the manuscript he copied) made a different distinction, between 112 poems of petition addressed to the Lord, which he designated *karuṇā*, and 23 poems of inner dialogue and remonstration, which he called *pramodh*—the poet's attempt to instruct and correct himself.[14]

There are other early manuscripts which conform, seemingly, to the Vallabhite perspective on Sur and contain either only a very few *vinaya* poems (Bikaner 3 has four; Kota 1, six) or none at all (Bikaner 1 and two related manuscripts, Jaipur 3 and 4). Given that this is sometimes the case, however, it is striking that when the *vinaya* poems do appear they are present in considerable numbers. They account for anywhere

11. The *Rām gītāvalī*, on which see F.R. Allchin's introduction to his translation of Tulsi Das, *The Petition to Rām* (London: George Allen and Unwin, 1966), pp. 37ff.

12. NPS 4.14, 42.1, 162.5, 170.2, and 201.2. The NPS edition has *vinaya* in 124.12, but the manuscripts read *binatī* or *vinatī* (B2: *vanatī*).

13. The *Sūrpachīsī* couplets were different enough from the rest that they were sometimes anthologized separately, as in Hindi MS no. 70 in the Anup Sanskrit Library in Bikaner (Vikram 1752) and Hindi MS no. 6/3/3 in the Sarasvati Bhandar at Kankarauli (Vikram 1751).

14. These bear general comparison to some of the poems of Kabir. See e.g., *pads* 48, 50, 53, 55, 86, and 93 in Charlotte Vaudeville, *Kabīr*, vol. 2 (Oxford: Clarendon Press, forthcoming).

from 10 percent to 22 percent of the total number of poems, and in the case of Jaipur 5 we have a text that is entirely devoted to the *vinaya* genre. Furthermore, the middle portion of the oldest dated Sur manuscript, Jaipur 1, is an independently numbered *vinaya* anthology that intersperses some of Sur's *vinaya* poems with those of other poets. Only one manuscript of the *Sūr sāgar* adopts the scheme that was later to become orthodox and places the *vinaya* poems at the beginning of the collection, as if they were to be understood as superseded by a conversion at the hands of Vallabhacharya. Not surprisingly, this manuscript is one of the most recent in the group and was compiled at Pachor, near the important Vallabhite seat at Kota, in which city it is now housed (Kota 1). In all other cases the *vinaya* poems are either distributed throughout the collection, as in manuscripts organized by raga, or, more commonly, placed precisely where they should not be from a sectarian Vallabhite point of view: at or near the end.

In the early manuscripts, then, we seem to have a clear difference of opinion as to whether Sur's *vinaya* poems were to be regarded as an integral part of the poet's message, with the majority feeling that they were. This would tend to give credence to the argument that in the early years most people did not regard Sur as being of an entirely different stripe from those of his contemporaries who are now known as Sants. Other evidence bears on the same point. A number of anthologies, many of them small but some more extensive, survive from this early period,[15] and in not a few of them the compositions of poets who were later to be called *saguṇa* bhaktas are included along with the compositions of those whom we have come to think of as Sants. Sur and Tulsi appear alongside Namdev and Kabir, and in varying orders. Those who made collections of the poetry of various bhakta/Sants in this early period had a natural tendency to include a significant number of *vinaya* poems, usually a higher proportion than one typically finds in independent collections. Both the fact of such groupings and their content, then, call into question too strong a dichotomy between Sant and Vaishnava.

It was some years before this dichotomy was widely observed. By the middle of the seventeenth century the Vallabha *sampradāy* was insisting that when Sur met Vallabhacharya he left behind all of his poetry that was not specifically bounded in the world of Krishna-*līlā*—

15. Such manuscripts are usually untitled and referred to in the catalogues under headings such as *phuṭkar pad, padāvalī,* or *khaṇḍit prati.*

that is, he gave up the very poetry that had tied him most directly to the Sants. Nonetheless poems continued to be contributed to the less sectarian, *vinaya* portions of the *Sūr sāgar*. These later poems, in fact, make clearer and more frequent reference to such marks of the Sant tradition as *satguru, satsaṅg* and *sabad* than one finds in earlier poems of the same group.[16] In such poems one observes a tendency for the poet to be 'routinized' along Sant lines.

But the bulk of the development and routinizing of the *Sūr sāgar* after 1700 came, of course, from the sectarian Vaishnava side. This leaves us with the odd and notable fact that of all the sections of the NPS *Sūr sāgar*, the one containing the highest proportion of poems from the early manuscripts is precisely the *vinaya* section, the part that fits so uneasily into the structure of the work as the NPS editors conceived it. And this is particularly the case for the poems which lie at its core, the boasts and complaints of Sur the sinner. It is a rare occasion when one can open the NPS *Sūr sāgar* and be confident that all of what one reads is attested in the early manuscript, but that does happen in the *vinaya* section. If one opens to pp. 44-45 of the 1972 edition, all nine poems (*pad*s 131-139) date to about 1700 or before.

Common Sant Themes in the Early Vinaya *Poetry*

The most numerous, and in many ways the most impressive, of Sur's *vinaya* poems are those that merit the name strictly speaking, *pad*s in which the poet calls upon the Lord of salvation. To assume that they are in the same vein as the petitions of the *Vinaya patrikā*. however, is to miss the distinctive characteristic of many of them, for they bespeak anything but the humility (however measured and confident) of a Tulsi Das. These are poems of bitter complaint and strenuous contest in which the poet demands that the Lord follow through on promise and precedent and save him, a sinner, or relinquish any claim to being known as savior of the fallen. Other moods, represented in somewhat less numerous poems, array themselves around this theme.

16. In NPS 407.2, for instance, the term *satguru* is explicitly associated with the concept of *sabad*. In NPS 360.7-8 *satsaṅg* is praised in the most familiar sort of way. The earlier *sādhi samādhi* (B4) becomes the formulaic *sahaj samādhi* in later readings of the same poem (NPS 312.2), and a similar shift toward familiar usage may be observed in NPS 356.8. In its only manuscript reading (J4, a relatively late attestation) it has the Sants as the objects or beneficiaries of songs to be sung in praise of Hari (*santana ko*); in the NPS version they are rather, as one would expect, the context in which such songs might be sung (*santana mili*).

There are poems in which some of the protagonists of the *Mahābhārata* also call upon the Lord — particularly Draupadi, whose situation is the most extreme and the most scandalous. There are poems of reassurance that such petitions as these will be heard: the NPS labels these *bhakta-vatsaltā* (Krishna's solicitude for his devotees, like a parent's for a child). And in quite the opposite vein there are poems of deep remorse, in which the poet laments a life wasted in absorption with the things of this world, contemplates death, and finds that it is too late to change. These are poems of an unusual sobriety, and unlike most later additions to the genre, they are not often relieved by a message of hope. The very act of giving voice to one's condition before the Lord provides the only glimmer.[17] In a companion series, the poet's reflections turn to self-accusation and he remonstrates with his own heart.

Among these outpourings are several motifs that place Sur firmly in the company of the Sants. There is the frequent mention of death, particularly as Yama[18] or as the devouring 'snake of time' (*kāl-vyāl*)[19], accompanied in both cases by the plea to be released. And because death is so pressing a concern, those whom the Lord has saved from its noose and jaws, Ajamil and Gajendra respectively, figure with special prominence when Sur is listing the recipients of the Lord's grace. When the poet is lamenting his wasted life, figures of speech common in poems of the Sants appear: the dogs, jackals, and vultures that symbolize the voracious world of the senses, for instance,[20] or the bird of the soul that has been so callously entrapped.[21] Then too there is the parrot who watches carefully over the ripening of the silk-cotton fruit until it appears juicy and full, and pecks it at last only to have the inedible cottony substance inside fly away in the breeze.[22] So

17. In commenting on a parallel genre in Bengali, poems of self-deprecation called *kākuvāda* or *kākukti*, Joseph T. O'Connell proposes that the act of throwing oneself at the Lord's feet has a hidden and intrinsic salvific power because it reveals the proper ontological relation of humans to the divine, namely servanthood. O'Connell, "Gaudiya Vaisnava Symbolism of Deliverance (*uddhara nistara...*) from Evil." *Journal of Asian and African Studies* 15:1-2 (1980), pp. 126-27, 131-32.

18. E.g., NPS 67.6, 111.2 and 334.6 Attention to the last moment of life as such, however, is more a feature of later additions to the *Sūr sāgar* than of these early poems. E.g. NPS 80.4 and 85.4.

19. E.g., NPS 117.12 in B4 and 312.12 (B4, J5: *kāl var vyāl*; U2: *kāl bal vyāl*; cf. J2: *byāl*, B3: *jam jāl*; also 326.8.

20. E.g., NPS 150.6.

21. E.g., NPS 337.

22. E.g., NPS 59.2. Cf. Vaudeville, *Kabir* 2: *pad* 50.

do we nurture our affections in this world, but they are ultimately indigestible.[23]

Graphic as some of these poems are in depicting the extremity of the human condition with a telling metaphor, most stop well short of attempting to convert the hearer with a gruesome catalogue of the ugly details of old age and death such as one finds in Kabir. Later compilers of the *Sūr sāgar*, it is true, transgressed these limits of Sur's sensibility; hence one does occasionally find such poems in current editions.[24] But for Sur it was the spiritual consequences of life in this world that were so horrifying, not the physical realities. He does refer to bodily decay, but it is more a sign of inner decrepitude than a matter of concern in its own right, and it is in depicting the state of the heart that Sur employs such familiar Sant sayings as that a blanket, once died black, will never turn another color[25] or that an arrow can never pierce a stone.[26] He does not, however, explicitly identify the arrow with the *sabad*, as Kabir does,[27] and his fondness for the black cloth or blanket has much to do with the fact that black is also Krishna's color and the *gopīs* are hopelessly dyed.[28] Sur and the Sants share much, but he retains (as do many of them, individually) a particular perspective.

A comparable difference emerges in regard to the issue of equality before God, with its implicit criticism of social hierarchies. Sur believes this as much as Kabir, but his style of exposition is different. Instead of lashing out at the meaninglessness of social distinctions and the hypocrisy of the great, Sur cites example after example in which the Lord, primarily as Krishna, has preferred the company of the low and outcaste to that of the pure and well-placed.[29] Indeed, the poet ridicules his own pretensions.

The Sants, especially Kabir, are remembered for their trenchant perceptions about human depravity. Their perspective is tough and

23. *Sākhīs* 163-165 of the *Bījak*, each of which concerns the image of the parrot and the *semar* tree, are translated by Linda Hess in collaboration with Shukdev Singh, in *The Bījak of Kabir* (San Francisco: North Point Press, 1983), p. 108. For the original, see Kabir, *Bījak*, with commentary by Khemraj Shrikrishnadas (Bombay: Shrivenkateshvar Press, 1968), pp. 466-67.

24. E.g., NPS 86.

25. NPS 332.8. Cf. Vaudeville, *Kabīr* 1: 24.17, p. 279.

26. NPS 332.7. Cf. Vaudeville, *Kabīr* 1: 22.2, p. 272.

27. Loc. cit. Cf. Vaudeville, *Kabīr* 1: p. 274.

28. E.g., NPS 2276.5-6. Cf. 4380.5-6 and many other poems in the *bhramargīt* section on blackness.

29. NPS 12, 19, and a great many others.

realistic, and the path to salvation that they describe is often regarded as more difficult than that presented by Vaishnava poets.[30] But there is a sense in which Sur's assessment of the nature of human need in the *vinaya* poems is even more radical than Kabir's, particularly in what he says about himself. In Kabir, especially as we meet him in the *Bījak*, there is a definite self-confidence.[31] Not so Sur. In the old poems of the *Sūr sāgar*, he never places himself in the position of criticizing others; it is only himself he ventures to call a fool. He does that and leaves his listeners to draw their own conclusions about themselves.[32] It is the very occasional poem in which he is confident enough to declare himself a servant bought by the Lord.[33] Sur leaves that sort of affirmation to Tulsi.[34] And the question of having attained an experience of plenitude (*pūrā*), a state Kabir knows, does not arise for Sur in the *vinaya* context.[35] Similarly it is uncharacteristic for him to praise any quality of the human heart save for its ability to call upon the Lord. This is true even for love (*prem, prīti*), which Kabir so openly praises.[36] Very rarely is it singled out as that element in people to which God responds.[37] For Sur it is the fact of Krishna that equalizes all beings before him, not any quality inherent in people. Likewise Sur emphasizes the unique privilege of the human condition, namely the potential availability of salvation, far less than one would think from reading the NPS edition. Poems that make a point of the countless births it takes to be born human are rare in the earlier layers of the Sur tradition.[38] Sur is sus-

30. See, for example, McLeod, *Nānak*, p. 152: "the easy path of traditional bhakti."

31. See Hess, "Studies in Kabir," chapter 2, section 11, pp. 63-68.

32. E.g. NPS 77.8; 103.8 in U1, B4, J4; and *man pramodh* poems such as NPS 337, where this is the general theme.

33. NPS 171.1. In general servitude is not a sufficient definition of lowliness for Sur; it must be depravity.

34. Tulsi Das, *Vinaya patrikā* [hereafter VP], with the '*Hari-toṣiṇī ṭīkā*' (Allahabad: Lokbharati Prakashan, 1977), 154.3, 155.5, 249.3, 263.1, 271.1, 271.4, 274.4, etc.

35. Vaudeville, *Kabīr* 2: *pad* 133.4. The poem in which this affirmation occurs is strikingly different from its counterpart in the *Sūr sāgar*, NPS 153. Both poets take the role of the dancer who has performed so long that there is not another step left in him. For Kabir, however, this emptying of every human desire and versatility yields, paradoxically, plenitude, *pūrā*, the presence of Ram. For Sur, however, there is no such release, and the poem ends in a devastated petition to the Lord to do away with this ignorant, misguided life (*avidyā*).

36. E.g., ibid. 1: 1.21, 14.15 and 14.31-35, on pp. 157, 222, and 225-26.

37. NPS 13.1 (*prīti*, B3, J2, cf. A1) and 19.2-30.

38. As against later entries such as NPS 68.8 or 317.5; cf. VP 83.1, 84.2. On

picious of all status, even Darwinian hierarchies: what matters in life has nothing to do with one's position. When Sur talks of status there is irony in his voice, as when, paradigmatically, he styles himself the best of sinners. If one must have hierarchy, better to be low than high.

Sur on the Sants

In accord with all this there is little praise for the Sants as such. Hari is Sur's refuge, not they; what importance they have derives purely from the fact that they sing the Lord's name(s). In this respect Sur is measurably different from his Sant compeers. Kabir, for example, frequently plays on the meaning of the word *sādh* (*sādhu*) so as to point his listener toward the original designation of the term. It means not the ascetics of this world but the good; their company, says Kabir, is heaven.[39] This interiorizing conception of true religion is by no means foreign to Sur, but one meets it by and large in the *bhramargīt*, where the *gopīs* are the models, rather than in the *vinaya* poems where the human *satsaṅg* might have been expected to play such an exemplary role.

The NPS *Sūr sāgar* does contain poems that praise the Sants as such, but they are overwhelmingly more recent additions to the corpus. Kabir's redefinition of *sādhu*, for instance, is echoed in a poem which proposes that *satsaṅg* is the true form of *sanyās*, giving life rather than leading to death, and offering to those who practise it the trackless forest into which they should truly abandon themselves — the endless singing of the name of Ram.[40] One can also read that to offer hospitality to a Sant (the term means here a religious specialist, a wanderer) is to perform an action as worthy as countless pilgrimages.[41] Such statements are entirely foreign to the early strata of the *Sūr sāgar*. Nor is there much emphasis on the notion, so frequent in later poems, that the Lord is the benefactor particularly of the Sants, that he comes into the world to tear away the net of death for their sake.[42] Such praise of a person

the contrary, Sur is likely to be found, in the earlier poems, lamenting how many lives — human, presumably — he has wasted cursing others or otherwise misbehaving, e.g., NPS 52.2.

39. Vaudeville, *Kabīr* 2: *pad* 103.5.

40. NPS 340.

41. NPS 360.

42. NPS 282 and 74.6. A version of the former poem does occur in B2, but the phrase *santani ke hitakārī* is tellingly absent. Nor, in a similar case, does one find in

or community is quite beside the point. Sur does recommend good company (*satsaṅg*, or rather *santa-samāgama* or *sādha-samāgama* as he more usually calls it),[43] but what he means by that has nothing to do with virtue of any sort. That company is made good by the simple fact that it provides the place where Hari's name is sung and heard. In perhaps the earliest instance in which Sur recommends the company of the Sants, the mention of the Lord's name directly precedes that of his devotees: *Hari bhajana sādhu samāgama*[44] and, in a locution that would be awkward but for the need of the Lord's Name as this point, *prabhu sādha samāgama.*[45] Another early citation calls the Sants *sujān* ('wise', 'knowing') but once again the reason is immediately at hand. It is the hearing of the glory of the Lord that renders them so: *nigama jākau sujasa gāvata sunata santa sujāna.*[46] This pattern begins to relax only in the most recent of the manuscripts we have been considering. In Allahabad 1 the poet states that without the devotion (or singing) that is possible in the company of the Sants this body is useless (*sādhu saṅgati bhakti binā tanu akārathu jāya*).[47]

In these early poems the virtues of the Sants are extolled derivatively or negatively. Sur does, on occasion, advise himself to keep away from those who turn their backs on Hari (*Hari bimukhana*) but this never becomes the frequent refrain it is for Tulsi Das.[48] Such clichés as *satsaṅgati karau* ('do *satsaṅg*'), which become common in poems more recently added to the Sur *vinaya* collection,[49] are entirely absent. In these earlier layers the Sants figure more as part of the religious landscape than anything else. Twice we find them as part of a series with Vedas, Puranas and the like, and in both cases pointing to Hari as the central figure. On one occasion, the poet praises the name of Hari as

the old manuscripts the notion evidently propounded in later manuscripts and reproduced by the NPS that the influence of the Sants (*saṅgati-pratāpa*) had anything to do with persuading the Lord to come to the aid of Gajendra. The old manuscripts omit the phrase, mentioning instead the thought of the elephant itself when it found itself in a situation of such extremity (e.g., U1: *chhina chitavata śrāpa sankaṭa te*). This focuses the matter directly upon Krishna.

43. E.g., NPS 233.6 (B4).

44. NPS 292.4.

45. NPS 233.6.

46. NPS 235.7.

47. NPS 330.3.

48. NPS 332.1. Certainly Sur has no category such as Tulsi's *kusaṅgati* or *ku-path* (VP 84.2) against whose example the *satsaṅg* are held up for praise. At best he speaks of the *asata-saṅgati* (NPS 144.6 in J4) in order to place himself at their head!

49. NPS 86.10, 360.8, etc. Cf. *bhakti karihau* in NPS 329.1.

"Shiva's wealth, the subject matter of the Vedas and Puranas, and everything the Sants have to their name (*santana kau sarabasa*)."[50] On the other, he asks to be given the grace of Krishna's presence, a foundation as basic for the Vedas, Puranas, and Smriti as water is to a fish.[51]

Similarly, references to the guru in these early poems are rare and tend to be nontechnical.[52] One line makes the guru the source of that illumination by means of which the heart is able to churn its raw material, curd, to ghee and eliminate the inessential buttermilk;[53] another, appearing only at the end of the period we are calling 'early', makes the guru responsible for urging the bhakta to sing the name of Govinda, perhaps implying that he had transmitted it as a mantra.[54] But not until much later additions are made to the *Sūr sāgar* is the guru himself singled out for special adulation,[55] or mentioned in the same breath as Govinda, as in the famous *sākhī* attributed to Kabir.[56] The term *satguru* does occur once (certainly there is no anathema attached to the concept, as if it represented the theology of a distinctly rival camp), but again it is a casual reference. The *satguru* is not the object of worship or reverence. Rather, says Sur addressing his own heart (*man*) in desperation, "The *satguru*'s told you and I'm telling you again: the Ram-jewel is the [only] true wealth."[57] All this is slightly offhanded, indicating a generally understood environment rather than an object of direct concentration. It is not the Sants or their *satsaṅg* as such that is essential for Sur, but the presence of the Lord that they may make possible. That is the ultimate *satsaṅg*, and the poet rails against himself for not having

50. NPS 114.5.

51. NPS 204.3.

52. For instance, Sur characterizes himself rather formulaically as *guru-drohī* ('insubordinate to the guru') in NPS 124.5.

53. NPS 351.3 (B4, U1, J4, J5). This imagery occurs also (but, as it happens, without mention of the guru) in a *pad* of Kabir. See Vaudeville, *Kabīr* 2: *pad* 84.

54. NPS 311.6 (A1). Cf. NPS 375.4 (J4).

55. NPS 417. Cf. also NPS 155.2, where the service of the guru (*guru sevā*) is seemingly placed on the same plane as the remembering of Hari (*Hari sumiran*). The earliest hint of such a notion comes in NPS 208.2, where gurus are described as divinely sent in order to facilitate the crossing over the sea of existence. The passage appears in J4 and J5.

56. NPS 65.3. The best known formulation attributed to Kabir occurs, for example, as the first poem in the selection of *sākhī*s given in Balkrishna Sharma 'Navin', ed., *Chayanikā* (Calcutta: Macmillan, 1973), p. 27. A presumably older version may be found in Vaudeville, *Kabīr* 1:*pad* 1.28.

57. NPS 59.5.

recognized that this more radically intimate companion (*suhṛd*) has been at his side through his entire life.[58]

The Quintessential Sinner

Sur is loath to describe himself as anything but a stranger to virtuous company,[59] so it is a good thing for him that the Lord to whom he appeals is not the Lord of the good and faithful—of *sādhs*, *sants*, and *bhagats*, as later poems in the *Sūr sāgar* tend to picture him—but rather the Lord of sinners.[60] Obviously Sur is, at least in part, reaching for a dramatic effect when he characterizes himself as the worst (or as he rather says, the best!) of sinners. But the underlying point, as with Luther's famous dictum, "Sin boldly!", is a serious one, and one that seems to have fit ill with the more routinized, less scandalous predispositions of later generations. Later versions of earlier poems are often sharply reoriented through the alteration of a few words. Evidently, later singers and scribes could not quite believe what they heard or read.

NPS 19 is such a poem. Its older versions praise the Lord who comes to the aid of those who seem least to deserve it, the meek and outcast of this world. In Bikaner 2 and Udaipur 1, these people are ultimately called 'the true', the Sants, but it is because of their unyielding devotion to Krishna. Their goodness—their Sant-hood—is inextricably bound up with their humility. In Bikaner 4, where the position of several lines is altered, the point emerges even more clearly. In this version the final, summary line focuses not on the worthiness of the recipients of the Lord's mercy but upon the extremity of their condition (*ārat ke dukh*, not *santan ke dukh*). Sur implicitly includes himself in their number; he joins them in appealing to a common Lord (*prabhu*).

Several minor alterations in later versions of the poem, reflected in the NPS edition, change the meaning appreciably. In the last line the vocative *saṭh* ('fool') appears. Whereas in earlier poems Sur seems to affirm his likeness to the fools of this world, here we find him castigating them and setting himself apart:

> Sing, fools, says Sur, a song to the Lord
> who burns away the trials of the low.

In the same vein, the NPS version fails to mention the hunchback

58. NPS 77.8. This too, however, is a familiar notion with Sants such as Kabir.
59. NPS 124.9-12, 130.7 in B4, J4.
60. NPS 124.9-10.

of Mathura, probably the most repellent among those who receive Krishna's ministrations and therefore one particularly deserving of mention in earlier versions of the poem: her need underscores his grace. Instead we find a reiteration of the comfortable sentiment that Hari is drawn to true love (or alternatively, truth and love: *satya prīti*). Inadvertently or not, the scandal has been removed.

In the early *Sūr sāgar*, Sur welcomes this scandal. It is the Lord of the unfortunate, the poor, the deformed and the evil that Sur feels he can address himself to, not the Lord of the good. And the style of the appeal, while consistent in some respects with that of the prayers of Kabir and Tulsi, has a pointedness uniquely his own. It is not typical for Sur merely to confess that he has fallen away from constant devotion, as Tulsi does, and hope confidently that the Lord of the fallen (*patita-pāvana*) will accept him back in the fold of the faithful.[61] He does not send a letter of petition from a respectful distance to the resplendency of the divine throne. The motif of the petitionary letter (*vinaya-patrikā*), which became so famous at the hands of Tulsi Das, does not appear in the old *pad*s of the *Sūr sāgar*.[62] Instead one has the opposite: not a letter sent from afar, from the outer fringes of the 'community of saints' that surrounds the heavenly throne, but a petition addressed to God at closest range, as if the poet has burst in upon the holy audience; a personal challenge that bypasses the community of the saints altogether; the wails and contortions of a desperate and unruly beggar; even the lewd dance of a transvestite (or nonvestite!) who refuses to go away until he is paid.[63]

Sur's access to God is an outsider's access: that of a sinner, not that of a saint. Tulsi Das, even when he is calling upon the Lord on the basis of his fallenness, cannot refrain from summarizing his plea in terms of the many ties (*nāte aneka*) that bind the Lord to him.[64] Sur's approach, in contrast to such complementarities, is all contest and combat. In poem after poem he singles himself out as a hero among sinners, the king, the great one among them, the crest-jewel, the best, the lord of them all, the one whose renown in the community of the fallen is unequalled, the head performer of the group, the one who has danced to

61. E.g., VP 92.7.

62. Nor, so far as I have been able to ascertain, does it occur in the *vinaya* poetry of Namdev, Kabir, Raidas, Dadu, or Dhanna. Contrast NPS 142 and 143, later poems in which the petitionary letter does figure.

63. E.g., NPS 134.4.

64. VP 79.4.

the tune of *māyā* as no one else has.[65] And that status (such as it is!) provides him his leverage on Hari, for Sur as the unredeemed offender stands to falsify the very core of Hari's claim to lordship: *prabhu kī prabhutā* as one poem calls it,[66] 'what makes the Lord the Lord,' namely, his capacity to save sinners. This is why he is so often called *patita-pāvana*, 'rescuer of the fallen'. It is not one name, really, but many which collectively constitute the divine name, or to put it another way, many versions of the same name. The Lord as *patita-pāvana* is also the merciful (*karunāmaya*), the pitier or friend of the wretched (*dīna-dayālu, dīna-bandhu*), the lord of those who have no lord (*anātha-nātha*), the refuge of those who have no refuge (*asarana-sarana*), pitier of the poor (*garība-nivāja*), and so on. In addition there are many stories of salvation that seem almost to have become part of the name.

Sur shares with other bhaktas of the period, Sants especially, the perception that, as Tulsi was to put it, the name of God is more crucial than God himself;[67] but the meaning he attaches to that affirmation is rather different. Sur is uninterested in a mystique of the Name as such. By comparison with Tulsi or Kabir he is relatively unimpressed with the benefits that accrue from hewing to the name of Ram (*Rāma nāma*).[68] Only in later additions to the *Sūr sāgar* does one find poems that repeat and encourage the repetition of the names Hari or Ram as such. In older poems, the form of Sur's repetitions is more likely to be a detailing of acts of divine mercy or of names which refer to that quality than of the Name as name.[69] This is because for Sur what is transcendent about the name of God is not its sound but its meaning: radical salvation.

65. NPS 108.2, 131.2, 134.3 (cf. 138.2), 138.1, 139.1, 144.1, 146.1, 147.1, 149.1, 153.1, 192.1, 197.1, 198.1, 200.6. When Tulsi Das writes in the same genre the outcome is altogether different. In VP 82, for instance (and in the refrain, as in so many of these poems of Sur), he singles himself out as the worst. But he is the worst of the *mand*, the dullest, and his situation is the result of a lapse of knowledge (*ajānyo*) rather than an act of will. Tulsi apologizes for himself; Sur vaunts himself.

66. NPS 124.10.

67. Tulsi Das, *Rāmcharitmānas* (Gorakhpur: Gita Press, 1947), 1.23-25. On this point see F.R. Allchin, "The Place of Tulsī Dās in North Indian Devotional Tradition," *Journal of the Royal Asiatic Society* 1966, parts 3 and 4, pp. 128-29.

68. For a somewhat different assessment on this point. see R.S. McGregor, "Some Materials from the *Sūrsāgar* bearing on the Evolution of the Sūr Tradition," in W.M. Callewaert, ed., *Early Hindi Devotional Literature in Current Research* (Leuwen: Katholieke Universiteit, 1980), p. 109, cf. p. 111.

69. E.g., NPS 7, 120, 132, and 133.

Sur has little interest in identifying the Ultimate with a particular series of vocables; even 'Hari' and 'Ram' are not conclusively validated above any others.[70] Similarly, on the human side of the salvation formula, he does not believe that there is any quality that makes a person potentially a recipient of salvation. All that matters is the state of fallenness itself; the sheer fact of absence from the divine creates the conditions for the manifestation of the divine presence.

Sur's way of making this point is to style himself the worst of sinners and to force his audience to recognize that this and only this is at issue. As he does so, however, he employs a second sense of the divine name, 'name' not only in the sense of designation or description (of which *patita-pāvana*, with its sometimes performative overtone, is the most frequent), but 'name' in the sense of reputation as well. The Lord has a name to live up to so as to be the Lord. If he cannot save Sur, he loses his name, and there is no sense in the panegyrics (*birad*) that his worshippers (whom Sur often calls *sant*s or *sādh*s) address to him.[71] Thus on the one hand Sur sets himself over against these Sants, a lapsed soul separated from the just and convinced, and on the other he makes it clear that the entire logic of *satsaṅg* — the recalling of the divine name — is dependent on just such a one as he. For the Lord has named himself by sinners, and that good name, his reputation, depends on their salvation.

Just as Sur's recognition of his own distance from 'saints' such as these in one sense makes him their essential companion (indeed to the point that Sur's songs were and are sung in *satsaṅg*, redefining and deepening what it means to be a part of such an association), so his distance from the Lord is what brings him before the divine presence. In his 'best of sinner' poems, which stand at the core of the early Sur *vinaya* collections, the poet confronts the Lord with a direct challenge. He stages a contest, full of bitterness, complaint and irony, trying to shame Hari not only with his helplessness but also with his shamelessness in boasting of his sins.[72] Every evil quality he can recount puts a

70. This is not always apparent from the current editions of the *Sūr sāgar*. Many poems begin with variations of the formula *Hari Hari Hari Hari sumirana karau* (e.g., NPS 224, 236, 245, 306, 344, 348, 382, 394, 395, 397, 399, 416, 420), but none of them is old.

71. NPS 124.2, 130.12, 131.6, 132.2, 133.1, 137.3, 137.5, 157.1, 188.8.

72. E.g., NPS 111.2, 120.2 and 150.1. These bear contrasting with another mood, which becomes prominent in a different strand of poetry, somewhat more recent and less widely shared, in which the poet is ashamed to come before the divine presence, e.g., NPS 128.3 (B4, A1) and NPS 137.4 (B4, U2).

question mark after that long list of mercies his divine rival is supposed to possess.

Sometimes, individual lines of poetry square off the sides. In the following line, for instance, the familiar title *patita-pāvana* is pulled apart so that the repetition of *patita* in the section before the caesura creates the expectation that *pāvana* will follow in rebuttal:

> I'm a notorious sinner (*patita*) among sinners (*patitani*);
> you're supposed to be the savior (*pāvana*)![73]

Sometimes series of words are arranged so as to have the same answering, challenging effect, as when the Lord's ineffable 'non'-qualities (*ajit*, *anādi*: 'unconquerable, beginningless') are measured against the lapses that make Sur just as much a 'non' (*ajān*, *matihīn*: 'unknowing, mindless').[74] And sometimes entire poems take their implicit structure from this test of strength, as when the poet details excess after excess and leaves the Lord (and the hearer) to answer the challenge or, as one poem vividly concludes, come forth with the betel that signifies surrender.[75]

The Nirguṇa *Side of Sur's Sensibility*

The effect of this view of access to God is to recast the terms in which *satsaṅg* makes sense. Tulsi and Kabir emphasize how pointed and harsh the path of faith is by saying it in so many words, and Kabir tries to startle his listeners into believing it and joining the *satsaṅg*. Sur takes a different tack, not so much drawing his hearers away from their sin as acting out his own to show that before the Lord there is no retreat. That, for Sur, is the meaning of the blistering road of faith. Sur treats the matter in characteristically dramatic fashion — with implied

73. NPS 131.2.

74. NPS 181.5 in J1, U1, J2 (twice), and B3. This can be expanded to two full lines, as in NPS 128.3-4 and 111.10-11, where one line details Sur's depravity, and the other the Lord's transcendence.

75. NPS 134.6. Tulsi Das has a poem (VP 75) that employs this same motif, but in a radically and characteristically different way. Tulsi demands the *pān* (Sur's *bīrā*) not because he is the most victorious sinner but because he has been unswervingly faithful in coming to Ram and no other for refuge. Tulsi is confident that his Lord, unlike the other gods, will honor his part of the bargain and provide shelter. Sur, quite the contrary, suggests that the Lord himself is guilty of unfair dealings: he has saved everybody else but him! The motif of the contest is also employed by Kabir. Linda Hess contrasts two usages of this motif. See "Studies in Kabir," chapter 2, section 8, pp. 51-56.

dialogue, with outrageous confrontation and with style—as he dances in the presence of the magic-making Lord with a magic all his own. But it is crucial to note that this dramatic approach does not blunt or diffuse the directness of the message; rather, it concentrates it. One thinks habitually of the *nirguṇīs* as those who approach God most directly—without attending to the intermediating connections and qualifications that classical philosophies of *saguṇa brahman* described, and specifically without appropriating to advantage the points at which the Ultimate has made itself manifest in this world for human benefit. But in this *vinaya* poetry of Sur we have a message as barren of qualification as anything Kabir or any other voice of the *via negativa* ever broadcast. Sur's sense of unmediated confrontation with the divine can well be seen as the *saguṇa* bhakti analogue to the *nirguṇa* position. In that it flouts any real attention to the community of the faithful. In fact, it emerges as an even stronger denial of qualifying circumstance than Kabir was prepared to offer. True, Sur's position takes very seriously the Lord's qualities (or at least his reputation for such qualities!); in this objective sense it is *saguṇa* bhakti. But in the subjective sense, in the way in which those qualities are addressed, there is no sense of qualification or mediation whatever. As far as the transaction between humanity and divinity is concerned, Sur's faith might fittingly be called *nirguṇa*.

This peculiar '*nirguṇa*' side of Sur's sensibility is not confined to the *vinaya* poems; we meet it elsewhere as well. At the most obvious level, Sur uses clusters of negative *nirguṇa* adjectives to point up the irony and wonder of the Lord's particularity against the background of his ineffability.[76] But even on what would seem the *saguṇa* side of things there is a touch that bears analogy to the *nirguṇa* perspective. One expects in a *saguṇa* point of view an appreciation for the Lord's qualities, and this is understood to mean an appreciation of his good qualities. By the medieval period, in fact, the term *guṇa* itself had come to mean just that. There is a measure of that in the *Sūr sāgar*, of course. But there is also a fascination with everything that seems to contradict it.

We have seen how Sur holds Krishna's *saguṇa* reputation up to question in the *vinaya* poems. In other poems of the *Sūr sāgar* he goes

76. One example among many is provided by NPS 746 (B4). Later contributions to the *Sūr sāgar*, e.g. NPS 1719, 2138, 2221 or 3445, tend to play out this incarnational irony even more explicitly. On the coalescence of *nirguṇa* and *saguṇa* elements in the theology of Tulsi Das, see Allchin, "The Place of Tulsī Dās," p. 127.

even farther, describing Krishna's troublemaking mischief and unconcern for others in just the same terms as he uses to characterize human (and his own) misbehavior and selfishness.[77] There emerges the sense, very strange from the *saguṇa* point of view, that if Krishna is the Lord, then he must be so precisely in spite of quite a number of his qualities! Or to see the matter in a slightly different light, it is the very range of his qualities, both good and bad, and even the fact that they seem to contradict one another, that signals his lordship. An awareness of contradiction in the nature of things has often been understood as a significant stage along the path to an awareness of the qualityless reality that lies beneath the whole phenomenal edifice. In Sur's poems, this sense of divine self-contradiction becomes dramatically real. It should come as no surprise, then, that the tone and format of many of the *vinaya* poems echo the complaint and contest, the longing and irony, that stand at the center of the *Sūr sāgar* as a whole, particularly in its older versions. These are the poems which express the *gopī*s' (and the poet's) *viraha*, culminating in the *bhramargīt*.

For Sur, evidently, there was no question of choosing between being Sant or Vaishnava, *nirguṇī* or *saguṇī*. On the contrary, one of his most central convictions (and not only his) was that the *viyogī* (or rather *viyoginī*) is the true Yogi. Life in the *saguṇa* world does not have the effect of distancing its subjects from a qualityless God but rather, paradoxically, of bringing them in direct confrontation with the One whom they have lost. And this unmediated confrontation, whether it be on the part of Sur the sinner facing the Lord of sinners or of the *gopī*s facing their vagrant lover, is as stringent and stark as any that *nirguṇa* bhakti has to offer.

Kabir once complained that everyone calls upon the name of Ram, but each means something different.[78] He was criticizing the lapsed and fallen. But Sur, who aligns himself with just such people, shows that it is not always a bad thing. His sense of the Name may be different from Kabir's, but it is no less radical, and no less demanding for faith.

77. *Kapaṭ*, *jhūṭh*, *haṭh*, *ḍhīṭh* and event *naṭ* occur in both contexts. But there is not a complete overlapping. Only in the exceptional case is Krishna called *saṭh*, 'simpleton', as sinners are (NPS 1420:6 [K1]); and the sinners of this world, Sur included, are never quite clever enough to qualify for the title *ṭhag*, a favorite for Krishna.

78. Vaudeville, *Kabīr*, 1:28.1, p. 288.

SECTION III

MOVEMENTS

THE SHAIVA-VAISHNAVA SYNTHESIS IN MAHARASHTRIAN SANTISM*

CHARLOTTE VAUDEVILLE

Sant mat (the teachings of the Sants) and *sant paramparā* (the tradition of the Sants) are modern concepts. The term *sant* actually has no precise meaning. Parashuram Chaturvedi defines a Sant as one who observes *satya* ('truth') or *śuddha astitva* ('a pure way of being').[1] The characteristic quality of a Sant is often said to be *ekarasa*, the state of being entirely immersed in bhakti. A *sākhī* of Kabir gives the following very general definition of what a Sant is:

Absence of hatred and desire,
a tender love for the Lord,
Detachment from the pleasures of the senses —
such are the marks of the Sant. *KG sākhī* 4.24[2]

But such a definition only refers to a moral ideal — not to membership in any particular religious group. In the *Haripāṭh* of Jnaneshvar, for instance, all bhaktas who sing the praise of Hari are called *sant*, *sādhu* or *sajjana*.[3] Historically, however, the term *sant* has come to refer to the early non-sectarian poet-saints of northern India and Maharashtra — sometimes also the Vaishnava poets of Karnataka. Though non-sectarian, these poet-saints as a group are often considered 'liberal' Vaishnavas.[4]

*This paper is based on an earlier paper presented at the first International Conference on Maharashtra (Toronto, March 18-20, 1984) and published in N. K. Wagle and Milton Israel, eds., *Religion and Society in Maharashtra* (University of Toronto South Asian Studies Monograph Series, no. 1, 1985).

1. Parashuram Chaturvedi, *Uttarī Bhārat kī sant-paramparā* (Allahabad: Bharati Bhandar, 1950), pp. 3-9.

2. *KG* refers to the edition of the *Kabīr-granthāvalī* established by P.N. Tiwari (Allahabad: University of Allahabad, Hindi Parishad, 1961). Translations are by the author; see Charlotte Vaudeville, *Kabīr*, vol. 1 (Oxford: Clarendon Press, 1974).

3. Charlotte Vaudeville, *L'invocation: Le Haripāṭh de Dñyāndev* (Paris: Ecole Française d'Extrême-Orient, 1969), p. 58.

4. Curiously, the term 'Sant' is not used to refer to Shaiva bhaktas. The reason may be that in late medieval and modern India, Shaiva bhaktas are mostly sectarian. For example, the Virashaivas of Karnataka exclude the worship of any deity besides Shiva. The Maharashtrian Sants, by contrast, tend to include Shiva-worship in their practice even though they are worshippers of Krishna.

In the Maharashtrian tradition, the Sants are not only thought of and referred to as Vaishnava bhaktas or Bhagavatas, but are specifically identified as Varkaris, the devotees of Lord Vitthala of Pandharpur. According to R.D. Ranade, the Sants of Maharashtra all belong to the Vitthala-*sampradāy:* "not that the followers of other sampradayas are not Sants, but the followers of the Varkari Sampradaya are Sants *par excellence*."[5] Furthermore, though the Sant tradition as a whole is sometimes thought of as propounding *nirguṇa* bhakti, i.e. bhakti having as its object the quality-less, invisible, all-pervading supreme Reality, this formulation is more appropriate to the northern Sants than to the Sants of Maharashtra. The Varkaris are to a certain extent *saguṇa* bhaktas in that they are devoted to at least one visible *mūrti*, that of Vitthala, considered a *svarūpa* ('spontaneous manifestation') of the Godhead. It is indeed the popular cult of Vitthala that gives the Maharashtrian Sant tradition as a whole its characteristic Vaishnava flavor. The popular cult of Vitthala as a young cowherd boy merges into the cult of Krishna as cowherd, and Vitthala himself is identified with Krishna-Gopal.

Ultimately, however, it is not the Vitthala icon that grants salvation, but devotion to the Name of God, the invisible, all-pervading Godhead. It is this ardent devotion to the divine Name which is the rallying point of all the Sants, both northern and southern. This is well exemplified in two *sākhī*s attributed to Kabir in the *Ādi Granth* collection of the 'sayings' (*bāṇī*) of the 'Bhagats'. The *sākhī*s present a brief dialogue between two Maharashtrian Sants — Namdev (Nama), the tailor (*śimpī*) and his contemporary Trilochan:

O Nama, *māyā* has deceived you
  said his friend Trilochan:
Why do you keep printing cloth
  instead of meditating on Ram?
Said Nama: O Trilochan,
  with your mouth, invoke Ram,
With your hands and feet, do all your work,
  keeping your soul fixed on Niranjan.[6]

5. Ramchandra D. Ranade, *Mysticism in Maharashtra*, reprinted (Delhi: Motilal Banarsidass, 1982), p. 42.

6. *Salok Bhagat Kabīr jīu ke* 212-213, *Ādi Granth*, p. 1376. In the Tantric Buddhist tradition, i.e. the Sahajiya Siddhas and the Dharma cult of Bengal, *nirañjana* (literally 'the Stainless One') is said to be of the nature and form of the Void, like

Such an utterance, put by Kabir in the mouth of his illustrious predecessor Namdev, points to the convergence of the spiritual attitudes of the northern Sants and the Sants of Maharashtra. Whatever their particular religious tradition, the Sants are seekers of the 'Pure' (*nirañjan*), the Absolute, a Godhead which transcends their own traditional allegiances.

This spiritual attitude tends to blur not only the distinction between *nirguṇa* and *saguṇa*, but also the traditional distinction between Shaivism and Vaishnavism. In Maharashtra, as well as Gujarat and later on, in Karnataka, it is possible to follow step by step the gradual merging of the Shaiva faith into the nonsectarian Vaishnava bhakti of the Sants.

The Shaiva Background of Bhakti in Maharashtra

Traditionally, Shaivism was the basic faith in Maharashtra, and remained so throughout the medieval period. In early Marathi literature, it is not the orthodox Smarta or Vedantic tradition that dominates but the Tantric forms of Shaivism inherited from the Nath-panthi tradition[7] — which in turn may have inherited it from former unorthodox Shaiva sects such as the Kapalikas and Kalamukhas. The Naths hailed from the North, but their propaganda must have reached northern Maharashtra long before the onslaught of the Muslim invaders, and their prestige, at least with the low-caste masses, seems to have been considerable. The earliest texts composed in Marathi, the *Viveka-darpaṇa* and the *Gorakha-gīta*, belong to that tradition.[8] Moreover, the

---

the sky; see Shashi Bhushan Dasgupta, *Obscure Religious Cults*, 3rd ed. (Calcutta: K.L. Mukhopadhyay, 1976), p. 283. The word is commonly used in the Nath-panthi tradition and in the northern Sant tradition, especially by Kabir, to refer to the Ultimate Reality which can only be apprehended within. *Nirañjan* is a characteristic *nirguṇi* word.

7. The Nath *paramparā* traces its origin to Adinath, Lord Shiva himself, and to Matsyendranath or Minanath, who is still worshipped in Nepal as a form of Avalokiteshvara. In the Tibetan tradition, Matsyendranath is identified with Lui-pa, who is generally taken to be the first of the Buddhist Siddhacharyas; see Dasgupta, *Obscure Cults*, p. 198. The earliest historical guru of the Nath-panth is Gorakshanath or Gorakhnath. From Gorakhnath onward, the Naths are Shaiva, though they retain a strong link with the Buddhist Sahajiya Siddhas of northern India. For a discussion of the popular confusion of the Buddhist Siddhacharyas and the Nath Yogis, from which the tradition of the "eighty-four Siddhas" has arisen, see Dasgupta, *Obscure Cults*, pp. 206-10.

8. For information about the *Viveka-darpaṇa* and the *Gorakha-gīta*, see Shankar Gopal Tulpule, *Classical Marathi Literature: From the Beginning to A.D.* 1818 (Wiesbaden: Otto Harrassowitz, 1979), p. 314 and numbers 28, 30.

foundation of religious literature in Marathi was laid by two figures affiliated with the Nath tradition: Chakradhar, the founder of the Mahanubhav or Manbhau sect, and Jnaneshvar (Dnyandev), who is considered the fountainhead of the Sant movement in Maharashtra.[9] Even Mukundaraj, the author of the *Vivekasindhu*, the first Old Marathi work written on Vedantic lines, traces his spiritual heritage to Adinath (Shiva himself, as initiator of the Nath tradition), claiming as his own guru Raghunath, himself a disciple of Harinath, who has been identified as one with Chakradhar himself.[10] Dnyandev himself was the author of two treatises written from a Shaiva point of view, the *Amṛtānubhava* and the *Changadeva-pasasti*, a work in sixty-five verses addressed to the great Tantric Yogi Changadeva. Moreover, like Mukundaraj in the *Vivekasindhu*, Dnyandev traces his spiritual lineage to Adinath, followed by Matsyendranath.[11] Unlike Mukundaraj, however, Dnyandev claims Nivrittinath as his guru and Gahininath as his grand-guru.[12]

This parallelism in the *guru-paramparā* of the two *ādi-kavis* ('first poets') of Marathi literature is rather striking. For both of them, the original guru is Adinath (Lord Shiva himself), followed by Matsyendranath — both *divya* ('divine') gurus. The two divine gurus are then followed by two *mānav* ('human') gurus: Harinath and Raghunath for Mukundaraj, Gahininath and Nivrittinath for Dnyandev. It somehow

9. Though the Varkaris themselves consider Dnyandev the head of their lineage, textual criticism does not warrant this claim. It is more likely that the founder of the Varkari lineage was Namdev, who probably lived around the end of the fourteenth and the beginning of the fifteenth century. A number of modern Maharashtrian scholars accept the traditional view that Namdev and his group were contemporaries of Dnyandev and therefore belonged to the end of the thirteenth and the beginning of the fourteenth century. The present author, following Bharadvaj, Patwardhan, Bhandarkar, Macnicol and several other scholars, does not accept this hypothesis.

10. We know nothing about Raghunath, but Harinath appears in the *Tārarahasya*, where he is the third in the list of *mānav* or human Nath gurus. See Hazariprasad Dvivedi, *Nāth-sampradāy* (Varanasi: Naivedya Niketan, 1950), p. 26 and Tulpule, *Marathi Literature*, p. 316, n. 39.

11. For the lists of the Siddhas and Nath Yogis, see Dasgupta, *Obscure Cults*, pp. 202-10. The Nath *paramparā* according to Marathi tradition, as distinct from the Nath Siddha list, is given on p. 208. See also Dvivedi, *Nāth-sampradāy*, pp. 24-32.

12. Nivrittinath and Gahininath are unknown to the Nath tradition outside Maharashtra. In the *Gāthā* attributed to Jnaneshvar, Nivritti is called Nivrittidev or Nivrittidas, the latter name suggesting an affiliation to the Varkari congregation of Vitthala's devotees. In Tantric parlance, the word *nivṛtti* itself means the state of repose of the mind, as opposed to *pravṛtti*, the activity of the mind.

appears as if the shifting from Sanskrit to Marathi in religious literature—a bold step on the part of learned Brahmans such as Dnyandev and Mukundaraj — was determined by the will to establish a link with another tradition that was prestigious though non-Vedantic.[13]

Dnyandev's major work, however, completed in A.D., 1290, is the *Bhāvārtha-dīpika*, a kind of paraphrase on the *Bhagavad-gītā*, in which Dnyandev preaches through the mouth of Krishna himself. Popularly known as the *Jñāneśvarī*, it has stood as the main source of inspiration for all later Sant literature in Marathi. Most of the large body of Maharashtrian devotional literature that appears from the end of the fourteenth century onward has developed under the influence — and the spell — of Dnyandev's honeyed words on bhakti. As a result, the Sant tradition of Maharashtra is considered an offshoot of the great Vedantic tradition, and as belonging to the mainstream of Maharashtrian literature. By contrast, the Mahanubhav tradition remains largely beyond the pale, an eccentric religion from the start, and suspected of having later on imbibed a fair number of Muslim views and practices as well.[14]

In modern times, a renewed enthusiasm of the literate, and especially of the Brahman elite, for the Varkari poet-saints, has accentuated the tendency to view the medieval literary tradition of Maharashtra as essentially orthodox and Vaishnava. Furthermore, books were written from this point of view in both Marathi and Hindi, comparing the Sants of Maharashtra with their counterparts in northern India or in Karnataka. This has led to considerable confusion and to erroneous interpretations, particularly concerning the northern Sants, who cannot be said to fit into an orthodox Vaishnava pattern at all.

"*Nominal*" *Vaishnavism*

The interpenetration of the Nath-panthi and Vedantic traditions resulting in a form of nominal Vaishnavism or nominal Krishnaism is probably anterior to both Mukundaraj and Dnyandev. What is meant by "nominal" Krishnaism is a tendency to transfer the role of Shiva as supreme Lord and Guru of the universe to Krishna, presumed to be

13. It is well known that the Nath Siddhas always preached and wrote in the vernaculars. Their role in the early development of Indo-Aryan literatures has not been sufficiently emphasized.

14. See Tulpule, *Marathi Literature*, who refers to R.C. Dhere, *Musalmān marāṭhī sant-kavi* (Poona: Jnanraj Prakashan 1967), p. 84. See also Dharmvir Bharati, *Siddha sāhitya* (Allahabad: Kitab Mahal, 1965), pp. 325-28.

one with the Krishna of the *Bhagavad-gītā*, and called upon by the names Shrikrishna, Govinda, Keshava, Madhava, Hari, Narayana, etc. This Krishna may also be conceived as an incarnation of Shiva himself, a representation in human form of the supreme Lord.

In the Maharashtrian Nath-panthi tradition, this shifting from Shaiva to Vaishnava names is suggested in a late work, the *Yogī-sampradāya-viṣkṛti*, which gives an account of the incarnation of the "nine Narayanas" as the "nine Naths." Shiva, moved to pity by the sad plight of the earth at the end of the Dvapara Yuga, calls the "nine Narayanas" to Kailasa for a briefing and orders them to incarnate themselves as the nine Naths. According to Shashi Bhushan Dasgupta, the list includes Matsyendra, Goraksha, Gahini, Jvalendra, Karina-pa, Charpata, Revana, Bhartr and Gopichandra, and "it was settled that Matsyendra would be initiated by the Lord himself (Siva), Goraksa, Carpata and Revana by Matsyendra, and Gahini by Goraksa."[15] Hazariprasad Dvivedi, however, remarks that "the list does not link Goraksha (Goraknath) with any of the nine Narayanas, and moreover, that Shiva created Goraksha *after* the descent of the nine Narayanas.[16] This implies that Gorakhnath — the earliest "historical" guru of the Naths and the one from whom the Shaiva *paramparā* of the Naths begins — is not simply one of the nine Naths, but rather that he corresponds to the "Avirhotra-Narayana" identified in the same passage with Naganatha. This Naganatha or Nagnath can be no other than Lord Shiva himself in the form of the Nagnath *jyotirliṅga* at Aundh, a deity famous in the Maharashtrian tradition.

In the Mahanubhav tradition, the shifting is even more evident. The divine pentad which stands as the pillar of the Mahanubhav faith is known as the "five Krishnas" (*pañcha-Kṛṣṇa*). The five Krishnas include: (a) Shrikrishna Chakravarti, (b) Dattatreya Prabhu, (c) Changadeva Raula of Dvaravati, (d) Gundama Raula of Ridhpur, and (e) Changadeva Raula, i.e. Chakradhar, of Pratishthana (Paithan). Only the last three are historical figures — the *mānav* gurus of the Mahanubhavs.[17] The first two are *divya* gurus. Shrikrishna Chakravarti belongs to the Dvapara Yuga and clearly corresponds to the Krishna of the *Bhagavad-gītā*, while Dattatreya, a great Yogi or *avadhūta* who supposedly lived in the Sahyadri mountain range, is a mysterious figure. Sometimes identified as an avatar or even a son of

15. Dasgupta, *Obscure Cults*, p. 207, n. 2.
16. Dvivedi, *Nāth-sampradāy*, pp. 24-25.
17. Tulpule, *Marathi Literature*, p. 316, n. 34.

Shiva, Dattatreya came to be included in the devotional synthesis of the Varkaris.

Changadeva Raula of Pratishthana, the last of the five Krishnas and the founder of the Mahanubhav sect, has a complicated prehistory which suggests that he might have been the same person as the first of the human Krishnas, Changadeva Raula of Dvaravati. Ultimately, according to tradition, he was initiated into Vaishnavism by Govindaprabhu (the former Gundama Raula of Ridhpur) and given the name Chakradhar, one of the epithets of Vishnu.[18] According to recent research, however, Chakradhar was none other than the Harinath who was the grandguru of Mukundaraj.[19] So, finally, we are left with only two human gurus: Chakradhar, *alias* Harinath, *alias* Changadeva Raula, and Govindaprabhu, *alias* Gundama Raula. Raula is the name of a very low caste of Bhairava worshippers in Maharashtra. Thus, clearly, the founders of the Mahanubhav sect belonged to that group and were traditionally Shaiva.[20] Furthermore, the name Harinath both suggests a link with the Nath-panthi tradition and, because it is a hybrid, suggests in itself a passage from Tantric (Nath-panthi) Shaivism to "nominal" Vaishnavism. Such a movement may have been initiated two generations before Mukundaraj, possibly in the first part of the thirteenth century (A.D.)

This blurring of sectarian lines between Shaivism and Vaishnavism is found in the *Jñāneśvarī* itself. Though it takes the form of a discourse on moral and spiritual matters on the pattern of the *Bhagavad-gītā*, with Krishna as the teacher and Arjuna as the listener, the identity of the *Bhagavad-gītā* Krishna is not clearly established. There is not a single allusion to Vishnu-Hari legends, nor to the Krishna-Gopal legend, and the kind of bhakti exemplified in the text implies no com-

18. This rather confusing story is summarized by Tulpule; see ibid., pp. 316-17.
19. See above, n. 10.
20. The word *caṅga* itself (meaning 'good') also refers to a particular Shiva *jyotirliṅga* and to the deity Bhairava. There is every reason to believe that the historical gurus of the Mahanubhavs belonged to the Raula caste. It is well known that the Nath Siddhas as a whole, far from trying to conceal their low origin, gloried in it. (For a similar stance on the part of the Siddhas of Tamilnad, see K. Kailasapathy, "The Writings of the Tamil Siddhas," later in this volume.) The name Bhairava is found in the lists of Siddhas (see Dasgupta, *Obscure Cults* p. 203, n. 1. no. 73), but the name Changa is not. However, according to Dasgupta, we find two 'Rahulas' in the list "available in the Tibetan sources" (Ibid., p. 203, n. 3): no. 6, Saraha (or Rahula Saraha) and no. 47, Rahula. The latter might be the Changa Rahula of the Mahanubhav sect and the Changa Vateshvar of the Maharashtrian tradition. (See p. 13 and footnote 27, below).

mitment to the Vaishnava faith as such. It is a preference of the heart rather than a shift of allegiance — therefore not incompatible with a Shaiva stance.

The Divine Name: Shaiva or Vaishnava

Harinath, the founder of the Mahanubhav sect, is also considered to have initiated the Vedantic tradition in Maharashtra, of which the *Jñāneśvarī* is the supreme expression. In the *Jñāneśvarī*, Dnyandev teaches the Bhagavata ideal through the mouth of Lord Krishna. Though seemingly Vaishnava, however, the text is in fact hybrid, since Dnyandev proclaims that he has received the very doctrine he preaches from his guru Nivrittinath, who himself held it from Shiva:

> That teaching which has come down to us from Shankara,
> the great Guru, through the tradition of his disciplies.
>
> *Jñāneśvarī* 18.1737[21]

In addition to exalting the divine Guru as the supreme benefactor of the faithful and the main object of bhakti, the *Jñāneśvarī* exalts the power of the divine Name. While Dnyandev stresses the spiritual benefit to be reaped from the practice of the invocation of the Name (*nāma-smaraṇa*), however, he seems to hesitate on the question of which name — that of Shiva or that of Krishna — is best for *japa* and *smaraṇa*. Bound by his double allegiance to the Tantric and the Vedantic tradition, Dnyandev leaves the options open:

> *nātarī ekadheṅ nāṅva*
> *techi śaiva kā vaiṣṇava*
> *vāche vase teṅ vāgbhava*
> *tapa jāṇaveṅ*

> Or let a single Name,
> be it Shaiva or Vaishnava,
> Dwell in his speech —
> such is austerity. *Jñāneśvarī* 17.223

In actuality, the object of bhakti in the *Jñāneśvarī* is the Guru and the Name.[22] The kind of bhakti expressed in the *Jñāneśvarī* is strictly

21. From V.G. Pradhan, trans., *Jnaneshvari* [*Bhāvārthadīpikā*], 2 vols. (London: George Allen and Unwin Ltd., 1967, 1969).

22. See Charlotte Vaudeville, "The Cult of the Divine Name in the Haripath of Dnyandev," *Wiener Zeitschrift für die Kunde Süd und Ostasiens* 12-13 (1968-69), pp. 401-02.

along ancient Bhagavata lines, and is made compatible with both Shaiva and Vaishnava allegiances through the mediation of the Name, which concentrates in itself the full power of the Godhead — an idea clearly inspired by the Tantric notion of the Word as *bīja*. Emotional sectarian Vaishnavism or Krishnaism of the later medieval and modern type does not appear in the *Jñāneśvarī* or in any of the other Maharashtrian Sant texts.

The Shaiva Origins of the God Vitthala

The traditional cults of the low-caste people of Maharashtra, and especially the cults of the pastoral castes, center on Rudra-Shiva, Khandoba, Bhairava and a number of local goddesses.[23] These ancient cults were not abolished, but superseded, by the preaching of the bhakti cult centered on the god Vitthala of Pandharpur that began around the end of the fourteenth century. The *Tīrthāvalīgāthā*, a late text attributed to Namdev but in fact a collection of writings by several different Maharashtrian Sants, was designed to propagate Vaishnava bhakti centered on the cult of Vitthala. The cult, however, said to have been brought to Pandharpur by the merits of a mysterious holy man named Pundalik, is certainly older than Namdev. The famous icon of Vitthala — the object of ardent love and inspiration for the Varkaris and for the Maharashtrian Shudra masses as a whole — was originally a Kanarese deity. The mysterious apparition of Vitthala on the bank of the Bhima river at Pandharpur did not, however, result immediately in a conversion of the population to Vaishnavism. Shiva remained the supreme deity — as attested by the most ancient temple in Pandharpur, the Pundalik temple, now half submerged in the river bed. To this day, it remains a Shaiva temple, in the hands of low-caste Koli fishermen.

The original Shaiva character of the famous Vitthala icon itself is suggested by its bearing of the Shiva-*liṅga* as its headgear. Moreover, the akimbo position of the arms, which finds no equivalent in other Vaishnava icons, bears a striking similarity to the image of Bir Kuar, the cattle-god of the Ahirs of western Bihar. Further evidence concerning the identity of Vitthala is provided by a passage found in the *Līḷācharitra*, the earliest Marathi work of the Mahanubhav sect (ca. 1278), which recounts anecdotes from the life of Chakradhar. Replying

23. See Gunther Dietz Sontheimer, *Birobā Mhaskobā und Khaṇḍobā: Ursprung, Geschichte und Umwelt von pastoralen Gottheiten in Maharashtra* (Wiesbaden: Steiner, 1976).

to a question from his disciple Mahadaisa, Chakradhara states that a hero named Vitthala died while protecting the cows at Pandharpur and that a memorial stone (*bhaḍakhamba*) was erected in his memory. This stone was later "accepted as his own" by the deity, which means that the deity itself was identified with it. As S.G. Tulpule comments: "In short, the god Vitthala of Pandharpur is, according to Cakradhara, a deified hero-stone... It became *jāgṛta* (lit. "awake", i.e. "alive") and people started worshipping it. Its character was changed from a Saivite hero-cult to the Vaishnava cult of the Varakaris. It became, so to say, a quite different god."[24]

Despite the assimilation of Vitthala to Krishna-Gopal, important differences nevertheless remain. Though also regarded as a young boy, Vitthala, unlike Krishna, is rather innocent. The erotic element in the Krishna-Gopal legend, especially his dalliance with the milk-maids, is totally absent. Instead, the fundamental sentiment attributed to Vitthala is that of compassion, an infinite love and tenderness for his bhaktas that can only be compared to the love of a mother for her children. Vitthala is represented as pining for the presence of his devotees the way a cow pines for her far-away calf.[25]

Nama's "Conversion" to Vaishnavism

In light of the hybrid nature of Santism in Maharashtra, one may well ask what Namdev's own tradition was and what kind of Vaishnava bhakti he preached. According to tradition, Nama was originally a devotee of Sadashiva later converted to the cult of Hari. In one tradition, it is said that his own guru was Nagnath — a name that suggests a connection to the Nath-panthi tradition, though it may well have been the Nagnath of the *jyotirliṅga* at Aundh, i.e. Lord Shiva himself.[26]

24. Shankar Gopal Tulpule, "The Origin of Viṭṭhala: A New Interpretation," *Annals of the Bhandarkar Oriental Research Institute* Diamond Jubilee Volume (1977-78), pp. 1009-15. Tulpule quotes Guy A. Deleury, *The Cult of Vithoba* (Poona: Deccan College Postgraduate Research Institute. 1960), and Gunther Dietz Sontheimer (in collaboration with Dr. Settar), *Memorial Stones of India* (Dharwar, Karnataka: Karnataka University, 1978).

25. In the *Tiruvāśagam*, the Tamil Shaivite poet Manikka Vasagar (ninth century A.D.) already speaks of his heart which "unceasingly melts" for his Lord and compares his longing for Shiva with the longing of "the cow for her calf." The Maharashtrian Sant tradition reverses the roles: the Lord himself pines for the presence of his bhaktas just as they do for him. Already in the *Jñāneśvarī* (12.11), Dnyandev addresses the Guru, or the Guru's grace, as *ambe* ('mother').

26. See W.B. Patwardhan, Third Wilson Philological Lectures, *Fergusson College Magazine* (1917-19), pp. 52-53; also Vaudeville, *Haripāṭh*, p. 58. n. 1.

According to the most prevalent tradition in Maharashtra, however, Namdev's guru was a mysterious yogi named Visoba Khechara. R.C. Dhere accepts this tradition and traces Nama's *paramparā* to Gorakhnath, through Visoba Khechara, Krishnanath, Changa Vateshvar, and a yogini named Muktai.[27]

The link of Namdev with his purported guru, Visoba Khechara, is emphasized in the *Gāthā* attributed to Dnyandev.[28] Muktai and Dnyandev send Nama to the Nagnath of Aundh, and there, the famous episode of the meeting of Nama and Visoba takes place. Nama finds Visoba reclining at ease within the Nagnath temple, with his feet negligently placed on the top of the sacred Shiva-*liṅga*. When Nama expresses his dismay, Visoba, through his yogic powers, shows him the whole of the temple filled with the Shiva-*liṅga* in order to convince his would-be disciple that Shiva is the omnipresent, all-pervading Godhead.

The name Khechara (literally, 'one moving in the air') clearly refers to a Siddha, a Tantric Master endowed with magical powers. Though the name is not found in the traditional Nath-panthi lists of Siddhas, Khechara, along with Changa Vateshvar, may well have belonged to that tradition.[29] As to the name Visoba, derived from *viṣṇeṅ* ('to rest,

27. For the *paramparā* of Visoba Khechara according to the *Śilpaśāstra*, see Dhere, *Chakrapāṇī*, pp. 69ff.; for the *Yoginī Muktabāichī paramparā*, see ibid., p. 144. In the latter, Visoba Khechara is linked to the Nath *paramparā* through Krishnanath, Changa Vateshvar and Muktai, who herself is linked to Gorakhnath. The mystery of the *mahāyogī* Changa Vateshvar and of his link with the *Nath paramparā* through the *śivayoginī* Muktai, were investigated by R.C. Dhere in *Chakrapāṇī* (Pune: Vishvakarma Sahitya, 1977). The illustration facing page 160 reproduces an old Hindu image of Changadeva together with the Tibetan representation of the Siddha Dombi-pa. The resemblance is striking.

28. In the Dnyandev *Gāthā* compiled by Nanamaharaj Sakhare and edited by T.H. Avate (*Śrīsakalasantagāthā*, 2nd ed., Poona: Shrisamvadmay Prakashan Mandir, 1967, vol. 1, *Jñāndev-gāthā*), a meeting between Namdev and the four elders Nivritti, Dnyandev, Sopandev and Muktai is narrated from *abhaṅg* 1334 onward. Though a fervent bhakta of Hari, Namdev cannot be admitted into the group since, as Muktai says in *abhaṅg* 1341, "there is no sanctity without a guru" (*guruvīṇa santapaṇa ahe koṭheṅ.* In another, long *abhaṅg*, Dnyandev celebrates the greatness of the *satguru* and exhorts Nama to the practice of *satguru-sevā*, since there is "no *mukti* without a guru." Namdev asks about the guru he should seek and Dnyandev sends him to Visoba Khechara.

29. See above, note 27. In the later Varkari tradition as found in the Dnyandev *Gāthā* ("*Pandharīntil kālā*"—"The *kālā* [cowherd's festival] at Pandharpur", p. 128ff.), Khechara is mentioned several times as playing at the cowherd Kala festival in Pandharpur, along with Nivritti, Jñānadev and Sopandev (24.6, 27.6, 28.4, 29.4

to lie at ease'), it is apparently linked with the famous episode at Nagnath and the outrageously negligent pose adopted by the great Yogi.[30]

Why then did Namdev become a Vaishnava bhakta? First, he might have done so on the advice — or at least with the approval — of his guru. Secondly, his "conversion" may be related to the ascendancy of Krishna-Gopal, the child-god of the pastoral castes. Nama may simply have accepted the increasingly held view that his Shaiva *iṣṭadeva*, Vitthala, likewise a protector of cows, had assumed the personality of Krishna-Gopal. Finally, Nama may have found a particular sweetness in the Vaishnava bhakti and in the Vaishnava names of God already attributed to the supreme Godhead by Dnyandev in the *Jñāneśvarī*. Indeed, these names (Ram, Hari, Vishnu, Ramakrishna, Govinda, Keshava, Madhava, Narayana, Narahari, Gopala, Vitthala) were the very ones on which Nama based his own *kīrtan*.[31]

Namdev and Narsi Mehta

Another remarkable example of the process by which the early Sants shifted from Shaiva to Vaishnava bhakti is provided by Narsi Mehta, the first Vaishnava poet-saint of Gujarat (1414-1480?). He may have been an actual contemporary of Namdev. Narsi's "autobiography" consists of eight *pads* found at the opening of his *Putrano vivāha*, an account of the miracles worked by Krishna for Narsi on the occasion of the marriage of the latter's son.[32] In the opening *pads*, the Gujarati poet-saint tells of his conversion to Krishna-bhakti. Deeply affected by

---

and *passim*). This suggests that the great Yogi Khechara was himself a devotee of Vitthala of Pandharpur. Yet the name Visoba is not given in connection with the Kala episode, and the figure named Khechara remains somewhat anonymous.

30. Visoba might well be a nickname, which could be loosely translated as 'Relax-Baba'.

31. Narahari, Gopala and Vitthala are found only in the Dnyandev *Gāthā*, ("*Nāmamālā*", *abhang* 405-449). Dnyandev in the *Gāthā* and Namdev in general seem to have a preference for the name Hari. In the *Haripāṭh* attributed to Dnyandev, the name Hari is said to be Shiva's own mantra:

Hari Hari Hari, ha mantra śivāchā

Haripāṭh 14.3

32. See Françoise Mallison, "Notes on the Biography of Narasimha Mehta," *Annals of the Bhandarkar Oriental Research Institute* 55 (1974), pp. 189-201 and "The Conversion of Narasimha Mehta by Śiva," ibid., pp. 191-92. I am grateful to Françoise Mallison for providing me with detailed information about Narasimha Mehta and the literature on him.

his sister-in-law's sarcasm, Narsi went and meditated before Shiva for seven days, whereupon Shiva granted him *darśan*. Telling him, "Your bhakti delights me," Shiva placed his hand on Narsi's head, purified him from his sins and awakened his "sleeping speech." Narsi then asked for a boon:

> "O Lord, give me something agreeable to you and easy to attain: have pity on me!"
> Gopanath then gave me the gift of fearlessness (*abhaya*) —so Narsi for ever keeps singing Hari's praise.[33]

In the case of both Nama and Narsi, Shiva is the Guru. Either directly, as in the story of Narsi, or indirectly, as in the more popular version of Nama's "conversion", Shiva takes the initiative. He grants a boon to his humble devotee—and this boon is the joy of singing Krishna's praise forever. Shiva himself thus frees his bhaktas to become Hari-bhaktas. By singing Hari's praise, they will sing Shiva's own praise, but in a more joyful manner, because the name of Hari is sweeter to the mouth than any other name. Thus it appears as if Shiva himself could not resist the infinite charm of the Vaishnava *nāma-smaraṇa*, expressed most profoundly in *bhajan* and *kīrtan*. Lord Shiva's own "conversion" may well have been brought about by his experiencing the irresistible attraction of the devotional musical performances of the Vaishnava Sants. Considered sensuous, music had traditionally been frowned upon by the Shaiva ascetic tradition, while Vaishnavism, on the contrary, opened wide the gates of both emotion and music, seeing them as enrapturing the soul of the bhakta and delighting the deity as well.

In the Gujarati *pad* of Narsi Mehta's quoted above, Shiva is referred to as Gopanath ('Lord of the cowherds'), a name which recalls Shiva's ancient title 'Pasupati' ('Lord of the beasts or the cattle'). Another name of Shiva, often encountered in folk literature and attributed to several *liṅga*s, is Gopeshvar, which has the same meaning as Gopanath. What this suggests is that, out of love for his bhaktas, Shiva himself, the supreme Guru, has turned into an honorary cowherd like Krishna. Furthermore, while as Gopeshvar, Shiva is the Lord of the cowherds, he can also be Gopishvar, the Lord of the *gopī*s—the milk-maids of Braj—and thus in fact one with Krishna-Gopal himself.[34]

33. Narsi Mehta, *Putrano vivāha, pad* 8.

34. In Vrindavan, the holy city of the Gaudiya Vaishnavas in the Braj area, Gopeshvar is one of the four great Shiva-*liṅga*s. The *liṅga* is worshipped in the morn-

In Narsi's even more than in Nama's poetry, we find the Vaishnava names of God alternating with Shaiva or Vedantic names such as Jagadguru, Jagadish, Atmaram, Parabrahman, etc. Among the three names which appear most frequently in Narsi's *pad*s, besides Hari and Krishna, we find the name Vitthala, which apparently refers to the Pandharpur deity — and may be taken as an equivalent of Gopanath, a title which, as we have seen, fits both Shiva and Krishna. The names Hari, Krishna and Ram prevail in Narsi's *pad*s on the theme of "the greatness of the divine Names", but Narsi's own *chhāp* (a kind of signature which corresponds to the northern *bhaṇitā*) remains ambiguous. The formulas found in the last line of his *pad*s (*Nārāsaiṅyo no svāmī*, *Nārāsaiṅyo no nātha*, *Nārāsaiṅyo no prabhu*) may refer to Shiva as well as to Krishna.

To some extent, this ecumenical attitude typical of the early Sant tradition persists even among later Vaishnava poets more closely associated with sectarian movements. A remarkable example is found in Sur Das, the greatest of the Braj poets and an ardent exponent of Krishna-bhakti. Though tradition classifies him as a Krishnaite poet rather than a Sant, and identifies his poetry with the Vallabha sect, Sur himself, in a well-known *pad*, proclaims the identity of Shiva and Vishnu-Hari:

> To Hari-Hara, to Shankar, hail, hail!
> One makes the great snake into his couch,
> the other wears the snake as a necklace;
> One is a giver of boons,
> the other removes poison...
>
> Sur Das, both are the same
> under various names and forms —
> Different only
> are those who follow them.[35]

ing as Gopeshvar, in the traditional Shaiva manner. In the evening, Shiva becomes Gopishvar and the *liṅga* is draped in feminine attire, in order to allow Shiva to join in the mysterious *rās-līlā* which is supposed to be reenacted during the night by Krishna and the *gopī*s.

35. *Sūrsāgar*, 2 vols. (Banaras: Nagari Pracharini Sabha, 1948-50), vol. 1, p. 328, *pad* 789. For further discussion of Sant themes in Sur Das see J.S. Hawley, "The Sant in Sur Das," earlier in this volume.

THE DEVELOPMENT OF THE SIKH PANTH

W.H. McLEOD

Sant doctrine, with its strong emphasis upon the interior quality of religious devotion, offers no overt encouragement to the emergence of religious institutions or formally organized communities. On the contrary, one learns to expect from its proponents a persistent attack on the futility of institutional loyalties or sectarian allegiance. Truth transcends the various religious groupings which men have contrived. One may be a Hindu or a Muslim, but neither confers any particular insight or virtue, and salvation is certainly not earned by the rituals and conventions which they variously impose. To be a Sant is to be freed from the institutional obligations of organized religion.

For most people, however, actual practice necessarily differs from any theory which seeks to minimize the value of institutional forms. The first gathering of any group of disciples may flourish without acknowledging any formal organization, but if this first generation is followed by continuing family loyalties and widening influence, the pressure to institutionalize becomes irresistible. The Sant tradition has been no exception to this rule. The first acceptance of any Sant as an inspired teacher was inevitably accompanied by the rudimentary organization required by the giving of *darśan* and the assembling of disciples for *kīrtan*. A panth would thus come into being and if it grew in strength it would also grow in institutional definition.

Within the Sant tradition three panths command a particular importance, and of this select group one has achieved a unique status in terms of its numerical following, range of development, and sustained influence. We may acknowledge the claims to significance which are justly made on behalf of the Kabir-panth and the Dadu-panth. Neither, however, can remotely compare to the Nanak-panth. The purpose of this essay is to sketch the pattern of development which conferred on the Nanak-panth its uniquely important status, a status which entitles it to be known as simply the Panth.

The first emergence of the Nanak-panth is easily identified. This took place in central Punjab, early in the sixteenth century. Well-established tradition records that Nanak (1469-1539), following some years of itinerant preaching, eventually settled in Kartarpur, a village situated on the right bank of the Ravi river opposite the present town of Dera Baba Nanak. This village evidently became the focus of attention and devotion, earned by the appeal of his teachings and by the sanctity of his own life-style. The master thus attracted disciples. Nanak became Baba Nanak and those who were thus attracted to him became his disciples or *sikhs*. The Nanak-panth was born.

In these general terms, the emergence of the Nanak-panth can be viewed as conventional and the same might also be said of one of its major features. The renunciation of caste, or at least the degrading of caste from a religious to a purely social status, has been a characteristic element in the establishing of 'sectarian' movements or panths.[1] The fact that this will normally be a response to ideals rather than to a calculated opportunism should not obscure its practical importance in terms of the founding and growth of a panth. The persistence of an undiluted acceptance of caste distinctions must seriously inhibit panthic recruitment and, unless the leader or leaders of any particular panth are prepared to impose significant limitations on membership, the maintenance of such distinctions must be modified or wholly abandoned. The Sikh Gurus were certainly not prepared to restrict salvation to those with approved caste qualifications. Nanak is outspoken in his denunciation of caste and his successors plainly follow him in his belief. One may well argue that the intention was a renunciation only of those aspects of caste which accord privilege to some and impose discriminatory penalties on others.[2] This claim does not affect the inescapable fact that the Gurus were emphatic in their rejection of caste-based religious pretensions and that membership of the Panth was consequently seen to be open to people of all castes or none. In general terms, this insistence may be viewed as a characteristic feature of panthic development in its initial stage.

The first beginnings of the Panth accordingly follow what we may regard as a regular or standard pattern. Even at this initial stage, however, there are distinctive features which deserve to be noted as factors significantly contributing to its strength and longevity. At least three such factors can be identified. One was presumably the immediate

1. Louis Dumont, *Homo Hierarchicus* (Chicago: University of Chicago Press, 1970), p. 190. W.H. McLeod, "On the word *Panth*," *Contributions to Indian Sociology*, new series, 12:2 (1978), pp. 287-95.

2. W.H. McLeod, *The Evolution of the Sikh Community* (Oxford: Clarendon Press, 1976), pp. 87-91.

impact of Nanak's personality. A second was his *bānī*, the hymns which he composed in order to communicate to his disciples the message of salvation through devotion to the divine Name. The third was the nature of his early following.

Although the first of these is an assumption rather than a fact which can be conclusively documented, it is obviously a reasonable assumption. The charismatic appeal of either the initiator or one of his early successors is a feature typical of successful religious movements and there is no reason to suppose that the Nanak-panth was in any sense an exception to this rule.[3] It is an assumption strongly supported by the Panth's later hagiography (the *janam-sākhīs*) and also by the personality indicators which appear in Nanak's own works.

In the characteristic Sant style Nanak gave expression to his convictions in the form of religious songs and these hymns provide a second evident reason for the early strength and subsequent growth of the Nanak-panth. The actual function of Sant *bānī* is the provision of appropriate songs for communal singing (*kīrtan*), a corporate practice which serves to weld a group of disparate devotees into a society with a sense of common identity. This sense of identity will be encouraged or retarded by the nature of the materials which are used in such *kīrtan* sessions. Whereas the most banal of hymns can arouse at least a transient fervor, an inferior composition cannot reasonably expect to survive, and a dependence upon trivial thought or expression is unlikely to provide a secure foundation for any religious society. Nanak's work is at the opposite extreme. Its beauty is a simple beauty and the fact that the early Panth could build on such a foundation must surely be regarded as a major reason for its durable strength. It continues to serve this function even when the hymns are sung for their beauty rather than for their actual import, or when mere presence at *kīrtan* assumes greater importance than any understanding of what is being sung. The reputation of Nanak's *bānī* is too firmly established to permit serious questioning of its quality, even by those who might attach little importance to its status as scripture. A like quality is also to be found in the compositions of those of his successors who have left recorded works.

The third factor is perhaps the most important of all, for it helps to explain not merely the strength and longevity of the Panth but also

3. This point is convincingly made by Terry Thomas in *Sikhism: The Voice of the Guru*, Units 12-13 of the Open University series "Man's Religious Quest" (Milton Keynes: The Open University Press, 1978), p. 63.

the transformation which it subsequently experienced. This third feature concerns the distinctive response elicited by the early Gurus and the specific constituency thereby conferred on the Panth. Although some uncertainty still obscures the social foundations of the Nanak-panth, there are good grounds for supposing that a significant measure of the initial response came from the Jats of rural Punjab. As we shall see, the Jats of central Punjab eventually emerge to a strong numerical predominance within the Panth. The Nanak-panth certainly recruited in rural Punjab from its earliest days and it is therefore reasonable to suppose that the Jat response to the Gurus' teachings should be traced to its first beginnings. It is also reasonable to suppose that the Jat response owed much to the egalitarian emphasis made by Nanak and his successors. During the sixteenth-century period of Guru Nanak and his early successors, the Jats, though evidently growing stronger in terms of actual land control, were still viewed as comparatively humble in terms of ritual status. If this theory is correct, it means that there will have been a widening gap separating their ascending economic status and aspirations from their position within any national hierarchy of Punjab castes. Irfan Habib has suggested that the Jats would be strongly attracted to a panth which rejected caste as a religious institution.[4] This seems to be an eminently plausible conjecture, one which does much to explain both the actual constituency of the Panth and the vitality which it was to sustain.

It appears that even within the lifetime of Guru Nanak, divergent emphases had appeared within the emergent Panth. According to Sikh tradition, one of his sons, Siri Chand, rejected Nanak's insistence upon the futility of asceticism as a necessary means of salvation. The ascetic path of celibacy and austerities was, it seems, the mode of salvation affirmed by Siri Chand, and those of the Nanak-panth who accepted this view eventually took the form of the Udasi-panth without wholly renouncing their connection with the Nanak-panth. This proved, however, to be an early aberration from an established orthodoxy. The first Guru insisted upon the way of the householder (*grihast*) as the ideal and all-sufficient pattern of life for the seeker of salvation, rejecting in clear and unmistakable terms the ascetic alternative. His successors upheld the same ideal, expressing it in their own lives as well as in

4. Irfan Habib, "Jatts of Punjab and Sind," in Harbans Singh and N. Gerald Barrier, eds., *Essays in Honour of Dr. Ganda Singh* (Patiala: Punjabi University, 1976), p. 99.

their teachings. The doctrine, firmly established in the Panth's earliest days, was subsequently to be challenged but never with real strength and never with success.

The emergence of a separate Udasi-panth is of some interest, but the attention bestowed upon the sons of Guru Nanak in the *janam-sākhī* accounts of his death is appropriately fleeting. There was no necessary reason why either should have possessed particular claims to the succession, at least none which could be derived from their filial connection.[5] Such a relationship could well have strengthened claims which might be advanced on other grounds, but to regard them as sufficient in themselves would clearly have been unacceptable. Spiritual qualities would command much greater importance and the succession was accordingly bestowed upon a disciple who, according to tradition, had earned a reputation for single-minded devotion to his master. This was Bhai Lahina, known in his leadership role as Guru Angad.

Guru Angad succeeded to the *gaddī* following the first Guru's death in 1539. He was already associated with Khadur, a village situated near the right bank of the Beas river approximately thirty kilometers above its confluence with the Satluj. There was evidently no reason why he should remain in Kartarpur and the focus of the Panth's devotion accordingly transferred to a location very close to the point where the Majha, Malva and Doaba areas converge. His successor, Guru Amar Das, remained within the same vicinity, a choice which presumably helps account for the spread of the Panth's influence in all three regions.

Guru Angad's tenure of the *gaddī* appears, from the limited sources available to us, to have been a period of consolidation.[6] From the small collection of *śalok*s by him recorded in the *Ādi Granth* it is evident that his teachings faithfully reflected those of the first Guru. In them, he stresses the dangers inherent in attitudes which neglect spiritual concerns for worldly pursuits and, in the manner of his own preceptor, he insists that only through regular meditation on the divine Name can one attain to purity and salvation. To find and follow this path of salvation one must depend upon the grace of the Guru. For Nanak,

5. Siri Chand presumably disqualified himself as a successor to his father by reason of his ascetic views and his only brother, Lakhmi Das, evidently provided other reasons for suffering a similar rejection. This, at least, is the interpretation suggested by the *janam-sākhī*s. Bhai Gurdas, *Vār* 1:38. See also *Rāmkalī kī Vār, Rāi Balvaṇḍ tathā Sattā Ḍūm, Ādi Granth*, p. 967 (hereafter *AG*).

6. *Rāmkalī kī Vār, AG*, pp. 966-67. *Mahimā prakāś vārtak* and *Mahimā prakāś kavitā*.

the Guru had been the inner voice of God. Angad, however, perceives him as the one who having heard and comprehended that voice subsequently communicated its message in terms of unique clarity. For Angad, the supreme guide is the first Master, Guru Nanak.[7] The reference to Nanak in these terms confirms what we might legitimately have assumed, namely that by the end of the second Guru's lifetime the identity of the Nanak-panth must have been clearly established.

The impression which emerges from our sketchy understanding of the period of Guru Angad is one which implies a panth with a clear identity but an informal organization. Insofar as the Nanak-panth possessed a formal organization at this early stage it related exclusively to the person of the acknowledged Guru. He alone provided a focus for a continuing devotion to the memory and teachings of the Panth's founder. It is under his successor that a more formalized structure begins to appear. Guru Amar Das became the third incumbent in 1552 and directed the affairs of the developing Panth until his death in 1574. In terms of organization and of the increasing clarity of panthic definition his period is important for at least two major innovations and perhaps a third. As a result, the Panth which he left at the conclusion of his twenty-two years was evidently a more structured and more coherent company than the informal following which he had inherited from his predecessor.

The changes introduced by Guru Amar Das included the appointment of territorial deputies or vicars (*masand*) and the conferring of a distinctively Sikh status upon a specific place, specific occasions, and specific rituals.[8] These two innovations represent a distinct shift in emphasis, though it is not a development which one finds reflected in the recorded works of the third Guru. Here the emphases are still those of Guru Nanak, with the same insistence upon salvation through inward meditation on the divine Name. The difference is that the growth of the Panth has produced pressures which can only be relieved by institutional means. A first generation of adherents will identify with the fledgling Panth on the strength of a choice dictated by genuine devotion and direct personal contact with the Guru. For subsequent generations, however, more tangible patterns of allegiance will be required and if numbers significantly increase a greater measure of formal organization will be needed in order to maintain effective contact with the Panth's

7. *Vār Mājh*, 27:1, *AG*, p. 150. Two *śaloks* which together effectively summarize the message of Guru Angad are *Vār Mājh* 18:1-2, *AG*, p. 146.

8. McLeod, *Sikh Community*, pp. 7-8, 42.

expanding membership. An extension of the Panth's geographical outreach will emphasize this need still further. This, it seems, was the situation by the time of the third Guru. The measures which he took in order to sustain the Panth's coherence should therefore be viewed as important contributions to its development.

It is possible that Guru Amar Das may have been responsible for a third contribution to the formalizing of the Panth. Another of the many traditions upon which we must necessarily depend concerns the provision of a proto-scripture. According to this particular tradition, Guru Amar Das provided a collection of works subsequently utilized by Guru Arjan as his principal source for the *Ādi Granth*. This collection, the so-called 'Goindval *pothīs*', can be regarded as yet another step towards panthic definition and independence.[9]

Tendencies clearly established in the time of Guru Amar Das were further strengthened during the years of the fourth and fifth Gurus. Once again the actual location of the *gaddī* shifted, this time to the spot where Guru Ram Das established a new village. The village, first known as Guru ka Chak and later as Ramdaspur, was eventually to attain preeminence as the city of Amritsar. This status it largely owes to another of the significant steps in panthic development. It was here in 1603-04 that Guru Arjan compiled the sacred scripture variously known as the *Ādi Granth* or *Granth Sāhib* and subsequently as the *Gurū Granth Sāhib*.

It would be difficult to exaggerate the importance of the *Ādi Granth* in terms of the Panth's identity and coherence. Compiled under the close supervision of the fifth Guru, it acquired thereby a status which all loyal members of the Panth must necessarily acknowledge as sacrosanct and therefore as the object of profound veneration. It thus served to enhance the clarity of definition which distinguished the Nanak-panthi or Sikh from other men. The Panth now possessed a line of Gurus, a growing number of holy places, distinctive rituals, and its own sacred scripture. There could no longer be any question of vague definition nor of uncertain identity.

Two further developments served to emphasize this coherence still further during the period of Guru Arjan and his successors. The first was the occasional challenge to the *gaddī* offered by rival contestants. One of the most distinguished (or notorious) of these was Guru Arjan's elder brother, Prithi Chand. Another was Dhir Mal, grandson of the sixth Guru. Although it is difficult to evaluate their influence on the

9. *Ibid.*, pp. 60-61.

Panth, it seems reasonable to assume that the successful resisting of these challenges involved a heightened loyalty on the part of those who adhered to the orthodox line.

The same effect would also have been produced by external attack. Official concern on the part of Mughal administrators first became evident during the period of Guru Arjan and eventually led in 1606 to his death while in custody. Relations between the Panth and the Lahore administration deteriorated further during the time of Guru Hargobind (1606-44), so much so that fighting actually took place on three occasions. Considerable obscurity attends the death of Guru Arjan and neither the cause of the subsequent fighting nor its actual extent is altogether clear. The precise facts, however, are of less importance than the construction subsequently placed upon them. Guru Arjan's death came to be regarded as a martyrdom and tradition proceeds from this interpretation to the belief that it led directly to a deliberate arming of the Panth by his son Hargobind. This in turn heightened Mughal apprehension and the fighting which took place followed as a result of these growing fears.

An interpretation which views death as martyrdom and fighting as heroic struggle against an oppressor must contribute powerfully to a sense of identity. It is difficult to estimate the contemporary strength of this feeling and we must acknowledge that the traditional view of the early seventeenth century owes an indeterminate measure of its appeal to a period of later struggle. At the very least, however, one must acknowledge the development of genuine hostility, and there is no reason to suppose that the later tradition is wholly divorced from the early seventeenth-century Sikh's understanding of what was taking place in his own time. It must assuredly have involved an awareness of external threat, and such an awareness will normally contribute significantly to the cohesion of a society. We may therefore assume that the early decades of the seventeenth century contributed significantly to the growing sense of panthic identity. Sikhs were now united by a common threat as well as by a common devotion.

Precisely what happened to this sense of panthic identity during the quarter-century covered by the period of the seventh and eighth Gurus is impossible to determine. The seventh Guru remained in the Shivalik hills where his grandfather, the sixth Guru, had retired following the outbreak of hostilities with the Lahore administration; and although he occupied the *gaddī* for seventeen years, nothing of any striking importance marks the period. We can do little more than fall back on assumptions, one of which might well be the supposition that a period of prolonged absence from the plains must have produced a measure of weakening in panthic cohesion. This, however, would be an unsubstantiated deduction and even if it could be shown to be true its consequences are unlikely to have been significant. Anything that might have been lost during these years was later restored.

While the Guru remained in the hills relations between the Panth and the Mughal administration were largely uneventful. It was only when the ninth Guru moved to the plains again that serious tension returned. Eventually, this was to issue in the execution of Guru Tegh Bahadur and subsequently to a genuine re-awakening of hostilities during the period of his son, Guru Gobind Singh. Although the circumstances under which Guru Tegh Bahadur met his death have been the subject of some controversy, the question need not detain us. In its impact upon panthic self-awareness, true importance attaches to the construction placed upon his death rather than to the actual facts which led to it. As with the death of Guru Arjan, the execution of the ninth Guru was interpreted as martyrdom and the outcome an ultimate strengthening of panthic cohesion. Understandably, it also involved a considerable strengthening of the enmity which divided the Panth from the imperial administration.

Growing hostility finally led to open war. A struggle between Guru Gobind Singh and other local powers in the Shivaliks assumed a wider importance when a Mughal force from Sirhind entered against the Sikhs. The outcome of this conflict in military terms has plainly been of vastly inferior importance to its psychological impact. To this day the memory of the tenth Guru's struggles remains powerfully present in the Panth, sustaining within it a deep-rooted conviction of military prowess and the fulfilment of duty through the exercise of that calling. Concepts of panthic destiny were thereafter inextricably bound up with traditions of rights attained and protected through the exercise of arms. The ideal becomes the *sant sipāhī*, the servant of the Guru who combines devotion with valor. A history of intermittent warfare extending through the eighteenth century greatly strengthened this self-awareness.

The Panth which emerged from that turbulent century was in consequence one which confidently affirmed its identity as a society built upon the exercise of military power. It would, however, be false to suggest that this alone constituted the Panth's sense of identity. The name of Nanak has never been obscured and loyalty to the sacred scripture has retained its vigor, even if for many that loyalty has been to an external symbol rather than to an actual understanding of content.

But we are leaping ahead. Although warfare has certainly been of major significance in the development of the Panth, warfare alone will not serve to explain the identity which so clearly emerges at the end of the eighteenth century. At least three other issues are of fundamental importance in any attempt to analyze this identity. The first is the formal pattern of discipline and organization bestowed upon the Panth during the period of Guru Gobind Singh (the Khalsa and its *rahit*). The second is the social constituency of the following which formed the Panth, specifically those members who sustained their loyalty to it through the disturbed years of the eighteenth century. The third is the question of authority raised by the termination in 1708 of the line of personal Gurus.

As with all areas of the Panth's early history, there are aspects of the Khalsa's inauguration which remain obscure. The actual word is itself an example of this obscurity, for its etymology and original purport still remain open to some doubt. Although tradition implies that it was first introduced in 1699 at the actual ceremony of inauguration, it is evident that the term had already been used well before this date as a designation for the Panth.[10] The most attractive theory relates its introduction to the development of the *masand* system, and its apotheosis to the tenth Guru's eventual repudiation of the system. Whereas Sikhs living at a distance from the Guru had been grouped in territorial *sangat*s under individual *masand*s, those who were under the direct supervision of the Guru himself were his *khālsā* or 'royal domain'. During the latter part of the seventeenth century, many of the *masand*s progressively assumed an excessive independence and were finally anathematized by Guru Gobind Singh. Sikhs hitherto under the supervision of *masand*s were commanded to renounce their intermediate loyalty and attach themselves directly to the *khālsā*.[11]

Theories of this kind are harder to establish when we turn to the actual instituting of the Khalsa as a formal order with a defined code of conduct. Although no grounds exist for doubting that an event of critical

10. J.S. Grewal and S.S. Bal, *Guru Gobind Singh* (Chandigarh: Panjab University, 1967), p. 115.

11. *Ibid.* Also Ganda Singh, ed., *Hukam-nāme* (Patiala: Punjabi University, 1967), pp. 25-26; and J.S. Grewal, *From Guru Nanak to Maharaja Ranjit Singh* (Amritsar: Guru Nanak University, 1972), pp. 60-61.

significance took place on Baisakhi Day, 1699 (or at least on some specific date late in the seventeenth century), the actual details of the event are less clear. The problem indicated at this point is the conflict between belief in a definitive declaration on the one hand and a theory of extended evolution on the other. In other words, was the form of the Khalsa (and specifically its *rahit* or code of discipline) fully defined in 1699? Or did the 1699 event establish a basic pattern which attained its developed and settled form only after a post-1699 period extending well into the eighteenth century? The second of these possibilities raises a further issue. Was 1699 the beginning of the period of evolution? Or should the 1699 event be seen simply as an intermediate stage in a development which was already in progress by that date?

The intended role of the formally-constituted Khalsa is also open to debate. Tradition once again is clear. The Khalsa was established by Guru Gobind Singh in 1699 as a formal and defined order because the Panth in its earlier, looser form was inadequately equipped to resist forces of destruction which loomed threateningly and which were eventually to produce open conflict. The Panth consisted of sparrows which had to be transformed into hawks. The intention may indeed have been as simple as this, but there are other possibilities. A plausible alternative treats the establishment of the Khalsa as a result of militancy within the Panth rather than as its initiator. We have already noted the Panth's seventeenth-century experience of intermittent warfare and persecution, and it could be argued that the role of the Khalsa derived from the attitudes evoked by this experience. This claim would interpret the founding of the Khalsa brotherhood as a means of formalizing and disciplining an increasingly pervasive militancy within the Panth. The same claim could also be extended to cover the theory of a subsequent period of development. Founded as a means of formalizing a growing militancy, the Khalsa assumes its eventual form through the experience of persecution, struggle, and ultimate victory.

This, however, is speculation. It raises questions which we may never be able to answer and, expressed so summarily, it serves only to indicate major limitations on our present understanding of the development of the Panth. Such limitations are certainly important, but let it not be supposed that all is mist and obscurity. He have already stressed the fact that an event of great significance assuredly took place at the end of the seventeenth century and we can add to this the assurance that eventually, if not immediately, the Khalsa order assumed the status of a transformed orthodoxy. The Nanak-panth had produced the Khalsa, complete with a code of discipline which lay down the most explicit of rules concerning the external observances required of its baptized members. Although it would be incorrect to declare that the Nanak-panth has, in its entirety, been transformed into the Khalsa, there is no room for doubt concerning the Khalsa predominance within the wider Nanak-panth. It would be very difficult to deny that by the end of the eighteenth century it had become the Sikh orthodoxy.

The emergence of a defined and dominant Khalsa is thus plainly evident, and yet the important questions still remain unanswered. What conditions actually produced the Khalsa, and what process of development did they generate? Militancy, the threat of persecution and the actual experience of warfare have been noted as obvious contributors to its emergence. Alone, however, they are insufficient. For a fuller explanation, we must return to that most fundamental of all issues, the social constituency of the Panth.

All the Gurus were Khatris and the list of leading members of the early Panth provided by Bhai Gurdas in his eleventh *vār* indicates that during the period of early development, Khatri prominence extended beyond the Gurus' line. Other names given by Bhai Gurdas cover a sufficient range of castes to suggest that there must have been something resembling a cross-section of Punjab society in the Panth during the period covered by its first five or six Gurus. The lowest ranks in the order of Punjabi caste society are perhaps under-represented, but they are not absent. Moreover, a comparatively light representation in a list of prominent members does not necessarily imply a corresponding proportion of the actual adherents.

Three conclusions are thus indicated with regard to the constituency of the early Panth if we consider the evidence provided by Bhai Gurdas in conjunction with the theory of a Jat presence offered earlier in this essay. The first is the generally representative caste distribution of the Panth's more prominent members. The second is that if any caste group is to be accorded a particular prominence it must obviously be the Khatris. The third is that notwithstanding this Khatri prominence within a representative range, there was probably from the very earliest days of the Nanak-panth a substantial Jat constituency at the less conspicuous levels of membership.

If we are dealing with the early years of the Nanak-panth the third of these conclusions must necessarily be hedged with caution. It is, as we have already observed, a plausible theory, not an established fact.

If, however, we traverse three centuries and examine the constituency of the late nineteenth or early twentieth century, it emerges as a clear certainty and one which no longer concerns merely the less conspicuous orders of Sikh society. The censuses conducted by the British from 1881 onwards were by no means wholly accurate in terms of caste returns, but the general purport of their findings concerning membership of the Panth is beyond question. The first of the effective censuses (1881) clearly established that the Panth of the late nineteenth century was predominantly Jat in its constituency. An impressive 66% of Sikhs were returned as Jats, the next largest group (the Tarkhans) being a mere 6.5%.[12]

Although the change can be represented as dramatic, it did not cause much surprise. For many it merely confirmed widely-held impressions. Ever since their first arrival in the Punjab, British visitors and administrators had intermittently noted the preponderance of Jats amongst the Sikhs and if the 1881 returns revealed a discrepancy it was that the earlier impressions had been exaggerated. The first clear indication of Jat strength within the Panth actually goes back to the later years of Bhai Gurdas's own lifetime. The author of the *Dabistān-i-mazāhib*, writing during the period of Guru Hargobind, indicates that by the early seventeenth century Jats comprised, a significant section of the Panth,[13] and if it were true of this period it was probably also true of the preceding century.

The sixteenth century, however, does not concern us at this point. It is sufficient for present purposes if we can accept that a substantial proportion of the Panth's seventeenth-century membership was Jat and that a strong numerical presence implies a measure of influence within the Panth. Khatri influence had meanwhile begun to decline, a process which was evidently accelerated by Khatri reluctance to participate in the disturbances of the early eighteenth century.[14]

Once again the true nature of the argument must be made clear

12. McLeod, *Sikh Community*, p. 93.

13. Ganda Singh, English translation of relevant portion of the *Dabistān-i-mazāhib* in *The Panjab Past and Present* 1-1:1 (1967), p. 57.

14. Muzaffar Alam, "Sikh Uprisings under Banda Bahadur, 1708-1715," *Studies in History* 1:2 (1979), pp. 206-12. Muzaffar Alam also suggests that Khatri support for the Panth may well have been weakened by the tenth Guru's abolition of the Khatri-dominated *masand* system. He notes a tendency for the Khatris to support Mughals rather than Sikhs as a better means of defending their material interests during the time of turmoil. Ibid., pp. 207, 212.

before it is actually offered. The argument is still strictly a hypothesis and there can be no suggestion of definitive proof at this stage. It is, however, a line of reasoning which may prove more persuasive than a simple appeal to military threats and the need to forestall them.

The basis of the argument is the commonplace assumption that if a distinctive social group secures dominant status within a particular society it will inevitably exercise upon that society an influence which reflects its own mores. The Jats are unquestionably a distinctive group, manifesting a correspondingly distinctive range of ideals and conventions. These include strong martial traditions and, as an obvious corollary, the regular use of arms. The direction of the argument will by now be clear. If it be acknowledged that the Khalsa philosophy and code of discipline bear a striking resemblance to Jat ideals and conventions, the conclusion must surely be that an explanation for the rise of the Khalsa should be sought in any analysis of the Panth's dominant constituency.[15]

Does this mean, then, that having acknowledged the strength of Jat attitudes in the historical process which produced the Khalsa we must necessarily regard the Khalsa as an institutionalized conquest of the Panth by its Jat constituency? This, needless to say, would be a naive interpretation. Whereas we can certainly talk in terms of powerful Jat influences moulding the form and philosophy of the developing Panth, we must also retain a clear view of those features which the Panth carries forward from its origins and period of early growth. The reverence which attaches to the memory of the Gurus ought surely to warn us against exaggeration in this respect. Nanak and his teachings are still very much a part of the conscious inheritance of the Panth. The Khalsa may well incorporate powerful Jat influences, but they are certainly not exclusive. If that were true, it would be difficult to understand the survival of a practice such as *nām simraṇ* or the persistent refusal to abandon the honored conventions of *saṅgat* and *paṅgat*. Although the *Ardās* belongs to the later period of the evolving Khalsa, it scarcely reads as the petition of a caste-based community, particularly its concluding couplet:

Gurū Nānak nām chaṛhadī kalā
tere bhāne sarabat kā bhalā

15. This theory is argued in greater detail in McLeod, *Sikh Community*, especially chapter 3.

May Thy Name, taught by Guru Nanak,
ever increase;
And by Thy grace may all men prosper.

Such words are manifestly universalist in meaning and as such testify to the enduring strength of the Nanak-panthi ideal. It is an ideal which the Khalsa has retained, notwithstanding the powerful influence of martial affections.

Even those features which plainly derive from the martial experience of the Panth cannot be wholly explained in terms of Jat influence. The prominence given in the early *rahit* to the renunciation of Muslim contacts and example indicates another major element. In this period of strife Muslims come to be identified as the prime enemies of the Khalsa, and injunctions which reflect this hostility find their way into the evolving *rahit*. Some are subsequently shed or modified as changing circumstances affect attitudes towards the *rahit*; others survive to the present day. The clearest of all examples is provided by the ban on *halāl* meat. Another major precept which evidently reflects antagonism towards Muslims is the strict ban on the use of tobacco.

Social constituency and the experience of extended conflict thus combine to produce the all-important *rahit*, mutable with regard to many of its details but thoroughly consistent as an expression of the nature of the later Panth. The outcome is a paradoxical but nevertheless coherent blend of apparent contrasts. The Panth, represented now by the Khalsa, lays strong emphasis upon external forms without abandoning the earlier insistence upon inward devotion. Predominantly unicaste in constituency, it nevertheless preserves the concept of religious equality and freely admits men of other castes to its membership. Nurtured in warfare, it still affirms an eirenic ideal. It has, in other words, absorbed strong influences from its Jat connections and its experience of struggle without renouncing its avowedly religious inheritance from the early Nanak-panth.

An unaffected Nanak-panthi inheritance meanwhile continued to survive, sustained by devotees who perpetuated the old beliefs and practices without accepting the transforming requirements of the Khalsa discipline. Few have questioned their right to be regarded as Sikhs. Ever since the eighteenth-century rise of the Khalsa, however, their numbers appear to have been small and their caste affiliations predominantly non-Jat. The history of this section of the Panth is obscure until some notice is taken of them late in the nineteenth century. This is scarcely surprising for, as we have already noted, the eighteenth-century Khalsa had asserted a claim to orthodoxy which it has never since relinquished.

The final issue to be noted in connection with the eighteenth-century development of the Panth is the question of authority. Until the first decade of the eighteenth century, the nature of authority had presented no problem. Although the exercise of authority had been disputed by rival claimants from time to time, the actual form was acknowledged by all to be the personal leadership and direction of the Guru. Authority resided in the person of the Guru and, for all who acknowledged him as such, the sanctified will of the Guru was beyond challenge. This authority might be delegated to deputies, but never transferred. It was a clearly defined system and in spite of the recurrent disputes caused by rival claimants, it seems to have functioned effectively.

The system was, however, disrupted from 1708 onwards by the death of the tenth Guru without recognized heirs. The office had long since become hereditary and a succession problem now arose because the sons of Guru Gobind Singh had predeceased their father. Tradition records that the tenth Guru himself dictated the solution by declaring that after his death the Guru's authority would pass to the sacred scripture and the corporate Panth. The *Ādi Granth* thus becomes the *Gurū Granth Sāhib*, sharing divine authority with the Guru Panth.

Traditions as deeply rooted as this particular one cannot be lightly dismissed. There is, moreover, evidence which supports it, notably the testimony of the poet Sainapati whose *Srī Gur Sobhā* may date from 1711.[16] As opposed to the received tradition, one must consider the confusion which evidently attended the authority issue during the years following the death of Guru Gobind Singh. It is not possible to elicit from early eighteenth-century sources a clear awareness and consensus acceptance of the concept of dual authority. The impression is rather one of a continuing evolution which eventually issues in clearly defined doctrine. It may well be true that the tenth Guru explicitly conferred his authority on the Khalsa and it is certainly true that the scriptures had already acquired a sanctity which implied divine authority. There remains, however, a strong impression of inchoate rather than clearly defined doctrine. The latter form, implicit in the early eighteenth-cen-

16. Sainapati, *Srī Gur Sobhā*, ed. Ganda Singh (Patiala: Punjabi University, 1967), pp. 127-29.

tury situation emerges to clarity and practical application only after a period of uncertainty.

It is also evident that the theory of dual authority was applied in actual practice for a comparatively brief period. Sir John Malcolm's famous description of the Panth in corporate session vividly depicts a situation of genuine application, even if one which indicates that the greater weight of emphasis was attached to the Guru Panth aspect of the doctrine.[17] Even as Malcolm wrote, however, the balanced doctrine was well on the way to desuetude, sustained in theory but significantly amended in actual practice. Ranjit Singh, having achieved effective political authority in the Punjab by the end of the eighteenth century, was unlikely to look with favor upon a custom which left extensive power in the hands of a Khalsa assembly. Such assemblies were therefore suppressed and with them went the effective application of the Guru Panth doctrine. The ideal has remained a powerful one but in practice it has proved unworkable. The doctrine of the Guru Granth has accordingly advanced and to this day retains an unchallengeable authority if ever an issue is put to its arbitration. Within the Panth the word of the *Gurū Granth Sāhib* cannot be easily transgressed, at least not in an overt sense.

This does not mean, of course, that the question of authority is thereby solved. It is not possible to submit every issue to the arbitrament of scripture if only because many issues will not be covered by it. Even when this is theoretically possible the effect can commonly be negated by differing interpretations of meaning. In actual practice the scripture has been extensively used as a means of securing personal guidance by individuals, but rarely as an agent of corporate decision.

As a result the problem of authority has been a recurrent one. During the eighteenth century, the doctrine of the Guru Panth evidently possessed a measure of genuine if occasional authority, an authority which was consciously exercised in the physical presence of the sacred scripture. This authority was eventually superseded by an assertion of personal power on the part of Maharaja Ranjit Singh and during the first half of the nineteenth century effective authority was political. The destruction of the political base left a serious vacuum and for the next quarter-century the Panth drifted uncertainly amidst frequent prophecies of its impending break up. It was rescued from this fate largely

17. John Malcolm, *Sketch of the Sikhs* (London: John Murray, 1812), pp. 120-23. McLeod, *Sikh Community*, pp. 48-49.

as a result of the Singh Sabha renewal movement with its effective insistence upon a return to traditional panthic loyalties.

The impact of the Singh Sabha movement has been exaggerated by some, ignored by others. Whereas the latter response is indefensible we must nevertheless take care that the emphasis which is properly laid upon this phase in the Panth's development is not excessive. Its ideals were noble, but in terms of objectives, methods and membership it was distinctly elitist. The intention and procedures were very much those of the educated few, the small section of society which has been affected by Western models or by opportunities afforded by the British presence in India. It was no accident that the movement should have emphasised newspaper journalism, literature, educational conferences and modern schools, nor that it should be connected with such enterprises as business and banking. In general terms, the Singh Sabha was replicating a pattern which was emerging in similar circumstances elsewhere. Within the Punjab, some obvious parallels can be seen in the concurrent Arya Samaj development.

This is the first qualification which should be noted, though in itself it is of no great consequence. The importance of such movements must obviously depend upon their influence rather than their antecedents. A second qualification carries rather more weight. It is that the impact of the Singh Sabha can be easily exaggerated as a result of the movement's unquestionable influence in terms of articulate Sikh opinion. Those who depend for their understanding upon the printed word or upon contacts with acknowledged scholars can very easily get the impression that the movement's ideals secured a much greater influence than was actually the case. An understanding derived from such sources would need to be balanced by a representative view of the Singh Sabha influence at the village level. One should, for example, take heed of the significant participation of Khatri reformers, scholars, and entrepreneurs. It would obviously be absurd to brand the Singh Sabha as a Khatri movement, but equally it must be obvious that their prominence within it was substantially in excess of their numerical strength within the Panth. It was, in other words, a distinctly intellectual movement, one which stressed the importance of consistency in doctrine and in social observance.

A third qualification to be noted is the fact of division within the movement. This feature is perhaps less evident than it ought to be. The discord which separated the Lahore and Amritsar *dīvān*s is well known, but secondary sources offer little information concerning the Panch Khalsa Divan and its somewhat more radical notions.[18]

Having acknowledged these qualifications, we can repeat our insistence that the Singh Sabha was nevertheless a movement of great importance in the history of the Panth. This importance derives directly from the intellectual consistency which provided the true basis of the movement. Because it was consistent it laid rigorous stress upon observance of the *rahit*, affirming thereby precisely those features which provide the Panth with its distinctive identity. The same consistency also produced, by means of scriptural exegesis and other related literature, a revived concern for the patterns of devotion taught by the Gurus. Perhaps most impressive of all (and again a direct product of intellectual honesty and consistency) it campaigned for the full acceptance of men of all ranks and status within the Panth. The result was a significant accession of strength from outcaste sections of Punjab society.

The vigor of the Singh Sabha movement flagged during the early decades of the present century and its surviving descendant, the Chief Khalsa Divan, is now a shadow of its former self. The inheritance in terms of the Panth's self-awareness has, however, been considerable. A continuing insistence on the *rahit*, new or restored Sikh ceremonies, extensive adherence to devotional practices associated with the *Gurū Granth Sāhib*, and a genuine communal openness are all features which we properly associate with the twentieth-century Panth. Their continuing strength owes much to the Singh Sabha movement.

Although the influence of the Singh Sabha extended well into the twentieth century, it was not the last of the movements to exercise a perceptible influence on the development of the Panth. At least three others deserve to be noted. The first is the Gurdwara Reform Movement which in a sense grew out of the Singh Sabha concern for purified places of worship, but which moved forward into a pattern of political activity alien to the more restrained and gentlemanly procedures of its predecessor. The political approach stimulated by the Gurdwara Reform Movement carried through to the political activities of the Akali Party (the Shiromani Akali Dal) and to the phase which is still with us

18. An exception to this rule is an article by Harbans Singh, "The Bakapur Diwan and Babu Teja Singh of Bhasaur," *The Panjab Past and Present* 9-2:18 (1975), pp. 322-32. See also N. Gerald Barrier, *The Sikhs and Their Literature* (Delhi: Manohar, 1970), introduction, pp. *xxxiii-xxxiv*.

today. As a result of this development, the Panth of today is highly politicized and no description of its current condition could possibly ignore this feature. The resources of the Shiromani Gurdwara Prabandhak Committee and the rewards proffered by state politics have served to sustain and encourage political activity.

The second twentieth-century movement is actually an extension of a convention well established during the late nineteenth century and linked beyond that with the martial traditions of the Jat community. This has been the continued attachment to military service. As one of the so-called 'martial races' of India, the Sikhs (and particularly Jat Sikhs) were encouraged by the British to enlist in the Indian Army and having done so were required to retain their Khalsa insignia. Military service was both a response to traditional values and a strengthening of those values. It was also a comparatively profitable enterprise. Army remittances have contributed to the development of many Punjab villages.

Military service has also contributed to the third feature to be noted as a significant twentieth-century development for the Panth. This has been the Sikh diaspora, the migration overseas of numbers which no one has ever computed but which are obviously substantial. As a result of this movement Sikhs are now to be found in several countries outside India, notably in England, the United States, Canada, East Africa, and Malaysia. The impact upon the Panth of this mobility has yet to be made clear. In terms of economic betterment it has obviously succeeded in a large number of cases, particularly when we bear in mind the straitened circumstances from which so many of the migrants have come. Until recently, there were clear indications that overseas conditions acted as an effective solvent on the *rahit* and that the standard symbols of panthic identity could well be under serious threat. Although this still seems to be the case in the smaller expatriate communities, distinct signs are appearing within the larger groups of a reassertion of the traditional forms.

Inevitably we conclude on a note of uncertainty, for the future pattern of a dynamic society must always be uncertain. Four and a half centuries have now passed since the Nanak-panth made its first appearance in central Punjab. During that period it has developed from a loose cluster of disciples through a process of unusually explicit organization to the world-wide community which increasingly we are recognizing as the bearer of a major religion. It is a process which has carried the community a considerable distance from its Sant origins, yet not one which has involved any necessary renunciation of those origins. Sikh loyalty to the memory of the first Guru remains fiercely ardent and respect for his teachings continues undiminished. Although much may have been added during the intervening period, the inheritance which we trace to the Sant tradition still lives and thrives within the contemporary descendant of the Nanak-panth.

THE MEANING OF 'SANT' IN SIKH USAGE

W. H. McLEOD

The Sant whom we were seeking proved rather hard to find. Normally, Sant Hazara Singh remains in the village of Ghumani, ten kilometres from Batala. The day we had chosen for our visit happened, however, to be one of the rare occasions when importunity had triumphed and he had agreed to visit another village. There were already seven people in the Ambassador car and the addition of two guides from Ghumani slowed our progress still further. Eventually we located our quarry beyond Dhariwal in the village of Sujanpur and there had our brief *darśan* of the Sant. The inevitable *satsaṅg* had gathered and Sant Hazara Singh was all but invisible in the midst of the crowd assembled in the large courtyard. On such occasions there is advantage in being a foreigner, as Punjabi courtesy ensures that the stranger will receive special consideration. We soon found ourselves sitting in front of the Sant.

Although Punjabi courtesy confers special favors on the foreigner, such discrimination is no part of Hazara Singh's custom. All men are evidently equal in his sight and within this estimation he seems plainly to include himself. He is renowned (so we were assured) for the vigor and the color of the language which he uses whenever anyone tries to touch his feet. Anyone who offers him money will find it rejected with scant ceremony and the earnest seeker after enlightenment will be greeted either with the terse suggestion that he look elsewhere or (more commonly) by total silence. A request from one of our company for permission to take his photo produced an immediate refusal. The one gesture which he seems willing to accept is a gift of food, all of which will be distributed amongst those who happen to be present at the time.

The impression which Hazara Singh communicated was that of a decent and genuinely humble man who regards adulation as a sacrilegious bore. In this, of course, lies much of his appeal. The more offerings he rejects the wider spreads the fame of the (almost) silent Sant of Ghumani. We soon discovered that the local folklore concerning Hazara Singh laid heavy emphasis upon his reputation for curt, unpretentious common sense. Once, a couple came to him with the request that he should marry them. "Go," he said, "you are married." They protested that a marriage normally involved reciting of *Anand Sāhib* and circumambulating the *Gurū Granth Sāhib*. "Sit on your cycle," he replied, "that is enough—you are married." Such, at least, is the local tradition. Hazara Singh is something of a rarity in terms of his approach to 'santhood', but there is nothing untraditional in the response which he evokes.

We were not in the business of collecting Sants that day and so we resisted any temptation to linger as we entered the village of Naushehra Majha Singh on our way back to Batala. Naushehra Majha Singh is the abode of an even more famous Sant, Harnam Singh, and passing through the village one observes the distinctive blue turbans and sashes worn by his followers and the curious long-handled trowels which they carry.[1] We were, however, unable to resist another Sant whom we happened to spot. Our attention was actually caught by his garish minibus, bedecked with Khalsa flags and appropriate slogans. *Deg, teg, fateh* proclaimed the front of the wagon. *Rāj karegā khālsā* declared its rear,[2] and if one were to spend a few minutes on the task one could learn many things about the owner by reading the extensive inscriptions on either side of the vehicle. That, however, came later. The owner, sitting nearby on a charpoy, proved to be every bit as impressive as his chariot and the welcome which we received from this jovial soldier of the Khalsa was in the best traditions of rural Punjab. This time, there was no hesitation when the camera appeared, merely some small delay as a handsome sword was set at the best possible angle. Our new friend was Sant Jogindar Singh of Gurdwara Tahali Sahib in Bhangali Kalan, a village near the town of Jaintipur. He is, it seems, known far beyond the bounds of Bhangali Kalan, for he has paid a visit to England in his role as Sant. We departed amidst warmly insistent invitations to visit his *ḍerā*,[3]

1. Sant Harnam Singh and his following have been described by Gurdeep Singh Bajwa, "The New Namdhari Sect at Naushehra Majha Singh," in John C.B. Webster, ed., *Popular Religion in the Punjab Today* (Delhi: S.P.C.K., 1974), pp. 36-39. The long-handled trowel (rather like a blunt spear in appearance) has been prescribed in order that the disciple's daily excrement can be buried. The burying of excrement is a part of the rule prescribed by Sant Harnam Singh.

2. The two inscriptions are the most famous of Khalsa slogans, both dating from the eighteenth century. The first, 'Cauldron-sword-victory!', combines the ideal of charity with the promise of success in battle. The second declares the ultimate result: 'The Khalsa shall rule!'.

3. *ḍerā, ḍerāh*: 'camp', dwelling-place of a Sant and his followers. The term was also used for Kanphata Yogi establishments.

coupled with promises to drive us around the surrounding villages in the splendid minibus.

Within the space of a single morning we had encountered two extremes of the modern Sant movement in the Punjab. As we shall see, there are other varieties to be found within the range marked by these two extremes, and the extensive influence wielded by many of these men makes it a very important movement indeed. At first sight, the modern Sants of the Punjab may seem to represent a complete break with the earlier tradition which we associate with Sant literature and devotion, particularly if we focus our attention on political activity or emblazoned minibuses. A connection nevertheless exists and one of the two purposes of this essay is to trace the lineage linking the two. The second purpose is to extend the description, already initiated, of the Sant phenomenon in modern Punjab.

An examination of the early Punjabi usage of the term '*sant*' will inevitably carry us back to the works of Guru Nanak. This is the obvious place to begin, for Nanak is conventionally ranked as a distinguished representative of the *sant paramparā* of northern India.[4] In so doing, we immediately encounter the first hint that Punjabi usage of the term '*sant*' may perhaps bear connotations distinguishing it from the meaning attached to it elsewhere in North India. Although Nanak may be acknowledged as a representative of the *sant paramparā*, he will *never* be called 'Sant Nanak'. Sikhs and scholars join in agreeing that the title is inappropriate in his case. Whereas the latter presumably refrain from doing so in response to the dictates of convention,[5] the former would certainly regard it as altogether demeaning. Any reference to 'Sant Nanak' would be treated as an insult. The Sants of today may be accorded reverence in modern Punjab, but assuredly theirs is not the highest order in the conventional hierarchy of religious authority and piety. The proper title is '*Gurū*', and if one seeks a variant it will have

4. Parashuram Chaturvedi, *Kabīr-sāhitya kī parakh* (Allahabad: Bharati Bhandar, 1955), p. 15, and *Uttarī Bhārat kī sant-paramparā*, 2nd ed. (Allahabad: Bharati Bhandar, 1965), p. 421. Ramkumar Varma, *Hindī sāhitya kā ālochanātmak itihās*, 4th ed. (Allahabad: Ramnarayan Benimadhav, 1958), p. 57.

5. The distinction implied by the title is particularly striking in Parashuram Chaturvedi's edited selection of Sant works entitled *Sant-kāvya*, 3rd ed. (Allahabad: Kitab Mahal, 1967). A succession of thirteen poets, all bearing the title '*sant*', is eventually broken by '*Gurū*' Nanak Dev. Hazariprasad Dvivedi uses the same honorific form. See also Varma, *Hindī-sāhitya*, p. 270.

to be the '*Bābā*' of the *janam sākhīs* or the highly exalted title '*Satgurū*'.[6]

This, however, concerns a later perception of the figure of the Sikh Guru and does not necessarily imply that the word '*sant*' possesses a derogatory connotation if applied to individuals other than the actual Master. For Nanak himself, the word certainly possessed no derogatory overtones. When he uses it (and he does so with considerable frequency) he employs it in a sense corresponding precisely with the usage and understanding of the wider *paramparā*.

> *bhāī re santa janā kī renu*
> *santa sabhā gurū pāïai mukti padārathu dheṇu*
>
> Be as dust beneath the feet of Sants, brother.
> It is in an assembly of Sants that one finds the Guru;
> like the *kāmadhenu*, [a gathering of Sants] confers
> the blessing of salvation.[7]

The Sant is thus identified as the pious devotee, he who in consort with others of like mind and commitment gathers in a *satsaṅg* to sing the praises of God and seek the guidance of the eternal Guru within. Join them, Nanak repeatedly insists, for in their company salvation is attained. The same understanding is sustained by Nanak's successors and is most strongly asserted by the fifth Guru, Arjan.

> *jinā sāsi girāsi na visarai Harināma mani mantu*
> *dhanu si seī Nānakā pūranu soī santu*
>
> They who treasure the mantra of God's Name in their hearts and minds, remembering it with every breath and with every morsel,

6. This distinction in modern Punjab between '*sant*' and '*gurū*' is not confined to the Sikh Panth. Mark Juergensmeyer encountered the same feeling in the course of his work on the Ad Dharm movement. Some years ago, the Indian government issued a commemorative stamp honoring Sant Ravidas. This produced an objection in the Ad Dharm journal *Ravidās patrikā*, protesting the use of '*sant*' instead of '*gurū*'. Mark Juergensmeyer, "Political Hope: The Quest for Political Identity and Strategy in the Social Movement of North India's Untouchables, 1900-1970," (Ph.D. dissertation, University of California, Berkeley, 1974), p. 403.

7. *Sirī Rāg* 12, *Ādi Granth*, p. 18 (hereafter *AG*); see also *Prabhātī* 17 (1), *AG* p. 1332. The *gurū* to whom Nanak refers is the mystical presence of God. W.H. McLeod, *Gurū Nānak and the Sikh Religion* (Oxford: Clarendon Press, 1968), p. 199. The *kāmadhenu* is the 'wish-cow' which miraculously produced anything desired by her master, the rishi Vasistha.

Blessed are they, Nanak, for they are the true Sants.[8]

For the Gurus, the term '*sant*' thus designates any seeker after truth and salvation who pursues his objective by means of a particular range of activities. These include association with other devotees, regular participation in the singing of *kīrtan*, the individual practice of *nām simraṇ*, and pure living. Although the word recurs frequently in the *Ādi Granth*,[9] it is by no means the only term used to describe the Guru's followers, nor has it proved to be the most durable. In Sikh usage, the most popular of the several synonyms has been the word which tends to be overlooked by reason of its subsequent dominance — the word '*sikh*'. In the works of the Gurus, '*sikh*' and '*sant*' are normally interchangeable, and the meaning which they express is also covered by several other terms. One which seems to have been particularly favoured is '*gurmukh*', he who is 'turned towards the Guru' as opposed to the reprobate '*manmukh*'. Others which serve essentially the same purpose in the *Ādi Granth* are '*sādh*', '*sādhū*', '*bhagat*' (Hindi *bhakta*), '*sevak*' and (occasionally) '*gursikh*'. In this assembly '*sant*' takes its place as an important word, but certainly not one possessing a unique meaning or importance.

This usage, with the same variety of synonyms, is continued in the Sikh devotional literature of the seventeenth, eighteenth, and nineteenth centuries. The differences which one encounters are shifts in preference, with '*sikh*' surging strongly forward (accompanied by '*gursikh*') and '*sant*' dropping well behind it. The declining popularity of '*sant*' is emphasized by a shift in the meaning attached to '*bhagat*'. A particular distinction was conferred on '*bhagat*' by Guru Arjan who, when he compiled the *Ādi Granth* in 1603-1604, chose it as the term to be used when designating works which were not by one of the Gurus. These were hymns attributed to people whom most would probably call Sants, notably Kabir, Namdev, and Ravidas (Raidas). In the *Ādi Granth*,

8. *Gauṛī kī Vār* 8:1, *AG* p. 319. For another arresting definition see Guru Arjan's *Āsā* 88, *AG* p. 392. This latter *śabad* expounds the *sant rahit*, or 'way of life of a Sant'.

9. All examples of the *Ādi Granth* usage of the term are listed by Gurcharan Singh, ed., *Ādi Granth śabad-anukramaṇikā* (Patiala: Punjabi University, 1971), vol. 1, pp. 250-53. A comprehensive collection of *Ādi Granth* examples, giving the actual text in each case, is provided in Piara Singh Padam, ed., *Gurū Granth vichār-koś* (Patiala: Punjabi University, 1969), pp. 123-30. Kahn Singh Nabha, ed., *Gurumat mārtaṇḍ*, vol. 1 (Amritsar: Shiromani Gurduara Parbandahak Kamiti, 1962), pp. 196-204, provides a shorter collection, but adds to it examples from Bhai Gurdas, Nand Lal, and Mani Singh.

however, they are distinguished as '*bhagats*' and, since the compiling of the *Ādi Granth*, it is by this title that they have characteristically been known in Sikh parlance. This usage the *janam-sākhīs* naturally reflect on the rare occasions when reference is made to Kabir or to the *bhagat bāṇī*. No such distinction is bestowed upon '*sant*'. For most of the *janam-sākhī* narrators it commands no great popularity and, if it finds a place in their anecdotes concerning Guru Nanak, the reason is normally because it has been prompted by a quotation from the Guru's *bāṇī*. This is particularly marked in the case of those *janam-sākhīs* which concentrate on narrative rather than on scriptural exposition or exegesis. The B40 *janam-sākhī*, for example, has little use for the word.[10]

The same preferences are sustained by the authors of *rahit-nāmās*, the Khalsa 'codes of discipline' which first appear during the eighteenth century.[11] A partial exception to this rule is the *rahit-nāmā* attributed to Chaupa Singh, a work which employs the formula '*sant sākh*' when introducing an *Ādi Granth* quotation from the works of Kabir or Namdev. In other respects, however, the *rahit-nāmā* uses '*sant*' in the *janam-sākhī* sense, introducing it only occasionally[12] and demonstrating a much stronger preference for '*sikh*', '*gursikh*', and '*gurū kā sikh*'. The *rahit nāmā* known as the *Prem sumārg* offers the same pattern of preference, adding only an adjectival use which continues to the present day. In the *Prem sumārg*, descriptions of the Khalsa sometimes refer to it as the '*sant khālsā*'.[13]

By the time we reach the nineteenth century the trend seems to be clearly set. Although the term '*sant*' survives, it does so principally in the context of *Ādi Granth* usage and exposition. In the specifically *Ādi Granth* sense it continues, to the present day, to retain an intimate association with scriptural commentary and exegesis. Meanwhile, how-

10. For the *janam-sākhīs*, see W.H. McLeod, *The Evolution of the Sikh Community* (Oxford: Clarendon Press, 1976), chapter 2, and idem, *Early Sikh Tradition* (Oxford: Clarendon Press, 1980). See also Narindar Kaur Bhatia, ed., *Srī Satgurū jī de muhain dīān sākhīān* (Amritsar: by the Editor, 1978), pp. 41, 53, 59, for examples of seventeenth-century usage from works other than the *janam-sākhīs*. The last of these is particularly interesting as it sets '*sant*', '*bhagat*', and '*gurmukh*' in joint contrast to the supremely exalted '*mahā-purakh*'. The *janam-sākhīs* also use '*mahā-purakh*' as a means of distinguishing the Guru from ordinary people (*purakh*) or disciples (*sikh, sant*, etc.).

11. McLeod, *Sikh Community*, pp. 51-52.

12. Sikh Reference Library, Amritsar, manuscript no. 6124, ff. 45a, 49b, 89a.

13. Randhir Singh, ed., *Prem sumārg granth*, 2nd ed. (Jalandhar: New Book Company, 1965), pp. 3, 4, 8.

ever, it has assumed its new connotation. This new usage is a twentieth-century development and its period of growth is not yet over. We return now to the Sants of the modern Panth, to the variety of precept which they communicate and to the nature of the response which they attract.

Although the title is a twentieth-century style, the kind of person to whom it is applied has been a part of Punjabi society for much longer. Indeed, one might well argue that the antecedents of the modern Sants are as ancient as India's reverence for individuals distinguished by their piety, asceticism or supernatural powers. In general terms, this traditional reverence for gurus, *pīrs* and *mahants* is indeed a part of the modern Sant development. More specifically, the Sants of today represent a distinctive range of piety, one which can be clearly traced to earlier developments within the Sikh Panth. These earlier developments and the general change which they produce, explain the shift in meaning from the '*sant*' of Guru Nanak's hymns to Sant Jogindar Singh and his minibus.

An earlier essay in this collection describes the substantial changes which overtook the Sikh Panth as a result of its increasingly dominant Jat constituency and the disturbed conditions which it encountered during the eighteenth century.[14] A significant aspect of this transformation was a considerable shift in the popular understanding of piety, a shift which substituted strongly extrovert forms for the earlier insistence on interior devotion. Changes in notions of piety are naturally accompanied by corresponding changes in the meanings of associated terminology and the term '*sant*' seems plainly to provide a clear, if belated, example of this process. Whereas the extrovert forms are firmly established during the course of the eighteenth century, the actual application of the title '*sant*' to one such form does not achieve widespread popularity until the twentieth century.

The fact that such men existed within the Panth well before the twentieth century can be vividly illustrated by the career of Bhai Maharaj Singh during the period immediately following the British annexation of the Punjab in March, 1849. Maharaj Singh lived in a *ḍerā* and imparted religious instruction to his followers. As the British were to discover, however, his interests and ideals were certainly not those of a quietist ascetic. They incorporated, explicitly and actively, a determination to defend the honor of the Khalsa as perceived by a man of militant understanding. As such, Maharaj Singh embodied a concept

14. See W.H. McLeod, "The Development of the Sikh Panth," above, pp. 232, 240-43.

of religious duty corresponding closely to attitudes expressed by some of the modern Sants and a twentieth-century writer can refer to him as a Sant without any evident sense of incongruity.[15] Only the title '*bhāī*' is different.[16]

Maharaj Singh demonstrates that a pattern of militant religious leadership was current in the Punjab by the middle of the nineteenth century. In fact, it had been current within the Panth for generations earlier, as Maharaj Singh's own background shows. Prior to assuming a position of personal authority, Maharaj Singh had been the follower of another activist leader, Bhai Bir Singh of Naurangabad (1768-1844).[17] Bir Singh in turn had been the disciple of Baba Sahib Singh of Una (1756-1834), heir to a succession within the family of Guru Nanak's descendants.[18] Individuals in direct male descent from any of the Gurus had always been accorded reverence, and the lineage represented by Sahib Singh evidently received veneration from the time of the first Guru onwards.

The tradition of a subsidiary master-disciple relationship thus has a lengthy history within the Panth. Reverence for the Guru himself (or his subsequent embodiment in the scripture and the community[19]) remained the primary loyalty, but plainly it did not permanently displace the tradition of loyalty to a present and visible master. During the time of the later Gurus the role of immediate master was evidently discharged by the Gurus' appointed surrogates, the *masands*. The fact that these representatives were expressly disowned by Guru Gobind Singh did not destroy the pattern of allegiance to a present and visible master, as the lineage of Sahib Singh demonstrates. Although the *masands* were

15. M.L. Auluwalia, *Bhāī Mahar̄āj Siṅgh* (Patiala: Punjabi University, 1972), p. xiii. For Maharaj Singh's conflict with the British, see, in addition to Ahluwalia, Nahar Singh, ed., *Documents Relating to Bhai Maharaj Singh* (Gurdwara Karamsar, Punjab: Sikh History Source Material Search Association, 1968).

16. Maharaj Singh actually bore two titles. Originally his name had been Nihal Singh, a name which was subsequently abandoned as devotees insisted on addressing him as '*maharāj*'. To the new name of Maharaj Singh the honorific '*bhāī*' was subsequently added. Ahluwalia, *Mahar̄āj Singh*, p. 8.

17. Kahn Singh Nabha, *Guruśabad ratanākar mahān koś*, 2nd ed. (Patiala: Languages Department, Punjab Government, 1960), p. 658. Naurangabad is in the southern portion of Amritsar District.

18. Ibid., pp. 133, 658. Una is in the southern corner of Kangra District, near the Bhakra Dam.

19. See above pp. 244-46.

excommunicated and eventually destroyed, the tradition of fealty upon which they had depended was far too deeply rooted to disappear with them. Others attracted it, and thus sustained the convention to which the twentieth-century Sants are the present heirs.

In this manner, individuals continued to attract permanent followings. With his group of disciples each master lived in a *ḍerā*, almost always in a rural location. The following might be large or it might comprise a mere handful. Other adherents would visit the *ḍerā* from time to time, and individuals with no specific loyalty would come for *darśan*. Normally the benevolence of adherents, visitors, and neighboring villages would provide for the sustenance of a *ḍerā*, though some (such as the Una establishment) attracted official support in the form of land grants. Instruction in the principles of Sikh belief and practice was understood to be a function of the *ḍerā*, and for this reason its residents commonly included children.

This convention is as old as the Panth itself and, as we have observed, represents a tradition of much greater antiquity. What changes is not the essential form of the convention but the notion of piety which it communicates and the consequent behavior patterns which these ideals encourage. The fact that the *ḍerā* was a rural institution is important in this respect, for it was within the rural constituency of the Panth that the tradition of militant piety ascended to dominance during the eighteenth century. This ascendancy was faithfully reflected by many of the *ḍerā*s, and found expression in the teachings and example which they offered.

Today the tradition is continued by the modern Sants and as the ideal has changed, so too has the connotation of the term which has been appropriated to express it. The word '*sant*' seems to have found currency because each of its several competitors had meanwhile acquired a distinctive usage of its own. Its most intimate associate, '*sikh*', had long since assumed its present meaning as the general term applied to all members of the Panth, and '*gursikh*' is used to designate one who is strictly loyal to the '*rahit*'. The less common '*gurmukh*' applies to ordinary Sikhs of acknowledged piety and, as we have noted, '*bhagat*' has been firmly attached to poets such as Kabir whose works have been included in the *Ādi Granth*. Most people now regard a '*sādhū*' as an itinerant Hindu ascetic (commonly as a spurious pretender) and '*sevak*' implies *sevā* or 'service' in a *gurduārā*. This leaves *bābā*, *bhāī*, and *sant*. '*Bābā*' can still be used as an appropriate title, but only for the few who possess distinctly impressive credentials. It is too exalted to serve a generic purpose. '*Bhāī*' meanwhile has acquired a diversity of usage ranging from the highly respectful to the openly condescending. Scholars of traditional Sikh learning are still accorded the title of '*bhāī*' and when used in this context it expresses genuine respect. This is the upper end of the scale. At the lower end is the *gurduārā* musician (*rāgī*). He too may be addressed as '*bhāī*' and in some instances the title retains its deferential connotation. Commonly, however, it expresses a sense akin to 'hired servant'.

The process of elimination leaves us with '*sant*'. For whatever reason this is now the dominant title, though obviously not one with an agreed or static connotation. The response which the modern Sants elicit ranges from fervent devotion through indifference to outright condemnation. Some place total faith in their guidance; others regard them as ignorant exploiters of the credulous. There is, however, little doubt that the former greatly outnumber the latter and there is no visible indication that the popularity or authority of the Sants is waning.

The spectrum of response is well illustrated by the establishment developed during recent decades in the name of a famous Sant, Baba Nand Singh of Kaleran on the western edge of Ludhiana District. Nand Singh, originally from Sherpur village near Jagraon, earned a reputation as a devout ascetic by meditating for lengthy periods in holes dug underground. One of his caverns was located at Kaleran, five kilometers west of Jagraon, and it was here that he died. His successor, Sant Ishar Singh, commenced an ambitious *gurduārā* project at Kaleran in 1950, a plan which achieved a speedy and splendid success thanks to the reputation of the original Sant and the skill of his successor. Gurdwara Nanaksar is an expensive multistoried marble structure with gold-covered cupola and marble-paved tank. In the cellar marking Nand Singh's cavern, a portrait of the deceased Sant rests on a costly dais and elsewhere in the *gurduārā* his summer and winter clothes are preserved in a glass case as relics. Approximately one hundred attendants (*sevādār*) are permanently attached to the establishment and many thousands of devotees throng the *gurduārā* precincts during the annual celebrations of the Sant's birth.[20] There can be no ambiguity as far as these pilgrims are concerned. They come for a view of the great Sant's relics and thus combine in a conventional manner the benefits of *darśan* with the pleasures of a Punjabi outing. Others, however, are

20. *Punjab District Gazetteers: Ludhiana* (Chandigarh: Punjab State Government, 1970), pp. 660-61.

scornful and some plainly dismayed. Devotion of this order is due to the Guru alone, never to one of his disciples.

In another respect, of course, this particular example is far from typical. Most *ḍerās* are comparatively humble establishments. Sant Hazara Singh's abode in Ghumani is nothing more than a tiny mud hut attached to a mud-walled courtyard. The difference between multi-lakh grandeur and a mud hut illustrates the range of life-styles one encounters amongst the Sants, and one will also observe substantial differences in terms of their varying presentation of the Khalsa faith which all affirm. Four general categories can be recognised. First there are those like Hazara Singh who say little, but attract followings through a reputation for self-denying piety. Secondly, there are men with traditional *gurduārā* or *ḍerā* educations who emphasise the teaching of doctrine and *kīrtan*. Thirdly, there are those whose message is more concerned with the heroic traditions of the Panth. This third variety is, in a sense, the latter-day descendant of the *ḍhāḍhī*, the itinerant preacher who earned a meagre living by entertaining village audiences with stirring stories from the traditional history of the Panth. Sant Jogindar Singh, with his minibus, presumably belongs to this category, though he would probably regard the *ḍhāḍhī* tag as an insult. Finally, there are the muscular Sants who stress deeds rather than teaching and who today express their beliefs in political action.

The second of these groups attracts the most widespread sympathy, though it may be a sympathy without a notable fervor. One *silsilā* with a substantial and continuing reputation is the line of Sants who have successively occupied the *gaddī* in Bagrian village.[21] Even the skeptical pay a certain deference to the Bagrian reputation for panthic service, and likewise to a few individual Sants noted for what all recognise to be a genuine piety. A distinguished example from the early twentieth century was Sant Attar Singh of Mastuana (1886-1926), renowned as a teacher of the scriptures and of kirtan.[22]

In a few instances Sants of this second category have been associated

21. Bagrian is in Ludhiana District, seven and one half miles north-west of Nabha. Kahn Singh Nabha, *Mahān koś*, pp. 636, 783.

22. Ibid., p. 39. Like most of the famous Sants of his period, Attar Singh was a Malwai. Most Sants are Jats by caste, a feature which is scarcely surprising in view of the essentially rural nature of the modern Sant phenomenon. There are, however, some very important exceptions. Nand Singh of Kaleran was a Ramgarhia, and likewise the representatives of the Bagrian line. The Una line (descendants of Guru Nanak) are Khatris and so too is Sant Harnam Singh of Naushehra Majha Singh.

with the institution known as *ṭaksāl*. The *ṭaksāl* (literally 'mint') is a school or group of students attracted to a Sant of particular eminence. Anyone seeking an education in traditional Sikh learning may join a *ṭaksāl* and there receive instruction from its Sant without charge. A famous example is the Bhindranwala *ṭaksāl*, so named in 1906 after Sant Sundar Singh of Bhindran village. Although the *ṭaksāl* has a permanent base in Mehta Sahib village (Mehta Chowk) it spends much of its time on the move. The Sant, together with his students, settles for a few weeks in a *gurduārā*, thus enabling local Sikhs to hear the regular discourses in return for the hospitality which they provide. Having spent a period in one particular *gurduārā* the Bhindranwala *ṭaksāl* then moves on to another. A recent incumbent of the Bhindranwala *gaddī* was Jarnail Singh. Sant Jarnail Singh Bhindranwale achieved considerable prominence during the years following 1978 as a result of his involvement in Punjab politics and his eventual death during the Indian Army's assault on the Golden Temple complex in June 1984.[23]

Jarnail Singh's political involvement effectively translated him from the second to the fourth category, achieving for him a fame (or notoriety) equalled by no other Sant. As such, Jarnail Singh came to be regarded as an 'extremist', contending for panthic authority with the so-called 'moderate' leaders of the Akali Party. The most prominent of the 'moderates', Harchand Singh of Longowal, was another Sant who had moved from traditional religious leadership to highly conspicuous political activity.[24] Although his political style differed markedly from that of Jarnail Singh the two Sants shared a common conviction that political action is inseparable from panthic loyalty. An earlier example, one who achieved renown in the struggle for Punjabi Suba, was Sant Fateh Singh.

The term *sant* has thus travelled a considerable distance since the days of Guru Nanak, though the connection between the early usage

23. Narendra Aggarwal, "Portrait of a Religious Leader," *The Overseas Hindustan Times* 16:27 (3 July 1980), p. 11. The influence of the Bhindranwala *ṭaksāl* is attested by the fact that its alumni include a recent chief *granthī* at the Golden Temple and *jathedārs* of all the *takhts*. Ibid.

24. For an interesting if adulatory account of the life of Sant Harchand Singh, see Surjit Singh Gandhi, "Sant Harchand Singh Longowal" in *The Spokesman Weekly* 27:49 (31 July 1978), pp. 7-8. For a perceptive comment on the current political role of the Sants see Bhagawan Singh Josh, "New Dimensions in Sikh Politics" in the *Economic and Political Weekly* 13:4 (7 October 1978), p. 1697.

and its modern descendant is plainly visible. The path which it has followed is the path which the Panth itself has followed. As ideals have developed so too have important elements in the traditional terminology, and of these *sant* provides a prominent example. The process is by no means over. The Sants of today are a dynamic group and it would be naive to suggest that their days of influence are numbered.

SANTS AND THE SANT TRADITION IN THE CONTEXT OF OVERSEAS SIKH COMMUNITIES

BRUCE LaBRACK

The Sant as a religious figure in South Asian life is both ancient and revered. In addition to the term '*sant*' having a Sanskrit etymology, its bearers are part of a long religious tradition within Hinduism. However, as outlined by W.H. McLeod in an earlier essay in this volume, the Sikh Sants of recent times have had a slightly different orientation from their medieval predecessors. The conception of the Sant in medieval tradition is not totally congruent with Sikh doctrines as they have developed since then. Nevertheless, there have been, and continue to be, men referred to as Sants who adhere to and promulgate traditional Sikh ideals, values, and religious doctrine.

It is not my intention here to review the various 'types' of Sants found in the Punjab, nor to attempt to separate the 'real' Sants from the spurious, but rather to look at what roles men considered to be Sikh Sants play in overseas communities. Specifically, their behavior and the behavior of their audience will be examined to determine in some general way how the Sant role represents a continuity of traditional norms and ideas and to what extent it is undergoing change.

The observations upon which this paper is based are drawn from fifteen months of intensive field-work in Sikh communities of the northern Sacramento Valley of California, followed by an additional five years of periodic contact with Sikh groups in the San Francisco Bay area, Los Angeles, Fresno, and other California cities of the Central Valley.[1] The interpretations which will be made from these experiences are further informed by correspondence with scholars of Sikhism interested in the religious life of the Punjabi enclaves in their countries.

1. Portions of this research were funded by the National Science Foundation, Faculty Research Grants (1977, 1978) from the University of the Pacific, Stockton, and a University Fellowship from Syracuse University. All support is gratefully acknowledged. I also wish to thank W.H. McLeod, Harold Jacoby and Mark Juergensmeyer for reading and critically commenting upon earlier versions of this paper. However, responsibility for the final version is mine alone.

However, it should be understood that the conclusions herein are offered tentatively and with some reservations.

There are three reasons for this. First, I was only able to observe four visiting Sants directly during the period of my initial field-work in 1974-75, although I have gathered information on an additional seven Sants who have come to the West Coast since then.[2] Second, since the primary thrust of my ongoing work was concerned with the effect of culture change and differential adaptation, the Sants' role was not investigated per se, although their visits formed a part of the very active religious life of the Punjabi community. At one time, I considered them almost epiphenomenal to the adjustment process of the Punjabi immigrants, but later came to see how important they were as travelling affirmations of both a special spiritual tradition and as representatives of a cultural world which the Punjabi Sikhs had left but not forgotten. Finally, much of my material concerning attitudinal data was gathered ex post facto, long after the specific Sant had come and gone, a circumstance which may have colored the responses. Some of what I consider my most interesting examples of cultural continuity and expressions of deep emotional and cultural feelings were related in anecdotal form by community members and not personally witnessed by me. Thus, there always remains some doubt as to the validity or accuracy of such reports.[3] Even with these reservations, the fact remains that the role of the Sant in the lives of overseas Sikhs is a fascinating one with many dimensions and, since little is currently available on the subject, this paper is offered as a preliminary contribution which may help focus attention and promote interest in a more comprehensive and in-depth study of Sants, those religious figures whose contemporary incarnation is only the most recent manifestation of a very old tradition.

2. Because of the nature of this discussion and the fact that various Sants are differentially evaluated by community members I have not identified any of these men by name, as it would serve no useful purpose.

3. The responses of some Sikhs varied significantly depending on when they were interviewed. For example, one shaven Sikh man was enthusiastically looking forward to the impending visit of a particular Sant of whom he had heard very positive reports. However, a month after the actual visit, this same gentleman was quite adamant in his revised and negative opinion that the Sant was a trouble-maker and not the kind of man he had expected. No doubt the shaven Sikh's attitude was colored by the Sant's strong and vocal position on the maintenance of the beard and turban.

The Sant and Sikhism

From the beginnings of the Sikh religion there are mentions of men called Sants, Guru Nanak himself using the term to describe a person who is a realized being (the *Siddha goṣṭī* discourse in the *Ādi Granth*). This ideal self is also referred to in Sikh religious literature as '*sachiārā*', '*gurmukh*', and later as '*braham giānī*'.[4] Some recent commentators believe all these terms, including '*sant*', to be synonymous, the implication being that a Sant is simply a person who has achieved a higher spiritual plane, an enlightened individual.

This contrasts somewhat with the more exalted place which the Sant holds in Hinduism. It is also reasonably clear that in terms of Sikh organizational ideals (*khālsā, panth, saṅgat*), the free-lance Hindu Sant who is essentially, in theory at least, a charismatic teacher or guru without institutional portfolio, is incongruent with the more tightly organized and self-consciously communal nature of Sikh social and religious life. However, within the Sikh tradition, a number of Sant-centered panths have arisen, the Nanak-panth being the central and most important. Of course, Guru Nanak himself is considered by many as firmly within the Sant tradition.[5]

The Sant and Sikhism seem, at least to me, to be somewhat in opposition, since the personal worship of the Sant found so universally in Hinduism is anathema for the orthodox Sikh who holds that such veneration is due only to the Sikh Gurus and the *Gurū Granth Sāhib*. Thus, there is an apparent duality in the situation of contemporary Sikh Sants who are accepted within an institutional framework more rigid than the arena within which many Hindu Sants operate.

Yet, Sikh Sants often have large followings of members who are personally committed to them, and *ḍerā* centers to which pilgrimage-like visits are made. These Sants offer teachings and advice which are often accepted by their devotees not only as guides to behavior but literally as dictums. The Sikh Sant is, like all members of the Khalsa, an instrument of the Guru, subject to the will of the Panth and circumscribed in what teachings he can promulgate not only by the weight of tradition and the scriptural record, but by the monitoring and feedback

4. See Avtar Singh, *Ethics of the Sikhs* (Patiala: Punjabi University, 1970), pp. 25-26.

5. See Charlotte Vaudeville, "*Sant Mat*: Santism as the Universal Path to Sanctity", and W.H. McLeod, "The Development of the Sikh Panth" earlier in this volume.

of the local Sikh community. Therefore, the Sant of the Sikh tradition seems somewhat more constrained than some of his Hindu counterparts. The Sikh Sant is also generally more intimately linked to larger institutional segments within the Sikh religion.

It is not my intention to review the evolution or continuance of Sants within Sikhism, as that has been done by W.H. McLeod, but only to note that although the title 'Sant' has remained in Sikhism, some of the connotations of the term as used to describe Hindu Sants may be inappropriate. Doctrinal orthodoxy within the Sikh religion holds that the Sant, while learned and perhaps 'realized', is not himself a source of divine power or authority.

Nevertheless, the social and emotional attitudes surrounding many Sikh Sants are difficult to qualitatively distinguish from similar phenomena indulged in by followers of Sants from Hindu or Muslim traditions. The personal nature of the Sant-devotee relationship is a variation of the classic South Asian *guru-chelā* combination, with all the hierarchy, deference, obligation, and commitment implied. There is the same stress on affective worship that is at the core of all bhakti and which is so easily expressed through the ragas and *bānīs* that are an integral part of every Sikh service. The same concern for personal qualities and character is notable in discussions of Sikh Sants, although many highly-praised behaviors (vegetarianism, celibacy, personal poverty) are derived more from Hindu than from Sikh tradition. Theoretically, the difference between a Sikh Sant and a Sant outside the Sikh tradition is not too difficult to define, but operationally the lines are blurred and seem to meld together. Therefore, watching the interaction between a Sikh Sant and a California *saṅgat* seems comparable to any number of patterns seen in North India at non-Sikh worship centers. And this is the major question examined here: "What do Sikh Sants do in overseas settings and how are they perceived?"

That one finds a wide range of personalities among contemporary Sikh Sants is to be expected, particularly when the entire social and religious system emerged from within a society where the mechanisms for the validation of religious credentials are often nebulous or, in the case of practitioners of bhakti, uncheckable. 'Sant-hood' itself is publicly attained through a variety of avenues, most of which center around securing the recognition of a local group, some of whom become followers. The means range from self-declaration, conferral by another Sant or, in extreme cases, even by the denial of Sant status — in spite of the presence of an adoring constituency which proclaims that status in spite of their object's apparent reticence.

This ambiguity of criteria in ascertaining just who is a Sant is mentioned here because the role of a Sant in overseas communities is, in part, predicated upon and evaluated by means of perceptions of what a Sant should be, say, and do. The models themselves are derived from a combination of traditional, orthodox expectations and the community's prior experiences. Of course, these 'ideal' models are modified to an extent by the perceived needs of the community and its aspirations, social as well as religious. This combination of ambiguity and expectation can lead to thorny problems for the community, such as an individual being accepted as a *bona fide* Sant by some members of the community and not by others, or the evaluation of a particular Sant by some as a "wonderful, learned man who has preserved his ideals in the face of opposition," and a "conservative, backward fanatic" by others.

While this kind of public debate over religious issues is not unusual in India (or anywhere else for that matter), that it is taking place outside the Punjab is important, particularly as the Sikh communities participating in it are now, for the most part, rooted in English-speaking countries. This is what makes the overseas Sant a new element in expatriate Sikh life. As Sants have played a role in Sikhism for centuries, it is natural that as the people of the Punjab became participants in the world-wide population relocations which characterize the twentieth century, eventually Sikh Sants will enlarge their pastoral horizons and assume a role in Sikh religious life abroad.

The Sant Outside India

This paper examines the role of the Sant and his tradition from the point of view of a specific group of people who interact with the Sant rather than from a more removed viewpoint. What will be sketched is the social matrix within which Sants and their traditions function. The examination will focus upon the behavior and attitudes of the 'consumers', in this case communities of Sikhs who live abroad, particularly the North American Punjabi Sikh enclaves in California and their counterparts in England, East Africa, and Fiji. This is, therefore, a view from the sociological/anthropological rather than the philosophical/theological perspective. Specifically, an attempt will be made to delineate what functions these Sants serve in their periodic appearances in overseas Sikh *gurduārās*, and how their presence is both manipulated and extolled for purposes sometimes only marginally connected with their traditional social positions or religious duties. I will contend that the behavior and attitudes towards travelling Sants are rather different from those found in India. To jump somewhat ahead, I will argue that the major role played by travelling Sants in relation to overseas communities, at least up to the present, is the reinforcement of a generalized positive cultural identity and the renewal or revitalization of a commitment to the religious heritage, not necessarily devotion to a specific Sant nor even adherence to his view of religious orthodoxy. Under these circumstances, even a Sant who is intellectually or personally marginal can serve as a positive image, invoking a whole set of culturally charged associations which may have nothing to do with his personal qualities or the appeal of his spiritual message.

In order to understand how this situation evolved, it is necessary to sketch minimally the types of overseas social contexts within which the travelling Sant operates. Beginning in the 1830s and continuing up to the present, South Asian groups have emigrated out of the Indian subcontinent and taken up residence in a wide variety of social and geographical environments. Primarily an economic response to British colonial expansion, the movement of Indians as both indentured laborers and passenger migrants created an interesting natural laboratory for the study of social, economic, political, and religious change.[6] This situation developed due to varying conditions of immigration and certain social factors. The main ones include the fact that most early immigrants were indentured immigrants working in plantation economies under difficult circumstances where neither the complexity nor the subtlety of caste and *jāti* practices could be maintained. This simplification extended to all other areas of life as well: atrophy of *jajmānī*-like economic obligations, breakdown of endogamic barriers, rapid decline in the frequency of religious observances and general loss of what may be called orthodoxy. Such situations were prevalent in Trinidad, British Guiana, Surinam, Malaysia and other tropical areas.

In contrast, the passenger migrations of South Asians to areas of North America, Canada, England, Europe, the Far East, and Africa

6. A general orientation to the possibilities for study in overseas Sikh communities and some of the important social factors may be found in Bruce LaBrack, "Sikhs Real and Ideal: Discussion of Text and Context in the Description of Overseas Sikh Communities," in Mark Juergensmeyer and N. Gerald Barrier, eds., *Sikh Studies: Comparative Perspectives on a Changing Tradition* (Berkeley: Berkeley Religious Studies Series, 1979), pp. 127-42.

were undertaken by passenger migrants who were sojourners looking for financial gain and an eventual return to India, at least in the initial stages. Such groups tended to remain aloof from the host populations and retain many of the more rigid and traditional aspects of their Indian social and religious backgrounds. In addition, early overseas Indian population profiles were extremely skewed, the bulk of the populations often coming from one area, such as South Indians and Bengalis in the Carribbean, Punjabi Sikhs in Canada and the United States, or large numbers of single caste groups such as Gujarati Patels. This wide geographic dispersal of various socio-religious groups under quite different migration conditions gives an unusual opportunity to study social variability and to weigh the force of tradition and continuity against adaptation and cultural transformation. One small but fascinating aspect of such studies should include the role of religious specialists and the role they play in both cultural and religious continuity as well as social change. Sikh Sants are both living links with the Sikh religious tradition as it exists in India and representatives of the Punjabi cultural world.

The Gurduārā as Focal Center

In the West, as in India, the *gurduārā* is the nexus for Sikh religious (and much social) activity. Of course, Sikhism existed in many world areas for decades without the imposing edifices associated with Sikh shrines and holy places such as Amritsar, but as soon as it was financially feasible, *gurduārā*s were constructed. Built at great sacrifice and in a strong spirit of *sevā*, the *gurduārā*s often served as the primary social, religious, and political centers for the Punjabi migrant community. In California, for example, the first *gurduārā* was established in 1912 in Stockton and served for over three decades as the only Sikh worship facility in the United States. Other than occasional visits from Indian dignitaries or political figures, the Stockton *gurduārā* hosted few, if any, Sants. *Gurduārā* religious affairs and social issues were handled by local Sikhs, older retired men acting as *granthī*s. In essence, the Stockton *gurduārā* was a self-maintaining and self-contained entity, a condition made necessary by the legal and immigration status of East Indians in the period 1917-1947. After the end of World War II, other *gurduārā*s were established in El Centro (1948), Yuba City (1969 and 1978), several in the Los Angeles area and Live Oak (1979), with others planned in San Francisco and southern California.

The immediate results of the re-opening of immigration from India in 1947 were primarily the re-building of Sikh family life with increased immigration after 1965. But by the late 1960s, Sants had also begun to appear on the scene with some frequency. In most cases, the visit was part of a world or North American tour of which the primary destination was Vancouver, British Columbia, because of the large number of Punjabi Sikhs located there and the presence of several *gurduārās*. Such Sants would periodically add the Stockton facility to their itinerary, although it was seldom the primary destination. During this regeneration phase in California Sikh life, visits from Sants were relatively rare and special occasions which are remembered as much for their *melā* atmosphere as for the message of the Sant. With the construction of several *gurduārās* in California, the increased wealth and physical growth of the Sikh community, and a growing desire to establish stronger links with the base of Sikhism in India, the visits of Sants became more frequent. With this rise in number also came a parallel increase in duration and the effect of the Sants' visits on the community.

The frequency of visits by Sants to contemporary overseas communities is dependent on several variables. Normally, a community must be fairly well-established and organized, with proper facilities for the Sant and those accompanying him (most do not travel alone). It must, of course, be able to pay any travel and living expenses, which are usually raised by a combination of subscriptions and donations, and it must feel that such a visit will be beneficial to the community. Today, the most common mode of obtaining such a spiritual visitor is what I will refer to as 'becoming a stop in the circuit'. Word is received by someone in the community that a certain Sant is coming to the United States or Canada or would like to come to North America as part of a world tour. The matter is then discussed. In Sikh circles this is usually done by members of the *gurduārā* managing committee. If they feel that they desire a visit, then they correspond with the head of the group (in some cases there is literally a 'manager' who arranges 'bookings') and work out the timetable and estimate of expenses. If the money can be raised and the community supports the venture, the Sant will add Yuba City, California, for example, to a tour that might take him to Southall in England, Vancouver in Canada, Malaysia, and Fiji.

Therefore, in contrast to the wandering holy man of traditional India or the Sant who is either affiliated with a religious center or constitutes the nucleus of an institutionalized cult, the Sant who goes abroad to visit overseas communities is likely to arrive by air on Pan Am and to be treated as an international religious celebrity, being met at the airport by followers and community members, swept away in an air-conditioned car to some sort of reception, and generally accorded treatment which is a mixture of East and West or, in this specific case, West Coast. This sets a tone which, while not negative, is sometimes bewildering to Sants who have not been to America before. Others seem to enjoy and even expect this sort of V.I.P. status.

The criteria for selecting which Sants will visit California seems unclear or at least variegated. In one case, the musical accomplishments of a group were considered so outstanding that it seemed to me that the theological discussions and edifying lectures of their Sant leader were secondary to the requests for *bāṇīs*, ragas and *kīrtans*. In another situation, the selection seems to have been directly correlated to the degree of familial relationship the Sant had to a particular member of the community. This Sant, it turned out, tried very hard to get citizenship once in this country, but was refused because he entered on a ministerial visa which is not convertible to 'green card' or U.S. resident immigrant status, Yet another Sant used the temple platform primarily for political speeches in support of 'Khalsastan'[7] which were so radical that he was finally asked to leave lest he stir up some legal and political problems for the community. In short, the theological message of the Sants sometimes seems of less importance than a number of other considerations including musical ability, kinship to a community member and, if we can permit a Hollywood allusion, the 'drawing' power of his name.

This does not mean that the medium is the entire message, but to paraphase McLuhan, the medium is a *medium* in the sense of a cultural arbiter and the representative of a venerated, if imperfectly understood, tradition. The presence of a Sant is in itself edifying and a spiritual boost to the community. The ideas and concepts associated with *darśan* are still very much alive, even among second-generation American-born Punjabi Sikh children — at least among those who have been raised by parents who are tradition-oriented. It is very strong in older women immigrants who have not resided in the United States for an extended period and the recently-arrived immigrants. But this in itself is a problem. There is a tension associated with the visits of Sants which has several dimensions. The first, is the question of keeping up a good image of the community for the Sant, partially by providing him with gracious hospitality including fulfilment of any reasonable wish. In-

7. Khalsastan (now Khalistan) the demand for an independent Sikh state.

deed, there is a certain social one-upmanship involved in who is going to have the Sant to dinner and who will sponsor the *akhaṇḍ* and *sādhāraṇ pāṭhs*[8] he will participate in, as well as who will underwrite the costs of the various *laṅgar* meals provided during his stay. This does lead, occasionally, to minor rifts in the community over real or imagined slights in who will provide for the Sants and a certain vying for that honor. When this occurs, the more cynical members of the Sikh community point to what they call 'Brahmanism' and disparage the Sant who allows this divisiveness to occur. "A holy man should not start strife" is the dominant response.

The second dimension and a perhaps more revealing source of tension, is the desire on the part of some 'progressive' individuals in the community for the Sant himself to appear modern, in the sense that his presentation of Sikh teachings and his exhortations for community action should not be old-fashioned, orthodox in a narrow sense, or somehow socially atavistic. For example, if a Sikh Sant dwells too long on the whole question of the maintenance of the *pañj kakke*[9] or intimates that you cannot be a good Sikh without the turban and beard, he may receive a cool reception from many community members who are *sahaj dhārī*. Additionally, the more progressive parents are afraid that the Sant will appear a strict, forbidding, and antiquated figure to their children, further alienating them from a heritage which may already seem somewhat removed, exotic, or mythical.

Such fears are compounded when certain behaviors become apparent, behaviors which, in India, are acceptable, but which in the American context are looked upon as distasteful and 'primitive'. A case in point was a dispute which broke out when it became known to a small number in the community that several of the older women who were preparing and serving the Sant's food in the *gurduārā* kitchen were actually arguing over who had the right to eat the leftovers as an act of devotion. Some of the young adults and children were rather upset at this obviously 'backward' practice and the men became angry at the women for this public display of subservience and bad health practices.

8. An *akaṇḍ pāṭh*, or 'unbroken reading', is a complete reading of the *Ādi Granth* conducted without intermission by a relay of readers. The rite is invariably conducted for a specific purpose, perhaps to seek a special blessing or to celebrate an auspicious event. A *sādhāraṇ pāṭh*, or 'ordinary reading' is performed at intervals and need not be associated with a particular purpose.

9. *pañj kakke*: 'the five K's' or five external symbols which must be worn by all baptized members of the Khalsa.

What this seems to illustrate to me is the presence of a kind of cultural limit, a behavioral barrier which, when exceeded, clearly shows the limits of tolerance. It also highlights a value shift among some overseas Sikhs who now question certain practices and ideas which are generally not questioned in India. Of course, such negative occurrences cannot be blamed directly on the Sant. His presence may precipitate or incur certain kinds of behavior, but it is not he who created the cultural conception of appropriate behavior, although he may neither approve or disapprove such actions.

In another instance it became known that a certain Sant was distributing, for a not insubstantial remuneration, an elixir, which when accompanied with certain ritual formulas and prayers, was said to guarantee a male child. Some community members were scandalized. It was not only that they felt embarrased that some of the women were, as they put it, "being taken in" by this holy man, but they were concerned that under U.S. law the Sant himself could be liable for criminal prosecution for "prescribing drugs" (which this nostrum patently was not). Since it is fairly routine for Indian religious figures to sell all manner of items to promote or restore fertility and virility, many of the women ignored their husbands' advice and the transactions did not stop until the Sant was approached by several community members who, it was said, "explained the situation to him." Whether he actually understood the potential seriousness of what he may have considered, at worst, a harmless act is unknown, but he did cease distributing any further medicine.

Such new limits show a change in the cultural ideas about acceptable normative behavior and the proper role for the follower of a Sant. I would venture that a Sant generally receives more overt attention in overseas communities than in India, but engenders less personal commitment on the part of his audiences and must, to some extent, watch not only what he says and does but perhaps even what he permits others to do for him. An example of this arose when a Sant who was feeling ill received a therapeutic massage from the wife of a San Francisco Sikh man, a normal and perfectly acceptable Ayurvedic practice in India, but a devotional act which was not appreciated in the least by the woman's husband, who had to be talked out of confronting the Sant by his friends.

Thus far, the picture presented has been rather one-sided for, in spite of all the tensions and problems the visits of Sants can engender, they continue to be sponsored by communities who must make financial sacrifices to bring them over. Why? The traditional role of the Sant in India has had many facets, not the least of which is that of a transmission agent of religion and culture. While many South Asian individuals and groups are deeply concerned with the theological and philosophical hair-splitting which forms the basis of the differences between various Hindu and Sikh sects, the majority of Indians, Sikhs included, have a profound sense of religion which more often than not expresses itself somewhat non-critically and eclectically. The overseas communities generally have been less orthodox than their Indian counterparts; at least up to the present, I believe this to be true of Sikhs in North America and elsewhere. By this I do not mean that they are unaware of the foundations of their faith or that they value it any less; but from a practical standpoint, the particular doctrinal espousal of a particular Sant is far less important to them than what he represents. Just by being present, speaking in Punjabi, addressing the problems of the Panth, extolling the virtues of the Khalsa, singing the poetry of the *Gurū Granth Sāhib* and the works of the other Sants in the tradition such as Kabir, and by simply being from India, he is valued.

The itinerant Sant is as much a symbol of the Sikh faith as he is a cultural representative from contemporary India. A Sant abroad is possibly a more powerful (if temporary) icon and cultural image than he ever was in India, if only because of his relative scarcity and the limited time he spends in any one place. Because of this status as visitor, he will attract attention and often a measure of devotion, but this is somewhat tempered by the fact that his behavior is being critically monitored and community feedback can be immediate. One Sant let it be known that he ate beef. Coupled with the self-evident fact that he was clean-shaven, this would probably have led to a drop in attendance and public approbation in India, but in California it made him all the more acceptable to some of the Sikh community because here was a learned Sant who could be held up to a younger generation as a reasonable holy man who upheld the Sikh beliefs without being a 'fanatic'.

In overseas communities located in the West this whole problem of how to modernize one's social patterns without seriously altering the bases of the belief system is a serious one. The type of Sant who is selected to come to overseas *gurduārās* is to some extent one index of how the community perceives itself and what kind of image it wants to present. Certain Sants who offered to come to California were turned down for various reasons, but the most common ones were that they were too provincial, ultra-orthodox, or that they were not really Sants at all but only greedy *mahant*s who had failed as *granthī*s in the Punjab.

This last remark points to a somewhat delicate question which arises from time to time in overseas communities when a person presents himself as a Sant. In India there is some possibility for verification of, so to speak, 'credentials'; but it becomes more difficult abroad. Although it is easy enough to write relatives in India and inquire about a certain individual's reputation prior to his arrival, on occasion a man will appear at a *gurduārā* and claim to be a Sant. He is generally given the benefit of the doubt, but is cautiously questioned and there is a feeling of unease over his presence, particularly if he voices disapproval over religious conditions or some lack of devotional attitudes he might detect. If a traveler seems too critical of the local situation, he may be made to feel most uncomfortable. This could also be interpreted as a change in attitude from Indian practice, where lectures amounting to harangues are reasonably common and people do not seem to be unduly disturbed by diffuse criticism of life-styles or past behavior. The overseas community seems to be more sensitive to such charges and does not react kindly to intimations of backsliding and loss of faith. They have, in one sense, conflicting desires. On the one hand they want to perpetuate the ideals and ideas of their religion; on the other they may also wish to be selective in doing so. The presence of a Sant can therefore be seen as potentially both a positive and a negative force. As already mentioned, his simple presence is symbolically important, yet he can quickly become a divisive force if the thrust of his homilies and his exegesis of sacred literature moves from devotional commentary to social criticism which is deemed excessive and unwarranted. This seems to be true not only in California, but to an extent in East Africa, Fiji and England, which are on the regular routes for Punjabi Sikh Sants. Those Sants who are most appreciated seem to be those who have led by example and gentle persuasion, rather than the more politically-oriented or socially critical.

Recently, there is some evidence that this low-profile approach which, as I have indicated, existed in the mid-1960s and through much of the 1970s, may be phasing out to be replaced by a much more orthodox and militant style. As communities grow ever larger and begin to assert aspects of their identity, particularly in hostile environments, it seems natural that the patient counseling and homilies may give way to the other side of the Sikh character, namely the *sipāhī* or 'soldier' of the Sikh ideal of *sant-sipāhī*. A number of Sikh Sants in England have been very successful with what can only be described as revitalistic or revivalistic approaches which center around dedication (or re-dedication) to the Khalsa and maintenance of the *pañj kakke*. One can only speculate about the reasons for this upswing in Sikh intra-community proselytizing, but it certainly is comparable in a superficial way to the fundamentalist Christian 'born again' fervor now so in vogue in the West. There are undoubtedly many contributory factors, including a renewed desire of Sikhs everywhere to set themselves apart from other South Asian religious communities coupled with the belief, documented again and again in Sikh history, that a unified community is the best assurance of individual survival. To follow the exhortations of a Sant and undergo *pāhul* is literally standing up and being counted, the *keś-dhārī* being not only unwilling but unable to deny his affiliation.

Under the influence of ever-increasing numbers of newly-arrived Punjabi Sikhs directly from India, many overseas communities are undergoing a shift in the balance of power as the older generations, who underwent some degree of acculturation, become a smaller and smaller percentage of the entire group. There is another side to this Sant-led revivalism, which is that a significant number (how large is unknown) of the second-generation foreign-born children are reaching majority and many are opting for a stronger identification with the externals of orthodox Sikhism than their parents evidenced. In any event, it seems that Punjabi Sants will play an ever more active role in the religious leadership of Sikh communities around the world, if not by direct intervention, then by example and exhortation. In some areas, such as Great Britain, some Sants are taking up permanent residence, or spending a majority of their time there, making the presence of the Sant more than a fleeting visit.[10] Under such conditions, the perception of the individual Sant may shift increasingly from symbolic modes to a more personal/devotional aspect, as he gains both a retinue and a reputation.

Of course, such increased and close interaction between the Sant and the community could also result in his deliberate or unintentional involvement in the often vicious local *gurduārā* politics, a problem he could choose to overlook or underplay when a temporary guest. How effectively he can continue to be a link between India and the overseas community remains to be seen, but his role will certainly include acting

10. The increasingly orthodox fervor which I have noted in California is paraleled in other overseas communities, particularly England. Personal communication W.H. McLeod, October 17, 1979, and T.A.T. Thomas, December 11, 1979).

as spiritual advisor and channel of devotion for many overseas Punjabi Sikhs, just as his predecessors did in India for hundreds of years.

The Sant in overseas communities is still largely an iconic figure who embodies an entire cultural and religious tradition. The irony is that there are many aspects of that tradition which may be deemed inappropriate or unnecessary in the new foreign setting. This leaves the various communities in the rather ambiguous position of having to affirm the status of the Sant but also desiring a certain amount of control over what he says and does. This 'cultural censorship' syndrome often exacerbates already existing political, social, and doctrinal divisions within the community. The Sant is honored as an exemplar of a culturally-valued religious position, but is simultaneously a potential social or political problem.

This kind of ambiguity is not altogether new for South Asian religious leaders, although it seems particularly delicate when their access to overseas communities depends upon not only being perceived as a *bona fide* Sant but as one with an acceptable outlook on community matters which may have very little to do with doctrine or theology.

It is a dialectic, the investigation of which is likely to reveal a great deal about the overseas community. How much light it will shed on the Sant or his tradition (at least in a Great Tradition context), is not entirely clear.

THE KABIR-PANTH AND SOCIAL PROTEST*

DAVID N. LORENZEN

No ideology can be properly understood without analytically locating it in its specific historical, social, and economic-political context. However common-sensical this statement may appear, academic discussions of Indian religion often seem to delight perversely in ignoring its strictures and consequences. Nowhere is this more evident than in the chronic tendency to exaggerate the undoubtedly real and remarkable continuity of Hindu tradition and to correspondingly minimize its discontinuities. For instance, while few modern scholars wholly accept the traditional view that the essence of Hinduism is to be found in the four Vedas, many do not hesitate to accept the incredible theory that the mother-goddess worship of medieval Tantric cults represents a resurgence of the popular religion of the pre-Aryan Indus Valley civilization, notwithstanding the lapse of some two to three *thousand* years in which no serious evidence for the continuity of such a cult exists.

The concept of bhakti or devotion is a frequent victim of such anachronistic or de-contextualized analysis. Some form of devotion is obviously central to—or at least present in—all religions. The superficial similarity of the devotional sentiments expressed in different stages of Hindu tradition, in say the Vedas and Puranas, tends to disguise serious contextual and functional differences. Nonetheless, from the time of the *Bhagavad-Gītā*, we can identify a set or field of associated characteristics which makes bhakti Hinduism a legitimate category of analysis. These characteristics, not all of which are necessarily present

*I would like to thank the participants of the 1978 Berkeley Conference on the Sant Tradition and my colleagues in El Colegio de Mexico, particularly our then visiting professor Sabyasachi Bhattacharya, for their many comments on the ideas expressed in this paper. My field work in India in the spring of 1976 and the fall of 1979 was financially supported by El Colegio de Mexico and the Indian government under the auspices of the Mexico-India cultural exchange agreement. In Banaras, especially in 1976, Mr. Virendra Singh provided invaluable help as an interviewer, interpreter and research assistant. Dr. Shukdeo Singh of Banaras Hindu University and the monks of the Kabir Chaura *maṭh* in Banaras — above all Acharya Amritdas, Gangasharan Shastri, and Vivekdas — have given unstinting advice and cooperation throughout.

in any given manifestation of bhakti, include: (1) the doctrine of avatars or incarnations of the principal gods, usually Vishnu; (2) a defined contrast between different paths to salvation, only one of which is devotion; (3) the notion that, although the various paths to salvation are partly complementary, bhakti is in some sense the best and certainly the only one easily accesible to a wide range of social classes and to women; (4) a concept of salvation (*mukti*, *mokṣa*) implying a release from the cycle of rebirth (*saṃsāra*), determined by the moral fruits of past actions (*karma*), as well as some sort of permanent union or association (*sāyujya*, *sahaja*, etc.) with the object of devotion by means of some form of grace (*prasāda*); (5) varying degrees of elaboration and definition of different psychological attitudes of devotion based on human relationships such as child to parent, woman to lover, slave to master, friend to friend, etc.

The mere existence of this set of characteristics does not, however, tell us how it is used and interpreted in specific historical cases. To understand any particular manifestation of bhakti religiosity we must ask a number of specific questions about both content and context. First, what is the message? In other words, how is bhakti defined? Which aspects of the concept receive special emphasis and which are passed over more lightly? In many cases, including many studies of Kabir, the analysis gets little further than this. Secondly, who is transmitting the message? What is the socio-economic position and personal history of the transmitters? Why do they act as they do? Are they sincere or do they have ulterior motives? Thirdly, to whom is the message being transmitted? What is the social makeup and class base of the audience? Fourthly, when and where and how is the message transmitted? In other words, what is the total historical context of the message its exponents and its receivers? Finally, how is the message accepted and interpreted by the audience? How popular is it and how is it understood and utilized?

Milton Singer has aptly described this type of analysis as "the articulation of textual and contextual studies" and has rightly lamented its absence in most studies of contemporary Hinduism, not to mention studies of premodern Hinduism, where it is much more difficult to apply. For the most part, historians of religion, linguists, philosophers, sociologists and anthropologists have studiously avoided crossing supposed disciplinary boundaries to incorporate the findings of each other's research. The result has been the sacrifice of breadth for depth and the creation of distorted views of the significance of the objects of study. As Singer notes, "whatever its source, this cleavage must be transcended if our understanding of religion is to be advanced."[1]

In this essay I would like to examine the role of social and religious dissent in the bhakti movement associated with the name of Kabir. For practical reasons, largely having to do with the nature of the possible sources, the discussion will treat Kabir and the songs attributed to him in a somewhat separate fashion from the modern Kabir sect or panth. For the panth, I will rely on information collected during field work in the monasteries (*maṭh*) of the panth in Banaras in the spring of 1976 and the fall of 1979 as well as on the researches of other scholars such as G.H. Westcott, R.V. Russell and Hira Lal, F.E. Keay, Parashuram Chaturvedi, and Kedarnath Dvivedi.

The basic hypothesis of this paper is that the strong element of social and religious dissent in Kabir's teachings, whatever its original intent and function, has been used by the adherents of the panth—mostly marginal groups such as Shudras, Untouchables and Tribals—to express their rejection of certain aspects of hierarchical caste ideology, at the same time that their membership in the Kabir-panth has fostered their actual assimilation within that same society. Insofar as they do internalize large portions of higher caste ideology, they also attempt to raise the social status that others assign to them by adopting Sanskritized customs. Nonetheless these groups cannot realistically hope that this will dramatically raise their caste ranking in the eyes of others. Even so, the more egalitarian ideology of the Kabir-panth does provide them with a positive self-image, one which rejects the innate and absolute character of the inferior status to which they are relegated by more orthodox Brahmanical Hinduism. Their membership in the Kabir-panth indicates a general acceptance of caste society, but it is an acceptance conditioned by another vision of the ultimate nature of that society and of their own innate worth within it. In this vision the absolute value of the Untouchable is not inferior to that of the Brahman. They accept that it is difficult to change social customs, and that it is generally necessary to respect them, but the true human reality is a different one, one in which each human being is judged on his own merits, not those of his birth in a particular family. The social ideology of Kabir, as transmitted both within and without the Kabir-panth, clearly expresses what Jayant Lele has called the "liberating moments" of bhakti tradi-

1. Milton Singer, *When a Great Tradition Modernizes* (New York: Praeger Publishers, 1972), pp. 39-40.

tion and offers an indirect but sharp refutation of Michael Moffatt's dangerously mistaken view of the nature of Untouchable acceptance of caste society.[2]

Kabir has been commonly portrayed as a religious and social reformer who sought a spiritual reconciliation and purification of Islam and Hinduism, as well as the propounder of an exalted mystical religion of the heart which aimed to do away with vulgar exterior rites and noxious social practices and prejudices. J.E. Carpenter, for instance, has written that Kabir's age "was ripening for a great spiritual movement through the approach of the higher thought and practice of Hinduism and Islam.... The first serious effort towards mutual appreciation and sympathy was made by the greatest of Indian mystics, Kabir."[3] Tara Chand has praised Kabir enthusiastically to much the same effect: "He has gazed into the mystery of life and seen the vision of the ineffable light. He brings from the world of beyond a new message for the individual and for society.... He is a mighty warner, an intrepid pathfinder, the great pioneer of the unity of the Hindu and Muslim communities of India and the apostle of the faith of Humanity."[4]

Other scholars such as P.D. Barthwal and Hazariprasad Dvivedi, who examined the texts attributed to Kabir with somewhat more caution and attention, early noted that these texts owe considerably more to Hindu than to Islamic tradition, and that they were extensively influenced by the Tantric doctrines of the heterodox Nath sect. Barthwal and, later on, Dvivedi, Charlotte Vaudeville and W.H. McLeod, have suggested that Kabir's family may have been only nominally converted to Islam from the Nath tradition, or possibly even from Tantric Buddhism.[5] In any case, Kabir was not himself a Nath Yogi, however much

2. See Jayant Lele's introduction to his (ed.), *Tradition and Modernity in Bhakti Movements* (Leiden: E.J. Brill, 1981), pp. 1-15, and Michael Moffat, *An Untouchable Community in South India: Structure and Consensus* (Princeton: Princeton University Press, 1979). See also David N. Lorenzen, "The Kabir Panth and Politics," *Political Science Review* (Jaipur) 20:3 (1982), and "The Kabir Panth: Heretics to Hindus," in Lorenzen (ed.), *Religious Change and Cultural Domination* (Mexico: El Colegio de Mexico, 1981), pp. 151-72.

3. J.E. Carpenter, *Theism in Medieval India* (London: Williams and Norgate, 1921), p. 456.

4. Tara Chand, *Influence of Islam on Indian Culture* (Allahabad: Indian Press, 1954), pp. 145-46.

5. P.D. Barthwal, *The Nirguṇa School of Hindi Poetry* (Benares: Indian Book Shop, 1936), pp. 250-51. The Hindi translation, *Hindī kāvya meṅ nirguṇ samparadāy* (Lucknow: Avadh Publishing House, S. 2007, A.D. 1950) is much altered by the

he may have borrowed from this tradition. Rather, as McLeod has noted, Kabir represents in many ways the culmination of the Sant or *nirguṇa* tradition (*sampradāy*) which was "a synthesis of the three principal dissenting movements, a compound of elements drawn mainly from Vaiṣṇava bhakti and the *haṭha-yoga* of the Nath Yogis, with a marginal contribution from Sufism."[6]

Although it may be true that Sufism exercised less influence on Kabir than the Nath and Vaishnava traditions, it is still debatable whether he can be considered essentially a Hindu. I have argued elsewhere that, by their very ferocity, Kabir's satires against both Islam and Hinduism go beyond mere attacks on the hypocrisy of their external rites and suggest that he was attempting to stake out an ideological position basically independent of both.[7] A consideration of Kabir's own social background, however imperfectly known, lends support to this suggestion. Whether or not Kabir's family had been steeped in Nath tradition, it is certain that they were Julahas, a Muslim weaver caste of low status. Like most low-caste Muslims, they were undoubtedly indigenous converts to Islam and not immigrants, though when this conversion took place is not known. The fact that Kabir based his religious message more on Hindu traditions than on Muslim ones at least shows that he had little use for Islam. Granted that he was born in this faith, however, it would have been virtually impossible for him to directly re-enter the Hindu fold as an individual, and almost as impossible for him to have secured the re-entrance of his family or local caste group, since Hindu tradition has generally discouraged conversions from Islam. Furthermore, even when non-Hindu groups have been permitted to join Hindu caste society, they have generally been admitted as castes of the lowest status (ruling groups which became Kshatriya castes are

---

translator Parashuram Chaturvedi. According to Charlotte Vaudeville in her *Kabīr*, vol. 1 (Oxford: Clarendon Press, 1974), p. 24, the connection between Kabir's verses and the Naths was first pointed out by Barthwal in his article, "*Hindī kāvya meṅ yog-pravāh*," published in the *Nāgaṟī Prachāriṇī Sabhā Pattrikā*," 11 (S. 1987, A.D. 1930). See also Hazariprasad Dvivedi, *Kabīr* (Delhi: Rajakamal Prakashan, 1941), pp. 24-25; *Nāth-sampradāy* (Banaras: Naivedya Niketan, 1950); Vaudeville, trans., *Kabīr Granthāvalī* (*Dohā*) (Pondichery: Institut Français d'Indologie, 1957) and *Kabīr*, vol 1; Parashuram Chaturvedi, *Uttarī Bhārat kī sant-paramparā*, 2nd ed. (Allahabad: Leader Press, 1964); W.H. McLeod, *Gurū Nānak and the Sikh Religion* (Oxford: Clarendon Press, 1968).

6. McLeod, *Nānak*, p. 152. See also Hazariprasad Dvivedi, *Hindī sāhitya kī bhūmikā*, new ed. (Bombay: Hindi Granth-Ratnakar, 1963), p. 41.

7. Lorenzen, "Heretics to Hindus."

of course an exception). An independent spirit like Kabir is unlikely to have willingly accepted such a status even if it were offered.

This view of Kabir's social situation perhaps can also help to explain the choice of an impersonal (*nirguṇa*) deity as his sole object of worship. Although we know nothing of the social makeup of Kabir's listeners, it is reasonable to assume that they included mostly little-educated members from low castes such as Kabir's own. In the traditional Hindu view, such persons are best suited to a religion based on simple devotion to a thoroughly anthropomorphized deity. The classic example is Vaishnava devotion directed to the avatars of Vishnu such as Krishna and Ram, a religion which has had great success among the common people. Why did Kabir insist on a more difficult and arduous devotion to an impersonal godhead? Some scholars have simply argued that this choice simply shows the intuitive subtlety of Kabir's mind, or even the direct influence of *advaita* Vedanta. Others, with rather more plausibility, have argued that Kabir is merely developing a line of thought present in the teachings of his Sant predecessors. This explanation, however, simply broadens the question. Why did Kabir's predecessors also tend toward the worship of an impersonal deity?

Here we encounter a very interesting fact, namely that nearly all the better known Sants of the *nirguṇa* tradition were non-Brahmans, many from quite low castes. According to tradition, Kabir was one of twelve disciples of the Brahman Ramananda. Several of these disciples represent what Barthwal calls "an intermediate position between the Saguna [personal or with-attributes] and Nirguna Schools." They include Pipaji, the Khichi king of Gagaraunagadh; Sen, a barber (*nāī*); Ravidas or Raidas, a leatherworker (*chamār*); and Dhanna, a Jat. Among Kabir's more important predecessors should be mentioned Namdev (*c.* 1300), a cotton-printer (*chīpī*) and Sadhan or Sadan (c. 1350), a butcher (*kasāī*). Most of the prominent *nirguṇa* Sants who came after Kabir were also non-Brahmans. These include Guru Nanak (1469-1538), a Khatri; Dadu Dayal (1544-1603), a cotton carder (*dhuniyā*) and possibly born as a Muslim with the name Daud; Maluk Das (1574-1682), a *kakkaḍ* Khatri; Dariya of Bihar (1674-1780), the son of a Kshatriya (possibly converted to Islam) and the daughter of a seamstress; Charan Das (b. 1703), a *dhūsar* Bania; and others.[8] For Kabir, and these *nir-*

8. See Barthwal, *Nirguṇa School*, pp. 249-69. See also Chaturvedi, *Sant-paramparā*.

guṇa Sants as well, *saguṇa* worship implied worship of gods and avatars whose mythology was controlled by Brahmans and authoritatively codified in Sanskrit texts such as the Puranas. Given this situation, it is not surprising that an impersonal deity would be preferred in spite of the intellectual and psychological difficulties It (or He) presented.

The analysis of the interrelations between Kabir, his message, his audience and the socio-historical environment unfortunately cannot be carried much further without confronting a number of formidable obstacles. About the man Kabir we know virtually nothing apart from his having belonged to a family of Muslim weavers of Banaras. His dates are uncertain, with scholars about equally divided between 1448-50 and 1518 (or possibly 1504) as the year of his death.[9] As for his message, most independent scholars accept that all of the three major collections of writings attributed to Kabir—the songs contained in the *Ādi Granth*, the Rajasthani *Kabīr-granthāvalī* collection, and the Kabir-panth's own *Bījak*—contain interpolations of material from other sources.[10] In this regard, the *Bījak* collection seems particularly suspect although it has had the greatest historical impact among the members of the panth since most branches (*śākhās*) of the panth accept only it as authoritative. About Kabir's audience, as has been noted, little can be said apart from the supposition that it must have appealed primarily to people of marginal social status like Kabir himself. In any case, by the end of the sixteenth century or even earlier, Kabir's verses had become popular among the common people over wide parts of North India as is evident from the large number of later Sants who directly or indirectly acknowledge their debt to him.

As far as the Kabir-panth is concerned, its history before the nineteenth century is known almost exclusively from tendentious sectarian traditions. Nonetheless, there exist a sizable number of early references to legends of Kabir's life that may possibly be products of the early panth. Most are today accepted as true by all branches of the panth. They are found in such early texts as Nabhadas's *Bhaktamāl* (ca. 1600), its commentaries by Priyadas (1712) and others, Anantadas's *Kabīr parichay* [or *parachaī*] (ca. 1588), the *Dabistān-i-mazāhib* (ca. 1650),

9. The most complete discussion of his date is found in ibid., pp. 845-70. See also Vaudeville, *Kabīr* 1:36-39.

10. For a discussion of the different text collections see Barthwal, *Nirguṇa School*, pp. 273-82, and also Vaudeville, *Kabīr* 1:56-63.

Raghodas's *Bhaktamālā* (1660) and its commentary by Chaturdas (1794), and a number of Kabir-panth texts of uncertain age.[11]

The general tendency of these legends, which need not be discussed in detail here, is to make Kabir more Hindu and less Muslim. The principal legends are those which claim that Kabir (1) descended from heaven onto a lotus leaf in the Lahartara pond as an avatar of Vishnu (or alternately was the son of a virgin Brahman widow); (2) became, by a trick, the disciple of the Brahman Ramananda; (3) was persecuted by Sikandar Lodi, the Muslim Sultan (d. 1517) and disputed with a Muslim divine named Shaikh Taqi; (4) saved the temple of Jagannath in Puri from the wrath of the Lord of the Ocean who instead vented it on Dwarka in Gujarat. Another frequently cited legend relates how his Muslim and Hindu disciples fought over how to dispose of his body after his death but then discovered under his shroud only a pile of flowers which they evenly divided.[12]

In one respect, there exists an important difference between the legends accepted by the Kabir-panth and those accepted by the Sikh tradition. In the songs attributed to Kabir in the *Ādi Granth* and the *Kabīr-granthāvalī*, reasonably clear allusions are made to his wife or wives, to a son named Kamal, and possibly to a daughter named Kamali. Various legends about Kabir and these family members are current in Sikh tradition.[13] The monks of the Kabir-panth, on the other hand, insist that Kabir remained all his life an unmarried ascetic. They either deny the authenticity of the songs in question or interpret them away rather in the same fashion that certain Christian churches do the various biblical allusions to Jesus's brothers. Songs referring to Kabir's wives and children are noticeably absent from the panth's own *Bījak*.

However mythologized all these legends may be, they do clearly illustrate the rapid Hinduization of Kabir tradition. Except in the case of the stories of his family life, or its absence, however, it is not clear to what extent these stories are the product of diffused popular tradition as opposed to being relatively conscious creations of the Kabir-panth.

11. On these texts see especially Kedarnath Dvivedi, *Kabīr aur Kabīr-panth* (Allahabad: Hindi Sahitya Sammelan, 1965), and Chaturvedi, *Sant-paramparā*.

12. On these legends see Kedarnath Dvivedi, Chaturvedi and Lorenzen, "Heretics to Hindus."

13. Many of these legends are found in M.A. Macauliffe's translation of the *Ādi Granth*, *The Sikh Religion*, 6 vols. (Oxford: Clarendon Press, 1909). For the hagiographic literature and oral traditions of the Sikhs see W.H. McLeod, *The Evolution of the Sikh Community* (Oxford: Clarendon Press, 1976), pp. 20-36, and *Early Sikh Tradition* (Oxford: Clarendon Press, 1980).

The most that we can say is that today each branch of the panth actively fosters them, each in its own variants, often together with fanciful stories of Kabir's former births and a matching, rather eccentric theology. This is particularly true of various works of the Dharmadas *śākhā* such as Paramanandadas's *Kabīr-i-manshūr* (first published in Urdu in 1887) and Brahmalinamuni's Sanskrit *Sadguruśrīkavīracaritam* (1960). The Surat Gopal or Kabir Chaura *śākhā* has recently countered with the more reserved Hindi *Kabīr kā jīvancharitra* (1976) by Gangasharan Shastri, the current *adhikārī* of the Banaras Kabir Chaura *maṭh*.[14]

The first serious attempt at an academic description of the Kabir-panth seems to be that of H.H. Wilson in his famous study of Hindu sects first published in *Asiatick Researches* in 1828 and 1832.[15] Apart from brief discussions in various district gazetteers and the 1891 census report, the panth attracted little other attention from outsiders during the nineteenth century. In 1907, Bishop G.H. Westcott published his *Kabir and the Kabir Panth*, which became a principal source for much subsequent writing on the panth.[16] Also valuable is R.V. Russell's and Hira Lal's *Tribes and Castes of the Central Provinces* (1916).[17] No significant improvement on Westcott's work was published until F.E. Keay's *Kabir and His Followers* (1931), a detailed study based on first hand observation and extensive examination of Kabir-panthi literature.[18] Keay's work has since been partly superseded by Kedarnath Dvivedi's excellent *Kabīr aur Kabīr-panth*, first published in 1965. The revised second edition of Parashuram Chaturvedi's important *Uttarī Bhārat kī Sant paramparā*, though published a year earlier, relies in part on Kedarnath Dvivedi's work for its discussion of the panth.[19] Recently, the anthropologist Baidyanath Saraswati has done field work on the

14. For Paramanandadas's *Kabīr-i-manshur* I have have had access only to a Hindi translation by Sudhadas, *Kabīr manśūr*, part I (Baroda: Pandit Shri Motidasji Chetandasji, 1956). Brahmalinamuni, *Sadguruśrīkaviracaritam* (Surat: Svami Shri Brahmalinamuni, 1960); Gangasharan Shastri, *Kabīr kā jīvancharitra* (Varanasi: Kabir Vani Prakashan Kendra, 1976). See also *Kabīr-kasauṭī* (Bombay: Gangavishnu Shrikrishnadas, 1962).

15. H.H. Wilson, *Religious Sects of the Hindus* (Varanasi: Indological Book House, 1972), pp. 36-54.

16. G.H. Westcott, *Kabir and the Kabir Panth* (Calcutta: Susil Gupta, 1953).

17. Robert V. Russell and Rai Bahadur Hira Lal, *The Tribes and Castes of the Central Provinces of India*, 4 vols. (London: Macmillan and Co., 1916; reprint ed., Oosterhout, N.B.: Anthropological Publications, 1969). See especially 1:232-44.

18. F.E. Keay, *Kabir and His Followers* (Calcutta: Association Press, 1931).

19. For Kedarnath Dvivedi and Parashuram Chaturvedi, see notes 11 and 5 above.

panth, but as far as I am aware, he has as yet published very little.[20] A number of anthropologists, historians and government writers have made passing observations about the activities of the panth in different contexts but do not make it their central object of concern.

Considering the numerical strength of the panth and its strategic social and religious importance, its relative neglect by scholars is somewhat surprising, all the more so when compared to the ample material published on the person, language and literature of Kabir himself. In the remainder of this paper I would like first to briefly describe the organization and distribution of the panth, and then to argue the hypothesis that the panth has functioned primarily as a Hinduizing agent for marginal groups, mainly Untouchables, Shudras and Tribals.

According to Kabir-panthi tradition, four of the principal disciples of Kabir founded four distinct branches (*śākhā*) of the panth. Surat Gopal (or Sruti Gopal) founded the Kabir Chaura *śākhā* centered at Banaras; Dharmadas the Chhattisgarh *śākhā* centered in eastern Madhya Pradesh; Jagudas (or Jagodas) the *śākhā* centered at Bidupur (Muzaffarpur District, Bihar) and at Shivpur (near Banaras); and Bhagodas (also Bhagudas or Bhagavan Gusain), the Bhagatahi *śākhā* centered at Dhanauti (Chapra District, Bihar). In fact, this historical tradition is very dubious and omits another important *śākhā* of the panth, the Phatuha *śākhā* centered near Patna, said to have been founded by two other direct disciples of Kabir, the brothers Tattva and Jiva. Some scholars have suggested that all these branches of the Kabir-panth may date from a time considerably later than Kabir himself. Another important *śākhā* of the contemporary panth is that centered at Burhanpur in southwestern Madhya Pradesh and founded by Puran Sahab in about 1835. Independent monasteries, some with subsidiary centers elsewhere, exist at Puri in Orissa (apparently quite an old monastery), at Hatakesar in Madhya Pradesh, at Badaiya village about 37 miles west of Banaras, and two separate monasteries at Rusera (Rusada) in Darbhanga District, Bihar.[21]

The two principal branches of the panth are the Kabir Chaura *śākhā* of Banaras and the Chhattisgarh *śākhā* with rival headquarters in Damakheda and Kharasiya, both in eastern Madhya Pradesh. The

20. See Baidyanath Saraswati, "Notes on Kabir: A Non-Literate Intellectual," in S.C. Malik, ed., *Dissent, Protest and Reform in Indian Civilization* (Simla: Indian Institute of Advanced Study, 1977), pp. 167-87.

21. On this general topic see especially Kedarnath Dvivedi. Also see Keay and Parashuram Chaturvedi.

Kabir Chaura *maṭh* in Banaras is situated on the reputed site of Kabir's family house and claims to be the original seat (*mūl gaddī*) of the panth from which all the other branches derive. The members of the Kabir Chaura *śākhā*, both laymen and monks, on the average come from castes of somewhat higher status than those of the Chhattisgarh *śākhā*. The Kabir Chaura *maṭh* at Banaras maintains its authority over a large number of subsidiary monasteries located in northern Bihar, eastern U.P., and Gujarat.[22] It is not clear just how much contact the monks of this *śākhā* maintain with lay members of the panth. The Chhattisgarh *śākhā* seems, in this respect, to be much more active. Its chief area of operations is in Madhya Pradesh, especially the eastern (Chhattisgarh) and northwestern (Bundelkhand) districts, although it also controls a few centers in Gujarat and elsewhere. The Burhanpur *śākhā* is active chiefly in eastern Madhya Pradesh while the Bhagatahi and Phatuha *śākhā*s control numerous subsidiary monasteries in central and northern Bihar and even Nepal. The reason for this rather curious geographical distribution of the panth has not been adequately explained. Mostly it seems to stem from historical accident, although the relative absence of the panth from the Punjab and Rajasthan may result from the appropriation of the songs of Kabir by the religious traditions of the Sikhs and Dadu respectively. The absence of the Kabir-panth from all but extreme eastern U.P. may reflect the historical competition of Islam for the allegiance of the lower castes in this region.

The present size of the total Kabir-panthi population is somewhat difficult to estimate. In the 1901 census the number of Kabir-panthis in the Central Provinces (Madhya Pradesh) was recorded as about

22. Although I was never able to obtain a complete catalogue of these subsidiary establishments, the most important are probably those whose *mahant*s are on the eleven-member Supervisory Committee (*nirīkṣak maṇḍal*) of the Kabir Chaura *maṭh*. These include: (1) Sadguru Kabir Mandir Pani Daravaja, Baroda, Gujarat; (2) Sadguru Kabir Math, Satmalpur Post Office, Samastipur District, Bihar; (3) Sadguru Kabir Math, Samanpur, Chaitpur Post Office, Motihari District, Bihar; (4) Kabir Mandir, Phattesagar, Jodhpur, Rajasthan; (5) Kabir Math, Mehadi Ganj, Dali Ganj, Lucknow, U.P.; (6) Sadguru Kabir Mandir, Nayi Gharati, Baroda, Gujarat; (7) Sadguru Kabir Math, Balua Manjhariya, Sahajnama Post Office, Gorakhpur, U.P.; (8) Kabir Mandir, Pitariya Bamba, Ghi Kanta Road, Ahmedabad, Gujarat; (9) Sadguru Kabir Math, Rasalpur, Samastipur District, Bihar; (10) Sadguru Kabir Math, Rauna, Alauli Post Office, Monghyr District, Bihar; (11) Kabir Math, Hanumanghat, Gola Gopalpur Post Office, Gorakhpur District, U. P. The organizational structure of the Kabir Chaura *maṭh* is described in a pamphlet it published in about 1975 entitled *Śrīsadguru Kabīr mandir Kabīr Chaurā maṭh* (Banaras: Shri Kabir-Vani Prakashan Kendra).

500,000 and in India as a whole as about 850,000. In the 1911 census the number of Kabir-panthis in the Central Provinces was about 600,000.[23] The all-India census figure is probably a serious underestimate since, in at least some districts, the census-takers seem to have registered as Kabir-panthis only those who claimed this as their caste, a status generally applicable only to Kabir-panthi monks (*bairāgīs*) and not to the lay followers of the panth. If the relative percentage of Kabir-panthis in the total population has remained constant since 1901 the 850,000 Kabir-panthis of that date should have become by today (1986) some 2,500,000. Considering that the original figure is probably too low, the total numbers may well be much larger, especially if the panth's proselytizing activities have met with any success.

The question of the social composition and ideology of the Kabir-panth has also been investigated systematically only rarely if at all. The common scholarly consensus is that the panth represents merely one of a large number of heterodox sects which have arisen periodically in India to challenge the established religious and social and even political order. According to this view, these sects are in essence movements of social protest in the religious guise appropriate to the population of a pre-modern, traditional culture. It is correctly pointed out that most of these movements, including the Kabir-panth, tend to denounce — with varying degrees of severity — the so-called 'exterior' practices of religion such as elaborate sacrifices, idolatry and pilgrimages, as well as the degrading social inequalities fostered by the caste system. Instead, they preach a simpler and purer religion of the heart in which ceremony is minimized and all men are considered theoretically equal and individual. K.N. Panikkar has further suggested that the appearance of a large number of such movements in the eighteenth century tends to argue against the theory that "the emergence of modern ideas and the development of social protest and religious dissent in the nineteenth century...[was] a consequence of the introduction of European ideas and institutions into India." In his view, this theory "overlooks the elements of protest and dissent in the Indian intellectual tradition and the potentialities of social development in the eighteenth century before the intervention of the British."[24]

This general scholarly consensus, which classes the Kabir-panth and

23. Russell and Hira Lal, *Central Provinces*, 1:237 and 242.

24. K.N. Panikkar, "Presidential Address: Section III," *Proceedings of the Indian History Congress*, thirty-sixth session, Aligarh, 1975, p. 3.

other sects as indigenous movements of social dissent and protest, undoubtedly contains a large measure of truth. Unfortunately, it also tends toward oversimplification and at times contains an element of wishful thinking. Nearly all new religious movements necessarily arise within a context of serious changes in economic and social conditions, that is to say a situation of socio-economic dislocation and conflict. In part they are protests against these changes and against the social and economic injustices that accompany them. They also, however, embody attempts to come to terms with these changes, to create new value systems in which they can be accommodated and their negative, exploitative impact made bearable. In each movement, the relative strength and specific characteristics of the elements of social protest and social accommodation will be different. They also tend to change as the movements progress.

From this perspective, it is clearly a mistake to evaluate religious (and other) movements simply according to the degree of overt social protest they manifest. Social discontent and the striving toward change are always present, though they may take very different forms and directions. The essential character of any movement basically depends on the values and aims it expounds and the effectiveness of the means it uses to achieve them. In the final analysis, each movement must be considered on its own merits in its own material and ideological context.

The scholarly consensus which classes religious movements such as the Kabir-panth as pre-secular or pre-political social protest movements is often supplemented by a complementary theory which seeks to explain their evident change over the course of time. A number of scholars, especially anthropologists and sociologists, have noted that the element of overt social dissidence in new religious movements soon tends to get dissipated via a process that Max Weber called the institutionalization of charisma and Ernst Troeltsch the transition from sect to church. In the case of India, this process is often identified as the transition from cult or sect to caste. Clearly implied is the idea that the process represents a sort of spiritual hardening of the arteries leading to eventual senility. Nirmal Kumar Bose has asserted this hypothesis with bald clarity:

> If we pursue the history of nonconformist reformatory sects of the past, like those associated with the names of Caitanya-Nityānanda, or of Kabīr or Nānak (and this may even be stretched back to the time of Buddha and the Jaina Tīrthankaras), whenever there was a

> revolt against caste, and men were drawn into a new brotherhood on the basis of individual merits instead of birth, such groups slowly became converted, first into a sect, and eventually into a caste in which marriage was restricted to people of the same faith. So that, instead of weakening the bonds of caste, such revolts only succeeded in the end in adding one or more to the number of castes which already existed.[25]

Several objections must be raised to this statement. First, I seriously doubt the usefulness of a comparison of specific religious movements (as opposed to theoretical ideal types) in which these movements are abstracted from their specific socio-historical contexts. When this comparison is "stretched back" to the time of the Buddha and Jain Tirthankaras, a time when the caste system existed at best in quite rudimentary form, the result is startlingly anachronistic. Secondly, on a simple factual level, the view that the movements mentioned have been converted into one or several new castes is no more than partly true. In at least the case of the Kabir-panth, in most cases intermarriage is permitted between Kabir-panthi and non-Kabir-panthi members of the same caste. Only in one or two cases have they formed endogamous subcastes. Thirdly, as we have seen, it is highly questionable to what extent the Kabir-panth and other panths represented, even in their original stages, an individualistic, anticorporatist rebellion against caste. Likewise the passage of time has not meant the total evaporation of the element of social protest in these movements to the extent that this view implies. Rather, this element has been modified and institutionalized to serve the changing needs of their followers.

In another paper I have discussed how the monks of the Kabir-panth have Hinduized and Sanskritized the panth so that today it is flatly a Vaishnava Hindu sect. As Gangasharan Shastri (formerly Gangasharandas), the *adhikārī* of the Kabir Chaura *maṭh* remarked to me: "*Maiṅ Hindū hūṅ, maiṅ Vaiṣṇav hūṅ.*" Since my field work was principally among the monks of the panth, the paper did not make a serious effort to relate these Hinduizing and Sanskritizing tendencies (nor the partly contradictory 'Westernizing' tendency) to the ideological and social needs of its lay adherents. In spite of the fact that sustained field work on this question has not yet been attempted, a clear general

25. Nirmal Kumar Bose, "Some Aspects of Caste in Bengal," in Milton Singer, ed., *Traditional India: Structure and Change* (Philadelphia: American Folklore Society, 1959), pp. 191-206. See especially p. 203.

profile can be obtained from brief references to the proselytizing activities of the panth by anthropologists and sociologists and from a few more detailed studies of analogous cases.

The Kabir-panth has two principal sorts of clientele: (1) lower class Hindus who seek an ideology which offers them a more positive status and self image, certainly in their own eyes and if possible in the eyes of others as well, and (2) tribal peoples who are being socially and culturally assimilated into the lower levels of the caste hierarchy and are trying to preserve their self-esteem against almost hopeless odds. In both cases membership in the panth embodies an element of social protest against the hierarchical structure of the Hindu socio-religious order at the same time that it represents a general acceptance of the hegemony of that same order.

The only well-documented example of Kabir-panth activity among tribal populations is that of the Kabir-panthi Bhagats (*bhakta*s) among the Oraon, one of the principal tribes of Chhotanagpur in southern Bihar (especially Ranchi District). In the 1961 census this tribe numbered about one and a half million persons, of whom about one half lived in Bihar. In Ranchi District, they have coexisted peacefully for more than two hundred years with the Mundas. Although the two tribes are linguistically and culturally distinct, they have often joined forces to protest, with limited success, against foreign penetration and domination of their region. Early in this century, the direct religious influence of the alien Hindu social system began to make itself felt in the so-called Bhagat movements. N.K. Bose distinguishes as most significant: (1) the Nemha Bhagats, native Oraons who were instructed in visions to introduce Hinduized customs; (2) the Kabir-panthi Bhagats, initially non-Oraon outsiders from the Chhattisgarh region; (3) the Vaishnava or Bacchidan Bhagats, also outsiders from other regions; (4) the followers of the month-long Manda Parab ceremony (which includes a fire-walking finale); and (5) the Tana Bhagat or Kurukh Dharam movement, which actively got involved in nationalist politics.[26]

26. Nirmal Kumar Bose, *Some Indian Tribes* (New Delhi: National Book Trust, 1972), pp. 124-49. The original anthropological work on the Bhagat movements was done by Sarat Chandra Roy early in the century. See his *Oraon Religion and Customs* (Ranchi: Man in India Office, 1928). See also Stephen Fuchs, *Rebellious Prophets* (Bombay: Asia Publishing House, 1965), pp. 35-46; Edward Jay "Revitalization Movement in Tribal India," in L.P. Vidyarthi, ed., *Aspects of Religion in Indian Society* (Meerut: Kedar Nath Ram Nath, 1961), pp. 282-322; and Sachchidanand, *Culture Change in Tribal Bihar* (Calcutta: Bookland, 1964), pp. 96-104.

All these movements have inculcated observance of essentially Hindu customs and a corresponding rejection of certain traditional Oraon behavior. The new movements did not completely reject tribal culture, however, and preserved or tolerated many traditional beliefs and practices. They remained distinctively Oraon versions of Hinduism. The Kabir-panthi Bhagats abstain from the worship of idols and other visible symbols of divinity; abandon the drinking of alcoholic beverages or their use as libations; practise vegetarianism and abstain from animal sacrifice; reject the worship of spirits and minor deities; offer devotional worship (bhakti) to a single god; adopt strict personal morality with regard to truthfulness, honesty, non-violence to animals, and religious and social tolerance; employ and respect gurus as spiritual advisors and priests; and wear a rosary with a bead of *tulsī* wood which is given to the devotee at the time of his initiation. Although traditional Oraon life crisis rites have continued to be practised among the followers of the Kabir-panthi Bhagats, they are accompanied by a distinctive Kabir-panthi ceremony known as the *chaukā*. The Kabir-panthi Oraons also have continued to intermarry with non-Kabir-panthi fellow tribesmen although marriage with Kabir-panthis is preferred.[27]

These Oraon Bhagats are mostly attached to the Chhattisgarh *śākhā*, but in 1976 the lone *pujārī* at the Kabir Chaura *śākhā* shrine at Lahartara near Banaras was also an Oraon.

The other Hindu-influenced Bhagat movements among the Oraon preached a similar message stressing vegetarianism, rejection of animal sacrifice, abstention from alcohol, and a stricter personal morality, especially with regard to interaction between the sexes. The Tana Bhagat movement, in many respects the most influential, also sought the recovery of economic and political rights and powers lost during the long-term progressive alienation of the Oraons from their lands by outsiders.

A less well-documented case of Kabir-panth proselytization among the Mundas of Ranchi District is mentioned in P.C. Tallents's 1921 census report for Bihar and Orissa. The sect was introduced "about ten years" earlier by "a *guru* named Kristo Mohan" from the Chhattisgarh region. This guru made converts of about seventeen families among the Khangar Mundas of the Ranchi and Khunti subdivisions. Tallents remarks:

> Conversion does not appear to affect their outward way of life to any serious extent, for the converts continue to eat and intermarry with other Khangar Mundas and observe the same marriage and

27. Jay, "Revitalization Movement," pp. 293-94.

funeral ceremonies. But they believe in one God, they have ceased to believe in witchcraft or to worship their ancestors, and they have given up dancing. They tell their beads when opportunity offers and sing the hymns of Kabir after their evening meals. Once a year, when their *guru* visits them, they hold a feast and offer sweetmeats, spices, nuts and a piece of white cloth to the deity. The son of a Kabir panthi is not born a Kabir panthi but has to be initiated. Apart from the fact that they usually wear yellow clothes and, unlike other Mundas, salute one another with an embrace there is little to distinguish the Kabir panthis outwardly from their fellows. It is however reported that their conversion has made a marked change in their outlook and manner.[28]

Although only the Tana Bhagat movement directly pressed for economic and political justice, the appearance of these Hindu or Hindu-influenced movements among the Oraons and Mundas cannot be properly understood except against the background of political and economic changes which occurred in this region during the nineteenth century and even before. In his sharp analysis of the effects of these events on these two tribes (with a comparison to the Santals of the nearby Santal Parganas District), John MacDougall has argued that the nineteenth century saw an incomplete peasantization of the tribes.[29] Though the Oraons apparently practised rice cultivation even before the takeover of the district by the British between 1770 and 1810, earlier they did *not* constitute a peasant society, understood by MacDougall as a society where:

> (1) most of the members are peasants, i.e. settled cultivators with a household mode of production; and (2) there are other groups that (a) extract economic surplus from the peasants, (b) are organized into a state..., (c) are accorded at least some prestige by peasants, and (d) participate in a civilization to which peasants are linked albeit tenuously.[30]

28. P.C. Tallents, *Report* (Patna: Superintendent, Government Printing, Bihar and Orissa, 1923), Part 1 of vol. 8, *Bihar and Orissa*, Census of India, 1921, p. 131.

29. John MacDougall, "Agrarian Reform vs. Religious Revitalization: Collective Resistance to Peasantization Among the Mundas, Oraons and Santals, 1858-95," *Contributions to Indian Sociology*, new series, 11 (1977): 295-327. See also Susana B.C. Devalle, *La palabra de la tierra* (*protesta campesina en India, siglo XIX* (Mexico: El Colegio de Mexico, 1977) and R.O. Dhan, "Tribal Movements in Chotanagpur," in Malik, *Dissent*, pp. 199-213.

30. MacDougall, "Agrarian Reform," p. 311.

In MacDougall's opinion, this profile is not applicable to the Oraons (nor to the Mundas and Santals) before British rule since the tribes did not contribute a significant surplus to the Maharaja of Chhotanagpur, nor did they participate in any meaningful way in the Hindu civilization to which the Maharaja's family was oriented. "Above all," he notes, "*adivasi* social structure was not organized on the basis of religiously-legitimated hierarchy. Rather, the major feature of *adivasi* society was that it consisted of isolated, egalitarian villages."[31]

During the nineteenth century, the British dramatically increased land revenue taxes and made extensive changes in the laws governing land tenure. These measures indirectly fostered the flooding of the region by outsiders, or *diku*s as the tribals called them, who were mostly caste Hindus. The net result was that the Tribals rapidly fell into debt and lost control of their ancestral lands to the *diku*s. The Tribals were forced to work as day laborers on these lands or to sell themselves into virtual slavery on British tea plantations outside the region. Not surprisingly, this situation led to a variety of protest movements, some of which ended in open rebellion against British-*diku* rule. Although many of these movements had a strong religious coloring, economic and political demands remained central to them. The climax came with the millenarian rebellion of Mundas and Oraons led by Birsa Munda in 1895-1900. All the movements which turned to armed rebellion, including Birsa's were put down with brutal force by the British government. Although partial attempts at reform were sometimes made in the aftermath of the rebellions, in general, the situation of the Tribals continued to deteriorate. The several Christian missions active in the region also made sporadic efforts to help the Tribals, at least the converts, buti nvariably retreated whenever the Tribals' demands threatened a vital interest of the government. Successful proselytization also seriously weakened tribal unity, a side effect recognized and appreciated by the government.

What seems to have happened to the Tribals in the course of the nineteenth century is that their society became extensively peasantized in the spheres of economics and politics while their traditional social structure and culture retained considerable vitality.[32] By the early twentieth century, especially in the wake of the defeat of the Birsa movement, the cultural ramparts could no longer hold. Their collapse was signaled by the appearance of the several Bhagat movements and

31. Ibid., pp. 311, 300.
32. Ibid., p. 316.

proselytization by various Hindu sects. Through conversion to these movements and sects the Tribals attempted an accommodation with Hindu society on terms they found more or less acceptable. The new cults did introduce several cultural values at odds with the traditional tribal ones, but they permitted the converts to retain a tribal identity and to preserve as much tribal tradition as possible.

The majority of Kabir-panthis belong not to tribal groups but to castes low in the status hierarchy of Hindu society. Although these people are not culturally on the margins of Hindu society in the same way as the Tribals, they do share many of the same economic and political disabilities, and, at least in the case of the Untouchables, they hold a socio-religious status inferior even to that of the Tribals. Although the functioning of society depends on their labor, on the whole, they receive in exchange a disproportionately small recompense in terms of money, status, education, and power. In all these senses they too are marginalized human beings.

That the Kabir-panth should appeal to people of this class is not surprising and needs less historical analysis than in the case of the Tribals. It would nevertheless help enormously if we could determine to which castes the Kabir-panthis belong and in what proportions, which *śākhā*s are associated with each caste, and whether or not the Kabir-panthis in each caste form endogamous subcastes. Unfortunately, this information for the most part will have to remain unavailable until more extensive field work can be undertaken. From my work among the Kabir-panthi monks, especially those in Banaras, however, it is possible to say a little more about the monks' own caste perceptions.

The considerable extent to which the Kabir-panthi monks are sensitive to the values of higher caste society was evident from their reluctance to talk about their own caste origins. The *adhikārī* of the Kabir Chaura *maṭh* would only say that most of the twenty-five to thirty monks living there were of Vaishya or "clean" Shudra origin, but he would not let them talk to me about their family backgrounds on the pretext that they had abandoned all family ties when they became monks. The monks at the other *maṭh*s in Banaras, Bihar and Madhya Pradesh on the whole were equally reluctant to broach this subject.

Nonetheless other sources provide partial confirmation of the *adhikārī*'s statements. It is common knowledge that the *mahant*s of several of the major *maṭh*s of the Kabir-panth in Bihar and eastern U.P. come from the Koiri and Yadav (Ahir) castes, two peasant castes whose members are often owners of their own land. For example, the present *mahant* of the Kabir Chaura *maṭh* in Banaras is said to be from a Koiri family, while his predecessor was probably a Yadav. I did learn subsequently that two or three of the approximately forty monks resident in this *maṭh* were in fact from Untouchable families. They do not receive treatment different from that given to the other monks, including the obligation to work as cooks in the kitchen of the *maṭh*.

About the lay members of the panth, the *adhikārī* of the Kabir Chaura *maṭh* claimed that the majority of those attached to the Kabir Chaura *śākhā*, or as he prefers the *mūl gaddī*, were of "clean" castes. My subsequent field work in northwestern Bihar has tended to confirm this estimate. The principal castes with large numbers of followers of the Kabir-panth in this region are the Koiris, the Yadavs (Ahirs), and the Kurmis. In some areas the Mahuris, Sonars, Malis, Gaderis, Kahars, Kumhars, Mallahs, and Tharus provide substantial numbers of followers as well. Among the Untouchables only the Chamars, Dusadhs and Pasis are important in this regard.

In the Chhattisgarh *śākhā* the lay members of the Kabir-panth seem to on average belong to castes of slightly lower status. In Bilaspur, Rai garh and Raipur Districts my interviewees said that members of the panth were particularly numerous among the agricultural castes of the Chandnahus (or Chandranahus), the Gabels and the Kurmis. The Sahus, Banias, Panikas, Bairagis, Ravats, Telis, and Kostas were also mentioned, together with the Harijan castes of the Satnamis and Chamars and the tribal groups of the Kamvars and Gonds. For the whole of the Chhattisgarh region Russell and Hira Lal add the names of the Baghel Rajputs, the Lodhis and Kachhis, the Balahis and Koris, the Kevats, the Dhobis, and the Mahars.[33]

One of the strongest supports of the Kabir-panth in Madhya Pradesh is the Panka caste. Russell and Hira Lal identify it as "a Dravidian caste of weavers and labourers found in Mandla, Raipur and Bilāspur, and numbering 215,000 persons in 1911".[34] Today they can be estimated at about 600,000. They seem to be related to "the Pān tribe of Orissa and Chota Nāgpur, who are also known as Panika, Chīk, Gānda and by various other designations." In 1911, 84% of the caste were members of the Kabir-panth. The Kabir-panthis form one subcaste who are contrasted with other Pankas who are called Saktaha (*śākta*). In contrast to the Kabirhas, the Saktahas eat meat, drink liquor and ignore

33. Russell and Hira Lal, *Central Provinces*, 1:242-43. See also Lorenzen, "Politics."

34. Russell and Hira Lal, *Central Provinces* 3:324.

other restrictive customs. Intermarriage between the Kabirhas and Saktahas is discouraged but apparently does occur.[35] Among the related Gandas in Orissa (especially near Sambalpur) there are four subdivisions, one of which is composed of Kabir-panthis who do not normally intermarry with the other three subdivisions.[36]

In most cases, however, Kabir-panthis do not form endogamous subcastes. When asked about the possibility of intermarriage between Kabir-panthi and non-Kabir-panthi members of the same caste, the *adhikārī* of the Kabir Chaura *maṭh* said that it could and did occur although marriage with other Kabir-panthis of the same caste was generally preferred. Intercaste marriages are not permitted even if both persons are Kabir-panthis. In the case of a Kabir-panthi marrying a non-Kabir-panthi, the wife is expected to follow the religion of her husband. If the wife is the Kabir-panthi and the husband is not, however, she is encouraged to attempt to convert him by persuasion. The *adhikārī* stressed that above all this meant abstention from alcohol and meat, for as Kabir supposedly said in one of his verses: "On account of eating meat and fish and drinking liquor, men will go to hell and their parents as well."[37]

Most low-caste Kabir-panthis distinguish themselves from other members of their castes first and foremost by their vegetarianism and their abstention from alcohol (and usually tobacco). Kabir's rejection of idolatry and other 'external' religious practices is only party honored. The Kabir Chaura monks encourage pilgrimages to the *maṭh* at Banaras as well as to the subsidiary centers at Lahartara (Kabir's birthplace) and Magahar (the site of his death). The daily service at the Kabir Chaura *maṭh* has also taken on many of the characteristics of Hindu temple worship, while the Chhattisgarh *śākhā maṭh* in Banaras gives pride of place to a large image of Kabir which is daily offered *prasād* in the traditional Hindu manner. Although the monks of all *śākhā*s do express some verbal support for Kabir's attacks on caste pride, few of them I talked to rejected the caste system itself in favor of any idea that all men were created equal.

The emphasis the Kabir-panth gives to vegetarianism and abstention from alcohol needs little explanation. From a Hindu point of view the consumption of alcohol and meat are degrading and polluting practices.

35. Ibid., 324-29.

36. L.S.S. O'Malley, *Report* (Calcutta: Bengal Secretariat Book Depot, 1913), Part 1 of vol. 5, *Bengal, Bihar and Orissa*, Census of India, 1911, p. 497.

37. See Lorenzen, "Heretics to Hindus," for more details.

Low castes that wish to secure a higher socio-religious status in the eyes of other castes have little other option than to abandon them. A respondent in Sachchidananda's recent *The Harijan Elite* makes this point with simple clarity:

> Under the influence of Kabirpanth a large number of scheduled caste villagers have changed their food habits. Some fifty years ago some Kabirpanthis...came to my village. They suggested to the Harijans that the adoption of vegetarianism would bring the end of their troubles and disabilities. Due to their preaching the entire community became vegetarian. Even now the situation is the same.[38]

To see the religious insight and biting social criticism of Kabir's verses reduced to little more than vegetarianism can hardly help but inspire cynicism. We must bear in mind, however, that except in a very few cases — most notably those of Basava, Kabir and Nanak (and perhaps the early materialists) — no influential religious and social critic in pre-colonial India directly questioned the overall legitimacy of the Hindu socio-religious order. Romila Thapar has aptly remarked with regard to the early heterodox groups, that they objected "not to the system (which was a workable, socio-economic system) but to the brahmanical interpretation of it."[39] Even in the cases of Basava, Kabir and Nanak, the extent to which they questioned the legitimacy of the system is debatable. With some exceptions, this also holds true for the social and religious reformers of the nineteenth and twentieth centuries.

Although this paper is not the place to initiate a full-scale discussion of why this should be the case, I would like to conclude with one or two speculative remarks about this problem. The answer must lie, of course, in the nature of the socio-religious order and in its interaction with the political and economic aspects of Indian society. Although both these aspects periodically underwent fundamental changes in the course of history, in two important respects they have preserved a significant continuity since very early times. First, the basic economic unit of the society has remained, to some extent even today, the relatively self-sufficient village. This has been true even through transformations in the dominant mode of production. Secondly, political authority has remained relatively divorced from religious and social concerns. For the

38. Sachchidanand, *The Harijan Elite* (Faridabad, Haryana: Thomson Press, 1977), p. 123.

39. Romila Thapar, *Ancient Indian Social History* (New Delhi: Orient Longman, 1978), p. 35.

most part (and for somewhat different reasons) Hindu, Muslim and British rulers have been content to extract the economic surplus of the villages and leave them to their own religious and social devices. Each sect and caste has been allowed to maintain its own values and social customs so long as they have not attempted to directly interfere with the practical day to day functioning of the rules and customs which govern the interaction of different groups within the hierarchical socio-religious system as a whole. By the time a group somehow managed to win enough economic and political power to be able to successfully challenge the system, it had also gained a status near the top of the hierarchy and lost any interest in overthrowing it. As a result, the only feasible strategy of religious and social critics has been to preach their more egalitarian social vision exclusively to the oppressed lower classes, and to confine the institutional expression of this vision to pacifistic religious sects, usually with a limited caste, class and regional base. The political leaders of independent India have pledged to finally sweep the societal configuration based on high caste hegemony into the dust-bin of history. If and when this happens, the liberating potential of Kabir's message may yet find a more concrete expression.

CLAN AND LINEAGE AMONG THE SANTS: SEED, SUBSTANCE, SERVICE

DANIEL GOLD

Introduction: The Coherence of Sant Tradition as a Problem in the History of Religions

Sharing almost as few conventions with each other as with the adherents of the orthodoxies they sometimes mocked, the North Indian Sants appear more as a diverse collection of spiritual personalities than as a distinct religious tradition. Such a tradition was, nevertheless, recognized by the Sants themselves. Though their common spiritual roots derive ultimately from forms of Yoga and devotion long practised in India, the coherence they saw in their tradition had little grounding in any developed Indian ritual or mythology. Indeed, identifying closely with neither the Hindu heritage nor Islam, the Sants sang of a Lord who transcended the established traditions of both — a Lord approached through no traditionally established *image*, but through the more 'formless' saving power of *śabda*, divine *sound*. Frequently referred to as *satguru*, the True Guru, the Lord could find a focus on earth in the figure of the Sant as guru; and his sanctified personality, standing independent of conflicting bases of Hindu and Muslim authority, could then serve for some as an object of devotion both readily believable and close at hand.

Since they felt bound to no orthodoxy, individual Sants were free to adopt the spiritual resources available to them according to their various personal religious visions and styles. Understanding the coherence of Sant tradition, then, means understanding the ways its often highly individual constituent figures perceived their relationships to one another and the socio-religious patterns such perceptions entailed. The coherence that did develop, I will argue, derives from two basic principles: first, a concept of the organic relationship between guru and disciple, which generated self-perpetuating *lineages*; second, a sense that 'genuine' Sants of any lineage formed a vaguely related spiritual *clan*. Underlying these principles of lineage and clan are important cultural presuppositions. Most basic is an Indian world-view in which the varied orders of the created universe form a continuous, substantial whole.

Within this context, the Sants could readily see parallels to their own interrelationships in the worlds of (1) Indian family life and (2) medieval Indian politics.

Different implications of what it can mean for an Indian to perceive the universe in such substantial terms have recently been examined by anthropologists and historians.[1] In this paper I will look at what such a world-view might imply for the coherence of Sant tradition as a problem in the history of religions. Thus the notions of 'lineage' and 'clan' I use will be self-consciously religio-historical, though they do, in fact, derive from a standard anthropological usage noted by Graburn: "Generally speaking lineages are descent groups leading back to a known ancestor, whereas clans are groups descending from a common *mythical* ancestor."[2] In the present religio-historical context 'clan' will refer to a consciousness of kinship through broad, historically untraceable, generic relationships; 'lineage' will refer to a sense of kinship which identifies definite relationships to specific persons. While notions of both clan and lineage appear throughout the tradition, their relative significance varies in the different socio-religious forms they can together entail. These different socio-religious forms are marked by changes in the nature of the guru-disciple relationship which yield corresponding perceptions of the '*satguru*' who looms so large in most Sant texts.

Most Sants sometimes sing of the 'guru' in terms which seem very human. But just which Sants normally did have a living person in mind when they so sang is not always clear. Particularly problematic in this respect are the well-known early Sants, most of whom are sources of significant lineages. Western scholars today usually see the 'guru' referred to by Kabir, Nanak, and Dadu as bearing little reference to any one living person, though Indian scholars, with some good reasons of their own, tend to see otherwise.[3] In any case, though the earliest Sants

1. See McKim Marriott, "Hindu Transactions," in B. Kapferer, ed., *Transaction and Meaning* (Philadelphia: Institute for the Study of Human Issues, 1976), pp. 109-42; Ronald Inden, *Marriage and Rank in Bengali Culture* (Berkeley: University of California Press, 1976); Ronald Inden and Ralph Nicholas, *Kinship in Bengali Culture* (Chicago: University of Chicago Press, 1977).

2. Nelson Graburn, *Readings in Kinship and Social Structure* (New York: Harper and Row, 1971), p. 2.

3. The arguments from Vaishnava authority sometimes cited by Indian scholars to find Kabir's lineage in Ramananda certainly do not appear to the present writer "good reasons" as such. But the nearly universal Tantric insistence on the necessity of a living guru at key stages of spiritual development seems convincing. If the Sants' inner experience was indeed of the general Tantric variety, then it follows that most

did not seem to have maintained extended contact with individual preceptors of their own, in singing as they did of the Lord as *satguru*, they were — no doubt consciously — offering *themselves* to be taken in place of the traditional objects of worship they are often seen as rejecting. Yet, as is usually the case as well with later figures taken as the source of lineages, while normally giving the name of no one guru as specically theirs, they often make specific reference to other Sants.[4] Thus, not clear about any lineage of their own, such figures certainly provide a basis for the future elaboration of the notion, and demonstrate a definite awareness of a larger Sant clan.

The tradition takes a significantly different form with the first several successors of well-known Sants. Aware of the *satguru* as also a unique individual at hand, their references to him seem more patently human, and they sometimes sing of the paradoxes involved in devotion to a living person.[5] While retaining a significant awareness of a larger Sant clan, these figures, many illustrious in their own right, also saw their

---

Sants should have had significant contacts with living gurus. In *Sant sāhitya ke preraṇā srot* (Delhi: Rajpal and Sons, 1975), Parashuram Chaturvedi refers to considerable discussion in Sant texts of the guru (pp. 109-21) and the *satguru* (pp. 122-31). For Western scholarly opinion, see W.H. McLeod, *Guru Nanak and the Sikh Religion* (Oxford: Clarendon Press, 1968), pp. 196-99; Charlotte Vaudeville, *Kabīr*, vol. 1 (Oxford: Clarendon Press, 1974), pp. 116-17.

4. Thus in a short verse given by Parashuram Chaturvedi in his *Sant kāvya* (Allahabad: Kitab Mahal, 1952), pp. 200-01, Dhanna Bhagat, an early Rajasthani Sant, mentions Kabir, Ravidas (Raidas), Namdev, and Sena Nai. See also the excerpt from Tulsi Sahib below.

5. For example, the following example from Paltu Sahib, an eighteenth-century Sant from Ayodhya taken as the disciple of Govind Sahib in the lineage of Bauri Sahiba:

> These, says Paltu, are the Sant's distinctive signs...
> At times his words are humble;
>   At times he sits up proud.
> At times he sings our Hari's play;
>   At times he says the name of Ram within.
> At times he says the world is true;
>   At times he holds it false.
> At times he talks about the Lord with Form;
>   At times he shows the Formless,
> At times he talks about the dualistic path;
>   At times he becomes non-dual....

(Another twenty-four parallel lines follow). *Palṭū sāhib kī bānī*, 3 vols. (Allahabad: Belvedere Press, 1965), 3:59.

own status as gurus deriving in large part from the fact of their lineage. As we shall see, moreover, they began to give this perception socio-religious and theological expression. It is then the form Sant tradition takes within the first several generations of a lineage with which this study will be principally concerned. This form differs significantly not only from that seen in the relatively lineageless early Sants, but also from that seen in the elaborate growth of lineage traditions called the Sant panths, whose members are more often aware of a particular Sant of the past as the 'true' guru than of any living person today.

The particular notions of lineage we will be examining are those found among gurus of the Radhasoami tradition. With its source in Sant Shiv Dayal Singh, known as Soamiji, who flourished in Agra in the mid-nineteenth century, its history is relatively clear and can reveal important implications of concepts that develop among the immediate successors of a well-known Sant. Like most of the Sants we know about, the Radhasoami gurus not only had significant popular followings but also spoke — in their own variant of a common 'Tantric' esoteric jargon — of specific inner 'experiences' which came to them somehow from 'the guru'. Now the nature of the living guru as mediator is usually presented in Indian esoteric traditions in terms of mystery: the guru, himself identified with the divine, is able to offer something of this identity to the disciple. The different specific traditions offer their various solutions to this mystery, which the disciple is to realize according to his level of spiritual maturity. The problem of the guru's *real* identity, though perhaps not of pressing concern to the wider circle of devotees, was certainly significant for the few who could qualify as successors. Understanding the perceptions behind Sant lineages, then, involves getting some sense of the more esoteric aspects of the guru as mediator. These aspects are, in fact, presented in a clearly delineated, if perhaps unusually bare, form in the Radhasoami literature, which identifies the living guru with the highest Lord in particularly outspoken and unambiguous terms.

Depicted as hierarchies of matter which interpenetrate and present continuity of pattern, the hidden worlds of the Radhasoamis resemble many found in later Indian metaphysical texts. Thus the familiar examples of the heavenly Vrindavan (and Kashi, and Ganga), with their earthly extensions and points of access within the human body, are usually subsumed by Radhasoami gurus into a complex cosmology: they can become part of a universe containing eighteen subtle planes taken in three groups of six — all accessible by means of Yoga through progressively higher centers in the body.[6] Whether, and in what ways, kindred notions of continuous substance might be significant in the everyday perceptions of most Indians is a question being pursued by Marriott, Inden, and others who take an ethno-scientific approach to cultural studies.[7] But some such notions probably did in fact color the general perception of serious practitioners of later esoteric *sādhanās*. When transposed into the more mundane world, the perception that like modes of substance tend to be organized along similar lines implies that aspects of culture taken as significantly related to one another are internally coherent in similar ways. As principles of internal coherence, notions of lineage and clan among the Sants then present parallels first to concepts of lineage and clan seen as basic to ordinary biological kinship; and second, to the extension of such kinship concepts into the world of medieval Indian politics — which bears significant socio-religious implications for Sant tradition.

Figures of speech stemming from these parallels are then employed in the Sant literature. Particularly important in the discourses of the Radhasoami gurus is the figure of the seed and the field, a biological metaphor which occurs with much the same force among the disciples of spiritual masters in India generally.[8] Linked to the political developments are injunctions of service to the master, found throughout the

6. Different representatives of Radhasoami tradition can differ, however, in just how they interpret the three sets of six stages each. For detailed accounts of Radhasoami cosmology from the two major branches of the lineage, see Maharaj Saheb, *Discourses on Radhasoami Faith* (Soamibagh, Agra: Radhasoami Satsang, 1973), pp. 179-287; Lekh Raj Puri, *Radha Swami Teachings* (Beas: Radha Soami Satsang Beas, 1972), pp. 167-224. Puri gives a chart outlining his interpretation of the "three sets of six" in *Mysticism: The Spiritual Path* (Beas: Radha Soami Satsang Beas, 1974), p. 386.

7. See note 1 above.

8. Thus Rajjab, a disciple of Dadu, in a verse of his from the section of the *Sarvāṅgī* entitled "The Importance of the Guru's Presence or Absence," uses the figure in an elaborate metaphor which begins: "The *śabda* has the nature (*sarūp*) of a seed; the guru — a farmer; the chela — a field..." W.M. Callewaert, *The Sarvāṅgī of the Dādūpanthī Rajab* (Leuven: Department Orientalistiek, Katholieke Universiteit, 1978) p. 122, v. 8.19. See also his poetic translation and analysis of the metaphor (Ibid., p. 188). The occurrence of the seed and field metaphor thus used seems to coincide more with a stress on aspects of the master-disciple relationship than with any specific Indian tradition. Shaikh Ahmad Sirhindi, for example, perhaps the most orthodox of Indian Sufis but one clearly concerned with the development of the figure, talks about worthless *pīrs* as providing bad seed. See the Urdu translation of his collection of his letters called *Tajalliyāt-e-rabbānī*, ed. Maulana Naim Ahmad Faridi Amrohi (Lucknow: Kutub Khana Al-Furgan, 1978), p. 42.

tradition. The coherence of the Sant tradition can then be approached by examining the significance of 'seed' and 'service' within a substantial Indian world-view and the specific aspects of these concepts drawn upon by Sants generally and Radhasoami gurus in particular.

Seed, Substance, and Spiritual Family

1. *The Substantial Basis of Kinship*

Within the Indian universe, taken as continuous matter, spiritual power normally moves through established channels. Men's access to these channels then comes through specific mediating sources: a sacred object, for example, a divine image, or a holy man. The Sant in his esoteric aspect as a holy man who mediates spiritual power should be differentiated both from the priest in Brahmanic tradition and from the officiant in most Hindu *sampradāy*s and some Sant panths, both of which are institutions arising to preserve the teachings and distribute the grace of specific spiritual personalities. Unlike these figures, who normally manipulate the power of a divine being through some sort of ritual channels, the living Sant as esoteric guru—standing outside ritual traditions—delivers grace and power directly through his own person. The guru's image is what remains as a distinct object of worship for his disciples, who can then perceive the divine *satguru* as the real nature of the living master himself.[9]

The following song, attributed to Kabir, can be readily interpreted to depict the devotee's interaction with the divine as an assimilation of the personal spiritual substance of a living master. It comes from a popular anthology well respected among the Radhasoamis, which makes it more relevant to the present discussion than the fact that it may indeed be Kabir's.[10] Here the guru, portrayed as a dyer, draws the devotee's oath through the liquid colors he provides.

9. Thus Kirpal Singh, a Radhasoami Guru, can tell his disciples: "I'm only a channel and nothing else..." (Kirpal Singh, *Heart to Heart Talks*, vol. 1 (Delhi: Ruhani Satsang, 1975), p. 198. The significance of the Master's form in other Radhasoami groups is treated in Puri, *Teachings*, p. 232; and Babuji Maharaj, *Discourses of Babuji Maharaj*, vol. 2, trans. S.D. Maheshwari (Soamibagh, Agra: S.D. Maheshwari, 1977), p. 404.

10. The song appears on page 2 of the second volume of *Sant bānī saṅgrah*, an anthology of verses culled from the *Sant bānī pustak mālā* series of the Belvedere Press, Allahabad. This series, which consists of editions of all the major, and many rather obscure Hindi Sants, has enough scriptural authority for the Radhasoami group at Soami Bagh to specifically include it along with the works of its own gurus as the basis for its useful glossary, *Śabda koś—sant mat bānī* (Soamibagh, Agra: Radhasoami Satsang, 1970).

The *satguru*'s a dyer — he's dyed my spotted cloth.[11]
(refrain)
He got out all the black and colored it vermillion.
Washing by itself won't do the job;
Still, every day the color of my cloth gets better.
In the reservoir of feeling, in the water of affection,
He drew my cloth through colors of love.
Applying good, thick starch he shook it out,
All brightly colored.
The *satguru* has dyed my cloth,
The *satguru*, so clever and so wise.
To him I offer everything —
My mind and body, wealth and life.
So says Kabir: the dyer-guru has shown mercy towards me.
I put on my cool cloth and lose myself in bliss.

The 'colors' here clearly derive from a 'blissful' divine source, which the poet — particularly if he really was Kabir — may have seen first of all as the Lord above. But the disciple can simultaneously see these 'colors' as the distinct emanation of a living guru, someone "clever and wise"[12] — attributes not normally given to the highest — to whom the disciple offers the stuff of his own being. The ways in which the disciple shares the distinct spiritual substance of his guru can then be seen as parallel to the more densely substantial bonds of everyday biological kinship.

Behind the relevant concepts of both biological and spiritual kinship lies the traditional Indian notion of the relationship between the 'seed' and the 'field'. A child is conceived out of the mixing of two reproductive substances: the father's, thought of as 'seed' (*bīja*) and that of the mother, who is likened to the 'field' (*kṣetra*). The 'seed' carries the child's distinctive attributes; the 'field' merely nourishes the seed, without supplying significant attributes of its own. From the understanding that the man's distinctive substance dominates the woman's, two theoretical consequences follow: (1) upon marriage the

11. Throughout the song the word for cloth is *chunarī*, a cloth which is tie-dyed to have the spots left in it, thus suggesting perhaps the imperfect 'spotted' state of the devotee. The cloth's 'blackness' (*syāhī*) has a specificmetaphorical sense of 'stigma', and works well with the imagery of fluid colors: *syāhī* is the normal Hindi word for ink. I am grateful to K.C. Bahl for help in construing line 2

12. *chatur, sujān*.

husband is able to transform the distinctive substance of his wife into that of his own, and (2) children inherit the distinctive attributes of their father, not of their mother. Within many medieval perceptions of kinship and caste relations this meant that (1) on marriage the wife is transformed into a member of her husband's specific exogamous descent group, and (2) children were born into their *father's* descent group.[13] Within the medieval Indian soteriological context, the terms 'seed' and 'field' can have much the same force they do in the parable of Jesus.[14] A fundamental mantra as seed, *bīja-mantra*, is a familiar concept in Tantric traditions. But among the Sants, the mantra, name, or sound comes from the guru. In the Radhasoami literature, then, we find the perception of the guru as (1) 'husband', who *transforms* the nature of the disciple's personal substance into that of his own, and (2) 'father', whose 'seed' provides the particular pattern for his spiritual growth.

In the following verses of Soaṁiji, founder of the Radhasoami line, the seed and field metaphor is developed to assert the permanence of the guru-disciple relationship through successive incarnations. The guru's spiritual 'seed' here is seen as something powerful and indestructible.

> Once the Sant has placed the seed in the soil of the *jīva*'s body[15]
> Who is strong enough to burn it out?
>
> In time the seed will sprout;
> When Sants come into the world, the ones with
> sprouted seeds stay with them.
>
> The Sant waters the plant, his own,
> and the devotee becomes as a tree...

13. The descent groups referred to here are the *gotra*s found in most subcastes. Inden, (*Marriage and Rank*, pp. 92-98) presents a more detailed treatment of the seed and field metaphor for perceptions of kinship; the metaphor can be found in Manu 10.69-72. Georg Bühler, trans., *The Laws of Manu*, reprint ed. (Delhi: Motilal Banarsidass, 1964), p. 418.

14. Matthew 13:18-23 provides an interesting comparison.

15. The word for body here is *ghaṭ* ('pot'), a technical term in Sant practice. The passage is from the seventh section of *bachan* 38 of Soamiji Maharaj, *Sār bachan Rādhāsvāmī* (Beas: Radha Soami Satsang Beas, 1967), p. 344 and is commented on frequently. See, for example, Puri, *Teachings*, p. 133; Maharaj Saheb, *Discourses of Maharaj Saheb*, trans. S.D. Maheshwari (Soamibagh, Agra: S.D. Maheshwari, 1978), p. 360.

While the seed and field metaphor has roots in a few occurrences in Soamiji's verses, it blossoms in the discourses of his successors. Its importance is stressed by Sawan Singh of Beas, probably one of the most influential Radhasoami gurus of the present century:

> I have said many a time before and repeat it again that once the seed of Nam (Sound Current) has been sown in a soil (heart) it will sprout one day, grow, become a tree and bear fruit. It is impossible to destroy this seed.[16]

As bearer of the Sant's seed, the disciple's task is to nurture it and make it grow. Thus, in the Radhasoami literature we find alongside images of conjugal bliss common to many forms of bhakti references to the faithful wife's duties. Maharaj Saheb, the third major Radhasoami guru at Agra, has presented a Hindi discourse entitled "Faithfulness to the Husband as a Description of Service to the Guru."[17] Here the ways in which the chaste wife remains intent on adapting to her husband's wishes are developed as "an example in all respects complete and proper"[18] for the disciple. Telling the story of how Kabir's wife unquestioningly obeyed his outlandish, seemingly insane commands, Maharaj Saheb concludes that "in this way the mind becomes firm."[19] Thus he points out the need for the disciple's deliberate *transformation* through submission to the guru's will, for "without [the guru's stern] 'fashioning' [*gaṛhat*] the mind will in no way become 'straight' [*sīdhā*]."[20]

In another passage, Maharaj Saheb reveals the implications of the principles behind such a transformation, in a development of feminine imagery unusual among the Radhasoamis: the one who bears the seed as faithful wife herself turns into a child. Maharaj Saheb, having begun a discourse entitled "Stages of Devotion" by comparing the dependence of the devotee on the Lord to that of the child on his mother, now proceeds to describe the creation of the spiritual child. The language of the published sectarian translation, adopted here with slight modi-

16. Huzur Maharaj Sawan Singh, *Spiritual Gems* (Beas: Radha Soami Satsang Beas, 1965), p. 367.

17. Maharaj Saheb, *Bachan* (Soamibagh, Agra: Radhasoami Satsang, 1972), pp. 202-06.

18. Ibid., p. 202.

19. Ibid., p. 206.

20. Ibid., p. 204; *gaṛhat* carries the specific connotation of 'beating and mending', the work of the iron forger.

fication,[21] unmistakably evokes a world of flowing substance in which spiritual and biological phenomena present natural parallels.

> When does one become a child in spiritual development? It is when one becomes solely dependent on the current of the Holy Feet. One becomes dependent when the current of the Holy Feet envelopes [*sic*] one in its fold...when the child is in the womb, its body is formed with the mother's blood, and externally, the milk, which is the product of her blood, becomes the main food and sustenance for its growth and nourishment. Similarly in spiritual development, when the current of the Holy Feet envelopes [*sic*] one in its fold and sustenance and one comes under its influence, then does one become a child. In the former case, the relation, both internally and externally is of blood, whereas in the latter, it is the relation with the current of spirituality or nectar. And he in whom the seed has fallen definitely becomes a child one day. Without the seed a child cannot be born.

"He in whom the seed has fallen..." Even in the midst of such maternal imagery, Maharaj Saheb finally describes both the disciple and the child as males, and soon invokes the father, who is consistently depicted in Radhasoami literature as an attractive, guiding center, as the normative parental figure. Continuing his discussion of "Stages of Devotion," Maharaj Saheb turns immediately to the *bhāva*s or devotional 'attitudes', of which he considers three out of the set of five well-known to later Indian devotion. Omitting both the *śānta* or peaceful *bhāva*, and the *vātsalya bhāva* (devotion to the Lord as a child), he notes: "There are three kinds of attitudes in devotion: the first is that of the servant to the master, the second — the son to his father, and the third — the wife to her husband..."[22] These three attitudes, in contrast to the traditional ones omitted, all definitely suggest the affectionate *service* of a subordinate, an ideal which, as we shall see, has important implications for Sant socio-religious formations. The following passage

21. I have retained the somewhat cumbersome rendering of the Soami Bagh translation to illustrate that Radhasoamis do in fact find language of fluid substance appropriate when expressing themselves in English. The only significant changes I have made involve rendering rather more literally terms derived from the seed and field metaphor: for *bālak*, 'child' instead of 'child-like'; for *jismeṅ bīj paṛā hai* 'in whom the seed has fallen' instead of 'in whom the seed is present'. The passage is from Maharaj Saheb, *Discourses*, pp. 365-66.

22. Ibid., p. 366.

illustrates how the more normative Radhasoami devotional attitude of son to father, together with some natural generational 'transformations', can indeed be linked to a perception of self-perpetuating lineages. An English devotee relates how Charan Singh, whom she calls Maharaj Ji, the present guru of the Radhasoami group at Beas, presents the ideals of an ordered and affectionate Indian household.

> Maharaj Ji gave us a revealing glimpse of family life as it has been customarily observed in India for hundreds of years, and of His family experiences in particular. He spoke of the habitual respect of the younger members for the older, the unswerving obedience... This attitude of habitual respect becomes so established that it is passed down the family automatically; when young each is the recipient of love and the giver of obedience, and later the recipient of obedience and the receiver, and giver, of love.[23]

Thus the 'family' (of good lineage) works 'automatically' to 'pass down' spiritual values.

2. *Clan, Lineage, and Scriptural Collections*

While particular spiritual attributes can be transmitted through principles of lineage, the distinctive religious qualities of the Sant are also seen to inhere in a number of figures and lineages among whom no traceable historical relationships are claimed. Thus we find the notion of a 'clan' of Sants who, ultimately sharing the nature of the divine *satguru*, are composed of the same type of spiritual fibre. The notion of such a 'clan' of Sants is tacit in these verses of Tulsi Sahib of Hathras, a late eighteenth-century Sant and immediate predecessor of the Radhasoami revival:

> Now we find one separate nameless Lord
> Beyond the void and great void.
> That Lord is beloved of the Sants;
> Sants make their court at his abode.
> No one knows the secrets there,
> Though Nanak and Kabir Das tell us,

23. Flora Wood, *In Search of the Way* (Beas: Radha Soami Satsang Beas, 1965), pp. 67-68. Inden and Nicholas point out that the father as head of household manifests a specific kind of 'love' capable of expanding indefinitely to encompass a widening circle of dependents (*Kinship*, p. 33). Compare the attitude of the guru toward his circle of disciples.

And Dadu, Dariya, and Raidas;
Inapproachable enjoyment for Nabha and Mira.
And many other Sants have sung about the inapproachable path
After having reached its rank.[24]

The highest of all possible spiritual 'ranks' (*pada*) is, within the tradition as a whole, naturally held by the Sant. But individual lineages and their branches differ both as to the question of just who is a fully accomplished Sant, and who among the true Sants is particularly their own. We can see some of these differences reflected in the choice of texts read and commented upon among specific groups. As short, 'independent verses'[25] the Sant-*bānī* are normally gathered together as collections. When we look at the factors which seem to order these collections we can gain some insight into the way an individual devotee can make distinctions within the 'clan' of Sants as a whole and see his own place within it.

Both the Dadu-panthis and the Sikhs have put together from the sayings of a number of Sants compilations which have been given special canonical status. Among the Dadu-panthis, we see two important principles of compilation operating in separate scriptural collections. The *Pañchvāṇī* collections represent an attempt to gather together *all* the genuine verses of a set of five particular Sants which have, for whatever reasons,[26] been singled out within the tradition as particularly its own. The *Sarvāṅgī*, on the other hand, represents an attempt by Rajjab, an important disciple of Dadu, to cull out of the entire Sant tradition a large number of verses he felt were particularly important for understanding specific spiritual topics. Naturally, Rajjab's own verses figure prominently in the *Sarvāṅgī*, as well as those of Dadu and other *Pañchvāṇī* Sants.

24. Tulsi Sahib, *Ghaṭ Rāmāyaṇa*, vol. 1 (Allahabad: Belvedere Press, 1973), p. 59.

25. For an important discussion of the significance of 'independent verses' (*muktaka kāvya*) as literary forms and their elaboration and collection in medieval India, see Richard Williams, "The Dholā Mārū rā Dūhā and the Rise of Hindi Literary Tradition," unpublished Ph.D. dissertation (University of Chicago, 1976), especially chapter 3.

26. All the *Pañchvāṇī* Sants are important either universally in Sant tradition or locally in Rajasthan, where Dadu lived and the tradition has been centered. Thus besides Dadu they include Namdev and Kabir, illustrious universally, and Haridas and Raidas, key figures in Rajasthani Sant tradition. Except for Haridas, who is a somewhat obscure figure, and Dadu himself, they are early Sants whose authority antedates the beginning of the lineage.

In the *Guru Granth* of the Sikhs, both these principles operate: it contains all the verses of a set of particular figures—in this case gurus of the Sikh lineage—and a selection from the tradition as a whole. The image in Sikh hagiography of Guru Arjan compiling the *Granth* reveals the importance attached to the guru's power of spiritual discrimination in this process of selection: people approach him and propose various *bānī* of different Sants, and the guru passes judgement according to his particular divinely-attuned religious perceptions and tastes.[27]

When a compiler selects a finite number of verses out of a vast tradition, we can understand him to be in fact acknowledging certain aspects of it as particularly his own. We have seen three factors contributing to his choice: the compiler's lineage; what he accepts as generally authoritative; and an individual, but discriminating, spiritual taste. *Sant saṅgrah* (A Collection of Sants) and *Santoṅ ki bānī* (Sants' Sayings),[28] are compilations published by different Radhasoami groups which reveal how these factors can work in different branches of a single lineage.

Sant saṅgrah was compiled in two volumes by Rai Salig Ram, known as Huzur Maharaj, Soamiji's immediate successor at Agra. In this collection, Huzur Maharaj presents his guru in continuity with authoritative and familiar Sants, but gives him a singularly important position. In each volume, then, Soamiji's verses, coming at the beginning, take pride of place. But the great bulk of the first volume, made up of the brief verses called *sākhīs*, is devoted to Kabir—who, besides being authoritative, is universally considered the master of *sākhīs par excellence*. In the second volume, containing the longer *śabdas*, Soamiji's verses not only come first but are also most numerous. Soamiji's *śabdas* are followed by comparatively lengthy selections from Kabir and Tulsi Sahib, the latter having been familiar locally and exerting direct spiritual influence if not on Soamiji, then clearly on his family. Included in both volumes are at least a few verses of a number of other well-known Sants, including Paltu, a popular eighteenth-century Sant, and

27. See, for example, M. A. Macauliffe, *The Sikh Religion*, 6 vols., reprinted (New Delhi: S. Chand and Co., 1963), 3:59ff. For a critical study of the 'selection' of Kabir's *sākhīs* in the *Gurū Granth*, see Karine Schomer, "Kabir in the *Gurū Granth Sāhib*: An Exploratory Essay" in Mark Juergensmeyer and N. Gerald Barrier, eds., *Sikh Studies: Comparative Perspectives on a Changing Tradition* (Berkeley: Berkeley Religious Studies Series, 1979), pp. 75-86

28. Huzur Maharaj, *Sant saṅgrah*, 2 vols. (Soamibagh, Agra: Radhasoami Satsang, 1978, 1976); Charan Singh, *Santoṅ kī bānī* (Beas: Radha Soami Satsang Beas, 1978).

Guru Nanak of the Sikhs. The significance given to the role of the guru's discriminating taste is seen on the title page of both volumes, which inform the devotee that he is reading "a collection of Sants, which the highest Sant and true guru (*param sant satguru*) Huzur Maharaj selected from several books."

Santoṅ kī bānī, is published by the Beas *satsaṅg*—a well-established group in the traditionally Sikh Punjab—and bears the name of Charan Singh, the present guru at Beas, as author. Here we see the same attention drawn to the role of the guru's power of discrimination, and his concern with lineage. But what is taken as generally authoritative is somewhat different, as is presumably the guru's discriminating taste. In a preface, the chairman of the executive committee at Beas notes that these verses are often taken as the basis for the guru's public discourse and that they "shed great light on the principles of *sant mat*." As in the two volumes of *Sant saṅgrah*, here also Soamiji's verses come first. The group of verses which immediately follows, however, by far the longest in the book, is from the Sikh scriptures, generally authoritative in the Punjab. And only after these comes, as in *Sant saṅgrah*, a rather lengthy set of verses by Kabir, followed shortly by one from Tulsi Sahib. Amid the remaining mostly rather short selections which follow is a long one from Paltu, whom Charan Singh presumably likes and whose songs he finds suitable for expressing his teaching. (Discourses on verses by Paltu have been published separately and figure significantly—together with those on verses by gurus in the lineage and Sikh gurus—in a published collection.)[29]

The passages that the guru selects as a basis for his public discourse are no doubt ones he likes and with which he feels comfortable. He has, moreover, probably realized their more profound aspects in his private meditative experience. Providing structure for both his public discourse and his inner experience, the verses a guru adopts as his own reflect an important component of his personal religious identity. Judging from the selection criteria we have seen, this identity has an articulated place for individual uniqueness, but at the same time is also deeply informed by the individual's identification with his guru and lineage, and the members of the Sant clan he particularly knows and respects.

29. Maharaj Charan Singh Ji, *Discourses on Two Poems of Saint Paltu* (Beas: Radha Soami Satsang Beas, 1977); Maharaj Charan Singh, *Light on Sant Mat* (Beas: Radha Soami Satsang Beas, 1964). Of the eleven songs discussed in *Light on Sant Mat*, four are by Soamiji, one is by Tulsi Sahib, four by various Sikh gurus and two by Paltu.

Service to the Master in Theory and Practice

1. *Spiritual and Political Lineages*

This identification of the disciple with his guru and lineage finds a socio-religious articulation in the principles of loyalty and allegiance current in the medieval political culture. The virtues of unqualified service to one's master are extolled in the ballads of the Rajputs, who not only maintained Hindu kingdoms in Rajasthan during the Muslim period, but also spread out as princes into the Gangetic plain.[30] The power of the ruler, earned through devotion to a deity, was ideally conceived as a manifestation of the deity; and as the deputy of the deity, the ruler had deputies of his own, connected to him through bonds of kinship, contracted political alliance, or both. The word *ṭhākur*, referring both to the lord of the land and the Lord as the Supreme Being, can have the same sort of ambiguous, human and divine implications as the 'guru' of Sant texts. Service to one's immediate master, seen as service to the 'Lord', could entail ideals of self-giving, sometimes to the point of death, which recall the recurrent Sant theme we saw above in Kabir's offering "everything" to the *satguru*, his "body, mind, wealth, and life."

Employing imagery similar to the Radhasoamis' 'seed and field,' the Rajput bard could draw on kinship metaphors to describe the power of his Lord. The ruler is spoken of as 'husband' of the land and 'parent' of his subjects. Thus linked to notions of deity and paternal authority, trappings from the medieval court could naturally find their way into

30. The ideals of service we describe seem to hold for Rajput culture generally, but the political forms here offered as parallel to Sant socio-religious structures seem to be more typical of the relatively more dynamic Rajput lineages outside Rajasthan proper. There is room, incidentally, for specific acknowledgement of the Rajput ideal in Sant poetry. Thus Paltu Sahib, when referring to the spiritual 'warrior' (*sūramā*), alludes more than once to the 'Rajput' (*Bānī* 1:34, 2:11). For a study of the Rajput ethic as reflected in the ballads, see Norman Ziegler, "Notes on Rajput Loyalties During the Mughal Period" in J.F. Richards, ed., *Kingship and Authority in South Asia* (Madison: South Asian Studies, University of Wisconsin, 1978), pp. 215-51, where support for the particulars in our text can be found (pp. 233-34). A.M. Shah and R.G. Shroff, "The Vahivanca Barots of Gujarat" in Milton Singer, ed., *Traditional India: Structure and Change* (Philadelphia: American Folklore Society, 1959) reveals some general similarities between Rajput bards in Rajasthan and Gujarat. Useful treatments of Rajput political structures are Susanne Rudolph, "The Princely States of Rajputana," *Indian Journal of Political Science*, January-March, 1963, pp. 14-32; and Richard G. Fox, *Kin, Clan Raja, and Rule* (Berkeley: University of California Press, 1971), who treats U.P. lineages.

Sant literature. Tulsi Sahib in the second line of the extract of his cited above sings of the Sant's court (*darbār* in Hindi). The *gaddī* (cushion) as seat of authority could be used for speaking of the succession of gurus as well as rajas; and the Sikh hagiography gives us ample description of 'court politics' taking place around the person of the guru.[31]

Parallels between the religious and political norms extend to the *contractual* aspect of the relationship between the Rajput and his lord as well. The disciple, offering service, and the guru, pledging protection, are often understood to be entering into a set of 'voluntary' mutual obligations. And in religion as well as politics, such relationships were seen as taking place between specific persons: allegiance was generally due to one's immediate master and to no one else, including figures in the lineage senior even to him.[32]

Now mutual assimilation of the figures of deity, ruler, and paterfamilias and parallel forms of political and religious order are common enough both in Indian religion and the history of religion generally. But what we usually find is assimilation of the ruler to some unique supreme deity, along with relatively stable parallel hierarchies of religious and temporal authority. What is of particular interest in late medieval India is the diffused and fragmented nature of Hindu political power — often subordinate to foreign authority — and its echo in the loose, multifocused and adaptable socio-religious forms which typically emerge during that time. In both such orders, notions of clan and lineage play central formative roles and can reveal the kind of continuity seen between the biological, the political, and the spiritual.

In somewhat different ways, a general notion of 'clan' provides both Sants and Rajputs with a sense of their tradition as a whole, an orientation to the wider Indian heritage, and some broad internal discriminative categories. The Sants' consciousness of themselves as all sharing a common type of spiritual substance derived ultimately from the divine *satguru* parallels the Rajputs' seeing themselves as all 'sons of Rajas', their biological substance derived ultimately from the heroes of the Hindu epics. This group derivation gives the Rajputs a link to the

31. Macauliffe, *Sikh Religion*, 2:1-45 on the career of Angad, a figure still close to the early Sant tradition, provides an apt example.

32. Thus Soamiji tells the story of a fakir stranded on a raft in the sea who refuses first the proffered hand of Muhammad, then that of God, and then of his guru's guru, whereupon "the Guru Himself came, embraced the disciple and took him immediately to his house." *Sār Bachan* (*Prose*), trans., S.D. Maheshwari (Soamibagh, Agra: S.D. Maheshwari, 1958), pp. 218-21.

respectable past which the Sants can find (when they want to) by seeing Kabir's (no doubt non-historical) connection with Ramananda and orthodox Vaishnava bhakti. But both Sants and Rajputs did discriminate among their numbers as to just who they took in as their own. Just as Sants distinguish different spiritually akin groups of figures in compiling their scriptural collections, so Rajputs distinguish locally ranked sub-clans when they accept women in the biological — and often political — alliance of marriage.[33]

In both politics and religion concrete relationships between individuals were informed by the concepts of lineage that link the members of the extended Indian family, and exhibited both the familiarity and the tensions these imply. Thus the normal Hindi term for fellow-disciple is *guru bhāī* (guru-brother) or *guru bahan* (guru-sister), and in certain Kabir-panthi groups marriages between guru-brothers and guru-sisters have been forbidden as incestuous.[34] Similarly, the term *chāchā guru* (father's-younger-brother-guru), is sometimes used to refer to a respected (though junior) brother disciple of one's own guru. Like the sons of a raja, qualified disciples of the same guru could branch out and establish centers of their own (often thought of in terms of their locality as well as their founder), while one disciple would inherit the master's *gaddī*. And like the sons of a raja, guru-brothers could often find themselves at odds with one another, especially over matters of succession.

In religion as in many other aspects of Indian society, such typically medieval patterns have persisted to the present day, and the relationships among some of the important Radhasoami gurus afford an historically traceable account of how a lineage can develop. Published sources mention at least four qualified successors to Soamiji, the lineage founder, who passed away in Agra in 1878. Although no one of these sources is apt to describe all four as perfect gurus, each tends, while singling out one, to treat the others as respected elders.[35] Of these, two eventually left Agra — Garib Das going to Delhi, Jaimal Singh to Beas. The other two, each with a rightful, but somewhat different, claim to the place,

33. See Fox, *Kin, Clan, Raja*, pp. 37-38.

34. George H. Westcott, *Kabir and the Kabir Panth* (Cawnpore: Christ Church Mission Press, 1907), p. 109 f., 23.

35. Kirpal Singh, *Talks* 1:30; B.M. Sahai and R.K. Khanna, *The Saint and His Master* (Delhi: Ruhani Satsang, 1968), p. 42; Puri, *Teachings*, p. 126; S.D. Maheshwari, *Jīvan charitra Bābūji Mahārāj* (Soamibagh: Agra, Radhasoami Satsang, 1968), pp. 327 ff., 406 ff.

stayed on in Agra. Seth Pratap Singh, called Chachaji Maharaj, was Soamiji's younger natural brother, while Huzur Maharaj was generally recognized as Soamiji's chief disciple. From the last figure, two important lines of succession become established at Agra, between which there has been considerable hostility, extended court cases, and lingering bad feeling.

Jaimal Singh's line too has undergone a major split. The issues attendant on this split can give rise to heated feelings among those concerned, but when examined with respect, they also can reveal significant principles involved in perceiving legitimacy of succession. As the true son obeys his father and the prince serves his lord, so a guru's legitimate spiritual son is seen to be following the command of his master. Thus after the death in 1948 of Jaimal Singh's successor Sawan Singh, two figures, Charan Singh and Kirpal Singh, eventually gained substantial followings—each understanding himself to be 'serving' as guru under the explicit direction of his predecessor.

Disciples of Charan Singh, who presently holds the *gaddī* at Beas, affirm that Sawan Singh not only definitely selected his successor before his passing, but also specifically designated him in a formal will. This successor, they say, was Jagat Singh, who before his death left a will nominating Charan Singh. Though such formal written designation was a normal practice among Indian Sufis, it has little precedent in Sant tradition. So disciples of Charan Singh sometimes say that Sawan Singh provided for a will because he foresaw the problems that would follow upon Kirpal Singh's claim. But the will's lack of precedent can at the same time give Kirpal Singh's disciples some justification to question the circumstances surrounding its composition and signing; and Kirpal Singh understands that Sawan Singh, during the days of his final illness, gave him clear verbal directions to carry on his work.[36] His disciples also make reference to more public events: remarks suggestive of Kirpal Singh's successorship made by Sawan Singh in front of witnesses, jealousies aroused on his using Kirpal Singh as initiator during his own lifetime, and his giving him a mantle (symbolic of succession among Indian Sufis).[37]

In addition to such external criteria of legitimacy, both Charan Singh and Kirpal Singh speak of certain internal signs. In answer to a

36. Kirpal Singh's version of the events is narrated in Kirpal Singh, *A Brief Life Sketch of Hazur Baba Sawan Singh ji Maharaj* (Delhi: Ruhani Satsang, 1973), pp. 20-35. His death in 1974 has led to further branching in the lineage.

37. Sahai and Khanna, *Saint and Master*, pp. 65-66.

disciple's question about Kirpal Singh, Charan Singh mentions in addition to Sawan Singh's will such an internal 'key' given "at the time of initiation." While he retains a diplomatic reserve, his feelings are clear:

> As regards S. Kirpal Singh, let him say or do anything he likes. Sooner or later he will have to render account for his actions. You have been given the key at the time of Initiation and can satisfy yourself as to whether or not he is a true Master. It would not be in good taste for me to go into detail, but I will say this much, that the Great Master Sawan Singh Ji never gave him permission to initiate anyone, and duly appointed Sardar Bahadur Maharaj Jagat Singh Ji as His Successor by a legally executed will, in writing and duly witnessed, so as to leave no doubt about the matter ...[38]

While Charan Singh's disciples can look to a public "legally executed will" to resolve any doubts as to the legitimacy of their guru, those of Kirpal Singh stress the importance of internal criteria. Kirpal Singh is emphatic that a true Master should be able to give his disciples some spiritual experience at the time of initiation, and this, he gives reason to believe, does not usually occur at Beas. When a disciple questions him about initiation at Beas he replies matter-of-factly:

> The other day I gave initiation to six hundred and fifty-three people. All saw Light—about two hundred saw the Master's Form. The teachings at Beas are the same, but the words given at initiation now *are not charged*. That is the difference. I got a letter from Dr. Stone; he is now what you say, a forerunner of the Beas group ... they're afraid of asking for any experience ...[39]

Thus, while the basic grounds for legitimacy in succession are designation by the previous guru, the criteria used for recognizing that designation are both internal and external and can be stated in terms of 'formal' evidence (the wills, the mantle, the 'inner key') or as the successor's evident spiritual power. The disciples of Charan Singh, who in fact holds the *gaddī* at Beas, seem to look to criteria involving trustworthy forms. Those attracted by the spiritual personality of Kirpal Singh—for whom formal public evidence is undeniably more tenuous—cite instead the guru's demonstrated power.

38. Maharaj Charan Singh, *Divine Light* (Beas: Radha Soami Satsang Beas, 1967), pp. 221-22.
39. Kirpal Singh, *Talks* 2:157-58.

2. *Institutional Developments: "The Problem of the Historical Guru"*

The central issue of succession at stake between Charan Singh and Kirpal Singh is grounded in two important presuppositions. First, it assumes that a qualified disciple can indeed serve the same functions as his guru and thus perpetuate the lineage in similar form. Second, it implies that a Sant lineage normally does possess imposing religious figures with perceptible charismatic powers. But as Sant traditions become older and more established, a central issue of debate can turn out to be the understanding of the Sant lineage itself. Is it an unstructured *paramparā*—a simple succession of guru and disciple, all of whom are in a basic sense equal as 'true' Sants? Or is its proper function to propagate the teachings of an originator seen as in some way uniquely divine? Thus a central point of debate turns on the status of the figure standing at the head of the lineage. Was he a Sant like any other, perhaps a particularly great one, but still one among many? Or was he a divine figure of a special order, peerless and guruless? Among the Radhasoami groups at present, this issue is a live one, and reveals both different perceptions of the lineage within Sant tradition and the type of role it should play as a religious institution.

L.R. Puri, a prominent disciple from the Beas group, while tactfully not affirming outright that Soamiji, the lineage founder, actually had a guru, emphasizes his "intimate association" with Tulsi Sahib, to whom he payed "the same sort of love and respect" "as one does to one's spiritual master."[40] Soamiji thus stands as one in the tradition of the Sants: "*Radha Swami Mat*," says Puri, "*is Sant Mat pure and simple*" (Puri's italics).[41] On the other hand, A.P. Mathur, a great-great-grandson of Huzur Maharaj, whom he sees as important in the systematization of the tradition at Agra, has written a book appropriately enough entitled *Radhasoami Faith*.[42] Here he characterizes the tradition as "*a new religion* (my italics) based on sant traditions."[43] He is emphatic that Soamiji had no guru: " ... for, if Soamiji was born 'Almighty', as Shri Kripal Singh himself admits, there was hardly any need for him to have accepted the discipleship of anyone."[44]

40. Puri, *Teachings*, p. 7.
41. Ibid., p. 17.
42. Agam Prasad Mathur, *Radhasoami Faith: A Historical Study* (Delhi: Vikas Publishing House, 1974), p. 75.
43. Ibid., p. 24.
44. Ibid.

This perception of a lineage as fundamentally unique, "a new religion," also lies behind the formation of panth traditions around the teachings of particular Sants. Like the members of Vaishnava *sampradāys*, who are clearly within Hinduism, panthis generally recognize a fixed scripture and employ some ritual forms. Unlike the Vaishnavas, however, who generally try to find an ultimate source for their tradition in the Vedic heritage, panthis normally look to their particular Sant alone. And their ritual, not so fundamental an aspect of *nirguṇa* devotion as of Krishna worship, is generally less elaborate.

Still, during the later stages of Sant tradition, figures have arisen who have spoken out against the established panths as providing little access to the true Sant teaching, which is perceived as leading to inner experience. Soamīji was one. Tulsi Sahib, his predecessor, argues sharply with panthi characters in his *Ghaṭ Rāmāyaṇa*.[45] Earlier, in Bihar, Dariya Sahib was taken as an incarnation of Kabir, come again to spread the true teaching on seeing the degeneration of his panth.[46] Today we see Charan Singh wary of letting institutions develop too far from the guru's immediate range of influence. To an American disciple who asks about setting up a colony for his devotees, whom he refers to here as 'Satsangis', Charan Singh replies:

> ... Without the guiding hand of the Master on the spot, it is extremely difficult to run such institutions smoothly. I feel that since the time of the creation of the Corporation Sole [*sic*] in America the old harmony and understanding that existed among the Satsangis there is gradually disappearing. For the present you may postpone the idea of such a scheme ... [47]

Since members of a panth often justify its existence through its being able to preserve the teachings of a particular Sant, they tend to minimize the importance of any wider Sant clan. They do retain such a notion, however, and employ it in different ways to articulate their own religious identities. Thus members of the various branches of the Kabir-panth, undoubtedly the oldest and largest panth tradition, gene-

45. Tulsi Sahib, *Ghaṭ Rāmāyana* 1:169ff., 2:123-81.

46. P. Chaturvedi, *Uttarī Bhārat kī sant paramparā* (Allahabad: Leader Press, 1972), p. 660 gives an account of the way in which Dariya took himself as 'non-separate' from Kabir. Dariya-panthi publications speak of him simply as "Kabir's other avatar". See introductory page to *Dariyā vachanāmṛt*, a periodical published from the Dariya Ashram, Kashi.

47. Charan Singh, *Divine Light*, p. 335.

rally see their extended lineage as being the basis for all other panths. Present day Kabir-panthis will then sometimes talk about members of other panths as "really Kabir-panthis," and one contemporary writer gives a list of ten major and minor Sant lineages (including the Radhasoamis) which he calls Kabir-panth 'sub-branches' (*upaśākhāeṅ*).[48] This attitude is given some implicit support by the Dariya-panthis, who, seeing Dariya as an incarnation of Kabir, can take their lineage as the *real* Kabir panth.

Whereas Kabir was probably the most iconoclastic of the Sants and his panth the most self-contained, Dadu was more tolerant of existing traditions and his panth today takes itself as less independent of the larger Indian heritage.[49] Its sectarian literature is correspondingly less imperialistic toward other panths and attempts instead to reveal the Sant clan generally as occupying a significant place in Indian religious tradition. Thus Raghavadas, a seventeenth-century Dadu-panthi, has written a *bhaktamāl*, (a 'garland' of biographical sketches of medieval devotees) in which the treatment of Dadu and his extended lineage, though full, figures only as a relatively short section. According to Dadu-panthi tradition, Raghavadas wrote his work at the command of his guru's guru to supplement the famous *Bhaktamāl* of Nabhaji, which was weighted toward devotees of the Lord with form and ignored too many of the Sants. "You write a *bhaktamāl*," the guru is said to have instructed him, "in which you record without bias the stories of devotees to the Lord both with form and without ... all indeed are devotees by reason of devotion alone."[50]

48. Sukrit Das Barari, *Satkabīr mahāpurāṇa* (Bangalore: Satkabir Sahitya Prakashan Samiti, 1977), introductory page *ṭh*.

49. The differences between the attitudes of Kabir-panthis and Dadu-panthis in this respect can be illustrated in a set of interviews the present writer conducted at the Pushkar *melā* in 1979. At the time of the *melā* the waters of Pushkar lake are said to yield special benefit, and pilgrims come from all over the region to bathe. While both Kabir-panthis and Dadu-panthis were to be found at their respective temples at Pushkar, when asked if they were going to bathe in the lake they gave different kinds of replies. The Kabir-panthis consistently answered no, there was no benefit in bathing in the lake — they'd use tap water. They had come to get together with other Kabir-panthis at the fair, they said, and perhaps do some proselytization among the crowds of pilgrims. Many of the Dadu-panthis did go to bathe, however, and Hariramji of Narayana, an important Dadu-panthi *mahant*, explained that for people who approached it with the right attitude bathing in the lake could indeed be of benefit.

50. Swami Narayandas, ed. *Śrī Rāghavadās jī virachit bhaktamāl* (Jaipur: Shri Dadudayalu Mahasabha, 1969), p. 4.

Thus the way was open for panths still identifying with the larger Sant clan to adopt clear-cut Vaishnava forms. Perhaps those who have gone furthest in this direction are the Charandasis, a fairly small group centered at Delhi who practise regular ritual worship of Krishna. They derive from Charan Das, an eighteenth-century figure, who appears to have been influenced distinctly both by Sant tradition and Krishna bhakti.[51] Since the larger Indian tradition sees the Sant panths generally as within the Vaishnava fold, the Charandasis can reconcile their two heritages without difficulty and will, when questioned, point out with satisfaction their position vis-a-vis the other panths. "We worship Krishna," this writer was told by Charandasi *mahants* at Delhi and Jaipur, "the Dadu-panthis worship a book."[52] Thus drawing on different aspects of Indian tradition and developing in different ways, the panths as individual lineages within an extended clan have been able to maintain distinct religious identities — much, indeed, as did the diverse spiritual personalities taken as their source.

51. Sectarian biographies report him as having taken initiation into a Sant *sādhanā* early in life, and then later to have travelled to Vrindavan. See Triloki Narayan Dixit, *Charandās* (Allahabad: Hindustani Academy, 1961), pp. 25-72. The major collection of his writings, *Bhaktisāgar*, presents both Hatha Yoga practices and a description of the Internal Mathura. See Charandas, *Bhaktisāgar* (Lucknow: Naval Kishore Press, 1975).

52. The *mahants* are referring to the important place of handwritten copies of Dadu's saying in Dadu-panthi ceremonial, which many Dadu-panthis will matter-of-factly refer to as *granth pūjā* ('book worship'). A further conversation with the Jaipur *mahant* about the death of a Charandasi *mahant* whom the present writer had met some years before illustrates what seeing the Sant panths as constituting an extended 'clan' can practically imply. In describing the customary convocation of dignitaries that followed to affirm and consecrate the deceased *mahant*'s successor, the Jaipuri *mahant* spontaneously used a kinship analogy: the convocation was compared to what happens when the head of a family dies and all the family members come together to decide what to do. Who came to the convocation? All the Charandasi *mahants*, as well as some others with whom they kept up a relationship (*sambandha*). When questioned as to just who these others were, the first people he mentioned were Kabir-panthis and Dadu-panthis, who would then be seen as significant members of an 'extended family'.

THE RADHASOAMI REVIVAL OF THE SANT TRADITION

MARK JUERGENSMEYER

Where may the Sant tradition be found today? In one sense everywhere, for throughout the popular religious culture of modern India the presence of the medieval Sants is ubiquitous. One finds Kabir quoted by politicians as embellishments to their campaign appeals, Guru Nanak brandished as the brand-name of water-pumps sold in the Punjab, and pictures of Ravi Das (Raidas) vibrantly displayed on the calendars of lower-caste households as a mark of spiritual devotion and lower-caste pride. On the facade of an arched gazebo in the gardens of the headquarters of the Harijan Sevak Sangh in Delhi is a sort of honor roll of the Sants—Kabir, Nanak, Namdev, Dadu, Mirabai, Ravi Das—those regarded as preceding Gandhi in India's indigenous struggle against inequality and the prejudices of caste. And Gandhi himself is sometimes regarded as a modern Sant. The veneration of particular Sants is taken as the solemn obligation of the members of those movements that bear Sants' names (the Kabir-panthis, the Dadu-panthis, the Raidasis, the Nanak-panthis) and it is found also in the Sikh tradition which is built upon, and continues to be indebted to, the teachings of Guru Nanak and the nine other spiritual masters who followed in his lineage.

But there is one movement in North India today that regards itself as the main repository of the heritage of the Sants, their teachings and their approach to religious knowledge. That movement is Radhasoami. It boldly proclaims itself to be the manifestation of *sant mat* (the Sant tradition) for the present day, not simply by repeating the teachings of the medieval Sants and honoring their memories, but through lineages

The preparation of this article was made possible, in part, through the labors of Jack Hawley of the University of Washington, who translated some of the Hindi language materials and helped me wend my way through others, especially the *Ghāṭ Rāmāyaṇa* and the *Anurāg sāgar*. My thanks also to Janak Raj Puri of the Radhasoami Satsang, Beas, and Prof. A.P. Mathur of Agra University for commenting on an earlier draft. This article excerpts and summarizes portions of my forthcoming *Radhasoami Reality: The Logic of a Modern Faith*. Financial assistance for research in India was provided by the American Institute of Indian Studies and the Indo-American Fellowship Program, to whom I am most grateful.

of spiritual masters who embody within themselves that same power of guruship that the Sants are reputed to have had in their times. Thus, the Radhasoami movement presents itself literally as the living incarnation of the Sant tradition, an unbroken continuation not only of the teachings of the Sants but of the Sants themselves.

It is a strong claim, but one that is repeated by some outside the movement as well. P.D. Barthwal, in his often-cited study of the Sant tradition, *The Nirguṇa School of Hindi Poetry*,[1] ends his list of Sants with Shiv Dayal Singh, the nineteenth-century teacher and poet from Agra who is regarded by the Radhasoami movement as the first guru in their lineages and the founder of their faith. Much of Barthwal's interpretation of *nirguṇa* theology relies upon Radhasoami writings, moreover, and his description of the Sant tradition as a whole is much indebted to the Radhasoami interpretations of it. Parashuram Chaturvedi, in his encyclopaedic survey of the Sant tradition, also depicts Radhasoami as the most impressive Sant movement in the modern age, devoting more space to it than to any other current Sant phenomenon.[2]

Can Radhasoami be regarded as *sant mat* for our generation? Two matters must be settled before we can decide. The first is the more vexing: the problem of identifying the Sant elements in Radhasoami. We have to agree upon what the Sant tradition *was*, before we can decide whether it continues to be, and that means coming to some agreement about the major contours of philosophy and style that unite such diverse figures as Kabir and Ravi Das, Dadu and Nanak. Whether such agreement is ever possible among those who revere and hold those figures in high esteem is questionable, but we should at least consider the possibility that a distillation of Sant teachings may be created and take seriously some of the attempts that have been made to do so, including that of the Radhasoami movement itself. The other matter, conceptually more simple, is as a practical matter more difficult: the task of tracing the actual linkages of Radhasoami lineage and teachings back to the early Sant tradition. But before we can undertake either of these projects, we should briefly consider the growth and teachings of the Radhasoami movement itself.

1. Pitambar Datta Barthwal, *The Nirguṇa School of Hindi Poetry* (Banaras: Indian Book Shop, 1936).

2. Parashuram Chaturvedi, *Uttarī Bhārat kī sant-paramparā* (Allahabad: Leader Press, 1952), pp. 789-811.

The Radhasoami Movement

The movement's own memory places the founding date at 1861, when Swami Shiv Dayal Singh began publicly proclaiming his interpretations of Nanak and Kabir with the spiritual force of one who had been specially enlightened.[3] His family, Punjabis of mercantile caste who had settled in Agra as money lenders, were devotees of a guru who had been teaching in the nearby town of Hathras. This guru, Tulsi Sahib, had composed a sort of *nirguṇa Rāmāyaṇa* purporting to be the philosophical essence of the *Rāmāyaṇa* with all of the characters and stories left out. Shiv Dayal, influenced by these and other esoteric writings, and strongly conscious of the poetry of Kabir, Nanak, and other Sants, formulated his own insights regarding the spiritual journey of the soul through increasingly rarefied regions of consciousness until it reaches the highest state, which he called the realm of Radhasoami. Dayal made much of the importance of latching onto a sound current to facilitate such journeys, an accomplishment to be achieved through a distinctive spiritual discipline, a sort of Yoga aimed at awakening and exercising one's internal sound energy. These and other doctrines are propounded in his own collection of prose and poetry, the *Sār bachan* (Essential Teachings), which continues to be regarded within the Radhasoami movement as its primal document.[4]

The systematization of the movement — its beliefs and its organization — came in the next generation through the separate efforts of two of Dayal's chief disciples, Rai Saligram and Jaimal Singh. Saligram was Dayal's successor at Agra following Dayal's death in 1878. Before becoming a guru, Saligram had risen to distinction in government service, serving as the first Indian Postmaster-General of the United Provinces. According to Max Müller, Saligram's journey from the high offices of government bureaucracy to religious obedience was prompted by his experience of the social chaos accompanying the Mutiny of 1857.[5] Perhaps for that reason, he was determined to eradicate disorder from within the Radhasoami movement. He drew up an administrative system, formalized the *satsaṅg* worship services, and codified the

3. The standard biography of Shiv Dayal Singh is the one written by his relative Seth Partap Singh, *Jīvan charitra Soāmijī Mahārāj* (Soamibagh, Agra: Radhasoami Satsang, 1902).

4. Shiv Dayal (Soamiji Maharaj), *Sār Bachan* (*Essential Teachings*), trans. S. D. Maheshwari (Agra: Radhasoami Satsang, Soamibagh; prose version 1958, poetry in 2 vols. 1970).

5. Friedrich Max Müller, *Ramakrishna: His Life and Sayings* (London: Longmans, Green and Co., 1898), p. 20.

theology of the movement under the rubric of *surat śabda yoga*, 'the discipline of concentrating on the divine word through one's inner current.'[6]

At the same time that Saligram was busily at work building the movement in Agra, another devotee of Dayal's, Jaimal Singh, had returned to his native Punjab to establish a separate branch of the movement there on the banks of the Beas river near Amritsar. The theological differences between the two major branches of Radhasoami are only slight. The Beas branch reveals five sacred names at the time of a member's initiation, whereas the Agra branch reveals only one; and the Beas view of the spiritual nature of Shiv Dayal is a bit more modest than Agra's.[7] From the Agra point of view, Shiv Dayal was a *paramātmā satguru* — a Sant of Sants, a unique revelation in human history — whereas the Beas followers, although hardly underestimating Dayal's significance, see him as part of an unbroken chain of *satguru* manifestations, from the current holders of the chairs of guruship back to ancient religious figures such as Jesus and the Buddha. But the basic teachings of all branches of Radhasoami are much the same. The current master of the Beas branch, Charan Singh, summarizes those basic elements in the Radhasoami 'method of God-realization' in three words:

> First is the *simran* or the repetition of the Lord's Holy Names. It brings back our scattered attention to the Tisra Til — Third Eye (behind our eyes) which is the headquarters of our mind and soul, in the waking state, whence it has scattered.
>
> Second is the *dhyan* or contemplation on the immortal form of the Master. This helps in keeping the attention fixed at that centre.
>
> Third is the *bhajan* or listening to the *anhad shabd* or Celestial Music that is constantly reverberating within us. With the help of this Divine Melody, the soul ascends to higher regions and ultimately reaches the Feet of the Lord.[8]

6. Rai Saligram's systematization of the faith is found in his *Rādhāsoāmī mat prakāś* (Banaras: Radhasoami Satsang, 1896); English translation published by Radhasoami Satsang, Soamibagh, Agra, 1957. His own biography is found in Rai Ajudhia Prasad, *Jīvan charitra Hūzur Mahārāj* (Soamibagh, Agra: Radhasoami Satsang, 1908).

7. Jaimal Singh's perspective on Radhasoami teachings is to be found in his *Spiritual Letters* (Beas: Radhasoami Satsang Beas, 1976). The preface to this edition of his writings gives a brief biography of Jaimal Singh.

8. Charan Singh (Maharaj Ji), foreword to Sawan Singh (Huzur Maharaj), *Spiritual Gems* (Beas: Radhasoami Satsang Beas, 1965), p. iii.

More telling than the doctrinal differences among the several branches of Radhasoami are those of organizational structures and leadership style. During this century, strong leaders in both the Agra and Beas branches have created imposing organizations. In 1903, Jaimal Singh, the Beas founder, was succeeded by Sawan Singh, who is remembered as 'the Great Master': his training as a senior engineer in the Military Engineering Service eminently qualified him for forty-five years of efficient and thorough leadership in an expanding organization.[9] Over the years he initiated 124,000 devotees into the fellowship. Most were urban folk, some of them were his former army comrades and other government officials, and a few were villagers from lower castes. He also used his military engineering abilities to good effect. The major construction for the modern city built and dedicated to the memory of his guru, Dera Baba Jaimal Singh, was his singular achievement, including the design of its buildings. The Dera is a dream city on the banks of the Beas river, centered around Sawan Singh's masterpiece, an imposing temple (or *satsaṅg ghar*, 'meeting house for the community') which creates a distinctive landmark on the Punjab plains. The Beas Dera functions as a residential community as well as a sort of Radhasoami Vatican, although most of its residents have settled there after retirement. Beas has some agricultural holdings, but not much industry.

The Agra branch has developed in quite a different way. Several schisms have fragmented its lineages, but the group that has emerged strongest is the one located at a residential colony it calls Dayalbagh on the outskirts of Agra. Founded by Anand Swarup, a visionary who had once been a member of the Arya Samaj, Dayalbagh marshalled its manpower into small industries which allowed Swarup's followers to "earn their living through honest labor" and provided an occupation for those who wished to live near him "for spiritual benefit."[10] The

9. Sawan Singh's major statements about the teachings of the Radhasoami and Sant traditions are in his *Discourses on Sant Mat* (Beas: Radhasoami Satsang Beas, 1939) and *Gurmat siddhānta* (Philosophy of the Masters), 5 vols. (Beas: Radhasoami Satsang Beas, 1963). Accounts of the life and teachings of Sawan Singh are to be found in Daryai Lal Kapur, *Call of the Great Master* (Beas: Radhasoami Satsang Beas, 1964); Julian P. Johnson, *With a Great Master in India* (Delhi: The National Journals Press, 1934); and Rai Sahib Munshi Ram, *With the Three Masters*, 3 vols. (Beas: Radhasoami Satsang Beas, 1967).

10. From the testimony of the leader of the Dayalbagh branch who founded the colony, Anand Sarup, before the Lindsey Commission, an investigatory commission sponsored by Christian missions. Quoted in *Souvenir in Commemoration of the First Centenary of the Radhasoami Satsang* 1861-1961 (Dayalbagh: Radhasoami Satsang, 1962), p. 200.

great growth of Dayalbagh climaxed at the time of the ascension of Gursarandas Mehta to the position of guru in 1937. Mehta, like his rival in Beas, Sawan Singh, was also an engineer (Chief of the Public Works Department of the Punjab Government, a position he retained for a while even after assuming his spiritual duties).

On taking office, Mehta established a five-year industrial program for the Dayalbagh community. He targeted a gross income of ten million rupees annually and in two years actually managed to realize this ambitious goal.[11] Included in the rapidly developing industrial complex he inherited from Swarup were the Research Laboratories which manufactured toilet goods, the Everyday Footwear Factory, a hosiery plant, and in Amritsar the huge Dayalbagh Spinning and Weaving Mills. Ultimately the community manufactured everything from handkerchiefs to hunting knives, microscopes to toilet soaps, and created their own banks to handle their investments. Surrounding the colony of Dayalbagh were 3,000 acres of choice farmland which the movement developed as a model of modern scientific collective agriculture. The several colleges established in and near the Dayalbagh colony have pioneered in modern educational techniques.

Today the Dayalbagh industrial and agricultural cartel is much less impressive, in part because of new limitations imposed by the Indian government on the commercial ventures of religious institutions. But the center has undergone a revival of enthusiasm since 1976 when M.B. Lal, the former head of Lucknow University, was installed as the new spiritual Master.[12] Other offshoots of the Agra branch of Radhasoami—two with headquarters in Agra, at Soamibagh and Peepalmandi, and others at Hyderabad, Gwalior, and Hoshiarpur—continue their stable, settled circles of devotees.[13]

By far the most active branches of the Radhasoami family tree are those on the Beas side of the original Agra/Beas division. The Beas

11. *First Centenary Souvenir*. For the teachings and history of the Agra branches see Agam Prasad Mathur, *Radhasoami Faith: A Historical Study* (Delhi: Vikas Publishing House, 1974).

12. M.B. Lal has expanded the Dayalbagh colony's already impressive collection of educational institutions with a new university which emphasizes agricultural technology.

13. These are only the larger centers. David Lane has identified approximately thirty different lineages of gurus which have branched out from the Radhasoami tradition, and which may be traced directly to Swami Shiv Dayal. David Lane, "Genealogical Tree of Sant Mat Gurus and Gaddis," (unpublished chart, Graduate Theological Union, Berkeley, 1979).

center itself has become the hub of an international network of some 360 local organizations from Texas to South Africa.[14] A similarly large international following pursues a major offshoot of the Beas center which was established by Kirpal Singh, a close associate of the Great Master of Beas, Sawan Singh, who had been led to believe that he would himself be installed as the Beas Master following Sawan Singh's death. But when the mantle passed over him and fell instead on a chemistry teacher, Jagat Singh, Kirpal Singh repaired to Delhi, where he established his own organization, the Ruhani Satsang ('Spiritual Community'), eschewing the term 'Radhasoami'. He found a fertile field of growth in America.[15] Other disciples of Beas masters have founded organizations explicitly directed toward a Western clientele. Among the best known are the popular Divine Light Mission of the boy guru, Maharaj-ji, whose family members were followers of the Great Master of Beas; and the eclectic American movement Eckankar whose founder, Paul Twitchell, was also an initiate of Kirpal Singh. The teachings of Eckankar are essentially those of Ruhani Satsang and the other branches of Radhasoami.[16]

Despite the remarkable industrial and organizational growth of the various branches of the movement, and despite their appropriation of the metaphors of science[17] and the images of the New Testament,[18] the teachings of the major branches of the movement are fundamentally the same as those propounded by Swami Shiv Dayal Singh some one hundred and twenty years ago. And the movement continues to insist, as he did, on giving those teachings a name that recalls the prestige of some of the greatest figures in medieval Hindi religious literature. *sant mat.*

14. Mark Juergensmeyer, "Radhasoami as a Trans-National Movement," in Jacob Needleman and George Baker, eds., *Understanding the New Religions* (New York: Seabury Press, 1978), pp. 190-200.

15. For the issues separating Kirpal Singh from the Beas lineage see Daniel Gold, "Clan and Lineage among the Sants: Seed, Service, Substance," earlier in this volume, pp. 322-24.

16. See David Lane, *The Making of a Spiritual Movement: The Untold Story of Paul Twitchell and Eckankar* (Berkeley: B. William Walsh, 1979).

17. See Jagat Singh (Sardar Bahadur Maharaj), *The Science of the Soul* (Beas: Radhasoami Satsang Beas, 1952).

18. See Charan Singh (Maharaj Ji), *Light on Saint Matthew* (Beas: Radhasoami Satsang Beas, 1978); and *Saint John: The Great Mystic* (Beas: Radhasoami Satsang Beas, 1979).

The Elements of Sant Mat *in Radhasoami*

A new series of books at the Beas center presents a conspicuous departure from their pattern of publishing the wisdom of recent Masters in the movement. These new books are concerned solely with the writings and lives of the medieval Sants; but they are promoted in the general lists of works on the science of Radhasoami. Literally, then, as well as implicitly, the movement has claimed the Sant tradition as its own: "Radhasoami Mat and Sant Mat are the same thing," it proclaims.[19]

Members of the movement may take such a statement as an article of faith, but outsiders will need to be assured by some other means. Are they the same? The first step in answering this question is to determine which figures one includes when one talks about the Sant tradition, and which of their teachings can be said to display a common, homogenous Sant perspective.

The Radhasoami movement provides its own geneology of Sants, "the perfect and true Saints" who have, in preparing the way for Radhasoami's lineages of perfect masters, "manifested themselves in the last seven centuries."[20] The roll call includes "Kabir Sahib, Tulsi Sahib, Jagjiwan Sahib, Gharib Das Ji, Paltoo Sahib, Guru Nanak, Dadoo Ji, Tulsi Das Ji, Nabha Ji, Swami Hardas Ji, Surdas Ji, and Raidas Ji, and among the Mohammedans: Shams Tabriz, Maulana Roomi, Hafiz, Sarmad, and Muhaddid Alif Sani."[21] The Hindu side of the list seems more or less in line with the popular conception of the Sant tradition in India. P.D. Barthwal, for example, includes the first seven of the Radhasoami list in his survey of the *nirguṇa* school of Hindi poetry, adding to them some eleven more, including Bulle Shah and Shiv Narayan.[22] The differences between the lists indicate the imprecision of the term. Are such revered figures as Sur Das, Tulsi Das, and Ravi Das to be regarded as Sants or not? It depends upon one's starting point and one's standard. If Kabir, Nanak and Dadu set the standard, and that standard is devotion to a formless divinity (*nirguṇa*) rather than to one with definable attributes (*saguṇa*), Ravi Das is near their number, and Tulsi Das and Sur Das are progressively less so. This suggests,

19. Lekh Raj Puri, *Radha Swami Teachings* (Beas: Radhasoami Satsang Beas, 1965), p. 17, quoting the founding Master, Shiv Dayal Singh.
20. Shiv Dayal, *Sār bachan*, p. 46.
21. Ibid.
22. Barthwal, *Nirguṇa School*, pp. 249-69.

perhaps, that there is a Sant — or rather a *nirguṇa* — dimension to many medieval Hindi religious poets, rather than a specific, separate lineage of *nirguṇa* Sants.

Yet the idea that there are Sants, a Sant tradition, and specifically Sant teachings (*sant mat*) persists. It is obviously to the benefit of movements such as Radhasoami which rely upon connections to the Sant tradition for their legitimacy that such a tradition in fact existed. Indeed, there is some evidence that the term *sant mat* originated in movements that immediately preceded the origins of Radhasoami in the mid-nineteenth century, and that the concept was crystallized and broadcast by the Radhasoami movement itself.[23] But Radhasoami certainly did not create Kabir, Nanak, Dadu or Ravi Das. Such figures are facts of Indian history and are part of India's common inheritance. It is also historically inescapable that there are similarities among their teachings. The attempts to collect together the Sant writings is itself an important facet of the tradition, going back as far as the sacred Sant anthologies of the sixteenth and seventeenth centuries — the *Granth Sāhib* of the Sikhs and the *Sarvāṅgī* of the Dadu-panthis — and continuing to the present century with the attempts by Radhasoamis and scholars of literature to present syntheses of Sant ideas. One can attribute to a movement such as Radhasoami the service of pointing out these connections, but not the manufacture of the connections themselves. There is something there. Call it *sant mat*, the Sant tradition, the *nirguṇa* school — a common albeit tenuous and sometimes fuzzy thread exists and ties the major figures together.

What are these common Sant elements? One is tempted to avoid theological controversy by speaking of a common Sant style, rather than common Sant ideas. Yet the dominant style of religious expression that unites them — bhakti — is an idea as well: devotion and spiritual love. As a genre of religion, bhakti encompasses much more than the Sant tradition since it is at the heart of the non-Brahmanical piety that characterizes medieval Hinduism — *saguṇa* Vaishnavas and Shaivas and *nirguṇa* Sants alike. Nonetheless, there is a certain cast to Sant bhakti which distinguishes it from the rest, and much of that distinction has to do with the central ideas that are common to all the Sants. And that

23. Tulsi Sahib uses the term in his *Ghaṭ Rāmāyaṇa*, 2 vols. (Allahabad: Belvedere Press, 1911), *passim*. The notion that he originated the term is implied by Parashuram Chaturvedi in *Sant-paramparā*, p. 783, and claimed outright by Janak Raj Puri, *Tulsi Sahib: Saint of Hathras* (Beas: Radhasoami Satsang Beas, 1978), p. 17.

leads us back to the problem of having to specify precisely what they are.

One such scholarly attempt to establish the central Sant motifs has been made by P.D. Barthwal, whose pioneering effort in the 1930s to identify the major themes of Kabir, Nanak, Dadu and others of the '*nirguṇa* school' has not yet been superseded. These themes include, of course, the concept of the divine as formless (*nirguṇa*). But they also embrace the importance of a spiritual master (a guru) in one's spiritual progress; a conviction that such spirituality is essentially interior rather than bound up with the external forms of piety and religiosity that characterize both Hindu and Muslim customs; and the tendency of those who follow a particular spiritual path to enjoy a spiritual fellowship (*satsaṅg*) with one another. The Radhasoami movement displays an allegiance to each of these elements of spiritual belief and practice, though developing each one in its own way.

1. *The Absolute as* Nirguṇa

A clear message of the '*nirguṇa* school' is its rejection of the plurality of forms of God as commonly understood in the Hindu pantheon. As Kabir asked:

> For the sake of one life
> why worship a thousand gods?
> Why not worship Ram alone
> whom even Shiva adores?[24]

The one God, for Kabir, was Ram, by which he usually meant not the physical Ram who is the dashing, active subject of the legendary *Rāmāyaṇa*, but an ineffable, transcendent Ram, a God-force. For Nanak, and also often for Kabir, not even this name is given, only the actual 'name' itself: *nām*, the divine energy and grace which permeates the world, yet transcends its crassest aspects.

The Radhasoami tradition affirms this notion that the Absolute is an essence beyond the pantheon of gods. But the Radhasoami Masters go a step further: they give a name to the nameless essence. A publication of the Dayalbagh branch of the movement explains its theological departure from the Sant tradition on this point:

24. *Kabīr-granthāvalī*, ed. Shyamsundar Das (Banaras: Nagari Pracharini Sabha, 1928), p. 129.

The Teachings of the Radhasoami Faith are similar to those of other Faiths, collectively and separately known as the Religion of Saints, but with a marked difference. This difference consists in the fact that the Message of the Radhasoami Faith is the Message of the Highest Region of creation...(and) it is for the first time only that the Holy Name of the Supreme Being has been explicitly revealed...[25]

That holy name is Radhasoami. In the theology of the movement, the eternal essence of God resides in the form of pure energy: light and sound of matchless and incredible purity. The name Radhasoami both describes that fact and exemplifies it. The term Radha is taken to mean not the physical Radha, the consort of Krishna, but Radha as she is sometimes theologically interpreted in Vaishnava circles, as the pure spiritual energy (*śakti*) of Krishna, or the energy center, the soul, within oneself. Radhasoami, then, as the 'swami of Radha', refers to the control of the soul, or the mastery of spiritual energy. And it so happens that the very sound of the name, Radhasoami, is for the Agra branches like a *mūl-mantra:* it is the vessel of that purest essence of energy itself. In the Beas branches of the movement, the names of the five Lords of the interior regions provide the syllables for the mantra. For these branches Radhasoami is still a central term, however, for it describes the highest stage of god-realization, and is the name of the Lord of the ultimate realm.

2. *The Interior Path of Spirituality.*

A logical corollary to the concept of the Absolute as formless is the notion that the external forms of religious expression, which so frequently are attempts to please and placate the moods of the gods, are useless. Rituals, sacrifices, chants and festivals — all are dashed upon the dungheap of spiritual devices. Like the Protestant response to the high church's spiritual apparatus at the time of the European Reformation, the Sant message to Brahmanical theism is a call for a radical, uncompromising submission to faith. The externals are irrelevant. Only the interior transformation of the soul matters.

Differences arise among the Sants in describing the nature of this interior spirituality. Kabir's spirituality seems to be both simple and obscure. Through abrupt and mind-churning conjunctions of images

25. *First Centenary Souvenir*, pp. i-ii.

Kabir would jolt the listener out of a complacent exteriority into a sharply different but indescribable realm within. Nanak goes further in demarcating the landscape of this internal realm, defining five interior levels through which the devout soul passes in its search for the highest, which he calls the realm of truth (*sach-khaṇḍ*). But in Radhasoami teachings the landscape has become a jungle, each interior level described in geographical and floral detail; and not just each level, but each sub-level of each level, from that residing just behind the worldly senses, the realm of *piṇḍ*, to that glorious and dazzling spectacle that awaits the soul upon its transit to the inner realms of *anāmī lok*, that highest level also known, again, as the Radhasoami realm.

3. *The Necessity of a Guru*

The Sants have rendered most of the well-known religious offices obsolete, for, from the Sant point of view, those offices are engaged only in the externals of religion. Brahmans, *sanyāsīs*, yogis and the like are not only useless, they are positively misleading. Yet the spiritually-minded person has some need for a guide to steer him or her away from the excesses of this world toward the richer rewards of the internal spiritual realms. Those services are provided by a guru, who is more than simply a guide. He (or she, for there are no sexual prerogatives for this role) is the primary access that a devotee has to the spiritual world. The mediary function of the guru is itself a form of divine grace.

Perhaps this is a good point to consider a paradox in the idea of *nirguṇa* bhakti which the concept of guru helps to resolve. The notion of the Absolute as *nirguṇa*, without form, and the notion of bhakti, loving devotion, as the appropriate response to the Absolute, make an odd juxtaposition; for, if the Absolute has no personal qualities, who or what can one be loving towards and devoted to? To some extent, *nirguṇa* bhakti is love for the sake of love, devotion to devotion itself. Yet the role of guru is helpful here. As a manifestation of a higher form of spirituality than most devotees possess, the guru is both an exemplar of behavior and a revelation of the divine itself. The guru provides an accessible form of divinity towards which the *nirguṇa* bhakta can express his or her devotion; he gives form to the formless. *Nirguṇa* bhakti becomes, in effect, guru-bhakti: devotion to the guru.

But is this guru an actual person? In Sant writings — the sayings of Kabir, for instance — much is made of the *satguru* (the 'True Guru') and the necessity of adhering to the *satguru*'s dictates. Yet this *satguru*, from

Kabir's perspective, dwells within, a sort of spiritual conscience, an inner voice. The early Sants displayed considerable awe in response to this internal *satguru*, and it is unclear whether they felt themselves worthy of the appellation or the veneration it implies. The movements which came to be established in the Sants' names, however, regarded the matter with greater certainty. To the Kabir-panthis, Kabir was as close to a full manifestation of God as one would hope to achieve. The Nanak-panthis regarded Nanak similarly. After Nanak yet another twist was added to the evolving concept of guruship: a lineage of spiritual authority that passed from one guru to another and which laid the basis for the new religious tradition of the Sikhs.

To the Sikhs the concept of guru is paramount. Nanak and the other nine Gurus in the lineage he established are regarded as manifestations of the divine. Miraculous occurrences are attributed to them, both in legend and in the present day.[26] According to a commandment said to have been proclaimed by the tenth Guru, Gobind Singh, their spiritual energy has been transferred to two entities: the sacred book (the *Ādi Granth*, a compilation of the poetry of the first five Gurus, Kabir, Ravi Das and other Sants) and the community (the Khalsa). Since the book is a form of the guru, some pious Sikhs treat it in an anthropomorphized way. Like the images worshipped in *saguṇa* bhakti devotion, the Sikhs' sacred book is refreshed with fans, placed to sleep under gentle silks, and awakened by the tinkling of bells and the softest of voices.

The Radhasoami devotees, if anything, surpass the Sikhs in their enthusiasm for gurus, but they have no need for such obeisance to a book. They have the living guru himself. Like the later Sant movements, they have come to regard the Sants — and especially their own lineages of Masters — as incarnate forms of the Absolute. In the poetry and other writings of the Radhasoami Masters one detects a certain self-consciousness about the role that they command in the spiritual lives of their readers. There is very little of the abandon and play of Kabir, for instance: rather, the Radhasoami style tends to be more didactic, promulgatory, exalted. And no wonder, considering the slavish attention with which their followers honor every utterance of the living Masters. Each word is taken as a pearl of revelation.

26. For the development of the Sikh legendry surrounding Guru Nanak, see W.H. McLeod, *Gurū Nānak and the Sikh Religion* (Oxford: Clarendon Press, 1968) and *Early Sikh Tradition: A Study of the Janam-sākhīs* (Oxford: Clarendon Press, 1980).

The guru-bhakti in Radhasoami can sometimes be seen in extreme forms. Many of the devotees pray to their living Master and expect his intercession in their daily affairs, and a few have reported seemingly magical occurences as a result of his presence or his gaze upon them.[27] The story told by J.N. Farquhar about Swami Dayal's devotees treating his excrement as if it were a sacrament is probably apocryphal,[28] but the present-day devotees in the Soamibagh branch of the movement proudly display and venerate finger-nail clippings of the original Master as sacred relics. Among village followers of the movement especially, the sacred sight (*darśan*) of the living Master has powerful, even healing qualities. I have seen mothers rush to hold up their sick children as the automobile of the present Master of the Beas branch hurries past, hoping that even such a brief exposure to such powerful spiritual energy would work its healing effects.

The continuation of living Masters is guaranteed by Radhasoami theology. There is not likely to be the sort of lacuna in the spiritual lineages which has required the Sikhs, for example, to seek their masters in history or on some trans-physical plane. The Radhasoami teachings require that a guru be alive and present for the devotee's spiritual quest to be efficacious. That this insistence is a departure from the early Sant tradition is noted by the leaders of the Dayalbagh branch, who cite their belief that "the Supreme Sound Current...would take abode in one Satguru after another until the entire creation is redeemed," as another of the "marked differences" between themselves and "the Religion of Saints."[29]

4. *The Fellowship of* Satsaṅg

The term *satsaṅg* can be translated as the 'fellowship of the true' or even 'the communion of saints', with all the spiritual enjoyment which that phrase implies to a practising Christian. In the early Sant writings the term seems to be taken in its loosest sense: the actual meetings of bhaktas to share their spiritual delight and common dedication

27. See for example Johnson, *With a Great Master*, *passim*.

28. J.N. Farquhar, *Modern Religious Movements in India* (New York: Macmillan Co., 1924), p. 169. See also his entry on Radhasoami in James Hastings, ed., *Encyclopaedia of Religion and Ethics* (New York: C. Scribner's Sons, 1955-58). For an excellent recent analysis of the Radhasoami veneration of the guru, see Lawrence A. Babb, "The Physiology of Redemption," *History of Religions* 22:4 (1983).

29. See *First Centenary Souvenir*, pp. i-ii.

with one another. It seems that any devoted person was, in that early context, a Sant. Later, as only the major poets such as Kabir were so regarded, the concept of *satsaṅg* seems to have shifted to the fellowships which were created when two or more persons came together as mutual followers of the same Sant. Such meetings must have been very much like similar situations in modern India, where two persons who follow the spiritual discipline of the same master will sometimes refer to each other as '*guru bhāī*' or '*guru bahin*', guru-brother or guru-sister of one another. Such relationships were most likely the beginnings of the fellowships which outlasted the lives of the medieval Sants themselves, and which have continued over generations as panthic movements: the Kabir-panthis, Nanak-panthis, Raidasis and Dadu-panthis.

In most cases these associations have been fairly informal. A Raidasi, for instance, is virtually anyone who reveres the name of Ravi Das, and in some areas of North India the term has been appropriated as the caste name for the lower-caste Chamars.[30] At the other extreme, the Sikh tradition, which has evolved out of the Nanak-panth, is regarded as a separate religion, one that has its own distinctive marks of identity and elicits fierce loyalties from its membership.

The Radhasoami movement has taken a somewhat different tack. On the one hand it claims not to be a religion like the Sikhs: followers may retain their old ties to Hindu, Sikh or Christian communities. On the other hand, it empties those religious traditions of their meanings by suggesting that Radhasoami teachings contain a higher science and by providing a community and a set of traditions that effectively rival those of other religions. Yet the term religion (*dharma*) is avoided by the movement in describing itself. Radhasoami adherents prefer to be known instead by the Sant terminology: *satsaṅg*.

In Radhasoami parlance a Sant is only that person who has reached the final stage of god-realization. Those rare souls are the true gurus. A *satsaṅg*, following this definition of Sant, is any fellowship with, or on behalf of, the living spiritual master. The Radhasoami Satsang, as it is officially called, might not be easily recognized as a *satsaṅg* by Kabir or any of the other early Sants. Part of the reason would be organizational: the modern penchant for communicating the word and stren-

30. See the discussion of the use of Ravi Das as a symbol for lower-caste unity in the Ad Dharm movement in Mark Juergensmeyer, *Religion as Social Vision: The Movement Againts Untouchability in 20th Century Punjab* (Berkeley: University of California Press, 1982), chapter 8.

gthening the community through large administrative networks was simply unknown to the early Sants. But another reason is theological: not everyone can become admitted into the fellowship by his or her own choice. The living Master himself makes the selection, following a lengthy trial period, a selection based upon the Master's alleged ability to determine the internal spiritual readiness of each candidate. Upon selection, the initiate (an adult, usually, and a married one at that) is inducted into the fellowship by receiving the secret mantra — five sacred names in the case of the Beas branch, one name or phrase in the case of the Agra branches — and is thereafter a member of the Satsang and is known as a *satsaṅgī*. *Satsaṅg*, however, as the members of the Radhasoami Satsang use it, is a word like 'church', denoting both a fellowship (or rather, local fellowships) and an event. Thus the local *satsaṅg* of, say, Jalandhar or Bombay, will hold its *satsaṅg* on certain Sundays, and this *satsaṅg* as an event will consist of a collective service of worship usually involving readings from the Sants and the Masters in the Radhasoami tradition, and some homily delivered in interpretation and exposition of the readings. It is *satsaṅg* all right, but of a definite Radhasoami organizational stripe.

5. *The Radhasoami Form of* Sant Mat

Thus it appears that in Radhasoami tradition each of the essential Sant characteristics has been replicated — even self-consciously so. Yet it also appears that there is a certain Radhasoami way of interpreting and embodying each of them. Exactly what that Radhasoami style is, however, cannot easily be said. P.D. Barthwal has made a theological distinction between the teachings of Shiv Dayal and those of the early Sants. He regards Shiv Dayal as a *viśiṣṭādvaitin*, one whom he describes as believing that God resides in each person but that the whole of God is not contained therein, as opposed to what he regards as the strict *advaita* position of Kabir and the *bhedābheda* position of Nanak.[31] These distinctions are not wholly convincing, however; and the difference is more than theological. Perhaps ultimately it is a difference of generations, a modern style contrasted to a late medieval one. As Wilfred Cantwell Smith has observed, when a tradition ages there is a general tendency towards a reification of religion — the self-conscious setting apart, through organization and doctrine, of the religious things

31. Barthwal, *Nirguṇa School*, pp. 32-56.

of life.[32] Perhaps this tendency alone would explain what appears to be a more orderly and less spontaneous form of religious expression in the writings and life-style of the Radhasoami movement as over against the mood captured in the vibrant poetry of the early Sants.

Yet other explanations may be offered as well. The Radhasoami movement, after all, has developed in particular places at particular times, and has been subject to the historical circumstances of those places and times. The origins of the movement in Agra — at the edge of the Braj pilgrimage region, famed for being the boyhood home of Lord Krishna — might explain some of the Vaishnava elements which have permeated the otherwise solid *nirguṇa* philosophy of Radhasoami.[33] The use of the name Radhasoami itself, for example, is said to have been especially encouraged by the second guru at Agra, Rai Saligram, whose family were devotees of a Krishna temple in Brindavan.[34] The frequent similarities between Radhasoami beliefs and practices and their Sikh counterparts — especially those regarding the semi-divine nature of the guru and the cohesiveness of the community — might be attributed to the Punjabi family background of Shiv Dayal. In addition, each of the Masters of the Beas branch of the movement has come from a Sikh background, and all have retained Sikh customs. The penchant for organization and ideological systematization may be understood against the background of the aggressive models of religious organization displayed throughout North India since the mid-nineteenth century. These include the Arya Samaj (which appealed to the same caste community, the urban Khatris, who constitute much of the Radhasoami leadership) and the various institutions of the Christian missions.[35]

32. Wilfred Cantwell Smith, *The Meaning and End of Religion* (New York: Harper and Row, 1978).

33. Examples of some of the Vaishnava elements include the use of the flute as a spiritual metaphor (recalling Krishna's use of that instrument), stories of ladies flocking to the feet of the Master (recalling the lure of Krishna for the cow-maidens) and, of course, the name 'Radhasoami' itself, which is a name for Krishna, the lord of his consort, Radha. The stories of Shiv Dayal and his wife dressing up as Krishna and Radha are probably apocryphal although they are reported as fact by Farquhar, *Modern Religious Movements*, p. 170.

34. Interview with Dr. Agam Prasad Mathur, Chairman of the History Department, Agra College, at Peepalmandi, Agra, August 8, 1978. Mathur is the great-grandson of Rai Saligram, the author of an historical work on Radhasoami (see above, footnote 11, *Radhasoami Faith*) and is also serving as the spiritual master of a branch of the Radhasoami movement which traces its lineage directly to Rai Saligram.

35. There were some leaders of the Arya Samaj who switched over to the Dayal-

More difficult to understand is how this organizational style fits the Radhasoami bent towards esoteric practices, a tendency seen in the movement's appropriation of a special Yoga, its emphasis on secret initiation and the efficacy of cosmic knowledge in accomplishing an interior journey, and in its attribution of almost magical powers to the guru. Some of these same elements have been identified with the medieval Nath Yoga tradition, but the Nath elements in North Indian religion are usually thought of as having been supplanted by or suffused with more moderate notions of spirituality, so it is somewhat surprising to see in Radhasoami a resurgence of an earlier, more radical mysticism. Yet elsewhere in India, spiritual organizations have recently arisen which embody this same combination of elements, so it may be that the spirit of modern times calls for forceful, interior forms of religious experience, presented in a systematic organizational manner.[36]

Together, all of these factors help us to understand the complexity of the Radhasoami tradition, how the simple bhakti of the early Sants has been complicated by the offer of a more elaborate path to spiritual fulfilment, and a more meticulous doctrine and organization to surround it. Ultimately, not everyone who reveres and follows the early Sants will be easily persuaded that *sant mat* is Radhasoami *mat*, that the two are one and the same. Yet one would be hard pressed to deny that Radhasoami *mat* is indeed a kind of replication of *sant mat*, one that is appropriate for its own time. The only matters remaining to be determined are the historical connections between the Sants and Radhasoami, and the question of how and where the esoteric interpretation of the Sant teachings emerged.

The Historical Links to the Sant Tradition

A search for the antecedents to the Radhasoami movement must begin with the writings of Shiv Dayal Singh. His is regarded as the founding genius of the tradition, and although later Masters have refined, interpreted and expanded his ideas, few have felt the need to alter them in a major way. For most branches of the Radhasoami movement,

---

bagh branch of Radhasoami during the 1930s, including Baba Ram Jadoun, General Secretary of the branch. (Interview with Baba Ram Jadoun, November 9, 1973 at Dayalbagh.)

36. See Charles S.J. White, "The Sai Baba Movement: Approaches to the Study of Indian Saints," in *Journal of Asian Studies* 31:4 (1972), in which he traces the origins of that movement to both Nath and Sant elements.

his writings have canonical authority, and in at least one of those branches his presence in history is regarded as having been an occasion of divine revelation without parallel. This branch of the movement possesses the original location of the garden at the edge of Agra where Dayal achieved enlightenment. At this place, now called Soamibagh, it is constructing an enormous granite and marble edifice. Intended to be a *satsaṅg ghar* (meeting place for the community) as well as a *samādhi* (tomb) for the remains of the first Master, the half-finished structure gives evidence of a mixed architectural heritage. To the Westerner, the design appears to be much like a cathedral with minarets, surmounted by a giant webbed dome. Its builders hope that when completed the building will rival in popularity Agra's other major tourist attraction, the Taj Mahal.[37]

Shiv Dayal — or Swamiji, as he is known — began life in much less pretentious surroundings. He was born in the crowded Pannigali section of Agra sometime early in the nineteenth century to a Punjabi family of Khatri caste who had come to Agra as money lenders.[38] He is said to have begun the practice of *surat śabda yoga*[39] at a very early age, and in January 1861 began teaching in public to a gradually expanding group of devotees from varying religious backgrounds. These he initiated into '*sant mat*'. In 1878, after seventeen years of this ministry, he 'sloughed off the mortal coil', as Radhasoami biographers, quoting *Hamlet*, usually put it.

His *Sār bachan*, written in versified Hindi, gives no indication as to the origins of the ideas it presents, except to attribute them to Swami Dayal's own spiritual insights; and although there are vague references

37. See Raghu Rai, "Twentieth Century Taj Mahal," *Illustrated Weekly o, India*, August 15, 1979.

38. Singh, *Jīvan charitra.* The birth date is given as 1818. Barthwal suggests 1828. The writers of the Beas branch of Radhasoami agree with Agra on the earlier date, 1818. See for example Puri, *Teachings* and Puri, *Tulsi Sahib.* The earlier date, if authentic, would make the claim of Swamiji's relationship with Tulsi Sahib more convincing, assuming that the death date usually asserted for Tulsi Sahib (1843) is correct.

39. Earlier in this article I have translated the difficult phrase *surat śabda yoga* as 'the discipline of concentrating on the divine word through one's inner current'. *Surat* most likely comes from either the sanskrit *śrota,* consciousness or mental flow, or from *śruti,* that which has been heard; but in Radhasoami terminology it means one's internal sound current, or simply one's soul. Radhasoami authors have translated the whole phrase variously, including 'the yoga of the audible life stream' (Puri, *Tulsi Sahib* introduction) and 'the practice of merging the soul in the Divine Current of the Supreme Being's Melody and Power' (Puri, *Teachings*, p. 5).

to the importance of having the guidance of a spiritual master, Swamiji does not tell us who his own master was, nor whether indeed he ever had one, at least in physical form. He does claim the whole of the Sant tradition as his antecedent, however, and at times refers to specific Sants as having corroborated his points with similar insights of their own. The following is one of the longer enumerations of Sants with whom he claims a relationship:

> If in your mind you do not believe what I say, then consult the sayings of Kabir and Guru Nanak. Tulsi's persuasion is just the same, and so is that of Paltu and Jagjivan. These saints I take as my authority, and I witness to what they teach.[40]

The connections with Kabir and Nanak are clear enough. These we have discussed earlier. All of the major contours of the teachings may be found there — the interior realms of consciousness, the importance of the spiritual sound or *nāma*, and the necessity of finding the *satguru* — although in somewhat less elaborate form than that propounded by Swami Dayal. Of the two, Nanak seems more directly related to Dayal's thoughts than Kabir (at least the Kabir we know through those writings regarded as authoritatively his). The specifications of the internal realms, the centrality of *nāma*, the deification of the guru — all are characteristically Nanak-panthi, even Sikh. Since Dayal's family came from the Punjab, the transmission of Nanak's ideas to him could have been quite direct. Farquhar reports Dayal as having originally preached from the Sikh scriptures, the *Ādi Granth*, and the family name Singh makes one wonder whether Dayal's family might not at some time in their past have been Sikhs. Against such a background it would be plausible to regard Dayal's teachings as a sort of revised Sikhism for an Agra audience.

Yet there is more to Swami Dayal's teachings than that which Kabir or Nanak could have provided, and the other Sants mentioned by Dayal were historically even more accessible to him than the medieval ones. He knew of Jagjivan (or Jagjivan Das as he is also known) who founded the Satnami sect around the end of the eighteenth century, and Paltu who composed poetry at Ayodhya in the same period and warred against the Hindu *vairāgīs*, whom he considered to be idolatrous. Both of them are regarded as Sants by Barthwal and both enlarged upon the

40. Shiv Dayal, *Sār bachan* (Hindi version), p. 36. My appreciation to J.S. Hawley for translating this passage.

nirguṇa bhakti ideas of the early Sant tradition.[41] How Swami Dayal became aware of them and their writings is not known. His connections with another of these latter-day Sants are, however, well established, for this holy man lived only a few miles away from Dayal. Dayal's parents were his devotees and Swamiji himself is said to have had with him an association "of great love."[42] That Sant was Tulsi Sahib.

Tulsi Sahib lived and taught in Hathras, twenty miles from Agra, early in the nineteenth century. His vital dates are uncertain,[43] and so too is his place of origin. A biographical introduction provided in Tulsi Sahib's versified book of teachings, the *Ghaṭ Rāmāyaṇa*, claims that he was born a Brahman, son of a Peshwa in Poona, in 1763. His original name was Shyam Rao. Disgusted with the affairs of the Maratha court, he is said to have eventually wandered to Banaras, where he successfully challenged the spiritual authorities. After that he repaired to the town of Hathras and adopted the name Tulsi Sahib. The Maratha origins of Tulsi Sahib can be neither proven nor disproven, although it is notable that his compositions seem to be quite unencumbered by words of Marathi origin, even though the polyglot vocabulary contains words from other North Indian languages that were current in the region of Western Uttar Pradesh at that time.[44] No reason is given for his adopting the name Tulsi Sahib, although at one point the *Ghaṭ Rāmāyaṇa* claims him to be one and the same as Tulsi Das, author of the great vernacular *Rāmāyaṇa*. It is said that Tulsi Sahib, in the person of his famous namesake, first offered the interior *Ghaṭ Rāmāyaṇa* to Banaras society, but hid it away when its message proved too rarified for the tastes of the day. Then and only then did he bother to compose a lesser, more exterior representation of the same truths, the book the world knows as the *Rāmāyaṇa* of Tulsi Das.[45]

41. Barthwal, *Nirguṇa School*, pp. 264-65.

42. Puri, *Teachings*, p. 6.

43. According to the editors of the Belvedere Press, who have provided a biographical introduction to their edition of Tulsi Sahib's *Śabdāvalī*, he died in 1842 or 1843 at the age of 80. This does not correspond with the dates of his life (1791-1848) given in another of their introductions, that prefacing their edition of Tulsi Sahib's *Ratan sāgar*. According to Parashuram Chaturvedi, others have placed his dates at 1760 to 1763 for the birth date, and 1842 or 1843 for his death date (*Sant-paramparā*, p. 782). The latter dates are those given in the introduction to Tulsi Sahib's *Ghaṭ Rāmāyaṇa* and relied upon by Janak Raj Puri in *Tulsi Sahib*, p. 1.

44. Puri, *Tulsi Sahib*, p. 18.

45. Both Chaturvedi, *Sant-paramparā*, pp. 779-80, and Barthwal, *Nirguṇa School*, pp. 268-69, argue that Tulsi Sahib's claim to authorship of the *Rāmāyaṇa* is

The teachings of Tulsi Sahib are remarkably similar to those of Shiv Dayal. They are couched in the context of the struggle against *kāl*, time or mortality, the negative power. The major vehicle available for the avoidance of this power is a positive one of even greater force: the words (*śruti*) of the *satguru*. This *śruti* (or *surat* or *surati*) seems to be not a sound framed by ordinary words, but a remarkable sound which is discovered within the soul of each person. Tulsi Sahib admonishes the seeker to find that sound, fix on it, and follow its path as a devotee might follow the sound of Krishna's flute. The regions into which the soul enters as it makes its transit through the 'tenth door', or the third eye, are described in glorious detail. Tulsi Sahib seems obsessed with enumeration: the reader is treated to lists of everything—the thirty-six waters of creation, the eighty-five winds, the sixteen skies, the eighty-four spiritual attainments, the nine inner channels, the twenty-two names of *sunna*, emptiness. The point of all this is to lend credence to Tulsi Sahib's account of the soul's ascent to the highest of the high regions, the fourth part of the realm of *satlok*: *anāmī*. The ultimate moment is described as follows:

> The soul hears a wave of sound and rhythm that becomes visible from the west. It opens the door—unspeakable, indescribable. Going beyond rhythm and sight, one enters the gate of the tower of emptiness, where by means of the doors of sight and sound one finds the level of highest reality (*parabrahma*). Then one sees the sound-current (*surati-sail*) issuing forth hundreds of thousands of universes (literally, 'heaven eggs'), and sound (*surat*) penetrates to the middle of them all, their crown jewel, which is tiny as an insect.[46]

The *satguru* is essential for the proper accomplishment of this spiritual journey. He is the guide out of the lower regions, the administrator of the higher ones and, in some indescribable manner, he seems to be himself the sound current vehicle of spiritual transportation. Thus, much is made of the *satguru*, and for that matter much also is made of the other key terms that cluster around the term Sant: the Sants themselves, their *satsaṅg*, and *sant mat*. Sants such as Kabir, Nanak, Dadu and

---

a spurious interpolation from some later hand. Quite aside from their textual arguments for its spurious authorship, the very idea of such a claim is clearly an affront to their literary sensibilities. Says Barthwal: "The author of this fabrication (the interpolation) stands guilty of an unpardonable crime for he has called...the literary jewel that has won the heart of all humanity the work of an impostor" (p. 269).

46. Tulsi Sahib, *Ghaṭ Rāmāyaṇa*: 1:159. Translation by J.S. Hawley.

others are regarded not only as intellectual precursors of these ideas but as persons who have embodied within themselves the special *satguru* energies. The *satsaṅg*, then, the communion of saints, is a matter of assembling all of this spiritual energy from past ages, and amounts to nothing less than the creation of a sort of spiritual critical mass. For Tulsi Sahib there is spiritual as well as intellectual significance to the notion that the Sants are interconnected, and he relies upon the authority of this collective *sant mat* for his insights. As we have noted, some claim that the term *sant mat* was his.[47]

Swami Shiv Dayal apparently received all of this first hand as a disciple of Tulsi Sahib's. I say 'apparently', for neither Tulsi Sahib nor Swami Dayal record that relationship as a fact, but the biographies of Swamiji describe many touching stories of their affectionate friendship.[48] According to some memories within the Radhasoami movement, the followers of Tulsi Sahib shifted to Swami Dayal after the former's death, which would imply a guru-succession.[49] But there is no indication that Tulsi Sahib had actually initiated Swamiji. Some Radhasoami members, however, interpret the *Ghaṭ Rāmāyaṇa* as having forecast Swamiji's coming, in the manner of John the Baptist.[50] The present incumbent of the lineage established by Tulsi Sahib at Hathras, one Sant Prakash Das, adamantly denies that Swamiji's lineage carries Tulsi Sahib's authority, although he concurs that Swamiji was a disciple of Tulsi Sahib.[51]

Whatever its nature, some sort of relationship between Shiv Dayal and Tulsi Sahib seems likely to have existed and the similarities in their teachings reflect that. Thus we may be persuaded that in Tulsi Sahib we have discovered an earlier generation of what became the Radhasoami tradition. The next question follows naturally. What preceded Tulsi Sahib, and are there links through him to the earlier Sants?[52] No

47. Puri, *Tulsi Sahib*, p. 17.
48. See for example Puri, *Teachings*, pp. 6-7.
49. Interview with K.L. Khanna, General Secretary of the Radhasoami Satsang, Beas, May 25, 1971, and others at the Beas Dera.
50. Puri, *Tulsi Sahib*, p. 6.
51. Interview with Sant Prakash Das, the *mahant* of Tulsi Sahib's ashram and *samādhi*, Hathras, August 9, 1978.
52. One branch of the Radhasoami movement provides its own solution. According to Kirpal Singh, founder of the Ruhani Satsang, the linkage was accomplished as follows: Gobind Singh, tenth and final guru in the Sikh lineage, did not die in 1699 as is reported, but moved to Bengal where he was succeeded by one Rat

definitive answer can be given to either part of this question, but there are some intriguing hints in Tulsi Sahib's writings themselves. In the *Ghaṭ Rāmāyaṇa* he mentions his acquaintance with many of the early Sants—no surprises there. But then he singles out individuals whom he engages in argument and among them is one he calls Phul Das, a representative of the Kabir-panth. This in itself might indicate some sort of ambivalent relationship between Tulsi Sahib and the Kabir-panthis, but a further clue is offered in Tulsi Sahib's favorable mention of an esoteric writing attributed to Kabir, the *Anurāg sāgar*.[53]

Although of uncertain origin, the *Anurāg sāgar* ('Sea of Love') purports to be principally a dialogue between Kabir and one of his best-known disciples, Dharamdas, who is said to have founded the Chhattisgarh branch of the Kabir-panth sometime in the late sixteenth century.[54] It is doubtful that the *Anurāg sāgar* was actually written by Dharamdas or anyone of his time — the language of the text seems to suggest at best an eighteenth-century date — but the use of his name and other names associated with him would indicate that the actual writer had some association with his branch of the Kabir-panth. In fact, the discussions in the text reveal a dispute over the sixth-generation succession to the leadership of the Dharamdasi branch, and an enumeration of rival panths that venerate Kabir but which the author of the *Anurāg sāgar* regards as illicit.[55] Therefore, if we can find strong similarities between Tulsi Sahib's writings and the *Anurāg sāgar*, we may be able to posit some connection to Kabir via the branch of the Kabir-panth that produced the esoteric work. This leads us to a consideration of the substance of the *Anurāg sāgar* itself.

The *Anurāg sāgar* is one of forty works spuriously attributed to Kabir and collected together by a Kabir-panthi in the eleven-volume *Kabīr sāgar* ('Ocean of Kabir'). Behind all of these works lies a common mythological core, which Barthwal describes as follows.[56] At the begin-

---

Nagan Rao, who in turn went to the Maratha country and initiated as his successor the man who eventually came to Hathras and became known to the world as Tulsi Sahib. After him came Dayal, and so on to the present day.

53. Tulsi Sahib, *Ghaṭ Rāmāyaṇa* 2:23.

54. Chaturvedi, *Sant-paramparā*, p. 282. Since Chaturvedi places Kabir's death in 1505 he doubts that Dharamdas knew Kabir personally.

55. *Kabīr sāhib kā anurāg sāgar* (Allahabad: Belvedere Press, 1975), pp. 87-88. A recent translation has been published under the title *The Ocean of Love: The Anurāg Sāgar of Kabir*, trans. Raj Kumar Bagga, Partap Singh and Kent Bicknell, Sanbornton, New Hampshire: Sant Bani Ashram, 1982).

56. Barthwal, *Nirguṇa School*, pp. 278-82.

ning of time, the Primal Being begat a number of sons, two of whom were Kabir and Niranjan, who were destined to be rivals for eternity. Kabir was identified with the forces of good and of life, the positive power in the world. Niranjan was linked with evil and death, the negative force. (Niranjan was also a name connected with a school of Nath Yogis with whom the Kabir-panthis quarrelled; hence their name may have been deliberately adopted for this demonic role.) Through deceit, Niranjan (also known as Kal, the Lord of Death) takes possession of the physical world and, through the seduction of *māyā*, illusion, he fathers Brahma, Vishnu and Shiva, the three major gods of the Hindu pantheon. Together with his *saguṇa* sons, then, Niranjan rules the world and keeps it bound to negativity, darkness and death. There is one flaw in his malign and macabre rule, however: Kabir. In the background of world history, Kabir, the force of life, stands ready to intercede. It was he, for example, who constructed the bridge from India to Sri Lanka that allowed Ram to cross over and rescue Sita, as described in the *Rāmāyaṇa*. In this present *Kali* age (the age of darkness in the traditional Hindu division of history), just as it appears that Niranjan is finally about to deliver the *coup de grâce* in his conquest of the world, the divine force of goodness, Kabir, appears himself in human history, incarnate as the Sant we know by the same name.

The *Anurāg sāgar* does not repeat this story in detail, although it does reflect many of its salient points, especially the general background of the cosmic conflict between Niranjan, or Kal, and the forces of good enshrined in the transcendent Kabir. The *Anurāg sāgar*, however, is particularly concerned with the succession of Kabir's spiritual energy in the teachers and panths that follow after him. With ritualistic detail, the author describes how Kabir transmits his power to the founder of the Chhattisgarh Kabir-panth, Dharamdas.[57] Ultimately, Kabir grants to Dharamadas two essential parts of himself: the *nād* (the deep sound made by blowing a conch shell) and the *bind* (a point, such as the point on one's forehead above and between the eyes). These are also described as the two aspects of spiritual sound (*śabda*) that will be manifest in Dharamdas's Kabir-panth: the *nād* is the force that propels the panth, and the point (the eye-point?) will always accompany the presence of the sound. In this way, "thousands will be led into salvation (*mukti*)."[58] The knowledge contained in the sound (*śabda*) that is thus

57. *Anurāg sāgar*, pp. 92-95.
58. Ibid., p. 93.

transmitted from Kabir to Dharamdas is a potent thing; it can be distributed to others only through initiation. On that account care must be taken to withhold it from the wrong sorts of persons. Examples given of the latter are those who are merciless, those with shifty eyes, those whose chins jut out too far and whose heads are too heavy, and those whose middle eye is blocked by even the tiniest thing.[59] In general, then, it may be said that the *Anurāg sāgar* is concerned with the transmission of a secret knowledge which is incarnate in sound, received through panths and spiritual leaders, and which issues originally from the merciful Kabir, the *satguru* who banishes the negative forces of death.

The *Anurāg sāgar* and similar cosmological writings attributed to Kabir amount to an esoteric Santism which appears to have been rife within at least one branch of the Kabir-panth during the eighteenth century. Whether this esoteric Santism was more widespread, and whether its origins can be traced even earlier, is not known. What is clear, however, is that a direct line can be drawn from the ideas of Shiv Dayal, the founding Master in the Radhasoami lineages, back through Tulsi Sahib and finally to the esoteric Santism manifest in the *Anurāg sāgar*. The concepts of the cosmic conflict between the forces of life and death, the availability of the life force in the form of sound, the incarnation of such a sound current in the *satguru*, the transmission of this sound through an organization (panth) and through lineages of spiritual Masters, the access into this realm of salvific sound through the central eye-point, and the barriers to that entrance posed by the selection and secret initiation provided by the panth itself—all these concepts survive intact, though in somewhat altered forms, from the time of the *Anurāg sāgar* onward. They are cardinal features of Radhasoami teachings even in the present day.

There is much more to Radhasoami than this, however, and the discovery of coincidental elements does not mean that we have located the sole origins of the tradition. Like all traditions, it has many origins, absorbing and synthesizing a variety of elements as they endure over time. In the case of Radhasoami, these other elements include the Sikh and Vaishnava contexts; modern influences such as the ideas of the Arya Samaj, Christian missions, and scientific knowledge; and, of course, the unique contributions of Tulsi Sahib, Swami Dayal and the other Radhasoami Masters themselves. We should also not discount the possibility that many ideas were assimilated directly from the extant

59. Ibid., p. 95.

writings of the early Sants — Kabir, Nanak and the others — unmediated through esoteric Santism.

What, then, can be said about Radhasoami's claim to have revived the Sant tradition? No doubt it revives a certain kind of Sant tradition. Whether this can be claimed as authentic to the Sants depends on the way in which one regards a tradition. If one expects a tradition throughout its history to retain the ideas of its originators in a pure, unaltered form, then the answer is no, for Radhasoami's *sant mat* is of a certain kind. But if one regards traditions as flowing, flexible entities, at once true to themselves and changeable in the same way that a river or some organic being is both the same and different over time, then the Radhasoami movement, which owes virtually all of its vocabulary and ideas to the tradition which venerates the Sants, has as much claim to being *sant mat* for our day as do the Kabir-panthis, the Sikhs, or any others who continue to find the insights from the Sant tradition valid for our modern context. Surely the vitality of the one hundred and twenty-year-old history of the Radhasoami movement is to be explained not only by its ability to keep pace with the shifts in moods from generation to generation, but also by the broad popularity which the ideas and images of the whole Sant tradition is able to elicit in each new age. It is this enthusiasm for the Sants that the Radhasoami movement, in its own way, has both affirmed and revived.

SECTION IV

RELATED TRADITIONS

THE SANT MOVEMENT AND NORTH INDIAN SUFIS

BRUCE B. LAWRENCE

Considering the vast popularity of the Sant movement, the number of important figures which it produced, and the lives of countless devotees (both Hindu and Muslim) whom it affected, one must marvel that so little can be said with assurance about the origin, early development and geographical provenance of the Sants. Most attempts to construct a defensible historical preamble to the literary legacy of the Sant movement focus on the biographies of medieval figures who presaged the beginning of a new direction in Indian spirituality. Notwithstanding the importance of Maharashtrian and Kashmiri poets (of whom Namdev and Lalla, respectively, rank as the major lyrical exemplars) the majority of early Sants belonged to that part of present-day India known as the Punjab and Uttar Pradesh, and in its barest outline the formative period of the Sant movement seems to have been shaped by two fifteenth/sixteenth century figures, Kabir and Guru Nanak. Both have assumed legendary status in the literary and religious history of the South Asian subcontinent. Recently, new luster has been added to their names by the critical studies of two contemporary Western scholars, Charlotte Vaudeville and W.H. McLeod.

Yet neither Kabir nor Nanak can be described historically with a modicum of the satisfaction that derives from tracing their legendary attainments. In each case the legend dwarfs, even as it distends, the kernel of historical truth. Preliminarily, it might be asked: why are Western scholars so preoccupied with 'historical' questions in the face of a tradition which until quite recently never concerned itself with the problem of ascertaining what is factual and capable of objective verification? That problem, as it applies to the study of religious texts and traditions, derives from the European Enlightenment and the methodology introduced into Biblical scholarship by late nineteenth/early twentieth-century giants such as Julius Wellhausen and Albert Schweitzer. The very assumption of an implicit opposition between 'legend' and 'fact', for instance, derives from Western investigations of canonical scripture.

Hence McLeod, in his brilliant but cautious reconstruction of Guru Nanak's biographical profile, notes that legends do have significance since they "serve to communicate, in some measure, an impression of the power [of great religious figures] to attract and inspire," yet he quickly adds that in his own study, "legend must wherever possible be identified and set aside" since "the strict, at times ruthless, approach is as much required in a quest for the historical Nanak as it has been required in the quest of the historical Jesus."[1]

Despite the tacit theological assumptions that inform McLeod's (and also Vaudeville's) investigations of non-Biblical, non-Western religious texts, one must applaud their efforts to answer the unanswerable questions about the seminal figures of the Sant movement. Vaudeville bravely titles the second chapter of her major book on the Sant of Magahar, "Kabir's Biography in History and Legend." In effect, however, she is compelled to compare legends about Kabir in order to reconstruct an internally consistent calendar of his major activities, for there is *no* kernel of historical fact apart from the myriad legend about Kabir. Summing up the results of her investigation, Vaudeville deduces that "the hinduization of Kabīr's legend" has tended "to make him conform to the ideal of Vaiṣṇava sanctity as depicted in sectarian writings from the seventeenth century onwards."[2] Similarly, McLeod concludes his biography of Guru Nanak by lamenting "the [cycle of] assumption and conjecture" that has plagued his attempt to periodize the life of the Sikh leader.[3]

Underlying the historical uncertainty of both Kabir and Guru Nanak are two issues — one methodological, the other contextual — which must be treated before the relationship of either of these Sants to individual Sufis and the Sufi tradition can be evaluated. The methodological issue concerns the disparity between poetry and prose as literary media. All the primary evidence for reconstructing the life of Kabir is set forth in *sākhī*s or *dohā*s which, as Vaudeville explains, are short, rhymed poems of didactic quality that were set to music.[4] How does one decide which verses are authentic compositions of the fifteenth-century Sant of Maga-

1. W.H. McLeod, *Gurū Nānak and the Sikh Religion* (Oxford: Clarendon Press, 1968), p. 68. The concluding remark is an oblique reference to Albert Schweitzer's *The Quest of the Historical Jesus*, the first English edition of which was published in 1911 (London: A. and C. Black).

2. Charlotte Vaudeville, *Kabīr*, vol. 1 (Oxford: Clarendon Press, 1974), p. 47.

3. McLeod, *Gurū Nānak*, p. 229.

4. Vaudeville, *Kabīr*, pp. 51-54.

har and which are the spurious inventions of later devotees? The magnitude of the problem in analyzing the *sākhīs* of Kabir has led Vaudeville to assert that "there is no evidence that Kabīr ever composed a single work or even wrote a single verse — though a large number of works have been attributed to him by the Kabir-panthis."[5] All a biographer of Kabir can do, therefore, is to try to determine which of the verses attributed to him have the ring of authenticity. In analyzing material from the *Bījak* and the *Ādi Granth* (the *Gurū Granth Ṣāhib*), Vaudeville applies internal criteria to decipher what appears to be Kabir's own verse. Diligently, she assembles the least legendary elements of his biography, not siphoning off history from legend but rather choosing among the autobiographical verses (none of which may actually have been spoken by Kabir) those which sound most plausible to her, at the same time as she rejects the evidence of other verses in which a too literal or fanciful portrait has been projected by Kabir's followers.

Unlike the life of Kabir, the life of Guru Nanak may be gleaned from prose accounts in the Sikh *janam-sākhīs* or hagiographic accounts composed in Punjabi and written in the Gurmukhi script. The language of the *janam-sākhīs*, however, is both inflated and opaque, with the result that McLeod, following Vaudeville, has been compelled to adopt a set of internally consistent criteria for separating true from false passages, accepting those biographical details which can be regarded as probable, while discarding the improbable. (Only in the case of Guru Nanak's alleged encounters with the Lodi monarch Daulat Khan and the Mughal Emperor Babar — leaving aside the facetious Baghdad inscription — can McLeod apply external criteria to his evaluation of the *janam-sākhīs*.)[6] Yet McLeod does enjoy a relative certainty in the wealth of genealogical material which he can and does use to trace both the ancestry and the offspring of Guru Nanak. He is also aided by the proximity of the last decades of Nanak's life to the time when the earliest *janam-sākhīs* were authored (the beginning of the seventeenth century). However, like the Kabir-panthis' eulogistic accounts of Kabir (which Vaudeville discounts in their entirety), the *janam-sākhīs* of Nanak were all composed within the Sikh community for the benefit of those who were loyal to, and engaged in worship of, Guru Nanak. For this reason, as McLeod himself avers,[7] they are highly unsatisfactory as historical sources.

5. Ibid., p. 49.
6. McLeod, *Gurū Nānak*, pp. 68-69.
7. Ibid., pp. 8ff.

In sum, there is an obvious and a less obvious aspect to the methodological issue raised by Sant hagiographic sources. The inescapable, basic point is that neither the *sākhī*s of Kabir nor the *janam-sākhī*s of Nanak provide apt grist for objectively-minded, fact-oriented historical biographers. Of the two bodies of material, however, the accounts of Nanak appear to be more plausible than the anecdotes about Kabir. The latter are all narrated in poetry, as noted above, and to the extent that they were good poetry, they were intentionally anagogic and ambiguous, relying more on suggestive undertones than public declarations. The merit of the Kabir *sākhī*s requires, even as it offsets, their concomitant inadequacies as biographical source material and theological proof texts.[8] It is to be expected therefore that, of the two, Kabir is the more baffling figure. Vaudeville has noted "the strangely allusive, esoteric language in which many of his [Kabir's] utterances were couched;"[9] while McLeod, in describing the difference between their respective notions of ultimate union (*sahaja*), has suggested that in Guru Nanak's works "one can distinguish with much greater clarity the means whereby this spiritual sight is acquired and the path to God followed. There is in his thought relative clarity at a point where in tne thought of Kabir we are obliged to grapple with mystery."[10]

Beyond the methodological problem of reconstructing biographies out of verses (Kabir) or inflated prose texts (Nanak), there is the contextual problem posed by Indian biographical literature. What antecedents are there in the religious traditions of the South Asian subcontinent for compiling a quasi-historical biography, however much it may be distorted by legendizing propensities within a particular religious community? Other than the Buddha (whose biography is dependent on Chinese as well as Indian records), Ashoka (who left his own edicts on stone tablets), and certain royal personages from the first millenium A.D., e.g., Harshavardhana, (who are known from court chronicles they commissioned about themselves), are there extant historical biographies that describe major Hindu or Buddhist religious figures? Shankara's life is shrouded in mythical obscurity, as is Ramanuja's and Madhava's. Can one locate any Indian religious leader prior to Kabir

8. Concerning the theological 'inconsistencies' which both Kabir and Nanak exhibit (though in a different degree, according to McLeod, p. 149), consult the brilliant discussion of love and death in Vaudeville, *Kabīr*, pp. 143-48 and the comprehensive doctrinal survey in McLeod, *Gurū Nānak*, pp. 148ff.

9. Vaudeville, *Kabīr*, p. 23.

10. McLeod, *Gurū Nānak*, p. 194.

and Guru Nanak whose biography can be more securely traced than either of theirs?

The thrust of these rhetorical questions is to underscore the fact that hagiography, rather than religious biography based on a modicum of factual data, was characteristic of medieval Indian society — with one exception. We do have information of verifiable correctness about the lives of many of the earliest Sufi saints in northern India. Some of the data has been gathered from epigraphic and inscriptional records.[11] Most of it is derived from literary documents produced not only within the community loyal to a particular saint by his followers but also outside that community by those attracted to him and/or his tomb.

As in the cases of Kabir and Guru Nanak, there is also legendary material, some of it originating from a date almost contemporaneous with the Sufi saint in question.[12] The legendary material about Indo-Muslim Sufis does not, however, swallow up or distort beyond recognition the non-legendary details of their lives, and that itself is astonishing. Since there was no fixed standard for historical writing in the medieval Islamic world, one must ask why the biographies of Sufi saints came to be compiled with what can only be termed, in the Indian context, a scrupulous concern for factual accuracy. Part of the motivation lies with the trans-Indian, inter-continental loyalties of Muslims: it was important, at least for the elite members of the pre-Mughal, Mughal and provincial Islamic ruling dynasties, to be able to trace their ancestry through to a non-Indian, preferably Arab, lineage. Genealogical charts required accuracy with respect to names, dates and places, and the same care was taken in compiling spiritual biographies.

Another motivation for accurate biographical writing among Muslims relates to the discipline of *ḥadīṯẖ* collection. The problem which Vaudeville and McLeod faced in determining the legitimate 'sayings' of Kabir and Guru Nanak, respectively, confronted members of the Muslim community in the early centuries after Muhammad's death. The

11. The best source for epigraphic and inscriptional data on the entire Indo-Muslim period is Zia ud-din Desai, ed., *Epigraphia Indica: Arabic and Persian Supplement*, published annually by the Archaeological Survey of India.

12. For spurious material presented in the form of *malfuzāt*, see Mohammad Habib "Chishti Mystics' Records of the Sultanate Period," in Khaliq A. Nizami, ed., *Politics and Society during the Early Medieval Period*, vol. 1 (New Delhi: People's Publishing House, 1974), pp. 401-33; and Bruce Lawrence, "Afzal al-fawaid—A Reassessment," in Zoe Ansari, ed., *The Life, Times and Works of Amir Khusrau Dehlavi* (New Delhi: National Amir Khusrau Society, 1975), pp. 119-31.

science of *ḥadīth* criticism evolved precisely to distinguish true from questionable statements attributed to, or reported about, the Prophet Muhammad. By compiling a generation to generation list of *bona fide* transmitters of a particular *ḥadīth* or tradition, Muslim scholars strove to assemble a composite profile of the *sunnah* or custom of Muhammad that could be defended as accurate historical data and cited as valid legal evidence.

It is no accident that the most widely accepted biography of Indo-Muslim Sufis was authored by a scholar whose primary renown was in the field of *ḥadīth* collection and criticism. In the late sixteenth century, out of a concern for accuracy abetted by genuine affection for Sufis, 'Abd al-Haqq Muhaddith Dehlawi compiled the *Akhbār al-akhyār (fī asrār al-abrār)*, giving full biographical details of the major Sufi *shaikhs* of medieval Hindustan but also including legendary material which he marked as dubious by adding *Allāh ā 'lam* "God is the most wise, i.e., God knows best" at the end of each questionable narrative. The *Akhbār al-akhyār* still contains errors and even occasional miracles that are reported without qualifying rejoinders, but on the whole the book is a trustworthy assessment of the earliest Indo-Muslim Sufi saints, their families, their followers and their literary as well as spiritual testaments.[13]

Since there is no counterpart to *Akhbār al-khyār* in the Sant movement, it is difficult to relate particular Sants to the Sufi tradition or particular Sufi *shaikhs* to their Sant contemporaries. The equilibrium of historical truth claims is too heavily tilted toward the medieval Sufis. Yet there have been numerous attempts to link Kabir with the Muslim mystical tradition as well as its organizational representatives. One of the most ingenious was made by a late nineteenth-century Punjabi hagiographer and litterateur, Ghulam Sarvar Lahori. His extensive *tadhkira* entitled *Khazīnat al-asfiyā* has been frequently cited in connection with Kabir. Ironically, though the *Khazīnat al-asfiyā* was the last of the comprehensive Sufi *tadhkiras* produced in the South Asian subcontinent, it was the first to identify Kabir as a Sufi, however questionable his orthodoxy. Vaudeville has pointed out that Lahori's source

13. Mohammad Mujeeb, *The Indian Muslims* (Toronto and London: McGill University Press, 1967), for instance, relies mainly on *Akhbār al-akhkhyār* for the biographical data he provides of major medieval Indo-Muslim Sufis. A concise description of *Akhbār al-akhyār* and Abd-al-Haqq's numerous other writings is to be found in Khaliq A. Nizami, *Hayat-i Shaykh 'Abd al-Haqq Muhaddith Dehlavi* (Delhi: Nadwat al-Musannifin, 1964), pp. 158-219.

of information may not have been the antecedent Muslim tradition but rather a modern and Western appraisal of the Sikhs, viz., Malcolm's *Sketch of the Sikhs*.[14] Her conjecture is supported by the fact that Lahori places Shaykh Kabir Julaha, as he is titled in the *Khazīnat al-asfiyā*, within the Chishti family division, linking him to Shaykh Taqi Manikpuri and through Taqi to Shaykh Salim bin Baha ud-din Chishti, who is none other than the famed Salim Chishti of Fatehpur Sikri, a contemporary of the Mughal Emperor Akbar (reigned 1556-1605)! On chronological grounds alone the alleged affiliations of Kabir with the Chishtis must be discredited. It seems likely that Lahori was prompted to add Kabir's name to the band of Taqi's disciples because of the latter's occupation: like Kabir, he was allegedly a *hā'ik* or weaver. In Lahori's defense one ought to note that he does describe Kabir's teaching with moderate accuracy, despite his transparent ploy to provide still another hagiographical dimension to the weaver-bard of Magahar.

Kabir's fictitious affiliation with organizational Sufis did not end with Malcolm and Lahori. Westcott discussed two Shaikh Taqis and conjectured, along with Yusuf Husain, that Kabir was actually a disciple of Shaikh Taqi of Jhusi.[15] Shaikh Taqi of Jhusi is more plausible as Kabir's Sufi mentor than Shaikh Taqi of Manikpur (who may also have been from Jhusi!) since affiliation with the former moves Kabir back into the fifteenth century where most contemporary biographers want to place him. Yet whichever Shaikh Taqi is advocated, scholars are plagued by the adamantine obscurity of their sources: the sole reference to any Shaikh Taqi is in a poem of the *Bījak* containing references to Kabir visiting a number of Sufi centers. As with all poetry, as we have stated above, the factual content of this poem is shaded with ambiguity. If we follow Vaudeville's reasoning, it is also laced with sarcasm.[16] The *Bījak* references may echo a real historical relationship, but it is too remote to reconstruct and too tangential to merit the effort required even to trace it.

In the case of Guru Nanak, there are also encounters with Sufi *shaikhs*. They are described in the *janam-sākhīs* and at first glance appear

14. Vaudeville, *Kabīr*, p. 35.

15. Yusuf Husain, *Glimpses of Medieval Indian Culture*, reprint ed. (New Delhi: Asia Publishing House, 1973), p. 16, gives no source reference for his conjecture, but it may have been Westcott since he is the authority acknowledged by Muhammad Hedayetullah for the same identification. Idem, *Kabir: The Apostle of Hindu-Muslim Unity* (Delhi: Vikas, 1977), pp. 182-83.

16. Vaudeville, *Kabīr*, p. 92.

to have more historical substance than Kabir's dalliance with Shaykh Taqi. Because Guru Nanak's life is so closely linked to the Punjab, there is compelling reason for him to be accepted as a holy man by Muslims as well as Hindus.

Even without the testimony of the *janam-sākhīs*, McLeod argues,[17] we could assume that Guru Nanak visited both Pakpattan and Multan, two major loci for the Chishti and Suhrawardi orders of the Punjab, respectively. The only meeting with an actual *shaikh* of either place that can be deemed probable on McLeod's rating scale, however, is the encounter with Shaikh Ibrahim, the *sajjādahnashīn* or successor to the *khānqāh* of Baba Farid in Pakpattan. Can we assume that the exchange between the two holy men, if it did take place, proved mutually beneficial, as the *janam-sākhīs* imply? No, for the story, in its sundry versions, serves more as a patterned validation of Guru Nanak's spiritual quest than as an expression of the Sufi humanitarian impulse, even though certain modern writers, such as Lajwanti Rama Krishna, wish to portray Ibrahim and all the medieval Sufi Saints of the Punjab as itinerant ambassadors of ecumenical good-will, suggesting an all too convenient contrast between them and the militant, exclusivistic, conversionary Muslims whom such writers see elsewhere.[18]

Nothing of lasting value can finally be gained from examining the accounts of direct contacts between major Sant figures and their Sufi contemporaries. The accounts, like the contacts, are fictionalized in their content. They serve a legitimating function for followers of a particular Sant figure. They have no parallel in Muslim literature either contemporary or later, except in those rare instances where a modern Muslim writer chooses to comment on the claims about Sufi *shaikhs* advanced by Sant hagiographers.[19]

17. McLeod, *Gurū Nānak*, pp. 140-42.

18. In *Panjabi Sufi Poets A.D. 1460-1900* (New Delhi: Ashajanak Publications, 1973), Dr. Lajwanti Krishna laments that it was not till the end of his life that Shaikh Ibrahim was able to dispense with "the fanatical side of Islam" (p. 30). On the other hand, she eulogizes Bulle Shah because his pantheism overpowered his dedication to Islamic beliefs and practices and, therefore, unlike other Sufis, "he never took part in the work of conversion" (p. 80). The communal bias — and subsequent distortion — evident in both statements undermines Krishna's attempt at historical objectivity, though her work continues to be of value for its wealth of poetical citations from obscure, largely unavailable and seldom translated primary sources.

19. One sample of such contemporary comment by a Muslim scholar is Khaliq A. Nizami, *The Life and Times of Shaikh Farid-u'd-din Ganj-i-Shakar*, reprint ed.

What is more interesting and fruitful to explore is the indirect influence of North Indian Sufis on the Sant movement. Methodologically it would seem plausible to gauge such an influence on three planes: (1) through references to Sufis in the extant Sant literature, (2) through the use of Sufi technical terms by Sant writers and (3) through thematic novelties in the Sant distichs that are suggestive of the outlook of Muslim rather than Hindu mystics. However, neither (1) nor (2) proves to be of high numerical frequency, even though one might expect the Sants to make laudatory references to holy men — whether Hindu or Muslim — or at least to pose contrasts between Sufis and the '*ulamā*, those stalwarts of Islamic formalism. Yet Nanak places "Sufis under the same condemnation as the conventional *qāzīs* and *mullahs*,"[20] while Kabir scarcely refers to Sufis by name anywhere in his allegedly authentic sayings. Technical terms of Sufi provenance are similarly rare in Kabir's work, and the one term that claims conspicuous attention because of its centrality in Guru Nanak's thought, namely, *hukam*, can only be fitted into the Sufi technical lexicon by imputing a far-fetched and uncharacteristic emphasis to the Perso-Arabic word *hukm*, meaning 'regulation, belief, wisdom'.[21]

It is (3), the thematic correspondence between Sufi and Sant poetry, that presents the largest and potentially most significant field of exploration. It is also, by its elusive nature, the major aspect of Hindu-Muslim interaction in the medieval period that continues to evoke conjecture, as well as provoke debate, up to the present time. McLeod has recently adopted an extreme position. Defining the Sant movement as a synthesis primarily shaped by two decisive elements, Vaishnava bhakti and the Gorakhnathi or Nath tradition, he minimizes the influence of Sufi thought on the emergent Sants. He defends his devaluation of Sufi influence with the argument that affinities of thought (between Sants

(Delhi: Idarah-i Adabiyat-i Delli, 1973), Appendix C, "*Shaikh* Farīd and the *Guru Granth*," pp. 121-22.

20. McLeod, *Gurū Nānak*, p. 158.

21. Ibid., pp. 199-203. On another lexical parallel McLeod seems to have overstated the case, however, in arguing (pp. 221-24) that the five *khaṇḍs* or realms mentioned in *Japjī* 34.7 do not have possible Sufi antecedents. It is not the *maqāmāt* but the cosmological hierarchy of Sufi speculative treatises that approaches Nanak's quintuple. They are commonly labeled as *nāsūt*, *malakūt*, *jabarūt*, *lāhūt* and *hāhūt*. Like the fourth syllable (*turiyā*) of the mantra '*aum*' (see, e.g., the *Māṇḍukya Upaniṣad*), the final or fifth level is often not mentioned by name since it lies beyond the lower levels of speech and attribution.

and Sufis) need not be indicative of historical dependency.[22] But the accumulation of such affinities, especially in a time period markedly different from the period preceding it, cannot be lightly dismissed. Indeed, the conceptual overlap between Sant and Sufi poetry is so pervasive that it is difficult to agree with McLeod that "Muslim beliefs, both Sufi and orthodox, had at most a marginal effect."[23] Vaudeville, by contrast, has noted that "Sufi preachings had already spread all over Northern India in Kabir's [and, therefore, also in Nanak's] time, and. . .Sufi mysticism had impregnated the religious sensibility of the elite as well as the whole composite culture of the time."[24] Her assessment of the socio-religious climate of Hindustan during the fifteenth and sixteenth centuries strongly implies the likelihood of indirect Sufi influences on the emergent Sant movement of northern India.

If we accept Vaudeville's assessment, can we then trace the nature and extent of indirect Sufi influences on the Sants? Negatively, there was the common rejection of ceremonial and scriptural authorities. The Sufis emphasized the inadequacy of Muslim formalism (though they continued to uphold the revelatory truth of the Qur'an), while the Sants derided as ineffectual both Muslim and Hindu external authorities. The Sufi/Sant displacement of ritual and literary props to religious experience, however, already presupposed a positive redefinition of the basis for spiritual development: it was the intense, interior vision of the ineffable God either communicated directly to the devout believer or mediated through the agency of an efficacious preceptor. While McLeod goes to great lengths to show that concepts of unity, interiority and mystical ascent from the Nath tradition combined with the practice of loving devotion in the Vaishnava community to produce the Sant synthesis of interior devotion to a formless, immanent, non-incarnated God i.e., *nirguṇa* bhakti, it is evident that both elements were already present in, and widely known through, the Sufi movement of northern India.

It is impossible to verify the extent of the Sufi influence on the Sants of Uttar Pradesh and the Punjab because the spiritual evolution of the latter was almost entirely shaped within a predominantly Hindu-oriented, Hindi-speaking environment, no matter how drastic the changes to which that environment was subject in the fifteenth and sixteenth

22. McLeod, *Gurū Nānak*, p. 159.

23. Idem, *The Evolution of the Sikh Community* (Oxford: Clarendon Press, 1976), p. 6.

24. Vaudeville, *Kabīr*, p. 94.

centuries. And the religious/poetical language of the Sants reflects their environment. As Simon Digby has noted, "the expression of religious ideas must depend largely on the linguistic tradition in which they are put forth."[25] Hence, what we find in investigating the literary legacy of the Sants are thematic parallels that suggest lexical equivalences to the language of the Sufis, even though the Sant poets use mainly Hindi/Sanskrit terms in their verse while the Sufis rely on a Perso-Arabic vocabulary. The ineffable deity, for instance, is often described by Sants as *aparampāra* ('beyond the beyond'), for which the Sufi equivalent, often found in Indo-Persian verse of the medieval period, is *wāra'l-wāra* ('behind the behind'). Other parallels include *karma* and *qadr* ('fate'), *prapatti* and *aslama/tawakkul* ('total dependence on, and surrender to, God'), and, of course, *japa* and *dhikr* ('efficacious means of invoking the divine names').[26]

But the major thematic equivalence between Sants and Sufis concerns the love relationship. It is fundamental to both groups, and in its intensity it supersedes all other relationships and ritual/scriptural requirements. Not only the love relationship but its special manifestation through the pain and suffering of the devotee are articulated and extolled as indispensable experiences in Sant and Sufi poetry alike. Yet the theme of love as intense suffering is not common to all religious traditions of the subcontinent: it is absent from the Nath tradition, and cannot be traced in Vaishnava bhakti poetry prior to the Sant movement. McLeod hints at the possible indebtedness of Kabir to the Sufis for his vivid expression of love as a way of suffering. The thematic overlap may be even stronger than he allows. "In Kabir's poetry and in the Sant tradition generally, "according to Vaudeville, "the notion of *viraha*, a tormenting desire of the soul for the absent Beloved, bears a resemblance to the Sufi notion of *'ishq*."[27] However, one must be careful to note differences between Kabirian and Indo-Persian love poetry.

The *dramâtis persona* of the former, for instance, is invariably a

25. S. Digby, review of McLeod, *Gurū Nānak and the Sikh Religion*, in *The Indian Economic and Social History Review* 7:2 (1970), p. 311. Digby's lengthy review (pp. 301-13) has been of immense help to the present writer in evaluating the full extent of Sufi-Sant interaction during the Mughal period.

26. The last point of correspondence is explored in Vaudeville, *Kabīr*, p. 140. The first two have been broached by Hedayetullah (*Kabīr*, pp. 233, 235), though in these instances, as in others, the author substitutes quotation of translated excerpts from primary sources for a critical analysis of their content.

27. Vaudeville, *Kabīr*, p. 146.

woman lamenting her departed husband; of the latter, a man in quest of an unseen, previously unknown Beloved. Despite the differences, however, the common emphasis on passionate love (*'ishq/prem*), as communicated through pain, agony, anxiety and grief (*dard/viraha*) and symbolized by blazing fire (*ātish/agni*), is recurrent in the verse of both Kabir and Indo-Persian lyricists. The collection of *sākhī*s which Vaudeville has published under the title "Love in Separation" harks back to the impassioned but eternally frustrated Sufi lover. In one *dohā* Kabir even speaks of the moths which flutter and burn, an image so familiar to Sufi poetry that it seems more plausible to trace its origin to Kabir's Muslim contemporaries than to the Sanskrit poets Ashvaghosa and Kalidasa, as Vaudeville has suggested.[28] In another *dohā* Kabir declares:

Within the heart a fire is burning
  yet no smoke is visible;
He whom it consumes knows that flame
  and He who kindled it![29]

Is its mere coincidence that Indo-Persian poets from the thirteenth century on, echoing a celebrated Qur'anic passage (104.6.7), speak of "a flame in the midst of the heart which reduces us to ashes"?[30]

Kabir's mystical insights are nowhere so dazzling as in those passages where he argues that suffering is not merely possible but necessary, because only those who suffer separation can learn the true meaning of love. In verses like the following, he rings out the paradox of love's agony:

By laughter the soul cannot meet the Husband,
  they found Him only who wept:
If by merry-making the Beloved were found,
  there would be no deserted wife![31]

Corresponding verses in the rich Indo-Persian poetic corpus are legion. Two may be quoted here to illustrate the thematic affinity between Sant

28. Ibid., p. 157, fn. 145.

29. Ibid., p. 162. For the original Hindi and a French rendition of the same *dohā*, see Charlotte Vaudeville, trans., *Kabīr Granthāvalī* (*Dohā*) (Pondichery: Institut Français d'Indologie, 1957), p. 11.

30. An early and typical Indo-Muslim elaboration of this image is set forth in Bruce Lawrence, "The *Lawa'ih* of Qazi Hamid ud-din Nagauri," *Indo-Iranica* 28 (1975), p. 42.

31. Vaudeville, *Kabīr*, p. 168; *Kabīr Granthāvalī*, p. 9.

and Sufi. One is often attributed to the first Islamic martyr to mystical love, Mansur al-Hallaj, the ninth-century Baghdadian who was mutilated, hung, and burned for his daring language:

Hāsil-e 'ishq az in se so<u>kh</u>ān pesh nīst
so<u>kh</u>tam o-so<u>kh</u>tam o-so<u>kh</u>tam.

The sum total of love is nought but these three words:
I-burn and I-burn and I-burn.[32]

The other verse, from Qazi Hamid ad-din Nagauri, a thirteenth-century Suhrawardi Sufi of Delhi, states the lover's dilemma in an extreme manner that poignantly foreshadows Kabir and the Sant movement:

Be-'āshiq o-'ishq kār-e ma 'shūq hubā' st.
Tā 'āshiq nīst nāz-e ma 'shūq kojā'st?

Without a lover and love the labor of the Beloved is lost.
If there be no lover, where is the coquetry of the Beloved?[33]

Since the *nirguṇa* bhakti tradition, however much it stresses the transcendent and formless quality of the Beloved, always posits *a* Beloved, what Hamid ad-din Nagauri has declared in a Sufi context also applies to the Sants: without Bhagvān and *bhagat*, Lord and devotee, how can there be bhakti or devotion?

In short, an extensive comparison of both Sant and Sufi poetry would indicate many more similar passages than could be adduced if one were seeking only to find explicit points of lexical or doctrinal relatedness between the two systems, points such as exist, for instance, between the Sants and the Vaishnava bhaktas or between the Sants and the Gorakhnathis. At the same time, none of the parallel citations from the literary legacy of Sants and Sufis needs to be traced to a chain-link pattern of historical dependency. As distinctive poetical outpourings from spiritual giants of a common age in a shared space, they warrant the attention of Sant and Sufi scholars alike.

There is one realm in which the Sants are indisputably dependent on, and indebted to, the Sufis: the concept of a hagiographical tradition. We noted earlier that writing religious biography — no matter how

32. The verse, often quoted by South Asian Sufis, has been immortalized by Jalal al-Din Rumi in *Dīvān-i Shams-i Tabrīz* 1768. For a variant English translation, see Annemarie Schimmel, *Mystical Dimensions of Islam* (Chapel Hill: University of North Carolina Press, 1975), p. 324.

33. Lawrence, "The *Lawa'ih*," p. 50.

legendary its content — was an uncharacteristic activity of pious scholars in pre-Muslim Indian society. Vaudeville has observed that manuscripts containing a biographical sketch of Kabir cannot be dated earlier than the seventeenth century. Most manuscripts, in fact, are much later, while the popular hagiographies of the Kabir-panthis (*Kabīr-charitra* and *Kabīr-kasauṭī*) quote from a late eighteenth century biography in verse.[34] Similarly, some manuscripts of the *janam-sākhī*s of Guru Nanak date from the seventeenth century, but the most extensive seem to have been copied in the late nineteenth century. As Digby has suggested in his review of McLeod's book on Guru Nanak,

> the obvious and close parallel to the *janam-sakhi* hagiographical tradition is not the ornate and sanskritised form of the Vaishnava *bhaktamalas* but rather that of the Indo-Persian Sufi *tazkiras*, particularly those more fanciful *tazkiras* of the sixteenth or seventeenth centuries dealing with single Pirs or a few related Pirs. Like the *janam-sakhi* collections these *tazkiras* are not biographies but anecdotal collections, and any anecdotes in them are of similar content to those of the *janam-sakhis*.[35]

It is difficult to escape the conclusion, therefore, that the Sufi *tadhkira* tradition, which was already well established in Delhi by the early sixteenth century and flourished under the patronage of the Mughals, was influential in molding the hagiographical writing of the early Sant leaders. In fact, it may even have provided the impetus for Sant devotees to compile anecdotal collections as supplements to the sayings and verses that initially (and, for the mass of their followers, continuously) established the spiritual preeminence of the Sants over their Sufi contemporaries, who, as Digby has pointed out, were also often their rivals.

A clear demarcation between biography and hagiography is no more possible in medieval India than it is in primitive or medieval Christendom. Concerning the biography of Saint Francis, for instance, Edward Armstrong has demonstrated that the lineaments of the saint can only be discerned "through the rosy mists of hagiographical adulation."[36] Like Saint Francis, the early Sants will never be knowable as

34. Vaudeville, *Kabīr*, p. 28, fn. 1.

35. Digby, review of McLeod, *Gurū Nānak*, p. 305.

36. Edward A. Armstrong, *Saint Francis: Nature Mystic* (Berkeley: University of California Press, 1973), p. 218. The entire book, published by the University of California Press in the imaginative series "Hermeneutics: Studies in the History of

reconstructed historical persons, but we can study the traditions which influenced devotees attempting to project a successful image of the particular Sant, they followed, and we can analyze the topical as well as historical content of anecdotes exemplifying spiritual, magical, territorial and also lyrical prowess, especially those which bear a resemblance to contemporary or earlier anecdotes of similar tone in the Sufi *tadhkira* literature.

Religions," marks a major advance in understanding the process of legend formation as it has evolved within religious communities and been subject to the changing interests of constituent groups.

THE BAULS AND THE ISLAMIC TRADITION

EDWARD C. DIMOCK, JR.

A mild kind of controversy has lately risen again around those curious mendicant singers and folk poets of Bengal called Bauls. Some time ago there was a good deal of speculation about the origin of their name. Some felt that the word *bāul* was derived from the Arabic *auliyā*, 'friend' [of God]; others, whose view became more widely accepted, felt that the derivation of the name was a normal one from the Sanskrit *vātula*, 'affected by the wind disease', i.e. mad. And cultivatedly mad they do seem to be: their way of life is deliberately *ulṭo*, 'contrary' to the current of accepted custom. And the etymology would be regular, as the intervocalic consonant would be lost in Middle Bengali, the final vowel dropped, and the *v* would go to *b*. But a recent article by Harendra Chandra Pal seems again to want to argue that the proper etymology is Arabic, and that Baul doctrine (if indeed one can use such a term) must be interpreted through the Islamic, and specifically through the Sufi, tradition.[1]

It seemed for a long time too that Rabindranath Tagore's view of the Bauls and of their songs would be the accepted one. Tagore not only found their peculiar musical forms appealing, but also found in their humanistic impulses a strong echo of his own. Their sometimes mournful, always poignant, longing for the 'man of the heart', the God within man who is at the same time unknown and the object of a long, anguished, and pointless search through religious forms and rituals, spoke not only to his own iconoclasm but to his sense of separation. So pure a chord did this poignancy strike in the heart of Tagore, say some later writers, that he either missed or was too embarrassed to notice publicly the strong element of sexual and Tantric symbolism in the songs. Upendranath Bhattacharya, in the long, erudite, and persuasive introduction to his extensive collection of Baul songs, *Bāṅglār Bāul o Bāul*

1. Harendra Chandra Pal, "*Bāul-tattver pūrbābhāsā*," *Sāhitya patrikā* (Journal of the Bengali Department, Dacca University) Winter 1969. The title of the article means "Hints about the Doctrine of the Bauls."

gān,[2] has put forward this position and, more recently, it has been taken up by younger American scholars as well.[3] According to this position, one must keep Tantric symbolism clearly in mind when reading or listening to the songs. One must realize that the *rasa* so often spoken of is semen; that the river so prominent in many of the songs is not only the river of life, but also the menstrual flux which is important for the esoteric ritual of the Bauls; and that, far from scorning all ritual activity — as held by Tagore and others — the Bauls have at the very base of their religious way of life the Yogic practice of control of breath and sphincters.[4] This position would also claim that the Sufi interpretation is an error.[5]

The Tantric arguments, it must be confessed, are persuasive, and seem to be gaining currency — not only for the reason just stated, but for two others as well. The first and most obvious reason is no doubt the growing interest in Tantrism generally, perhaps because of its esoteric quality, or perhaps because it is a system in which the individual is at the center, controlling his own destiny. The second, more mundane, may have to do with the fact that not many years ago a group of these mendicant Baul singers were brought to this country to give public concerts and appear on the covers of Bob Dylan albums. This visit had its effect in a variety of ways. Not only did these Bauls become known to Americans already interested in the subject and arouse the interest of other Americans, but they became sought after as informants when American scholars visited Bengal. And the Bauls in this particular network are indeed Tantric, as has been shown in a recent paper by Carol Salomon.[6]

It would be exceedingly foolish to try to deny a strong Tantric

2. Upendranath Bhattacharya, *Bānglār Bāul o Bāul gān* (Calcutta: Orient Book Company, 1969).

3. For example, Charles Capwell in his article "The Esoteric Belief of the Bauls of Bengal," *Journal of Asian Studies* 32:2 (1974), pp. 255-64.

4. Ibid., p. 259.

5. Muhammad Mansur-ud-din makes a statement difficult to dispute: "Some say that the Bauls are Vaishnava. That is an error. Among the Bauls there is a group which could certainly be called Vaishnava, but because that is so they are not all Vaishnavas. And in the same way that they are not Vaishnavas, they are not Muslim Sufis. They are all Bauls." See his *Hārāmani* (Calcutta: Calcutta University, 1942), p. 12.

6. Carol Salomon, "A Sahajiyā Interpretation of the Bilvamaṅgal-Cintāmani Legend as Sung by Sanātan Dās," unpublished paper given at the Bengal Conference, Ann Arbor, Michigan, April 1976.

element in the Baul tradition. A Baul, essentially, is one who says he is a Baul, and who has taken initiation from a guru, or *murshid*, recognized by other Bauls. It would be equally foolish to suggest that any Baul does not have the right to sing the songs, and to interpret them, as he chooses. But the problem in trying to identify, much less generalize about, the doctrines of a group of people on the basis of a collection of short songs, are many. One would have to have the complete, or nearly complete, corpus of each poet, for only a small part of any doctrinal system will be treated in a short song. And one would have to have many such corpora, for the beliefs of one individual may differ sometimes widely from those of the next. And even then, the Bauls pose the problem of being unabashedly heterodox. Not only do they draw from, and to that extent participate in, three religious traditions (Islam, Tantrism, and Vaishnavism), but they consciously deviate from the orthodoxy of all three; one might say that they are doctrinally heterodox. And finally, there is the perpetual anthropologists' problem of distinguishing between text and ritual in practice. These are not always consistent with one another, and are sometimes not at all so.

The following is an excerpt from a song by a Baul called Lalan Shah or Lalan Fakir, who lived in the late eighteenth and early nineteenth centuries:[7]

> Whether the Lord God has form or is formless:
> if one distinguishes between these, *āhād* and *āhamad*,
> knowledge is lost.
> I see that in the name *āhamad*
> [the name of] the Prophet is written by the letter *mīm*.
> If one takes away the *mīm*, *āhād* remains
> and the name *āhamad* is no more.[8]

The text is reasonably dense, and is based partly on a problem in Islamic theology, and partly on a play with the Arabic language,[9] though the language of the song is Bengali. The problem of the form of the formless God has long been of great interest to Bengali Muslim

7. 1890 is usually accepted as the date of his death, his age being at that time 116. See for example *Lālan-gītikā*, ed. Matilal Das and Piyushakanti Mahapatra (Calcutta: Calcutta University, 1958), p. 3. I would like to be somewhat more conservative.

8. Pal, *Pūrbābhāsā*, p. 13.

9. *āhād*, 'the One'; *āḥamad* or *āḥmad*, 'most laudable,' one of the names of the Prophet.

writers and, it might be added, to Vaishnava writers as well. The much earlier Saiyid Sultan,[10] perhaps not himself a Baul, finds God "ever concealed as the formless in the form (*rūpeta nirūpa rūpa*), like heat in the fire, hardness in clay, drops in water, and rays in the sun and moon."[11] The Vaishnavas add, "like the scent in the flower, and the music in the flute," the sense being that the music is real, even though one may not see the flute-player.

But even more interesting is the word-play. Another older writer, Hayat Mahmud, says: "Allah is the supreme one, *āhād*, without a second. . . . he made *āhammad* [a name of the Prophet] from *āhād*...you should know both *āhād* and *āhammad* as one."[12] The mere *mīm* distinguishes God the One, *āḥād*, the Creator, and his creation *āḥamad*; (or, with the addition of another *mīm*, Muhammad). *Mīm* is the principle of incarnation, and the relationship it states is that God is within man, *āḥād* within *āḥamad*. God is both formed and formless. To this we shall return.

That God is within man is of course a proposition perfectly acceptable to Bauls of all varieties. It is an important, even necessary, proposition for the Tantrics, for whom recognition and experience of divine bliss, the restoration of the primal unity within the microcosm of the body, is all. It is so, though less clearly so, for the Vaishnavas, whose doctrine of *bhedābheda*, separation and non-separation, the simultaneous immanence and transcendence of God, allows them to have it both ways. And it is of course familiar to the Sufis. The Bauls in fact make much of the "*an-al-haq*" dictum of Al-Hallaj,[13] who is in fact a kind of *ādi-guru* for them. There is for example this portion of a song by a Baul called Duddu, one of Lalan's pupils:

> If one knows the self, he knows Him who fosters;
> the Lord, formless, plays eternally, and the play has form.
> God is not distinct from God;
> he is on his throne in the throne-room of the heart.
> That palace is surrounded by ten walls;
> you will gain sight of it, by the power of fate.[14]

10. A poet of the mid-sixteenth century. Abdul Karim, *A Social History of the Muslims in Bengal* (Dacca: the Asiatic Society of Pakistan, 1959), p. 150, fn.

11. For this passage see Asim Roy's exceptional dissertation, "Islam in the Environment of Medieval Bengal," unpublished Ph.D. dissertation. Australian National University, Canberra, 1970), p. 189.

12. Ibid., p. 268.

13. "I am the truth." Al-Hallaj was executed in A.D. 922.

14. Pal, *Pūrbābhāsā*, p. 9.

The language is interesting: "God is on his throne in the room of the heart," *ārśe khodā deler ghare*, is almost pure Persian. And the other term used here, and usually, for 'God' or 'Lord' is *sāi*, derived from *svāmi*, which is analysed as *sva*+*āmi*, 'I am the self, I am the truth.'

Bauls often love to play with language, and especially with Persian. As *mīm* is the principle of incarnation, so the first letter of the alphabet, *alif*, is the principle of breath or of life. The term breath used in the following excerpt is not the Sanskrit or Bengali *prāṇa*, but the Persian *dam*, and the basic play is clear: *ā*+*dam* is the primal man, into whom God breathed life. The lines are from a song by a Baul named Naran or perhaps Narayan:

> He summons Dam Madar by breath, O mind, believe in that.
> Before *dam* mankind arises, and goes forth on the wind.
> If you would seize the fugitive moon, try the touch-stone breath,
> perform the *sādhan* of the breath.[15]

What I have translated as 'fugitive' is a rather complicated Bengali pun. The term is *a*+*dhar*, 'uncaught", suggēstive of the God for whom the Baul searches fruitlessly until he realizes that he is within. 'The uncaught moon' also suggests the Bengali proverb for ultimate futility: the dwarf standing on tip-toes to catch the moon. *Adhar* also means 'lower lip', suggestive in another context. And the moon is often a symbol of the mind. But even more interesting is the mention of the name of Dam Madar, a *pīr* or Sufi saint to whom, according to Bengali and perhaps other traditions, Muhammad gave the gift of long life. Madar, the more usual name of the saint, is a curiously frequent character in Middle Bengali texts.[16] And 'breath-*sādhan*' is the Yogic, and Sufi, practice of breath-control as one of the means of realization.

In any case, God breathes His breath, and man arises, and goes forth upon the wind — the wind which, traditionally, is the only home and shelter of the Baul. The breath is the wind of heaven, and the breath in man is the cosmic wind. But it is not only the divine breath which is

15. Ibid., p. 20.

16. For example, the following passage appears in the *Śūnya-purāṇa*, attributed to Ramai Pandit, a text dated variously between the tenth and fifteenth centuries: "The formless Niranjana became incarnated in heaven [the word is *bhest*—*behist*], and from his mouth spoke Dambadar [*mukheto boleto dambādār*]; all the gods there were agreed, and in delight donned trousers. Brahma became Muhammad, Vishnu the Paigambar, Shiva Adampha..." (Calcutta: Bangiya Sahitya Parishad, 1908), p. 141.

in man, not only *rūḥ* or *rūḥu'l-lāh,* but other parts of the physical and spiritual universe are within him as well:

> The primal Mecca[17] is in this human body;
> don't you see it, O my mind?
> Why do you run now from land to alien land
> and die, gasping for breath?
> He has made a most wonderful city,
> the Lord has built that human Mecca
> with his most wonderful creative light.
> And its four gates are four prophets of light,
> and among them sits the Lord.
> The human Mecca is a most wonderful thing.[18]

The Baul runs frantically about the world in search of the God within and dies, gasping, his breath out of control, a mere reflex of the lungs after exertion. This breath has only a tenuous relationship to the serene, supreme, breath of God, which man must realize. The contrast is also to the 'breath-*sādhan*' of the other verse. For by control of the breath, man, being in some sense God, realizes by emulation the divine element and divine gift, the truth, and life. Asim Roy gives the following summary of a text called *Chāri mukām bhed,* ("The Four Divisions of the *Muqāms,* or stages of Sufi Spiritual Progress") by 'Abd ul-Hakim:

> The *z̲ikr* [i.e., repetitions of the name of Allah] are followed by the sound *hū hū.* The *sādhaka* assumes an *āsana* [i.e. yogic posture] and performs *kumbhakā* [i.e., the yogic practice of the retention of the inhaled air]: air is drawn from the lower region of the navel towards the heart. The *z̲ikr* goes on incessantly in the heart. This is happening in the first *muqām* of *sharī'at* [i.e. formal prescribed practice; the writer uses the term *muqām* for both the stages and the practices associated with those stages]. In the second of the four stages, *tariqāt,* wind blows incessantly [the term is *paban,* which is literally wind]; the wind is the vehicle of the *ātmā.* The wind blows through the body, out the nostrils, either to the right, which is the abode of the sun, or to left, which contains the moon [c.f. the Tantric notion that in Hatha Yoga, *hā* is *chandra, ṭha* is *sūrya*]. *Kumbhakā* is practised, and while retaining the inhaled air, *lā ilāha* is repeated, and *illāllāh* when the air is exhaled. Longevity is increased as long as

17. *ādi Makka.*
18. Bhattacharya, *Baul gān,* song 43 of Lalan Fakir.

the air is retained. All of this brings, among other things, luster to the body and the power of true speech (*vākya-siddhi*).[19]

The themes running through this passage — the breath as cosmic wind and the body as microcosm — have a clear relationship to Tantric teachings. But equally clear is the Sufi idea that what was the gift of God to Adam, the gift of Muhammad to Madar, is now attainable by man himself. It is not usual to hear the Bauls speak of eternal corporeal life, as the Nath Yogis do. But they do speak of *jiyānta-morā*, 'being dead while yet alive,' which is the *jīvan-mukti* of other thought. The 'breath-*sādhan*' is one means of attaining it.

There are other interesting things about the last poem cited. For example, "the Lord has built that human Mecca/ with his most wonderful creative light" suggests yet another Baul view of the relationship of man to God. There is a couplet in a song by a Baul named Panja which reads:

By the light of Allah the Prophet is born; by the light of the Prophet
the world is complete;
Existence dwells in the body of Adam, and knows the light.[20]

The term 'light,' of course, is the Persian *nūr*, not the Bengali *ālo* or *jyoti*, and the theme is the creation of the universe directly by the light of Muhammad.[21] The concept of the *nūr-i-Muḥammadī* might be familiar to the Sufi tradition; the thorough anthropomorphization of it in Bengal might be less so. Muhammad is produced from the light of God, and the rest of creation is produced by the light of Muhammad, and in a very interesting way; by exudations from his body in sweat, *ghām*, or simply in *bindu*, 'drops.'[22] The light of Muhammad is spoken of as the friend or the lover of God. God, unable to realize or enjoy himself in the infinite void, brought Nur Muhammad into existence.[23] The formulation is the three-stage gradual descent or revelation of God

19. Roy, "Islam in Bengal," pp. 225 ff. The interpolations are mine.
20. Bhattacharya, *Baulgān*, song 232.
21. Annemarie Schimmel, in her *Mystical Dimensions of Islam* (Chapel Hill: University of North Carolina Press, 1975), discusses this interesting idea on pp. 214ff. On p. 215 she writes: "The idea of the 'Muhammadan light' seems to have been fully developed about 900 — Sal at Tustarī speaks of the three lights of God, the first one being Muhammad, his special friend: 'When he wanted to create Muhammad He showed a light from His light which illuminated the whole kingdom.' "
22. Ibid., p. 222.
23. Roy, "Islam in Bengal," p. 264.

familiar to Sufi thought, which is stated in another way by the colorful theory of the introduction of *mīm*: God, in perfect unity and stability, is agitated by the creative impulse, and *mīm* brings form to the formless One. But the third stage of creation, that of differentiation into the particulars of the world, is the most curious. A writer named Sayid Sultan puts forth the following:

> Seeing himself in the form of Muhammad, God contemplates his form as the *sādhaka*.... The formless one [*nirākāra*] becomes immersed in love.... As he enters [*prabeśila*] softly in love, slowly there arises perspiration from love, and from the perspiration of Muhammad everything comes into existence.[24]

Similarly, according to Shaikh Paran, the Lord creates *nūr* and gazes steadfastly at it; they look at one another like two mirrors, and the gaze of Niranjan (sic) makes Nur Muhammad perspire all over his body. Other causes for the sweat may be stated; for example, the *nūr* flees from God, and perspiration breaks out all over his body because of the exertion. Or, says a writer named Shaikh Chand, Muhammad is unable to see God and, because of the separation, his tears flow and cause the stream from which creation comes. The theme, incidentally, is a common one in Hindu *maṅgal* texts of the medieval period as well; in the *Dharma-maṅgal*, for example, the cosmic water, source of creation, comes from the sweat of Ishvara.

It is not necessary to belabor the possibilities here, but it should be at least noted that the concept of *bindu* is cardinal to the Tantric systems. *Bindu* is the point of origin. *Bindu* is also semen. But most important, the supreme *bindu*, *parabindu*, is the essential unity of universal forces, which is differentiated into multiple *bindu*s by the process called *sadṛśapariṇāma*. In the process, the seeming multiplicity of aspects of the created world, which constitutes the immanence of the deity, comes about. But the multiplicity of forms in no way affects the essential unity of the One. The thesis is also, it might be added, congenial to the Vaishnavas.

In all this discussion, I have neither proven nor disproven that the Bauls are Sufis, or that they are Tantrics, or that they are Vaishnavas. And this is perhaps the point: that they can be any, or all, or even none of these things. It would be possible, of course, and maybe even instructive, to speculate at length about the sexual aspects of all three tradi-

24. Ibid., p. 274.

tions and the place of ritual sexual intercourse in *sādhan*; or about the possible relationships between the Sufi idea of the *muqāms* and the Tantric idea of the *chakras* in the body; or about such symbolisms as that of the moon;[25] or of the nature and critical importance of the *murshid* to Sufis and the guru to Tantrics and for that matter to Vaishnavas; or about the ideas of *zikr* (*d̲h̲ikr*), *dhyāna*, mantra and the psychological as well as ritual importance of these, and so on. But perhaps enough has been said to bolster the simple-minded suggestion that some Bauls draw heavily on the Islamic tradition, and that it is difficult, or perhaps impossible, to interpret them apart from that tradition. One could find Baul songs, I expect, which draw almost exclusively on the Tantric and Vaishnava traditions, about which the same could be said. The most, I think, that can be safely inferred is that the various traditions flowed into a pool, bringing with them ideas that the human self, even the human body, is the repository of truth. What is common to them is this *deha-tattva*. The pool that was formed and colored by the soil of Bengal was, and is, available to all.

25. When the Bauls speak of the moon, or the four moons, as the mind, or of the *chandra-bheda*, one is reminded of the passage in Qur'an 54.1 when the moment of judgment draws near and the moon is divided. The Baul interpretation is that when the moment of the true perception of the self is approaching, the moon-mind is destroyed.

THE WRITINGS OF THE TAMIL SIDDHAS

K. KAILASAPATHY

In 1856 the Rev. Robert Caldwell published his *Comparative Grammar of Dravidian Languages*, a work which in many ways ushered in what has come to be called Dravidian Studies. Although it was basically a philological work, the author wrote a lengthy introduction to it endeavoring to place Dravidian culture and literatures in their historical perspective. In the course of his survey of Tamil literature, "the earliest cultivated and most highly developed of the Dravidian languages," he referred to what he described as "the Anti-Brahmanical Cycle" of compositions in Tamil, i.e. the songs of the Siddhas or Cittars, as they are called. These he discussed at some length.[1] Caldwell's observations are important because they illustrate the ideas held about the Siddhas by Christian missionary writers, especially those of the nineteenth century, and because these ideas were echoed by many Tamil researchers who took their cue from them in scholarly matters.[2] From his treatment

1. Robert Caldwell, *A Comparative Grammar of the Dravidian or South-Indian Family of Languages*, 2nd ed., revised and enlarged (London: Trübner and Co., 1875), pp. 146-49. Caldwell was mistaken in believing the Tamil Siddhas to be extinct. What is in fact remarkable about the Siddha school is its continuity to the present day. Both in Tamilnadu and Sri Lanka numerous Siddhas have lived and continue to live unnoticed by those uninterested in them. A few modern writers have written about their encounters with Siddhas. V. Balaramayya, *Cittar meipporul*, (Madras: Arudperumcoti Publishers, 1969), p. ix; Kamil V. Zvelebil, *The Poets of the Powers* (London: Rider and Company, 1973), p. 14; David C. Buck, *Dance, Snake! Dance!* (Calcutta: Writers Workshop, 1976), p. vi. On the Siddha tradition in Sri Lanka, see V. Muttucumaraswamy, *Tamil Sages Seers of Ceylon* (Jaffna: Saiva Prakasa Press, 1971); N. Muttiah, *Mupperum cittarkal* (Nawalapitiya, Sri Lanka: Atmajothi Nilayam, 1973); S. Ambihaipahan, "Yogar swamikalum cittar marapum," *Hindu Dharma*, Silver Jublee Number of the Hindu Students Union (Peradeniya: Hindu Students Union, 1978), pp. 51ff. Yogar Swami, who passed away in 1964, was considered by many to be a modern Siddha. He was a poet too. Popular belief held him to have lived more than a hundred years. His verses are no doubt in the Siddha mold. They have been published under the title *Natcintanai* (Jaffna: Sivathondan Nilayam, 1962). For an English translation and study of his poems, see Ratna C. Navaratnam, *Saint Yogaswami and the Testament of Truth* (Colombo: Times of Ceylon Publishers, 1972).

2. Cf. T. Isaac Tambyah, *Psalms of a Saiva Saint* (London: Luzac and Co., 1925), *passim.*

it is evident that he considered the language of the Siddhas unpolished and colloquial; that he took them to be of relatively late date (probably the seventeenth century A.D.); and that he believed their 'liberal' ideas and their ideals of universal love to be a result of direct Christian influence.

Although, as a result of researches done since the time of Caldwell's pioneering work, we know that his views on the Siddhas and their writings are untenable, we should hasten to add that we still do not know enough about them. In fact serious studies on the Siddhas have been rather scarce. It is only with the rise of socio-political movements like the Rationalist Association, the DK, the DMK and others that some of the overtly anti-Brahmanical and anti-hierarchical features of the poems have come to be highlighted. One of the best illustrations of such a usage is an oft-quoted line from Tirumular (verse 2104):

Caste is one and god is one.

The sixth-century mystic sang in the context of the caste system and a hierarchy of gods. What he actually meant was that, insofar as religious worship was concerned, all castes are equal and the only god is Shiva. But modern social reformers read more into it:

Mankind is one and God is one.

It is an interpretation of the old epigram in terms of the cultural ideas and socio-religious philosophies of the present age. 'God' is explained not as Shiva but as a nameless, universal God, the idea being to get away from any implications of sect and divisions. But in the process certain aspects tend to be exaggerated.

It is generally accepted by scholars that the Siddhas came in a line of wandering saints and *sanyāsīs* whose earliest forerunner Tirumular (also known as Sundara Natha in certain Puranas) could be ascribed to the sixth or the seventh century A.D. He is remembered for his work *Tirumantiram*[3] which deals primarily with Yoga and Tantra. It may be recalled that the period referred to marks the beginning of the bhakti movement in Tamil — a movement characterized by not only the extreme antagonism between the Vedic religions (Shaivism, Vaishnavism) and the non-Vedic or heterodox religions (Buddhism, Jainism and the

3. *Tirumantiram,* although said to contain 3000 verses, has in current editions 3081 verses. Probably several interpolations have crept in. I have used the Kasi Mutt edition (Tiruppanantal: Sri Kasi Mutt, 1951).

Ajivika faith) but also a sort of internecine conflict between Shaivism and Vaishnavism themselves. Shaivism of that period, which later crystallized into the metaphysical system of Shaiva Siddhanta, was hostile to Shankara's school of Vedanta too. In fact some of the most trenchant diatribes of the Shaiva Siddhanta polemic writers have always been reserved for the Vedantists, disparagingly called *ēkātmavādins* and *māyāvādins*. In the midst of such virulent sectarianism and dogmatism, Tirumular decried bigotry and preached equanimity and universal love.

> Those who follow the six religions know him not
> Nor is he confined to those six faiths.
> Seek and having sought cogitate in your mind
> And then without doubt you will gain salvation.[4]

Thus, it is in the songs of Tirumular that we see the beginnings of the Siddha *mārga* (way of the Siddhas) in Tamil. In other words, the Siddha tradition appears to have evolved *pari passu* with the growth of the various religious sects and the resultant conflicts. Although Tirumular belonged to the sixth century, most of the Siddhas seem to have flourished between the fourteenth and eighteenth centuries. Except for one or two, the others cannot be ascribed to definite dates.

There is a popular tradition in Tamil which speaks of eighteen Siddhas. But in fact there are more than fifty names associated with the Siddha school of poetry.[5] It is likely that different attempts were made to enumerate and clasify them at later dates. In medieval times almost all writers on medicine, astronomy, magic, alchemy, astrology, Tantra and Yoga were grouped together as Siddhas. Since they were supposed to have possessed supernatural powers, they were also considered to be adepts in esoteric knowledge. It is even possible that the number eighteen itself had some mystical significance.

Perhaps what is of particular interest here is the curious fact that in almost all the lists of Tamil Siddhas, Gorakh appears as one of them.[6]

4. Ibid., verte 1533.

5. R. Manikkavacakam, "Cittarkal," in *Perunthamizh: The Third Ten Days' Seminar Papers*, University of Madras. (Madras: Madras University Press, 1975) pp. 138-69.

6. Gorakhnath, who was the chief disciple of Matsyendranath, is one of the Nath Yogis who are well known throughout India. Gorakhnath is supposed to have learned Yoga from his guru who in turn learnt it from Adinath or Shiva himself. It may be remembered that Tirumoolar is said to have learnt the secret knowledge

Tradition has it that among the Tamil Siddhas were Arabs, Chinese and others from distant lands. Tirumular himself is supposed to have come from Kashmir.[7] Hence it is not impossible that the Naths too were thought to be connected. Although the Siddha school flourished in Tamilnadu over a long period, evolving its own ethos and claiming indigenous origins, it cannot be ruled out that it had an all-India basis and framework. But it is not possible to say more on this in the present state of our knowledge.

The main problem in the study of the Siddhas is the absence of reliable editions of all the literature concerned. Except for an soliated attempt by Pandit M.V. Venugopala Pillai,[8] the few editions available now vary in size and mode of selection. One edition includes even some poems of Ramalinga Swami (1823-1874), considered to be a modern Siddha.[9] Such an inclusion, while illustrating the continuity and vitality of the tradition, makes the task of the textual critic exasperating. Under the circumstances it is doubtful if a critical edition can be brought out. Paucity of copies resulting from the wanton and wilful destruction of manuscripts containing Siddha poems by Shaivite fanatics have rendered the task of textual critics even more difficult.

We get some idea of the continuing process of corruptions and interpolations in the Siddha texts not only by comparing the references to them in earlier manuscripts, especially those that quote them extensively, but also by comparing specific poems that got into print during the last century. For instance, Kasi Viswanatha Mudaliar (1806-1871),

---

from Nandhi Deva who in turn had been instructed by Lord Shiva himself. A comparative study of the Nath Yogis and the Tamil Siddhas will prove to be most fruitful. On the Nath Yogis, see Kalyani Mallik, *Siddha-Siddhanta-Paddhati and Other Works of the Natha Yogis* (Poona: Oriental Book House, 1954); also George W. Briggs, *Gorakhnāth and the Kānphaṭa Yogīs* (Delhi, Motilal Banarsidass, 1980).

7. T.P. Meenakshisundaran, *A History of Tamil Literature* (Annamalainagar: Annamalai University Press, 1965), p. 65.

8. M.V. Venugopala Pillai, *Cittar gnānakkōvai* (Madras: Premier Art Press, 1947).

9. Ramalinga himself claimed to have come "in the line of the great Siddhas." In his rejection of sectarianism, emphasis on universal love and compassion and avowed eclecticism he was following in the footsteps of the Siddhas. His disciples claimed that he performed miracles. Like some of the earlier Siddhas he too sang of "the glorious life without death." A prolific singer, his collected writings were published by his disciples. It may be mentioned in passing that there is considerable interest in him among contemporary Tamils. For a brief account, see S.R.V. Arasu, *Voice of Vallalar* (Madras: South India Saiva Siddhanta Works Publishing Society, 1974).

one of the earliest adherents of the Brahmo Samaj movement in Madras Presidency, published *Brāhma Samāja Nāṭakam* (1871)—a Tamil play extolling the virtues of Brahmoism. One of the characters in the play quotes at length several poems of Civavakkiyar—without doubt the most powerful poetic voice in the entire galaxy of Siddhas—to expose, criticize and ridicule Hindu orthodoxy. A comparison of the verses quoted in the play with present day versions of the same poems shows astonishing variations. Similarly, Siddha poems cited in Christian missionary tracts of the last century show striking differences from modern readings in print. For example, Henry Martyn Scudder's 1865 *A Companion to Native Preachers* quotes many Siddha poems approvingly.[10] Texts of the same poems in current editions show numerous variations. Furthermore, till very recent times, the corpus of Siddha poetry has been transmitted orally by the initiates and kept alive by the common people. As Menakshisundaran observes, "their poems have been left to the common man to preserve them as best as he can."[11]

The question then is: What is the intrinsic quality of these songs that has enabled them to surmount conscious derision and persistent persecution by the establishment? Orthodox Shaiva Siddhantists held the Siddhas to be "religious *pañchamas*" (religious outcastes), beyond the pale.[12] The reason for such anger and antagonism is not hard to guess. The Siddhas challenged the very foundations of medieval Hinduism: the authority of the Shastras, the validity of rituals and the basis of the caste system were often questioned by the Siddhas. It is true that the Siddhas did not constitute a well-defined school of thought and differed in their attitudes towards society and religion. However, "almost all of them manifest a protest, expressed often in very strong terms, against the formalities of life and religion; denial of religious practices and beliefs of the ruling classes."[13]

10. Henry Martyn Scudder, *A Companion to Native Preachers* (Madras: American Mission Press, 1865).

11. Meenakshisundaran, *Tamil Literature*, p. 70. Other writers too have mentioned this important fact: "They are most popular works in Tamil and there is no pure Tamilian, educated or uneducated who has not committed to memory at least a few stanzas from one or other of them." M.S. Purnalingam Pillai *Tamil Literature*, 2nd ed. (Tinnevely: The Bibliotheca, 1929), p. 263.

12. M. Sambasiva Pillai, *Tirunānmarai Vilakka Ārāyci* (Trichinopoly: Jegam and Co., Dodson Press, 1926), pp. 32, 210ff.

13. Zvelebil, *Poets of Powers*, p. 8. For a fuller discussion of the social implications of the teachings of the Siddhas in Tamil, see K. Kailasapathy, *Oppiyal ilakkiyam* (Madras: Pari Nilayam, 1969), pp. 183-212.

Civavakkiyar's poems express these sentiments clearly and forcefully:

The chanting of the four Vedas
The meticulous study of the sacred scripts,
The smearing of the holy ashes,
And the muttering of prayers,
Will not lead you to the Lord!
Let your heart melt within you.
And if you can be true to yourself
Then you will join the limitless light
and lead an endless life.

You dumb fools performing the rituals
With care and in leisureliness.
Do gods ever become stone?
What can I do but laugh?[14]

Of what use are temples,
And of what use are sacred tanks?
Slavishly you gather to worship
In temples and tanks![15]

Equally emphatic and blunt is the voice of Pambatti Cittar:[16]

The Four Vedas, six kinds of Shastras,
The many Tantras and Puranas,
The Agamas which speak of the arts,
And various kinds of other books
Are of no use; just in vain.
So dance snake, dance!

In a statue of stone whanged with a chisel
D'ya think there's understanding?
D'ya think the idiots of the world
Have any understanding?
Will a flaw in a pan go away

14. *Cittar gnānakkovai*, Civavakiyar, verse 121.

15. Ibid., verse 29.

16. The entire work of Pambatti Cittar is translated in David Buck's book *Dance, Snake! Dance!* cited above in fn. 1. It should provide invaluable help to readers in English. The notes explaining 'technical' terms and a perceptive introduction enhance the value of the book.

If you rub it with tamarind?
Ignorance won't go away from the idiots
So dance snake, dance![17]

We'll set fire to divisions of caste,
We'll debate philosophical questions in the market place,
We'll have dealings with despised households,
We'll go around in different paths.[18]

One could multiply the instances. The stanzas quoted above illustrate the mood of the Siddhas and their mode of expression. These poems are a "grand remonstrance against almost everything that was held sacred" in their time. The Siddhas were "implacable opponents of the caste system and the gradations of orthodoxy and respectability that it gave rise to."[19]

This leads us to another important fact: many of the Siddhas came from low castes. While we should exercise caution in accepting the 'historical' information provided by anthologists in later times about the place and date of birth of the Siddhas and their social status (caste), we cannot reject them outright. It is obvious that often facts are mixed with fiction, especially in matters relating to the fantastic longevity of life of the Siddhas and their metamorphoses. But considering the fact that the caste origins of persons were vital information in medieval India and the Siddha school has preserved its traditions remarkably well, the data must be given due credence. The lists of Siddhas describe some of them as being shepherds, temple-drummers, artificers, robbers, potters, fishermen, hunters, etc., clearly indicating their social position. They were well below the Brahmans and Vellalas (agriculturalists) who along with Vanigas (merchants) constituted the ruling castes in those times. There are of course a few Brahmans and Vellalas among the Siddhas, but the very fact that a considerable number of them were from lower castes underlines the special attraction the Siddha way of life had for the outcastes. It shows the openness of the Siddha school. We must not say that the Siddhas were conscious egalitarians, for that

17. Pambatti Cittar, in Buck, *Dance, Snake! Dance!*, pp. 107-08.

18. *Cittar gnānakkōvai*, Pambatti Cittar, verse 123.

19. A.V. Subramania Iyer, *The Poetry and the Philosophy of the Tamil Siddhas* (Chidambaram: Manivacagar Noolakam, 1969), pp. 47-48. Cf. K.M. Sen, *Hinduism* (London: Penguin Books, 1961), p. 97: "The outstanding aspect of Indian medieval mysticism is its complete independence from sectarian organizations and orthodox scriptures."

would be pitching it too high. But it must be pointed out that "in direct opposition to Hindu orthodoxy, no distinction at all was made with regard to caste" within their fraternity.[20]

There is an interesting parallel to this in an earlier work. *Periyapurānam*, 'the Great Purana', a hagiographical work of the twelfth century which narrates the lives of sixty-three Shaiva saints who were all natives of Tamilnadu, delineates in detail the various castes into which these saints were born. These saints were supposed to have lived during the heyday of the South Indian bhakti movement (some time between the sixth and ninth centuries) and were canonized later. Sekkilar, the author of *Periyapurānam*, who was himself a minister in the Chola court, wove the biographies of sixty-two saints around the life of Sundara, who emerges as the 'hero' of the epic. "These saints belong to all kinds of castes and tribes, classes and creeds."[21] Among them too we find potters, hunters, washermen, fishermen, shepherds, weavers, oil-pressers, pariahs and others who, by their work, were classified as belonging to low castes. The bhakti movement was a great equalizer of men, at least in the eyes of God.[22] Moved by the great ideal of absolute devotion to God and its logical consequence of reverence for human life — an idea that was not too common nor widespread in caste-bound medieval India — Sekkilar portrays the saints overcoming their caste origins and attaining spiritual glory through a life of dedication and love. Some modern scholars have described the *Periyapurānam* as a 'national epic' of the Tamils. A student of Tamil literature is compelled to see certain parallels between these two groups of religious men, even though they belonged to different periods.

Notwithstanding these precedents from the past, the Siddhas have always been measured against an alien set of norms. Consequently they have been stigmatized as a deviation from the caste Hindu conformist model, which itself has never been clearly defined. This relentless refusal to consider the Siddhas as part and parcel of the variegated historical and cultural contributions to religious experience has, without doubt, been the main reason Shaivism has excluded the Siddha view

20. Zvelebil, *Poets of Powers*, p. 133.

21. Meenakshisundaran, *Tamil Literature*, p. 122.

22. For a socio-economic interpretation of the bhakti movement in Tamilnadu see K. Kailasapathy, *Pandai Tamilar vālvum valipādum* (Madras: Pari Nilayam, 1968), pp. 84-197. On the impact of *Periyapurānam* on other South Indian literatures see T.P. Meenakshisundaran, *Tamil and Other Cultures* (Madurai: Madurai University Press, 1970), pp. 15-23.

from both its vast canonical corpus and socio-philosophic theories. It may be argued that in proportion to their castigation by the establishment the Siddhas too, true to their origins, rebelled against polite behavior.

There is a real danger here of oversimplification. As has been remarked earlier, not all the Siddhas were equally vehement in their condemnation of caste fissions and orthodoxy. Some of them were oblique in their ridicule. A Siddha like Pattinattar was concerned with the question of morality and other human virtues like love, compassion and equality. Yet others were eloquent by their silence on such matters. But basically they were all theists and believed in a transcendental God and his grace towards man. In that sense they were, without doubt, exemplary devotees in the best of Hindu tradition. However, the Siddhas were not devotees in the sense of idol-worshippers or believers in a supreme Person. They believed in a supreme Abstraction. The recurrent use by the Siddhas of the word *civam* (an abstract noun meaning 'goodness', 'auspiciousness' and the highest state of God, in which he exists as pure intelligence) in preference to the common term *civan* (meaning Shiva) makes this point very clear. In other words, they believed in an abstract idea of Godhead rather than a personal God. In so believing they freed themselves from rituals and other observances that had swamped the religious life of the average Hindu. If one were to adopt the framework of the three Hindu religious paths for gaining salvation (*jñāna*, the way of knowledge; *karma*, the way of work; and *bhakti*, the way of devotion), the Siddhas would be closer to the path of knowledge. But being eclectic, they never confined themselves to any one path or school and were, in practice, followers of the path of devotion and Yoga too. Since the Siddhas strove to effect a synthesis of apparently diverse elements, most of them held the different paths to be of more or less equal value. Naturally, emphasis on any one of these varied according to the temperament, background and personality of an individual Siddha. But by and large they were open in such matters. One of Tirumoolar's verse makes this clear:

> The bhakta with the help of guru's grace,
> instructed in *caryā* and *kriyā*,
> practising the blameless *Yoga* by the grace [of the Lord],
> realizing by *jñāna* [the nature of *Siva*],
> will in his mind become *Siva*.[23]

23. *Tirumantiram*, verse 1455. It should be pointed out here that in spite of it

Rejecting the mechanical and dreary aspects of bhakti, they cherished love, tenderness and compassion that were the human expression of the path of bhakti. With a unique combination or blend of both knowledge and love, the Siddhas were seeking Yogic or spiritual experience leading to unadulterated consciousness. Strictly speaking, at its best it was mysticism of the highest order. Like all mystics they used symbols to convey their personal knowledge.

It has been said of the Siddhas that "many of them use a language which is very imaginative, ambiguous, obscure, puzzling, often vulgar and even obscene," and that it is a "language in which words are on purpose semantically polyvalent."[24] The language of the Siddhas has often been described as a paradox. Mainstream Tamil literature, especially poetry, has consistently eschewed the spoken idiom almost until the beginning of the twentieth century. It is in the writings of Subramania Bharathi (1882-1921) that we find for the first time a radical rupture with the past as far as the diction of poetry is concerned.[25] The diction of classical poetry has reigned supreme uninterrupted for nearly two millennia. In stark contrast, the poetry of the Siddhas is sustained

---

being considered the source book for South Indian Siddhism, existing exegesis and modern commentaries on it are exclusively from the Shaiva Siddhanta viewpoint. Given the condition of the texts and the consistent suppression of unorthodox (Siddha) views, it is not surprising that the commentaries have interpreted the book in an impeccably orthodox vein. This need not surprise us since it is common knowledge that cryptic statements can be made to fit a thousand different theories. Nonetheless perceptive readers have often seen many glaring discrepancies between the verses and the tortured, tendentious arguments of the Shaivite commentators. There has been increasing awareness of this matter among serious scholars. But before attempting any new commentaries, the fundamental task will be to bring out a critical edition. The translation of the verse quoted here is from Mariasusai Dhavamony, *Love of God According to Saiva Siddhanta* (Oxford: Clarendon Press, 1971), p. 129.

24. Zvelebil, *Poets of Powers*, p. 21. In his *Smile of Murgan* (Leiden: E.J. Brill, 1973), a general survey of Tamil literature, Zvelebil had a chapter "The Cittar: An Enigma." The same idea had been expressed by M. Arunachalam, *History of Tamil Literature: XIV Century* (Tanjore: Gandhi Vidyalayam, 1969), p. 339, in which he said "The position of the Siddhas in Tamil literature is still an enigma."

25. Like his predecessor Ramalinga Swami, Bharathi too refers to the Siddhas. In his autobiographical poem "*Suya charitai*" he says, "There were many Siddhas before me, I too am one in their line." He and Tagore are probably the two most outstanding poetic voices in twentieth-century India. The Tamils consider him to have ushered in the modern era. In form he was greatly indebted to the Siddhas. He was also influenced by European Romantic poets. See Kailasapathy, *Oppiyal ilakkiyam*, pp. 213-59; also *Iru mahākavikal*, 4th ed. (Madras: New Century Book House, 1974).

by the simple colloquial expressions and speech patterns of the common people. It lacks in every way the 'grammatical finesse' exalted in traditional poetry. In fact it would appear that they were sung by persons unlettered and 'uneducated'. On its face value it can be read and understood by any native speaker of the language. And yet these poems are, to be sure, full of obscurities and peculiarities that baffle the best of literary minds. There are many reasons for this situation.

First, it must be remembered that a Siddha becomes one by being initiated into the fold by a guru, a 'preceptor'. The novice emerges after initiation "endowed with a totally different being from that which he possessed before his initiation; he has become *another*."[26] As a result of protracted and secret instructions from his preceptor and his participation in a number of rites, ceremonies and ordeals, the novice encounters the experience of the sacred. This unique experience and the ecstatic vision of the world has to be articulated by the Siddha not only in terms of his own personal experiences, but also within the framework of his traditional knowledge—images, symbols and myths, and histories—to which he gains access. It is here that symbolic language comes into play. The language used at the time of initiation itself is cryptic and is coded. This coded language is jealously guarded by the Siddhas and is explained only to the tested and the worthy. They in turn adopt the same strict methods. As a result the Siddhas had developed over the centuries a secret language of their own, best suited for the propagation and transmission—invariably orally—of their lore. Further, the Siddhas held their original guru to be Shiva himself and as such believed their knowledge to be even more sacred and esoteric.[27] These considerations made them use a diction that was difficult to penetrate except by the initiates.

Secondly, like all persons with deep religious experience, particularly those with mystical visions, at least some of the Siddhas considered their experience to be ineffable. They felt it impossible to describe their

26. Wendell C. Beane and William G. Doty, eds., *Myths, Rites, Symbols: Mircea Eliade Reader*, vol. 1 (New York: Harper Colophon Books, 1976), p. 164.

27. The concept of a preceptor is crucial in the Siddha system. *Tirumanturam* says "The guru is *civam*; the guru is the ineffable One" (verse 1581). Despite many fundamental doctrinal differences, Shaiva Siddhanta and Siddhism agree on the importance of a guru for a person's spiritual progress. In the biography of Manikkavackar it is said Shiva himself appeared in the guise of a Brahman sage and initiated him. *Gurutaricanam*, 'the vision of the guru', plays a pivotal role in the Siddhanta scheme of enlightenment.

consciousness in any language, let alone the common speech. Nevertheless, as behooves singers, they attempted to express themselves in various ways and used different techniques, even as they kept insisting that what they were talking about was beyond description.[28] As a Siddha put it laconically, "those who have seen describe it not; those who describe have seen it not."[29] This genuine difficulty in conveying their experience naturally tended to make their diction abstruse.

Thirdly, the core of the Siddha orientation is Tantric, in which sexuality plays a crucial role. In fact sexuality is the very basis of Tantric teaching and practices. As with the Tantrics, the ultimate ideal of the Siddha is the apprehension of an 'undifferentiated unity'. This unity is often explained in terms of the perfect sexual union (like the oneness of Shiva and Shakti) and appropriate myths and rituals are invoked to legitimize such a 'spiritual union'. In other words, sexual union is both a symbol and a reality. Myths and ritual sanctifies the principle of sexual union and sexual union in turn provides the rationale for certain myths and rituals. As Eliade says in a different context, "rituals are symbols in acted reality."[30]

Here again one can perceive the close connections between Siddha sexuality and the Tantric union of Shiva and Shakti. There is no doubt that they were representatives of a pan-Indian tradition that probably predates the Vedic religion and was widespread in India. In general terms, it came to be called Tantric Yoga. The Siddhas gave powerful poetic voice to some of the salient features of this tradition. In so doing they remain at the same time both all-Indian and specifically Tamilian.

It may be pointed out that Shiva Siddhanta literature (and Vaishnava poetry too) uses the vivid imagery of man-woman intimacy to express the God-soul relationship. The soul is in intense love with the supreme Being — the Lord — and passionately seeks a union which can only be compared to sexual intercourse or 'confluence'. *Tirukkōvaiyār*, a dramatic poem by the celebrated Shiva saint and hymnist Manikkavacakar (ca. ninth century A.D.), is perhaps the best example of this type of poetry.[31] The poem, which is part of the Shiva canonical lite-

28. Cf. Walter T. Stace, *The Teachings of the Mystics* (New York: Mentor Books, 1960), p. 13.

29. *Cittār gnanakkōvai*, Pambatti Cittar verse 105.

30. Beane and Doty, *Eliade Reader* 1:164.

31. *Kōvai* (literally 'string', 'arrangement', 'scheme') is the name of this genre. Basically a literary form used for erotic themes, especially of pre-marital situations, it has been considered a touchstone for poetic ability. *Tiru kōvai* means 'the sacred

rature, treats the heroine as God (a point to be noted, since it glorifies the female principle) and the hero as soul. In the tradition of the earliest Tamil love poetry, the hero and heroine of this poem meet each other by chance, undergo the thrill of first love, see their fondness grow, suffer the pangs of separation, enjoy a protracted period of courtship and illicit love, and finally experience the indescribable bliss of nuptial union. The poem is undoubtedly a *tour de force* and its perfection is beyond all criticism. And yet traditional Shaiva scholars, particularly the commentators, have always gone to great lengths to argue that it is mystic poetry and that the sexual union portrayed in it should be construed allegorically. For them, relating these poetic situations to sexuality would be preposterous if not blasphemy, and everything in the poem has an allegorical spiritual significance. That Manikkavacakar's poem is to be read at more than one level may be readily granted. The presence of symbolism in the poem is obvious. But to argue, as the scholars do, that sexuality is just not there is to totally misunderstand the poem, if not distort its profound emotional tone and essential eroticism. Only a person utterly insensitive to language can miss the pointedly sex-linked vocabulary that is so pervasive in the poem. Of course the poem is composed in traditional meter, accepted and approved by the grammarians of the establishment. The language is chaste and classical. Furthermore, the author was a minister in the Pandyan court and naturally had 'correct' and conservative views on religion and society. Besides this narrative poem, he also composed many exquisite lyrics.[32] He was thus part of the mainstream bhakti

---

kovai'. For a brief sketch of this genre, see Kamil V. Zvelebil, *Tamil Literature*, vol. 10, fasc. 1 in *A History of Indian Literature*, ed. Jan Gonda (Wiesbaden: Otto Harrassowitz, 1974), pp. 202-03.

32. That the erotic theme is present in some of the lyrics too can be seen from the following paraphrase of a well known verse:

> "I shall adorn myself with *konrai* 'cassia' flowers [so dear to him] and when he comes I will hug his broad shoulders; and hugging him tight, I shall be united with him; I shall lose myself completely in the ecstasy of [sexual] union. Enjoying the kisses from his fragrant-red lips, and wanting it more I will pretend to be angry and sulk. Being with him my entire body and soul will be enthralled. I shall always contemplate the holy feet of my Lord [Shiva], who holds the fire in his palm and whose feet dance eternally."

Manikkavacakar, *Tiruvācakam*, with commentary and notes by K. Subramania Pillai (Madras: B. Ratnanayagar and Sons, 1949), p. 226. For an English translation of the poems, see G.U. Pope, *Tiruvācakam* (Oxford: Clarendon Press, 1900). For

school in spite of the apparent eroticism,[33] which in any case was explained away or easily rarefied.

In contrast, the Siddhas suffered on all counts. Having cut themselves off from orthodox and ostentatious devotionalism and rituals and also social conformity, they had to lead a life of seclusion and vagrancy. As a result they developed a strong sense of detachment. Mystics in many cultural traditions emphasize the necessity of detachment "from desires for sensations."[34] The Siddhas too spoke of this. But they also developed a detachment from social life. Their form of protest was indifference to existing norms and behavior patterns. It was both a spiritual and a social attitude. This self-exclusion was a necessary condition for their moral improvement.[35] Here again the detachment from society and concern for personal purification influenced the language of the Siddhas. They were indifferent to accepted language or respectability in modes of expression, hence they spoke the common idiom. But they also spoke among themselves on the basis of certain basic assumptions and understandings born of shared experience. Hence they used cryptic phrases, enigmatic sounds and other verbal formulae that were known only to themselves. In that sense it was a private or group diction.

We may summarize the facts about the 'paradox' of the language of the Siddhas. On the one hand, as outcastes and itinerant recluses rebelling against all forms of establishment including the literary, which was particularly oppressive in Tamil, they had a predilection for the ordinary language — the colloquial. On the other hand, because of the

recent studies on Manikkavacakar's poems, see Glenn E. Yocum, "The Goddess in a Tamil Saiva Devotional Text: Manikkavacakar's *Tiruvācakam*." *Journal of the American Academy of Religion* 45:1 (March 1977), pp. 369-88; and "Mānikkavācakar's Image of Siva," *History of Religions* 16:1 (August 1976), pp. 20-41.

33. For more on the origin and development of sexuality in Tamil literature see K. Kailasapathy, "Erotic Themes in Tamil Poetry," a paper presented at the Ninth Annual Workshop of the Conference on Religion in South India, Chambersburg, PA, U.S.A. (1978).

34. Stace, *Teachings*, p. 19.

35. Compare: "A necessary condition for their moral improvement was detachment from all earthly things: 'we are weighed down here on earth by sin and temptation'. Christian morality therefore concentrates upon the adoration of God and upon an attitude of resignation towards existing evils as a means of expiation; hence the exclusive importance given to individual purification." Gaetano Salvemini, *Mazzini*, 3rd ed. (London: Jonathan Cape, 1956), p. 44. This observation could equally apply to the majority of the medieval mystics of India, including some of the Siddhas.

'private', eccentric and esoteric nature of their knowledge, they invariably adopted a vocabulary or diction that was highly specialized and related to their life-style.

It was in effect a sort of 'technical language'. This peculiar combination of the ordinary and the occult, the readily recognizable and the recondite, is at the source of both their life-style and their literary style. The overtly simple colloquialisms proved attractive to ordinary people who intuitively responded to the sentiments so casually expressed in the poems. They made these poems their own: wisecracks, witticisms, epigrams and earthy adages that echoed their own vague yearnings or unresolved doubts. Such terse and telling phrases became part and parcel of the everyday language. They were neither fully aware nor particularly interested in the hidden meanings of the words and the intricacies of the extended metaphors and figurative language. But both elements were intrinsic to the poems. In short, the so called 'paradox' evidenced in these poems is not a paradox at all. Rather, it is a unique blend of the abstract and the concrete through the agency of symbolism, which is the special characteristic of their writings. The nature of the metaphors in the poems is such as to render physical immediacy to abstractions and conceptual dimensions to concrete objects.

In terms of literary craft and conventions, the Siddhas revolutionized Tamil poetry, especially religio-philosophic poetry, by bringing into its world the language of folklore. This bold device became irrevocable. Although mainstream scholars preferred to ignore it or pretended not to see it, the yoking of the high and the low was there to stay and to be seized upon by successive poets and singers who, in spite of their fewness, kept the tradition burning until it became sufficiently fecund to impregnate the modern Romantics. Beginning from Subramania Bharathi, Turaiyappa Pillai (1872-1929)[36] and others generally adopted most of the 'folk' meters used by the Siddhas while increasingly relying upon the current idiom for fashioning their poetic language. They thus vindicated the persistence and perspicacity of the prophetic Siddhas.

36. T.A. Turaiyappa Pillai was a Sri Lankan contemporary of Subramania Bharathi and, like him, ushered in the modern phase in Tamil poetry. He used the *kummi* form for patriotic content. He was an educationist and social reformer. For a brief account of the poetical achievement of Turaiyappa Pillai, see K. Kailasapathy, "A Century of Tamil Poetry in Sri Lanka," *Silver Jublilee Souvenir of the Calcutta Tamil Association* (Calcutta: Calcutta Tamil Association, 1978), pp. 41-51; for a fuller account, see *Turaiyappa Pillai Centenary Volume* (Tellippalai, Jaffna: Mahajana College, 1972).

The poems of the Siddhas are of necessity always about ideas as well as things, about the sacred as well as the profane. In the best tradition of mystics who want to do away with all forms of duality and multiplicity, transcend the various polarizations that life and literature have helped create and perpetuate, and see nothing but unity, the Siddhas too gave expression to their experience of the undifferentiated unity. Their language naturally reflects this apprehension of the Oneness. The following verses exemplify the peculiar use of language by the Siddhas:

> In a park there was a mendicant.
> He beseeched the potter for ten long months
> And came away with a water-pot.
> He danced and leaped and dropped it.
> The pot was smashed to pieces.[37]

The original which is full of music and is in fact sung by illiterate Tamils for its sheer sound effects is perhaps one of the most popular songs in the Siddha collection. One can hear beggars singing this song all over Tamilnadu. The reason is obvious. The listener does not require any profound knowledge to understand the significance of the poem. As he sings or repeats the words and lines he can intuitively feel that the poem has moved from a simple physical external event into a complex inner spiritual experience. The details of the metaphor employed are certainly interesting but not essential to the understanding of the general purport. The waste of this precious life and the failure to make use of it for spiritual gain comes through the words quite clearly. But we can be more specific. The poem speaks of the soul (mendicant) longing to be born at the end of the period of pregnancy (ten months) into a human body (water-pot). Overjoyed by its existence, it leads a hectic life (dancing and leaping) and throws away a rare opportunity for self-improvement and spiritual progress.

The author, Kaduveli Cittar, called his poem "*Ānantha kalippu*" (Ecstatic Joy), meaning that it was a poem expressive of ecstatic delight. Due to the immense popularity of the poem, the phrase 'ecstatic joy' came to denote the metrical form in which the poem was composed.[38] It may be appropriate to say that the phrase aptly describes a state of mind: the poet pouring forth his insights into the meaning of life in a

37. *Cittār gnanakkōvai*, Kaduveli Cittar, verse 4.
38. Arunachalam, *Tamil Literature*, p. 325

state of serenity. This manner of expression, inchoate in Kaduveli Cittar, was taken up by Tayumanavar (ca. seventeenth century A.D.), who made great poetry out of it. His personality found a perfect outlet in this type of verse in which philosophy, literature and devotion blended in absolute harmony. He was not a Siddha in the strict sense of the term. But attuned as he was to eclecticism, he had imbibed the best and positive aspects of the Siddha teachings and made them his own. The result was a flow of mellifluous poems that have remained unrivalled.

Civavakkiyar dares to refute the theory of transmigration which is so deeply entrenched in the Indian mind.

> Milk does not return to the udder,
> Likewise butter can never become butter-milk;
> The sound of the conch does not exist once it is broken;
> The blown flower, the fallen fruit do not go back to the tree;
> The dead are never born again, never![39]

In his characteristic style the author adduces simple similes to drive home his message. The instances he cites are commonplace, yet the effect is dramatic. A stanza from Tirumoolar uses the same technique. It is also an example of a poem with double meanings.

> I sowed eggplant seed; jack sprouted.
> I dug the dust; the pumpkin blossomed.
> The garden folk took it away merrily;
> What was fully ripe was the banana fruit.[40]

Although the objects referred to are within everybody's experience, the poem is no doubt puzzling. The things mentioned are symbolic and intended to convey some other meaning: the eggplant seed is yogic practice; the jack tree connotes freedom from worldly desires; digging the dust means philosophical speculations; the pumpkin flower signifies *civam* manifesting itself; by 'the garden folk' is meant the sense organs; ripening means obtaining; and the banana fruit represents spiritual gain.

It is a truism that artistic form is a revelation of content. The main points of the content of the poetry of the Siddhas reveal themselves in the forms that they created or adopted. Inasmuch as their content was unorthodox, rebellious, non-conformist and incisive, the meters they

39. *Cittār gnanakkōvai*, Civavakkiyar, verse 43.
40. *Tirumantiram*, verse 2869.

frequently used and the experiments they made with the formal aspects of poetry were designed to maximize the efficacy of their expression. True to their spirit of eclecticism, they were not averse to choosing certain traditional meters that had come down from the earliest times. The earliest known grammatical treatise *Tolkāppiyam*[41] which is usually assigned to the pre-Christian era (ca. second century B.C.) enumerates four basic meters deemed suitable for literary compositions: *akaval* (used in narratives), *vancippā* (used in descriptive situations), *venpā* (used in didactic works), and *kalippā* (ideal for love poetry and choral music). Since the ancient bards who sang of the Heroic Age came to be venerated as the 'Noble Ones', these meters used by them became established as the standard ones. Given the extreme dominance of tradition in mainstream Tamil literature, these four have remained to this day the meters *par excellence* — at least according to grammatical works. However, in course of time new meters arose which were held to be derivatives by the later prosodists. With their penchant for tracing the origin of things to earlier sources, the medieval grammarians argued, at times even in the face of irrefutable evidence, that almost all the later meters were subsidiaries of the original four. The new ones were called 'related meters'. The argument of the medieval prosodists need not delay us here. Suffice to say it could not have been true. But the later meters, despite many differences, had one common point: they were all used in poetry that came in the classical tradition, which emphasized the perfection of style. Hence they were described and prescribed by writers on poetics and prosody.

The Siddhas used some of these meters, especially the *akaval*, *venpā* and some variations of the *kalippā*. On the whole, however, they exploited metrical forms that had no literary or grammatical sanction. It is to be surmised that besides their own innovations in these matters, they adapted melodies, tunes and meters that were in vogue among the people, particularly the working populace. Many of them would have been folk songs. For instance, most of the songs of Idaikkattu Cittar or 'the Siddha of the Pasture-Forest' are composed in the form of a dialogue between two shepherds, though of course the poem as we have it is more than a shephered's dialogue. Tradition has it that he

41. On the *Tolkāppiyam* and early Tamil meters, see K. Kailasapathy, *Tamil Heroic Poetry* (Oxford: Oxford University Press, 1968), pp. 48-51 and 139-46; also George L. Hart, *The Poems of Ancient Tamil* (Berkeley: University of California Press, 1975), pp. 197ff.

was born in the Idaiyar or cowherd caste and hence was full of the pastoral ethos. Whatever may be the case, there is no doubt that "the tone and imagery of his poetry suggest a pastoral milieu."[42] It is reasonable to think that he adapted certain songs that were prevalent among shepherds during his time and in the process of handling the tunes, raised the level of the content of the songs. Similarly the poems of Pambatti Cittar or 'the Snake-Charmer Siddha' are modelled on the songs of professional snake charmers. A modern writer thinks that the Siddha "may be taken to be a true representative of his tribe."[43] What is of particular interest to us is the fact that for centuries the songs of this Siddha have been on the lips of every Tamilian to whom these are the exemplary songs of snake-charmers.[44] It is to the credit of the Siddha that his song, whether a copy or an original, has superseded the authentic one.

A majority of the Siddha poems seem to be composed in a metrical form called *cintu.* It is a kind of musical composition. Some modern writers see it as an offshoot of a medieval meter which in turn is traced to the ancient *kalippā.* This is yet another instance of a tenacious argument betraying the pernicious influence of literary tradition. *Cintu* is a composition in which the stanzas are generally two lines long with either initial or end rhyme. Each line may have two to four metrical feet, though occasionally we come across a cintu with five metrical feet. The two lines are usually broken into four half lines. Sometimes the stanzas are four lines long, making a total of eight half-lines. At the end of a half-line comes a detached word which has the measure of a metrical foot. The two detached words at the end of two half lines have rhyme. These detached words, when they are nouns, take the form of the vocative case: persons, animals, birds and things are directly addressed by the poet. Akappey Cittar, for instance, repeats the vocative *akappēy*, 'the devil of the mind'. Since his poems are primarily concerned with the problem of cleansing the mind which is the root of all illusions, he addresses the mind. This catchy expression *akappēy* has in fact supplanted his proper name which we do not know.

42. Zvelebil, *Poets of Powers*, p. 107.

43. Subramania Iyer, *Tamil Siddhars*, p. 64.

44. Since snake-charmers are a common sight to this day in India, their music is very familiar to the people. Further, generations of Bharata Natyam dancers have contributed much to the popularity of these songs by including a snake dance in their regular repertoire. The Tamil cinema too has used the Cittar songs, including this one, in song and dance situations.

Similarly, Kutampai Cittar uses the word *kutampai* in its vocative form. It literally means a kind of ear-ring but by metonymy becomes the substitute for a girl wearing the ear-ring. Kutampai Cittar has left behind only thirty-two stanzas but is considered one of the more complex Siddhas. His language is at once simple and highly symbolic. It is said that the girl he addresses is for him the female symbol of the soul. He seems to draw his terminology partly from the Siddha medicinal system. This Siddha is also known by the refrain he uses in his poem "*Kutampai*". His proper name is not known.[45] Idaikkattu Cittar addresses a shepherd, a cow, a peacock, etc., in his poems. A later Siddha, Valaisamy, addresses a 'wise woman' and Konkana Cittar addresses 'a young girl', posing philosophic questions to her. Alukani Cittar repeats the expression 'my darling', the literal meaning of the Tamil phrase being 'she who is like the apple of the eye'. Sometimes the detached word is an exclamation expressive of wonder. About ten stanzas of Alukani Cittar's poem have such an expression.

Cintu is probably the most widespread musical form in Tamil folk literature. Many songs connected with rituals among the Tamils are in this meter. In utilizing this common form of composition the Siddhas did two things. First, by investing it with serious content, especially pertaining to societal issues and mystical insights, they raised its value and made it possible for future poets to treat it with respect and esteem. Secondly, by the very process of using it for overtly intellectual purposes, they divested it of its essentially musical function and made it pliable for literary composition. As has been mentioned earlier, both these trends found their fruition in the works of the modern poet Bharathi and his followers. In an encomium which is certainly not misplaced, Bharathidasan (1891-1964), called Bharathi 'the father of *Cintu*' meaning that he ushered into mainstream Tamil poetry the *cintu* which had till then been largely confined to the substream. By using it for modern

45. The practice of naming poets after their suggestive phrases has a long history. Already in the Sangam period we see numerous poets named after "suggestive and beautiful, eloquent and living phrases." Very often these phrases are similes. For instance '*Kal-poru-ciru-nuraiyār*' is the name of a Sangam poet which is derived from an arresting simile in one of his poems; the phrase means 'the foam dashing on the rock'. For more on this matter see M. Varadarajan, *The Treatment of Nature in Sangam Literature* (Madras: South India Saiva Siddhanta Works Publishing Society, 1957), p. 169, *passim* and T.P. Meenakshisundaran, *Collected Papers: Sixty-First Birthday Commemoration Volume* (Annamalainagar: Annamalai University Press, 1961), pp. 34-37.

poetry there is no doubt that Bharathi completed the process begun by the Siddhas, divesting it of its musical quality and giving it a descriptive and analytical applicability.

Another form of composition used with mastery by the Siddhas is *kummi,* a poem composed in a meter meant for the *kummi* dance, in which young girls clap hands to time and sing. By its very nature it is a communal dance that is doubtless very old, since we have reference to it in ancient literature. Beat and rhythm are its chief characteristics and the Siddhas have used it to convey thoughts and feelings that could be shared by their listeners. End rhyme is one of its distinguishing features and a person like Kaduveli Cittar uses it with great effect. His two-line stanzas have become well known maxims. For example:

> Know the body is a bubble atop water,
> The illusion will float away sooner or later.

Using the same metaphor of bodily life as a momentary bubble, Tayumanavar says:

> Why in this water-bubble,
> this unabiding clay,
> Should there be all this suffering
> And all this sorrow, say, Lord of all?[46]

Just as Bharathi used the *cintu* meter with alacrity and undoubted success, Ramalinga Swami, who just preceded him, adopted the *kummi* with great zeal and wrote some scintillating songs in this meter. His *Natecar kummi* is widely known.

Kanni is another metrical form that was fully explored by the Siddha poets. It is a poem of two-line stanzas with initial rhyme, each stanza self-contained in meaning. The word *kanni* also has the meaning of 'flower garland', and the poem could be compared to a garland in which flowers are strung together. Pattinattar, regarded by some as the greatest poet among the Siddhas,[47] perfected this form, exploiting all its potentialities. Along with Tayumanawar, whose *Parāparak kanni* (Lord of All), is a fine example of poetic achievement, Pattinattar is often associated with this meter.

These two-line stanzas, used so effectively by most of the Siddhas, seem to have common features with the *dohā* verses one encounters in

46. Tambyah, *Psalms of a Saiva,* p. 37.
47. Zvelebil, *Poets of Powers,* p. 90.

Tantric literature elsewhere. Guiseppe Tucci's observation on them seems apposite here. Such pithy stanzas are "initiatic lyrics in which the mystic, with a terminology understandable only by his brethren, sings of his ecstasies and hints in devious terms at his laborious and blissful conquests."[48] Here again we see the universality of the Siddha way.

The metrical compositions mentioned above, are all descriptively called *canda kavi* (Skt. *chandas*), meaning musical flow, rhythmic movement of verse, etc. In the case of the poetry of the Siddhas, as with all inspired writings, it is impossible to separate form and content. The two elements have an integral function. Given the circumstances under which the Siddhas lived and wrote, their songs survived because of their inherent strength. It was as much from the vitality of ideas as from the manner in which the ideas were communicated. Both are inseparable. Because the Siddhas came from various walks of life and kept close to their origins, they were successful in describing their inner visions in terms of their own backgrounds and linguistic experience, though constantly intensifying and heightening the function of that language. What touched them most profoundly and generated their strongest powers was "the sense of spiritual reality at work in all living things."[49] Their deep mysticism and the strong desire for self-purification never took them away from the people. They had enough humility to see their own shortcomings and sins. Says a modern writer: "No one can read Tayumanavar's psalms without being struck by the reality of the saint's conflicts with 'a sin-burdened I', a selfhood as rebellious as you see in the hymns of Kabir or Tukaram."[50]

This brings us to another aspect of the Siddhas. We have referred to the belief among the Siddhas that some of them came from other cultural traditions, such as the Chinese, the Arabic, etc. The connections seem to have been strong in the fields of medicine, alchemy and astronomy. Attention has also been drawn to the belief that the first known Tamil Siddha Tirumoolar came from Kashmir. Whatever the authenticity of these stories, it is obvious that there has been a certain amount of intermingling of Muslim and Hindu saints at the popular

48. Guiseppe Tucci, *Tibetan Printed Scrolls* (Rome: Libreria dello Stato, 1949), p. 226.

49. Cf. Cecil M. Bowra, *The Romantic Imagination* (London: Oxford University Press 1961), p. 14.

50. Tambyah, *Psalms of a Saiva* p. cli.

level. Two Muslim Sufis are included in the lists of Siddhas. One is Pir Muhamed who composed "*Gnānaratina kuravanci,*" a short poem in the form of a dialogue between a husband and wife belonging to the Kuravas, wandering gypsies who eke out a living by selling simple herbal medicines, semi-precious stones and perfumes and tell fortunes by reading the palm.[51] This literary form which came into prominence during and after the sixteenth century was originally a folk dance treating erotic themes. Later it was adapted for other subjects too. The *dramatis personae* in Pir Muhamed's poem discuss philosophical questions but, because of the relative simplicity of the language, they sound quite natural. The poem has sixty-four stanzas or couplets. The other Muslim is Mastan Sahib, a Sufi poet in his own right. Literary critics associate his name with Tayumanavar, because their poems have striking similarities. But Mastan's verses, being simpler and more colloquial, are closer to the Siddha strain.

Apart from the inclusion of Muslim Sufis and poets in the company of the Siddhas, medieval Tamilnadu and Sri Lanka have many cult sites that are the graves of Muslim Sufi saints and *pīr*s. Many celebrated Hindu shrines of the god Skanda are believed to have been constructed on or near the tombs of Muslim Sufi saints. The common people believe that dead Sufi saints are propitious; hence their tombs are of immediate importance. Further, it is reasonable to think that Sufi mysticism had no difficulty in coexisting with the Siddha way. In the final analysis, both schools of mysticism were responding to numerous varieties of local cultures in Tamilnadu and taking up similar stances. As a result, the reaction of the masses to both Hindu and Muslim mysticism was similar. The Muslim Siddhas were not differentiated in any way. Rather, they were sometimes respected even more, since they had transcended sectarianism and joined the brotherhood of universal faith. Perhaps the most tangible result of the teachings of the Siddhas was the progressive realization by the poeple that the rivalry and conflicts between Vaishnavism and Shaivism — which was very much visible and into which they were drawn — were futile and meaningless. A popular saying reflects this:

> Hari and Hara are one:
> Those not realizing this know none.

51. For details on this genre, see Zvelebil, *Tamil Literature*, p. 224.

Having discussed the salient features of the philosophy, religion and literature of the Siddhas, one thing remains to be shown. What was it that made them so close to the common people, binding them with their expectations and inner thoughts? That the Siddhas were non-sectarian, anti-establishment and unflinchingly critical of smug religiosity is evident from their poems. The aggressive tirades of Civavakkiyar and the outbursts of Pambatti Cittar are proof of it. That they used the colloquial language and popular expressions, and experimented with folk meters and melodies, is also equally clear. Even the illiterates were at home with their catchy lines. But these were, in a sense, negativistic acts done (often consciously) in opposition to the dominant cultural values of their times. They registered their protests by acting contrary to prevailing norms. But there must have been something more positive in their possession that endeared them to the voiceless people. This is not so clear from their songs that are considered 'poetry', but a persual of their works on astrology, medicine, physiognomy and Yoga gives us some insight into the matter.

Some of the Siddhas were great physicians. It is not within the scope of this paper to discuss this aspect. Suffice to say that the traditional system of medicine among the Tamils, both in Tamilnadu and Sri Lanka, has been called Cittavaittiyam, 'Siddha medicine'.[52] The Siddhas trace their system to the sage Agastya, to whom are ascribed numerous medical treatises. Among the Siddhas, Teraiyar, Pokar, Roma Rishi and Puli Pani are reputed to have been great healers. Teraiyar is supposed to have practised surgery. Since the Siddhas were constantly on the move and were inveterate travellers (visiting cult sites like Palni in Tamilnadu and meeting fellow mystics), they were always in contact with people. The bonds were indeed close. As healers they were respected, admired and even loved more than the priests who in any case led an exclusive life and were beyond the reach of ordinary people because of caste distinctions. Furthermore, as a corollary of their interest in medicine, the Siddhas held the human body to be sacred and divine. "The body is no longer a source of pain and temptation,

52. For an introduction to the subject, see A. Kanagaratnam, *Citta maruttuvam* (Colombo: Ceylon Printers, 1949); *Proceedings of the Siddha Medical Conference* (Coimbatore, 1959); Lalitha Kameswaran, *A Study of References to Medicine in Literature in Tamilnad* (Madurai: By the Author, 1968). The above three are written by persons qualified in Siddha medicine. For a general view see, Cami Citamparanar, *Cittarkal kanda vignānam-tattuvam* (Madras: New Century Book House, 1961), pp. 19-32.

but the most reliable and effective instrument of man in his quest to conquer death and bondage. Since liberation can be gained even in this life, the body must be preserved as long as possible, and in perfect condition."[53] Tirumular asserts this time and again:

> Mistakenly I had believed the body to be imperfect,
> But within it I realized the Ultimate Reality.[54]
>
> Those who let the body decay, destroy the spirit;
> They will not attain the true, powerful knowledge.
> I have learned the art of how to foster the body;
> I fostered the body, and I fostered the soul.[55]

Elsewhere Tirumular goes further in describing the divine nature of the human body. Not only is it a fit instrument for the progress of the soul in its spiritual journey but it is the actual abode of God. In a celebrated verse that has wide currency in Tamil he says:

> The mind is the sacred chamber,
> The physical body is the temple;
> For my gracious Lord the mouth is the tower gate,
> The enlightened ones know the soul to be Shiva's *liṅga*
> The guileful senses are truly lamps that illuminate.[56]

This is in contrast to much of the mainstream religious teachings which decried the body as evil and full of defects and characterized life itself as a 'dreadful dream'. Though a few singers connected to the Siddha school did sing in a tragic vein and emphasized a negative attitude towards the body and consequently about life itself, the majority of the Siddhas took a more cheerful attitude. This too must have been a solace to the people whose life of drudgery and tedium was bad enough without being harangued about it. In other words, the central teachings of the Siddhas and their reverence for the human body had very little to do with the spirit of 'world and life negation' which Schweitzer found so depressing in Indian religious thought.[57] To put it differently, the

53. Zvelebil, *Poets of Powers*, p. 31.
54. *Tirumantiram*, verse 725.
55. Zvelebil, *Poets of Powers*, p. 76.
56. *Tirumantiram*, verse 1823.
57. Schweitzer took the view that much of Brahmanic thought is governed by world and life negation, in contrast to European thought which is governed by world and life affirmation. Although he conceded that in the Upanishads and in some other

drab and dreadful routine of life was tragic enough already for the people. A pessimistic philosophy of life could only aggravate it. The philosophy of the Siddhas even at its saddest moments helped to accept the world with a kind of stoical resignation, which was a great comfort. In this respect the Siddhas resembled the primitive prophets and shamans who were singers, magicians, healers, ministers — all in one person. Their boundless love for humanity manifested itself in every word and act of theirs. A much quoted line of Tirumular aptly reflects this:

May the world be as happy as I am.[58]

Inasmuch as the Siddhas were striving for liberation, they were able to instill that ideal into the minds of the people who were "tormented by

---

writings in Indian literature one finds strong expression of world and life affirmation, world and life negation occupies a predominant position in Indian thought. Having thus generalized, he sees a significant exception in the *Kural*, the ancient ethical work in Tamil. After adumbrating its cardinal teachings, especially the idea of active love, he concludes thus: "So a natural and ethical world and life affirmation of this kind was present among the people of India at the beginning of our era, although nothing of it can be found in Brahmanism, Buddhism and Bhagavad Gita Hinduism. It gradually penetrates into Hindu thought through the great religious teachers who had sprung from the lower castes and lived among and felt with the people." One is not sure if Schweitzer was familiar with the writings of the Tamil Siddhas, but he could as well have had them in mind in making this remark. See Albert Schweitzer, *Indian Thought and Its Development* (London: Adam and Charles Black, 1951), pp. 3, 200-05. The *Kural* cherished by the Tamils as the Dravidian Bible has been translated into several languages. Early Christian missionaries thought the book showed Christian influences. Doubtless they were mistaken. It is interesting to note that according to tradition its author Valluvar was of low caste and his profession was weaving. He too was an eclectic in religion and philosophy, although the work as a whole has a Jain flavor. For a balanced view on the *Kural* and its author see Meenakshisundaran, *Tamil Literature*, pp. 52-59. According to some traditional scholars, "even Valluvar is included among the Siddha mystics." N. Subrahmanian, *History of Tamilnad*, 2nd ed. (Madurai: Koodal Publishers, 1976), p. 403. There is no doubt that the Siddhas drew spiritual sustenance from the *Kural*. Besides being the most quoted and revered book in Tamil, the *Kural* is also the one book that is interpreted to reflect different religious tenets: Jains Buddhists, Vaishnavites, Shaivites, Christians and even atheists have with equal vigor and credibility claimed the author to be one of them. Likewise almost all the modern socio-political movements in Tamilnadu have used his maxims to argue their causes. All these indicate if not prove that the book is essentially eclectic in content. For an interesting attempt to see the work in terms of 'syncretism', see S. Ramakrishnan, *Valluvan kanda Vālviyal* (Madras: Star Publishers, 1957).

58. *Tirumantiram*, verse 85.

unsatisfied longings which they cannot explain, cannot express."[59] The Siddhas were like the poet described by Belinsky:

> Society wants him to be a representative of its spiritual, ideal life; an oracle who can answer the most difficult questions; a physician who discovers in himself, before discovering them in others, man's common pains and sufferings and heals them by reproducing them in poetic form.[60]

One could not have captured the essential qualities of the Siddhas better.

Recent studies show that interest in the Siddhas is growing both from an Indian perspective and from a comparative viewpoint. It would appear that any serious study of Indian Yoga, Tantricism, mysticism and religious nonconformity will be incomplete without taking into account the phenomenon of the Siddhas. One could go even further. At a time when provincialisms are breaking down and an increasing world-wide interest in the dynamics of counter-traditions is becoming evident, the life and teachings of the hitherto little-known Siddhas can turn out to be a truly exciting discovery. The Siddhas are not only inheritors of a literary heritage as old as any in the world, but also the harbingers of a counter-tradition as vigorous and germane as any that the world has seen. This makes their contribution assume a broader significance. Louis Kampf's definition of counter-tradition seems apt here to place the Siddhas in a universal perspective:

> The impulse to oppose cultural norms appears as inarticulate revolt, as social criticism, as vision, as ideology, as completed revolution; it may spring from logic, disillusionment, or the experience of oppression. In short, it is part of the continuing dialectic of history, as much our cultural heritage as what it opposes. What I mean, then, by 'counter-tradition' is not 'that which opposes tradition', but, 'the tradition which opposes'.[61]

A similar approach to the study of the Siddhas would seem to be a *sine qua non* at the present time.

59. George Thomson, *Marxism and Poetry* (New York: International Publishers, 1946), p. 46.

60. V.G. Belinsky, *Selected Philosophical Works* (Moscow: Foreign Languages Publishing House, 1948), p. xiv.

61. Sheila Delany, ed. *Counter-Tradition: The Literature of Dissent and Alternatives* (New York: Basic Books, 1971), p. 4.

APPENDIX

NOTE ON THE FRONTISPIECE

ELINOR W. GADON

The miniature painting reproduced here in the frontispiece is from the collection of the Victoria and Albert Museum in London.[1] It is unique among Mughal miniatures in that it includes inscribed portraits of Sants and Yogis who can be identified as historical, legendary or symbolic figures associated with these two unorthodox movements of medieval Hinduism. The work of an unknown artist, these individual studies of Hindu holy men are of extraordinary beauty and reveal a great empathy and understanding, each figure delineated with great dignity and naturalness. Above the frieze of Hindu holy men, we find a group of Sufi saints and Mughal court familiars watching *sama'*, the ecstatic singing and dancing of Muslim mystics. This miniature, of superb quality, an obvious product of the imperial Mughal workshops, illustrates a vision of common religious experience among Muslim and Hindu mystics and strongly suggests the patronage of Prince Dara Shikoh.

The setting can be identified as Ajmer, home of the Dargah Khwaja Sahib, the shrine of the Sufi saint Mu'inuddin Chishti, and the scene of the annual *urs melā*, the anniversary of the saint's death, held in the Muslim month of Rajab. In the background, against the green hills, the artist, with a lively, finely drawn hand, has sketched some details of the popular activities associated with this festival, such as wrestling, snake charming, and trained animal performances. Both the style of his backgrounding, known as *dur-nāmā* or 'distant scene', and the grandiose buildings show the influence of the European prints and drawings that the Jesuits and ambassadors had brought to the Mughal court.

1. I.S. 94-1965. This has been previously published in L. Binyon, *The Court Painters of the Great Moguls*, with historical introduction and notes by T.W. Arnold (London: Oxford University Press, 1921), plates XVIII and XIX, pp. 61, 72-73. Also, in Leigh Ashton, ed., *The Art of India and Pakistan*, a commemorative catalog of the exhibition held at the Royal Academy of Arts, London, 1947-1948 (London: Faber and Faber, 1950), no. 780.

The architecture can be read as the magnificent marble structures that the emperor Jahangir built in the city in honor of the Chishtiyya order. The Chishtis had been closely associated with the Mughal dynasty since the days of its founder, Babar. Akbar made a special pilgrimage on foot from Agra to the shrine at Ajmer in 1579, thereby fulfilling his vow of thanksgiving for the birth of his first son, Jahangir. Jahangir was born in Ajmer in the house of a Chishtiyya Sufi, Shaikh Salim, after whom he was named, and made frequent pilgrimages to Ajmer, attending the annual festival in 1613, 1615 and 1618. Years later, Jahangir's own son, the future emperor Shah Jahan, also prayed for the birth of a son at the tomb of Mu'inuddin Chishti. Dara Shikoh, who was born in Ajmer in 1615, notes this in his biographical account of Mu'inuddin Chishti:

> Thus, it is a happy coincidence that Dārā, born at the city of a great mystic and divine, turned out to be a devout Sufi and a 'man of the Path' throughout his life.[2]

In the upper portion of the painting, we can identify three of the Muslim saints standing in line in front of the colonnaded buildings. The strong-faced, black-bearded figure leaning on his stick at the center left is Qutbuddin Bakhtiyar Kaki (d. 1235). His name is inscribed in Persian over his pompomed turban. The dark-robed figure directly opposite Kaki and the man next in line to the right with a light shawl over his shoulder can be identified by comparison with inscribed portraits in other miniatures as Mu'inuddin Chishti (d. 1236) and Mulla Shah Bakhshi (d. 1661). Mu'inuddin Chishti was the outstanding figure in the movement which brought Sufism to India. His order, the Chishtiyya, became a major force in the Islamization of central and southern India, and his tomb in Ajmer is still an important pilgrimage site visited by Hindus and Muslims alike. Kaki was his friend and successor who came with him to India. Mulla Shah, the spiritual guide of Dara Shikoh, was the head of the Qadiriyya order into which he initiated the prince in 1640. The representations of Kaki and Mu'inuddin are not portraits from life: the saints had long been dead. Their presence here in a con-

2. Dara Shikoh, *Majma' ul-bahrain*, ed. in the original Persian with English translation, notes and variants by Mahfuzul-Haw (Calcutta: The Asiatic Society of Bengal, 1929).

temporaneous scene suggests the concept of *silsilā* or spiritual chain through which generations of Sufis are linked to the Prophet Muhammad and through him to God.

Below the main body of the painting, in a separate compositional space, we find twelve figures seated informally in front of a series of stone arcades. Eleven of them can be identified by their inscription. From left to right, they are: (1) Ravidas or Raidas (fl. 1470), a cobbler from Banares, a member of the Untouchable caste of leatherworkers, known for his great holiness and as the guru of Mira Bai; (2) Pipa (1353-1403), said to have been a raja who abdicated his sovereignty and distributed his wealth among the poor; (3) Namdev (latter half of the fourteenth century), who exemplifies the Maharashtrian Sant-Vaishnava tradition in his total devotion to the god Vithoba, and whose name probably comes from his extraordinary faith in the name of God; (4) Sena, a barber from the court of the raja of Rewa, who wrote hymns and, according to popular tradition, performed menial offices for holy men, believing that the service of holy men was equivalent to the service of God himself; (5) Kamal, the supposed son of Kabir, who was the founder of one of the twelve branches of the Kabir-panthis; (6) a figure labeled 'Aughar', which is not a personal name, but rather the name of a class of Shaivite ascetics, followers of Gorakhnath, who have not undergone the final Nath initiation ceremony of having their ears split; (7) Kabir; (8) Pir Muchhandar, the Punjabi form of Matsyendranath, the mythical figure known in the traditions of the Nath Yogis as their first teacher and also as the guru of Gorakhnath; (9) Gorakhnath (twelfth century), the foremost guru of the Nath Yogi sect, said to have been converted to Shaivism from Tantric Buddhism and traditionally associated with both Kabir and Nanak; (10) Jadrup,[3] a Hindu sadhu from Ujjain referred to at some length by Jahangir in his *Memoirs* in connection with mystic ideas common to both Hinduism and Islam,[4] (11) Lal Swami, popularly called Babalal Das Vairagi, a

3. Sukumar Sen identifies this portrait as that of Jiva Goswami (1511?-1556) but does not give his reasons for doing so. Sukumar Sen, *A History of Braja Buli* (Calcutta: University of Calcutta, 1935), opposite pp. 380-84.

4. Jahangir describes his visit to the saint in February 1617 at the place where he lived in a hole in the side of a hill, and says of him that "he was throughly mastered the science of Vedanta, which is the science of Sufism." Jahangir, *The Tuzuk-i-Jahangiri*; or Memoirs of Jahangir, trans. A. Rogers and ed. H. Beveridge, 2 vols. in 1 (London: Royal Asiatic Society, 1909-1914), 1:355-59, 2:49, 52, 104-05, 108.

Hindu reformer and teacher best remembered for his dialogues with Dara Shikoh;[5] (12) a figure whose identification is problematical, as the inscribed name is badly rubbed and only the latter part, '...*svāmī*', can be read. It might be Chitan Swami, the teacher of Babalal who is seated next to him, and if so, this would follow the existing pattern here of representing a disciple with his guru.

This panel of twelve figures can roughly be divided into Sants on the left and Yogis on the right, further subdivided into four discrete groupings loosely contained by the arches behind. The first group at the far left—Ravidas, Pipa, Sena and Namdev, along with Kabir in the next group—are all, according to the *Bhaktamāl* of Nabhaji (c. 1600), followers of Ramanand. The second grouping is more problematical: Kabir and his son/disciple, Kamal, are to be included with the Sants, while the Aughar figure belongs with the unorthodox Shaivite yogis, the first group on the right. Sitting apart on the far right are Babalal and his guru, who are yogis associated with Vaishnavism.

This frieze of Sants and Yogis has no compositional relationship to what is depicted above, and can be considered, as in the case with the predella of Renaissance altarpieces, as a less formal commentary on the more hieratic scene illustrated above, the assembly of saints watching *sama'*. Essentially, the miniature pictures three levels of religious experience. Above, the Muslim saints, heads of Sufi orders, symbolize the *silsilā*, the unbroken chain linking one master to another, going back to the Prophet himself. In the middle ground, we see the actual ritual practice of Muslim mystics, *dhikr*, the chanting of the names of God to the accompaniment of music and dance. Below, we find a varied group of unorthodox Hindus, members of eclectic movements which reflect the popular religious experience of the Indian masses, and whose common association is their devotion to the name of God and their rejection of Brahmanical ritual and authority.

5. These were recorded by the prince's private secretary, Chandar Bhan, who was present at these interviews, perhaps acting as interpreter. The manuscript account of these interviews, written in Persian, *Mukalana Baba Lāl was Dārā Shikoh*, contains a summary of questions that were asked by Dara Shikoh on various aspects of Hindu religion and ascetic life, as well as the replies that were given by Babalal, the only Hindu whose aphorisms he quotes in *Majma' ul-bahrain*, his speculative work on the unity of Muslim and Hindu metaphysics (see fn. 2).

Despite the very real genre details of the *sama'* and the *melā*, and the authenticity of the Ajmer setting, the scene represented cannot be considered as an actual historical event. Kaki and Mu'inuddin Chishti are long dead, and, among the Sants and Yogis, only Babalal is alive. Their representation together in the historical time and space of the mid-seventeenth century at the *urs melā* suggests a vision of Hindu-Muslim synthesis associated in the popular imagination with Dara Shikoh, who is remembered in Indian tradition as a martyr for the cause of Indian cultural unity.

Dara Shikoh's spiritual commitment to Sufi mysticism grew out of his visit at the age of nineteen with Mian Mir, the saintly head of the Qadiriyya order. Deeply depressed, following the death of his infant daughter, he was taken by his father, Shah Jahan, to the saint, who provided the necessary solace for his recovery and introduced the prince to the mysteries of the faith. When Mian Mir died the following year, his follower, Mulla Shah, became the prince's spiritual guide. For the next six years, Dara Shikoh devoted himself to studying the lives and miracles of the Sufi saints. In 1640, he completed his first book, *Safīnat-ul-Awliyā*, an authoritative work of Sufi hagiography and, on January 21, 1640, he was initiated into the Qadiriyya order. Contemporary chronicles report that he had a great curiosity about all kinds of spiritual matters, sought out *sanyāsīs* and yogis as well as Muslim ascetics. He is credited with other books on religious subjects and in the later years of his life attempted to formulate a basic philosophical syncretism between Muslim and Hindu metaphysics.

We have ample contemporary evidence of the prince's converse with mystics, Hindu and Muslim, in the many paintings from his lifetime identifying him as visiting with ascetics or seated in an assembly of Sufi saints. One miniature, showing Dara Shikoh seated on the carpet with his master Mulla Shah and his master's master, Mian Mir, all three haloed, may have been commissioned to commemorate the Prince's initiation into the Qadiriyya order.[6] The frequent copying of this painting continued until the demise of Mughal art in the nineteenth century, which suggests a popular appreciation of Dara as a Sufi mystic.

What do we know about Dara Shikoh as a patron of art? The only documentation we have for the existence of his personal atelier is a signature on a miniature in the Bibliotheque Nationale, '*manohar Dārā*

6. Reproduced in Yetta A. Godard, "Un Album de Portraits des Princes Timuri des de l'Inde," *Athar-e-Iran* 2 (1937), pp. 179-277.

Shikoh'.[7] However, it was well within Mughal imperial tradition for a prince to have painters attached to his service. Jahangir, for instance, had his own artists during his years of exile in Allahabad. The renowned Dara Shikoh album, now in the India Office Library, is testimony to the range of the prince's interests as an art collector as well as to his tastes as a connoisseur. This collection of miniatures and calligraphy was a present to his wife, Nadira Begum, in A.H. 1051 (A.D. 1641-42) and contains paintings from the Akbar to the Shah Jahan periods on the range of themes characteristic of the Mughal School: imperial family portraits, religious figures, nature studies, copies after Persian and European art.

Our miniature is undated. However, its date can be reliably established through stylistic comparisons with miniatures of the late Shah Jahani period, ca. 1650-1658.[8] Dara Shikoh is suggested as likely patron for two reasons. First, the painting is a visual complement to the metaphysical speculation in which Dara Shikoh was involved in the later years of his life, through which he attempted to identify the philosophic essence of Hinduism with that of Islam. The last original work attributed to him, *Majma' ul-bahrain*, translated into Sanskrit under the title *Samudra saṅgam* (The Mingling of the Two Oceans), was written in 1655. The work is a pretentious collection of correspondences between Sufi and Upanishadic cosmologies, esoteric beliefs and practices. Whatever the weakness of his speculation, Dara's intent was to find common religious experience between the two faiths. He himself writes in the preface to the *Majma'* that "he did not find any difference except verbal, in the way in which they (Sufis and Indian monotheists) sought and comprehended Truth."[9]. As a patron, his philosophic speculation could have provided inspiration for the gifted unknown artist who created this singular painting, which, through its compositional structure, identifies Sants and Yogis, the unorthodox monotheists of Hinduism, with the esoteric liberal Sufis of Indian Islam. Secondly, the later half of the

7. Ibid., p. 181.

8. There is an identifiable character which distinguishes Shah Jahani period painting from Jahangiri. In the earlier period the focus is on naturalism and realism, in the later on technical virtuosity. Shah Jahani painting is more formal, more dramatic, full of spatial ambiguities, rather static even when movement is indicated. There is also a certain airlessness about the whole. The keen observation of details and psychological character, so remarkable in the Jahangiri work, continues but is romanticized, less real, rather like in a stage play.

9. Dara Shikoh, *Majma' ul-bahrain*, p. 38.

1650s was a period of fratricidal warfare between the sons of Shah Jahan for the imperial succession, which culminated in the victory of the ultra-orthodox Aurangzeb and Dara's execution for apostasy. Dara was officially charged with frequenting with *sanyāsīs* and yogis, regarding their scriptures as the work of God and having them translated into Persian. In a climate so intolerant of religious exploration, it seems unlikely that any other member of the imperial circle would commission this painting.

GLOSSARY

abhaṅg: Short lyric composed in the Marathi language, similar to the North Indian *pad* (q.v.).

acharaj: wonderful; a marvel, a miracle.

āchārya, ācārya: person of exemplary conduct and authoritative doctrine.

adhikārī: one who possesses authority; governor, ruler; superior.

Ādi Granth: the Sikh sacred scripture compiled by Guru Arjan, 1603-1604.

ādi-guru: the primal Guru, the supreme Guru; Shiva.

Ādi-nāth: the primal *Nāth* (q.v.), Shiva.

Ādivāsī: tribal, aborigine.

advaita: 'non-dual'; monism.

Āgamas: Hindu sectarian texts.

agnicayana: fire-altar rite.

agochar, agocara: mysterious, secret, unseen.

Ahīr: member of a herding and agrarian caste.

ahiṃsa: non-injury to all living creatures.

alaṅkār, alaṅkāra: ornament, embellishment; figure of speech.

alaukik, alaukika: other-worldly.

anāmī lok: condition of supreme beatitude.

ardhālī: one of the two identical lines which make up a quatrain, each *ardhālī* itself being divided in two.

āsan, āsana: yogic posture.

ātmā: spirit, soul.

ātman: the Self, the soul.

avatār: a 'descent'; incarnation of a deity, usually Vishnu.

bābā: 'father', a title of respect applied to holy men.

bachan, vacana: utterance, statement, dictum.

bairāgī, vairāgī: Hindu renunciant.

bālama: lover; beloved person.

bānī, vāṇī: speech, sound; divine utterance.

bhagat: See *bhakta*.

bhagat bānī: the works of *bhagat*s recorded in the *Ādi Granth*.

Bhāgavata: 'one devoted to the Lord (*Bhagavān*)'; a devotional tradition worshipping Narayana, identified with Vishnu and Krishna.

bhāī: 'brother'; a title applied to Sikhs of acknowledged learning and piety.

bhajan: religious song.

bhakta, bhagat: an exponent of *bhakti* (q.v.), especially one with a particular reputation for piety and spiritual wisdom.

bhaktamāl: 'garland of *bhaktas*'; collection of hagiographic narratives.

bhakti, bhagati: loving devotion; belief in and adoration of a personal god.

bhaṇitā: statement of author's identity at the conclusion of a poem.

bhāruḍ: dramatic poem in the Marathi language.

bhāva: emotional state; devotional attitude.

bhedābheda: 'distinct (yet) not distinct'; doctrine that the divine is both separate from the human soul and present within it.

bhramargīt: 'songs of the bee'; *pads* (q.v.) describing the hostile reactions of the *gopīs* (q.v.) to Krishna's messenger Udho.

bīj-mantra, bīja-mantra: 'seed-*mantra*', a fundamental *mantra* (q.v.).

bindu: drop, point, dot, semen.

braham gyānī: one who possesses divine wisdom.

brahman: the Absolute; Ultimate Reality.

Brāhman: member of the highest section of the four-fold classical caste hierarchy.

chakra: disc; in *haṭha-yoga* (q.v.) theory, 'lotuses' spaced along the spinal chord which release psychic energy as they are pierced by the ascending *kuṇḍalinī* (q.v.).

Chamār: member of the leather-worker caste.

chandra: moon.

charyā, caryā: observance of rituals; austerities.

chaupāī: verse comprising four lines.

chelā: disciple.

cintu: Tamil lyric, usually comprising two-line stanzas with either initial or end rhyme.

Cittar: Tamil *Siddha* (q.v.).

civam: goodness, auspiciousness; God as pure intelligence.

darbār: royal court; religious assembly; entourage of a Sant.

dard: pain.

darśan, darśana: view, vision; audience with a person of regal or spiritual stature, visit to a holy shrine or object; the six systems of Brahmanical philosophy.

deha-tattva: the spirit or reality within the human body.

ḍerā: encampment; dwelling-place of a Sikh Sant.

dharma: duty, the appropriate moral and religious obligations attached to any particular status in Hindu society.

dhikr, *zikr*: repetition of the name of Allah, the Sufi discipline of 'remembrance' of God.

dhuniyā: cotton-carder.

dhyān, *dhyāna*: meditation.

dīkṣā: initiation.

dīvān: royal court; Sikh assembly; series of poems based on the alphabet.

dohā: couplet.

fakīr, *faqīr*: 'poor man', Muslim ascetic; Sufi.

gaddī: cushion; seat of authority.

garbha-gṛha: the inmost sanctuary of a Hindu temple; cell in a temple where the idol or sacred emblem is installed.

gopī: cowherd woman, milkmaid (especially associated with Krishna).

gopuram: tower over the gate of a South Indian temple.

Gorakhnāthī: *Nāth* (q.v.).

gotra: exogamous caste grouping within a *jāti* (q.v.).

granth, *grantha*: book, volume.

granthī: professional reader of the *Ādi Granth*; the custodian of a *gurduārā* (q.v.).

guṇa: the three vital 'qualities' or constituents of cosmic substance which by their varying proportions determine the nature of all that exists.

gurduārā: Sikh temple.

gurmukh: one who is loyal to the Guru; a devout Sikh.

Gurmukhī: the script used in the *Ādi Granth* and for modern Punjabi.

gursikh: a devout Sikh, a follower of the Guru.

ḥadīth: reported sayings or actions of Muhammad.

halāl: 'lawful'; in accordance with Muslim law.

haṭha-yoga: 'yoga of force', a variety of yoga requiring physical postures and processes of extreme difficulty.

'ishq: love for God. (Islamic term).

Īshvar, *Īśvara*: Shiva, God.

jajmānī: reciprocal service; the prescriptive patron/client relationship between different castes.

janam-sākhī: traditional account of the life of Guru Nanak.

jap, *japa*: repetition of a word or *mantra* (q.v.) representing the *nām* (q.v.).

Jaṭ: member of an agrarian caste with strong military traditions.

jathedār: leader of a *jathā* (military detachment).
jāti, zāt: endogamous caste grouping.
jīv, jīva: life, self, soul.
jīvan-mukti: the attainment of release from transmigration while still living the life of a mortal.
jñāna, giān: knowledge, wisdom.
Julāhā: member of a Muslim weaver caste.
kalippā: metre used for Tamil love poetry.
kaliyuga: the *Kali* age, the 'age of strife', the fourth and last of the cosmic eras; the age of degeneracy; the present age.
Kāma, Kāma-deva: the Hindu god of love.
kāmadhenu: the legendary cow of plenty.
kāmin: a lustful man.
kāminī: a beautiful woman.
karma: the destiny or fate of an individual generated in accordance with the deeds performed in his present and past existences; deed, action.
kavi: poet.
kāvya: poem.
kāyā-sādhanā: 'culture of the body', *sādhanā* (q.v.) based on the physical body; *haṭha-yoga* (q.v.).
kes-dhārī: a Sikh who maintains his *kes* (uncut hair).
Khālsā: the Sikh order or brotherhood, instituted by Guru Gobind Singh in 1699.
Khatrī: member of the Punjabi mercantile caste.
Khudā: God (Islamic term).
kīrtan: corporate singing of hymns.
kriyā: pious deed, religious ceremony.
kumbhak, kumbhaka: breath restraint.
kuṇḍalinī: the coiled serpent which, according to *haṭha-yoga* (q.v.) doctrine, resides at the base of the human spine.
laṅgar: the dining hall attached to a *gurduārā* (q.v.) where meals are regularly served free of charge.
liṅga: the phallus as a symbol of Shiva.
mahant: head of a religious order or institution.
maṅgal, maṅgala: auspicious; blessing, bliss.
manmukh: one who follows his own self-willed impulses rather than the guidance of the Guru (cf. *gurmukh*, q.v.).
mantra: sacred Vedic formula; a verse, phrase, word or syllable of particular religious import.

maqām, muqām (pl. *maqāmāt*): resting-place, abode; stage of spiritual development in the Sufi ascent to mystical union.
mārga: path, way.
masand: territorial deputies appointed by the Sikh Gurus to supervise congregations and collect tithes.
mat: mind; counsel; doctrine; creed.
maṭh: monastery.
māyā: cosmic illusion; the corruptible and corrupting world.
melā: fair, assembly.
mīm: the letter 'M' in Arabic.
mleccha: foreigner, non-Aryan, non-Hindu, barbarian.
moha: attachment to worldly things.
mokṣa: deliverance, release from transmigration, salvation.
momin: Muslim weaver.
mukti: release from the round of transmigration; salvation.
mūl gaddī: original seat of authority.
mūl mantra, mūla mantra: fundamental *mantra* (q.v.).
mullah: a teacher of the law and doctrines of Islam.
murshid: guide, preceptor (Islamic term).
mūrti: body, tangible form; idol.
nām, nāma: the divine Name, the expression of the nature and being of God in terms comprehensible to human understanding.
nām simaraṇ: see *simaraṇ*.
nārī: woman, wife.
Nāth: 'master'. A yogic sect of considerable influence until comparatively recent times. Its members, who are also known as Kanphata yogis, practise *haṭha-yoga* (q.v.) in order to attain immortality.
nirākār, niraṅkār: without form or material substance.
nirgranth, nirgrantha: 'book-less', not possessing a sacred scripture.
nirguṇa: without 'qualities' or attributes, unconditioned (cf. *saguṇa*, q.v.).
nirguru: without a guru; uninitiated, uninstructed by a qualified preceptor.
nirvikalpa: undifferentiated, at one with the divine spirit.
nūr: light, refulgence (Arabic word).
Nyāya: a tradition of logic and epistemology, one of the six systems of Brahmanical philosophy.
pad, pada: short lyric, hymn.
pāhul: baptism, initiation into the *Khālsā* (q.v.).

Pañchvāṇī: the recorded utterances of five Sants (Kabir, Namdev, Raidas, Dadu and Haridas).
paṇḍit: learned person; Brahman.
pāṇḍitya: scholarship; the traditional teachings and practices of Brahmans.
paṅgat: row; the practice of sitting in a row in order to obliterate notions of status and precedence.
pañj kakke (*pañj kakār*): 'the five K's', the five external symbols worn by all members of the *Khālsā* (q.v.).
panth: path, road; the community of those observing a distinctive pattern of religious belief and practice.
panthī: adherent of a *panth* (q.v.).
paramparā: spiritual succession, lineage.
piṇḍa: the body.
piñjārī: cotton-carder, *dhuniyā* (q.v.).
pīr: the head of a Sufi order; a Sufi saint.
pothī: volume, tome.
prabhu: Lord.
prakṛti: primeval matter, that which has material existence.
prasād, prasāda: food offered to a god; divine grace.
prem, prema: love.
pūjā: worship, adoration.
pūjārī: one who performs *pūjā* (q.v.); temple custodian and officiant.
purakh: person.
Purāṇas: 'ancient'; Hindu texts, compendia of myth and ritual lore.
qāzī: Muslim judge, administrator of Muslim law.
rāg, rāga: a series of five or more notes on which a melody is based.
Rahīm: the Merciful One, God (Islamic term).
rahit: the *Khālsā* (q.v.) code of conduct.
rahit-nāmā: recorded version of the *rahit* (q.v.).
Rām, Rāma: the hero of the *Rāmāyaṇa*, an *avatār* (q.v.) of Vishnu; God.
Rāmgaṛhiā: member of a Sikh artisan caste.
ras, rasa: juice, taste, flavor.
rath, ratha: carriage, chariot.
rūḥ: breath, spirit (Arabic word).
rūḥu'l-lāh: the spirit of God (Islamic term).
śabda, śabad: the divine Word, the divine self-communication.
sachiārā: one who lives according to the truth.
sadguru: see *satguru*.

sādh, sādhu: one who has attained spiritual excellence; holy man; renunciant.

sādhak, sādhaka: one who practises a *sādhanā* (q.v.).

sādhanā, sādhan: method of attaining or 'realizing' an ultimate spiritual objective.

sādha-samāgama: see *satsaṅg*.

saguṇa: possessing 'qualities' or attributes; manifested, usually as an *avatār* (q.v.). Cf. *nirguṇa* (q.v.).

sahaj, sahaja: the condition of ultimate beatitude, the ineffable state of mystical union.

sahaj-dhārī: a Sikh who neither receives initiation into the *Khālsā* (q.v.) nor observes its *rahit* (q.v.) in full.

śākhā: branch, section.

sākhī: couplet; brief verse; *dohā* (q.v.); section of a *janam-sākhī* (q.v.).

śalagrām, śālagrāma: ammonite incorporating spiral patterns, regarded as representations of Vishnu.

sama': ecstatic singing and dancing (Sufi).

samādhi: contemplation, mystical trance; place of burial or cremation; structure marking such a place; tomb, cenotaph.

sampradāy, sampradāya: tradition, school of religious thought and practice.

saṃsār, saṃsāra: the world, the universe; transmigration, the round of death and rebirth.

saṃvat: a year in the *Vikramī* (q.v.) era.

saṅgat: assembly, religious congregation.

sant mat: the way of the Sants; the doctrine and practices of the Sants.

sanyās, sanyāsa: renunciation.

sanyāsī: renunciant.

satguru, sadguru: the 'True Guru', the supreme preceptor.

satī: the burning of a widow on her husband's pyre; a woman so burned.

satsaṅg: fellowship of true believers, congregation.

sevā: service.

sevak, sevaka: devotee.

shaikh: leader; venerable man; prominent Sufi.

Shaiva, Śaiva: Shaivite, relating to Shiva; a devotee of Shiva.

Shākta, Śākta: practitioner of *Shakti* (q.v.) rituals.

Shakti, Śakti: the energy or potency of a god (usually Shiva) expressed in his feminine counterpart; rituals performed by Tantric sects (Hindu and Buddhist), commonly involving magical *mantras* (q.v.) and symbols, and, in the case of so-called 'left-handed' Tantrism, including sexual practices and the consumption of flesh and alcohol as well.

sharī'at: the sacred law of Islam governing ethics, behavior, etc.

Shāstras, *Śāstras*: Hindu sacred scriptures.

Shūdra, Śūdra: member of the fourth and lowest section of the classical caste hierarchy; a menial.

Siddhas: eighty-four exalted personages believed to have attained immortality through the practice of *haṭha-yoga* (q.v.) and to be dwelling on the distant heights of the Himalayas; anti-Brahman Tamil poets from the sixth century onwards.

silsilā: succession, lineage.

simaraṇ, sumiraṇ: repeating or 'remembering' the *nām* (q.v.).

sipāhī: soldier.

skandha: section, chapter.

smṛti: 'remembered'; Hindu literature comprising lawbooks, epics and *Purāṇas* (q.v.).

Śruti: 'heard'; revealed knowledge; the Vedas.

stotra: hymn of praise.

śūnya: emptiness, void.

śūnyavāda: nihilism.

surat, surati: 'hearing' the divine Word (*śabda*, q.v.); the faculty with which one 'hears' the *śabda.*

sūrya: the sun.

svāmī, swāmī: spiritual preceptor.

ta<u>dh</u>kira, tazkira: hagiographic anecdote concerrning a Sufi *pīr* (q.v.).

Tantras: texts enunciating the forms of *Shakti* (q.v.) worship.

ṭek, ṭeka: refrain of a *pad* (q.v.).

ṭhākur: lord, master; deity.

tīrtha: sacred place; place of pilgrimage.

tīrtha-yātra: tour of pilgrimage centres.

'*ulamā* (sing. '*ālim*): 'learned men', men educated in traditional Muslim learning.

vacana: see *bachan.*

vairāgī: see *bairāgī.*

Vaishnava, Vaiṣṇava: worshipper of Vishnu; associated with the worship of Vishnu.

vāmamārga: 'left-handed' Tantrism (see *Tantras*, *Shakti*).

vaṇī: see *bānī.*

vār: heroic ode; song of praise; dirge.

vārkarī: pilgrim, devotee.

Vikram, Vikramī: dating according to the *Vikramī* era (commencing in 57-56 B.C.).
vinaya: reverence; humble submission; petition, intercession.
viraha: separation from one's beloved; the pain of separation.
virahiṇī: woman suffering the pangs of *viraha* (q.v.).
viśiṣṭādvaita: qualified monism, doctrine that the human soul is a distinct but subordinate reality.
viyogī: separated; a man separated from his beloved.
viyoginī: a woman separated from her husband or lover.
Yama: the god of the dead.
zikr: see *d̲hikr*.

SELECT BIBLIOGRAPHY

A. Primary Sources in Indian Languages

Ādi Granth. Ādi Srī Gurū Granth Sāhib Jī. Amritsar: Shiromani Gurduara Parbandhak Committee, various editions. Standard version of the *Ādi Granth.*

Bānglār Bāul o Bāul gān. Collected by Upendranath Bhattacharya. Calcutta: Orient Book Company, 1969. An extensive collection of Baul songs, with a scholarly introduction stressing the Tantric element in Baul belief.

Charandas. *Bhaktisāgar.* Lucknow: Naval Kishore Press, 1975. One of the major works of Charandas.

Cittar gnānakkōvai. Edited by M.V. Venugopala Pillai. Madras: Premier Art Press, 1947. Best collection of Tamil Siddha poetry currently available.

Dadu. *Śrī Dādū charitāmṛt.* Edited by Swami Narayandas. 2 vols. Jaipur: Swami Jayaramdas Smriti Granthamala, 1975.

Dariya Sahab (of Bihar). *Dariyā-granthāvalī.* Edited by Dharmendra Brahmachari Shastri. 2 vols. Patna: Bihar-Rashtrabhasha-Parishad, 1962.

Eknath. *Śrī Eknāth mahārāj yāñchā abhaṅgañchī gāthā.* Collected and edited by Brahmibhut Shrinanamaharaj Sakhare. Pune: Indira Prakashan, 1952. Collected *abhaṅg*s and *bhārūḍ*s of Eknath.

Gorakhnath. *Gorakh-bāṇī.* Edited by Pitambar D. Barthwal. 4th ed. Allahabad: Hindi Sahitya Sammelan, 1979. (Original ed., 1946.) Critical edition of the Hindi utterances of Gorakhnath.

Kabir. *Anurāg sāgar. Kabīr sāhib kā anurāg sāgar.* Allahabad: Belvedere Press, 1975. 18th-century cosmological work of the Chhattisgarh branch of the Kabir-panth spuriously attributed to Kabir. An important text for late esoteric Santism.

Kabir. *Bījak. Kabīr sāhab kā bījak.* Edited by Hansdas Shastri and Mahabir Prasad. Barabanki: Kabir Granth Prakashan Samiti, 1950. For long the standard text of the *Bījak* referred to in most scholarly work.

Kabir. *Bījak.* Edited by Shukdev Singh. Allahabad: Nilabh Prakashan, 1972. The first attempt at a critical edition of the *Bījak.*

Kabir. *Kabīr-granthāvalī*. Edited by Parasnath Tiwari. Allahabad: University of Allahabad, Hindi Parishad, 1961. Edition of Kabir's utterances now accepted by scholars as the most authoritative. Though based on a systematic comparison of all the principal textual traditions, is heavily weighted towards the *Pañchvāṇī* or Rajasthani tradition.

Kabir. *Kabīr granthāvalī*. Edited by Shyamsundar Das. 14th impr. Varanasi: Nagari Pracharini Sabha, 1976. (Original ed., 1928). First edition of the utterances of Kabir preserved in the *Pañchvāṇī* manuscript tradition of the Dadu-panth. Until the appearance of Parasnath Tiwari's *Kabīr-granthāvalī* this was the standard edition in use among academic scholars.

Kabir. *Sant Kabīr*. Edited by Ramkumar Varma. 4th impr. Allahabad: Sahitya Bhavan, 1957. Standard text for the Kabir materials contained in the *Ādi Granth*.

Kabīr kā jīvancharitra. Edited by Gangasharan Shastri. Varanasi: Kabir Vani Prakashan Kendra, 1976. A recent biography of Kabir produced by the Kabir Chaura branch of the Kabir-panth. Most of its material comes from the Urdu *Kabīr-i-manshūr*.

Kanha and Saraha. *Les chants mystiques de Kāṇha et de Saraha*. Édités et traduits par Muhammad Shahidullah. Paris: Adrien-Maisonneuve, 1928. Contains the Apabhramsa and Tibetan texts and a French translation of the *dohā-koṣa*s (couplet collections) and *charyāpada*s (song-lyrics) of the Buddhist Siddhas Kanha and Saraha.

Lalan Fakir. *Lālan-gītikā*. Edited by Matilal Das and Piyushakanti Mahapatra. Calcutta: Calcutta University, 1958. Collection of the songs of Lalan Fakir (also called Lalan Shah), a well-known late 18th-century Baul.

Nabhaji. *Śrī bhaktamāl*, with the commentary of Priyadas. Edited by Sitaramsharan Bhagavanprasad. Lucknow: Tejkumar Press, 1961. Vaishnava hagiographic work composed around 1600 A.D. Includes accounts of Kabir and other early Sants.

Paramanandadas. *Kabīr-i-manshur. Kabīr manśūr*. Translated into Hindi by Sudhadas. Baroda: Pandit Shri Motidasji Chetandasji, 1956. (Original ed. 1887.) Highly mythologized late 19th-century biography of Kabir, a product of the Chhattisgarh branch of the Kabir-panth.

Raghavadas. *Śrī Rāghavadāsjī virachit bhaktamāl*. Edited by Svami Narayandas. Jaipur: Shri Dadudayalu Mahasabha, 1969. Early

18th-century Dadu-panthi hagiographic work modeled on the *Bhaktamāl* of Nabhadas.

Raidas. *Sant guru Ravidās-vāṇī*. Edited by P.B. Sharma. New Delhi: Surya Prakashan, 1978. First attempt at a critical edition of the utterances of Raidas, the 16th-century Chamar Sant.

Rajjab. *Śrī Rajjab vāṇī*. Edited with a commentary by Svami Narayandas. Ajmer: Narayansingh Shekhavat, n.d., 1967? Most recent edition of the *bānī* of the Dadu-panthi Sant Rajjab. The language of the text has been simplified to help the modern reader.

Sakalasantagrantha. Edited by Nanamaharaj Sakhare. Poona: Indian Printing Press, 1961. Standard compilation of Sant literature from Maharashtra.

Sant Bani Pustak Mala Series. Allahabad: Belvedere Press, various editions. Popular collections of the *bānī* of North Indian Sants.

——— Bhikha Sahab. *Bhikhā sāhab kī bānī aur jīvan charitra*. 1974.

——— Bulla Saheb. *Bullā sāheb kā śabdasāgar*. 1973.

——— Dariya Sahab (of Bihar). *Dariyā sāheb Bihārvāle ke chune hue pad aur sākhī*. 3rd impr. 1968.

——— Dariya Sahab (of Rajasthan). *Dariyā sāhab* (*Mārvāṛ ke prasiddha mahātmā*) *kī bānī aur jīvan-charitra*. 7th impr. 1973.

——— Daya Bai. *Dayābāī kī bānī*. 2nd impr. 1967.

——— Dhani Dharamdas. *Mahātmā Dhanī Dharamdāsjī kī śabdāvalī*. 5th impr. 1971.

——— Dharanidas. *Dharanīdās jī kī bānī*. 2nd impr. n.d.

——— Dulandas. *Dūlandās jī ki bānī*. 1964.

——— Garibdas. *Garībdās jī kī bānī*. 1969.

——— Gulal Saheb. *Gulāl sāheb kī bānī*. 1975.

——— Jagjivan Sahab. *Jagjīvan sāhab kī bānī*. 3rd impr. 2 vols. 1967.

——— Maluk Das, *Malūk dās jī kī bānī*. 4th impr. 1971.

——— Paltu Sahib. *Palṭū sāhib kī bānī*. 3 vols. 1965.

——— Sahajobai. *Sahajobāī kī bānī*. 1975.

——— Tulsi Sahib. *Tulsī sāhib Hāthras vāle kī śabdāvalī aur jīvan-charitra*. 2 vols. 1966, 1964.

Sant-kāvya. Compiled by Parashuram Chaturvedi. 3rd ed. Allahabad: Kitab Mahal, 1967. (Original ed., 1952.) Selected utterances from all the major northern Sants. Intended as a companion volume to the compiler's *Uttarī-Bhārat kī sant-paramparā*.

Sant saṅgrah. Compiled by Rai Saligram (Huzur Maharaj). 2 vols. Soamibagh, Agra: Radhasoami Satsang, 1978, 1976. A compilation of Sant utterances made by the second guru of the Radhasoami movement.

Santō kī bānī. Compiled by Charan Singh. Beas: Radha Soami Satsang Beas, 1978. A compilation of Sant utterances made by the present guru of the Radhasoami movement's Beas branch.

Sundar Das. *Sundar-granthāvalī*. Edited by Purohit Harinarayan Sharma. 2vols. Calcutta: Rajasthan Research Society, 1936. Critical edition of the complete works of Sundar Das, Dadu's youngest disciple and the greatest poet of the Dadu-panth.

Śūnya-purāṇa. Edited by N.N. Vasu. Calcutta: Bangiya Sahitya Parishad, 1908. Principal text of the esoteric Dharma cult of Bengal, ca. 13th-15th century. Attributed to Ramai Pandit, the founder of the cult. Important source for medieval cosmological ideas.

Tirumular. *Tirumantiram*. Tiruppanantal: Sri Kasi Mutt, 1951. Collection of three thousand verses by the 6th-century poet-saint Tirumular, considered the major source book for the South Indian Siddha tradition.

Tulsi Sahib. *Ghaṭ Rāmāyaṇa*. 2 vols. Allahabad: Belvedere Press, 1911. A versified book of teachings by the late 18th-century Sant Tulsi Sahib. It purports to be a *nirguṇa Rāmāyaṇa* expressing the philosophical essence of the *Rāmāyaṇa* with all the characters and stories lett out.

Tukaram. *Śrī Tukārāmañchā gāthā* 2 vols. Bombay: Government Central Press, 1950. Standard government-sponsored edition of Tukaram.

Tukaram. *Viśvavandh Śrītukārāmmahārāj yāñchī sampurṇa abhaṅg gāthā*. Poona: Panshikar Prakashan, 1968. The complete *abhaṅg* collection of Tukaram.

B. Primary Sources in Translation

Adi Granth. *Selections from the Sacred Writings of the Sikhs*. Translated by Trilochan Singh *et al.* London: George Allen and Unwin, 1960. Selections from both the *Ādi Granth* and the *Dasam Granth*.

Adi Granth. *The Sikh Religion: Its Gurus, Sacred Writings and Authors*. Edited by Max Arthur Macauliffe. Reprint ed. 6 vols. in 3. New Delhi: S. Chand and Co., 1963. (Original ed., 1909.) Major collection of translations of the *Ādi Granth*. Includes some historiographic and critical commentary, generally reflecting the "neo-Sikh" perspective of the early 20th century.

Bahina Bai. *Bahinā Bāī*. A Translation of her Autobiography and Verses by Justin E. Abbott. The Poet-Saints of Maharashtra, vol. 5. Poona: Scottish Mission Industries, 1929. Selections from an important 17th-century woman Sant of Maharashtra. The autobiography is of special interest. Marathi text is provided in appendix.

Baul songs. *Songs of the Bards of Bengal*. Translated by Deben Bhattacharya. New York: Grove Press, 1969. Free translations of Baul songs, some recorded by the translator, others obtained from published collections. Sources for individual poems are not indicated.

Buddhist Siddha lyrics. *An Anthology of Buddhist Tantric Songs*. Translated by Per Kvaerne. Oslo: Norwegian Research Council, 1977. Apabhramsa and Tibetan texts with English translation. The introduction contains a useful section on the vocabulary of the Siddhas.

Buddhist Siddha lyrics. *Buddhist Mystic Songs: Oldest Bengali and Other Eastern Vernaculars*. Translated and annotated by Muhammad Shahidullah. 2nd revised ed. Dacca: Bengali Academy, 1966. (Original ed., 1960.) English translation of the author's 1928 edition of the texts of Kanha and Saraha (q.v.).

Charan Singh. *Light on Sant Mat*. 3rd ed. Beas: Radhasoami Satsang Beas, 1964. Contains translations of twelve discourses in Hindi by the present guru of the Beas branch of the Radhasoamis.

Dara Shikoh. *Majma' ul-bahrain*. Edited in the original Persian with English translation, notes and variants by Mahfuzul-Haw. Calcutta: The Asiatic Society of Bengal, 1929. The last original work attributed to Prince Dara Shikoh. Attempts to identify the philosophic essence of Hinduism with that of Islam.

Eknath. *Eknāthī Bhāgavata*. Chapter 23. *Bhikshugita: The Mendicant's Song*. Translated by Justin E. Abbott. The Poet-Saints of Maharashtra, vol. 3. Poona: Scottish Mission Industries, 1928. Eknath's Marathi rendering of chapter 23 of the 11th book of the *Bhāgavata Purāṇa*. One of the most popular texts of Maharashtrian bhakti.

Garibdas. *Anabhay-prabodh*. "The Anabhay-Prabodha of the Dādū-Panthī Garībdās" and "Key for Understanding Mystic Literature". Translated by Winand M. Callewaert. *Orientalia Lovaniensia Periodica* 5 (1974), pp. 162-85; 8 (1977), pp. 309-30. A text composed in 1608 by Dadu's successor Garibdas as an aid for disciples.

In 141 couplets, it gives a series of synonyms for the most frequently used terms in *nirguṇa* Sant literature.

Jnaneshvar. *Jnāneshvari* [*Bhāvārthadīpikā*]. Translated from the Marathi by V.G. Pradhan. Edited and with an introduction by H.M. Lambert. 2 vols. London: George Allen & Unwin Ltd., 1967, 1969. Jnaneshvar's ten thousand verse Marathi commentary on the *Bhāgavadgītā*, composed in 1290 A.D. Fundamental text of Maharashtrian bhakti.

Jnaneshvar. *L'Invocation: Le Haripāth de Dnyāndev*. Translated by Charlotte Vaudeville. Paris: École Francaise d' Extrême-Orient, 1969. French translation of the *Haripāṭh*, a collection of twenty-eight *abhaṅg*s by Jnaneshvar.

Kabir. *Anurāg sāgar. The Ocean of Love: The Anurāg Sāgar of Kabir*. Translated by Raj Kumar Bagga, with the assistance of Partap Singh and Kent Bicknell, with introduction and notes by Russell Perkins, under the direction of Sant Ajaib Singh Ji. Sanbornton, New Hampshire: Sant Bani Ashram, 1982.

Kabir. *Au Cabaret de l'amour*. Traduit du Hindi, préfacé et annoté par Charlotte Vaudeville. Paris: Gallimand, 1959. French translation of *pad*s of Kabir selected from the *Bījak*, the *Ādi Granth* and the Shyamsundar Das edition of the *Kabīr-granthāvalī*.

Kabir. *The Kabir Book: Forty-Four of the Ecstatic Poems of Kabir*. Versions by Robert Bly. Boston: Beacon Press, 1977. Adaptations of selected poems from Tagore's *One Hundred Poems of Kabir*, currently enjoying considerable popularity in the United States because of Bly's prominence as a contemporary poet.

Kabir. *One Hundred Poems of Kabir*. Translated by Rabindranath Tagore. Reprint ed. London: Macmillan, 1973. Also reprinted as *Songs of Kabir*. New York: Samuel Weiser, 1975. (Original ed., 1915.) A translation of selected *pad*s of Kabir from the collection made by Kshiti Mohan Sen. The best known English translation of Kabir, it has in turn been translated into many other languages.

Kabir. *Bījak. The Bījak of Kabir*. Translated by Linda Hess and Shukdev Singh. San Francisco: North Point Press, 1983. A translation of selected *pad*s and *sākhī*s from the Shukdev Singh edition of the *Bījak*. Effectively captures the terseness, power and immediacy of Kabir's style. The best poetic rendering of Kabir so far in any Western language. An insightful appendix elucidates Kabir's obscure *ulaṭbāṃsī* utterances.

Kabir. *Bījak. The Bijak of Kabir.* Translated into English by the Rev. Ahmad Shah. Hamirpur, U.P.: By the Author, 1917. A reasonably accurate but not very literary translation of the entire *Bījak*, from a 1911 edition based on earlier printed source.

Kabir. *Kabīr-granthāvalī. Kabir.* Translated by Charlotte Vaudeville. Vol 1. Oxford: Clarendon Press, 1974. The first of a two-volume translation of Parasnath Tiwari's critical edition of the *Kabīr-granthāvalī*. Includes an annotated translation of the *sākhī*s and a lengthy introduction to Kabir and Kabir studies. One of the major recent scholarly contributions to the field.

Kabir. *Kabīr-granthāvalī. Kabīr Granthāvalī (Dohā).* Pondichéry: Institut Français d'Indologie, 1957. A French translation of the entire *dohā* section of the Shyamsundar Das edition of the *Kabīr-granthāvalī.*

Lal Ded. *Lallā Vākyānī or the Wise Sayings of Lālded, a Mystic Poetess of Ancient Kashmir.* Translated by George A. Grierson and L.D. Barnett. London: Royal Asiatic Society, 1920. Scholarly translation of *vākh* or utterances of the 14th-century yogini-poetess Lal Ded, obtained orally from an oral source and supplemented by manuscript sources.

Mahipati. *Bhaktalīlāmṛt.* Chapters 13-24. *The Life of Eknāth: Śrī Eknāth Charitra.* Translated by Justin E. Abbott. The Poet-Saints of Maharashtra, vol. 2. Reprint ed. Delhi: Motilal Banarsidass, 1983. (Original ed., 1927.) Translation of the section devoted to Eknath in Mahipati's 1774 hagiographic work. The basis for modern popular accounts of Eknath.

Mahipati. *Bhaktalīlāmṛt.* Chapters 25-30. *Tukārām.* Translated by Justin E. Abbott. The Poet-Saints of Maharashtra, vol. 7. Reprint ed. Delhi: Motilal Banarsidass, 1980. (Original ed., 1930.) Translation of the section devoted to Tukaram in Mahipati's 1774 hagiographic work.

Mahipati. *Bhaktavijaya. Stories of Indian Saints: Translation of Mahipati's Marathi Bhaktavijaya.* Translated by Justin E. Abbott and Pandit Narhar R. Godbole. The Poet-Saints of Maharashtra, vols. 9-10. Reprint ed. 2 vols. in 1. Delhi: Motilal Banarsidass, 1982. (Original ed., 1933-34.)

Maratha Sant lyrics. *Psalms of the Marāṭhā Saints.* Translated by Nicol Macnicol. Calcutta: Association Press, 1919. Translation into rhymed English verse of 108 *abhaṅg*s by Maratha Sants, selected for their popularity and regular use in worship.

Maratha Sant lyrics. *Stotramālā: A Garland of Hindu Prayers*. Translated by Justin E. Abbott. The Poet-Saints of Maharashtra, vol. 6. Poona: Scottish Mission Industries, 1929. A collection of Maratha Sant lyrics from Jnaneshvar to Mahipati.

Maratha Sant lyrics. "Translations from Tukaram and Other Saint-Poets," by Arun Kolatkar. *Journal of South Asian Literature* 17:1 (1982), pp. 111-14. Excellent modern translations.

Mohsin Fani. *Dabistān-i-mazāhib. Oriental Literature or the Dabistan*. Translated from the original Persian by David Shea and Anthony Troyer. Reprint ed. Lahore: Khalil & Co., 1973. (Original ed., 1843.) Late 17th-century Muslim work giving an account of the major religions of the day. Includes an extensive discussion of the Nanak-panth as well as comments on Kabir and Dadu.

Pampatti Cittar. *Dance, Snake! Dance!* A Translation with Comments of the *Song of Pāmpāṭṭi-Cittar*, by David C. Buck. Calcutta: Writers Workshop, 1976. Effective and sensitive translation of the entire 129 stanzas of Pampatti Cittar's work. Includes a knowledgeable introduction and notes elucidating technical terms.

Rajjab. *The Sarvāṅgī of the Dādūpanthī Rajab*. Edited and translated by Winand M. Callewaert. Orientalia Lovaniensia Analecta, vol. 4. Leuven: Departement Orientalistiek, Katholieke Universiteit, 1978. A thorough study of the *Sarvāṅgī* manuscript tradition. Contains the text and an annotated translation of Rajjab's own *sākhī*s included in the *Sarvāṅgī*. An introductory essay discusses the sources for the study of the Dadu-panth.

Shiv Dayal Singh (Soamiji Maharaj). *Sār Bachan* (*Essential Teachings*). Translated by Sewa Singh. 2nd ed. Beas: Radhasoami Satsang Beas, 1955. Shiv Dayal Singh's collection of his own prose and poetry, regarded within the Radhasoami movement as its primal document.

Sikh literature. *Textual Sources for the Study of Sikhism*. Selections translated by W.H. McLeod. Manchester: Manchester University Press, 1984. Includes portions from the Adi Granth and the Dasam Granth, the works of Bhai Gurdas and Nand Lal, the *janam-sākhī*s, the *rahit-nāmā*s, popular Sikh history, sectarian texts, and modern Sikh theologians.

Tulsi Sahib: Saint of Hathras. Trans. by Janak Raj Puri, with assistance of Chandrawati Rajwade and Virendra Kumar Sethi. Beas: Radhasoami Satsang Beas, 1978. Selected poems by Tulsi Sahib.

Tukaram. *The Poems of Tukārām*. Translated and re-arranged with notes and introduction by J. Nelson Fraser and K.B. Marathe. 3 vols. Reprint ed. Delhi: Motilal Banarsidass, 1981. (Original ed., 1909-1915.) Translation of the entire corpus of Tukaram as preserved in the 1869 edition of his poems by S.P. Pandit. Includes a long introductory essay on the life of Tukaram.

Tukaram. *Psaumes du pélerin*. Traduction, introduction et commentaires de G.A. Deleury. Paris: Gallimard, 1956. French translation of 101 *abhaṅg*s of Tukaram. One third of the poems selected are those used in the liturgy at Pandharpur.

Virashaiva lyrics. *Speaking of Śiva*. Translated by A.K. Ramanujan. Baltimore: Penguin Books, 1973. Brilliant translations of selected Kannada *vachana*s of the 10th to 12th-century Virashaiva saints of Karnataka. The introduction contains an important discussion of the oral poetics of the *vachana* form.

C. Secondary Sources

Barrier, N. Gerald. *The Sikhs and Their Literature*. Delhi: Manohar, 1970. A basic guide to 19th and early 20th-century Sikh literature.

Barthwal, Pitambar D. *The Nirguṇa School of Hindi Poetry: An Exposition of Medieval Indian Santa Mysticism*. Benares: Indian Book Shop, 1936. Reprint ed.: *Traditions of Indian Mysticism Based upon the Nirguna School of Hindi Poetry*. New Delhi: Heritage Publishers, 1978. Hindi translation: *Hindī kāvya meṅ nirguṇa sampradāy*. New Delhi: Heritage Publishers, 1974. Pioneering work on the Sant tradition in North India, responsible for the formulation of many of the basic issues in the study of Sant religion.

Briggs, George Weston. *Gorakhnāth and the Kānphaṭa Yogīs*. Reprint ed. Delhi: Motilal Banarsidass, 1973. (Original ed., 1938.) An excellent ethnographic and historical study of the Nath Yogis.

Bryant, Kenneth E. "*Sant* and *Vaiṣṇava* Poetry: Some Observations on Method," in Mark Juergensmeyer and N. Gerald Barrier, eds., *Sikh Studies: Comparative Perspectives on a Changing Tradition*. Berkeley: Berkeley Religious Studies Series, 1979. A rhetorical analysis of the contrast between *saguṇa* Vaishnava poetry as dramatic and *nirguṇa* Sant poetry as dialectical.

Callewaert, W.M. "Life and Works of the Dādū-Panthī Rajjab." *Orientalia Lovaniensia Periodica* 4(1973), pp. 141-53.

Capwell, Charles. "The Esoteric Belief of the Bauls of Bengal." *Journal of Asian Studies* 32:2 (1974), pp. 255-64.

Chaturvedi, Parashuram. *Kabīr-sāhitya kī parakh* (Hindi) 3rd ed. Allahabad: Bharati Bhandar, 1972. Literary analysis of Kabir's poetry.

Chaturvedi, Parashuram. *Sant sāhitya ke preraṇā srot* (Hindi). Delhi: Rajpal and Sons, 1975. A treatment of some of the historical issues in the Sant tradition.

Chaturvedi, Parashuram. *Uttarī Bhārat kī sant-paramparā* (Hindi). 3rd ed. Allahabad: Bharati Bhandar, 1972. (Original ed., 1952.) Principal source for the historical study of the Sant tradition in North India.

Chaturvedi, Parashuram and Mahendra, eds. *Kabīr-koś* (Hindi). Allahabad: Smriti Prakashan, 1973. A dictionary of Kabir based primarily on the Shyamsundar Das edition of the *Kabīr-granthāvalī*. A useful aid in reading Kabir.

Darshan Singh. *Indian Bhakti Tradition and the Sikh Gurus*. Chandigarh: Panjab Publishers, 1968. A study of traditional bhakti and the attitudes of the Sikh Gurus towards it.

Darshan Singh. *A Study of Bhakta Ravidāsa*. Patiala: Punjabi University, 1981.

Dasgupta, Shashi Bhushan. *Obscure Religious Cults*. 3rd ed. Reprint ed. Calcutta: K.L. Mukopadhyay, 1976. (Original ed., 1946.) Pioneering work on the esoteric religious cults of medieval Bengal and their interrelations. Discusses the Buddhist and Vaishnava Sahajiyas, the Bauls, the Naths, and the Dharma cult. An essay in the appendix shows the link between the doctrines of these cults and those of the Sants of North India.

Date, V.H. *Spiritual Treasure of Sant Rāmadāsa*. Delhi: Motilal Banarsidass, 1975. Study of the Marathi Sant Ramdas, with special attention to his *Dāsabodha*.

Deleury, G.A. *The Cult of Vithoba*. Poona: Deccan College, 1960. Excellent ethnographic and historical study of the Varkari-panth of Maharashtra. Includes maps and plates.

Deming, Wilbur Stone. *Eknath: A Maratha Bhakta*. Bombay: Karnatak Printing Press, 1931.

Digby, Simon. "Abd Al-Quddus Gangohi (1456-1537 A.D.): The Personality and Attitudes of a Medieval Indian Sufi," in K.A. Nizami, ed., *Medieval India: A Miscellany*. Bombay: Asia Publishing House, 1975, vol. 3, pp. 1-66. Study of a prominent Chishti

Sufi whose thought was influenced by Nath-panthi yogic ideas and who interspersed his own compositions with Hindi *pads* and *dohās*.

Dikshit, Triloki Narayan. *Charandās* (Hindi), Allahabad: Hindustani Academy, 1961.

Dvivedi, Hazariprasad. *Kabīr* (Hindi). 2nd ed. Delhi: Rajkamal Prakashan, 1973. (Original ed., 1955.) Erudite and persuasive study of Kabir with emphasis on his link to the esoteric Nath-panthi tradition.

Dvivedi, Hazariprasad. *Nāth-sampradāy* (Hindi). Varanasi: Naivedya Niketan, 1950. Important historical and textual study of the Nath-panth based on primary sources in Sanskrit, Prakrit and Apabhramsa.

Dvivedi, Kedarnath. *Kabīr aur Kabīr-panth* (Hindi). Allahabad: Hindi Sahitya Sammelan, 1965. A comprehensive study of Kabir and the Kabir-panth based on both written sources and field research. Partly supersedes Keay's 1931 work.

Dwyer, William. *Kabīr kī bhakti bhāvanā* (Hindi). Delhi: Macmillan, 1976. A study of Kabir's devotional mysticism.

Eliade, Mircea. *Yoga: Immortality and Freedom.* Translated by Willard R. Trask. London: Routledge and Kegan Paul, 1958. Authoritative study of the ideas, symbolism and methods of Yoga.

Farquhar, J.N. *Modern Religious Movements in India.* New York: Macmillan, 1924. Includes an account of the Radhasoami movement.

Fraser, J. Nelson and J.F. Edwards. *The Life and Teachings of Tukaram.* Madras: Christian Literature for India, 1922.

Grewal, J.S. *From Guru Nanak to Maharaja Ranjit Singh.* 2nd revised ed. Amritsar: Guru Nanak University, 1982. (Original ed., 1972.) Essays on aspects of Sikh history from the late 15th to the mid-19th centuries.

Grewal, J.S. *Guru Nanak in History.* Chandigarh: Panjab University, 1969. A study of Guru Nanak's work as a response to his political, social and religious environment.

Grewal, J.S. "The Sikh Panth: 1500-1850," in David N. Lorenzen, ed., *Religious Change and Cultural Domination.* Mexico: El Colegio de Mexico, 1981, pp. 193-97.

Gurcharan Singh. *Ādi Granth Śabad-anukramaṇikā* (Punjabi). Patiala: Punjabi University, 1971. Concordance of the Ādi Granth.

Habib, Mohammad. "Chisti Mystics' Records of the Sultanate Period," in Khaliq A. Nizami, ed., *Politics and Society during the Early Medieval Period.* New Delhi: People's Publishing House, 1974, vol. 1, pp. 401-33.

Hedayetullah, Muhammad. *Kabīr: The Apostle of Hindu-Muslim Unity.* Delhi: Motilal Banarsidass, 1977. A study of Kabir as a figure who helped bring the religious outlooks of Hinduism and Islam into a position of mutual adaptation and interaction.

Hess, Linda. "Studies in Kabir: Texts, Traditions, Styles and Skills." Ph.D. dissertation, University of California (Berkeley), 1980.

Jayasval, Matabadal. *Kabīr kī bhāṣā* (Hindi). Allahabad: Kailash Brothers, 1965. A study of Kabir's language as a problem in historical linguistics.

Jodh Singh. *Kabir.* Patiala: Punjabi University, 1971.

Johnson, Julian P. *With a Great Master in India.* Delhi: the National Journals Press, 1934. A series of letters to friends and fellow seekers in the United States from an American surgeon who spent several years in India as a follower of the Radhasoami guru Sawan Singh (Huzur Maharaj). First-hand account of a modern guru in the Sant tradition.

Juergensmeyer, Mark. "Radhasoami as a Trans-National Movement," in Jacob Needleman and George Baker, eds., *Understanding the New Religions.* New York: Seabury Press, 1978, pp. 190-200.

Juergensmeyer, Mark. *Religion as Social Vision: the Movement against Untouchability in 20th-Century Punjab.* Berkeley: University of California Press, 1982. A study of the modern Ad Dharm movement of Untouchables in the Punjab. Discusses the movement's appropriation to its cause of the figure of the 16th-century Chamar Sant Raidas.

Juergensmeyer, Mark and N. Gerald Barrier, eds. *Sikh Studies: Comparative Perspectives on a Changing Tradition.* Berkeley: Berkeley Religious Studies Series, 1979. Papers from the Conference on Sikh Studies held in Berkeley in 1976.

Kahn Singh Nabha. *Guruśabad ratanākar mahān koś* (Punjabi). 4th ed. Patiala: Languages Department, Punjab Government, 1981. (Original ed., 1930). A comprehensive encyclopedia of Sikh history, religion and literature.

Kailasapathy, K. *Oppiyal ilakkiyam.* (Tamil). Madras: Pari Nilayam, 1969. Includes a discussion of the Tamil Siddhas.

Karve, Irawati. "On the Road: A Maharashtrian Pilgrimage." *Journal of Asian Studies* 22:1 (1962), pp. 13-29. A lively first-person account of the pilgrimage to Pandharpur.

Keay, F.E. *Kabīr and His Followers*. Calcutta: Association Press, 1931. A detailed study of the Kabir-panth based on first-hand observation and an exhaustive examination of Kabir-panthi literature.

Khushwant Singh. *A History of the Sikhs*. 2 vols. Princeton: Princeton University Press, 1963, 1966.

Lawrence, Bruce. "The *Lawa'ih* of Qazi Hamid ud-din Nagauri." *Indo-Iranica* 28 (1975). An account of a well-known fourteenth-century Indian work on Sufi mystical doctrine. A translation of the extant portion of the text is included.

Lele, Jayant, ed. *Tradition and Modernity in Bhakti Movements*. Leiden: E.J. Brill, 1981.

Lorenzen, David N. "The Kabir Panth and Politics." *Political Science Review* (Jaipur) 20:3 (1982).

Lorenzen, David N. "The Kabir Panth: Heretics to Hindus," in David N. Lorenzen, ed., *Religious Change and Cultural Domination*. Mexico: El Colegio de Mexico, 1981, pp. 151-71. Historical study of the Kabir-panth from the point of view of pressures toward Sanskritization.

McCormack, William. "Liṅgāyats as a Sect." *Journal of the Royal Anthropological Institute* 93:1 (1963), pp. 59-71.

McLeod, W.H. *Early Sikh Tradition: A Study of the Janam-sākhīs*. Oxford: Clarendon Press, 1980. A detailed study of the origins and content of the traditional accounts of Guru Nanak's life.

McLeod, W.H. *The Evolution of the Sikh Community: Five Essays*. Delhi: Oxford University Press, 1975. Critical essays on major theological and socio-religious issues concerning the origin and historical development of Sikhism. Outlines the current state of research and suggests new questions and approaches.

McLeod, W.H. *Gurū Nānak and the Sikh Religion*. 2nd ed. Delhi: Oxford University Press, 1976. (Original ed., 1968.) Basic work on source materials and critical issues concerning Guru Nanak and his times.

McLeod, W.H. "Kabīr, Nānak and the Early Sikh Panth," in David N. Lorenzen, ed., *Religious Change and Cultural Domination*. Mexico: El Colegio de Mexico, 1981, pp. 173-91.

McLeod, W.H. "Sikhism." In A.L. Basham, ed., *A Cultural History of India*. Oxford: Clarendon Press, 1975, pp. 294-302.

Machwe, Prabhakar. *Namdev: Life and Philosophy*. Patiala: Punjabi University, 1968.

Maharaj Sahib. *Discourses on Radhasoami Faith*. Soamibagh, Agra: Radhasoami Satsang, 1973. An exposition of Radhasoami teachings from the perspective of the Agra branch of the movement.

Mahendra. *Kabīr kī bhāṣā* (Hindi). Delhi: By the Author, 1969. A study of Kabir's language with emphasis on his style.

Mathur, Agam Prasad. *Radhasoami Faith: A Historical Study*. Delhi: Vikas Publishing House, 1974. A critical history of the Radhasoami movement based on original source materials. Best source for an understanding of the movement.

Mazumdar, B.P. "Divine Love in Indian Sufism and Vaisnavism." *Journal of the Bihar Research Society* 1968 (Special Issue: Prof. Syed Hasan Askari Felicitation Volume), pp. 69-80.

Mishra, Vijay Chandra. "The Devotional Poetics of Kabir: A Study of Kabir's Poetry and its Tradition with an Annotated Translation of his Songs." 2 vols. Ph.D. dissertation, Australian National University, 1981.

Muttucumaraswamy, V. *Tamil Sages and Seers of Ceylon*. Jaffna: Saiva Prakasha Press, 1971. A study of the Siddha tradition in Sri Lanka.

Nandimath. S.C. *A Handbook of Viraśaivism*. 2nd revised ed. Delhi: Motilal Banarsidass, 1978. (Original ed., 1953.)

Nirbhai Singh. *Bhagata Nāmadeva in the Guru Grantha*. Patiala: Punjabi University, 1981.

Nizami, Khaliq A. *The Life and Times of Shaikh Farid-u'd-din Ganj-i-Shakar*. Reprint ed. Delhi: Idarah-i Adabiyat-i Delli, 1973. A study of Baba Farid, the 13th-century Sufi of the Chishti order some of whose verses are included in the *Ādi Granth*.

Orr, W.G. *A Sixteenth-Century Indian Mystic: Dadu and His Followers*. London: Butterworth Press, 1947. A study of Dadu and the Dadu-panth. Includes translations of selected passages from a 1907 printed edition of Dadu's *bānī*.

Pal, Harendra Chandra. "*Bāul-tattver pūrbābhāsā*" (Bengali). *Sāhitya patrikā* (Journal of the Bengali Department, Dacca University) Winter 1969. Argues for the Sufi antecedents of Baul doctrine.

Partap Singh, Seth. *Jīvan charitra Soāmījī mahārāj* (Hindi). Soamibagh, Agra: Radhasoami Satsang, 1902. Standard biography of Shiv Dayal Singh, the founder of the Radhasoami movement.

Prasad, Rai Ajudhia. *Jīvan charitra Huzūr mahārāj* (Hindi). Soamibagh, Agra: Radhasoami Satsang, 1908. A biography of Rai Saligram,

Shivdayal Singh's successor as head of the Agra branch of the Radhasoami movement.

Puri, Lekh Raj. *Radha Swami Teachings*. Beas: Radhasoami Satsang Beas, 1965. An exposition of Radhasoami teachings from the perspective of the Beas branch of the movement. Provides a lucid inside perspective on Radhasoami religious literature.

Raghavan, V. *The Great Integrators: The Saint Singers of India*. Delhi: Ministry of Information and Broadcasting, 1966. An overview of all the devotional poet-saints of India, with emphasis on their elements of commonality across regions and across the *saguṇa-nirguṇa* distinction.

Ranade, Ramchandra D. *Mysticism in Maharashtra: Indian Mysticism*. Reprint ed, Delhi: Motilal Banarsidass, 1982. (Original ed. 1933.)

Rizvi, S. Athar Abbas. "Sufis and Natha Yogis in Medieval Northern India (12th-16th Centuries)." *Journal of the Oriental Society of Australia* 7:1-2 (1970), pp. 119-33.

Śabda koś santmat bānī (Hindi). Agra: Radhasoami Satsang, 1970. A glossary of obscure or technical terms found in the Radhasoami gurus and in the Sant Bani Pustak Mala series of the Belvedere Press (Allahabad).

Saligram, Rai. *Rādhā Soamī mat prakāś* (Hindi). Banaras: Radha Soami Satsang, 1896. English translation published by Radhasoami Satsang, Soamibagh, Agra, 1957. Presents Rai Saligram's systematization of Radhasoami belief.

Sant mahātmāoṅ kā jīvan charitra saṅgraha (Hindi). Allahabad: Belvedere Press, 1969. Popular biographical accounts of the North Indian Sants.

Saraswati, Baidyanath. "Notes on Kabir: A Non-Literate Intellectual," in S.C. Malik, ed., *Dissent, Protest and Reform in Indian Civilization*. Simla: Indian Institute of Advanced Study, 1977.

Sardar, Gangadhar Balkrishna. *The Saint-Poets of Maharashtra: Their Impact on Society*. Translated by Kumudini A. Mehta. Bombay: Orient Longman's, 1969.

Sawan Singh (Huzur Maharaj). *Gurmat siddhānta* (Hindi). 5 vols. Beas: Radhasoami Satsang Beas, 1963. One of the major statements about the Radhasoami and Sant traditions by the second guru of the Beas branch of the Radhasoamis.

Schimmel, Annemarie. *Pain and Grace: A Study of Two Mystical Writers of Eighteenth-Century Muslim India*. Leiden: E.J. Brill, 1976. In-depth study of the poetry of Shah Abdul Latif and

Khwaja Mir, two important Indian Sufi poets of the 18th century.

Schomer, Karine. "Kabir in the *Guru Granth Sahib:* An Exploratory Essay," in Mark Juergensmeyer and N. Gerald Barrier, eds., *Sikh Studies: Comparative Perspectives on a Changing Tradition.* Berkeley: Berkeley Religious Studies Series, 1979, pp. 75-86. Contrasts the Kabir corpus of *dohās* in the *Ādi Granth* with that in the *Pañchvāṇī* or Rajasthani tradition in terms of the relative importance given to different religious themes.

Sharma, Vasudev. *Sant-kavi Dādū aur unkā panth* (Hindi). New Delhi: Shodhaprabandha Prakashan, 1969.

Simha, K.P. *Dādūpanth evaṃ uske sāhitya kā samīkṣātmak adhyayan* (Hindi). Banaras: Kashi Vidyapith, 1971.

Smith, Wilfred Cantwell. "The Crystallization of Religious Communities in Mughal India," in Mojtaba Minovi and Iraj Afshar, editors, *Yād-nāme-ye Irānī-ye Minorsky.* Tehran: Tehran University, 1969, pp. 1-24.

Subhan, John. *Sufism: Its Saints and Shrines.* An Introduction to the Study of Sufism with Special Reference to India. Reprint ed. New York: Samuel Weiser, 1970. (Original ed., 1938.)

Subramania Iyer, A.V. *The Poetry and the Philosophy of the Tamil Siddhars.* Chidambaram: Manivacagar Noolakam, 1969.

Surjit Singh Hans. "Historical Analysis of Sikh Literature (A.D. 1500-1850)." Ph.D. dissertation, Guru Nanak Dev University, 1980.

Tikku, G.L. "Mysticism in Kashmir in the Fourteenth and Fifteenth Centuries." *Muslim World* 53 (1963), pp. 226-33.

Tulpule, Shankar Gopal. *Classical Marāṭhī Literature.* A History of Indian Literature, vol. 9, fasc. 4. Wiesbaden: Otto Harrassowitz, 1979. Includes extensive discussion of the Maratha Sants and their works.

Varma, Ramkumar. *Kabīr kā rahasyavād* (Hindi). Allahabad: Sahitya Bhavan, 1955. Study of Kabir's mysticism, including comparisons with Hatha Yoga and Sufism.

Vaudeville, Charlotte. "Cokhameḷā: An Untouchable Saint of Maharashtra." *South Asian Digest of Regional Writing* 6. Heidelberg: University of Heidelberg, 1977.

Vaudeville, Charlotte. "Kabīr and Interior Religion." *History of Religions* 3:2 (1964), pp. 191-201. Succinct and sensitive statement of Kabir's religious stance.

Vaudeville, Charlotte. "La Conception de l'amour divin chez Muhammad Jāyasī: *virah* et *ishq.*" *Journal Asiatique* 1962, pp. 351-67.

Approaches the theme of *viraha* in Jayasi from the point of view of parallelisms between Sufi and Yoga mysticism.

Vaudeville, Charlotte. "Paṇḍharpūr: The City of Saints," in Harry M. Buck and Glenn E. Yocum, eds., *Structural Approaches to South India Studies*. Chambersburg, Pennsylvania: Wilson Books, 1974, pp. 137-61. A study of Pandharpur as the pilgrimage center for the Sant movement in Maharashtra.

Webster, John C.B. *Popular Religion in the Punjab Today*. Delhi: S.P.C.K., 1974. Twenty descriptive essays, of which half deal directly with Sikh organizations, sects and religious issues.

Westcott, G.H. *Kabir and the Kabir Panth*. Reprint ed. Delhi: Bharatiya Publishing House, 1974. (Original ed., 1907.) First major Western work on the Kabir-panth since H.H. Wilson's comments in *Religious Sects of the Hindus*. Was for long the principal source for the study of the panth.

Wilson, H.H. *Religious Sects of the Hindus*. Reprint ed. Calcutta: Sushil Gupta, 1958. (Original ed., 1861.) The first attempt at serious academic description of Hindu sects, it was first published in article form in 1828 and 1832. Includes accounts of Kabir, Dadu and other Sants.

Zelliot, Eleanor. "The Medieval Bhakti Movement in History: An Essay on the Literature in English," in Bardwell L. Smith, ed., *Hinduism: New Essays in the History of Religions*. Leiden: E.J. Brill, 1976, pp. 143-68. Useful bibliographic essay.

Zvelebil, Kamil V. *The Poets of the Powers*. London: Rider and Company, 1973. Excellent study of the Tamil Siddhas. Includes translations from some of the principal Siddha poets.

Zvelebil, Kamil V. *The Smile of Murugan*. Leiden: E.J. Brill, 1973. Contains a chapter on the Tamil Siddhas.

NOTES ON THE CONTRIBUTORS

WINAND M. CALLEWAERT is a Research Associate in the Department Orientalistiek of the Katholieke Universiteit of Leuven. His research has been in the area of early Hindi *nirguṇa* literature, particularly the literature of the Dadu-panth. His publications include *The Sarvāṅgī of the Dādūpanthī Rajab* (Leuven, 1978), the edited volume *Early Hindī Devotional Literature in Current Research* (Leuven, 1980) and *Bhagavadgītānuvāda: a Study in Transcultural Translation* (Ranchi, 1982).

EDWARD C. DIMOCK is Distinguished Professor of Bengali and South Asian Studies at the University of Chicago. His publications, principally in the area of Bengali Vaishnavism, include *The Place of the Hidden Moon* (University of Chicago Press, 1966), *In Praise of Krishna* (with Denise Levertov, Doubleday, 1967) and *The Sound of Silent Guns and Other Essays* (Oxford University Press, New Delhi, 1986). He is also one of the editors of *The Literatures of India* (University of Chicago Press, 1975).

ELINOR W. GADON has interests in art history, the history of religions, cultural anthropology and women's studies. She has taught at Harvard University, the University of California at Santa Barbara, the New School of Social Research and the University of Massachussetts. She is currently completing a book on the iconography of the *Bālagopālastuti* manuscripts and early Krishna bhakti in Gujarat.

DANIEL GOLD holds a Ph.D. degree in the History of Religions from the University of Chicago. He is completing a book on guru devotion in the Sant tradition and, in collaboration with his wife, Ann Grodzins Gold, is pursuing ongoing research on the popularization of esoteric tradition among the Naths of Rajasthan. He has taught at Vassar College and Oberlin College, and is currently a Mellon Fellow in the Department of Religious Studies at Stanford University.

JOHN STRATTON HAWLEY is Professor of Asian Languages and Literature at the University of Washington. His books include *At Play with Krishna* (in association with Shrivatsa Goswami, Princeton University Press, 1981 and 1985), *Krishna, The Butter Thief* (Princeton University Press, 1983) and *Sūr Dās : Poet, Singer, Saint* (University of Washington

Press and Oxford University Press, 1984). Together with Donna M. Wulff, he edited volume 3 of the Berkeley Religious Studies Series, *The Divine Consort: Rādhā and the Goddesses of India* (1982).

LINDA HESS holds a Ph.D. in Comparative Literature from the University of California at Berkeley. She has taught at Barnard College and Dartmouth College, and is currently a Bunting Fellow of Radcliffe College, Harvard University. Her publications include *The Bījak of Kabir* (North Point Press, 1983) and a forthcoming book on the Ram Lila in collaboration with Richard Schechner.

K. KAILASAPATHY (1933-1982) was Dean of the Faculty of Arts and Professor of Tamil at the University of Sri Lanka in Jaffna. In 1978, he was Visiting Professor in the Department of South and Southeast Asian Studies at the University of California, Berkeley. In addition to his numerous publications on Tamil literature in Tamil, he is the author of *Tamil Heroic Poetry* (Clarendon Press, 1968).

MARK JUERGENSMEYER is Associate Professor of Religious Studies at the Graduate Theological Union and the University of California, Berkeley. He has also taught at Panjab University. His publications include *Religion as Social Vision: the Movement against Untouchability in 20th-Century Punjab* (University of California Press, 1981), *Fighting with Gandhi* (Harper and Row, 1984) and *Radhasoami Reality: the Logic of a Modern Faith* (in press). He is editor-in-chief of the Berkeley Religious Studies Series and, with N. Gerald Barrier, edited volume 1, *Sikh Studies: Comparative Studies in a Changing Tradition* (1979).

BRUCE LABRACK, Associate Professor of Anthropology and International Studies at the University of the Pacific, has conducted research in India and among South Asians overseas. He has contributed on Sikhs to *Sikh Studies* (Berkeley Religious Studies Series, 1979) and *Overseas Indians* (Vikas, 1983), as well as articles to *Amerasia Journal* (1982), *Population Review* (1983) and *Journal of Marriage and Family* (1984). He is currently editing a forthcoming volume on overseas Sikh migration and an annotated bibliography of the Sikhs in North America.

BRUCE B. LAWRENCE is Professor of Islamic Studies and History of Religions at Duke University. His areas of research are South Asian Islam and contemporary Islamic movements. His publications include *Shaharastānī on the Indian Religions* (Mouton, 1976), *Notes from a*

Distant Flute: Sufi Literature in Pre-Mughal India (Great Eastern, 1979), and the edited volumes *The Rose and the Rock: Mystical Elements in the Intellectual History of South Asian Islam* (Duke University Press, 1979) and *Ibn Khaldun and Islamic Ideology* (E.J. Brill, 1984). He is presently completing a book on Jewish, Christian and Islamic fundamentalism.

DAVID N. LORENZEN is a member of the Center of Oriental Studies at El Colegio de Mexico in Mexico City. His publications in the area of heterodox religious movements in India include *The Kapalikas and Kalamukhas: Two Lost Saivite Sects* (University of California Press, 1972) and several articles on aspects of the Kabir-panth. He edited the volume *Religious Change and Cultural Domination* (El Colegio de Mexico, 1981).

WILLIAM HEWAT MCLEOD, Professor of History at the University of Otago, New Zealand, has interests in Sikh history, textual studies and Sikhs overseas. His major works in Sikh studies are *Gurū Nānak and the Sikh Religion* (Clarendon Press, 1968), *The Evolution of the Sikh Community* (Clarendon Press, 1976) and *Early Sikh Tradition: A Study of the Janam-sakhis* (Clarendon Press, 1980). He has also published a volume of translations entitled *Textual Sources for the Study of Sikhism* (Manchester University Press, 1984).

VIJAY C. MISHRA is currently Chairman of the Department of Comparative Literature at Murdoch University in Perth, Australia. He has written extensively on Indian religious literature, particularly the poetry of Kabir. His publications include *Rama's Banishment: A Centenary Tribute to the Fiji Indians* (Heinemann, New Zealand, 1980) and a forthcoming book on the devotional poetics of Kabir. For a number of years, he was the co-editor of the *Journal of Studies in Mysticism*.

WENDY DONIGER O'FLAHERTY is Professor of History of Religions and Indian Studies at the University of Chicago. She has done research on comparative religion and the ancient Indian tradition, with particular focus on Hindu mythology. Her publications include *Śiva: The Erotic Ascetic* (Oxford University Press, 1973 and 1981), *Hindu Myths* (Penguin, 1975), *The Origins of Evil in Hindu Mythology* (University of California Press, 1976), *Women, Androgynes and Other Mythical Beasts* (University of Chicago Press, 1980), *Dreams, Illusions and Other Realities* (University of Chicago Press, 1984) and *Tales of Sex and Violence* (University of Chicago Press, 1985). She edited volume 2 of the Berkeley Religious Studies Series, *The Critical Study of Sacred Texts* (1980).

ANDREW RAWLINSON is Lecturer in Buddhism at the University of Lancaster. His research is in the area of Mahayana Buddhism and comparative mysticism. He was Visiting Lecturer in Religious Studies at the University of California, Berkeley in 1979.

KARINE SCHOMER has interests in the medieval, modern and folk literature of the Hindi area and Rajasthan. She taught Hindi and South Asian Studies at the University of California, Berkeley for a decade and is currently a Research Associate of the Center for South and Southeast Asia Studies. Her publications include *Mahadevi Varma and the Chhayavad Age of Modern Hindi Poetry* (University of California Press, 1983), and contributions to *The Oral Epics of India* (forthcoming) and volumes 1 and 2 of the Berkeley Religious Studies Series.

FRITS STAAL, Professor of Philosophy and South Asian Studies at the University of California, Berkeley, is author of several books, including *Advaita and Neoplatonism* (Madras, 1961), *Exploring Mysticism* (Penguin and University of California Press, 1975), and *Agni: The Vedic Ritual of the Fire Altar* (Asian Humanities Press, 1983), which sets in context the Vedic ritual portrayed in his film *The Altar of Fire*.

CHARLOTTE VAUDEVILLE, Professor at the Sorbonne and Director of Studies in the IVth section of the École Pratique des Hautes Études, is a specialist in the literature and religion of medieval North India. Her works include *Étude sur les sources et la composition du Rāmāyaṇa de Tulsī-dās* (Adrien-Maisonneuve, 1955), *Les duhā de Ḍholā Mārū: une ancienne ballade du Rajasthan* (Institut Français d' Indologie, 1962), *Soūr-Dās: Pastorales* (Gallimard, 1971), *Le Rāmāyaṇa de Tulsī-Dās* (Belles Lettres, 1978) and *Kabīr*, volume 1 (Clarendon Press, 1974). *Kabīr*, volume 2 is currently in press. She has also written a series of articles on Braj culture in the *Indo-Iranian Journal* (1976 and 1980).

ELEANOR ZELLIOTT is Professor of History at Carleton College. She has published widely on the Untouchables of Maharashtra, the Buddhist conversion movement, Chokhamela and Eknath, the Sants of Maharashtra and contemporary Marathi literature of protest. She and Philip Engblom edited the Marathi Sampler issue of the *Journal of South Asian Literature* (1982). She was also a major contributor to the *Historical Atlas of South Asia* (University of Chicago Press, 1978).

INDEX

Brahmanical learning, 21, 51, 93, 95
Brahmanical tradition. See Brahmanical Hinduism
Brahmo Samaj, 389
Braj: region, 123, 227 *n*34, 345; language, 66, 228
Breath-control, 379-81 *passim*
Bryant, Kenneth, 74, 193, 195
Buddha, 294, 332, 362
Buddhan, 183-84, 189
Buddhism, 36 *n*21, 39, 62, 66, 108 *n*29, 109, 386, 410 *n*57; Tantric, 28, 216 *n*6, 284, 417
Buddhists, 71, 148, 410 *n*57; and Sants, 8, 10, 24, 25, 66-69
Buddhist Siddhas. See Siddhas, Buddhist
Bulle Shah, 336, 366 *n*18
Burhanpur, Kabir-panth in, 291

Caldwell, Robert, 385
Callewaert, Winand M., 112 *n*6
charyā-pada, 113 *n*9
Caste: among Sikhs, 230, 232, 240-41, 243; and Kabir-panth, 14, 293-94, 299-301; and tribals, 283-84, 295; exclusiveness, 2, 4, 8, 25, 37, 38, 270, 292; in Eknath's *bhāruḍs*, 91, 97, 103, 107; of Sants, 8, 93, 187, 189, 194, 285, 286; Sant attitude towards, 8, 24, 139 *n*67, 158, 187, 291, 329; specific castes, 36 *n*21, 95 *n*12, 286, 291, 303, 343, 345,
Chachaji Maharaj. See Pratap Singh, Seth
Chaitanya, 2, 54, 55, 56, 123, 293
Chaitanya sect. 37, 118 *n*24, 192, 227 *n*34
chakra, 383
Chakradas, 288
Chakradhar, 218, 220, 221, 223-24. See also Changadeva Raula; Harinath
Chamars, 343
Chand, Shaikh, 382
Chandidas, 123 *n*33
Changa Vateshvar, 221 *n*20, 225, 225 *n*27
Changadeva Raula, 220, 221, 221 *n*20. See also Chakradhar; Harinath
Chaṅgadeva-pasasti, 218
Charan Das, 6-7, 286, 327, 327 *n*51
Charandasis, 327, 327 *n*52
Charan Singh, 315, 318, 322-23, 325, 332
Charpata, 220
Chaturadas, 185, 186
Chaturvedi, Parashuram, 3, 6, 215, 283, 289, 307 *n*3, 330
Chaupa Singh, 256
chaupāī, 74, 88, 114
Chaurāsī vaiṣṇavan kī vārtā, 195
Chhattisgarh, Kabir-panth in, 290-91, 296, 300, 301, 352, 353
Chishtiyyas, 365, 366, 416
Chitan Swami, 418
Chokhamela, 24, 24 *n*7, 93, 108 *n*29, 109, 187
Christian missions, 298, 345, 354, 385, 410 *n*57
cintu meter, 403-05
Cittars. See Siddhas, Tamil
Cittavaittiyam, 408
Civavakkiyar, 389, 390, 401, 408
Clan, in Sant tradition, 14, 305, 315, 320-21, 327 *n*52
Code of discipline. See *rahit*

Dabistān-i-mazāhib, 187, 241, 287
Dadu Dayal, 6, 69, 316 *n*26, 329, 338, 350; Akbar and, 182; and Kabir, 138, 147, 326; as cotton-carder, 183, 185, 187-88, 189, 286; as Sant, 31, 330, 336, 337; biography of, 12, 181-89, 181 *n*2; Brahmanization of, 183, 189; guru of, 183-84, 189, 306; Rajab as disciple of, 75, 112 *n*6, 309-*n*8, 316; utterances of, 76 *n*51, 112 *n*5, 193, 206 *n*62
Dādū janma līlā, 181, 182-84, 185, 186, 189
Dadu-panth, 181, 184, 186, 188, 192, 229, 326; and Kabir, 6, 11, 27 *n*9, 76 *n*51, 112, 112 *n*6, 291; literature of, 76, 76 *n*51, 112 *n*6, 182, 188 *n*21; Nagas, 188; Western sources on, 188-89
Dadu-panthis, 123, 316, 326 *n*49, 327, 327 *n*52, 329, 337, 343